# Contents

# How to use the Guide

❶ **Location** Place names are listed alphabetically within each county.

❷ **Map reference** Each site is given a map reference for use in conjunction with the atlas section at the back of the guide. The map reference comprises the guide map page number, the National Grid location square and a two-figure map location reference.
For Example: **MAP 03 SX47**
**03** refers to the page number of the map section at the back of the guide
**SX** is the National Grid lettered square (representing 100,000sq metres) in which the location will be found
**4** is the figure reading across the top or bottom of the map page
**7** is the figure reading down each side of the map page

❸ **Site name & Rating** Campsites are listed in descending order of their Pennant/Holiday Centre rating (see pages 8 & 9). Sites are rated from one to five pennants and are also awarded a Merit Score ranging from 50%-100% according to how they compare with other parks within the same pennant rating. Some sites are also given a Holiday Centre grading. For a fuller explanation see page 8. A new category for parks catering only for recreational vehicles (**RV**) has been created, (no toilet facilities are provided at these sites).

**NEW** indicates that the site is new in the guide this year. Where the name appears in italic type the information that follows has not been confirmed by the establishment for 2008.

❶ TAVISTOCK MAP 03 SX47

❸ ►►► 80% **Langstone Manor Camping & Caravan Park**

❹ *(SX524738)*

Moortown PL19 9JZ

☎ 01822 613371 📠 01822 613371

❺ **email:** jane@langstone-manor.co.uk

**web:** www.langstone-manor.co.uk

❻ **dir:** *Take B3357 from Tavistock to Princetown. Approx 1.5m turn right at x-rds, follow signs*

❼ ★ £10-£12 £10-£12 ▲ £10-£12

❽ Open 15 Mar-Oct (rs week days in low season restricted hours in bar & restaurant) Booking advisable BH & Jul-Aug Last arrival 22.00hrs Last departure 11.00hrs

❾ A secluded site set in the well-maintained grounds of a manor house in Dartmoor National Park. Many attractive mature trees provide a screen within the park, and there is a popular lounge bar with a menu of reasonably priced evening meals. Plenty of activities and places of interest can be found within the surrounding moorland. A 5.5-acre site with 40 touring pitches, 5 hardstandings and 25 statics.

❿ **Leisure:**

**Facilities:**

**Services:**

⓫ **Notes:** No skateboards, scooters, cycles, ball games

❹ **Six figure map reference** Each entry also includes a 6-figure National Grid reference as many sites are in remote locations. To help you find the precise location of a site the 6-figure map reference, based on the National Grid, can be used with the relevant Ordnance Survey maps in conjunction with the atlas at the back of the guide.

❺ **Contact details** This will always include location, postcode and telephone numbers and email and website addresses as available. (see page 2 for website explanation)

❻ **Directions** Brief directions from a recognisable point, such as a main road, are included in each entry. Please contact the individual site for more detailed directions or try the online AA Route Planner, **www.theAA.com**, and insert the postcode.

7 **Charges** Rates are given after each appropriate symbol (Caravan, Campervan, Tent) and are the overnight cost for one caravan or tent, one car and two adults, or one motorhome and two adults. The prices vary according to the number of people in the party, but some parks have a fixed fee per pitch regardless of the number of people. Please note that some sites charge separately for certain facilities, including showers; and some sites charge a different rate for pitches with or without electricity. Prices are supplied to us in good faith by the site operators and are as accurate as possible. They are, however, only a guide and are subject to change during the currency of this publication.
★ If this symbol appears before the prices, it indicates that the site has not advised us of the prices for 2008; they relate to 2007.

8 **Opening, Arrival & Departure times** Sites and parks are not necessarily open all year and while most sites permit arrivals at any time, checking beforehand is advised (see page 10).

9 **Description** These are based on information supplied by the AA inspector at the time of the last visit. The brief description of the site includes the number of touring pitches and hardstandings. We include the number of static caravan pitches available for holiday rental in order to give an indication of the nature and size of the site.
**Please note:** The AA pennant classification is based on the touring pitches and the facilities only. AA inspectors do not visit or report on rented caravans or chalets. The AA takes no responsibility for the condition of rented accommodation and can take no action in the event of complaints relating to them.

10 **Symbols and Abbreviations** These are divided into Leisure, Facilities and Services sections and the explanations can be found on page 7 and at the bottom of the pages throughout the guide.
→ Any symbol that follows the red arrow represents a facility found within 3 miles of the site.

11 **Notes** This includes information about any restrictions the site would like their visitors to be aware of. As most sites now accept credit and debit cards - we have only indicated those that don't accept cards.

12 **Photograph** Many caravan parks and camping sites choose to include a photograph within their entry. These are supplied to the AA by the caravan park or campsite and accepted in good faith.

13 **Countryside Discovery** A group of over 30 family-run parks with fewer than 150 pitches, each sharing a common theme of tranquillity. **www.countryside-discovery.co.uk**

14 **Best of British** A group of over 40 parks, both large and small, which focus on high quality facilities and amenities. **www.bob.org.uk**

15 **David Bellamy award** Many AA recognised sites are also recipients of a David Bellamy Award for Conservation. The awards are graded Gold, Silver and Bronze. The symbols we show indicate the 2006/7 winners as this was the most up-to-date information at the time of going to press. For the 2007/8 winners please contact:
British Holiday & Homes Parks Association
Tel: 01452 526911.

**Facilities for disabled visitors**

The final stage (Part III) of the Disability Discrimination Act came into force in 2004. This means that service providers may be required to make permanent physical adjustments and adaptations to their premises; for example, the installation of ramps, hand rails and toilet and shower facilities suitable for use by visitors with restricted mobility.
♿ If a site has told us that they provide facilities for disabled visitors their entry in the guide will include this symbol. The sites in this guide should be aware of their responsibilities under the Act. However, we recommend that you always telephone in advance to ensure the site you have chosen has facilities to suit your needs. For further information see the government website **www.disability.gov.uk.dda**

# Symbols and Abbreviations

## Facilities

| | |
|---|---|
| | Bath |
| | Shower |
| | Electric Shaver |
| | Hairdryer |
| | Ice Pack Facility |
| | Disabled Facilities |
| | Public Telephone |
| | Shop on Site or within 200yds |
| | Mobile Shop (calling at least 5 days per week) |
| | BBQ Area |
| | Picnic Area |
| | Dog Exercise Area |
| → | Facilities found within 3 miles of site |

## Leisure

| | |
|---|---|
| | Indoor Swimming Pool |
| | Outdoor Swimming Pool |
| | Tennis Court |
| | Games Room |
| | Children's Playground |
| | Stables & Horse Riding |
| | 9/18 hole Golf Course |
| | Boats for Hire |
| | Cinema |
| | Fishing |
| | Mini Golf |
| | Watersports |
| | Separate TV room |

## Services

| | |
|---|---|
| | Toilet Fluid |
| | Café or Restaurant |
| | Fast Food/Takeaway |
| | Baby Care |
| | Electric Hook Up |
| | Motorvan Service Point |
| | Launderette |
| | Licensed Bar |
| | Calor Gas |
| | Camping Gaz |
| | Battery Charging |

## Abbreviations

| | |
|---|---|
| **BH** | bank holiday/s |
| **Etr** | Easter |
| **Whit** | Whitsun |
| **dep** | departure |
| **fr** | from |
| **hrs** | hours |
| **m** | mile |
| **mdnt** | midnight |
| **rdbt** | roundabout |
| **rs** | restricted service |
| **RV** | Recreational Vehicles |
| **U** | rating not confirmed |
| **wk** | week |
| **wknd** | weekend |

| | |
|---|---|
| | no dogs |
| | no credit or debit cards |

# AA Pennant Classification

## AA Pennant Rating and Holiday Centres

AA parks are classified on a 5-point scale according to their style and the range of facilities they offer. As the number of pennants increases, so the quality and variety of facilities is generally greater. There is also a separate category for Holiday Centres which provide full day and night holiday entertainment as well as offering complete touring facilities for campers and for caravanners.

## What can you expect at an AA-rated park?

All AA parks must meet a minimum standard: they should be clean, well maintained and welcoming. In addition they must have a local authority site licence (unless specially exempted), and satisfy local authority fire regulations.

## The AA inspection

Every year one of a team of highly-qualified inspectors pays an unannounced visit to each campsite in Great Britain in the guide to make a thorough check on its facilities, services and hospitality. Establishments pay an annual fee for the inspection, recognition and rating, and receive a basic text entry in the AA Caravan and Camping Guide. AA inspectors pay when they stay overnight on a park. The criteria used by AA inspectors in awarding the AA pennant rating is shown on the opposite page.

## AA Merit % Score

AA Rated Campsites, Caravan Parks and Holiday Centres are awarded a percentage score alongside their pennant rating or holiday centre status. This is a qualitative assessment of various factors including customer care and hospitality, toilet facilities and park landscaping. The % score runs from 50% to 100% and indicates the relative quality of parks with the same number of pennants. For example, one 3-pennant park may score 60%, while another 3-pennant park may achieve 70%. Holiday Centres also receive a % score between 50% and 100% to differentiate between quality levels within this grading. Like the pennant rating, the percentage is reassessed annually.

## Holiday Centres

In this category we distinguish parks which cater for all holiday needs including cooked meals and entertainment. They provide:

- A wide range of on-site sports, leisure and recreational facilities
- Supervision and security at a very high level
- A choice of eating outlets
- Facilities for touring caravans that equal those available to rented holiday acommodation
- A maximum density of 30 pitches per acre
- Clubhouse with entertainment provided
- Laundry with automatic washing machines

# AA Pennant Rating Guidelines

## One Pennant Parks

These parks offer a fairly simple standard of facilities including:

- No more than 30 pitches per acre
- At least 6 pitches or 10% of the total pitches allocated to touring caravans
- An adequate drinking water supply and reasonable drainage
- Washroom with flush toilets and toilet paper provided, unless no sanitary facilities are provided in which case this should be clearly stated
- Chemical disposal arrangements, ideally with running water, unless tents only
- Adequate refuse disposal arrangements that are clearly signed
- Well-drained ground, and some level pitches
- Entrance and access roads of adequate width and surface
- Location of emergency telephone clearly signed
- Emergency telephone numbers fully displayed

## Two Pennant Parks

Parks in this category should meet all of the above requirements, but offer an increased level of facilities, services, customer care, security and ground maintenance. They should include the following:

- Separate washrooms, including at least 2 male and 2 female WCs and washbasins per 30 pitches
- Hot and cold water direct to each basin
- Externally-lit toilet blocks
- Warden available during day, times to be indicated
- Whereabouts of shop/chemist clearly signed
- Dish-washing facilities, covered and lit
- Reception area

## Three Pennant Parks

Many parks come within this rating and the range of facilities is wide. All parks will be of a very good standard and will meet the following minimum criteria:

- Facilities, services and park grounds are clean and well maintained, with buildings in good repair and attention paid to customer care and park security
- Evenly-surfaced roads and paths
- Clean modern toilet blocks with all-night lighting and containing toilet seats in good condition, soap and hand dryers or paper towels, mirrors, shelves and hooks, shaver & hairdryer points, and lidded waste bins in female toilets
- Modern shower cubicles with sufficient hot water and attached and private changing space, allowing 1 male and 1 female shower per 35 pitches
- Electric hook-ups
- Some hardstanding/wheel runs/firm, level ground
- Laundry with automatic washing and drying facilities, separate from toilets
- Children's playground with safe equipment
- 24 hours public telephone on site or nearby
- Warden availability and 24-hour contact number clearly signed

## Four Pennant Parks

These parks have achieved an excellent standard in all areas, including landscaping of grounds, natural screening and attractive park buildings, and customer care and park security. Toilets are smart, modern and immaculately maintained, offer the following facilities:

- Spacious vanitory-style washbasins including some in washbasins in lockable cubicles, at least 2 male and 2 female per 25 pitches
- Fully-tiled shower cubicles with doors, dry areas, shelves and hooks, at least 1 male and 1 female per 30 pitches
- Availability of combined toilet/washing cubicles, or shower/toilet/washing cubicles

Other requirements are:

- A shop on site, or within reasonable distance
- Warden available 24 hours
- Reception area open during the day, with tourist information available
- Internal roads, paths and toilet blocks lit at night
- Maximum 25 pitches per campable acre
- Toilet blocks heated October to Easter
- Minimum 50% electric hook-ups
- Minimum 10% hardstandings where necessary
- Late arrivals enclosure

## Five Pennant Premier Parks

Premier parks are of an extremely high standard, set in attractive surroundings with superb mature landscaping. Facilities, security and customer care are of an exceptional quality. As well as the above they will also offer:

- Some fully-serviced 'super' pitches: of larger size and with water and electricity supplies connected
- Electricity to most pitches
- First-class toilet facilities including several designated self-contained cubicles, ideally with WC, washbasin and shower.

Many Premier Parks will also provide:

- Heated swimming pool
- Well-equipped shop
- Café or restaurant and bar
- Sports and entertainment facilities, both indoors and outdoors for young people
- A designated walking area for dogs (if accepted)

# Useful Information

## Booking Information
It is advisable to book in advance during peak holiday seasons and in school or public holidays. Where an individual park requires advance booking, **advance bookings accepted** or **booking advisable** (followed by dates) appears in the guide entry. It is also wise to check whether or not a reservation entitles you to a particular pitch. It does not necessarily follow that an early booking will secure the best pitch; you may simply have the choice of what is available at the time you check in.

Some parks may require a deposit on booking which may be non-returnable if you have to cancel your holiday. If you do have to cancel, notify the proprietor at once because you may be held legally responsible for partial or full payment unless the pitch can be re-let. Consider taking out insurance such as AA Travel Insurance, tel: 0800 085 7240 or visit the AA website: **www.theAA.com** for details to cover a lost deposit or compensation. Some parks will not accept overnight bookings unless payment for the full minimum period (e.g. two or three days) is made.

**Advance bookings not accepted** indicates that a park does not accept reservations.

**Last Arrival** – Unless otherwise stated, parks will usually accept arrivals at any time of the day or night, but some have a special 'late arrivals' enclosure where you have to make temporary camp to avoid disturbing other people on the park. Please note that on some parks access to the toilet block is by key or pass card only, so if you know you will be late, do check what arrangements can be made.

**Last Departure** – As with hotel rooms and self-catering accommodation, most parks will specify their overnight period – e.g. noon to noon. If you overstay the departure time you can be charged for an extra day. Do make sure you know what the regulations are.

## Chemical Closet Disposal Point (cdp)
You will usually find one on every park, except those catering only for tents. It must be a specially constructed unit, or a WC permanently set aside for the purpose of chemical disposal and with adjacent rinsing and soak-away facilities. However, some local authorities are concerned about the effect of chemicals on bacteria in cesspools etc, and may prohibit or restrict provision of CDPs in their areas.

## Complaints
Speak to the park proprietor or supervisor immediately if you have any complaints, so that the matter can be sorted out on the spot. If this personal approach fails, you may decide, if the matter is serious, to approach the local authority or tourist board. AA guide users may also write to:

The Editor,
The AA Caravan & Camping Guide,
AA Lifestyle Guides, 14th floor,
Fanum House, Basingstoke, RG21 4EA

The AA may at its sole discretion investigate any complaints received from guide users for the purpose of making any necessary amendments to the guide. The AA will not in any circumstances act as representative or negotiator or undertake to obtain compensation or enter into further correspondence or deal with the matter in any other way whatsoever. The AA will not guarantee to take any specific action.

## Dogs
Dogs may or may not be accepted at parks, and this is entirely at the owner's or warden's discretion. Even when the park states that they accept dogs, it is still discretionary, and certain breeds may not be considered as suitable, so we strongly advise that you check when you book.* Dogs should always be kept on a lead and under control, and letting them sleep in cars is not encouraged.

*Some sites have told us they do not accept dangerous breeds. The following breeds are covered under the dangerous Dogs Act 1991 – Pit Bull Terrier, Japanese Tosa, Dogo Argentino and Fila Brazilerio.

## Electric Hook-Up
This is becoming more generally available at parks with three or more pennants, but if it is important to you, you should check before booking. The voltage is generally 240v AC, 50 cycles, although variations between 200v and 250v may still be found. All parks in the AA scheme which provide electric hook-ups do so in accordance with International Electrotechnical Commission regulations. Outlets are coloured blue and take the form of a lidded plug with recessed contacts, making it impossible to touch a live point by accident. They are also waterproof. A similar plug, but with protruding contacts which hook into the recessed plug, is on the end of the cable which connects the caravan to the source of supply, and is dead. This equipment can usually be hired on site, or a plug connector supplied to fit your own cable. You

should ask for the male plug; the female plug is the one already fixed to the power supply. This supply is rated for either 5, 10 or 16 amps and this is usually displayed on a triangular yellow plate attached to source of supply. If it is not, be sure to check at the site reception. This is important because if you overload the circuit, the trip switch will operate to cut off the power supply. The trip switch can only be reset by a park official, who will first have to go round all the hook-ups on park to find the cause of the trip. This can take a long time and will make the culprit distinctly unpopular with all the other caravanners deprived of power, to say nothing of the park official. Tents and trailer tents are recommended to have a Residual Circuit Device (RCD) for safety reasons and to avoid overloading the circuit.

It is a relatively simple matter to calculate whether your appliances will overload the circuit. The amperage used by an appliance depends on its wattage and the total amperage used is the total of all the appliances in use at any one time.

If you are not sure whether your camping or caravanning equipment can be used at a park, check beforehand.

## Average amperage

**Portable black & white TV**
50 watts approx. — 0.2 amp

**Small colour TV**
90 watts approx. — 0.4 amp

**Small fan heater**
1000 watts (1kW) approx. — 4.2 amp

**One-bar electric fire**
NB each extra bar rates
1000 watts (1kW) — 4.2 amp

**60 watt table lamp**
approx. — 0.25 amp

**100 watt light bulb**
approx. — 0.4 amp

**Battery charger**
100 watts approx. — 0.4 amp

**Small refrigerator**
125 watts approx. — 0.4 amp

**Domestic microwave**
600 watts approx. — 2.5 amp

## Motor Caravans

At some parks motor caravans are only accepted if they remain static throughout the stay. Also check that there are suitable level pitches at the parks where you plan to stay.

## Overflow Pitches

Campsites are legally entitled to use an overflow field which is not a normal part of their camping area for up to 28 days in any one year as an emergency method of coping with additional numbers at busy periods. When this 28 day rule is being invoked site owners should increase the numbers of sanitary facilities accordingly. In these circumstances the extra facilities are sometimes no more than temporary portacabins.

## Parking

Some park operators insist that cars be put in a parking area separate from the pitches; others will not allow more than one car for each caravan or tent.

## Park Restrictions

Many parks in our guide are selective about the categories of people they will accept on their parks. In the caravan and camping world there are many restrictions and some categories of visitor are banned altogether. Where a park has told us of a restriction/s this is included in notes in their entry.

On many parks in this guide, unaccompanied young people, single-sex groups, single adults, and motorcycle groups will not be accepted. The AA takes no stance in this matter, basing its pennant classification on facilities, quality and maintenance. On the other hand, some parks cater well for teenagers and offer magnificent sporting and leisure facilities as well as discos; others have only very simple amenities. A small number of parks in our guide exclude all children creating an adults-only environment aiming for holiday makers in search of total peace and quiet. (See p.27)

Most parks display a set of rules which you should read on arrival.

## Pets Travel Scheme

The importation of animals into the UK is subject to strict controls. Penalties for trying to avoid these controls are severe. However, the Pet Travel Scheme (PETS) allows cats, dogs, ferrets and certain other pets coming from the EU and certain other countries to enter the UK without quarantine provided the appropriate conditions are met. Visitors intending to bring pets into the UK should consult The Department for Environment, Food & Rural Affairs (DEFRA) at least 7 months in advance of their proposed date of travel. Details of other qualifying countries and further information are available on the website: **www.defra.gov.uk/animalh/quarantine/index.htm**

PETS HELPLINE on 0870 241 1710
(08.30-17.00 Mon-Fri).
E-mail: pets.helpline@defra.gsi.gov.uk

Pets resident in the British Isles (UK, Republic of Ireland, Isle of Man and Channel Islands) are not subject to any quarantine or PETS rules when travelling within the British Isles.

## Shops

The range of food and equipment in shops is usually in proportion to the size of the park. As far as our pennant requirements are concerned, a mobile shop calling several times a week, or a general store within easy walking distance of the park entrance is acceptable.

# Before You Go

A useful tip is to have a checklist to ensure that nothing is left behind when setting off from home, or from park visits, with a towed caravan. It is all too easy to place things under the caravan and then drive away or to arrive home and find a broken vase with flowers and water all over the upholstery.

- Check that all interior caravan items are safely stored, cupboards are closed, loos have no moveable objects and all interior electrics are set correctly. Remember that vase of flowers!
- Check roof lights are closed and the windows are secure.
- Corner steadies should be wound-up tightly, blocks cleared away and steps stowed.
- Disconnect electric hook-ups to site and check that gas bottles are turned off.
- Make sure electrics to car are secure.
- Check that the tow-hook safety wire is clipped on, and, if used, that the anti-snake device is fitted correctly.
- Visually check that the caravan number plate is secure – and that it reads the same as the one on the car.
- Using a second person to stand behind the caravan and check that all lights and indicators are working correctly.
- Move forward about 15 metres, then stop, get out and inspect your pitch for any items which have been left under the caravan.
- Check that the caravan door is locked and secure.
- Another useful and potentially life-saving tip is to always travel with a small fire extinguisher, fire blanket or preferably both, and keep them easily accessible. Fires in caravans and tents are all too common, and once started can take hold very quickly. By the time help has arrived, or you have gone to find the site's fire-fighting equipment, a tent in particular can have burned down completely. Never treat fire risk lightly.

## Useful Addesses

**British Holiday & Home Parks Association**
6 Pulman Court, Great Western Road,
Gloucester, GL1 3ND
Tel: 01452 526911
**www.bhhpa.co.uk**

**Camping & Caravanning Club**
Greenfields House, Westwood Way,
Coventry, CV4 8JH
Tel: 0845 130 7631
**www.campingandcaravanningclub.co.uk**

**Caravan Club**
East Grinstead House, East Grinstead, RH19 1UA
Tel: 01342 326944
**www.caravanclub.co.uk**

**National Caravan Council**
Catherine House, Victoria Road,
Aldershot, GU11 1SS
Tel: 01252 318251
**www.nationalcaravan.co.uk**

**The Best of British Touring & Holiday Parks**
PO Box 28249, Edinburgh, EH9 2YZ
**www.bob.org.uk**

# Island Camping

## Channel Islands

Tight controls are operated because of the narrow width of the mainly rural roads. On all of the islands tents can be hired on recognized campsites.

**Alderney**

Neither caravans nor motor caravans are allowed, and campers must have a confirmed booking on the one official camp site before they arrive.

**Guernsey**

Only islanders may own and use towed caravans, though motor caravans are allowed under strict conditions. A permit must be sought and received in advance, the vehicle must not be used for sleeping, and when not in use for transport the van must be left under cover at a camping park with prior permission. Tents and trailer tents are allowed provided you stay on official campsites; booking is strongly recommended during July and August.

**Herm and Sark**

These two small islands are traffic free. Herm has a small campsite for tents, and these can also be hired. Sark has three campsites. New arrivals are met off the boat by a tractor which carries people and luggage up the steep hill from the harbour. All travel is by foot, on bicycle, or by horse and cart.

**Jersey**

Visiting caravans are now allowed into Jersey, provided they are to be used as holiday accommodation only. Caravans will require a permit for travelling to and from the port and campsite on their arrival and departure days only. Motorvans may travel around the island on a daily basis, but must return to the campsite each night. Bookings should be made through the chosen campsite, who will also arrange for a permit. Early booking is strongly recommended during July and August.

## Isle of Man

Motor caravans may enter with prior permission. Trailer caravans are generally only allowed in connection with trade shows and exhibitions, or for demonstration purposes, not for living accommodation. Written application for permission should be made to the Secretary, Planning Committee, Isle of Man Local Government Board, Murray House, Mount Havelock. The shipping line cannot accept caravans without this written permission.

## Isles of Scilly

Caravans and motor caravans are not allowed, and campers must stay at official sites. Booking is advisable on all sites, especially during school holidays.

## Scottish Islands

**Inner Isles (including Inner Hebrides)**

Skye is accessible to caravans and motor caravans, and has official camping sites, but its sister isles of Rhum and Eigg have no car ferries, and take only backpackers. Official camping only is allowed at Rothsay on the Isle of Bute. The islands of Mull, Islay, Coll and Arran have official campsites, and welcome caravans, motor caravans and tenters. Offsite camping is also allowed with the usual permission. Iona is car free, and a backpacker's paradise, while Tiree does not accept caravans or motor caravans, and has no official sites. Colonsay and Cumbrae allow no caravanning or camping, although organized groups such as the Guides or Scouts may stay with official permission. Jura and Gigha allow neither camping nor caravanning, and Lismore bans caravans but permits camping, although there are no official sites and few suitable places.

**Orkney**

There are no camping and caravanning restrictions, and plenty of beauty spots in which to pitch camp.

**Shetland**

There are four official campsites on the Shetlands, but visitors can camp anywhere with prior permission. Caravans and motor caravans must stick to the main roads. Camping 'böds' offer budget accommodation in unisex dormitories for campers with their own bed rolls and sleeping bags. There is no camping or caravanning on Noss and Fair Isle, and the Tresta Links in Fetlar.

**Western Isles (Outer Hebrides)**

There are official campsites on these islands, but 'wild' camping is allowed within reason, and with the landowner's prior permission.

# Full Circle – 40 Years of Camping

*by Denise Laing*

Camping has seen constant improvement over the last forty years but it's undergone a dramatic change in the last year or two, as many fashionable magazines keep telling us. More often prefixed with 'cool' it has even morphed into terms like 'glamping' to make sure we all understand that weekends and holidays under canvas can be an undeniably glamorous experience. Camping is still all things to all men – and women, but we can forget an inevitable prospect of spartan facilities, smelly tents and sweaty sleeping bags, unless that is your preferred camping experience! Now it's whatever level of comfort and sophistication you want to enjoy. Whether that is home-from-home family tents with separate bedrooms, heating and satellite TV; a sleek retro campervan in gleaming silver, complete with luxurious Egyptian cotton sheets and goosedown duvets, sheepskin rugs underfoot, fine wines and a hamper from the deli; an igloo tent in the corner of a field or maybe a yurt with a central woodburning stove; whatever takes your fancy – the choice is yours.

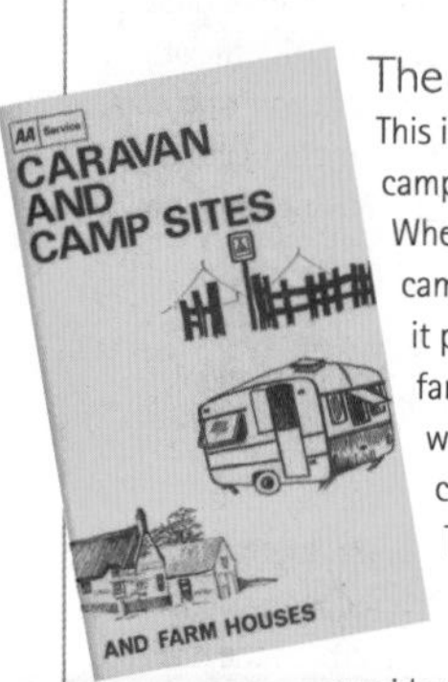


## The Early Years

This is all light years away from camping as most people knew it. When the AA first began providing camping information in 1939, it published a pamphlet on farmhouse B&B accommodation with a list of a few hundred camping fields at the back. These were in the more popular touring areas of the country, particularly the seaside resorts, and the health benefits of a holiday under canvas was a key attraction. AA membership was a significant factor, on arrival at the chosen campsite AA membership cards were presented as an introduction and the AA pamphlet exhorted the camping enthusiasts, among its then half a million members, to respect the countryside and behave in a cordial manner towards site owners. Rather quaintly, compliance with a list of military-style Do's and Don't's such as 'Air your bedding and tidy your tent on rising' was 'earnestly invited' by the AA of the late thirties. This pamphlet was supported by the services of AA patrolmen stationed throughout the country who offered advice and information on available campsites. These patrolmen also inspected the listed sites, and had knowledge of onsite facilities such as they were in those days. The abbreviation SA for 'Sanitary Accommodation' appears next to very few entries, suggesting that cooking and washing water was more often collected from cold standing taps and no doubt spades were an essential part of the toilet arrangements.

By the time the first edition of an AA guide dedicated to Caravan & Camp Sites was published for 1968, the number of campsites had increased and coverage was better spread around the country. In the late sixties campsite owners discovered the benefits of marketing and campsites were named more attractively as Riverside 'Camping Park', or Sunny Glen 'Holiday Park'.

*1969: AA patrols were on hand to help*

To make themselves more appealing they added some home-from-home necessities. Information about toilet blocks began to appear more often in the gazetteer listings, and showers with hot and cold water were less remarkable than a few years previously.

## Care and Consideration

While the reader of this early guidebook was no longer 'earnestly invited' to 'air the bedding' and 'tidy the tent' the guide did include a Code of Conduct at the front of the book. The message was much the same and advice is given to:

- place your caravan where it will not inconvenience others
- never leave rubbish lying around
- control your dog and keep noise down to a minimum
- hang laundry discreetly
- try at all times to be considerate and courteous

## The Grading Schemes

It took another four years of research and development before a national scheme for grading caravan parks was introduced by the AA. In 1972, 700 of the, much expanded, 1,000 campsites had been inspected and classified by the pennant scheme which is still in use today. As they do now, the pennants covered a wide range of camping possibilities. In those days campers with their own facilities who craved peace and seclusion could probably find it on a one pennant site, where nothing more than a tap, adequate refuse storage and collection, and well-drained ground were required for the grading. At the top end of the range just four campsites with five pennants were listed, and these offered the last word in camping luxury of the time, with automatic laundries, swimming pools and supermarkets available on site. Slightly down the scale at four pennants were a mere 28 sites, demonstrating the less sophisticated facilities of the vast majority of sites, rated at three pennants and below.

The pennant scheme was designed to reflect changes in public demand as camping and caravanning became more popular. In 1972 the AA estimated the numbers at around three million. More than half of the motorists arriving from the Continent, where the joys of camping were very firmly established, brought sophisticated camping gear with them and expectations grew. The pennant requirements also became more demanding. A 3-Pennant park, for example, had to provide a deep sink for the exclusive washing of clothes, though it was not for another 12 years that sinks were joined by spin dryers to hasten the hand washing process and it took a few more years to persuade some campsite owners that these changes were positive, indeed essential amenities.

By 1977 a new rating system had been added to the pennants, so that for the first time guide users could judge the standards of each site within its pennant rating. These were based on three categories: Environment, Sanitary Installations, and Equipment and Facilities. Sites were evaluated, where appropriate, with

1 – Adequate,
2 – Good, and
3 – Excellent.

A few years later this system was replaced by one that only rewarded outstanding achievement in one or more of these categories, with an appropriate logo shown beside a site entry. As standards of landscaping, maintenance and toilets improved, this system was abolished in 1998. However, the need to differentiate between campsites of the same pennant rating was recognised, and in 2003 the Merit percentage score used today was successfully adopted.

## Mod cons v back-to-basics

Consumer pressure forced the introduction of ever more sophisticated facilities. One that caused the most stir among top-of-the-range campsites was the demand for private washing facilities. Gone were the days when all campers happily stripped off in front of rows of washbasins, with many now preferring some

# Full Circle – 40 Years of Camping

*continued*

privacy during their daily ablutions. By 1998 four and five pennant parks not only had to provide some washbasins in cubicles to promote choice, but also at least one cubicle containing a washbasin and toilet. Early resistance from campsite owners was quickly overcome by the sheer popularity of these improved services, and nowadays the provision of family bathrooms with washbasin, toilet and bath/shower are quite normal, even on two and three pennant sites.

Less controversial has been the provision of electricity to the vast majority of pitches. Many sites have gone several stages further and created fully-serviced pitches, which can include fresh and waste water facilities, refuse points, TV, satellite and Wi-fi connections, and in some places even personal toilet facilities. A holiday under canvas or on wheels has become

*Camping in the New Forest 1968*

*Camping in the New Forest 2008*

*1969 and time for a roadside barbecue while the AA patrolman sorts out the route*

easier and more comfortable than the early pioneers could have imagined. For some however, such luxuries have been spurned in favour of an altogether different style of camping. The fashionable trend for designer equipped back-to-basics camping has brought the wilder side of outdoor holidays back into the mainstream, exalting those isolated sites in beautiful settings where Nature can be experienced in the raw.

Facilities on site may be lacking but there is no end to the range of designer accessories, not to mention basic equipment, that is now pretty as well as practical. One of the most popular campsites of 2007 has no toilet facilities at all. The return to cold water taps, with spades as the ultimate accessory, might be here again, but the spades will probably come in a pretty pastel shade and 'green' camping stoves powered by methane from local cow dung will heat the freezing water in no time. The traditionalists and purists are wavering between delight and disdain at these latest developments.

## ...and finally

One thing has never changed since the first Guide to Caravan & Camp Sites was published, it remains the best-selling guidebook within the AA's stable of Lifestyle Guides, and with the ever-increasing popularity of camping and caravanning, it looks likely to remain so.

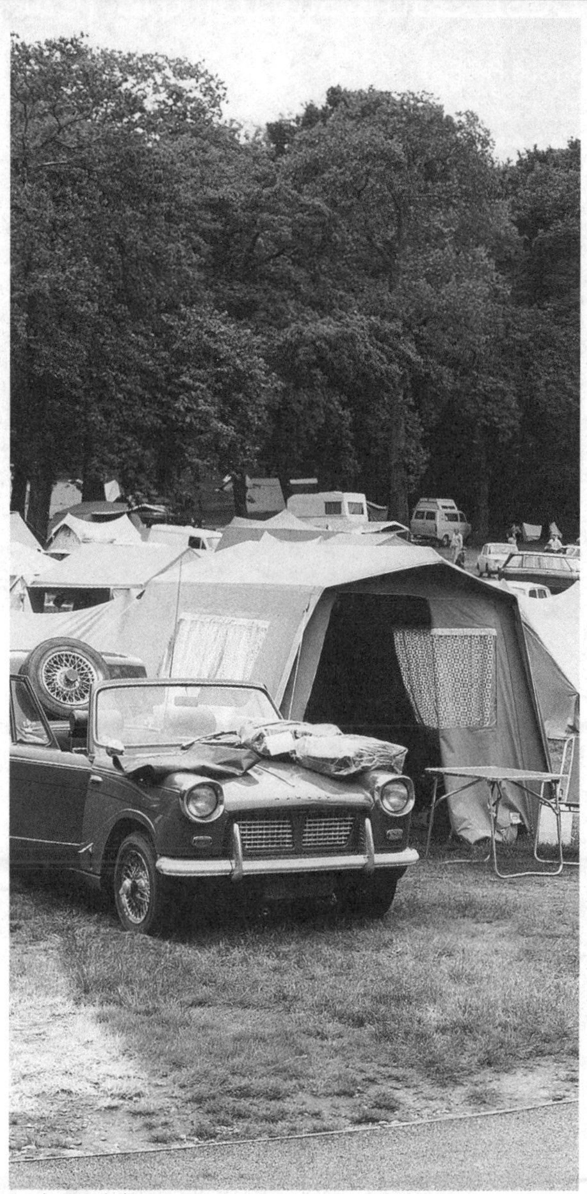

*Popular campsite in Kent, 1969*

# AA Campsites of the Year

## England & Overall Winner of the AA Best Campsite of the Year 2008

**Stroud Hill Park**

St Ives, Cambridgeshire

►►►►► Page 37

Stroud Hill Park is outstanding in every respect. Built entirely from scratch just a few years ago, it was the dream child of Jayne and David Newman who undertook thorough research before embarking on this project. The result is a distinctive park built to exacting standards, and it more than meets the expectations of the most discerning campers and caravanners. The facilities consist of just one large service building constructed in a rustic style from green oak. The building houses the toilets, bar and restaurant, shop, café and reception. The design, materials and finish all ooze exceptional quality.

The site is peacefully located in the Cambridgeshire countryside, a short drive from historic St Ives. All 60 pitches are fully serviced and sited on generously sized hardstandings across rising ground. Leisure facilities include a hard tennis court, and a large fishing lake containing rudd, roach, tench and bream, as well as large specimen carp. The park is open all year, and its out-of-season special themed weekend events are very popular; a wine weekend and a bonfire weekend complete with entertainment are just two that are offered. In order to maintain its tranquil atmosphere the park does not accept children.

Visitors can enjoy relaxing in the beautiful, spacious bar and the beamed and lofty first-floor restaurant. On warm evenings tables are arranged outside on the terrace. This is a special place, and Jayne and David are to be congratulated on their achievement.

# Scotland

## Huntly Castle Caravan Park

Huntly, Aberdeenshire

►►►► Page 292

There are many good reasons for visiting this very northerly part of Scotland, and one of them has got to be the chance to stay on this winning caravan park. It's set in parkland and surrounded by lovely countryside, within easy reach of the beautiful Moray coast, and the Cairngorm Mountains. No doubt the Speyside Malt Whisky Trail will also appeal to many visitors. Debbie and Hugh Ballantyne are the well-organised and thoughtful owners who put customer care at the very top of their list of priorities. They are especially welcoming to disabled visitors, providing level paths and fully accessible toilets and showers. Particular locations on site are willingly allocated on request.

The three toilet facilities are of a high quality, and include private washing and family shower cubicles. There are three dish washing and vegetable preparation areas, as well as a fully equipped laundry. Some fully serviced pitches offer a touch of luxury.

The park is further enhanced by an excellent indoor activity centre with a wide range of games including snooker, table tennis, short tennis and badminton. An extensive children's indoor play area has separate facilities for small and older children, and a small coffee bar offers more scope for relaxation. The attractive town of Huntly with its ruined castle and choice of shops and restaurants is a short walk away. So get motoring, and discover the joys of Huntly Castle for yourself.

# Wales

## River View Touring Park

Pontarddulais, Swansea

►►►► Page 359

Keith and Kath Brasnett have achieved remarkable results in their development of this park over the past four or five years. When they bought the park it consisted of just a small area by the river with a fairly small, old toilet block. It clearly had potential, but not many people could have envisaged these stunning results. Much of the work has been carried out by Keith and Kath themselves.

The park now has three separate areas: the original River Meadow caters only for adults and people with disability; in the upper levels, Gorse Meadow has 12 pitches, and Oakwoods Meadow has 22 pitches, five of them fully serviced. The layout and landscaping is excellent. In between the two levels is an award-winning solar-powered toilet block, with under floor heating, and quality fittings. Two rooms offer fully private facilities.

The park is a David Bellamy Gold award winner, which really sets the theme. The woodland boundaries consist of native trees and wildflowers, and the whole park is very neat and tidy with well cut grass. Recycling and energy conservation are taken seriously, and the Brasnetts are very proud of their Wales Business & Sustainability Award. All grey water and waste from the toilet block goes into a septic tank which is then pumped to a reed bed on site. It doesn't get more 'green' than that.

And to cap it all, the standard of customer care is second to none, resulting in many repeat visits. A true gem of a park.

# AA Regional Campsites of the Year

## South West

**Polmanter Tourist Park**

St Ives, Cornwall

►►►►► Page 84

This premier family park is close to the picturesque fishing port of St Ives, with stunning views of the Cornish coastline and beaches. Polmanter is divided into meadows with all pitches individually numbered and marked out. The excellent modern toilet blocks are well maintained and regularly inspected. Amenities are many and varied: a superb heated pool with sun loungers and sun-bathing terraces, a children's paddling pool, a games room with pool and table tennis tables, an outdoor sports field for ball games, a play area with swings and climbing frames, hard tennis courts and a putting green are just some of them. The lounge has a well stocked bar, and there is an attractive family room and conservatory for meals and drinks. There is also a takeaway food counter that can be found near the conservatory. In fact, everything you could ask from a holiday.

## South East

**Southland Camping Park**

Newchurch, Isle of Wight

►►►►► Page 254

This is a top quality park with excellent facilities. It belongs to the select Countryside Discovery group (see page 5 for details), which promotes a common theme of rural tranquillity. On top of its peaceful setting in the Arreton Valley, the park is beautifully landscaped with well-trimmed hedges, trees, shrubs and lawns all contributing to a feeling of privacy and peace, even when the park is full. The friendly, well-organised staff, headed by owners Viv and Vanessa McGuinness, are pleased to welcome back many customers year after year. Well-behaved children are welcome too, and there's a small playground for them, with space to kick a ball and to run around. Plans to increase the size and facilities of the park are sure to be of the same exacting standards, and will allow more people to share this holiday dream.

# Heart of England

**Stanmore Hall Touring Park**

Bridgnorth, Shropshire

►►►► Page 221

The peaceful grounds of Grade II listed Stanmore Hall make a lovely setting for this superb park. The pitches, many of them fully serviced, are arranged around the lake, where a sunny conservatory makes the most of the view. The house itself houses the Midland Motor Museum. The high quality facilities are a pleasure to use, and constantly monitored. Adults can choose an area away from children if they prefer even more peace and relaxation. The park is handy for touring Ironbridge and visiting the Severn Valley Railway, while the attractive old market town of Bridgnorth is also worth exploring. A delightful park to represent middle England.

# North West

**Stanwix Holiday Park**

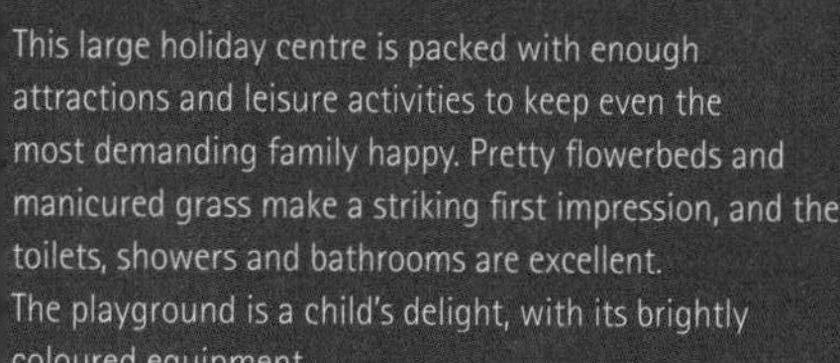


Silloth, Cumbria

Page 108

This large holiday centre is packed with enough attractions and leisure activities to keep even the most demanding family happy. Pretty flowerbeds and manicured grass make a striking first impression, and the toilets, showers and bathrooms are excellent. The playground is a child's delight, with its brightly coloured equipment.

Keeping to the same high standards is the leisure complex: it includes a self-service restaurant that is open from early morning until late at night, two adult-only bars, one with entertainment, and a family bar which also features live entertainment and discos. The sound, lighting and air conditioning systems here are all state-of-the-art. It comes as no surprise that the indoor swimming pool and gym are superb too.

# North East

**Riverside Caravan Park**

High Bentham, North Yorkshire

►►►► Page 272

This caravan park has the distinction of being in North Yorkshire while its nearest towns are in Cumbria, and its postal address is Lancaster! This wonderful position, amidst some of the north's most beautiful countryside, is an undoubted attraction. The park itself is another, with its shallow river meandering though, mature landscaping, grass pitches and immaculate service buildings.

The creation of a play area on steep banking has been a great success, and there is plenty of space for children to let off steam. The attention to detail at this park is quite exceptional.

# AA Premier Parks ►►►►►

## ENGLAND

### CAMBRIDGESHIRE

**St Ives**
Stroud Hill Park

### CORNWALL

**Bude**
Wooda Farm Park

**Mevagissey**
Sea View International Holiday Park

**Pentewan**
Sun Valley Holiday Park

**St Ives**
Polmanter Tourist Park

### CUMBRIA

**Appleby-in-Westmorland**
Wild Rose Park

**Windermere**
Limefitt Park

### DEVON

**Newton Abbot**
Dornafield
Ross Park

### DORSET

**Bridport**
Highlands End Holiday Park

**Charmouth**
Wood Farm C&C Park

**Wimborne Minster**
Merley Court
Wilksworth Farm Caravan Park

### HEREFORDSHIRE

**Peterchurch**
Poston Mill C&C Park

### LANCASHIRE

**Silverdale**
Holgate's Caravan Park

### NORFOLK

**Clippesby**
Clippesby Hall

### NORTHUMBERLAND

**Berwick-upon-Tweed**
Ord House Country Park

### OXFORDSHIRE

**Standlake**
Lincoln Farm Park Oxfordshire

### SHROPSHIRE

**Shrewsbury**
Beaconsfield Farm Caravan Park

### SOMERSET

**Cheddar**
Broadway House Holiday Caravan & Camping Park

**Glastonbury**
The Old Oaks Touring Park

### SUFFOLK

**Woodbridge**
Moon and Sixpence

### ISLE OF WIGHT

**Newbridge**
Orchards Holiday Caravan Park

**Newchurch**
Southland Camping Park

### YORKSHIRE, NORTH

**Harrogate**
Ripley Caravan Park
Rudding Holiday Park

**Scarborough**
Jacobs Mount Caravan Park

## CHANNEL ISLANDS

### JERSEY

**St Martins**
Beuvelande Camp Site

## SCOTLAND

### DUMFRIES & GALLOWAY

**Brighouse Bay**
Brighouse Bay Holiday Park

**Creetown**
Castle Cary Holiday Park

**Ecclefechan**
Hoddom Castle Caravan Park

### EAST LOTHIAN

**Dunbar**
Thurston Manor Holiday Home Park

### FIFE

**St Andrews**
Craigtoun Meadows Holiday Park

### HIGHLAND

**Corpach**
Linnhe Lochside Holidays

### PERTH & KINROSS

**Blair Atholl**
Blair Castle Caravan Park
River Tilt Caravan Park

## WALES

### CARMARTHENSHIRE

**Newcastle Emlyn**
Cenarth Falls Holiday Park

### WREXHAM

**Eyton**
The Plassey Leisure Park

# Adults – No Children

Over 40 of the parks in the AA pennant rating scheme have opted to provide facilities for adults only, and do not accept children. The minimum age for individual parks may be 18, or 21, while one or two pitch the limit is even higher. For more information please contact the individual parks.

## ENGLAND

CAMBRIDGESHIRE
Stanford Park, Burwell
Stroud Hill Park, St Ives

CHESHIRE
Lamb Cottage Caravan Park, Whitegate

CORNWALL
Wayfarers Caravan & Camping Park, St Hilary

CUMBRIA
Larches Caravan Park, Mealsgate

DERBYSHIRE
Peakland C&C Park, Ashbourne
Thornheyes Farm Campsite, Buxton

DEVON
Woodland Springs, Drewsteignton
Zeacombe House Caravan Park, East Anstey
Meadow View Touring Park, Lynton

DORSET
Back of Beyond Touring Park, St Leonards

GREATER MANCHESTER
Gelder Wood Country Park, Rochdale

LANCASHIRE
Rimington Caravan Park, Gisburn

LINCOLNSHIRE
Orchard Park, Boston
Saltfleetby Fisheries, Saltfleetby St Peter

NORFOLK
Fakenham Camp Site, Fakenham
Two Mills Touring Park, North Walsham
The Rickels C&C Park, Stanhoe
Breckland Meadows Touring Park, Swaffham

NOTTINGHAMSHIRE
New Hall Farm Touring Park, Southwell

SHROPSHIRE
Beaconsfield Farm Caravan Park, Shrewsbury

SOMERSET
Exe Valley Caravan Site, Bridgetown
Cheddar Bridge Touring Park, Cheddar
The Old Oaks Touring Park, Glastonbury
Long Hazel Park, Sparkford
Homestead Park, Wells
Waterrow Touring Park, Wiveliscombe

STAFFORDSHIRE
Longnor Wood C&C Park, Longnor

SUFFOLK
Beulah Hall, Beccles

WEST MIDLANDS
Somers Wood Caravan Park, Meriden

WILTSHIRE
Greenhill Farm C&C Park, Landford

YORKSHIRE, EAST RIDING OF
Croft Park, Little Weighton

YORKSHIRE, NORTH
Shaws Trailer Park, Harrogate
Foxholme C&C Park, Helmsley

YORKSHIRE, WEST
Moor Lodge Park, Bardsey
St Helena's Caravan Park, Horsforth

## SCOTLAND

HIGHLAND
Faichemard C&C Park, Invergarry

## WALES

DENBIGHSHIRE
Penddol Caravan Park, Llangollen

PEMBROKESHIRE
Rosebush Caravan Park, Rosebush

POWYS
Riverside C&C Park, Crickhowell
Dalmore C&C Park, Llandrindod Wells

# AA Holiday Centres

## ENGLAND

CORNWALL

**BUDE**

Sandymouth Bay Holiday Park

**HAYLE**

St Ives Bay Holiday Park

**HOLWELL BAY**

Holywell Bay Holiday Park

Trevornick Holiday Park

**LOOE**

Tencreek Holiday Park

**MULLION**

Mullion Holiday Park

**NEWQUAY**

Hendra Holiday Park

Newquay Holiday Park

**PENTEWAN**

Pentewan Sands Holiday Park

**PERRANPORTH**

Perran Sands Holiday Park

**POLPERRO**

Killigarth Manor Holiday Centre

**REJERRAH**

Monkey Tree Holiday Park

**ST MERRYN**

Harlyn Sands Holiday Park

**WHITECROSS**

White Acres Holiday Park

**WIDEMOUTH BAY**

Widemouth Bay Caravan Park

CUMBRIA

**FLOOKBURGH**

Lakeland Leisure Park

**POOLEY BRIDGE**

Park Foot Caravan & Camping Park

**SILLOTH**

Stanwix Park Holiday Centre

DEVON

**CROYDE BAY**

Ruda Holiday Park

**DAWLISH**

Golden Sands Holiday Park

Lady's Mile Holiday Park

Peppermint Park

**EXMOUTH**

Devon Cliffs Holiday Park

**MORTEHOE**

Twitchen House Holiday Parc

**PAIGNTON**

Beverley Parks C&C Park

**SHALDON**

Coast View Holiday Park

**WOOLACOMBE**

Golden Coast Holiday Park

Woolacombe Bay Holiday Village

Woolacombe Sands Holiday Park

DORSET

**BRIDPORT**

Freshwater Beach Holiday Park

West Bay Holiday Park

**HOLTON HEATH**

Sandford Holiday Park

**POOLE**

Rockley Park

**WAREHAM**

East Creech C&C Park

**WEYMOUTH**

Littlesea Holiday Park

Seaview Holiday Park

CO DURHAM
**BLACKHALL COLLIERY**
Crimdon Dene

ESSEX
**CLACTON-ON-SEA**
Martello Beach Holiday Park
Highfield Grange
**MERSEA ISLAND**
Waldegraves Holiday Park
**ST LAWRENCE**
Waterside St Lawrence Bay
**WALTON ON THE NAZE**
Naze Marine

HAMPSHIRE
**FORDINGBRIDGE**
Sandy Balls Holiday Centre

KENT
**EASTCHURCH**
Warden Springs Caravan Park

LANCASHIRE
**BLACKPOOL**
Marton Mere Holiday Village
**HEYSHAM**
Ocean Edge Leisure Park

LINCOLNSHIRE
**CLEETHORPES**
Thorpe Park Holiday Centre
**MABLETHORPE**
Golden Sands Holiday Park
**SALTFLEET**
Sunnydale

MERSEYSIDE
**SOUTHPORT**
Riverside Holiday Park

NORFOLK
**BELTON**
Wild Duck Holiday Park
**BURGH CASTLE**
Breydon Water
**GREAT YARMOUTH**
Vauxhall Holiday Park
**HUNSTANTON**
Searles Leisure Resort

NORTHUMBERLAND
**BERWICK-UPON-TWEED**
Haggerston Castle
**NORTH SEATON**
Sandy Bay

SOMERSET
**BREAN**
Warren Farm Holiday Centre
**BURNHAM-ON-SEA**
Burnham-on-Sea Holiday Village

SUFFOLK
**KESSINGLAND**
Kessingland Beach Holiday Park

SUSSEX, EAST
**CAMBER**
Camber Sands

SUSSEX, WEST
**SELSEY**
Warner Farm Touring Park

WIGHT, ISLE OF
**COWES**
Thorness Bay Holiday Park
**ST HELENS**
Nodes Point Holiday Park
**SHANKLIN**
Lower Hyde Holiday Park
**WHITECLIFF BAY**
Whitecliff Bay Holiday Park

YORKSHIRE, EAST RIDING OF
**SKIPSEA**
Low Skirlington Leisure Park
**WITHERNSEA**
Withernsea Sands

YORKSHIRE, NORTH
**FILEY**
Blue Dolphin Holiday Park
Flower of May Holiday Park
Primrose Valley Holiday park
Reighton Sands Holiday Park

## SCOTLAND

DUMFRIES & GALLOWAY
**GATEHOUSE-OF-FLEET**
Auchenlarie Holiday Park
**SOUTHERNESS**
Southerness Holiday Village

EAST LOTHIAN
**LONGNIDDRY**
Seton Sands Holiday Village

HIGHLAND
**DORNOCH**
Grannie's Heilan Hame HP
**NAIRN**
Nairn Lochroy Holiday Park

NORTH AYRSHIRE
**SALTCOATS**
Sandycoats

PERTH & KINROSS
**TUMMEL BRIDGE**
Tummel Bridge Holiday Park

SCOTTISH BORDERS
**EYEMOUTH**
Eyemouth

SOUTH AYRSHIRE
**AYR**
Craig Tara Holiday Park
**COLYTON**
Sandrum Castle Holiday Park

## WALES

CEREDIGION
**BORTH**
Brynowen Holiday Park

CONWY
**TOWYN**
Ty Mawr Holiday Park

DENBIGHSHIRE
**PRESTATYN**
Presthaven Sands

GWYNEDD
**PORTHMADOG**
Greenacres

PEMBROKESHIRE
**TENBY**
Kiln Park Holiday Centre

SWANSEA
**SWANSEA**
Riverside Caravan Park

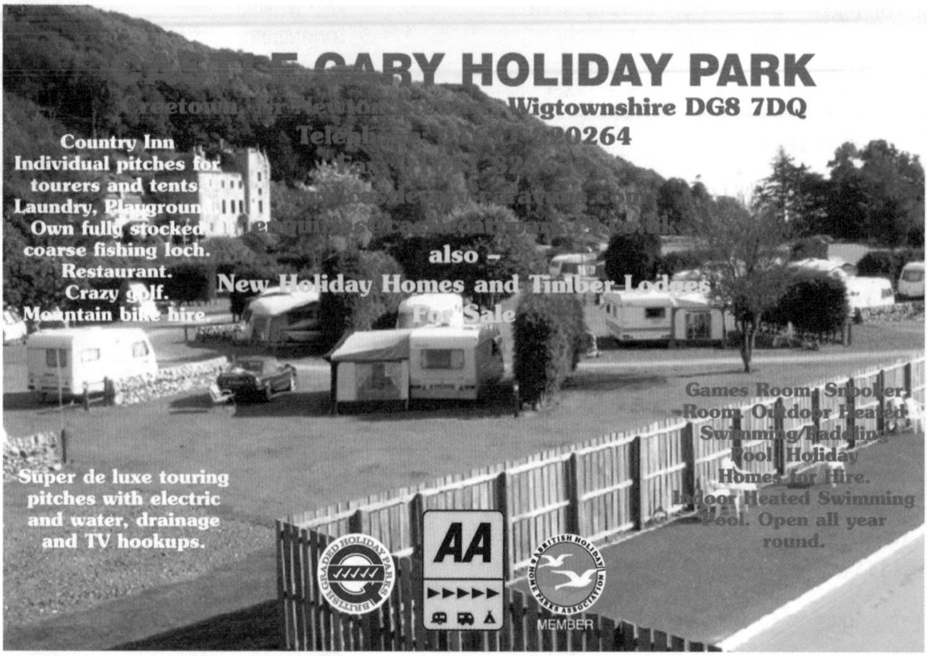

CARY HOLIDAY PARK
Wigtownshire DG8 7DQ
Country Inn
Individual pitches for tourers and tents.
Laundry, Playground.
Own fully stocked coarse fishing loch.
Restaurant.
Crazy golf.
Mountain bike hire.
also –
New Holiday Homes and Timber Lodges
For Sale
Games Room, Snooker Room, Outdoor Heated Swimming/Paddling Pool. Holiday Homes for Hire.
Indoor Heated Swimming Pool. Open all year round.
Super de luxe touring pitches with electric and water, drainage and TV hookups.
AA
MEMBER


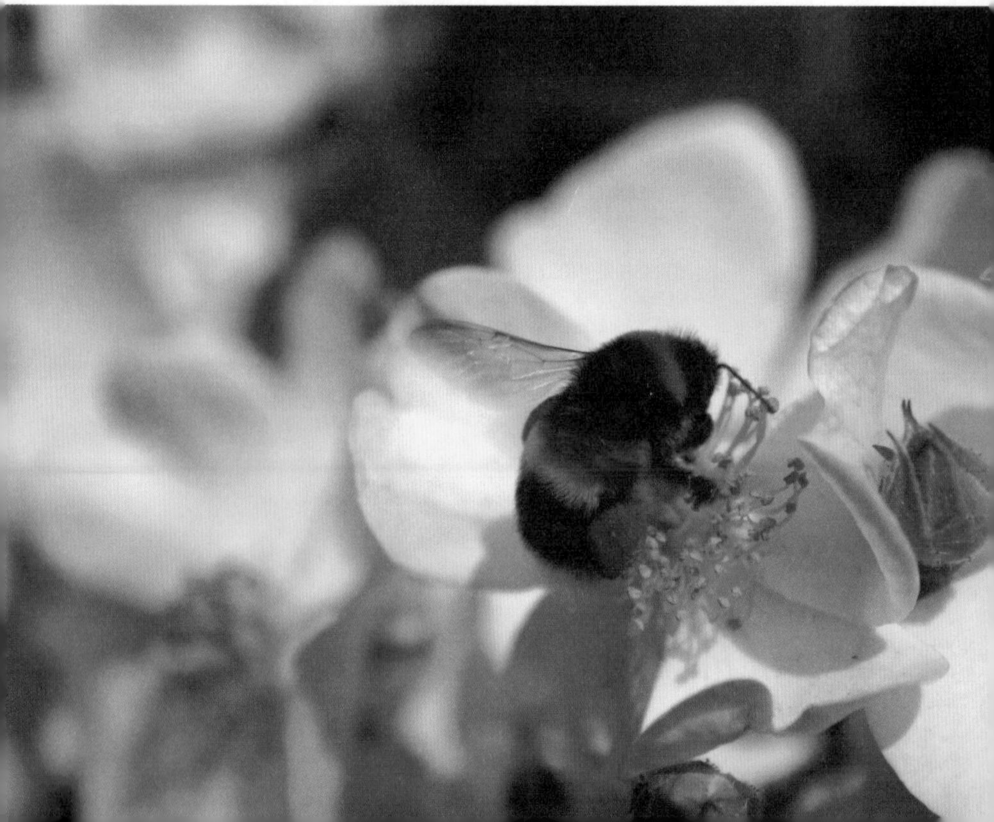

# England

Buttermere area, Lake District, Cumbria

ENGLAND

**ISLE OF** Places incorporating the words 'Isle of' or 'Isle' will be found under the actual name, eg Isle of Wight is listed under Wight, Isle of. Channel Islands and Isle of Man, however, are between England and Scotland and there is a section containing Scottish Islands at the end of the Scotland gazetteer.

# BERKSHIRE

## FINCHAMPSTEAD MAP 05 SU76

### ►►► 73% California Chalet & Touring Park

*(SU788651)*

Nine Mile Ride RG40 4HU

☎ 0118 973 3928 📠 0118 932 8720

**email:** enquiries@californiapark.co.uk

**web:** www.californiapark.co.uk

**Dir:** *From A321 (S of Wokingham), right onto B3016 to Finchampstead. Follow Country Park signs on Nine Mile Ride to site*

★ £16-£22 £10-£15

Open all year Booking advisable Jul & Aug Last arrival 20.00hrs Last departure noon

A peaceful woodland site with secluded pitches among the trees, adjacent to the country park. Several pitches have a prime position beside the lake with their own fishing area. A 5.5-acre site with 30 touring pitches, 30 hardstandings.

**Facilities:**

**Services:**

## HURLEY MAP 05 SU88

### ►►► 77% Hurley Riverside Park

GOLD

*(SU826839)*

Park Office SL6 5NE

☎ 01628 823501 & 824493 Bookings 📠 01628 825533

**email:** info@hurleyriversidepark.co.uk

**web:** www.hurleyriversidepark.co.uk

**Dir:** *Signed off A4130 (Henley to Maidenhead road), just W of Hurley village*

★ £10.50-£17 £10.50-£17 £8.50-£15

Open Mar-Oct Booking advisable BH, school hols & Henley Regatta Last arrival 20.00hrs Last departure noon



Large Thames-side site with good touring area close to river. Level grassy pitches in small, sectioned areas, and a generally peaceful setting. A 15-acre site with 200 touring pitches, 7 hardstandings and 290 statics.

**Facilities:**

**Services:**

**Notes:** No unsupervised children, dogs must be kept on leads. Fishing in season, slipway

*see advert on this page*

## NEWBURY MAP 05 SU46

### ►► 76% Bishops Green Farm Camp Site

*(SU502630)*

Bishops Green RG20 4JP

☎ 01635 268365

**Dir:** *Turn off A339 (opp New Greenham Park) towards Bishops Green & Ecchinswell. Site on left, approx 0.5m by barn*

Open Apr-Oct Booking advisable Last arrival 21.30hrs

A sheltered and secluded meadowland park close to the Hampshire/ Berkshire border, offering very clean and well-maintained facilities. There are woodland and riverside walks to be enjoyed around the farm, and coarse fishing is also available. A 1.5-acre site with 30 touring pitches.

**Facilities:**

**Services:**

**Notes:**

### RISELEY MAP 05 SU76

**►►► 77% Wellington Country Park**

*(SU728628)*

RG7 1SP

☎ 0118 932 6444 0118 932 6445

**email:** info@wellington-country-park.co.uk

**web:** www.wellington-country-park.co.uk

**Dir:** *Signed off A33 between Reading and Basingstoke, 4m S of M4 junct 11*

★ £15-£20 £15-£20 £13-£16

Open Mar-Nov Booking advisable peak periods Last arrival 17.30hrs Last departure 13.00hrs

A peaceful woodland site set within an extensive country park, which comes complete with lakes, nature trails, deer farm and boating. Ideal for M4 travellers. An 80-acre site with 72 touring pitches, 10 hardstandings.

**Leisure:**

**Facilities:**

**Services:**

**Notes:** No open fires. Miniature railway, crazy golf

## BRISTOL

### BRISTOL

*see Redhill (Somerset)*

## CAMBRIDGESHIRE

### BURWELL MAP 12 TL56

**►►► 69% Stanford Park** *(TL578675)*

Weirs Drove CB25 0BP

☎ 01638 741547 & 07802 439997

**email:** enquiries@stanfordcaravanpark.co.uk

**web:** www.stanfordcaravanpark.co.uk

**Dir:** *Signed from B1102*

★ £12 £12 £12

Open all year Booking advisable BH Last arrival 20.00hrs Last departure 11.00hrs

A secluded site on the outskirts of Burwell set in four large fields with several attractive trees. The amenities are modern and well kept, and there are hardstandings hedged with privet. A 20-acre site with 100

touring pitches, 20 hardstandings.

**Leisure:**

**Facilities:**

**Services:**

**Notes:** Adults only No group bookings

*see advert on this page*

### CAMBRIDGE MAP 12 TL45

*see also Burwell & Comberton*

**►►► 72% Cambridge Camping & Caravanning Club Site** *(TL455539)*

19 Cabbage Moor, Great Shelford CB2 5NB

☎ 01223 841185

**web:** www.campingandcaravanningclub.co.uk/cambridge

**Dir:** *M11 junct 11 onto A1309 signed Cambridge. At 1st lights turn right. After 0.5m follow site sign on left*

★ £15.45-£20.15 £15.45-£20.15 £15.45-£20.15

Open 13 Mar-3 Nov Booking advisable BH & peak periods Last arrival 21.00hrs Last departure noon

A popular, open site close to Cambridge and the M11, surrounded by high hedging and trees, with well-maintained toilet facilities. The large rally field is well used. An 11-acre site with 120 touring pitches.

**Leisure:**

**Facilities:**

**Services:**

**Notes:** Site gates closed 23.00-07.00

ENGLAND

## COMBERTON MAP 12 TL35

### ►►►► 91% Highfield Farm Touring Park *(TL389572)*

Long Rd CB23 7DG

☎ 01223 262308 🖷 01223 262308

**email:** enquiries@highfieldfarmtouringpark.co.uk

**web:** www.highfieldfarmtouringpark.co.uk

**Dir:** *From M11 junct 12, take A603 (Sandy) for 0.5m, then right onto B1046 to Comberton*

£10.50-£15.50 £10.50-£15.50 Ʌ £10-£15

Open Apr-Oct Booking advisable BH, wknds Last arrival 22.00hrs Last departure 14.00hrs

Run by a very efficient and friendly family, the park is on a well-sheltered hilltop, with spacious pitches including a cosy backpackers/cyclists area, and separate sections for couples and families. There is a 1.5m marked walk around the family farm, with stunning views. An 8-acre site with 120 touring pitches, 52 hardstandings.

**Leisure:** **Facilities:**

**Services:** →

**Notes:** Postbox

## HEMINGFORD ABBOTS MAP 12 TL27

### ►►► 77% Quiet Waters Caravan Park

*(TL283712)*

PE28 9AJ

☎ 01480 463405 🖷 01480 463405

**email:** quietwaters.park@btopenworld.com

**web:** www.quietwaterscaravanpark.co.uk

**Dir:** *Follow village signs off A14 junct 25, E of Huntingdon, site in village centre*

★ £12.50-£16 £12.50-£16 Ʌ £12.50-£16

Open Apr-Oct Booking advisable high season Last arrival 20.00hrs Last departure noon

This attractive little riverside site is found in a most charming village just one mile from the A14, making an ideal centre to tour the Cambridgeshire area. A 1-acre site with 20 touring pitches, 18 hardstandings and 40 statics.

**Facilities:**

**Services:** →

**Notes:** Pets must be kept on leads. Fishing & boating

## HUNTINGDON MAP 12 TL27

### ►►► 79% Huntingdon Boathaven & Caravan Park *(TL249706)*

The Avenue, Godmanchester PE29 2AF

☎ 01480 411977 🖷 01480 411977

**email:** boathaven.hunts@virgin.net

**web:** www.huntingdonboathaven.co.uk

**Dir:** *S of town. Exit A14 at Godmanchester junct, through Godmanchester on B1043 to site (on left by River Ouse)*

★ £14-£17 £14-£17 Ʌ £13-£16

Open all year (open in winter only when weather permits) Booking advisable Last arrival 21.00hrs

A small, well laid out site overlooking a boat marina and the River Ouse, set close to the A14 and within walking distance of Huntingdon town centre. Clean, well kept toilets. A pretty area has been created for tents beside the marina, with wide views across the Ouse Valley. Weekend family activities are organised throughout the season. A 2-acre site with 24 touring pitches, 18 hardstandings.

**Facilities:**

**Services:** →

**Notes:** No cars by tents

### ►►► 77% The Willows Caravan Park

*(TL224708)*

Bromholme Ln, Brampton PE28 4NE

☎ 01480 437566

**email:** willows@willows33.freeserve.co.uk

**web:** www.willowscaravanpark.com

**Dir:** *Exit A14/A1 signed Brampton, follow Huntingdon signs. Site on right close to Brampton Mill pub*

★ £14-£16 £14-£16 Ʌ £12-£16

Open all year (rs Nov-Feb 10 pitches only plus 6 storage spaces) Booking advisable BH & school hols Last arrival 22.00hrs Last departure noon

A small, friendly site in a pleasant setting beside the River Ouse, on the Ouse Valley Walk. Bay areas have been provided for caravans and motorhomes, and planting for screening is gradually maturing. There are launching facilities and free river fishing. A 4-acre site with 50 touring pitches.

**Leisure:** **Facilities:**

**Services:** →

**Notes:** No cars by tents, dogs must be on leads, ball games on field provided, no generators, one-way system 5mph, no groundsheets. Free book lending

## ST IVES MAP 12 TL37

AA Campsite of the Year for England and overall winner of the AA Best Campsite of the Year 2008

PREMIER PARK

### ►►►►► 92% Stroud Hill Park

*(TL335787)*

Fen Rd PE28 3DE

☎ 01487 741333 🖷 01487 741365

**email:** stroudhillpark@btconnect.com

**web:** www.stroudhillpark.co.uk

**Dir:** *Off B1040 in Pidley follow signs for Lakeside Lodge Complex, down Fen Road site on right*

★ £20 £20 Å £15

Open all year Booking advisable at all times Last arrival 20.00hrs Last departure noon

A superb adults-only caravan park purpose built to a very high specification in a secluded and sheltered spot not far from St Ives. A traditional timber-framed barn houses the exceptional facilities, including beautifully tiled toilets with spacious cubicles containing combined showers, washbasins and toilets. A bar and café, restaurant, small licensed shop, tennis court and course fishing are among the attractions, and there are three pay-as-you-go golf courses and a ten-pin bowling alley nearby. A 6-acre site with 60 touring pitches, 44 hardstandings.

**Leisure:**

**Facilities:**

**Services:**

**Notes:** Adults only. No large motorhomes

## ST NEOTS MAP 12 TL16

### ►►► 80% St Neots Camping & Caravanning Club Site *(TL182598)*

Hardwick Rd, Eynesbury PE19 2PR

☎ 01480 474404

**web:** www.campingandcaravanningclub.co.uk/stneots

**Dir:** *From A1 take A428 to Cambridge, 2nd rdbt left to Tesco's, past Sports Centre. Follow International Camping signs to site*

★ £15.45-£22.15 £15.45-£22.15 Å £15.45-£22.15

Open 13 Mar-3 Mar Booking advisable BH & peak periods Last arrival 21.00hrs Last departure noon

A level meadowland site adjacent to the River Ouse on the outskirts of St Neots, with well maintained and modern facilities, and helpful, attentive staff. An 11-acre site with 180 touring pitches, 33 hardstandings.

**Facilities:**

**Services:**

**Notes:** Gates closed 23.00-07.00

## WISBECH MAP 12 TF40

### ►►► 80% Little Ranch Leisure *(TF456062)*

Begdale, Elm PE14 0AZ

☎ 01945 860066 🖷 01945 860114

**web:** www.littleranchleisure.co.uk

**Dir:** *From rdbt on A47 (SW of Wisbech) take Redmoor Lane to Begdale*

fr £14 fr £14 Å fr £10

Open all year Booking advisable BH

A friendly family site set in an apple orchard, with 25 fully-serviced pitches and a beautifully designed, spacious toilet block. The site overlooks a large fishing lake, and the famous horticultural auctions at Wisbech are nearby. A 10-acre site with 25 touring pitches, 25 hardstandings.

**Facilities:**

**Services:**

**Notes:**

ENGLAND

# CHESHIRE

## CODDINGTON MAP 15 SJ45

### 86% Manor Wood Country Caravan Park (SJ453553)

Manor Wood CH3 9EN

01829 782990 & 782442 01829 782990

**email:** info@manorwoodcaravans.co.uk

**web:** www.cheshire-caravan-sites.co.uk

**Dir:** *From A534 at Barton, turn opposite Cock O'Barton pub signed Coddington. Left in 100yds. Site 0.5m on left*

★ £15-£17 £15-£17 £15-£17

Open all year (rs Oct-May swimming pool closed) Booking advisable Last arrival 20.30hrs Last departure 11.00hrs

A secluded landscaped park in a tranquil country setting with extensive views towards the Welsh Hills across the Cheshire Plain. This park offers fully serviced pitches, modern facilities, a heated outdoor pool and tennis courts. Wildlife is encouraged, and lake fishing with country walks and pubs are added attractions. An 8-acre site with 45 touring pitches, 38 hardstandings and 12 statics.

**Leisure:**

**Facilities:**

**Services:**

**Notes:** No cars by caravans or tents

## DELAMERE MAP 15 SJ56

### NEW 85% Delamere Forest Camping & Caravanning Club Site (SJ555704)

Station Rd CW8 2HZ

01606 889231

**web:** www.campingandcaravanningclub.co.uk/delamereforest

**Dir:** *M56 junct 12 take B5152 towards Frodsham. Park on left before train station.*

★ £18.15-£20.05 £18.15-£20.05 £18.15-£20.05

Open all year Booking advisable BH & peak periods Last arrival 21.00hrs Last departure noon

A newly created park adjacent to Delemere Forest with its miles of walking and cycling trails, and well-placed for visiting Chester. Excellent toilet facilities in a purpose-built, wood-clad block, spacious pitches and attractive landscaping and planting are some of the desirable features here. A 6-acre site with 80 touring pitches, 45 hardstandings.

**Facilities:**

**Services:**

**Notes:** Site gates closed 23.00-07.00 Go Ape! High Wire forest adventure

## KNUTSFORD MAP 15 SJ77

### 74% Woodlands Park (SJ743710)

Wash Ln, Allostock WA16 9LG

01565 723429 & 07976 702490

**Dir:** *From Holmes Chapel take A50 N for 3m, turn into Wash Lane by Boundary Water Park. Site 0.25m on left*

Open Mar-6 Jan Booking advisable BH Last arrival 21.00hrs Last departure 11.00hrs

A very attractive park in the heart of rural Cheshire, and set in 16 acres of mature woodland, 3m from Jodrell Bank. A 16-acre site with 40 touring pitches and 140 statics.

**Facilities:** **Services:** **Notes:**

## MACCLESFIELD MAP 16 SJ97

### 75% Capesthorne Hall (SJ840727)

Siddington SK11 9JY

01625 861221 01625 861619

**email:** info@capesthorne.com

**web:** www.capesthorne.com

**Dir:** *On A34, 1m S of A537*

★ £16-£20 £16-£20

Open Mar-Oct Booking advisable public hols Last arrival 16.30hrs Last departure noon

Set in the magnificent grounds of the historic Capesthorpe Hall, with access to the lakes, gardens and woodland walks free to site users. Pitches in the open parkland are spacious and can take the larger motorhomes, and the clean toilet facilities are housed in the old stable block. The beautiful Cheshire countryside is easily explored. No tents or trailer tents. A 5.5-acre site with 30 touring pitches, 5 hardstandings.

**Facilities:** **Services:**

**Notes:** No tents. Capesthorne Hall & Gardens

## WHITEGATE MAP 15 SJ66

### 90% Lamb Cottage Caravan Park (SJ613692)

GOLD

Dalefords Ln CW8 2BN

01606 882302 01606 888491

**email:** lynn@lccp.fsworld.co.uk

**web:** www.lambcottage.co.uk

**Dir:** *From A556, turn at Sandiway lights into Dalefords Lane, signed Winsford. Site 1m on right*

Open Mar-Oct Booking advisable all season Last arrival 20.00hrs Last departure noon

A secluded and attractively landscaped adults-only park with the emphasis on peace and relaxation. The serviced pitches are spacious with wide grass borders for sitting out. A good central base for exploring the surrounding countryside, with access to nearby woodland walks and cycle trails. A 6-acre site with 45 touring pitches, 28 hardstandings and 22 statics.

**Facilities:** **Services:**

**Notes:** Adults only. No tents (ex trailer tents), no commercial vehicles

ENGLAND

# CORNWALL & ISLES OF SCILLY

## ASHTON MAP 02 SW62

### ►►► 70% **Boscrege Caravan & Camping Park** *(SW595305)*

TR13 9TG

☎ 01736 762231

**email:** enquiries@caravanparkcornwall.com

**web:** www.caravanparkcornwall.com

**Dir:** *From Helston on A394 turn right at Ashton next to Post Office. 1.5m along lane signed Boscreage.*

Open Mar-Nov Booking advisable Jul-Aug Last arrival 22.00hrs Last departure 11.00hrs

A quiet and bright little touring park divided into small paddocks with hedges, and offering plenty of open spaces for children to play in. The family-owned park offers clean, well-painted toilets facilities and neatly trimmed grass. In an Area of Outstanding Natural Beauty at the foot of Tregonning Hill. A 14-acre site with 50 touring pitches and 26 statics.

**Leisure:**

**Facilities:**

**Services:**

**Notes:** Recreation fields, microwave, nature trail

*see advertisement under HELSTON*

## BLACKWATER MAP 02 SW74

### ►►► 90% **Chiverton Park** *(SW743468)*

East Hill TR4 8HS

☎ 01872 560667 01872 560667

**email:** chivertonpark@btopenworld.com

**web:** www.chivertonpark.co.uk

**Dir:** *Exit A30 at Chiverton rdbt (Little Chef) onto unclass road signed Blackwater (3rd exit). 1st right & park 300mtrs on right*

★ £13-£18 £13-£22 £13-£18

Open 3 Mar-3 Nov (rs Mar-May & mid Sep-Nov limited stock kept in shop) Booking advisable mid Jul-Aug Last arrival 21.00hrs Last departure noon

A small, well-maintained site with some mature hedges dividing pitches, sited midway between Truro and St Agnes. Facilities include a good toilet block and a steam room, sauna and gym. A games room with pool table, and children's outside play equipment prove popular with families. A 4-acre site with 12 touring pitches, 10 hardstandings and 50 statics.

**Leisure:** **Facilities:**

**Services:**

**Notes:** No ball games. Drying lines available

### ►►► 80% **Trevarth Holiday Park** *(SW744468)*

TR4 8HR

☎ 01872 560266 01872 560379

**email:** trevarth@lineone.net

**web:** www.trevarth.co.uk

**Dir:** *Leave A30 at Chiverton rdbt onto B3277 signed St Agnes. At next rdbt take road signed Blackwater. Site on right in 200mtrs.*

£10-£15 £10-£15 £10-£15

Open Apr-Oct Booking advisable Jul-Aug Last arrival 22.00hrs Last departure 11.30hrs

A neat and compact park with touring pitches laid out on attractive, well-screened high ground adjacent to A30/A39 junction. This pleasant little park is centrally located for touring, and is maintained to a very good standard. A 4-acre site with 30 touring pitches, 6 hardstandings and 21 statics.

**Leisure:** **Facilities:**

**Services:**

## BLISLAND MAP 02 SX17

### ► 81% **South Penquite Farm** *(SX108751)*

South Penquite PL30 4LH

☎ 01208 850491 0870 1367926

**email:** thefarm@bodminmoor.co.uk

**web:** www.southpenquite.co.uk

**Dir:** *From Exeter on A30 exit at 1st sign to St Breward on right, (from Bodmin 2nd sign on left). Follow narrow road across Bodmin Moor. Ignore left & right turns until South Penquite Farm Lane on right in 2m*

£10

Open May-Oct Booking advisable school hols Last departure 14.00hrs

Located on a working organic farm on Bodmin Moor, this fairly simple, tenting site is sheltered by mature trees and hedges. The two fields afford plenty of space, and the friendly conservation-conscious owners will give details of a lovely riverside walk past a Bronze Age settlement. A 4-acre site with 40 touring pitches.

**Leisure:** **Facilities:**

**Notes:** No caravans. Organic produce available

ENGLAND

## BODMIN MAP 02 SX06

*see also Lanivet*

### ►►► 71% Bodmin Camping & Caravanning Club Site *(SX081676)*

Old Callywith Rd PL31 2DZ

☎ 01208 73834

**web:** www.campingandcaravanningclub.co.uk/bodmin

**Dir:** *A30 from N, at sign for Bodmin turn right crossing dual carriageway in front of industrial estate, turn left at international sign, site left*

★ £14.05-£18.85 £14.05-£18.85 £14.05-£18.85

Open 13 Mar-3 Nov Booking advisable BH & peak periods Last arrival 21.00hrs Last departure noon

Undulating grassy site with trees and bushes set in meadowland close to the town of Bodmin with all its attractions. The site is close to the A30 and makes a very good touring base. An 11-acre site with 130 touring pitches, 12 hardstandings.

**Leisure:**

**Facilities:**

**Services:** →

**Notes:** Gates closed 23.00-07.00

## BOLVENTOR MAP 02 SX17

### ►►►► 78% Colliford Tavern Campsite *(SX171740)*

Colliford Lake, St Neot PL14 6PZ

☎ 01208 821335 01208 821335

**email:** info@colliford.com

**web:** www.colliford.com

**Dir:** *Exit A30 1.25m W of Bolventor onto unclass road signed Colliford Lake. Site 0.25m on left*

★ fr £13 fr £13 fr £13

Open Etr-Sep Booking advisable BH & Jul-Aug Last arrival 22.30hrs Last departure 11.00hrs

An oasis on Bodmin Moor, a small site with spacious grassy pitches and very good quality facilities. The park is surrounded by mature trees and very sheltered in the centre of the moor. Fly fishing is available at nearby Colliford Lake. A 3.5-acre site with 40 touring pitches.

**Leisure:**

**Facilities:**

**Services:** →

**Notes:** Dogs must be kept on leads

## BOSCASTLE MAP 02 SX09

### ► 76% Lower Pennycrocker Farm *(SX125927)*

PL35 0BY

☎ 01840 250257 01840 250613

**email:** karynheard@btinternet.com

**web:** www.pennycrocker.com

**Dir:** *Leave A39 at Marshgate onto B3263 towards Boscastle, site signed in 2m*

Open Etr-Oct Booking advisable Last arrival anytime Last departure anytime

Mature Cornish hedges provide shelter for this small, family-run site on a dairy farm. Spectacular scenery and the nearby coastal footpath are among the many attractions, along with fresh eggs, milk and home-made clotted cream for sale. The small toilet block is very clean if quite basic. A 6-acre site with 40 touring pitches.

**Facilities:**

**Services:** →

**Notes:**

## BRYHER MAP 02 SV81

*See Scilly, Isles of*

## BUDE MAP 02 SS20

*see also Kilkhampton & Bridgerule (Devon)*

### 76% *Sandymouth Bay Holiday Park* *(SS214104)*

Sandymouth Bay EX23 9HW

☎ 01288 352563 01288 354822

**web:** www.sandymouthbay.co.uk

**Dir:** *Signed off A39 approx 0.5m S of Kilkhampton, 4m N of Bude*

Open Apr-Oct Booking advisable Jul & Aug Last arrival 22.00hrs Last departure 10.00hrs

A friendly holiday park with glorious and extensive sea views. This well kept park boasts many on-site facilities, and an extensive entertainment programme for all ages. A 24-acre site with 100 touring pitches and 158 statics.

**Leisure:**

**Facilities:**

**Services:** →

**Notes:** Sauna, solarium, crazy golf

ENGLAND

## PREMIER PARK

### ►►►►► 84% *Wooda Farm Park* (SS229080)

GOLD

Poughill EX23 9HJ

☎ 01288 352069 🖷 01288 355258

**email:** enquiries@wooda.co.uk

**web:** www.wooda.co.uk

**Dir:** *2m E from A39 at edge of Stratton follow unclass road signed Coombe Valley/Poughill*

Open Apr-Oct (rs Apr-May & mid Sep-Oct shop hours limited) Booking advisable Jul-Aug Last arrival 20.00hrs Last departure noon

An attractive park set on raised ground overlooking Bude Bay, with lovely sea views. The park is divided into paddocks by hedges and mature trees, and offers high quality facilities in extensive colourful gardens. A variety of activities is provided by the large sports hall and hard tennis court, and there's a super children's playground. A 25-acre site with 200 touring pitches, 60 hardstandings and 55 statics.

**Leisure:**

**Facilities:**

**Services:**

**Notes:** Restrictions on certain breeds of dogs. Coarse fishing, clay pigeon shooting, pets corner

*see advert on this page*

### ►►►► 86% *Budemeadows Touring Holiday Park* (SS215012)

EX23 0NA

☎ 01288 361646

**email:** holiday@budemeadows.com

**web:** www.budemeadows.com

**Dir:** *3m S of Bude on A39. Park entered via layby*

Open all year (rs Sep-Spring BH shop, bar & pool closed) Booking advisable Jul-Aug Last arrival 21.00hrs Last departure 11.00hrs

A very well kept site of distinction, with good quality facilities. Budemeadows is set on a gentle sheltered slope in nine acres of naturally landscaped parkland, surrounded by mature hedges. Just one mile from Widemouth Bay, and three miles from the

CONTINUED

BUDE CONTINUED

unspoilt resort of Bude. A 9-acre site with 144 touring pitches, 24 hardstandings.

**Leisure:**

**Facilities:**

**Services:** → 

**Notes:** Table tennis, giant chess, baby changing facility

### ►►► 74% Upper Lynstone Caravan Park

*(SS205053)*

Lynstone EX23 0LP

☎ 01288 352017 01288 359034

**email:** reception@upperlynstone.co.uk

**web:** www.upperlynstone.co.uk

**Dir:** *0.75m S of Bude on coastal road to Widemouth Bay*

★ £8.50-£15.50 £8.50-£15.50 £8.50-£15.50

Open Apr-Oct Booking advisable Last arrival 22.00hrs Last departure 10.00hrs

There are extensive views over Bude to be enjoyed from this quiet family-run park set on sheltered ground. There is a small shop selling camping spares, and a children's playground. A path leads directly to the coastal footpath with its stunning sea views, and the old Bude Canal is a stroll away. A 6-acre site with 65 touring pitches and 41 statics.

**Leisure:**

**Facilities:**

**Services:** →

**Notes:** No groups. Baby changing room

### ►►► 76% Willow Valley Holiday Park

*(SS236078)*

Bush EX23 9LB

☎ 01288 353104

**email:** willowvalley@talk21.com

**web:** www.willowvalley.co.uk

**Dir:** *On A39, 0.5m N of junct with A3072 at Stratton*

Open Mar-Dec Booking advisable Jul & Aug Last arrival 21.00hrs Last departure noon

A small sheltered park in Strat Valley with a stream running through and level grassy pitches. The friendly family owners have improved all areas of this attractive park, which has direct access off the A39, and only 2 miles from the sandy beaches at Bude. A 4-acre site with 41 touring pitches and 4 statics.

**Leisure:**

**Facilities:**

**Services:** →

**Notes:**

## CAMELFORD MAP 02 SX18

### ►►► 75% Juliot's Well Holiday Park

*(SX095829)*

PL32 9RF

☎ 01840 213302 01840 212700

**email:** juliotswell@breaksincornwall.com

**web:** www.juliotswell.com

**Dir:** *Through Camelford, A39 at Valley Truckle turn right onto B3266, then 1st left signed Lanteglos, site 300yds on right*

★ £12-£19 £12-£19 £12-£19

Open Mar-Oct Booking advisable all year Last arrival 20.00hrs Last departure 11.00hrs

Set in the wooded grounds of an old manor house, this quiet site enjoys lovely and extensive views across the countryside. A rustic inn on site offers occasional entertainment, and there is plenty to do, both on the park and in the vicinity. A 33-acre site with 39 touring pitches and 52 statics.

**Leisure:**

**Facilities:**

**Services:** →

**Notes:** Unisex toilet block

### ►►► 77% Kings Acre *(SX090850)*

PL32 9UR

☎ 01840 213561 01840 213561

**email:** info@kings-acre.com

**web:** www.kingsacrecamping.co.uk

**Dir:** *On B3266, towards Boscastle, on right*

Open May-Sep (rs May-Jun No café or bar) Booking advisable Jul-Aug Last arrival 20.00hrs Last departure noon

Extensive rural views towards the rugged north Cornish coast can be enjoyed from this slightly sloping and sheltered park. Toilet facilities are to a very good standard. The site is handy for the ancient town of Camelford, while various beaches are within a 6-mile drive. A 1.5-acre site with 20 touring pitches and 1 static.

**Leisure:**

**Facilities:**

**Services:** →

**Notes:** No pets allowed. Wi-fi Internet access

### ►►► 70% Lakefield Caravan Park
*(SX095853)*
Lower Pendavey Farm PL32 9TX
☎ 01840 213279
**email:** lakefield@pendavey.fsnet.co.uk
**web:** www.lakefieldcaravanpark.co.uk
**Dir:** *From A39 in Camelford turn right onto B3266, then right at T-junct, site 1.5m on left*

Open Etr or Apr-Oct Booking advisable Jul-Aug Last arrival 22.00hrs Last departure noon

Set in a rural location, this friendly park is part of a specialist equestrian centre, and offers good quality services. Riding lessons and hacks always available, with BHS qualified instructor. A 5-acre site with 40 touring pitches.

**Facilities:**
**Services:** → 
**Notes:** Own lake & full equestrian centre

CARLYON BAY MAP 02 SX05

### ►►►► 84% *Carlyon Bay Caravan & Camping Park* *(SX052526)*
Bethesda, Cypress Av PL25 3RE
☎ 01726 812735 01726 815496
**email:** holidays@carlyonbay.net
**web:** www.carlyonbay.net
**Dir:** *Off A390 W of St Blazey, turn left onto A3092 for Par, right in 0.5m. On private road to Carlyon Bay*

Open Etr-3 Oct (rs Etr-mid May & mid Sep-3 Oct swimming pool, take-away & shop closed) Booking advisable mid Jul-mid Aug Last arrival 21.00hrs Last departure 11.00hrs

An attractive, secluded site set amongst a belt of trees with background woodland. The spacious grassy park offers plenty of on-site attractions, with occasional family entertainment, and it is less than 0.5m from a sandy beach. The Eden Project is only 2m away. A 35-acre site with 180 touring pitches, 6 hardstandings.

**Leisure:**
**Facilities:**
**Services:** → 
**Notes:** Crazy golf, children's entertainment in Jul & Aug

*see advert on this page*

### ►►► 79% East Crinnis Camping & Caravan Park *(SX062528)*
Lantyan, East Crinnis PL24 2SQ
☎ 01726 813023 01726 813023
**email:** eastcrinnis@btconnect.com
**web:** www.crinniscamping.co.uk
**Dir:** *From A390 (Lostwithiel to St Austell) take A3082 signed Fowey at rdbt by Britannia Inn, site on left*
★ £8-£15 £8-£15 £8-£15

Open Etr-Oct Booking advisable Jul & Aug Last arrival 21.00hrs Last departure 11.00hrs

A small rural park with spacious pitches set in individual bays about one mile from the beaches at Carlyon Bay. The friendly owners keep the site very clean, and the Eden Project is just 2m away. A 2-acre site with 25 touring pitches, 6 hardstandings.

CONTINUED

## CARLYON BAY CONTINUED

**Leisure:**

**Facilities:**

**Services:** →

**Notes:** Dogs must be kept on leads at all times. Coarse fishing, wildlife & pond area with dog walk

## COVERACK MAP 02 SW71

### ►►► 75% Little Trevothan Caravan & Camping Park *(SW772179)*

Trevothan TR12 6SD

☎ 01326 280260

**email:** sales@littletrevothan.co.uk

**web:** www.littletrevothan.co.uk

**Dir:** *From A3083 onto B3293 signed Coverack, approx 2m after Goonhilly ESS right at Zoar Garage on unclass road. Across Downs approx 1m then take 3rd left. Site 0.5m on left*

Open Mar-Oct Booking advisable Aug Last arrival 21.00hrs Last departure noon

A secluded site near the unspoilt fishing village of Coverack, with a large recreation area. The nearby sandy beach has lots of rock pools for children to play in, and the many walks both from the park and the village offer stunning scenery. A 10.5-acre site with 70 touring pitches and 40 statics.

**Leisure:**

**Facilities:**

**Services:** →

**Notes:** Dogs must be kept on a lead & waste picked up

## CRACKINGTON HAVEN MAP 02 SX19

### ►►► 73% Hentervene Holiday Park *(SX155944)*

EX23 0LF

☎ 01840 230365

**email:** contact@hentervene.co.uk

**web:** www.hentervene.co.uk

**Dir:** *Exit A39 approx 10m SW of Bude (1.5m beyond Wainhouse Corner) onto B3263 signed Boscastle & Crackington Haven. 0.75m to Tresparret Posts junct, right signed Hentervene. Site 0.75 on right*

Open Mar-Oct Booking advisable BH & school hols Last arrival 21.00hrs Last departure 11.00hrs

This much improved park is set in a rural location a short drive from a golden sandy beach. It is in an Area of Outstanding Natural Beauty, and pitches are in paddocks which are bordered by mature hedges, with a small stream running past. Some pitches are on level terraces, and there are also hardstandings. A 4.5-acre site with 43 touring pitches, 9 hardstandings and 24 statics.

**Leisure:**

**Facilities:**

**Services:** →

**Notes:** Baby bathroom, microwave & freezer for campers

## CRANTOCK (NEAR NEWQUAY) MAP 02 SW76

### ►►►► 80% Trevella Tourist Park *(SW801599)*

The Best of British Touring and Holiday Parks — David Bellamy Conservation Award GOLD

TR8 5EW

☎ 01637 830308 📠 01637 830155

**email:** trevellapark@aol.com

**web:** www.trevella.co.uk

**Dir:** *Between Crantock & A3075*

Open Etr-Oct Booking advisable BH & Jul-Aug

A well established and very well run family site, with outstanding floral displays. Set in a rural area close to Newquay, this attractive park boasts three teeming fishing lakes for the experienced and novice angler, and a superb outdoor swimming pool and paddling area. All areas are neat and clean. A 15-acre site with 313 touring pitches, 53 hardstandings.

**Leisure:**

**Facilities:**

**Services:** →

**Notes:** Crazy golf, badminton

*see advert on page 65*

### ►►► 76% Crantock Plains Touring Park *(SW805589)*

TR8 5PH

☎ 01637 830955 & 831273

**web:** www.crantock-plains.co.uk

**Dir:** *Leave Newquay on A3075, take 3rd right signed to park & Crantock. Park on left in 0.75m on narrow road*

Open Etr-Oct Booking advisable Jul-Aug Last arrival 22.00hrs Last departure noon

A small rural park with pitches on either side of a narrow lane, surrounded by mature trees for shelter. The family-run park has modern toilet facilities appointed to a good standard. A 6-acre site with 60 touring pitches.

**Leisure:**

**Facilities:**

**Services:** →

**Notes:** No skateboards

### ►►► 82% Higher Moor *(SW782600)*

Treago Rd TR8 5QS

☎ 01637 830928

**Dir:** *Turn off A3075 (Newquay to Redruth road) for Crantock. Follow brown signs for Treago, site 200mtrs beyond Treago Farm*

Open Apr-Oct Booking advisable Jul-Aug Last arrival 23.00hrs Last departure 11.00hrs

On the edge of the extensive National Trust Cubert Common, this site is one of Cornwall's best kept secrets. It is tucked away from the main tourist areas, and has excellent toilet facilities. There are lovely beaches nearby. A 2-acre site with 22 touring pitches.

**Leisure:**

**Facilities:**

**Services:**

**Notes:** No cars by caravans

## NEW ►►► 71% Quarryfield Holiday Park

*(SW793608)*

TR8 5RJ

01637 872792 01637 872792

**email:** quarryfield@crantockcaravans.arangehome.co.uk

**web:** www.quarryfield.co.uk

**Dir:** *From A3075 (Newquay-Redruth road) follow Crantock signs. Site signed*

£11-£15 £11-£15 £11-£15

Open Etr to end Oct (rs May/Sep pool closed) Booking advisable all year Last arrival 23.00hrs Last departure 10.00hrs

This park has a private path leading to the golden sand and dunes at Crantock Beach about 10 minutes away, and is within easy reach of all that Newquay has to offer the family. The park has a new toilet block, and offers plenty of amenities. A 10-acre site with 145 touring pitches and 43 statics.

**Leisure:**

**Facilities:**

**Services:**

**Notes:** No campfires, quiet after 22.30

## ►►► 81% Treago Farm Caravan Site

*(SW782601)*

TR8 5QS

01637 830277 01637 830277

**email:** treagofarm@aol.com

**web:** www.treagofarm.co.uk

**Dir:** *From A3075 (W of Newquay) turn right for Crantock. Site signed beyond village*

Open mid May-mid Sep (rs Apr-mid May & Oct no shop or bar) Booking advisable Jun-Aug Last arrival 22.00hrs Last departure 18.00hrs

A grass site in open farmland in a south-facing sheltered valley. This friendly family park has direct access to Crantock and Polly Joke beaches, National Trust land and many natural beauty spots. A 5-acre site with 90 touring pitches and 10 statics.

**Leisure:**

**Facilities:**

**Services:**

### CUBERT MAP 02 SW75

## ►►► 78% Cottage Farm Touring Park

*(SW786589)*

Treworgans TR8 5HH

01637 831083

**web:** www.cottagefarmpark.co.uk

**Dir:** *From A392 towards Newquay, left onto A3075 towards Redruth. In 2m turn right signed for Cubert, right again in 1.5m signed Crantock and left in 0.5m*

★ £10-£12 £10-£12 £10-£12

Open Apr-Oct Booking advisable late Jul-Aug Last arrival 22.30hrs Last departure noon

A small grassy touring park nestling in the tiny hamlet of Treworgans, in sheltered countryside close to a lovely beach at Holywell Bay. This quiet family-run park boasts very good quality facilities. A 2-acre site with 45 touring pitches, 2 hardstandings and 1 static.

**Facilities:**

**Services:**

**Notes:** No pets

### EDGCUMBE MAP 02 SW73

## ►►► 73% Retanna Holiday Park *(SW711327)*

TR13 OEJ

01326 340643 01326 340643

**email:** retannaholpark@lineone.net

**web:** www.retanna.co.uk

**Dir:** *100mtrs off A394, signed*

★ £11-£15 £11-£15 £11-£15

Open Apr-Sep extra toilet blocks open Aug. Booking advisable Jul & Aug Last arrival 21.00hrs Last departure noon

A small family-owned and run park in a rural location midway between Falmouth and Helston. Its well-sheltered grassy pitches make this an ideal location for visiting the lovely beaches and towns nearby. An 8-acre site with 24 touring pitches, 2 hardstandings and 29 statics.

**Leisure:**

**Facilities:**

**Services:**

**Notes:** No dogs allowed during school holidays. Free use of fridge/freezer in laundry room

ENGLAND

## FALMOUTH MAP 02 SW83

### ►►► 74% Pennance Mill Farm Touring Park *(SW792307)*

Maenporth TR11 5HJ

☎ 01326 317431 01326 317431

**web:** www.pennancemill.co.uk

**Dir:** *From A39 (Truro-Falmouth) follow brown camping signs towards Maenporth Beach. At Hill Head rdbt take 2nd exit for Maenporth Beach*

Open Etr-Xmas Booking advisable Last arrival 22.00hrs Last departure 10.00hrs

Set approximately half a mile from the safe, sandy Bay of Maenporth this is a mainly level, grassy park in a rural location sheltered by mature trees and shrubs and divided into three meadows. It has a modern toilet block. A 6-acre site with 75 touring pitches, 8 hardstandings and 4 statics.

**Leisure:**

**Facilities:**

**Services:**

**Notes:**

### ►► 78% Tregedna Farm Touring Caravan & Tent Park *(SW785305)*

Maenporth TR11 5HL

☎ 01326 250529

**email:** enquiries@tregednafarmholidays.co.uk

**web:** www.tregednafarmholidays.co.uk

**Dir:** *Take A39 from Truro to Falmouth. Turn right at Hill Head rdbt. Site 2.5m on right*

Open Apr-Sep Booking advisable Last arrival 22.00hrs Last departure 13.00hrs

Set in the picturesque Maen Valley, this gently-sloping, south-facing park is part of a 100-acre farm. It is surrounded by beautiful wooded countryside just minutes from the beach, with spacious pitches and well-kept facilities. A 12-acre site with 40 touring pitches.

**Leisure:**

**Facilities:**

**Services:**

**Notes:** One dog only per pitch

## FOWEY MAP 02 SX15

### ►►► 70% *Penhale Caravan & Camping Park* *(SX104526)*

DAVID BELLAMY CONSERVATION AWARD BRONZE

PL23 1JU

☎ 01726 833425 01726 833425

**email:** info@penhale-fowey.co.uk

**web:** www.penhale-fowey.co.uk

**Dir:** *Off A3082, 0.5m before junct with B3269*

Open Etr/Apr-Oct Booking advisable BH, Jul-Aug

Set on a working farm 1.5m from a sandy beach and the town of Fowey, this grassy park has stunning coastal and country views. Pitches are well spaced, and there is an indoor room for wet weather. A 4.5-acre site with 56 touring pitches and 15 statics.

**Leisure:**

**Facilities:**

**Services:**

### ►►► 79% Penmarlam Caravan & Camping Park *(SX134526)*

Bodinnick PL23 1LZ

☎ 01726 870088 01726 870082

**email:** info@penmarlampark.co.uk

**web:** www.penmarlampark.co.uk

**Dir:** *From A390 at East Taphouse take B3359 signed Looe & Polperro. Follow signs for Bodinnick & Fowey, via ferry. Site on right at entrance to Bodinnick*

★ £12-£18 £12-£18 £12-£18

Open Etr & Apr-Oct Booking advisable BH, Jul-Aug Last departure noon

A tranquil park set above the Fowey Estuary in an Area of Outstanding Natural Beauty, with access to the water. Pitches are level, and sheltered by trees and bushes in two paddocks; the toilets are well maintained. A 4-acre site with 65 touring pitches and 1 static.

**Facilities:**

**Services:** →

**Notes:** Wi-fi. Private slipway, small boat storage

## NEW ►► 74% Polglaze *(SX107529)*

Polglaze Farm PL23 1JZ

☎ 01726 833642

**email:** bookings@polglaze.co.uk

**web:** www.polglaze.co.uk

**Dir:** *1m from Fowey on B3269 towards Bodmin*

★ £6-£8 £6-£8 £6-£8

Open May-Oct Booking advisable Last arrival 21.00hrs Last departure noon

Set off the beaten track just a few minutes outside Fowey, a peaceful campsite in an Area of Outstanding Natural Beauty. Pitches can be found in a paddock or amongst the trees, and the toilet facilities are modern and well maintained. A 2.5-acre site with 30 touring pitches, 1 hardstanding and 1 static.

**Facilities:**

**Services:** →

**Notes:** No unaccompanied persons under 21, groups by prior agreement. Local bus service

## GOONHAVERN MAP 02 SW75

*see also Rejerrah*

### ►►►► 82% Penrose Farm Touring Park *(SW795534)*

TR4 9QF

☎ 01872 573185 01872 573185

**web:** www.penrosefarm.co.uk

**Dir:** *From Exeter take A30, past Bodmin and Indian Queens. Just after Wind Farm take B3285 towards Perranporth, site on left on entering Goonhavern*

Open Apr-Oct Booking advisable Jul & Aug Last arrival 21.30hrs

A quiet sheltered park set in five paddocks divided by hedges and shrubs, only a short walk from the village. Lovely floral displays enhance the park's appearance, and the grass and hedges are neatly trimmed. Four family rooms are very popular, and there is a good laundry. A 9-acre site with 100 touring pitches, 8 hardstandings and 3 statics.

**Leisure:**

**Facilities:**

**Services:** →

**Notes:** No skateboards/rollerskates. Families & couples only

*See advertisement under PERRANPORTH*



### ►►►► 80% Silverbow Park *(SW782531)*

GOLD

Perranwell TR4 9NX

☎ 01872 572347 01872 572347

**web:** www.chycor.co.uk/parks/silverbow

**Dir:** *Adjacent to A3075, 0.5m S of village*

★ £10-£20 £10-£20 £10-£20

Open May-mid Sep (rs mid Sep-Oct & Etr-mid May swimming pool & shop closed) Booking advisable Jun-Sep Last arrival 22.00hrs Last departure 10.30hrs

This park has a quiet garden atmosphere, and appeals to families with young children. The landscaped grounds and good quality toilet facilities - including four family rooms - are maintained to a very high standard with attention paid to detail. A 14-acre site with 100 touring pitches, 2 hardstandings and 15 statics.

**Leisure:**

**Facilities:**

**Services:** →

**Notes:** No cycling, no skateboards. Short mat bowls rink

*see advert on this page*

## GOONHAVERN CONTINUED

### ►►► 73% **Roseville Holiday Park**

*(SW787540)*
TR4 9LA
☎ 01872 572448 01872 572448
**web:** www.rosevilleholidaypark.co.uk
**Dir:** *From mini-rdbt in Goonhavern follow B3285 towards Perranporth, site 0.5m on right*

Open Whit-Oct (rs Apr-Jul, Sep-Oct shop closed) Booking advisable Jul-Aug Last arrival 21.30hrs Last departure 11.00hrs

A family park set in a rural location with sheltered grassy pitches, some gently sloping. The toilet facilities are modern, and there is an attractive outdoor swimming pool complex. Approximately 2 miles from the long sandy beach at Perranporth. An 8-acre site with 95 touring pitches and 5 statics.

**Leisure:**
**Facilities:**
**Services:** →
**Notes:** Families only site. Off-licence in shop

### ►►► 74% **Sunny Meadows Tourist Park**

*(SW782542)*
Rosehill TR4 9JT
☎ 01872 572548 & 571333 01872 571491
**Dir:** *From A30 onto B3285 signed Perranporth. At Goonhavern turn left at T-junct, then right at rdbt to Perranporth. Site on left*

Open Etr-Oct Booking advisable mid Jul-Aug

A gently sloping park, in a peaceful rural location, with mostly level pitches set into three small hedge-lined paddocks. Run by a friendly family, the park is just two miles from the long sandy beach at Perranporth. A 14.5-acre site with 60 touring pitches, 1 hardstanding.

**Leisure:**
**Facilities:**
**Services:** →
**Notes:** Dogs must be kept on leads. Pool table & family TV room

*See advertisement under PERRANPORTH*

### ►► 76% ***Little Treamble Farm Touring Park*** *(SW785560)*

Rose TR4 9PR
☎ 01872 573823 & 0797 1070760
**email:** info@treamble.co.uk
**web:** www.treamble.co.uk
**Dir:** *A30 onto B3285 signed Perranporth. Approx 0.5m right into Scotland Rd signed Newquay. Approx 2m to T-junct, right onto A3075 signed Newquay. 0.25m left at Rejerrah sign. Site signed 0.75m on right*

Open all year Booking advisable BH, Jun-Aug Last departure noon

This site is set in a quiet rural location with extensive countryside views across an undulating valley. There is a small toilet block and a well-stocked shop. This working farm is next to a Caravan Club site. A 1.5-acre site with 20 touring pitches.

**Facilities:**
**Services:** →
**Notes:**

## GORRAN MAP 02 SW94

### ►►► 75% **Treveague Farm Caravan & Camping Site** *(SX002410)*

PL26 6NY
☎ 01726 842295 01726 842295
**email:** treveague@btconnect.com
**web:** www.infotreveaguefarm.co.uk
**Dir:** *From St Austell take B3273 towards Mevagissey, past Pentewan at top of hill, turn right signed Gorran. Past Heligan Gardens towards Gorran Churchtown. Follow brown tourist signs from fork in road*

★ £8-£15 £8-£15 £6-£12

Open Apr-Oct Booking advisable at all times Last arrival 21.00hrs Last departure noon

Spectacular panoramic coastal views are a fine feature of this rural park, which is well equipped with modern facilities. A stone-faced toilet block with a Cornish slate roof is an attractive and welcome feature of the park. A footpath leads to the fishing village of Gorran Haven in one direction, and the secluded sandy Vault Beach in the other. A 4-acre site with 40 touring pitches.

**Leisure:**
**Facilities:**
**Services:** →
**Notes:** Wi-fi. Bird hide with observation cameras

### ►►► 74% **Treveor Farm Caravan & Camping Site** *(SW988418)*

PL26 6LW
☎ 01726 842387 01726 842387
**email:** info@treveorfarm.co.uk
**web:** www.treveorfarm.co.uk
**Dir:** *From St Austell bypass left onto B3273 for Mevagissey. On hilltop before descent to village turn right on unclass road for Gorran. Right in 3.5m, site on right*

★ £6.50-£15 £6.50-£15 £6-£13

Open Apr-Oct Booking advisable Last arrival 20.00hrs Last departure noon

A small family-run camping park set on a working farm, with grassy pitches backing onto mature hedging. This quiet park with good facilities is close to beaches, and offers a large coarse fishing lake. A 4-acre site with 50 touring pitches.

**Leisure:**

**Facilities:**

**Services:**

**Notes:**

## GORRAN HAVEN MAP 02 SX04

### ►► 67% Trelispen Caravan & Camping Park *(SX008421)*

PL26 6NT

☎ 01726 843501 01726 843501

**email:** trelispen@care4free.net

**web:** www.trelispen.co.uk

**Dir:** *B3273 from St Austell towards Mevagissey, on hilltop at x-roads before descent into Mevagissey turn right on unclass road to Gorran. Through village, 2nd right towards Gorran Haven, site signed on left in 250mtrs*

★ £12-£18 £12-£18 £12-£18

Open Etr & Apr-Oct Booking advisable Last arrival 22.00hrs Last departure noon

A quiet rural site set in three paddocks, and sheltered by mature trees and hedges. The simple toilets have plenty of hot water, and there is a small laundry. Sandy beaches, pubs and shops are nearby, and Mevagissey is two miles away. A 2-acre site with 40 touring pitches.

**Leisure:**

**Facilities:**

**Services:**

**Notes:** 30-acre nature reserve may be visited

## GWITHIAN MAP 02 SW54

### ►►► 80% Gwithian Farm Campsite *(SW586412)*

Gwithian Farm TR27 5BX

☎ 01736 753127

**email:** camping@gwithianfarm.co.uk

**web:** www.gwithianfarm.co.uk

**Dir:** *Exit A30 at Hayle rdbt, take 4th exit signed Hayle, 100mtrs. At 1st mini-rdbt turn right onto B3301 signed Portreath. Site 2m on left on entering village*

£13-£21 £13-£21 £10-£18

Open 31 Mar-1 Oct Booking advisable Jul-Aug Last arrival 22.00hrs Last departure 17.00hrs

An unspoilt site located behind the sand dunes of Gwithian's golden beach, which can be reached directly by footpath from the site. The site boasts a superb toilet block with excellent facilities including a bathroom and baby-changing unit. There is a good pub opposite. A 7.5-acre site with 87 touring pitches, 4 hardstandings.

**Facilities:**

**Services:**

**Notes:** Surf board & wet suit hire

## HAYLE MAP 02 SW53

### 75% St Ives Bay Holiday Park *(SW577398)*

73 Loggans Rd, Upton Towans TR27 5BH

☎ 01736 752274 01736 754523

**email:** stivesbay@btconnect.com

**web:** www.stivesbay.co.uk

**Dir:** *Leave A30 at Hayle then immediate right onto B3301 at mini-rdbts. Park entrance 0.5m on left*

Open May-1 Oct (rs Etr-1 May & 25 Sep-25 Oct no entertainment, food & bar service) Booking advisable Jan-Mar Last arrival 23.00hrs Last departure 09.00hrs

An extremely well maintained holiday park with a relaxed atmosphere, built on sand dunes adjacent to a 3-mile-long beach. The touring section forms a number of separate locations around this extensive park. This park is specially geared for families and couples, and as well as the large indoor swimming pool there are two pubs with seasonal entertainment. A 90-acre site with 240 touring pitches and 250 statics.

**Leisure:**

**Facilities:**

**Services:**

**Notes:** Crazy golf, video room

### ►►► 76% Atlantic Coast Caravan Park *(NW580400)*

SILVER

53 Upton Towans, Gwithian TR27 5BL

☎ 01736 752071 01736 758100

**email:** enquiries@atlanticcoast-caravanpark.co.uk

**web:** www.coastdaleparks.co.uk

**Dir:** *From A30 into Hayle, turn right at double rdbt. Park 1.5m on left*

Open Etr-end Oct Booking advisable Aug Last arrival 21.00hrs Last departure 11.00hrs

Fringed by the sand-dunes of St Ives Bay and close to the golden sands of Gwithian Beach, the small, friendly touring area offers all fully serviced pitches. There's freshly baked bread, a takeaway and a bar next door. This park is ideally situated for visitors to enjoy the natural coastal beauty and attractions of south-west Cornwall. A 4.5-acre site with 15 touring pitches and 50 statics.

**Facilities:**

**Services:**

**Notes:** Couples & families only

ENGLAND

HAYLE CONTINUED

### ►►► 75% Higher Trevaskis Caravan Park (SW611381)

Gwinear Rd, Connor Downs TR27 5JQ
☎ 01209 831736

**Dir:** *At Hayle rdbt on A30 take 1st exit signed Connor Downs, in 1m turn right signed Carnhell Green. Site 0.75m just past level crossing*

★ £10-£22 £10-£22 £10-£22

Open mid Apr-Sep Booking advisable May-Sep Last arrival 20.00hrs Last departure 10.30hrs

An attractive paddocked park in a sheltered rural position with views towards St Ives. This secluded park is personally run by owners who keep it quiet and welcoming. Three unisex showers are a great hit with visitors. Fluent German spoken. A 6.5-acre site with 82 touring pitches, 3 hardstandings.

**Leisure:**

**Facilities:**

**Services:**

**Notes:** Max speed 5mph, max 2 dogs, no dangerous dogs, balls on field only. Football/sport field

### ►►► 66% Parbola Holiday Park (SW612366)

Wall, Gwinear TR27 5LE
☎ 01209 831503 01209 831503
**email:** bookings@parbola.co.uk
**web:** www.parbola.co.uk

**Dir:** *At Hayle rdbt on A30 take Connor Downs exit. In 1m turn right signed Carnhell Green. In village turn right to Wall. Site in village on left*

Open Etr-Sep (rs Etr-end of Jun & Sep shop closed, pool unheated) Booking advisable Jul-Aug Last arrival 21.00hrs Last departure 10.00hrs

Pitches are provided in both woodland and open areas in this spacious park in Cornish downland. The park is centrally located for touring the seaside resorts and towns in the area, especially nearby Hayle with its three miles of golden sands. A 16.5-acre site with 110 touring pitches and 28 statics.

**Leisure:**

**Facilities:**

**Services:**

**Notes:** Dogs not allowed Jul-Aug. Crazy golf & table tennis, giant chess & draughts

### ►►► 74% Treglisson Camping & Caravan Park (SW581367)

Wheal Alfred Rd TR27 5JT
☎ 01736 753141
**email:** enquiries@treglisson.co.uk
**web:** www.treglisson.co.uk

**Dir:** *4th exit off rdbt on A30 at Hayle. 100mtrs, turn left at 1st mini-rdbt. 1.5km past golf course, site sign on left*

Open Etr-Oct Booking advisable Jul-Aug Last arrival 20.00hrs Last departure 11.00hrs

A small secluded site in a peaceful wooded meadow, a former apple and pear orchard. This quiet rural site has a well-planned modern toilet block and level grass pitches, and is just two miles from the glorious beach at Hayle with its vast stretch of golden sand. A 3-acre site with 30 touring pitches.

**Leisure:** **Facilities:**

**Services:**

**Notes:** Max 6 people to a pitch, dogs must be on lead at all times. Tourist information, milk deliveries

## HELSTON — MAP 02 SW62

*see also Ashton*

### ►►► 75% *Lower Polladras Touring Park* (SW617308)

DAVID BELLAMY CONSERVATION AWARD SILVER

Carleen, Breage TR13 9NX
☎ 01736 762220 01736 762220
**email:** lowerpolladras@btinternet.com
**web:** www.lower-polladras.co.uk

**Dir:** *From Helston take A394 then B3302 (Hayle road) at Hilltop Garage, 2nd left to Carleen, site 2m on right*

Open Apr-Oct Booking advisable Jul-Aug Last arrival 22.00hrs Last departure noon

A rural park with extensive views of surrounding fields, appealing to families who enjoy the countryside. The planted trees and shrubs are maturing, and help to divide the area into paddocks with spacious grassy pitches. A 4-acre site with 60 touring pitches, 13 hardstandings.

**Leisure:** **Facilities:**

**Services:**

**Notes:** Caravan and boat storage area

### ►►► 73% Poldown Caravan Park

*(SW629298)*
Poldown, Carleen TR13 9NN
☎ 01326 574560
**email:** stay@poldown.co.uk
**web:** www.poldown.co.uk
**Dir:** *From Helston follow Penzance signs for 1m then right onto B3302 to Hayle, 2nd left to Carleen, 0.5m to site*

★ £8.50-£12.50 £8.50-£12.50 £8.50-£12.50

Open Apr-Sep Booking advisable Jul-Aug Last arrival 22.00hrs Last departure noon

A small, quiet site set in attractive countryside with bright toilet facilities. All of the level grass pitches have electricity, and the sunny park is sheltered by mature trees and shrubs. A 2-acre site with 13 touring pitches and 7 statics.

**Leisure:**
**Facilities:**
**Services:**
**Notes:**

### ►►► 76% Skyburriowe Farm *(SW698227)*

Garras TR12 6LR
☎ 01326 221646
**email:** bkbenney@hotmail.co.uk
**web:** www.skyburriowefarm.co.uk
**Dir:** *From Helston take A3083 to The Lizard. After Culdrose naval airbase continue straight at rdbt, after 1m left at Skyburriowe Lane sign. In 0.5m right at sign Skyburriowe B&B/Campsite sign. Continue past bungalow to farmhouse. Site on left.*

£8-£16 £8-£16 £6-£14

Open Apr-Oct Booking advisable Last arrival 22.00hrs Last departure 11.00hrs

A leafy no-through road leads to this picturesque farm park in a rural location on the Lizard Peninsula. The facilities are fairly basic, but most pitches have electricity. There are some beautiful coves and beaches nearby. A 4-acre site with 30 touring pitches.

**Facilities:**
**Services:**
**Notes:** Dogs must be kept on leads, quiet after 23.00hrs

## HOLYWELL BAY MAP 02 SW75

### 71% Holywell Bay Holiday Park *(SW773582)*

TR8 5PR
☎ 01637 871111 & 0871 641 0199
01637 850818
**email:** enquiries@parkdeanholidays.co.uk
**web:** www.parkdeanholidays.co.uk
**Dir:** *Leave A30 onto A392, take A3075 signed Redruth, then right in 2m signed Holywell/Cubert. Follow road through Cubert past Trevornick to park on left*

★ £7-£25 £10-£28 £7-£25

Open Mar-Oct Booking advisable high season Last arrival 21.00hrs Last departure 10.00hrs

CONTINUED

ENGLAND

## HOLYWELL BAY CONTINUED

Close to lovely beaches in a rural location, this level grassy park borders on National Trust land, and is only a short distance from the Cornish Coastal Path. The park provides a popular entertainment programme for the whole family, and there is an outdoor pool with a waterslide, children's clubs and evening entertainment. Newquay is just a few miles away. A 40-acre site with 53 touring pitches and 162 statics.

**Leisure:**

**Facilities:**

**Services:** →

**Notes:** Family entertainment, surf school

### 92% Trevornick Holiday Park (SW776586)

TR8 5PW

☎ 01637 830531 01637 831000

**email:** info@trevornick.co.uk

**web:** www.trevornick.co.uk

**Dir:** *3m from Newquay off A3075 towards Redruth. Follow Cubert & Holywell Bay signs*

★ £11-£19.30 £11-£19.30 £11-£19.30

Open Etr & mid May-mid Sep Booking advisable Jul-Aug Last arrival 21.00hrs Last departure 10.00hrs

A large seaside holiday complex with excellent facilities and amenities. There is plenty of entertainment including a children's club and an evening cabaret, adding up to a full holiday experience for all the family. A sandy beach is a 15-minute footpath walk away. The park has 68 ready-erected tents for hire. A 20-acre site with 593 touring pitches, 6 hardstandings.

**Leisure:** **Facilities:**

**Services:** →

**Notes:** Families and couples only. Fishing, golf course.

*see advert on page 61*

## INDIAN QUEENS — MAP 02 SW95

### ►►► 70% *Gnome World Caravan & Camping Site* (SW890599)

Moorland Rd TR9 6HN

☎ 01726 860812 01726 860812

**Dir:** *Signed from slip road at A30 & A39 rdbt in village of Indian Queens - park on old A30, now unclassified road*

Open all year (rs Nov-Mar statics closed) Booking advisable Jul-Aug Last arrival 22.00hrs Last departure noon

Set in open countryside, this spacious park is set on level grassy land only 0.5m from the A30 (Cornwall's main artery route), in a central holiday location for touring the county. There are no narrow lanes to negotiate. A 4.5-acre site with 50 touring pitches and 60 statics.

**Leisure:**

**Facilities:**

**Services:** →

**Notes:** Dogs must be kept on leads. Nature trail

*see advert on opposite page*

## JACOBSTOW — MAP 02 SX19

### ►►► 72% *Edmore Tourist Park* (SX184955)

Edgar Rd, Wainhouse Corner EX23 0BJ

☎ 01840 230467 01840 230467

**email:** enquiries@cornwallvisited.co.uk

**web:** www.cornwallvisited.co.uk

**Dir:** *Leave A39 at Wainhouse Corner onto Edgar Rd, site signed on right in 200yds*

Open 1 wk before Etr-Oct Booking advisable BH & school hols Last arrival 21.00hrs Last departure noon

A quiet family-owned site in a rural location with extensive views, set close to the sandy surfing beaches of Bude, and the unspoilt sandy beach and rock pools at Crackington Haven. Friendly owners keep all facilities in a very good condition. A 3-acre site with 28 touring pitches.

**Leisure:**

**Facilities:**

**Services:**

**Notes:**

## KENNACK SANDS — MAP 02 SW71

### ►►► 70% Chy-Carne Holiday Park (SW725164)

Kuggar, Ruan Minor TR12 7LX

☎ 01326 290200 & 291161

**email:** enquiries@chy-carne.co.uk

**web:** www.chy-carne.co.uk

**Dir:** *From A3083 turn left on B3293 after Culdrose Naval Air Station. At Goonhilly ESS right onto unclass road signed Kennack Sands. Left in 3m at junct*

★ £14-£16.50 £14-£16.50 £10-£13

Open Etr-Oct Booking advisable Aug Last arrival dusk

Small but spacious park in quiet, sheltered spot, with extensive sea and coastal views from the grassy touring area. A village pub with a restaurant is a short walk by footpath from the touring area, and a sandy beach is less than 0.5 miles away. A 6-acre site with 14 touring pitches and 18 statics.

**Leisure:**

**Facilities:**

**Services:** →

*see advert on opposite page*

## ►►► 72% Gwendreath Farm Holiday Park

*(SW738168)*

TR12 7LZ

☎ 01326 290666

**email:** tom.gibson@virgin.net

**web:** www.tomandlinda.co.uk

**Dir:** *From A3083 turn left past Culdrose Naval Air Station onto B3293. Right past Goonhilly Earth Station signed Kennack Sands, left in 1m. At end of lane turn right over cattle grid. Right, through Seaview to 2nd reception*

Open Etr-Oct Booking advisable all times Last arrival 21.00hrs Last departure 10.00hrs

A grassy park in an elevated position with extensive sea and coastal views, and the beach just a short walk through the woods. Campers can use the bar and takeaway at an adjoining site. A 5-acre site with 10 touring pitches and 21 statics.

**Leisure:**

**Facilities:**

**Services:** →

**Notes:**

## KENNACK SANDS CONTINUED

### ►►► 74% **Silver Sands Holiday Park** *(SW727166)*

Gwendreath TR12 7LZ

☎ 01326 290631 01326 290631

**email:** enquiries@silversandsholidaypark.co.uk

**web:** www.silversandsholidaypark.co.uk

**Dir:** *From Helston follow signs to Goonhilly. 300yds after Goonhilly Earth Station turn right at x-roads signed Kennack Sands, 1.5m, left at Gwendreath sign, park 1m*

★ £11-£17 £11-£17 £10-£14

Open Etr-Sep Booking advisable Jul-Aug Last arrival 20.00hrs Last departure 11.00hrs

A small park in a remote location, with individually screened pitches providing sheltered suntraps. A footpath through the woods from the family-owned park leads to the beach and the local pub. A 9-acre site with 34 touring pitches and 16 statics.

**Leisure:**

**Facilities:**

**Services:**

**Notes:** No groups. First Aider on site

## KILKHAMPTON MAP 02 SS21

### ►► 72% **Tamar Lake** *(SS288118)*

Upper Tamar Lake

☎ 01288 321712

**email:** info@swlakestrust.org.uk

**web:** www.swlakestrust.org.uk

**Dir:** *From A39 at Kilkhampton onto B3254, left in 0.5m onto unclass road, follow signs approx 4m to site*

★ £10

Open 31 Mar-Oct Booking advisable

A well-trimmed, slightly sloping site overlooking the lake and surrounding countryside, with several signed walks. The site benefits from the excellent facilities provided for the watersports centre and coarse anglers, with a rescue launch on the lake when the flags are flying. A good family site, with Bude's beaches and surfing waves only 8m away. A 2-acre site with 36 touring pitches.

**Leisure:**

**Facilities:**

**Services:**

**Notes:** Dogs must be kept on a lead. Watersports centre, canoeing, sailing, windsurfing

## LANDRAKE MAP 03 SX36

### ►►► 82% **Dolbeare Caravan & Camping Park** *(SX363616)*

St Ive Rd PL12 5AF

☎ 01752 851332 01752 547871

**email:** reception@dolbeare.co.uk

**web:** www.dolbeare.co.uk

**Dir:** *A38 to Landrake, 4m W of Saltash. At footbridge over A38 turn N, follow signs to site (0.75m from A38)*

Open all year Booking advisable peak periods only Last arrival 23.00hrs Last departure noon

A mainly level grass site with trees and bushes set in meadowland. The keen and friendly owners set high standards, and the park is always neat and clean. A 9-acre site with 60 touring pitches, 54 hardstandings.

**Leisure:**

**Facilities:**

**Services:**

**Notes:** Wi-fi, Information centre, Off licence

*see advert on opposite page*

## LAND'S END MAP 02 SW32

### ►►► 87% **Sea View Holiday Park** *(SW357254)*

TR19 7AD

☎ 01736 871266 01736 871190

**email:** bookings@seaview.co.uk

**web:** www.seaview.org.uk

**Dir:** *From Penzance follow A30/Land's End signs to Sennen, through village until First & Last pub, site on left*

Open Mar-Nov Booking advisable Jul-Aug Last arrival 18.30hrs Last departure 10.00hrs

This park is set in unspoilt countryside with views of the sea. A Scandanavian-style timber building houses a children's playroom with soft toy play zone, a snack/soft drinks bar, and a restaurant and lounge bar. The outdoor swimming pool and sun terrace enjoy the wonderful views. An 11.5-acre site with 120 touring pitches, 6 hardstandings and 95 statics.

**Leisure:**

**Facilities:**

**Services:**

**Notes:** Family park, dogs only with permission. Bowling alley, Space maze

ENGLAND

## LANIVET MAP 02 SX06

### ►►► 78% Mena Caravan & Camping Site

*(SW041626)*
Mena Farm PL30 5HW
☎ 01208 831845
**email:** mena@campsitesincornwall.co.uk
**web:** www.campsitesincornwall.co.uk
**Dir:** *Exit A30 at Innes Downs rdbt onto A391 signed St Austell. 0.5m 1st left, then 0.75m turn right (before bridge) signed Fowey/Lanhydrock. 0.5m to staggered junct & monument stone, sharp right, 0.5m down hill, right into site*

£9-£11 £9-£11 £9-£19

Open Etr-Sep Booking advisable Jul-Aug Last arrival 22.00hrs Last departure noon

Set in a secluded, elevated location with high hedges for shelter, and plenty of peace. This grassy site is about 4 miles from the Eden Project, and midway between north and south coasts. On site is a small coarse fishing lake. A 4-acre site with 25 touring pitches and 2 statics.

**Leisure:**
**Facilities:**
**Services:**
**Notes:** Wi-fi, small fishing lake

## LEEDSTOWN (NEAR HAYLE) MAP 02 SW63

### ►►►► 74% Calloose Caravan & Camping Park *(SW597352)*

TR27 5ET
☎ 01736 850431 & 0800 328 7589 01736 850431
**email:** calloose@hotmail.com
**web:** www.calloose.co.uk
**Dir:** *From Hayle take B3302 to Leedstown, turn left opposite village hall, before entering village. Park 0.5m on left at bottom of hill*

★ £12-£18 £12-£18 £12-£18

Open Mar-Nov, Xmas & New Year (rs Mar-mid May & late Sep-Nov swimming pool closed) Booking advisable Etr, May BH & Jun-Aug Last arrival 22.00hrs Last departure 11.00hrs

A comprehensively equipped leisure park in a remote rural setting in a small river valley. This very good park is busy and bustling, and offers bright and clean facilities. A 12.5-acre site with 120 touring pitches and 17 statics.

**Leisure:**
**Facilities:**
**Services:**
**Notes:** Crazy golf, skittle alley

## LOOE MAP 02 SX25

### 68% Tencreek Holiday Park

*(SX233525)*
Polperro Rd PL13 2JR
☎ 01503 262447 01503 262760
**email:** reception@tencreek.co.uk
**web:** www.dolphinholidays.co.uk
**Dir:** *Take A387 1.25m from Looe. Site on left*

★ £9.20-£18 £9.20-£18 £9.20-£18

Open all year Booking advisable Jul & Aug Last arrival 23.00hrs Last departure 10.00hrs

Occupying a lovely position with extensive countryside and sea views, this holiday centre is in a rural spot but close to Looe and Polperro. There is a full family entertainment programme, with indoor and outdoor swimming pools, an adventure playground and an exciting children's club. A 14-acre site with 254 touring pitches and 101 statics.

**Leisure:**
**Facilities:**
**Services:**
**Notes:** Families & couples only. Nightly entertainment, solarium, 45mtr pool flume

*see advert on page 56*

ENGLAND

*LOOE* CONTINUED

### ►►►► 74% **Tregoad Park** *(SX272560)*

St Martin PL13 1PB

01503 262718 01503 264777

**email:** info@tregoadpark.co.uk

**web:** www.tregoadpark.co.uk

**Dir:** *Signed with direct access from B3253, or from E on A387 follow B3253 for 1.75m towards Looe. Site on left*

Open all year Bistro open in high and mid season Booking advisable Jul & Aug Last arrival 20.00hrs Last departure 11.00hrs

A smart terraced park with extensive sea and rural views, about 1.5m from Looe. All pitches are level, and the facilities are well maintained. There is a licensed bar with bar meals served in the conservatory. A 55-acre site with 200 touring pitches, 60 hardstandings and 3 statics.

**Leisure:**

**Facilities:**

**Services:**

**Notes:** Wi-fi, fishing lake, crazy golf, ball sports area

*see advert on opposite page*

### ►►► 80% **Camping Caradon Touring Park** *(SX218539)*

Trelawne PL13 2NA

01503 272388 01503 272858

**email:** enquiries@campingcaradon.co.uk

**web:** www.campingcaradon.co.uk

**Dir:** *Site signed from B3359 near junct with A387, between Looe and Polperro*

Open all year (rs Oct-Etr by booking only) Booking advisable Jul-Aug Last arrival 22.00hrs Last departure noon

Set in a quiet rural location between the popular coastal resorts of Looe and Polperro, this family-run park is just 1.5m from the beach at Talland Bay. The owners are continuing to improve the park. A 3.5-acre site with 85 touring pitches, 23 hardstandings.

**Leisure:**

**Facilities:**

**Services:**

### ►►► 77% **Polborder House Caravan & Camping Park** *(SX283557)*

Bucklawren Rd, St Martin PL13 1NZ

01503 240265

**email:** reception@peaceful-polborder.co.uk

**web:** www.peaceful-polborder.co.uk

**Dir:** *Approach Looe from E on A387, follow B3253 for 1m, left at Polborder & Monkey Sanctuary sign. Site 0.5m on right*

Open all year Booking advisable Jul-Aug Last arrival 22.00hrs Last departure 11.00hrs

A very neat and well-kept small grassy site on high ground above Looe in a peaceful rural setting. Friendly and enthusiastic owners. A 3.5-acre site with 31 touring pitches, 15 hardstandings and 5 statics.

**Leisure:** **Facilities:**

**Services:**

**Notes:** Dogs by prior notice. Info centre

### ►►► 74% ***Talland Caravan Park*** *(SX230516)*

Talland Bay PL13 2JA

01503 272715 01503 272224

**email:** tallandcaravan@btconnect.com

**web:** www.tallandcaravanpark.co.uk

**Dir:** *1m from A387 on unclass road to Talland Bay*

Open Apr-Oct Booking advisable school hols Last arrival 20.00hrs Last departure noon

Overlooking the sea just 300 yards from Talland Bay's two beaches, this quiet park has an elevated touring area with sea views. Surrounded by unspoilt countryside and with direct access to the coastal footpath, it is approximately halfway between Looe and Polperro. A 4-acre site with 80 touring pitches and 46 statics.

**Leisure:** **Facilities:**

**Services:**

### ►►► 78% ***Trelay Farmpark*** *(SX210544)*

Pelynt PL13 2JX

01503 220900 01503 220900

**email:** stay@trelay.co.uk

**web:** www.trelay.co.uk

**Dir:** *From A390 at East Taphouse, take B3359 S towards Looe. After Pelynt, site 0.5m on left*

Open Apr-Oct Booking advisable Jul & Aug Last arrival 21.00hrs Last departure noon

A small site with a friendly atmosphere set in a pretty rural area with extensive views. The good-size grass pitches are on slightly sloping ground; the toilets are immaculately kept. Looe and Polperro are 3 miles away. A 4.5-acre site with 55 touring pitches and 20 statics.

**Facilities:**

**Services:**

**Notes:** Baby bath & mat, fridge, freezer

ENGLAND

## LOSTWITHIEL MAP 02 SX15

### ►►► 77% Powderham Castle Holiday Park

*(SX083593)*

PL30 5BU

☎ 01208 872277 01208 871236

**email:** info@powderhamcastletouristpark.co.uk

**web:** www.powderhamcastletouristpark.co.uk

**Dir:** *1.5m SW of Lostwithiel on A390 turn right at brown/white sign in 400mtrs*

★ £11-£15 £11-£15 £11-£15

Open Etr or Apr-Oct Booking advisable Jul-Aug Last arrival 22.00hrs Last departure 11.30hrs

A grassy park set in attractive paddocks with mature trees. A gradual upgrading of facilities continues, and both buildings and grounds are carefully maintained. This park is ideally located for visiting the Eden Project, the nearby golden beaches and sailing at Fowey. A 12-acre site with 72 touring pitches, 12 hardstandings and 38 statics.

**Leisure:**

**Facilities:**

**Services:**

**Notes:** Badminton, soft tennis, putting green

## LUXULYAN MAP 02 SX05

### ►►► 75% Croft Farm Holiday Park *(SX044568)*

GOLD

PL30 5EQ

☎ 01726 850228 01726 850498

**email:** lynpick@ukonline.co.uk

**web:** www.croftfarm.co.uk

**Dir:** *Leave A30 at Bodmin for A391 towards St Austell. In 7m left at double rdbt onto unclass road towards Luxulyan/Eden Project, continue to T-junct, turn left signed Luxulyan. Park 1m on left. (NB Do not approach any other way as roads are very narrow)*

£10-£14.50 £10-£14.50 £10-£14.50

Open Etr-Oct Booking advisable Jul-Aug, BH & half term wks Last arrival 18.00hrs Last departure 11.00hrs

A peaceful, picturesque setting at the edge of a wooded valley, and only one mile from The Eden Project. A 10.5-acre site with 52 touring pitches, 20 hardstandings and 40 statics.

**Leisure:**

**Facilities:**

**Services:**

**Notes:** No skateboarding, ball games only in playing field, quiet between 23.00hrs-07.00hrs Woodland walk, crazy golf, information room

## MARAZION MAP 02 SW53

*see also St Hilary & Praa Sands*

### ►►► 76% Wheal Rodney Holiday Park

*(SW525315)*

Gwallon Ln TR17 0HL

☎ 01736 710605

**email:** reception@whealrodney.co.uk

**web:** www.whealrodney.co.uk

**Dir:** *Turn off A30 at Crowlas, signed Rospeath. Site 1.5m on right. From Marazion centre turn opposite Fire Engine Inn, site 500mtrs on left.*

Open Etr-Oct Booking advisable Xmas & Etr-Oct Last arrival 20.00hrs Last departure 11.00hrs

Set in a quiet rural location surrounded by farmland, with level grass pitches and well-kept facilities. Just half a mile away are the beach at Marazion and the causeway or ferry to St Michael's Mount. A cycle route is just 400yds away. A 2.5-acre site with 30 touring pitches.

**Leisure:**

**Facilities:**

**Services:**

**Notes:** Quiet after 22.00hrs, Wi-fi

## MAWGAN PORTH

### ►►►► 75% Sun Haven Valley Holiday Park *(SW861669)*

TR8 4BQ

☎ 01637 860373 01637 860373

**email:** sunhaven@sunhavenvalley.com

**web:** www.sunhavenvalley.com

**Dir:** *From B3276 in Newquay take Padstow road. Right onto unclass road just after shopping complex. Park in 1.75m*

Open Apr-Oct (rs Oct-Mar chalets only) Booking advisable Jul-Aug Last arrival 22.00hrs Last departure 10.30hrs

An attractive site with level pitches on the side of a river valley. The very high quality facilities include a TV lounge and a games room in a Swedish-style chalet, and a well-kept adventure playground. Trees and hedges fringe the park, and the ground is well drained. A 5-acre site with 118 touring pitches and 36 statics.

**Leisure:** **Facilities:**

**Services:**

**Notes:** Families and couples only

*See advert on page 64*

### ►►► 75% *Trevarrian Holiday Park*

*(SW853661)*
TR8 4AQ
☎ 01637 860381 & 0845 2255910
**email:** holiday@trevarrian.co.uk
**web:** www.trevarrian.co.uk

**Dir:** *From A39 at St Columb rdbt turn right onto A3059 towards Newquay. Fork right in approx 2m for St Mawgan onto B3276. Turn right, site on left*

Open Etr-Sep Booking advisable Jun-Aug Last arrival 22.00hrs Last departure 11.00hrs

A well-established and well-run holiday park overlooking Mawgan Porth beach. This park has a wide range of attractions including a free entertainment programme in peak season. A 7-acre site with 185 touring pitches.

**Leisure:**

**Facilities:**

**Services:**

**Notes:** Sports field, pitch 'n' putt

MEVAGISSEY MAP 02 SX04
*see also Gorran & Pentewan*

## PREMIER PARK

### ►►►►► 96% Seaview International Holiday Park *(SW990412)*

Boswinger PL26 6LL
☎ 01726 843425 01726 843358
**email:** holidays@seaviewinternational.com
**web:** www.seaviewinternational.com

**Dir:** *From St Austell take B3273 signed Mevagissey. Turn right before entering village. Follow brown tourist signs to site*

Open Mar-Oct Booking advisable Jul-Sep Last arrival 21.00hrs Last departure 10.00hrs

An attractive holiday park set in a beautiful environment overlooking Veryan Bay, with colourful landscaping including attractive flowers and shrubs. It continues to offer an outstanding holiday experience, with its luxury family pitches, super toilet facilities, takeaway, and shop. The beach and sea are just half a mile away. A 28-acre site with 189 touring pitches, 13 hardstandings and 38 statics.

**Leisure:**

**Facilities:**

**Services:** →

**Notes:** Restrictions on certain dog breeds, crazy golf, volleyball, badminton, scuba diving

*See advertisement in Preliminary Section, page 12*

### ►►► 72% Pensagillas Farm Touring C&C Park *(SW972467)*

Pensagillas Farm, Grampound TR2 4SR
☎ 01872 530808
**email:** info@pensagillas-park.co.uk
**web:** www.pensagillas-park.co.uk

**Dir:** *From St Austell take A390 towards Truro. 2-3m fork left onto B3287 signed Tregony. 2m to T-junct. Turn left. In 1m follow site signs*

£8-£15 £8-£15

Open all year Booking advisable Jul-Aug

Set in the heart of the Cornish countryside a few miles away from spectacular beaches and the beautiful fishing village of Mevagissey, this spacious grassy farm park with modern toilet facilities, has good on-site amenities including coarse fishing and an interesting farm trail. There is also a small bar, and a TV and games room. A 7-acre site with 50 touring pitches.

**Leisure:**

**Facilities:**

**Services:** →

## MULLION — MAP 02 SW61

### 74% Mullion Holiday Park

(SW699182)

Ruan Minor TR12 7LJ

☎ 01326 240428 & 0870 444 5344 🖷 01326 241141

**email:** bookings@weststarholidays.co.uk

**web:** www.weststartouring.co.uk/aa

**Dir:** *A30 onto A39 through Truro towards Falmouth. A394 to Helston, A3083 for The Lizard. Park 7m on left*

★ £12.75-£32 £12.75-£32 £12.75-£32

Open 5 Apr-28 Oct Booking advisable Jul-Aug & BH Last arrival 22.00hrs Last departure 10.00hrs

A comprehensively-equipped leisure park geared mainly for self-catering holidays, and set close to the sandy beaches, coves and fishing villages on the Lizard Peninsula. There is plenty of on-site entertainment for all ages, with indoor and outdoor swimming pools. A 49-acre site with 150 touring pitches, 8 hardstandings and 327 statics.

**Leisure:**

**Facilities:**

**Services:**

**Notes:** Family site. Wi-fi, Scuba diving, football pitch, surf & cycle hire, multi-sports court

*see advert on page 65*

### ►►► 70% 'Franchis' Holiday Park

(SW698203)

Cury Cross Lanes TR12 7AZ

☎ 01326 240301

**email:** enquiries@franchis.co.uk

**web:** www.franchis.co.uk

**Dir:** *Off A3083 on left 0.5m past Wheel Inn PH, between Helston & The Lizard*

★ £10-£15 £10-£15 £8-£13

Open Apr-Oct Booking advisable end Jul-Aug Last arrival 20.30hrs Last departure 11.00hrs

A grassy site surrounded by hedges and coppices, and divided into two paddocks for tourers, in an ideal position for exploring the Lizard Peninsula. Pitches are a mixture of level and slightly sloping. A 16-acre site with 70 touring pitches and 12 statics.

**Facilities:** **Services:**

**Notes:** Woodland walks

### ►► 78% *Teneriffe Farm Caravan Park*

*(SW674166)*

TR12 7EZ

☎ 01326 240293

**Dir:** *From Helston follow A3083 for 8m. Take B3296 through Mullion towards Mullion Cove. Turn left signed Predannack. Site on left in approx 1.5m*

A rural grassy touring park with sea views from some pitches. The park has fairly basic but clean and well maintained toilet and shower facilities, and most pitches have electric hookups. The Cornish coastal footpath is about half a mile walk from the park, and the attractive village of Mullion and Mullion Cove are both about one and a half miles. A 3-acre site with 20 touring pitches.

## NEWQUAY — MAP 02 SW86

*see also Rejerrah*

### 80% Hendra Holiday Park

(SW833601)

TR8 4NY

☎ 01637 875778 🖷 01637 879017

**email:** enquiries@hendra-holidays.com

**web:** www.hendra-holidays.com

**Dir:** *A30 onto A392 signed Newquay. At Quintrell Downs over rdbt, signed Lane, 0.5m on left*

★ £9.95-£18.25 £9.95-£18.25 £9.95-£18.25

Open Apr-Oct (rs Apr-Spring BH outdoor pool closed) Booking advisable Jul-Aug Last arrival dusk Last departure 10.00hrs

A large complex with superb facilities including an indoor fun pool and an outdoor pool. There is a children's club for the over 6s, and evening entertainment during high season. The touring pitches are set amongst mature trees and shrubs, and some have fully-serviced facilities. All amenities are open to the public. An 80-acre site with 600 touring pitches, 28 hardstandings and 283 statics.

**Leisure:**

**Facilities:**

**Services:**

**Notes:** Families and couples only. Solarium, fish bar, kids' club, train rides

*see advert on page 62*

ENGLAND

# Lookin' for five star smiles this summer

## "Best in the West!"

Proud to be a family park with a friendly relaxed atmosphere, specialising in touring and camping for families and couples only. Also Eurotents for hire.

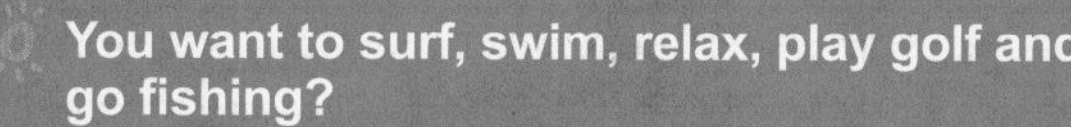

## You want to surf, swim, relax, play golf and go fishing?

Here at Trevornick Holiday Park we have on-site coarse fishing, golf, fun park, stunning pool, free full entertainment programme, children's club and a beautiful beach within walking distance.

## New for 2008

Stunning Club House, Restaurant and Takeaway.

**Check out our website and web cam!**

**www.trevornick.co.uk**

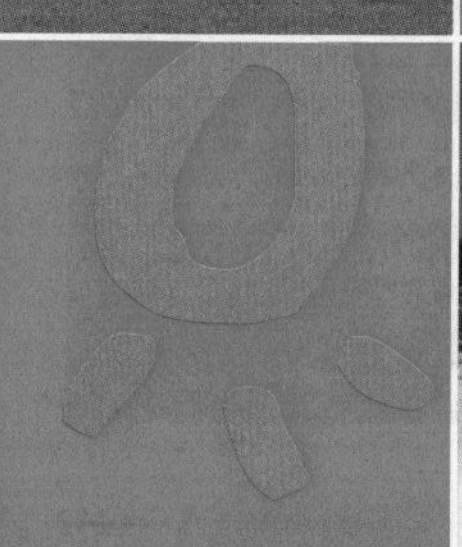

**Phone now for a brochure or email**

**bookings@trevornick.co.uk**

**0845 345 5531** (local rate)

HOLYWELL BAY • NEWQUAY • CORNWALL TR8 5PW

ENGLAND

ENGLAND

CHOOSE YOUR BEST HOLIDAY EVER FROM ONE OF NEWQUAY'S FINEST PARKS...

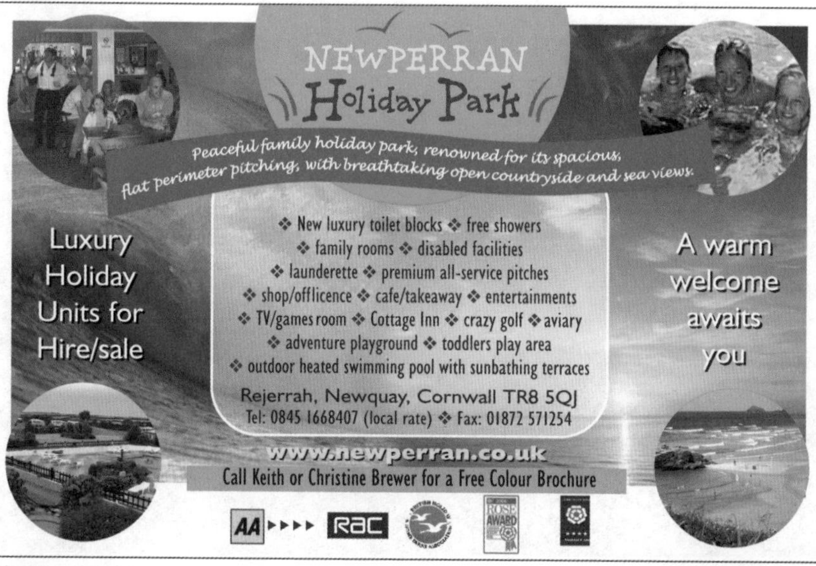

www.newquayfinestparks.co.uk

**Leisure:** Indoor swimming pool · Outdoor swimming pool · Tennis court · Games room · Children's playground · Stables · 9/18 hole golf course · Boats for hire · Cinema · Fishing · Mini golf · Watersports · Separate TV room

**Abbreviations:** BH-bank holiday/s Etr-Easter Whit-Whitsun dep-departure fr-from hrs-hours m-mile mdnt-midnight rdbt-roundabout rs-restricted service wk-week wknd-weekend no dogs No cards → following facilities within 3 miles of the site

ENGLAND

NEWQUAY MAP 02 SW86

## 75% Newquay Holiday Park (SW853626)

GOLD

TR8 4HS

☎ 01637 871111 & 0871 641 0199 🖷 01637 850818

**email:** enquiries@parkdeanholidays.co.uk

**web:** www.parkdeanholidays.co.uk

**Dir:** *From Bodmin on A30, under low bridge, turn right towards RAF St Mawgan. Take A3059 towards Newquay, site past Treloy Golf Club*

★ £10-£30 £10-£30 £7-£27

Open Mar-Oct Booking advisable at all times Last arrival 21.00hrs Last departure 10.00hrs

A well-maintained park with a wide range of indoor and outdoor activities. A children's playground and café/take-away enhance the facilities, and the club and bars offer quality entertainment. Three heated outdoor pools and a giant waterslide are very popular. A 60-acre site with 139 touring pitches, 10 hardstandings and 262 statics.

**Leisure:**

**Facilities:**

**Services:**

**Notes:** Snooker, family entertainment, children's club

## ►►►► 75% Trencreek Holiday Park

*(SW828609)*

Hillcrest, Higher Trencreek TR8 4NS

☎ 01637 874210 🖷 01637 874210

**email:** trencreek@btconnect.com

**web:** www.trencreekholidaypark.co.uk

**Dir:** *A392 to Quintrell Downs, turn right towards Newquay, left at 2 mini-rdbts into Trevenson Road to park*

★ £10.10-£14.50 £10.10-£14.50 £10.10-£14.50

Open Whit-mid Sep (rs Etr, Apr-May & late Sep swimming pool, café & bar closed) Booking advisable Jul-Aug Last arrival 22.00hrs Last departure noon

An attractively landscaped park in the village of Trencreek, with modern toilet facilities of a very high standard. Two well-stocked fishing lakes, and evening entertainment in the licensed clubhouse, are extra draws. Located about two miles from Newquay with its beaches and surfing. A 10-acre site with 194 touring pitches, 8 hardstandings and 6 statics.

**Leisure:**

**Facilities:**

**Services:**

**Notes:** Families and couples only. Free coarse fishing on site

## ►►► 85% Porth Beach Tourist Park

*(SW834629)*

Porth TR7 3NH

☎ 01637 876531 🖷 01637 871227

**email:** info@porthbeach.co.uk

**web:** www.porthbeach.co.uk

**Dir:** *1m NE off B3276 towards Padstow*

★ £10-£36 £10-£36 £8-£36

Open Mar-Nov Booking advisable Jul-Aug Last arrival 18.00hrs Last departure 10.00hrs

This attractive, popular park offers level, grassy pitches in neat and tidy surroundings. A well-run site set in meadowland and adjacent to sea and a fine sandy beach. A 6-acre site with 200 touring pitches, 19 hardstandings.

**Leisure:** **Facilities:**

**Services:**

**Notes:** Families and couples only

*see advert on page 63*

## ►►► 68% Riverside Holiday Park

*(SW829592)*

Gwills Ln TR8 4PE

☎ 01637 873617 🖷 01637 877051

**email:** info@riversideholidaypark.co.uk

**web:** www.riversideholidaypark.co.uk

**Dir:** *A30 onto A392 signed Newquay. At Quintrell Downs cross rdbt signed Lane. 2nd left in 0.5m onto unclass road signed Gwills. Park in 400yds*

Open Mar-Dec Booking advisable Jul-Aug Last arrival 22.00hrs Last departure 10.00hrs

A sheltered valley beside a river in a quiet location is the idyllic setting for this lightly wooded park. The fairly simple facilities are being gradually upgraded, and the park caters for families and couples only. The site is close to the wide variety of attractions offered by this major resort. An 11-acre site with 100 touring pitches and 65 statics.

**Leisure:**

**Facilities:**

**Services:**

**Notes:** Families and couples only.

## ►►► 74% Trebellan Park *(SW790571)*

Cubert TR8 5PY

☎ 01637 830522 🖷 01637 830277

**email:** treagofarm@aol.com

**web:** www.treagofarm.co.uk

**Dir:** *4m S of Newquay, turn W off A3075 at Cubert sign. Left in 0.75m onto unclass road*

★ £14-£20 £14-£20 £10-£16

Open May-Oct Booking advisable Jul-Aug Last arrival 21.00hrs Last departure 10.00hrs

A terraced grassy rural park within a picturesque valley with views of Cubert Common, and adjacent to the Smuggler's Den, a 16th-century thatched inn. This park has excellent coarse fishing on site on three well stocked lakes. An 8-acre site with 150 touring pitches and 7 statics.

**Leisure:**

**Facilities:**

**Services:**

**Notes:** Families and couples only

## ►►► 79% Treloy Touring Park

SILVER

*(SW858625)*

TR8 4JN

☎ 01637 872063 & 876279 🖷 01637 872063

**email:** treloy.tp@btconnect.com

**web:** www.treloy.co.uk

**Dir:** *Off A3059 (St Columb Major-Newquay road)*

Open 25 May-15 Sep (rs Apr & Sep pool, takeaway, shop & bar) Booking advisable Jul-Aug Last arrival 21.00hrs Last departure 10.00hrs

Attractive site with fine countryside views, within easy reach of resorts and beaches. The pitches are set in four paddocks with mainly level but some slightly sloping grassy areas. Maintenance and cleanliness are very high. A 12-acre site with 195 touring pitches, 24 hardstandings.

**Leisure:** **Facilities:**

**Services:**

**Notes:** Concessionary green fees for golf, entertainment

*see advert on page 64*

## ►►► 74% Trenance Holiday Park

*(SW818612)*

Edgcumbe Av TR7 2JY

☎ 01637 873447 🖷 01637 852677

**email:** enquiries@trenanceholidaypark.co.uk

**web:** www.trenanceholidaypark.co.uk

**Dir:** *Off A3075 near viaduct. Site by boating lake rdbt*

Open 26 May-Oct (rs Apr-25 May café, games room) Booking advisable Jul-Aug Last arrival 22.00hrs Last departure 10.00hrs

A mainly static park popular with tenters, close to Newquay's vibrant nightlife, and serving excellent breakfasts and takeaways. Set on high ground in an urban area of town, with cheerful owners and clean facilities. A 12-acre site with 50 touring pitches and 190 statics.

**Leisure:**

**Facilities:**

**Services:**

**Notes:**

*see advert on page 68*

ENGLAND



## NEWQUAY CONTINUED

### ►►► 75% Trethiggey Touring Park

GOLD

*(SW846596)*
Quintrell Downs TR8 4QR
☎ 01637 877672 01637 879706
**email:** enquiries@trethiggey.co.uk
**web:** www.trethiggey.co.uk
**Dir:** *From A30 take A392 signed Newquay at Quintrell Downs rdbt, turn left onto A3058 past pearl centre to site 0.5m on left*

★ £9.50-£14.70 £8.50-£13.70

Open Mar-Dec Booking advisable Jul-Aug Last arrival 22.00hrs Last departure 10.30hrs

A family-owned park in a rural setting that is ideal for touring this part of Cornwall. Pleasantly divided into paddocks with maturing trees and shrubs, and offering coarse fishing and tackle hire. A 15-acre site with 145 touring pitches, 35 hardstandings and 12 statics.

**Leisure:**

**Facilities:**

**Services:** →

**Notes:** Off licence, recreation field

## OTTERHAM — MAP 02 SX19

### ►►► 77% St Tinney Farm Holidays

GOLD

*(SX169906)*
PL32 9TA
☎ 01840 261274
**email:** info@st-tinney.co.uk
**web:** www.st-tinney.co.uk
**Dir:** *Signed 1m off A39 via unclass road signed Otterham*

Open Etr-Oct (rs Nov-Etr self catering lodges only) Booking advisable Spring BH & Jul-Aug Last arrival 21.00hrs Last departure 10.00hrs

A family-run farm site in a rural area with nature trails, lakes, valleys and offering complete seclusion. Visitors are free to walk around the farmland lakes and lose themselves in the countryside. A 34-acre site with 20 touring pitches and 15 statics.

**Leisure:**

**Facilities:**

**Services:** →

**Notes:** Wi-fi, coarse fishing

## PADSTOW — MAP 02 SW97

*see also Rumford*

### ►►► 70% Dennis Cove Camping *(SW919743)*

Dennis Ln PL28 8DR
☎ 01841 532349
**email:** denniscove@freeuk.com
**web:** www.denniscove.co.uk
**Dir:** *Approach Padstow on A389, turn right at Tesco into Sarah's Lane, 2nd right to Dennis Lane, follow lane to site at end*

★ £12.10-£15.90 £12.10-£15.90 £12.10-£15.90

Open Apr-Sep Booking advisable throughout season Last arrival 21.00hrs Last departure 11.00hrs

Set in meadowland with mature trees, this site overlooks Padstow Bay, with access to the Camel Estuary and the nearby beach. The centre of town is just a 10 minute walk away, and bike hire is available on site, with the famous Camel Trail beginning right outside. A 3-acre site with 42 touring pitches.

**Facilities:**

**Services:** →

**Notes:** Arrivals from 2pm

ENGLAND

### ►►► 84% **Padstow Touring Park**

*(SW913738)*
PL28 8LE
☎ 01841 532061
**email:** mail@padstowtouringpark.co.uk
**web:** www.padstowtouringpark.co.uk
**Dir:** *1m S of Padstow, on E side of A389 (Padstow to Wadebridge road)*

★ £10-£17.50 £10-£17.50 £10-£17.50

Open all year Booking advisable Jul-Aug Last arrival 21.30hrs Last departure 11.00hrs

Set in open countryside above the quaint fishing town of Padstow which can be approached by footpath directly from the park. This level grassy site is divided into paddocks by maturing bushes and hedges to create a peaceful and relaxing holiday atmosphere. A 13.5-acre site with 180 touring pitches, 14 hardstandings.

**Leisure:**

**Facilities:**

**Services:**

**Notes:** No groups. Wi-fi

### ►► 74% **Padstow Holiday Park** *(SW009073)*

Cliffdowne PL28 8LB
☎ 01841 532289 01841 532289
**email:** mail@padstowholidaypark.co.uk
**web:** www.padstowholidaypark.co.uk
**Dir:** *On B3274/A389 into Padstow. Signed 1.5m before Padstow*

★ £10-£14.50 £10-£14.50

Open Mar-Dec Booking advisable at all times Last arrival 17.00hrs Last departure noon

A mainly static park with some touring pitches in a small paddock and others in an open field. This quiet holiday site can be reached from Padstow (1m away) by a footpath. A 5.5-acre site with 27 touring pitches and 74 statics.

**Leisure:**

**Facilities:**

**Services:**

**Notes:** Wi-fi

## PENTEWAN MAP 02 SX04

### 80% **Pentewan Sands Holiday Park** *(SX018468)*

PL26 6BT
☎ 01726 843485 01726 844142
**email:** info@pentewan.co.uk
**web:** www.pentewan.co.uk
**Dir:** *On B3273 4m S of St Austell*

Open Apr-Oct (rs Apr-14 May & 15 Sep-Oct some facilities closed) Booking advisable May-Sep Last arrival 22.00hrs Last departure 10.30hrs

A large holiday park with a wide range of amenities, set on grassy pitches beside a private beach where plenty of aquatic activities are available. A short stroll leads to the pretty village of Pentewan, and other attractions are a short drive away. A club on site offers evening entertainment. A 32-acre site with 500 touring pitches and 120 statics.

**Leisure:**

**Facilities:**

**Services:**

**Notes:** No jet skis. Cycles, boat launch, water sports, caravan store

## PREMIER PARK

### ►►►►► 82% **Sun Valley Holiday Park** *(SX005486)*

The Best of British Touring and Holiday Parks — David Bellamy Conservation Award GOLD

Pentewan Rd PL26 6DJ
☎ 01726 843266 & 844393 01726 843266
**email:** reception@sunvalley-holidays.co.uk
**web:** www.sunvalleyholidays.co.uk
**Dir:** *From St Austell take B3273 towards Mevagissey. Park is 2m on right*

£16.50-£32.50 £16.50-£32.50 £13-£32.50

Open all year Booking advisable May-Sep Last arrival 22.00hrs Last departure noon

In a picturesque valley amongst woodland, this neat park is kept to an exceptionally high standard. The extensive amenities include tennis courts, indoor swimming pool, licensed clubhouse and restaurant. The sea is just a mile away, and can be accessed via a footpath and cycle path along the river bank. A 20-acre site with 29 touring pitches, 4 hardstandings and 75 statics.

**Leisure:**

**Facilities:**

**Services:**

**Notes:** Certain pet restrictions, please contact for details. No motorised scooters/skateboards or bikes at night. Pets corner, bike hire

ENGLAND

PENTEWAN CONTINUED

### ►►► 74% *Heligan Woods* (SW998470)

PL26 6BT

☎ 01726 842714 🖷 01726 844142

**email:** info@pentewan.co.uk

**web:** www.pentewan.co.uk

**Dir:** *From A390 take B3273 for Mevagissey at x-roads signed 'No caravans beyond this point'. Right onto unclass road towards Gorran, site 0.75m on left*

Open 1 wk before Good Fri-Nov Booking advisable late July & Aug Last arrival 22.30hrs Last departure 10.30hrs

A pleasant peaceful park adjacent to the Lost Gardens of Heligan, with views over St Austell Bay, and well-maintained facilities. Guests can also use the extensive amenities at the sister park, Pentewan Sands, and there's a new footpath with direct access to Heligan Gardens. A 12-acre site with 89 touring pitches and 30 statics.

**Leisure:**

**Facilities:**

**Services:**

### ►►► 67% *Penhaven Touring Park* (SX008481)

PL26 6DL

☎ 01726 843687 🖷 01726 843870

**email:** enquiries@penhaventouring.co.uk

**web:** www.penhaventouring.co.uk

**Dir:** *S from St Austell on B3273 towards Mevagissey. Site on left 1m after village of London Apprentice*

Open Apr-Oct Booking advisable public hols & end Jul-Aug Last arrival 21.00hrs Last departure 10.00hrs

An open park in a wooded valley with a river running past. The sandy beach at Pentewan is just a mile away, and can be accessed by a footpath and cycle path along the river bank directly from the park. A 13-acre site with 105 touring pitches, 12 hardstandings.

**Leisure:**

**Facilities:**

**Services:**

**Notes:** Off-licence

PENZANCE MAP 02 SW43

*see also Relubbus & Rosudgeon*

### ►►► 74% Bone Valley Caravan & Camping Park (SW472316)

Heamoor TR20 8UJ

☎ 01736 360313 🖷 01736 360313

**email:** enquiries@bonevalleycandcpark.co.uk

**Dir:** *A30 to Penzance, then towards Land's End, at 2nd rdbt right into Heamoor, 300yds right into Josephs Lane, 1st left, site 500yds on left*

★ £11-£15 £11-£15 £10-£15

Open all year Booking advisable Jul-Aug Last arrival 22.00hrs Last departure 11.00hrs

A compact grassy park on the outskirts of Penzance, with well maintained facilities. It is divided into paddocks by mature hedges, and a small stream runs alongside. A 1-acre site with 17 touring pitches, 2 hardstandings and 5 statics.

**Leisure:**

**Facilities:**

**Services:**

**Notes:** Baby changing facilities. Campers' kitchen

### ►►► 80% Higher Chellew Holiday Park (SW496353)

Higher Trenowin, Nancledra TR20 8BD

☎ 01736 364532 🖷 01736 332380

**email:** higherchellew@btinternet.com

**web:** www.higherchellewcamping.co.uk

**Dir:** *From A30 turn towards St Ives, left at mini-rdbt towards Nancledra. Left at B3311 junct, through Nancledra. Site 0.5m on left*

★ £9-£13 £9-£13 £9-£13

Open Fri before Etr-Oct Booking advisable mid Jul-Aug Arrivals from noon Last departure 10.30hrs

A small rural park quietly located just four miles from the golden beaches at St Ives, and a similar distance from Penzance. This well sheltered park occupies an elevated location, and all pitches are level. A 1.25-acre site with 30 touring pitches.

**Facilities:**

**Services:**

**Notes:** Microwave, freezer

ENGLAND

## PERRANPORTH MAP 02 SW75

### 76% Perran Sands Holiday Park *(SW767554)*

TR6 0AQ

☎ 01872 573742 📠 01872 571158

**web:** www.havenholidays.com

**Dir:** *A30 onto B3285 towards Perranporth. Park on right before descent on hill into Perranporth*

★ £12-£84 £12-£84 ▲ £12-£60

Open mid Mar-Oct (rs mid Mar-May & Sep-Oct some facilities may be reduced) Booking advisable school hols Last arrival 22.00hrs Last departure noon

Nestling amid 500 acres of protected dune grassland, and with a footpath through to the surf and 3 miles of golden sandy beach, this lively park is set in a large village-style complex. It offers a complete range of on-site facilities and entertainment for all the family which makes it an extremely popular park. A 550-acre site with 363 touring pitches, 19 hardstandings and 600 statics.

**Leisure:**

**Facilities:**

**Services:**

*see advert on this page*

### ►►► 69% Perranporth Camping & Touring Park *(SW768542)*

Budnick Rd TR6 0DB

☎ 01872 572174 📠 01872 572174

**Dir:** *0.5m E off B3285*

★ £15-£19 £15-£19 ▲ £15-£19

Open Etr-Sep (rs Etr-Whit & mid-end Sep shop & club facilities closed) Booking advisable Jul-Aug Last arrival 23.00hrs Last departure noon

A mainly tenting site with few level pitches, located high above a fine sandy beach which is much-frequented by surfers. The park proves attractive to young people, and is set in a lively town on a spectacular part of the coast. A 6-acre site with 120 touring pitches, 4 hardstandings and 9 statics.

**Leisure:**

**Facilities:**

**Services:**

*see advert on this page*

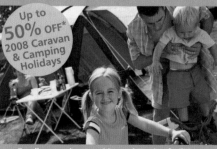

## PERRANPORTH CONTINUED

### ►►► 84% Tollgate Farm Caravan & Camping Park *(SW768547)*

Budnick Hill TR6 0AD
☎ 01872 572130 & 0845 1662126
**email:** enquiries@tollgatefarm.co.uk
**web:** www.tollgatefarm.co.uk
**Dir:** *Off A30 onto B3285 to Perranporth. Site on right 1.5m after Goonhavern*

Open Etr-Sep Booking advisable Whit, Jul-Aug Last arrival 21.00hrs Last departure 11.00hrs

A quiet site in a rural location with spectacular coastal views. Pitches are divided into four paddocks sheltered and screened by mature hedges. Children will enjoy the play equipment and pets' corner. The three miles of sand at Perran Bay are just a walk away through the sand dunes, or a 0.75m drive. A 10-acre site with 102 touring pitches, 10 hardstandings.

**Leisure:**

**Facilities:**

**Services:**

**Notes:** No large groups, 3 Family shower rooms

*see advert on opposite page*

### ► 84% Higher Golla Touring & Caravan Park *(SW756514)*

Penhallow TR4 9LZ

01872 573963 & 572116 01872 572116

**email:** trevor@cornishhairandbeautysupplies.co.uk

**web:** www.highergollatouringpark.co.uk

**Dir:** *A30 onto B3284 towards Perranporth. (Straight on at junct with A3075). Approx 2m. Site signed on right*

£8-£13

Open Etr-mid Oct Booking advisable Jul-Aug Last arrival 20.00hrs Last departure 10.30hrs

Extensive country views can be enjoyed from all pitches on this quietly located site. The facilities are very simple (2 WCs and 1 cold washbasin). Every pitch has electricity and a water tap. A 1.5-acre site with 12 touring pitches and 2 statics.

**Facilities:**

**Services:**

**Notes:** No kite flying, quiet between 21.00hrs & 08.00hrs

## POLPERRO MAP 02 SX25

### 69% *Killigarth Manor Holiday Centre* *(SX214519)*

PL13 2JQ

01503 272216 & 272409 01503 272065

**email:** killigarthmanor@breathemail.net

**web:** www.killigarth.co.uk

**Dir:** *From A38 at Trerulefoot rdbt onto A387, through Looe, over bridge signed Polperro. In 3.5m left past shelter/phone box. Park 400yds on left*

Open Etr-Oct Booking advisable 3rd wk Jul-Aug Last arrival 20.00hrs Last departure noon

Set on high ground at the approach to the historic fishing village, this large holiday centre offers a wide variety of leisure activities based around the indoor complex. In the evening the entertainment centres around the lively Harbour Lights Club. A 7-acre site with 202 touring pitches and 147 statics.

**Leisure:**

**Facilities:**

**Services:**

**Notes:** Amusement arcade, pool table, table tennis

### ►► 75% Great Kellow Farm Caravan & Camping Site *(SX201522)*

Lansallos PL13 2QL

01503 272387 01503 272387

**email:** kellow.farm@virgin.net

**web:** www.bestofsecornwall.co.uk

**Dir:** *From Looe towards Pelynt. In Pelynt left at church follow Lansallos sign. Left at x-rds, 0.75m. At staggered x-rds left and follow site signs*

★ £10-£12 £10-£12 £10-£12

Open Mar-3 Jan Booking advisable Jul-Aug Last arrival 22.00hrs Last departure noon

Set on a high level grassy paddock with extensive views of Polperro Bay, this attractive site is on a working dairy and beef farm, and close to National Trust properties and gardens. This very peaceful location is close to the fishing village of Polperro. A 3-acre site with 30 touring pitches and 10 statics.

**Facilities:**

**Services:**

**Notes:**

ENGLAND

## POLRUAN MAP 02 SX15

### ►►► 79% Polruan Holidays - Camping & Caravanning *(SX133509)*

Polruan-by-Fowey PL23 1QH
☎ 01726 870263 📠 01726 870263
**email:** polholiday@aol.com
**Dir:** *A38 to Dobwalls, left onto A390 to East Taphouse. Left onto B3359. Right in 4.5m signed Polruan*

Open Etr-Sep Booking advisable BH, Jul-Aug Last arrival 21.00hrs Last departure noon

A very rural and quiet site in a lovely elevated position above the village, with good views of the sea. The River Fowey passenger ferry is close by, and the site has a good shop, and barbecues to borrow. A 3-acre site with 47 touring pitches, 7 hardstandings and 10 statics.

**Leisure:**
**Facilities:**
**Services:**
**Notes:** No skateboards, rollerskates, bikes, water pistols, water bombs. Tourist information, off licence

## POLZEATH MAP 02 SW97

### ►►► 78% *South Winds Caravan & Camping Park* *(SW948790)*

Polzeath Rd PL27 6QU
☎ 01208 863267 📠 01208 862080
**email:** info@southwindcampsite.co.uk
**web:** www.rockinfo.co.uk
**Dir:** *Exit B3314 onto unclass road signed Polzeath, park on right just past turn to New Polzeath*

Open Mar-Oct Booking advisable Jul & Aug & school hols Last arrival 21.00hrs Last departure 10.30hrs

A peaceful site with beautiful sea and panoramic rural views, within walking distance of a golf complex, and 0.75m from beach and village. A 16-acre site with 100 touring pitches.

**Leisure:**
**Facilities:**
**Services:**
**Notes:** No disposable BBQs, no noise 23.00hrs-07.00hrs, dogs on leads at all times, families & couples only

*see advert on opposite page*

### ►►► 75% Tristram Caravan & Camping Park *(SW936790)*

PL27 6TP
☎ 01208 862215 📠 01208 862080
**email:** info@tristramcampsite.co.uk
**web:** www.polzeathcamping.co.uk
**Dir:** *From B3314 take unclass road signed Polzeath. Through village, up hill, site 2nd turn on right*

★ £22-£45 £22-£45 £14-£45

Open Mar-Nov Booking advisable Jul, Aug & school hols Last arrival 21.00hrs Last departure 10.00hrs

An ideal family site, positioned on a gently sloping cliff with grassy pitches and glorious sea views. There is direct, gated access to the beach, where surfing is very popular. The local amenities of the village are only a few hundred yards away. A 10-acre site with 100 touring pitches.

**Facilities:**
**Services:**
**Notes:** No ball games, no disposable BBQs, no noise between 23.00hrs-07.00hrs, dogs on leads at all times. Surf hire

*see advert on opposite page*

## PORTHTOWAN MAP 02 SW64

### ►►►► 81% Porthtowan Tourist Park *(SW693473)*

Mile Hill TR4 8TY
☎ 01209 890256
**email:** admin@porthtowantouristpark.co.uk
**web:** www.porthtowantouristpark.co.uk
**Dir:** *Exit A30 at junct signed Redruth/Porthtowan. Take 3rd exit from rdbt. 2m & right at T-junct. Park on left at top of hill*

★ £8.50-£14.50 £8.50-£14.50 £8.50-£14.50

Open Etr-Sep Booking advisable Jul-Aug Last arrival 21.30hrs Last departure 11.00hrs

A neat, level grassy site on high ground above Porthtowan, with plenty of shelter from mature trees and shrubs. The superb toilet facilities considerably enhance the appeal of this peaceful rural park, which is almost midway between the small seaside resorts of Portreath and Porthtowan, with their beaches and surfing. A 5-acre site with 80 touring pitches, 4 hardstandings.

**Leisure:**
**Facilities:**
**Services:**
**Notes:** No bikes/skateboards during Jul-Aug

ENGLAND

**Leisure:** Indoor swimming pool · Outdoor swimming pool · Tennis court · Games room · Children's playground · Stables · 9/18 hole golf course · Boats for hire · Cinema · Fishing · Mini golf · Watersports · Separate TV room

## PORTHTOWAN CONTINUED

### ►►► 79% Wheal Rose Caravan & Camping Park (SW717449)

Wheal Rose TR16 5DD

☎ 01209 891496

**email:** les@whealrosecaravanpark.co.uk

**web:** www.whealrosecaravanpark.co.uk

**Dir:** *Exit A30 at Scorrier sign, follow signs to Wheal Rose. Park 0.5m on left, Wheal Rose to Porthtowan road*

★ £8-£14 £8-£14 £8-£14

Open Mar-Dec Booking advisable Aug Last arrival 21.00hrs Last departure 11.00hrs

A quiet, peaceful park in a secluded valley setting, central for beaches and countryside, and 2 miles from the surfing beaches of Porthtowan. The friendly owners work hard to keep this park immaculate, with a bright toilet block and well-trimmed pitches. A 6-acre site with 50 touring pitches, 6 hardstandings and 3 statics.

**Leisure:**

**Facilities:**

**Services:** →

**Notes:** 5mph speed limit, dogs on leads, minimum noise after 23.00hrs, gates locked 23.00hrs

## PORTSCATHO — MAP 02 SW83

### ►►► 74% Trewince Farm Touring Park (SW868339)

TR2 5ET

☎ 01872 580430 01872 580430

**email:** info@trewincefarm.co.uk

**web:** www.trewincefarm.co.uk

**Dir:** *From St Austell take A390 towards Truro. Left on B3287 to Tregony, following signs to St Mawes. At Trewithian, turn left to St Anthony. Site 0.75m past church*

★ £10-£16 £10-£16 £10-£16

Open May-Sep Booking advisable high season Last arrival 23.00hrs Last departure 11.00hrs

A site on a working farm with spectacular sea views from its elevated position. There are many quiet golden sandy beaches close by, and boat launching facilities and mooring can be arranged at the nearby

*Trewince Farm Touring Park*

Percuil River Boatyard. The village of Portscatho with shops, pubs and attractive harbour is approximately 1 mile away. A 3-acre site with 25 touring pitches.

**Facilities:**

**Services:** →

**Notes:** Private quay & moorings

### ►► 70% *Treloan Coastal Farm Holidays* (SW876348)

Treloan Ln TR2 5EF

☎ 01872 580989 & 580888 01872 580888

**email:** enquiries@coastalfarmholidays.co.uk

**web:** www.coastalfarmholidays.co.uk

**Dir:** *From A3078 (Tregony to St Mawes road) take unclass road to Gerrans. Immediately after Gerrans church road divides take Treloan Lane, by Royal Standard pub, to park*

Open all year Booking advisable high season Last departure 11.00hrs

Set on a working farm where 1930's style organic farming methods are being recreated. This stunningly located, rather rustic coastal park has basic toilet facilities, but offers a friendly welcome and is near three secluded sandy coves. A 7-acre site with 57 touring pitches, 8 hardstandings and 8 statics.

**Facilities:**

**Services:** →

**Notes:** Coastal footpath on site

## PRAA SANDS MAP 02 SW52

### NEW ►►► 69% Higher Pentreath Farm Campsite *(SW570280)*

Higher Pentreath TR20 9TL
☎ 01736 763222
**email:** d.spencer@btinternet.com
**Dir:** *Off A394 approx midway between Helston & Penzance, signed on unclass rd to Pentreath.*

Set midway between Helston and Penzance, this simple campsite is set in two grassy paddocks, and enjoys extensive views over Praa Sands and its superb long sandy beach. The village also boasts a variety of cafés and gift shops, and a pub with adjoining restaurant. 90 touring pitches.

## REDRUTH MAP 02 SW64

### ►►► 75% Cambrose Touring Park *(SW684453)*

Portreath Rd TR16 4HT
☎ 01209 890747
**email:** cambrosetouringpark@supanet.com
**web:** www.cambrosetouringpark.co.uk
**Dir:** *A30 onto B3300 towards Portreath. Approx 0.75m at 1st rdbt right onto B3300. Take unclass road on right signed Porthtowan. Site 200yds on left*

★ £8.50-£14 £8.50-£14 £8.50-£14

Open Apr-Oct Booking advisable Jul-Aug Last arrival 22.00hrs Last departure 11.30hrs

Situated in a rural setting surrounded by trees and shrubs, this park is divided into grassy paddocks. About two miles from the harbour village of Portreath. A 6-acre site with 60 touring pitches.

**Leisure:**
**Facilities:**
**Services:**
**Notes:** Mini football pitch

### ►►► 76% Lanyon Holiday Park *(SW684387)*

Loscombe Ln, Four Lanes TR16 6LP
☎ 01209 313474
**email:** jamieriellу@btconnect.com
**web:** www.lanyonholidaypark.co.uk
**Dir:** *Signed 0.5m off B2397 on Helston side of Four Lanes village*

Open Mar-Oct Booking advisable Jul & Aug Last arrival 21.00hrs Last departure noon

Small, friendly rural park in an elevated position with fine views to distant St Ives Bay. This family owned and run park continues to be upgraded in all areas, and is close to a cycling trail. Stithian's Reservoir for fishing, sailing and windsurfing is two miles away. A 14-acre site with 25 touring pitches and 49 statics.

**Leisure:**
**Facilities:**
**Services:**
**Notes:** Take-away service, all-day games room

### ►►► 80% *Tehidy Holiday Park* *(SW682432)*

Harris Mill, Illogan TR16 4JQ
☎ 01209 216489 01209 216489
**email:** holiday@tehidy.co.uk
**web:** www.tehidy.co.uk
**Dir:** *Exit A30 at Redruth/Portreath junct onto A3047 to 1st rdbt. Left onto B3300. At junct straight over signed Tehidy Holiday Park. Past Cornish Arms pub, 800yds bottom of hill on left*

Open Apr-Oct Booking advisable Jul-Aug Last arrival 20.00hrs Last departure 10.00hrs

An attractive wooded location in a quiet rural area only 2.5m from popular beaches. Mostly level pitches on tiered ground, and the toilet facilities are bright and modern. A 4.5-acre site with 18 touring pitches, 2 hardstandings and 32 statics.

**Leisure:**
**Facilities:**
**Services:**
**Notes:** Dogs by arrangement only. Trampoline, off-licence

ENGLAND

AWARD WINNING
HOLIDAY PARK
For a great family holiday - minutes from Perranporth and Newquay and close to exciting visitor attractions!
Monkey Tree
HOLIDAY PARK
FREE heated pool
FREE kids club
FREE family entertainment
Restaurant, bar and shop
Monkey Tree Holiday Park, Rejerrah,
Newquay, Cornwall TR8 5QR
www.monkeytreeholidaypark.co.uk
enquiries@monkeytreeholidaypark.co.uk
Booking Hotline
01872 572032


**REJERRAH** **MAP 02 SW75**

79% **Monkey Tree Holiday Park** *(SW803545)*

Scotland Rd TR8 5QR

☎ 01872 572032 📠 01872 573577

**email:** enquiries@monkeytreeholidaypark.co.uk

**web:** www.monkeytreeholidaypark.co.uk

**Dir:** *Exit A30 onto B3285 to Perranporth, 0.25m right into Scotland Rd, site on left in 1.5m*

Open all year Booking advisable Jul & Aug Last arrival 22.00hrs Last departure 10.00hrs

A busy holiday park with plenty of activities and a jolly holiday atmosphere. Set close to lovely beaches between Newquay and Perranporth, it offers an outdoor swimming pool, children's playground, two bars with entertainment, and a good choice of eating outlets including a restaurant and a takeaway. A 56-acre site with 505 touring pitches.

**Leisure:**

**Facilities:**

**Services:**

**Notes:** Family park. Wi-fi, sauna, solarium, mountain bike hire, football pitch

*see advert on this page*

## ►►►► 84% **Newperran Holiday Park**

*(SW801555)*

TR8 5QJ

☎ 01872 572407 📠 01872 571254

**email:** holidays@newperran.co.uk

**web:** www.newperran.co.uk

**Dir:** *4m SE of Newquay & 1m S of Rejerrah on A3075. Or A30 Redruth, turn off B3275 Perranporth, at 1st T-junct turn right onto A3075 towards Newquay, site 300mtrs on left*

Open Etr-Oct Booking advisable Jul-Aug Last arrival mdnt Last departure 10.00hrs

A family site in a lovely rural position near several beaches and bays. This airy park offers screening to some pitches, which are set in paddocks on level ground. High season entertainment is available in the park's country inn, and the café has an extensive menu. A 25-acre site with 371 touring pitches, 14 hardstandings and 5 statics.

**Leisure:**

**Facilities:**

**Services:**

**Notes:** Crazy golf, adventure playground & pool

*see advert on page 63*

## ►►► 72% **Perran-Quay Tourist Park**

*(SW800554)*

Hendra Croft TR8 5QP

☎ 01872 572561 📠 01872 575043

**email:** rose@perran-quay.co.uk

**web:** www.perran-quay.co.uk

**Dir:** *Direct access off A3075 behind Braefel Inn*

Open all year (rs winter shop closed) Booking advisable Jul-Aug Last departure 10.00hrs

A friendly family-run site set in paddocks with mature trees and shrubs for shelter. The park has its own pub serving food and drink, and is close to the sandy beach at Holywell Bay. With its swimming pool and quiet surroundings midway between Newquay and Perranporth, it is popular with families. An 8.5-acre site with 110 touring pitches, 3 hardstandings and 16 statics.

**Leisure:**

**Facilities:**

**Services:**

**Services:** Toilet Fluid · Café/ Restaurant · Fast Food/Takeaway · Baby Care · Electric Hook Up · Motorvan Service Point · Launderette · Licensed Bar · Calor Gas · Camping Gaz · Battery Charging

## RELUBBUS MAP 02 SW53

### ►►►► 78% River Valley Country Park *(SW565326)*

SILVER

TR20 9ER

☎ 01736 763398 Fax 01736 763398

**email:** rivervalley@surfbay.dircon.co.uk

**web:** www.surfbayholidays.co.uk

**Dir:** *From A30 follow sign for Helston/A394. At next rbdt 1st left signed Relubbus*

★ £8.50-£17.50 £8.50-£17.50 £8.50-£17.50

Open Mar-Dec (rs Nov-4 Jan hardstanding & lodges only) Booking advisable Jul-Aug Last arrival 20.00hrs Last dep 11.00hrs

A quiet, attractive site in a picturesque river valley with direct access to a shallow trout stream. This level park has a good mix of grass and hard pitches, and is partly wooded with pleasant walks. It is surrounded by farmland, and just a few miles from the sandy beaches of both the north and south coasts, as well as St Michael's Mount at Marazion. An 18-acre site with 119 touring pitches and 48 statics.

**Facilities:**

**Services:**

**Notes:** No pets in tents Licensed shop, takeaway chip van twice weekly

## ROSUDGEON MAP 02 SW52

### ►►► 77% Kenneggy Cove Holiday Park *(SW562287)*

Higher Kenneggy TR20 9AU

☎ 01736 763453

**email:** enquiries@kenneggycove.co.uk

**web:** www.kenneggycove.co.uk

**Dir:** *On A394 between Penzance & Helston, turn S into signed lane to site & Higher Kenneggy*

Open 17 May-4 Oct Booking advisable Jul-Aug Last arrival 21.00hrs Last departure 11.00hrs

Set in an Area of Outstanding Natural Beauty with spectacular sea views, this family-owned park is quiet and well kept. A short walk along a country footpath leads to the Cornish Coastal Path, and on to the golden sandy beach at Kenneggy Cove. A 4-acre site with 50 touring pitches and 9 statics.

**Leisure:** **Facilities:**

**Services:**

**Notes:** No large groups. Fresh bakery items, homemade takeaway food

## RUMFORD MAP 02 SW87

### NEW ►►► 79% Music Water Touring Park *(SW906685)*

PL27 7SJ

☎ 01841 540257

**web:** www.caravancampingsites.co.uk

**Dir:** *A39 Winnards Perch rdbt on to B3274 signed Padstow. Left in 2m on to unclass rd signed Rumford & St Eval. Park 500mtrs on right*

★ £8-£11 £8-£11 £8-£11

Open Apr-Oct Booking advisable all year Last arrival 23.00hrs Last departure 11.00hrs

Set in a peaceful location yet only a short drive to the pretty fishing town of Padstow, and many sandy beaches and coves. This family owned and run park has grassy paddocks, and there is a quiet lounge bar and a separate children's games room. An 8-acre site with 55 touring pitches, 2 hardstandings and 2 statics.

**Leisure:** **Facilities:**

**Services:**

**Notes:** Maximum 2 dogs, one tent per pitch. Pets' corner - donkeys

## RUTHERNBRIDGE MAP 02 SX06

### ►►► 76% *Ruthern Valley Holidays* *(SX014665)*

COUNTRYSIDE DISCOVERY GOLD

PL30 5LU

☎ 01208 831395 Fax 01208 831395

**email:** ruthern.valley@btconnect.com

**web:** www.self-catering-ruthern.co.uk

**Dir:** *A389 through Bodmin, follow St Austell signs, then Lanivet signs. At top of hill turn right on unclass road signed Ruthernbridge. Follow signs*

Open Mar-New Year Booking advisable high season & BH Last arrival 20.30hrs Last departure noon

An attractive woodland site peacefully located in a small river valley west of Bodmin Moor. This away-from-it-all park is ideal for those wanting a quiet holiday, and the informal pitches are spread over four natural areas, with plenty of sheltered space. A 7.5-acre site with 29 touring pitches, 3 hardstandings and 18 statics.

**Leisure:** **Facilities:**

**Services:**

**Notes:** No pets in Jul & Aug, dogs only allowed in bungalows, lodges & static caravans. Woodland area, children's play area

**Leisure:** Indoor swimming pool Outdoor swimming pool Tennis court Games room Children's playground Stables 9/18 hole golf course Boats for hire Cinema Fishing Mini golf Watersports Separate TV room

## ST AGNES MAP 02 SW75

### 74% **Beacon Cottage Farm Touring Park** *(SW705502)*

Beacon Dr TR5 0NU

01872 552347 & 553381

**email:** beaconcottagefarm@lineone.net

**web:** www.beaconcottagefarmholidays.co.uk

**Dir:** *From A30 at Threeburrows rdbt, take B3277 to St Agnes, left into Goonvrea Road & right into Beacon Drive, follow brown sign to park*

★ £10-£20 £10-£20 £10-£20

Open Apr-Oct (rs Etr-Whit shop closed) Booking advisable Jul-Aug Last arrival 20.00hrs Last departure noon

A neat and compact site on a working farm, utilizing a cottage and outhouses, an old orchard and adjoining walled paddock. The unique location on a headland looking NE along the coast comes with stunning views towards St Ives, and the keen friendly family owners keep all areas very well maintained. A 5-acre site with 70 touring pitches.

**Leisure:**

**Facilities:**

**Services:** →

**Notes:** No large groups. Secure year-round caravan storage

### 70% ***Blue Hills Touring Park***

*(SW732521)*

Cross Combe TR5 0XP

01872 552999

**Dir:** *Pass through St Agnes towards Perranporth, turn left at Trevallas with brown sign to site in 1m*

Open Etr-Oct Booking advisable Aug Last arrival 23.30hrs Last departure 16.00hrs

Set in a beautiful rural position close to a coastal footpath, a small site with good toilets. A pleasant location for exploring nearby coves, beaches and villages. A 2-acre site with 30 touring pitches.

**Facilities:**

**Services:** →

**Notes:**

### 75% **Presingoll Farm Caravan & Camping Park** *(SW721494)*

TR5 0PB

01872 552333 01872 552333

**email:** pam@presingollfarm.fsbusiness.co.uk

**web:** www.presingollfarm.fsbusiness.co.uk

**Dir:** *From A30 Chiverton rdbt (Little Chef) take B3277 towards St Agnes. Park 3m on right*

★ fr £11 fr £11 fr £11

Open Etr/Apr-Oct Booking advisable Jul & Aug Last departure 10.00hrs

An attractive rural park adjoining farmland, with extensive views of the coast beyond. Family owned and run, with level grass pitches, and modernised toilet block in smart converted farm buildings. There is also a campers' room with microwave, freezer and free coffee and tea. A 5-acre site with 90 touring pitches.

**Leisure:**

**Facilities:**

**Services:** →

**Notes:** No large groups

## ST AUSTELL MAP 02 SX05

*see also Carlyon Bay*

### 83% **River Valley Holiday Park**

*(SX010503)*

London Apprentice PL26 7AP

01726 73533 01726 73533

**email:** river.valley@tesco.net

**web:** www.cornwall-holidays.co.uk

**Dir:** *Direct access to park signed on B3273 from St Austell at London Apprentice*

£10-£28 £10-£28 £10-£28

Open end Mar-end Sep Booking advisable Jul-Aug Last arrival 22.00hrs Last departure 11.00hrs

A neat, well-maintained family-run park set in a pleasant river valley. The quality toilet block and attractively landscaped grounds make this a delightful base for a holiday. A 2-acre site with 45 touring pitches and 40 statics.

**Leisure:**

**Facilities:**

**Services:** →

**Notes:** Wi-fi. Off-road cycle trail to beach

*see advert on opposite page*

### 78% **Court Farm Holidays** *(SW953524)*

St Stephen PL26 7LE

01726 823684 01726 823684

**email:** truscott@ctfarm.freeserve.co.uk

**web:** www.courtfarmcornwall.co.uk

**Dir:** *From St Austell take A3058 towards Newquay. Through St Stephen (pass Peugeot garage). Right at 'St Stephen/Coombe Hay/Langreth/Industrial site' sign. 400yds, site on right*

★ £11-£17.50 £15-£19.50 £9.50-£22.50

Open Apr-Sep Booking advisable Jul-mid Sep Last arrival by dark Last departure 11.00hrs

Set in a peaceful rural location, this large camping field offers plenty of space, and is handy for the Eden Project and the Lost Gardens of Heligan. Coarse fishing and use of a large telescope are among the attractions. A 4-acre site with 20 touring pitches, 5 hardstandings.

**Leisure:**

**Facilities:**

**Services:** →

**Notes:** No noisy behaviour after dark. Wi-fi, astronomy lectures, observatory, solar observatory

## ►►► 75% Old Kerrow Farm Holiday Park

*(SX020573)*

Stenalees PL26 8GD

☎ 01726 851651 📠 01726 852826

**email:** oldkerrowfarmholidaypark@hotmail.com

**web:** www.oldkerrowfarmholidaypark.co.uk

**Dir:** *Exit A30 at Innis Downs rdbt onto A391 to Bugle. Left at lights onto unclassified road. Site on right approx 1m just after sign for Kerrow Moor*

Open all year (closed until early Mar 2008 for refurbishment) Booking advisable at all times Last arrival 20.00hrs Last departure noon

A rapidly improving park set on a former working farm, with good toilet facilities. The touring area is divided into two paddocks - one especially for dog owners with an extensive dog walk. Cycle hire can be arranged, and there is a cycle track to the Eden Project four miles away. A 20-acre site with 50 touring pitches, 11 hardstandings.

**Leisure:**

**Facilities:**

**Services:**

**Notes:** No noise as quiet, peaceful location

*see advert on this page*

## ►►► 72% Trencreek Farm Country Holiday Park *(SW966485)*

SILVER

Hewas Water PL26 7JG

☎ 01726 882540 📠 01726 883254

**email:** reception@trencreek.co.uk

**web:** www.surfbayholidays.co.uk

**Dir:** *4m SW of St Austell on A390, fork left onto B3287. Continue for 1m, park is on left*

★ £10.45-£18 £10.45-£18 £8.50-£16

Open Mar-Dec (rs Mar-May, Sep-Oct various restrictions apply) Booking advisable Jul-Aug Last arrival 21.00hrs Last departure noon

Set in a quiet rural area, this park is divided into paddocks with mature hedges and trees, and with four coarse fishing lakes. This friendly, family park offers organised activities for children indoors and out in the summer holidays, and at other times caters for adult breaks. There are animals in pens which children can enter. A 56-acre site with 184 touring pitches, 18 hardstandings and 37 statics.

**Leisure:**

**Facilities:**

**Services:**

**Notes:** Under 15s must be accompanied by an adult around & in pool, farm animals

*see advert on page 82*

ENGLAND

## ST BLAZEY GATE — MAP 02 SX05

### ►►► 82% **Doubletrees Farm** *(SX060540)*

Luxulyan Rd PL24 2EH

☎ 01726 812266

**email:** doubletrees@eids.co.uk

**web:** www.eids.co.uk/doubletrees

**Dir:** *On A390 at Blazey Gate. Turn by Leek Seed Chapel, almost opposite BP filling station. After approx 300yds turn right by public bench into site.*

£12-£14 £12-£14 £11-£14

Open all year Booking advisable Last arrival 22.30hrs Last departure 11.30hrs

A popular park with terraced pitches offering superb sea and coastal views. Close to beaches, and the nearest park to the Eden Project, it is very well maintained by friendly owners. A 1.75-acre site with 32 touring pitches, 6 hardstandings.

**Facilities:**

**Services:** → 

**Notes:**

## ST BURYAN — MAP 02 SW42

### NEW ►►► 78% **Tower Park Caravans & Camping** *(SW406263)*

TR19 6BZ

☎ 01736 810286

**email:** enquiries@towerparkcamping.co.uk

**web:** www.towerparkcamping.co.uk

**Dir:** *On A30 towards Lands End, fork left onto B3283 signed St Buryan. Turn right at start of village, site 300yds on right.*

★ £9.75-£12.50 £10.75-£13.50 £7.75-£10.50

Open 7 Mar-Oct (rs low season breakfast not available) Booking advisable Etr, school hols & high season Last arrival 22.00hrs Last departure 10.00hrs

A rural campsite that is ideal for families and surfers, set just four miles from both Sennen Cove and Porthcurno. This grassy park is sheltered by mature trees and hedges, and surrounded by Areas of Outstanding Natural Beauty including unspoilt rugged coasts and sandy beaches. A 13-acre site with 102 touring pitches.

**Leisure:**

**Facilities:**

**Services:** → 

**Notes:** Takeaway breakfast

### ►►► 75% ***Treverven Touring Caravan & Camping Park*** *(SW410237)*

Treverven Farm TR19 6DL

☎ 01736 810200 & 810318 📠 01736 871977

**web:** www.chycor.co.uk/camping/treverven

**Dir:** *Leave A30 onto B3283 1.5m after St Buryan, left onto B3315. Site on right in 1m*

Open Etr-Oct Booking advisable Jul-Aug Last departure noon

Situated in a quiet Area of Outstanding Natural Beauty with panoramic views, this family-owned site is off a traffic-free lane leading directly to the coastal path. Toilet facilities are very good. Ideal for touring West Cornwall. A 6-acre site with 115 touring pitches.

**Leisure:**

**Facilities:**

**Services:** → 

## ST COLUMB MAJOR MAP 02 SW96

### ►►► 77% **Southleigh Manor Naturist Park**

*(SW918623)*
TR9 6HY
☎ 01637 880938 01637 881108
**email:** enquiries@southleigh-manor.com
**Dir:** *Leave A30 at junct with A39 signed Wadebridge. At Highgate Hill rdbt take A39. At Halloon rdbt take A39. At Trekenning rdbt take 4th exit 500mtrs along on right*

★ £17-£22.50 £17-£22.50 £17-£22.50

Open Etr-Oct (Shop open peak times only) Booking advisable Jun-Aug Last arrival 20.00hrs Last departure 10.30hrs

A very well maintained naturist park in the heart of the Cornish countryside, catering for families and couples only. Seclusion and security are very well planned, and the lovely gardens provide a calm setting. A 4-acre site with 50 touring pitches.

**Leisure:**
**Facilities:**
**Services:**
**Notes:** Sauna, spa bath, pool table, putting green

## ST DAY MAP 02 SW74

### ►►► 77% ***St Day Holiday Park*** *(SW733422)*

Church Hill TR16 5LE
☎ 01209 820459
**email:** holiday@stday.co.uk
**web:** www.stday.co.uk
**Dir:** *From A30 at Scorrier onto B3298 towards Falmouth. Site signed on right in 2m*

Open Etr & Apr-Oct Booking advisable Jul-Aug

A very good touring area and with modern toilet facilities. This rurally located park with keen friendly owners is situated in a quiet area between Falmouth and Newquay and within walking distance of the attractive village of St Day. A 4-acre site with 35 touring pitches, 11 hardstandings and 23 statics.

**Facilities:**
**Services:**
**Notes:**

## ST GENNYS MAP 02 SX19

### ►►► 74% **Bude Camping & Caravanning Club Site** *(SX176943)*

Gillards Moor EX23 0BG
☎ 01840 230650
**web:** www.campingandcaravanningclub.co.uk/bude
**Dir:** *From N on A39 site on right in lay-by, 9m from Bude. From S on A39 site on left in lay-by 9m from Camelford. Approx 3m from B3262 junct*

★ £15.45-£20.15 £15.45-£20.15 £15.45-£20.15

Open 28 Apr-29 Sep Booking advisable BH & peak periods Last arrival 21.00hrs Last departure noon

A well-kept, level grass site with good quality facilities. Located midway between Bude and Camelford in an area full of sandy coves and beaches with good surfing. A 6-acre site with 100 touring pitches, 9 hardstandings.

**Leisure:**
**Facilities:**
**Services:**
**Notes:** Site gates closed 23.00hrs-07.00hrs

## ST GILES-ON-THE-HEATH

*see Chapmans Well (Devon)*

## ST HILARY MAP 02 SW53

### ►►►► 78% **Wayfarers Caravan & Camping Park** *(SW558314)*

Relubbus Ln TR20 9EF
☎ 01736 763326
**email:** elaine@wayfarerspark.co.uk
**web:** www.wayfarerspark.co.uk
**Dir:** *Turn left off A30 onto A394 towards Helston. Turn left at rdbt onto B3280 after 2m. Site 1.5m on left*

£13-£19 £13-£19 £13-£19

Open Apr-Oct Booking advisable Jun-Sep Last arrival 20.00hrs Last departure 11.00hrs

A quiet sheltered park in a peaceful rural setting within 2.5 miles of St Michael's Mount. It offers spacious, well-drained pitches and very well cared for facilities. A 4.75-acre site with 45 touring pitches, 25 hardstandings and 4 statics.

**Facilities:**
**Services:**
**Notes:** Adults only Tourist information room

### ►►► 72% **Trevair Touring Park** *(SW548326)*

South Treveneague TR20 9BY
☎ 01736 740647
**email:** info@trevairtouringpark.co.uk
**web:** www.trevairtouringpark.co.uk
**Dir:** *A30 onto A394 signed Helston. 2m to rdbt, left onto B3280. Through Goldsithney. Left at brown site sign. Through 20mph zone to site, 1m on right*

Open Etr-Nov Booking advisable Jul-Aug Last arrival 22.00hrs Last departure 11.00hrs

Set in a rural location adjacent to woodland, this park is level and secluded, with grassy pitches. Marazion's beaches and the famous St Michael's Mount are just three miles away. The friendly owners live at the farmhouse on the park. A 3.5-acre site with 40 touring pitches and 2 statics.

**Facilities:**
**Services:**
**Notes:**

ENGLAND

## ST ISSEY

MAP 02 SW97

### ►►► 79% *Trewince Farm Holiday Park*

*(SW937715)*

PL27 7RL

☎ 01208 812830 01208 812835

**email:** holidays@trewincefarm.fsnet.co.uk

**Dir:** *From Wadebridge on A39 take A389 signed Padstow. Site 2m on left*

Open Etr-Oct Booking advisable at all times Last departure 11.00hrs

Set amongst rolling farmland close to the coast, this park is part of a working farm, and set in well landscaped grounds. It offers good facilities in a comfortable and friendly atmosphere, and is only three miles from Padstow. A 6-acre site with 120 touring pitches and 35 statics.

**Leisure:**

**Facilities:**

**Services:** →

**Notes:** Crazy golf, farm rides in summer, near Camel Trail

*See advertisement under WADEBRIDGE*

## ST IVES

MAP 02 SW54

**Regional Winner – AA South West of England Campsite of the Year 2008**

**PREMIER PARK**

### ►►►►► 85% Polmanter Tourist Park *(SW510388)*

The Best of British Touring and Holiday Parks

Halsetown TR26 3LX

☎ 01736 795640 01736 793607

**email:** reception@polmanter.com

**web:** www.polmanter.com

**Dir:** *Signed off B3311 at Halsetown*

Open Apr-end Oct (rs Apr-Whit & 12 Sep-Oct shop, pool, bar & takeaway food closed) Booking advisable Jul-Aug Last arrival 21.00hrs Last departure 10.00hrs

A well-developed touring park on high ground, Polmanter offers high quality in all areas, from the immaculate modern toilet blocks to the outdoor swimming pool and hard tennis courts. Pitches are individually marked and sited in meadows, and the park has been tastefully landscaped. The fishing port and beaches of St Ives are just 1.5m away, and there is a bus service in high season. A 20-acre site with 240 touring pitches, 24 hardstandings.

**Leisure:**

**Facilities:**

**Services:** →

**Notes:** Putting, sports field, 7 family shower rooms

### ►►►► 85% *Ayr Holiday Park*

David Bellamy Conservation Award GOLD

*(SW509408)*

TR26 1EJ

☎ 01736 795855 01736 798797

**email:** recept@ayrholidaypark.co.uk

**web:** www.ayrholidaypark.co.uk

**Dir:** *From A30 follow St Ives 'large vehicles' route via B3311 through Halsetown onto B3306. Park signed towards St Ives town centre*

Open all year Booking advisable Jun-Aug Last arrival 22.00hrs Last departure 10.00hrs

A well-established park on a cliffside overlooking St Ives Bay, with a heated toilet block making winter holidaying more attractive. There are stunning views from most pitches, and the town centre, harbour and beach are only 0.5m away, with direct access to the coastal footpath. A 4-acre site with 40 touring pitches, 20 hardstandings.

**Leisure:** **Facilities:**

**Services:** →

*see advert on opposite page*

### ►►► 87% Little Trevarrack Holiday Park

*(SW525379)*

Laity Ln, Carbis Bay TR26 3HW

☎ 01736 797580

**email:** info@littletrevarrack.co.uk

**web:** www.littletrevarrack.co.uk

**Dir:** *A30 onto A3074 signed 'Carbis Bay & St Ives'. Left opposite turn to beach. 150yds, over x-rds, site 2nd on right*

£11.50-£21 £11.50-£21 £11.50-£21

Open Etr-Sep (rs Etr-Whit, mid-end Sep games room & swimming pool closed) Booking advisable summer hols Last arrival 21.30hrs Last departure 10.00hrs

A pleasant grass park set in countryside but close to beaches and local amenities. Plenty of tree planting will result in more shelter and privacy in this landscaped park, and there are superb sea views. A private bus service runs to St Ives in high season. A 20-acre site with 200 touring pitches.

**Leisure:**

**Facilities:**

**Services:**

**Notes:** Wi-fi, sports area, recycling, night warden

## ►►► 77% Penderleath Caravan & Camping Park *(SW496375)*

Towednack TR26 3AF

☎ 01736 798403

**email:** holidays@penderleath.co.uk

**web:** www.penderleath.co.uk

**Dir:** *From A30 take A3074 towards St Ives. Left at 2nd mini-rdbt, approx 3m to T-junct. Left then immediately right. Left at next fork*

★ £11.50-£19.50 £11.50-£19.50 £11.50-£19.50

Open Etr-Oct Booking advisable Jul-Aug Last arrival 21.30hrs Last departure 10.30hrs

Set in a rugged rural location, this tranquil park has extensive views towards St Ives Bay and the north coast. Facilities are all housed in modernised granite barns, and include a quiet licensed bar with beer garden, breakfast room and bar meals. The owners are welcoming and helpful. A 10-acre site with 75 touring pitches.

**Leisure:**

**Facilities:**

**Services:**

**Notes:** Dogs must be well behaved & kept on a lead. Takeaway food

## ►►► 79% Trevalgan Touring Park *(SW490402)*

COUNTRYSIDE DISCOVERY

DAVID BELLAMY CONSERVATION AWARD SILVER

Trevalgan TR26 3BJ

☎ 01736 792048 🖷 01736 798797

**email:** recept@trevalgantouringpark.co.uk

**web:** www.trevalgantouringpark.co.uk

**Dir:** *From A30 follow holiday route to St Ives. B3311 through Halsetown to B3306. Left towards Land's End. Site signed 0.5m on right*

★ £12.50-£19 £12.50-£19 £12.50-£19

*Trevalgan Touring Park*

Open Etr-early Sep (rs Apr-May & Sep shop & takeaway closed) Booking advisable mid Jul-Aug Last arrival 22.00hrs Last departure 10.00hrs

An open park next to a working farm in a rural area on the coastal road from St Ives to Zennor. The park is surrounded by mature hedges, but there are extensive views out over the sea. There are very good toilet facilities including family rooms, and a large TV lounge and recreation room with drinks machine. A 4.75-acre site with 120 touring pitches.

**Leisure:**

**Facilities:**

**Services:**

**Notes:** Farm trail, crazy golf

ENGLAND

## ST IVES MAP 02 SW54

### ►► 85% Balnoon Camping Site (SW509382)

Halsetown TR26 3JA

☎ 01736 795431

**email:** nat@balnoon.fsnet.co.uk

**Dir:** *From A30 take A3074, at 2nd mini-rdbt take 1st left signed Tate St Ives. After 3m turn right after Balnoon Inn*

★ £8-£12

Open Etr-Oct Booking advisable Jul-Aug Last arrival 20.00hrs Last departure 11.00hrs

Small, quiet and friendly, this sheltered site offers superb views of the adjacent rolling hills. The two paddocks are surrounded by mature hedges, and the toilet facilities are kept spotlessly clean. The beaches of Carbis Bay and St Ives are about 2 miles away. A 1-acre site with 23 touring pitches.

**Facilities:**

**Services:** → 

**Notes:**

## ST JUST (NEAR LAND'S END) MAP 02 SW33

### ►►► 78% Kelynack Caravan & Camping Park (SW374301)

Kelynack TR19 7RE

☎ 01736 787633 01736 787633

**email:** kelynackholidays@tiscali.co.uk

**Dir:** *1m S of St Just, 5m N of Land's End on B3306*

Open Apr-Oct Booking advisable Jul-Aug Last arrival 22.00hrs Last departure 10.00hrs

A small secluded park nestling alongside a stream in an unspoilt rural location. The level grass pitches are in two areas, and the park is close to many coves, beaches and ancient villages. A 3-acre site with 20 touring pitches, 4 hardstandings and 13 statics.

**Leisure:**

**Facilities:**

**Services:** →

**Notes:** Dining & cooking shelter

### ►►► 76% Roselands Caravan Park (SW387305)

Dowran TR19 7RS

☎ 01736 788571

**email:** camping@roseland84.freeserve.co.uk

**web:** www.roselands.co.uk

**Dir:** *From A30 Penzance bypass turn right for St Just on A3071. 5m, turn left after tin mine chimney at sign, follow signs to park*

Open Etr-Oct Booking advisable Jun-Sep Last arrival 21.00hrs Last departure 11.00hrs

A small, friendly park in a sheltered rural setting, an ideal location for a quiet family holiday. The owners are continuing to upgrade the park, and in addition to the attractive little bar there is an indoor games room, children's playground, and good toilet facilities. A 3-acre site with 15 touring pitches and 15 statics.

**Leisure:**

**Facilities:**

**Services:** →

**Notes:** No cars by caravans. Cycle hire

### ►►► 75% Secret Garden Caravan & Camping Park (SW370305)

Bosavern House TR19 7RD

☎ 01736 788301

**email:** mail@bosavern.com

**web:** www.secretbosavern.com

**Dir:** *Turn off A3071 near St Just onto B3306 Land's End road. Park 0.5m on left*

★ £12-£16.50 £12-£16.50 £12-£16.50

Open Mar-Oct Booking advisable Jul-Aug Last arrival 22.00hrs Last departure noon

A neat little site in a walled garden behind a guest house, where visitors can enjoy breakfast, and snacks in the bar in the evening. This site is in a fairly sheltered location with all grassy pitches. There is no children's playground. A 1.5-acre site with 12 touring pitches.

**Leisure:**

**Facilities:**

**Services:** →

**Notes:** No pets

ENGLAND

►►► 76% **Trevaylor Caravan & Camping Park** *(SW368222)*

Botallack TR19 7PU

☎ 01736 787016

**email:** bookings@trevaylor.com

**web:** www.trevaylor.com

**Dir:** *On B3306 (St Just-St Ives road), site on right 0.75m from St Just*

★ £10-£12 £10-£12 £10-£12

Open Fri before Etr-Oct Booking advisable Jul & Aug Last departure noon

A sheltered grassy site located off the beaten track in a peaceful location at the western tip of Cornwall. The dramatic coastline and the pretty villages nearby are truly unspoilt. Clean, well-maintained facilities and a good shop are offered along with a bar serving bar meals. A 6-acre site with 50 touring pitches.

**Leisure:**

**Facilities:**

**Services:**

## ST JUST-IN-ROSELAND MAP 02 SW83

►►► 90% **Trethem Mill Touring Park** *(SW860365)*

The Best of British Touring and Holiday Parks

TR2 5JF

☎ 01872 580504 01872 580968

**email:** reception@trethem.com

**web:** www.trethem.com

**Dir:** *From Tregony on A3078 to St Mawes. 2m after Trewithian, follow signs to park*

★ £14-£20 £14-£20 £14-£20

Open Apr-Oct Booking advisable Jul-Aug Last arrival 20.00hrs Last departure 11.00hrs

A quality park in all areas, with upgraded amenities including a reception, shop, laundry, and disabled/family room. This carefully-tended and sheltered park is in a lovely rural setting, with spacious pitches separated by young trees and shrubs. The very keen family who own it are continually looking for ways to enhance its facilities. An 11-acre site with 84 touring pitches, 45 hardstandings.

**Leisure:**

**Facilities:**

**Services:**

**Notes:** Wi-fi, information centre

*See advertisement under ST MAWES*

## ST MABYN MAP 02 SX07

►►► 79% **Glenmorris Park** *(SX055733)*

David Bellamy Conservation Award SILVER

Longstone Rd PL30 3BY

☎ 01208 841677 01208 841514

**email:** info@glenmorris.co.uk

**web:** www.glenmorris.co.uk

**Dir:** *S of Camelford on A39, left after BP garage onto B3266 to Bodmin, 6m to Longstone, right at x-rds to St Mabyn, site approx 400mtrs on right*

★ £8-£14.30

Open Etr-Oct (rs Etr-mid May & mid Sep-Oct swimming pool closed) Booking advisable Jul-Aug (all year for statics) Last arrival 23.30hrs Last departure 10.30hrs

A very good, mainly level park in a peaceful rural location offering clean and well-maintained facilities - a small games room, heated outdoor swimming pool and sunbathing area, and shop. An ideal location for visiting this unspoilt area. An 11-acre site with 80 touring pitches and 11 statics.

**Leisure:**

**Facilities:**

**Services:**

**Notes:** Quiet after 22.00hrs

## ST MARY'S MAP 02 SV91

*See Scilly, Isles of. Page 90*

ENGLAND

## ST MAWES — MAP 02 SW83

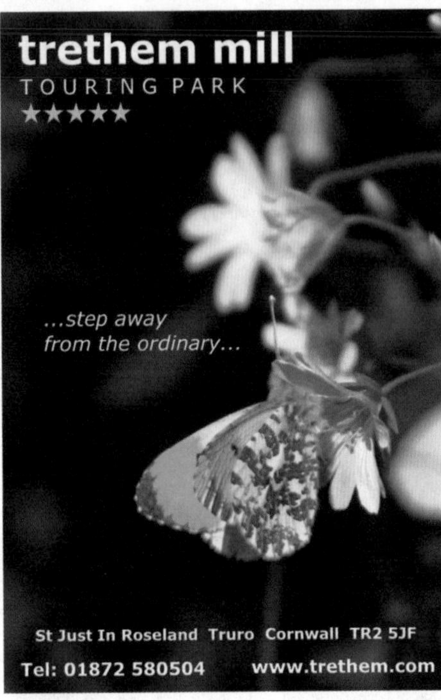

trethem mill
TOURING PARK
★★★★★
...step away
from the ordinary...
St Just In Roseland Truro Cornwall TR2 5JF
Tel: 01872 580504
www.trethem.com


## ST MERRYN (NEAR PADSTOW) — MAP 02 SW87

76% ***Harlyn Sands Holiday Park*** *(SW873752)*

Lighthouse Rd, Trevose Head PL28 8SQ

☎ 01841 520720 01841 521251

**email:** harlyn@freenet.co.uk

**web:** www.harlynsands.co.uk

**Dir:** *Exit B3276 in St Merryn centre onto unclassified road towards Harlyn Sands & Trevose Head. Follow brown park signs for approx 1m. (NB Do not turn right to Harlyn Sands)*

Open Etr-Nov Booking advisable Last arrival 22.00hrs Last departure 10.00hrs

A family park for 'bucket and spade' holidays, surrounded by seven bays each with its own sandy beach. On site entertainment for children and adults is extensive, and there is an indoor swimming pool complex, excellent restaurant and take-away, and a quiet over-30s lounge bar. A 21-acre site with 160 touring pitches, 6 hardstandings and 350 statics.

**Leisure:** **Facilities:**

**Services:** →

**Notes:** Families only. Arcade, clubhouse

►►►► 76% **Carnevas Holiday Park & Farm Cottages** *(SW862728)*

Carnevas Farm PL28 8PN

☎ 01841 520230 & 521209 01841 520230

**email:** carnevascampsite@aol.com

**web:** www.carnevasholidaypark.co.uk

**Dir:** *From St Merryn on B3276 towards Porthcothan Bay. Approx 2m turn right at site sign onto unclass road opposite Tredrea Inn. Site 0.25m on right*

★ £8-£15 £8-£15 £8-£15

Open Apr-Oct (rs Apr-Whit & mid Sep-Oct shop, bar & restaurant closed) Booking advisable Jul-Aug

A family-run park on a working farm, divided into four paddocks on slightly sloping grass. The toilets are central to all areas, and there is a small licensed bar serving bar meals. An 8-acre site with 195 touring pitches and 14 statics.

**Leisure:**

**Facilities:**

**Services:** →

**Notes:** No skateboards. Wi-fi, 2 family bathrooms

►►► 74% **Point Curlew Chalet & Touring Park** *(SW890717)*

St Merryn PL28 8PY

☎ 01841 520855 01841 521413

**web:** www.pointcurlew.com

**Dir:** *Take B3274 towards Padstow. In 3m turn left onto unclass road to St Merryn, follow brown signs to park*

£20-£22 £18-£20 £18-£20

Open Etr-Oct Booking advisable end Jun-early Sep Last arrival mdnt Last departure noon

This touring area, part of a larger chalet park set is in a quiet rural spot yet only two miles from seven popular bays. Free entertainment is available in high season and there are children's fun nights, and a quiet bar. A 4.5-acre site with 70 touring pitches and 220 statics.

**Leisure:**

**Facilities:**

**Services:** →

**Notes:** No pets

ENGLAND

## ►►► 74% Trevean Caravan & Camping Park (SW875724)

Trevean Ln PL28 8PR

☎ 01841 520772 🖷 01841 520772

**email:** trevean.info@virgin.net

**Dir:** *From St Merryn take B3276 to Newquay for 1m. Turn left for Rumford. Site 0.25m on right*

★ £8-£12 £8-£12 £8-£12

Open Apr-Oct (Shop open Whit-Sep) Booking advisable mid Jul-Aug Last arrival 22.00hrs Last departure 11.00hrs

A small working farm site with level grassy pitches in open countryside. The toilet facilities are clean and well kept, and there is a laundry and good children's playground. A 1.5-acre site with 36 touring pitches.

**Leisure:**  **Facilities:**

**Services:**

**Notes:** No teenage groups

## ►► 70% Tregavone Touring Park

(SW898732)

Tregavone Farm PL28 8JZ

☎ 01841 520148

**web:** www.tregavonefarm.co.uk

**Dir:** *From A389 towards Padstow, turn right after Little Petherick, in 1m just beyond Padstow Holiday Park turn left into unclass road signed Tregavone. Site on left in approx 1m.*

Open Mar-Oct Booking advisable end Jul-early Aug

Situated on a working farm with unspoilt country views, this spacious grassy park, run by friendly family owners, makes an ideal base for exploring the North Cornish Coast and the seven local golden beaches with surfing areas, or enjoying quiet country walks from the park. A 3-acre site with 40 touring pitches.

**Facilities:**

**Services:**

**Notes:**

### ST MINVER MAP 02 SW97

## ►►►► 74% Gunvenna Caravan Park

(SW969782)

PL27 6QN

☎ 01208 862405 🖷 01208 869107

**Dir:** *From A39 N of Wadebridge take B3314 (Port Isaac road), park 4m on right*

Open Etr-Oct Booking advisable Jul-Aug Last arrival 21.00hrs Last departure 11.00hrs

Attractive park with extensive rural views in a quiet country location, yet within three miles of Polzeath. This popular park is family owned and run, and provides good facilities in an ideal position for touring north Cornwall. A 10-acre site with 75 touring pitches, 5 hardstandings and 44 statics.

**Leisure:**

**Facilities:**

**Services:**

**Notes:**

### SCILLY, ISLES OF

### BRYHER MAP 02 SV81

## ►►► 76% Bryher Camp Site (SV880155)

TR23 0PR

☎ 01720 422886 🖷 01720 423092

**email:** brycamp@aol.com

**web:** www.bryhercampsite.co.uk

**Dir:** *Reached by boat from the main island of St Marys*

Open Apr-Oct Booking advisable summer months

Set on the smallest Scilly Isle with spectacular scenery and white beaches, this tent-only site is in a sheltered valley surrounded by hedges. Pitches are located in paddocks at the northern end of the island, and easily reached from the quay. There is a good modern toilet block, and plenty of peace and quiet. A 2.25-acre site with 38 touring pitches.

**Facilities:**

**Services:**

**Notes:** No pets

## ST MARY'S — MAP 02 SV91

### ►►► 74% **Garrison Campsite** *(SV897104)*

Tower Cottage, The Garrison TR21 0LS

☎ 01720 422670 Fax 01720 422670

**email:** tedmoulson@aol.com

**web:** www.garrisonholidays.com

**Dir:** *10 mins' walk from quay to site*

★ ▲ £12.60-£16.40

Open Etr-Oct Booking advisable Jul & Aug Last arrival 20.00hrs Last departure 19.00hrs

Set on the top of an old fort with superb views, this park offers tent-only pitches in a choice of well-sheltered paddocks. There are modern toilet facilities and a good shop at this attractive site, which is only 10 minutes from the town, the quay and the nearest beaches. A 9.5-acre site with 120 touring pitches.

**Facilities:**

**Services:**

**Notes:** No pets, no open fires, no cars on site. Playground adjacent to site

## SENNEN — MAP 02 SW32

### ►►► 72% **Sennen Cove Camping & Caravanning Club Site** *(SW378276)*

Higher Tregiffian Farm TR19 6JB

☎ 01736 871588

**web:** www.campingandcaravanningclub.co.uk/sennencove

**Dir:** *A30 towards Land's End. Right onto A3306 St Just/Pendeen Rd. Site 200yds on left*

★ £14.05-£18.85 £14.05-£18.85 ▲ £14.05-£18.85

Open 28 Mar-29 Sep Booking advisable BH & peak periods Last arrival 21.00hrs Last departure noon

Set in a rural area with distant views of Carn Brae and the coast just 2 miles from Land's End, this very good club site is well run with modern, clean facilities. It offers a children's playfield, late arrivals area and a dog-exercising paddock. A 4-acre site with 75 touring pitches, 6 hardstandings.

**Leisure:**

**Facilities:**

**Services:**

**Notes:** Gates closed 23.00-07.00

### ►►► 74% **Trevedra Farm Caravan & Camping Site** *(SW368276)*

TR19 7BE

☎ 01736 871818 & 871835 Fax 01736 871794

**email:** trevedra@btconnect.com

**web:** www.sennen-cove.com/trevedra.htm

**Dir:** *Take A30 towards Land's End. After junct with B3306 turn right into farm lane*

▲

Open Etr or Apr-Oct Booking advisable peak seasons Last arrival 19.00hrs Last departure 10.30hrs

A working farm with dramatic sea views over to the Scilly Isles, just a mile from Land's end. The popular campsite offers refurbished toilets, a well-stocked shop, and a cooked breakfast or evening meal from the food bar. There is direct access to the coastal footpath, and two beautiful beaches are a short walk away. An 8-acre site with 100 touring pitches.

**Facilities:**

**Services:**

**Notes:** Dogs must be kept on a lead at all times

## SUMMERCOURT — MAP 02 SW85

### RV 95% **Carvynick Country Club** *(SW878564)*

TR8 5AF

☎ 01872 510716 Fax 01872 510172

**email:** info@carvynick.co.uk

**web:** www.carvynick.co.uk

**Dir:** *Off B3058*

Open all year (rs Jan-early Feb Restricted leisure facilities) Booking advisable

Set within the gardens of an attractive country estate this spacious dedicated American RV Park (also home to the 'Itchy Feet' retail company) provides all full facility pitches on hard standings. The extensive on site amenities, shared by the high quality time share village, include an excellent restaurant with lounge bar, indoor leisure area with swimming pool, fitness suite and badminton court. 32 touring pitches.

**Leisure:**

**Services:**

**Notes:** Dogs must be exercised off site

## TINTAGEL — MAP 02 SX08

*see also Camelford*

### ►►► 70% *Headland Caravan & Camping Park* (SX056887)

Atlantic Rd PL34 0DE

☎ 01840 770239 Fax 01840 770925

**email:** headland.caravan@btconnect.com

**web:** www.headlandcaravanpark.co.uk

**Dir:** *From B3263 follow brown tourist signs through village to Headland*

Open Etr-Oct Booking advisable Jul-Aug Last arrival 21.00hrs

A peaceful family-run site in the mystical village of Tintagel, close to the ruins of King Arthur's Castle. The Cornish coastal path and the spectacular scenery are just two of the attractions here, and there are safe bathing beaches nearby. A 5-acre site with 62 touring pitches and 28 statics.

**Leisure:**

**Facilities:**

**Services:**

**Notes:** Dogs must be kept on short leads & exercised off park, quiet after 23.00hrs

## TORPOINT — MAP 03 SX45

### ►►►► 78% **Whitsand Bay Lodge & Touring Park** (SX410515)

Millbrook PL10 1JZ

☎ 01752 822597 Fax 01752 823444

**email:** enquiries@whitsandbayholidays.co.uk

**web:** www.whitsandbayholidays.co.uk

**Dir:** *From Torpoint take A374, turn left at Anthony onto B3247 for 1.25m to T-junct. Turn left, 0.25m then right onto Cliff Rd. Site 2m on left*

£12-£25 £12-£25

Open all year Booking advisable Jul-Sep Last departure 10.00hrs

A very well equipped park with panoramic coastal, sea and countryside views from its terraced pitches. An ambitious programme of development has resulted in a very high quality park with upmarket toilet facilities and other amenities. A 27-acre site with 17 touring pitches, 17 hardstandings and 5 statics.

**Leisure:** **Facilities:**

**Services:**

**Notes:** No cars by tents. Families & couples only. Sauna, sunbed, entertainment, putting, chapel, library

## TREGURRIAN — MAP 02 SW86

### ►►► 79% **Tregurrian Camping & Caravanning Club Site** (SW847654)

TR8 4AE

☎ 01637 860448

**web:** www.campingandcaravanningclub.co.uk/tregurrian

**Dir:** *A30 onto A3059, 1.5m turn right signed Newquay Airport. Left at junct after airport, then right at grass triangle, follow signs to Watergate Bay*

★ £15.45-£22.15 £15.45-£22.15 £15.45-£22.15

Open 28 Apr-29 Sep Booking advisable BH & peak periods Last arrival 21.00hrs Last departure noon

A level grassy site close to the famous beaches of Watergate Bay, with a modern amenity block. This club site is an excellent touring centre for the Padstow-Newquay coast. A 4.25-acre site with 90 touring pitches, 8 hardstandings.

**Facilities:**

**Services:**

**Notes:** Site gates closed 23.00hrs-07.00hrs

ENGLAND

## TRURO MAP 02 SW84

*see also Portscatho*

### ►►►► 90% Carnon Downs Caravan & Camping Park

*(SW805406)*

Carnon Downs TR3 6JJ

☎ 01872 862283 🖷 01872 870820

**email:** info@carnon-downs-caravanpark.co.uk

**web:** www.carnon-downs-caravanpark.co.uk

**Dir:** *Take A39 from Truro towards Falmouth. Site just off main Carnon Downs rdbt, on left*

Open all year Booking advisable Jul-Aug Last arrival 22.00hrs Last departure 11.00hrs

A mature park with a high standard of landscaping, set in meadowland and woodland close to the village amenities of Carnon Downs. The toilet facilities provide quality and comfort in private cubicles. A 33-acre site with 150 touring pitches, 67 hardstandings and 1 static.

**Leisure:**

**Facilities:**

**Services:** →

**Notes:** Baby & child bathroom, 3 family bathrooms

### ►►►► 77% Liskey Holiday Park *(SW772452)*

Greenbottom TR4 8QN

☎ 01872 560274 🖷 01872 561413

**email:** info@liskey.co.uk

**web:** www.liskey.co.uk

**Dir:** *Exit A390 at Threemilestone rdbt onto unclass road towards Chacewater. Site signed on right in 0.5m*

★ £9-£18 £9-£18 £9-£14

Open all year Booking advisable Jul-Aug Last arrival 21.00hrs Last departure 10.30hrs

An attractive south facing park divided into paddocks by mature hedging, and with quality modern toilets. It is located on the fringes of an urban area a few miles from the city, and almost equidistant from both the rugged north coast and the calmer south coastal areas. There is a bus from the gate to the city of Truro. An 8.5-acre site with 51 touring pitches, 26 hardstandings.

**Leisure:**

**Facilities:**

**Services:** →

**Notes:** No bicycles or skateboards. Wi-fi, serviced pitches, playbarn volleyball & badminton

### ►►► 76% Cosawes Caravan Park

*(SW768376)*

Perranarworthal TR3 7QS

☎ 01872 863724 🖷 01872 870268

**email:** info@cosawes.com

**web:** www.cosawes.com

**Dir:** *Turn off A39 midway between Truro & Falmouth, with direct access at park sign after Perranarworthal*

★ £11.50-£16 £11.50-£16 £9-£11

Open all year Booking advisable mid Jul-mid Aug Last departure noon

A small touring park in a peaceful wooded valley, midway between Truro and Falmouth. Its stunning location is ideal for visiting the many nearby hamlets and villages on the Carrick Roads, a stretch of tidal water which is a centre for sailing and other boats. A 2-acre site with 40 touring pitches, 25 hardstandings.

**Facilities:**

**Services:** →

**Notes:** Dogs must be kept on leads at all times

### ►►► 74% *Summer Valley*

*(SW800479)*

Shortlanesend TR4 9DW

☎ 01872 277878

**email:** res@summervalley.co.uk

**web:** www.summervalley.co.uk

**Dir:** *3m NW off B3284*

Open Apr-Oct Booking advisable Jul-Aug Last arrival 20.00hrs Last departure noon

A very attractive and secluded site in a rural setting midway between the A30 and the cathedral city of Truro. Keen owners maintain the facilities to a good standard. A 3-acre site with 60 touring pitches.

**Leisure:**

**Facilities:**

**Services:** →

**Notes:** Campers' lounge

## VERYAN MAP 02 SW93

### ►►► 76% Veryan Camping & Caravanning Club Site *(SW934414)*

SILVER

Tretheake Manor TR2 5PP

☎ 01872 501658

**web:** www.campingandcaravanningclub.co.uk/veryan

**Dir:** *Left off A3078 at filling station signed Veryan/Portloe on unclass road. Site signed on left*

★ £15.45-£20.15 £15.45-£20.15 £15.45-£20.15

Open 13 Mar-3 Nov Booking advisable BH & peak periods Last arrival 21.00hrs Last departure noon

A quiet park on slightly undulating land with pleasant views of the surrounding countryside. A tranquil fishing lake holds appeal for anglers, and the site is just 2.5 miles from one of Cornwall's finest sandy beaches. A 9-acre site with 150 touring pitches, 24 hardstandings.

**Leisure:**

**Facilities:**

**Services:** →

**Notes:** Site gates closed 23.00hrs-07.00hrs.

## WADEBRIDGE MAP 02 SW97

### ►►► 80% The Laurels Holiday Park *(SW957715)*

Padstow Rd, Whitecross PL27 7JQ

☎ 01209 313474

**email:** jamierielly@btconnect.com

**web:** www.thelaurelsholidaypark.co.uk

**Dir:** *Off A389 (Padstow road) near junct with A39, W of Wadebridge*

★ £14-£17 £14-£17 £14-£17

Open Apr/Etr-Oct Booking advisable Jun-Sep Last arrival 20.00hrs Last departure 10.00hrs

A very smart and well-equipped park with individual pitches screened by hedges and young shrubs. The dog walk is of great benefit to pet owners, and the Camel cycle trail and Padstow are not far away. A 2.25-acre site with 30 touring pitches.

**Leisure:**

**Facilities:**

**Services:** →

**Notes:** Dogs must be kept on leads



### ►►► 72% Little Bodieve Holiday Park *(SW995734)*

Bodieve Rd PL27 6EG

☎ 01208 812323

**email:** berry@littlebodieveholidaypark.fsnet.co.uk

**web:** www.littlebodieve.co.uk

**Dir:** *From A39 rdbt on Wadebridge by-pass take B3314 signed Rock/Port Isaac, site 0.25m on right*

Open Apr-Oct (rs early & late season pool, shop & clubhouse closed) Booking advisable Jul-Aug Last arrival 20.00hrs Last departure 11.00hrs

Rurally located with pitches in three large grassy paddocks, this family park is close to the Camel Estuary. The licensed clubhouse provides bar meals, with an entertainment programme in high season, and there is a swimming pool with sun terrace, and a separate waterslide and splash pool. A 22-acre site with 195 touring pitches and 75 statics.

**Leisure:**

**Facilities:**

**Services:** →

**Notes:** Families & couples only. Crazy golf, water shute/splash pool, pets' corner

**Facilities:** Bath · Shower · Electric Shaver · Hairdryer · Ice Pack Facility · Disabled Facilities · Public Telephone · Shop on Site or within 200yds · Mobile Shop (calls at least 5 days a week) · BBQ Area · Picnic Area · Dog Exercise Area

ENGLAND

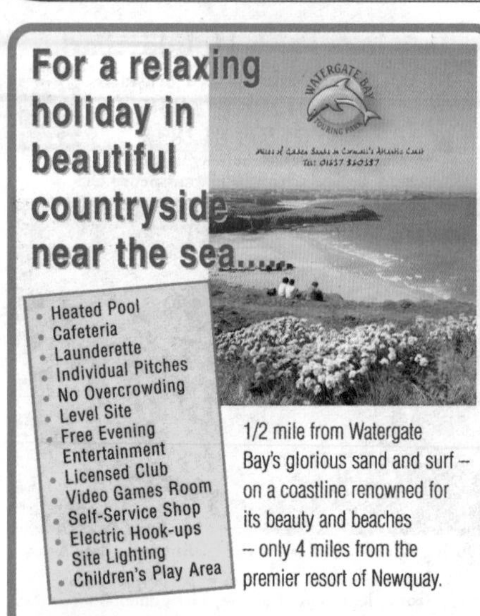


## WATERGATE BAY — MAP 02 SW86

### ►►►► 78% Watergate Bay Tourist Park

*(SW850653)*

Watergate Bay TR8 4AD

☎ 01637 860387 📠 01637 860387

**email:** email@watergatebaytouringpark.co.uk

**web:** www.watergatebaytouringpark.co.uk

**Dir:** *4m N of Newquay on B3276 (coast road)*

★ £9-£16 £9-£16 £9-£16

Open Mar-Oct (rs Mar-22 May & 13 Sep-Oct restricted bar, cafe, shop & swimming pool) Booking advisable Jul-Aug Last arrival 22.00hrs Last departure noon

A well-established park above Watergate Bay, where acres of golden sand, rock pools and surf are seen as a holidaymaker's paradise. Toilet facilities are to a high standard, and there is a wide range of activities including a regular entertainment programme in the clubhouse. A 30-acre site with 171 touring pitches, 14 hardstandings.

**Leisure:**

**Facilities:**

**Services:**

**Notes:** Entertainment, free minibus to beach.

*see advert on this page*

## WHITE CROSS — MAP 02 SW85

### 78% White Acres Holiday Park *(SW890599)*

GOLD

TR8 4LW

☎ 01726 862100 & 0871 641 0199 📠 01726 860777

**email:** enquiries@parkdeanholidays.co.uk

**web:** www.parkdeanholidays.co.uk

**Dir:** *From A30 at Indian Queens take A392 signed Newquay. Site 2m on right*

★ £13-£33 £15-£35 £10-£29

Open Mar-Oct Booking advisable high season Last arrival 21.00hrs Last departure 10.00hrs

A high quality holiday park with upmarket facilities and plenty of leisure activities and entertainment for the whole family. Boasting one of the best coarse fishing centres in the South West, it also offers a heated indoor swimming pool, sauna, jacuzzi and gym, coffee bar, restaurant and pub, and clubs for children. The touring area is partly terraced, and the setting of 100 rural acres is very attractive. A 167-acre site with 40 touring pitches, 6 hardstandings and 271 statics.

**Leisure:**

**Facilities:**

**Services:**

**Notes:** Entertainment, solarium, bowling

### ►►► 69% *Summer Lodge Holiday Park* *(SW890597)*

BRONZE

TR8 4LW

☎ 01726 860415 📠 01726 861490

**email:** summer.lodge@snootyfoxresorts.co.uk

**web:** www.snootyfoxresorts.co.uk

**Dir:** *From Indian Queens on A30 take A392 to Newquay. Site on left at Whitecross in 2.5m*

Open Mar-Oct (rs Etr-Whit & Sep-Oct shop café closed)

Small holiday complex offering use of good facilities. This park has a nightly cabaret in the licensed pub, plus other on-site entertainment. A 26-acre site with 100 touring pitches and 118 statics.

**Leisure:** **Facilities:**

**Services:** **Notes:** Crazy golf

## WIDEMOUTH BAY MAP 02 SS20

### 71% Widemouth Bay Caravan Park *(SS199008)*

EX23 0DF

01271 866766 01271 866791

**email:** bookings@jfhols.co.uk

**web:** www.johnfowlerholidays.com

**Dir:** *Take Widemouth Bay coastal road off A39, turn left. Park on left*

★ £7-£20 £7-£20 £7-£20

Open Etr-Oct Booking advisable all dates Last arrival dusk Last departure 10.00hrs

A partly sloping rural site set in countryside overlooking the sea and one of Cornwall's finest beaches. Nightly entertainment in high season with emphasis on children's and family club programmes. This park is located less than half a mile from the sandy beaches of Widemouth Bay. A 58-acre site with 220 touring pitches, 90 hardstandings and 200 statics.

**Leisure:**

**Facilities:**

**Services:** →

### ►►► 72% Cornish Coast Caravan & Camping *(SS202981)*

Aiddle Penlean, Poundstock EX23 0EE

01288 361380

**mail:** enquiries5@cornishcoasts.co.uk

**veb:** www.cornishcoasts.co.uk

**ir:** *5m S of Bude on A39, 0.5m S of Rebel Cinema on right*

)pen Apr-Oct Booking advisable school hols Last arrival 2.00hrs Last departure 10.30hrs

quiet family-run park, with terraced pitches making the most of the tunning views over the countryside to the sea at Widemouth Bay. eception is in a 13th-century cottage, and the park is well equipped nd tidy. A 3.5-acre site with 46 touring pitches, 2 hardstandings and statics.

**eisure:**

**acilities:**

**ervices:** →

**lotes:** Quiet after 22.00hrs

### ►►► 71% Penhalt Farm Holiday Park *(SS194003)*

EX23 0DG

01288 361210 01288 361210

**email:** denandjennie@penhaltfarm.fsnet.co.uk

**web:** www.holidaybank.co.uk/penhaltfarmholidaypark

**Dir:** *From Bude take 2nd turn right to Widemouth Bay road off A39, left at end by Widemouth Manor signed Millook onto coastal road. Site 0.75m on left*

Open Etr-Oct Booking advisable Jul & Aug

Splendid views of the sea and coast can be enjoyed from all pitches on this sloping but partly level site, set in a lovely rural area on a working farm. About one mile away is one of Cornwall's finest beaches which is popular with all the family as well as surfers. An 8-acre site with 100 touring pitches.

**Leisure:**

**Facilities:**

**Services:** →

**Notes:** Pool table, netball & football posts

**eisure:** Indoor swimming pool Outdoor swimming pool Tennis court Games room Children's playground Stables 9/18 hole golf course Boats for hire Cinema Fishing Mini golf Watersports Separate TV room

## CUMBRIA

**AMBLESIDE** MAP 18 NY30

### ►►►► 84% *Skelwith Fold Caravan Park* (NY355029)

LA22 0HX

☎ 015394 32277 015394 34344

**email:** info@skelwith.com

**web:** www.skelwith.com

**Dir:** *Leave Ambleside on A593 towards Coniston, turn left at Clappersgate onto B5286 Hawkshead road. Park 1m on right*

Open Mar-15 Nov Booking advisable public hols & Jul-Aug Last arrival dusk Last departure noon

In the grounds of a former mansion, this park is in a beautiful setting close to Lake Windermere. Touring areas are dotted in paddocks around the extensively wooded grounds, and the all-weather pitches are set close to the many facility buildings. There is a 5-acre family recreation area which has spectacular views of Loughrigg Fell. A 130-acre site with 150 touring pitches, 150 hardstandings and 300 statics.

**Leisure:**

**Facilities:**

**Services:** →

**Notes:** Family recreation area

*see advert on this page*

### ►►► 72% Low Wray National Trust Campsite (NY372013)

Low Wray LA22 0JA

☎ 015394 32810 015394 32684

**email:** lowwraycampsite@nationaltrust.org.uk

**web:** www.ntlakescampsites.org.uk

**Dir:** *3m SW of Ambleside on A593 to Clappersgate, then B5286. Approx 1m turn left at Wray sign. Site less than 1m on left*

★ £12-£12.60

Open wk before Etr-Oct Last arrival 20.00hrs Last departure 11.00hrs

Picturesquely set on the wooded shores of Lake Windermere, this site is a favourite with tenters and watersports enthusiasts. The well-maintained facilities are housed in wooden cabins, and tents can be pitched in wooded glades with lake views or open grassland. Off-road biking, walks and pub food are all nearby. A 10-acre site with 200 touring pitches.

**Leisure:**

**Facilities:** →

**Notes:** No cars by tents. No groups of more than 4 unless a family group with children. Launching for sailing craft

*see advert on this page*

## APPLEBY-IN-WESTMORLAND MAP 18 NY62

### PREMIER PARK

**►►►►► 94% Wild Rose Park** *(NY698165)*
Ormside CA16 6EJ
☎ 017683 51077 🖷 017683 52551
**email:** reception@wildrose.co.uk
**web:** www.wildrose.co.uk
**Dir:** *Signed on unclass road to Great Ormside, off B6260*

Open all year (rs Nov-Mar shop & swimming pool closed) Booking advisable BH & school hols Last arrival 22.00hrs Last departure noon

Situated in the Eden Valley, this large family-run park has been carefully landscaped and offers superb facilities maintained to an extremely high standard. There are several individual pitches, and extensive views from most areas of the park. Traditional stone walls and the planting of lots of indigenous trees help it to blend into the environment, and wildlife is actively encouraged. An 85-acre site with 240 touring pitches, 140 hardstandings and 273 statics.

**Leisure:**

**Facilities:**

**Services:**

**Notes:** No unaccompanied teenagers, no dangerous dogs, no group bookings. Tourist Information, pitch and putt

*see advert on this page*

Discover Eden's Caravanning Paradise
Multi-award winning camping and caravan park situated in the heart of the Eden Valley. Ideal for exploring the Lake District and Yorkshire Dales. Facilities include restaurant and take-away, mini market, launderette, play areas, tennis and badminton courts, TV and games rooms and heated outdoor pools.
Luxury holiday homes for sale – call for a brochure.
Tel: 017683 51077
Email: reception@wildrose.co.uk
www.wildrose.co.uk
AA
2006
Wild Rose Park


## AYSIDE MAP 18 SD38

**►►► 74% Oak Head Caravan Park**
*(SD389839)*
LA11 6JA
☎ 015395 31475
**web:** www.caravancampsites.co.uk/cumbria/oakhead.htm
**Dir:** *M6 junct 36, A590 towards Newby Bridge, 14m. Park sign on left, 1.25m past High Newton*

★ £14 £14 £12-£14

Open Mar-Oct Booking advisable BH Last arrival 22.00hrs Last departure noon

A pleasant terraced site with two separate areas - grass for tents and all gravel pitches for caravans and motorhomes. The site is enclosed within mature woodland and surrounded by hills. A 3-acre site with 60 touring pitches, 30 hardstandings and 71 statics.

**Facilities:**

**Services:**

**Notes:** No open fires

## BARROW-IN-FURNESS MAP 18 SD26

**►►► 82% South End Caravan Park**
*(SD208628)*
Walney Island LA14 3YQ
☎ 01229 472823 & 471556 🖷 01229 472822
**email:** kath.mulgrew@virgin.net
**web:** www.walney-island-caravan-park.co.uk
**Dir:** *M6 junct 36 onto A590 to Barrow follow signs for Walney Island. Turn left after crossing bridge. 4m S*

★ £16-£20 £16-£20

Open Mar-Oct Booking advisable Jul-Aug Last arrival 22.00hrs Last departure noon

A friendly family-owned and run park next to the sea and close to a nature reserve, on the southern end of Walney Island. It offers an

CONTINUED

## BARROW-IN-FURNESS CONTINUED

extensive range of quality amenities including an adult lounge, and high standards of cleanliness and maintenance. A 7-acre site with 50 touring pitches and 100 statics.

**Leisure:**

**Facilities:**

**Services:**

**Notes:** Bowling green, snooker table

## BASSENTHWAITE LAKE

*see map for locations of sites in the vicinity*

## BOOT MAP 18 NY10

### ►►► 92% Eskdale Camping & Caravanning Club Site (NY178011)

Hollins Farm CA19 1TH

☎ 019467 23253

**web:** www.campingandcaravanningclub.co.uk/eskdale

**Dir:** *Leave A595 at Gosforth or Holmbrook to Eskdale Green and on to Boot. Site on left towards Hardknott Pass after railway*

★ £18.15-£20.05 £18.15-£20.05 £18.15-£20.05

Open Mar-Oct Booking advisable BH & peak periods Last arrival 21.00hrs Last departure noon

A very pleasant site which has been extensively modernised and offers impressive facilities. The re-fitted toilets and showers, laundries and CDP are matched by an extensive reception and well stocked shop. The electric hook-ups are cleverly tucked away. The park is only 0.25m from Boot station on the Ravenglass/Eskdale railway ('Ratty').
An 8-acre site with 70 touring pitches.

**Leisure:**

**Facilities:**

**Services:**

**Notes:** Site gates closed 23.00hrs-07.00hrs

## BOWNESS-ON-WINDERMERE

*Sites are listed under Windermere*

## BRAITHWAITE MAP 18 NY22

### ►►► 76% Scotgate Holiday Park (NY235235)

CA12 5TF

☎ 017687 78343 017687 78099

**email:** info@scotgateholidaypark.co.uk

**web:** www.scotgateholidaypark.co.uk

**Dir:** *At junct of A66 and B5292, 2m from Keswick*

★ £15-£18.50 £12.40-£18.50 £9-£12.40

Open Mar-Oct Last arrival 22.00hrs Last departure 11.00hrs

Dramatic views of Skiddaw and the northern Fells dominate this pleasant rural site, which is frequented by tenters and close to the starting point of several walking routes. A popular café serves breakfast and other meals, and there is easy access to Whinlatter Forest,

*Scotgate Holiday Park*

Keswick, and Bassenthwaite Lake. An 8-acre site with 165 touring pitches and 35 statics.

**Leisure:**

**Facilities:**

**Services:**

## BRAMPTON MAP 21 NY56

### ►►► 68% Irthing Vale Holiday Park (NY522613)

Old Church Ln CA8 2AA

☎ 016977 3600

**email:** glennwndrby@aol.com

**web:** www.ukparks.co.uk/irthingvale

**Dir:** *From A69 take A6071 to site, 0.5m outside town. Turn opposite entrance to leisure centre by school. (NB take care in narrow lane)*

Open Mar-Oct Booking advisable public hols & Jul-Aug Last arrival 23.30hrs Last departure noon

A grassy site on the outskirts of the market town on the A6071. The friendly owners continue to gradually improve the facilities.
A 4.5-acre site with 20 touring pitches and 25 statics.

**Leisure:**

**Facilities:**

**Services:**

**Notes:**

## CARLISLE MAP 18 NY35

### ►►► 80% **Dandy Dinmont Caravan & Camping Park** *(NY399620)*

Blackford CA6 4EA

☎ 01228 674611 01228 674611

**email:** dandydinmont@btopenworld.com

**web:** www.caravan-camping-carlisle.itgo.com

**Dir:** *M6 junct 44, A7 N. Site 1.5m on right, after Blackford sign*

£10-£10.50 £10-£10.50 £8.50-£9.50

Open Mar-Oct Booking advisable BH Last arrival 22.00hrs Last departure 14.00hrs

A level sheltered site, screened on two sides by hedgerows. The grass pitches are immaculately kept, and there are some larger hardstandings for motor homes. Keen owners maintain good standards in all areas, and this rural park is only one mile from the M6 and Carlisle. A 4-acre site with 47 touring pitches, 20 hardstandings and 15 statics.

**Facilities:**

**Services:**

**Notes:** Dogs must be kept on leads at all times & exercised off site. Covered dishwashing area

### ►►► 84% **Green Acres Caravan Park**

*(NY416614)*

High Knells, Houghton CA6 4JW

☎ 01228 675418

**web:** www.caravanpark-cumbria.com

**Dir:** *Leave M6/A74(M) at junct 44, take A689 towards Brampton for 1m. Left at Scaleby sign and site 1m on left*

★ £11-£14 £11-£14 £8-£13

Open Etr-Oct Booking advisable BH Last arrival 21.00hrs Last departure noon

A small family touring park in rural surroundings with distant views of the fells. This pretty park is run by keen, friendly owners who maintain high standards throughout. A 3-acre site with 30 touring pitches, 25 hardstandings.

**Leisure:**

**Facilities:**

**Services:**

**Notes:**

## CARTMEL MAP 18 SD37

### ►►► 71% **Greaves Farm Caravan Park**

*(SD391823)*

Field Broughton LA11 6HU

☎ 015395 36329 & 36587

**Dir:** *From M6 junct 36 onto A590 signed Barrow. Approx 1m before Newby Bridge, turn left at x-roads signed Cartmel/ Staveley. Site 2m on left just before church*

★ £13-£15 £13-£15 £11-£14

Open Mar-Oct Booking advisable Last arrival 21.00hrs Last departure noon

A small family-owned park close to a working farm in a peaceful rural area. Motorhomes are parked in a paddock, and there is a large field for tents and caravans. This simple park is carefully maintained, and there is always a sparkle to the toilet facilities. A 3-acre site with 12 touring pitches and 20 statics.

**Facilities:**

**Services:**

**Notes:**

## CROOKLANDS MAP 18 SD58

### ►►► 82% **Waters Edge Caravan Park**

*(SD533838)*

LA7 7NN

☎ 015395 67708

**email:** dennis@watersedgecaravanpark.co.uk

**web:** www.watersedgecaravanpark.co.uk

**Dir:** *From M6 follow signs for Kirkby Lonsdale A65, at 2nd rdbt follow signs for Crooklands/Endmoor. Site 1m on right at Crooklands garage, just beyond 40mph limit*

★ £12.50-£18 £12.50-£18 £10.50-£18

Open Mar-14 Nov (rs low season bar not open on week days) Booking advisable BH Last arrival 22.00hrs Last departure noon

A peaceful, well-run park close to the M6, pleasantly bordered by streams and woodland. A Lakeland-style building houses a shop and bar, and the attractive toilet block is clean and modern. Ideal either as a stopover or for longer stays. A 3-acre site with 26 touring pitches and 20 statics.

**Leisure:**

**Facilities:**

**Services:**

**Notes:** Dogs must be kept on a lead at all times

ENGLAND

## CUMWHITTON MAP 18 NY55

### ►►► 72% Cairndale Caravan Park

*(NY518523)*

CA8 9BZ

☎ 01768 896280

**Dir:** *Off A69 at Warwick Bridge on unclass road through Great Corby to Cumwhitton, left at village sign, site 1m*

Open Mar-Oct Booking advisable school & public hols Last arrival 22.00hrs

Lovely grass site set in tranquil Eden Valley with good views to distant hills. The all-weather touring pitches have electricity, and are located close to the immaculate toilet facilities. A 2-acre site with 5 touring pitches, 5 hardstandings and 15 statics.

**Facilities:**

**Services:** →

**Notes:**

## DALSTON MAP 18 NY35

### ►►► 75% Dalston Hall Holiday Park

*(NY378519)*

Dalston Hall CA5 7JX

☎ 01228 710165

**web:** www.dalstonhall.co.uk

**Dir:** *M6 junct 42 signed for Dalston. 2.5m SW of Carlisle, just off B5299*

★ £12-£17 £12-£17 £8-£17

Open Mar-Oct Booking advisable BH, Jul-Aug Last arrival 22.00hrs Last departure noon

A neat, well-maintained site on level grass in the grounds of an estate located between Carlisle and Dalston. All facilities are to a very high standard, and amenities include a 9-hole golf course, a bar and clubhouse serving breakfast and bar meals, and salmon and trout fly fishing. A 5-acre site with 60 touring pitches, 26 hardstandings and 17 statics.

**Leisure:**

**Facilities:**

**Services:** →

**Notes:** No commercial vans, gates closed 22.00hrs-07.00hrs

## ESKDALE GREEN MAP 18 NY10

### ►►► 78% Fisherground Farm Campsite

*(NY152002)*

CA19 1TF

☎ 01946 723349 📠 01946 723349

**email:** camping@fishergroundcampsite.co.uk

**web:** www.fishergroundcampsite.co.uk

**Dir:** *Leave A595 at Gosforth or Holmrook, follow signs on unclass road to Eskdale Green then Boot. Site signed on left*

★ £12.50

Open Mar-Oct Booking advisable only for electric hook ups Last arrival 21.30hrs Last departure 11.00hrs

A mainly level grassy site on farmland amidst beautiful scenery, in Eskdale Valley below Hardknott Pass, between Eskdale and Boot. It has its own railway halt on the Eskdale-Ravenglass railway, 'The Ratty'. A large, heated boot-drying locker, offered free, in the laundry is an obvious bonus for walkers and climbers. A 9-acre site with 215 touring pitches.

**Leisure:**

**Facilities:**

**Services:** →

**Notes:** No caravans, dogs must be on a lead, no noise after 22.30hrs. Adventure playground, miniature railway, raft pond

## FLOOKBURGH MAP 18 SD37

### 77% Lakeland Leisure Park *(SD372743)*

Moor Ln LA11 7LT

☎ 01539 558556 📠 01539 558559

**web:** www.lakeland-park.co.uk

**Dir:** *On B5277 through Grange-over-Sands to Flookburgh. Left at village square, park 1m*

★ £9-£61 £9-£61 £9-£47

Open mid Mar-Oct Booking advisable Last departure 10.00hrs

A complete leisure park with full range of activities and entertainments, making this flat, grassy site ideal for families. The touring area is quietly situated away from the main amenities, but the swimming pools, all-weather bowling green and evening entertainment are just a short stroll away. A 105-acre site with 190 touring pitches and 800 statics.

**Leisure:**

**Facilities:**

**Services:** →

**Notes:** No cars by caravans or tents. Family park, no pets at Etr, May Day, Whitsun or summer hols. Wi-fi

*see advert on opposite page*

## GRANGE-OVER-SANDS

*see Cartmel*

ENGLAND

## GREAT LANGDALE MAP 18 NY20

### ►►► 71% Great Langdale National Trust Campsite *(NY286059)*

LA22 9JU

☎ 015394 37668 Fax 015394 37668

**email:** langdale.camp@nationaltrust.org.uk

**web:** www.langdalecampsite.org.uk

**Dir:** *A593 to Skelwith Bridge, right onto B5343, approx 5m to New Dungeon Ghyll Hotel. Site on left just before Hotel*

★ £12-£12.60

Open all year Last arrival 22.00hrs Last departure noon

Nestling in a green valley, sheltered by mature trees and surrounded by stunning fell views, this site is an ideal base for campers, climbers and fell walkers. The large grass tent area has some gravel parking for cars, and there is a separate area for groups and one for families with a children's play area. Attractive wooden cabins house the toilets, a shop, and drying rooms. A 9-acre site with 300 touring pitches.

**Leisure:**

**Facilities:** Shower, Electric Shaver, Ice Pack Facility, Disabled Facilities, Public Telephone, Shop on Site or within 200yds

**Services:**

**Notes:** No cars by tents. No noise between 23.00hrs-07.00hrs, numbers limited on group bookings

*see advert on page 96*

## HAVERTHWAITE MAP 18 SD38

### ►►► 72% Bigland Hall Caravan Park *(SD344833)*

LA12 8PJ

☎ 01539 531702 & 723339 Fax 01539 531702

**email:** biglandhallcaravanpark@hotmail.co.uk

**web:** www.biglandhallcaravanpark.com

**Dir:** *From A590 in Haverthwaite turn left opposite steam railway, left at T-junct signed B5278, park on left after 1.5m*

£15-£20 £15-£20

Open Mar-16 Nov Booking advisable public hols Last arrival 20.00hrs Last departure 13.00hrs

A wooded site in lovely countryside three miles from the southern end of Lake Windermere and near the Haverthwaite Steam Railway. The various touring areas are dotted around this large park, and the two toilet blocks are strategically placed. The site is suitable for large motorhomes. A 30-acre site with 36 touring pitches and 29 statics.

**Facilities:** Shower, Electric Shaver

**Services:**

**Notes:** Off-licence on site



## HOLMROOK MAP 18 SD09

### ►►► 71% Seven Acres Caravan Park *(NY078014)*

BRONZE

CA19 1YD

☎ 01946 822777

**Dir:** *Off A595 between Holmbrook & Gosforth*

This sheltered park is close to the quiet West Cumbrian coastal villages and beaches, and handy for Eskdale and Wasdale. There is a good choice of pitches, some with hedged bays for privacy, and some with coastal views. The park has a heated toilet block, and a children's play area, and there is plenty to do and see in the area. A 7-acre site with 37 touring pitches and 16 statics.

KENDAL MAP 18 SD59

### ►►► 76% Kendal Camping & Caravanning Club Site *(SD526948)*

Millcrest, Shap Rd LA9 6NY

☎ 01539 741363

**web:** www.campingandcaravanningclub.co.uk/kendal

**Dir:** *On A6, 1.5m N of Kendal. Site 100yds N of Skelsmergh sign*

★ £14.05-£18.85 £14.05-£18.85 £14.05-£18.85

Open 13 Mar-3 Nov Booking advisable BH & peak periods Last arrival 21.00hrs Last departure noon

A sloping grass site, set in hilly wood and meadowland, with some level all-weather pitches. Very clean, well kept facilities and attractive flower beds and tubs make a positive impression. The park is handy for nearby Kendal, with its shops and laundry (there is no laundry on site). A 3.5-acre site with 50 touring pitches, 6 hardstandings.

**Leisure:**

**Facilities:**

**Services:**

**Notes:** Site gates closed 23.00hrs-07.00hrs

KESWICK MAP 18 NY22

### ►►►► 92% Castlerigg Hall Caravan & Camping Park *(NY282227)*

Castlerigg Hall CA12 4TE

☎ 017687 74499 017687 74499

**email:** info@castlerigg.co.uk

**web:** www.castlerigg.co.uk

**Dir:** *1.5m SE of Keswick on A591, turn right at sign. Site 200mtrs on right past Heights Hotel*

£14.50-£16.95 £13.50-£15.50

Open mid Mar-7 Nov Booking advisable for touring caravans only Last arrival 21.00hrs Last departure 11.30hrs

Spectacular views over Derwentwater to the mountains beyond are among the many attractions at this lovely Lakeland park. Old farm buildings have been tastefully converted into excellent toilets with private washing and family bathroom, reception and a well-equipped shop, and there is a kitchen/dining area for campers with a courtyard tearoom which also serves breakfast. An 8-acre site with 48 touring pitches, 48 hardstandings and 30 statics.

**Leisure:** **Facilities:**

**Services:**

**Notes:** Dogs must be kept on a lead, no dogs left unattended. Wi-fi, campers' kitchen, sitting room

### ►►►► 76% Gill Head Farm Caravan & Camping Park *(NY380269)*

Troutbeck CA11 0ST

☎ 017687 79652 017687 79130

**email:** enquiries@gillheadfarm.co.uk

**web:** www.gillheadfarm.co.uk

**Dir:** *From M6 junct 40 take A66, then A5091 towards Troutbeck. Turn right after 100yds, then right again*

Open Apr-Oct Booking advisable BH Last arrival 22.30hrs Last departure noon

A family-run park on a working hill farm with lovely fell views. It has level touring pitches, and a log cabin dining room that is popular with families. Tent pitches are gently sloping in a separate field. A 5.5-acre site with 42 touring pitches and 17 statics.

**Leisure:** **Facilities:**

**Services:**

**Notes:** No fires

*see advert on this page*

### ►►► 80% Burns Farm Caravan Park

*(NY307244)*
St Johns in the Vale CA12 4RR
☎ 017687 79225 & 79112
**email:** linda@burns-farm.co.uk
**web:** www.burns-farm.co.uk
**Dir:** *Exit A66 signed Castlerigg Stone Circle/Youth Centre/Burns Farm. Site on right in 0.5m*

★ £10-£16 £10-£16 fr £10

Open Mar-4 Nov Booking advisable school hols, Jul-Aug Last departure noon

Lovely views of Blencathra and Skiddaw can be enjoyed from this secluded park, set on a working farm which extends a warm welcome to families. This is a good choice for exploring the beautiful and interesting countryside. Food can be found in the pub at Threlkeld. A 2.5-acre site with 32 touring pitches.

**Facilities:**

**Services:** →

**Notes:**

### ►►► 80% Castlerigg Farm Camping & Caravan Site *(NY283225)*

Castlerigg Farm CA12 4TE
☎ 017687 72479 017687 74718
**email:** info@castleriggfarm.com
**web:** www.castleriggfarm.com
**Dir:** *From Keswick on A591 towards Windermere, turn right at top of hill at camping sign. Farm 2nd site on left*

★ £10-£15

Open Mar-Nov Booking advisable Last arrival 21.30hrs Last departure 11.30hrs

Nestling at the foot of Walla Crag, this tranquil fellside park enjoys lake views, and is popular with families and couples seeking a quiet base for fell walking. The modern facilities include a shop, laundry and spotless toilet facilities. Castlerigg Stone Circle and the attractions of Keswick are nearby. A 3-acre site with 48 touring pitches.

**Facilities:**

**Services:** →

**Notes:** No noise after 22.30hrs, no fires on the ground, dogs must be kept on leads. Cycle storage

### ►►► 78% Derwentwater Camping & Caravanning Club Site *(NY262232)*

Crow Park Rd CA12 5EN
☎ 01768 772579
**web:** www.campingandcaravanningclub.co.uk/derwentwater
**Dir:** *Signed off B5289 in town centre*

★ £18.25-£22.15 £18.25-£22.15

Open Mar-14 Nov Booking advisable BH & peak periods Last arrival 21.00hrs Last departure noon

A peaceful location close to Derwentwater for this well-managed and popular park which is divided into two areas for tourers. Keswick, with its shops and pubs, is just a 5 minute walk away. A 16-acre site with 44 touring pitches, 17 hardstandings and 160 statics.

**Leisure:**

**Facilities:**

**Services:** →

**Notes:** Site gates closed 23.00hrs-07.00hrs

### ►►► 76% Keswick Camping & Caravanning Club Site *(NY258234)*

Crow Park Rd CA12 5EP
☎ 01768 772392
**web:** www.campingandcaravanningclub.co.uk/keswick
**Dir:** *From Penrith on A66 into Main Street (Keswick), right to pass 'Lakes' bus station, past rugby club, turn right, site on right*

★ £18.35-£23.25 £18.35-£23.25 £18.35-£23.25

Open Feb-Nov Booking advisable BH & peak period Last arrival 21.00hrs Last departure noon

A well situated lakeside site within walking distance of the town centre. Boat launching is available from the site onto Derwentwater, and this level grassy park also offers a number of all-weather pitches. A 14-acre site with 250 touring pitches, 95 hardstandings.

**Leisure:**

**Facilities:**

**Services:** →

**Notes:** Site gates closed 23.00hrs-07.00hrs

ENGLAND

## KIRKBY LONSDALE MAP 18 SD67

### ►►►► 77% New House Caravan Park

*(SD628774)*
LA6 2HR
☎ 015242 71590
**email:** colinpreece9@aol.com
**Dir:** *1m SE of Kirkby Lonsdale on A65, turn right into site entrance 300yds past Whoop-Hall Inn*

★ £13 £13

Open Mar-Oct Booking advisable BH, peak season Last arrival 22.00hrs

A very pleasant base in which to relax or tour the surrounding area, developed around a former farm. The excellent toilet facilities are purpose built, and there are good roads and hardstandings, all in a lovely rural setting. A 3-acre site with 50 touring pitches, 50 hardstandings.

**Facilities:**

**Services:** →

**Notes:**

### ►►►► 77% Woodclose Caravan Park *(SD618786)*

DAVID BELLAMY CONSERVATION AWARD GOLD

High Casterton LA6 2SE
☎ 01524 271597 01524 272301
**email:** info@woodclosepark.com
**web:** www.woodclosepark.com
**Dir:** *On A65, 0.25m after Kirkby Lonsdale towards Skipton, on left*

Open Mar-Oct Booking advisable BH, wknds & Jul-Sep Last arrival 21.00hrs Last departure noon

A peaceful park with excellent toilet facilities set in idyllic countryside in the beautiful Lune Valley. Ideal for those seeking quiet relaxation, and for visiting the Lakes and Dales, with the riverside walks at Devil's Bridge, and historic Kirkby Lonsdale both an easy walk from the park. Free view TV via a booster cable from reception is available. A 9-acre site with 29 touring pitches, 8 hardstandings and 54 statics.

**Leisure:**

**Facilities:**

**Services:** →

**Notes:** Cycle hire, internet access

## LAMPLUGH MAP 18 NY02

### ►►► 75% Inglenook Caravan Park *(NY084206)*

Fitz Bridge CA14 4SH
☎ 01946 861240 01946 861240
**email:** enquiry@inglenookcaravanpark.co.uk
**web:** www.inglenookcaravanpark.co.uk
**Dir:** *On left of A5086 towards Egremont*

Open all year Booking advisable at all times Last arrival 20.00hrs Last departure noon

An ideal touring site, well-maintained and situated in beautiful surroundings. The picturesque village of Lamplugh is close to the western lakes of Ennerdale, Buttermere and Loweswater, and a short drive from sandy beaches. A 3.5-acre site with 12 touring pitches, 12 hardstandings and 40 statics.

**Leisure:**

**Facilities:**

**Services:** →

## LONGTOWN MAP 21 NY36

### ►► 75% Camelot Caravan Park *(NY391666)*

CA6 5SZ
☎ 01228 791248 01228 791248
**Dir:** *Leave M6 junct 44. Site 5m N on A7, 1m S of Longtown*

Open Mar-Oct Booking advisable Jul-Aug Last arrival 22.00hrs Last departure noon

Very pleasant level grassy site in a wooded setting near the M6, with direct access from the A7. This park is an ideal stopover site. A 1.5-acre site with 20 touring pitches and 2 statics.

**Facilities:**

**Services:** →

**Notes:**

## MEALSGATE MAP 18 NY24

### ►►►► 75% Larches Caravan Park

*(NY205415)*
CA7 1LQ
☎ 016973 71379 & 71803 016973 71782
**Dir:** *On A595, Carlisle to Cockermouth road*

Open Mar-Oct (rs early & late season) Booking advisable Etr, Spring BH & Jul-Aug Last arrival 21.30hrs Last departure noon

This over 18s-only park is set in wooded rural surroundings on the fringe of the Lake District National Park. Touring units are spread out over two sections. The friendly family-run park offers well cared for facilities, and a small indoor swimming pool. A 20-acre site with 73 touring pitches, 30 hardstandings and 100 statics.

**Leisure:**

**Facilities:**

**Services:** →

**Notes:** Adults only

ENGLAND

MILNTHORPE MAP 18 SD48

### ►►► 73% Hall More Caravan Park

*(SD502771)*

Hale LA7 7BP

☎ 01524 781453 🖹 01524 782243

**email:** enquiries@pureleisure-holidays.co.uk

**web:** www.pureleisure-holidays.co.uk

**Dir:** *M6 junct 35 onto A6 towards Milnthorpe for 4m. Left at Lakeland Wildlife Oasis, follow brown signs*

★ £10-£12 £10-£12 £9-£10

Open Mar-Jan Booking advisable BH & school hols Last arrival 22.00hrs Last departure 10.00hrs

A pleasant meadowland site adjacent to the main road, with hardstanding and grass pitches. It is close to a farm and stables offering pony trekking, and there is trout fishing nearby. A 4-acre site with 44 touring pitches, 7 hardstandings and 60 statics.

**Facilities:**

**Services:**

PATTERDALE MAP 18 NY31

### ►►► 78% Sykeside Camping Park

*(NY403119)*

Brotherswater CA11 0NZ

☎ 017684 82239 🖹 017684 82239

**email:** info@sykeside.co.uk

**web:** www.sykeside.co.uk

**Dir:** *Direct access off A592 (Windermere to Ullswater road) at foot of Kirkstone Pass*

★ £16-£22 £16-£22 £12-£20

Open all year Booking advisable BH & Jul-Aug Last arrival 22.30hrs Last departure 14.00hrs

A camper's delight, this family-run park is sited at the foot of Kirkstone Pass, under the 2000ft Hartsop Dodd in a spectacular area with breathtaking views. The park has mainly grass pitches with a few hardstandings, and for those campers without a tent there is bunkhouse accommodation. A small campers' kitchen and bar serves breakfast and bar meals. There is abundant wildlife. A 5-acre site with 86 touring pitches, 5 hardstandings.

**Leisure:**

**Facilities:**

**Services:**

ENGLAND

## PENRITH MAP 18 NY53

### ►►►► 81% Lowther Holiday Park

GOLD

*(NY527265)*

Eamont Bridge CA10 2JB

☎ 01768 863631 01768 868126

**email:** sales@lowther-holidaypark.co.uk

**web:** www.lowther-holidaypark.co.uk

**Dir:** *3m S of Penrith on A6*

£22-£25 £22-£25 £22-£25

Open mid Mar-mid Nov Booking advisable BH Last arrival 22.00hrs Last departure 22.00hrs

A secluded natural woodland site with lovely riverside walks and glorious surrounding countryside. The park is home to a rare colony of red squirrels, and trout fishing is available on the 2-mile stretch of the River Lowther which runs through it. A 50-acre site with 180 touring pitches, 50 hardstandings and 403 statics.

**Leisure:**

**Facilities:**

**Services:**

**Notes:** Families only, no cats, rollerblades, skateboards, commercial vehicles

*see advert on page 105*

## PENRUDDOCK MAP 18 NY42

### ►►► 76% Beckses Caravan Park *(NY419278)*

CA11 0RX

☎ 01768 483224 01768 483006

**Dir:** *M6 junct 40 onto A66 towards Keswick. Approx 6m at caravan park sign turn right onto B5288. Site on right in 0.25m*

★ fr £10 fr £10 fr £10

Open Etr-Oct Booking advisable public hols Last arrival 20.00hrs Last departure 11.00hrs

A small, pleasant site on sloping ground with level pitches and views of distant fells, on the edge of the National Park. This sheltered park is in a good location for touring the North Lakes. A 4-acre site with 23 touring pitches and 18 statics.

**Leisure:**

**Facilities:**

**Services:**

**Notes:**

## POOLEY BRIDGE MAP 18 NY42

### 82% Park Foot Caravan & Camping Park *(NY469235)*

Howtown Rd CA10 2NA

☎ 017684 86309 017684 86041

**email:** holidays@parkfootullswater.co.uk

**web:** www.parkfootullswater.co.uk

**Dir:** *M6 junct 40, A66 towards Keswick, then A592 to Ullswater. Turn left for Pooley Bridge, right at church, right at x-roads signed Howtown*

★ £15-£29 £13-£25 £13.50-£25

Open Mar-Oct (rs Mar-May, mid Sep-Oct clubhouse open wknds only) Booking advisable BH Last arrival 22.00hrs Last departure noon

A lively park with good outdoor sports facilities, and boat launching directly onto Lake Ullswater. The attractive mainly tenting park has many mature trees and lovely views across the lake. The Country Club bar and restaurant provides good meals, as well as discos, live music and entertainment in a glorious location. An 18-acre site with 323 touring pitches and 131 statics.

**Leisure:**

**Facilities:**

**Services:**

**Notes:** Families & couples only. Boat launch, pony trekking, pool table, table tennis

**►►► 83% Waterfoot Caravan Park** *(NY462246)*

CA11 0JF

☎ 017684 86302 🖷 017684 86728

**email:** enquiries@waterfootpark.co.uk

**web:** www.waterfootpark.co.uk

**Dir:** *From M6 junct 40 take A66 for 1m, then A592 for 4m, site on right before lake. (NB Do not leave A592 until park entrance)*

★ £15-£21.50 £15-£21.50

Open Mar-14 Nov Booking advisable BH & school hols, tel bookings only Last arrival dusk Last departure noon

A quality touring park with neat pitches in a grassy glade within the wooded grounds of an elegant Georgian mansion. A lounge bar with a separate family room enjoys lake views, and there is a path to Ullswater. Aira Force waterfall, Dalemain House and garden, and Pooley Bridge are all close by. There is no access via Dacre. A 22-acre site with 34 touring pitches, 30 hardstandings and 146 statics.

**Leisure:**

**Facilities:**

**Services:**

**Notes:** Families only, no tents

## RAVENGLASS MAP 18 SD09

**►►► 83% Ravenglass Camping & Caravanning Club Site** *(SD087964)*

CA18 1SR

☎ 01229 717250

**web:** www.campingandcaravanningclub.co.uk/ravenglass

**Dir:** *From A595 turn W for Ravenglass. Before village turn left into site*

★ £18.25-£20.15 £18.25-£20.15 £18.25-£20.15

Open 12 Jan-Nov Booking advisable BH Last arrival 21.00hrs Last departure noon

A pleasant wooded park peacefully located in open countryside, a short stroll from the charming old fishing village of Ravenglass. This park is maintained to a high standard with level gravel pitches, a good toilet block and smart reception. Muncaster Castle and gardens, the Eskdale/Ravenglass Steam Railway and the coast are all within easy reach. A 5-acre site with 66 touring pitches, 56 hardstandings.

**Facilities:**

**Services:**

**Notes:** Site gates closed 23.00hrs-07.00hrs

## ST BEES MAP 18 NX91

**►►►► 78% Seacote Park** *(NX962117)*

The Beach CA27 0ET

☎ 01946 822777 🖷 01946 824442

**email:** reception@seacote.com

**web:** www.seacote.com

**Dir:** *From St Bees main street follow signs to beach. Take road past Seacote Hotel, through public car park to site*

★ £17 £17 £10-£17

Open Mar-14 Nov Booking advisable Last arrival 18.00hrs Last departure 11.00hrs

An ideal family holiday park with sweeping sea views, beach access and cliff walks, set in the charming village of St Bees. A smart toilet block with private cubicles is an obvious asset. The facilities of an adjacent hotel are open to park visitors, and include restaurant and bar meals, games room and live entertainment. A 20-acre site with 40 touring pitches, 40 hardstandings and 200 statics.

**Leisure:**

**Facilities:**

**Services:**

## SANTON BRIDGE MAP 18 NY10

### ►► 71% *The Old Post Office Campsite*

*(NY110016)*

CA19 1UY

☎ 01946 726286 🖷 01946 726125

**Dir:** *A595 to Holmbrook and Santon Bridge, 2.5m*

Open Mar-15 Nov Booking advisable BH & school hols Last departure noon

A family-run campsite in a delightful riverside setting next to an attractive stone bridge, with very pretty pitches. The simple, clean facilities include a disabled toilet, laundry and reception. Permits for salmon, sea and brown trout fishing are available, and there is an adjacent pub serving excellent meals. A 2.25-acre site with 40 touring pitches, 5 hardstandings.

**Leisure:** **Facilities:**

**Services:** → **Notes:**

## SILLOTH MAP 18 NY15

**Regional Winner – AA North West of England Campsite of the Year 2008**

### 90% **Stanwix Park Holiday Centre** *(NY108527)*

Greenrow CA7 4HH

☎ 016973 32666 🖷 016973 32555

**email:** enquiries@stanwix.com

**web:** www.stanwix.com

**Dir:** *1m SW on B5300. From A596 (Wigton bypass), follow signs to Silloth on B5302. In Silloth follow signs to site, approx 1m on B5300*

★ £17.60-£21.55 £17.60-£21.55 £17.60-£21.55

Open all year (rs Nov-Feb (ex New Year) no entertainment/shop closed) Booking advisable Etr, Spring BH, Jul-Aug & New Year Last arrival 22.00hrs Last departure 11.00hrs

A large well-run family park within easy reach of the Lake District. Attractively laid out, with lots of amenities to ensure a lively holiday, including a 4-lane, automatic, 10-pin bowling alley. A 4-acre site with 121 touring pitches, 100 hardstandings and 212 statics.

**Leisure:** **Facilities:**

**Services:** →

**Notes:** Amusement arcade, gym, kitchen

*see advert on opposite page*

### ►►►► 84% **Hylton Caravan Park** *(NY113533)*

Eden St CA7 4AY

☎ 016973 31707 🖷 016973 32555

**email:** enquiries@stanwix.com

**web:** www.stanwix.com

**Dir:** *On entering Silloth on B5302 follow signs Hylton Caravan Park, approx 0.5m on left, (end of Eden St)*

★ £17-£18.90 £17-£18.90 £17-£18.90

Open Mar-15 Nov Booking advisable school hols Last arrival 21.00hrs Last departure 11.00hrs

A smart, modern touring park with excellent toilet facilities including several bathrooms. This high quality park is a sister site to Stanwix Park, which is just a mile away and offers all the amenities of a holiday centre. An 18-acre site with 90 touring pitches and 213 statics.

**Leisure:**

**Facilities:**

**Services:** →

**Notes:** Families only. Use of facilities at Stanwix Park Holiday Centre

### ►►► 72% *Tanglewood Caravan Park*

*(NY131534)*

Causewayhead CA7 4PE

☎ 016973 31253

**email:** tanglewoodcaravanpark@hotmail.com

**web:** www.tanglewoodcaravanpark.co.uk

**Dir:** *Adjacent to B5302 (Wigton-Silloth), 4m from Abbeytown, site on left*

Open Mar-Jan Booking advisable Etr, Whit & Jul-Aug Last arrival 23.00hrs Last departure 10.00hrs

A pleasant park sheltered by mature trees and shrubs, set in meadowland close to the town. There is a clubhouse and bar, and two small toilet blocks for tourers, both with underfloor heating. A 7-acre site with 31 touring pitches, 21 hardstandings and 58 statics.

**Leisure:**

**Facilities:**

**Services:** →

## TEBAY MAP 18 NY60

**►►► 74% Westmorland Caravan Park** *(NY609060)*

GOLD

Orton CA10 3SB

☎ 01539 711322 015396 24944

**email:** caravans@westmorland.com

**web:** www.westmorland.com

**Dir:** *Exit M6 at Westmorland Services, 1m from junct 38. Site accessed through service area from either N'bound or S'bound carriageways. Follow park signs*

★ £15-£17 £15-£17

Open Mar-Oct Booking advisable Jul-Aug & wknds Last arrival anytime Last departure noon

An ideal stopover site adjacent to the Tebay service station on the M6, and handy for touring the Lake District. The park is screened by high grass banks, bushes and trees, and is within walking distance of a shop and restaurant. A 4-acre site with 70 touring pitches, 70 hardstandings and 7 statics.

**Facilities:**

**Services:** →

**Notes:** Wi-fi

## TROUTBECK (NEAR KESWICK) MAP 18 NY32

**►►►► 79% Troutbeck Camping and Caravanning Club Site** *(NY364270)*

Hutton Moor End CA11 0SX

☎ 01768 779615

**web:** www.campingandcaravanningclub.co.uk/troutbeck

**Dir:** *On A66 (Penrith to Keswick) turn left at Wallthwaite sign*

★ £18.25-£20.15 £18.25-£20.15 £18.25-£20.15

Open Mar-15 Nov Booking advisable BH Last arrival 21.00hrs Last departure noon

Beautifully situated between Penrith and Keswick, this quiet, pleasant Lakeland park offers a sheltered touring field with serviced pitches enjoying extensive views of the surrounding fells. The toilet block is of a very high standard and includes two family cubicles; the log cabin stocks local and organic produce. A 4.5-acre site with 30 touring pitches, 19 hardstandings and 20 statics.

**Leisure:** **Facilities:**

**Services:** →

**Notes:** Site gates closed 23.00hrs-07.00hrs

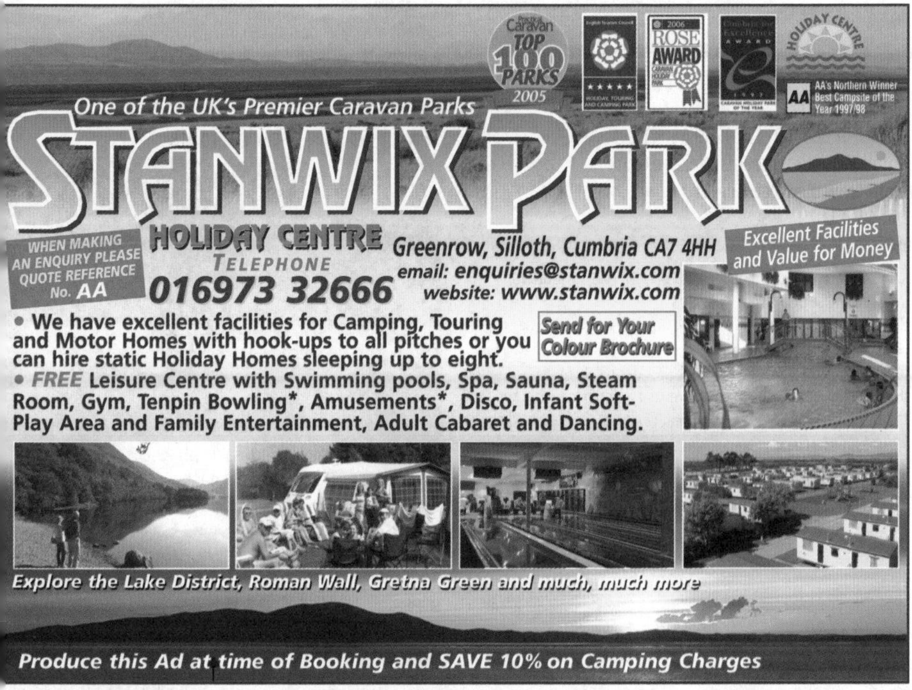

ENGLAND

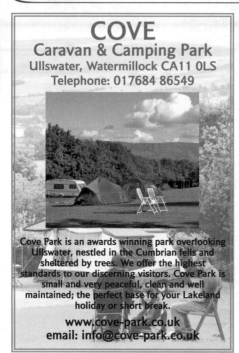



## ULVERSTON MAP 18 SD27

### ▶▶▶▶ 82% Bardsea Leisure Park

*(SD292765)*

Priory Rd LA12 9QE

☎ 01229 584712 01229 580413

**email:** reception@bardsealeisure.co.uk

**web:** www.bardsealeisure.co.uk

**Dir:** *Off A5087*

Open all year Booking advisable BH, Jul-Aug Last arrival 21.00hrs Last departure 18.00hrs

Attractively landscaped former quarry, making a quiet and very sheltered site. Many of the generously-sized pitches offer all-weather full facilities, and a luxury toilet block provides plenty of privacy. Set on the southern edge of the town, convenient for both the coast and the Lake District. A 5-acre site with 83 touring pitches, 83 hardstandings and 83 statics.

**Leisure:**

**Facilities:**

**Services:** →

## WASDALE HEAD MAP 18 NY1

### ▶▶▶ 72% Wasdale Head National Trust Campsite *(NY183076)*

CA20 1EX

☎ 019467 26220

**email:** wasdale.campsite@nationaltrust.org.uk

**web:** www.ntlakescampsites.org.uk

**Dir:** *From A595(N) left at Gosforth; from A595(S) right at Holmrook for Santon Bridge, follow signs to Wasdale Head*

★ £11.50-£12.30 £11.50-£12.30

Open all year (rs Nov-Mar shop open wknds only) Last arriva 22.00hrs Last departure noon

Set in a remote and beautiful spot at Wasdale Head, under the stunning Scafell peaks at the head of the deepest lake in England. Clean, well-kept facilities are set centrally amongst open grass pitches and trees. The renowned Wasdale Head Inn is close by. A 5-acre site with 126 touring pitches, 6 hardstandings.

**Facilities:**

**Services:** →

**Notes:** No cars by tents. No large groups

*see advert on page 96*

## WATERMILLOCK MAP 18 NY42

### ▶▶▶ 77% Cove Caravan & Camping Park

*(NY431236)*

Ullswater CA11 0LS

☎ 017684 86549 017684 86549

**email:** info@cove-park.co.uk

**web:** www.cove-park.co.uk

**Dir:** *M6 junct 40 take A592 for Ullswater. Right at lake junct, ther right at Brackenrigg Hotel. Site 1.5m on left*

★ £15-£21 £15-£21 £10-£18

Open Mar-Oct Booking advisable BH & school hols Last arrival 21.00hrs Last departure noon

A peaceful family site in an attractive and elevated position with extensive fell views and glimpses of Ullswater Lake. The ground is gently sloping grass, but there are also hardstandings for motorhomes and caravans. A 3-acre site with 50 touring pitches, 17 hardstandings and 39 statics.

**Leisure:** **Facilities:**

**Services:** →

**Notes:** No open fires

*see advert on this page*

▶▶▶ 88% **The Quiet Site** *(NY431236)*

Ullswater CA11 0LS

☎ 01768 486337 & 07768 727016

**email:** info@thequietsite.co.uk

**web:** www.thequietsite.co.uk

**Dir:** *M6 junct 40, A592 towards Ullswater. Right at lake junct, then right at Brackenrigg Hotel. Site 1.5m on right*

Open Feb-Nov Booking advisable BH, wknds, Jul-Aug Last arrival 22.00hrs Last departure noon

A well-maintained site in a lovely, peaceful location, with very good facilities, including a family bathroom. A charming olde-worlde bar is another attraction. A 6-acre site with 88 touring pitches, 50 hardstandings and 23 statics.

**Leisure:**

**Facilities:**

**Services:**

**Notes:** Quiet from 22.00hrs. Pets' corner, pool/darts (for adults), caravan storage

▶▶▶ 80% **Ullswater Caravan Camping Site & Marine Park** *(NY438232)*

High Longthwaite CA11 0LR

☎ 017684 86666 017684 86095

**email:** info@uccmp.co.uk

**web:** www.uccmp.co.uk

**Dir:** *M6 junct 40 take A592, W for Ullswater for 5m. Right alongside Ullswater for 2m, then right at phone box. Site 0.5m on right*

★ £17.50-£21 £17.50-£21 £15.50-£18

Open Mar-Nov (rs bar open wknds only in low season) Booking advisable public hols Last arrival 21.00hrs Last departure noon

A pleasant rural site with own nearby boat launching and marine storage facility making it ideal for sailors. The family-owned and run park enjoys fell and lake views, and there is a bar and café on site. Many of the pitches are fully serviced. A 12-acre site with 160 touring pitches, 58 hardstandings and 55 statics.

**Leisure:**

**Facilities:**

**Services:**

**Notes:** No open fires. Boat launching & moorings 1m

## WINDERMERE MAP 18 SD49

### PREMIER PARK

▶▶▶▶▶ 80% **Limefitt Park**

*(NY416032)*

LA23 1PA

☎ 015394 32300 015394 32848

**email:** enquiries@southlakeland-caravans.co.uk

**web:** www.southlakeland-caravans.co.uk/parks/1117/view

**Dir:** *From Windermere take A592 to Ullswater. Site 2.5m on right*

★ £16-£26 £16-£26 £18-£26

Open Mar-mid Nov Booking advisable BH, Jul-Aug Last arrival 22.00hrs Last departure noon

An attractive family site with superb facilities in a lovely location in the Lake District National Park. Buildings are well-integrated into the landscape, and the River Troutbeck runs through the grounds. From its valley setting there are spectacular views of the surrounding hills, with direct access to the fells and plenty of walks. A 20-acre site with 73 touring pitches, 38 hardstandings and 102 statics.

**Leisure:**

**Facilities:**

**Services:**

**Notes:** No pets, skateboards, roller skates/blades or electric scooters. Wi-fi

ENGLAND

ENGLAND

## WINDERMERE CONTINUED

### ►►►► 85% Fallbarrow Park (SD401973)

GOLD

Rayrigg Rd LA23 3DL

☎ 015394 44422 Fax 015394 88736

**email:** enquiries@southlakelandparks.co.uk

**web:** www.southlakelandparks.co.uk

**Dir:** *0.5m N of Windermere on A591. At mini-rdbt take road to Bowness Bay & the lake. Site 1.3m on right*

Open Mar-mid Nov Booking advisable BH, Jul-Aug Last arrival 22.00hrs Last departure 10.00hrs

A park set in impressive surroundings just a few minutes' walk from Bowness on the shore of Lake Windermere. There is direct access to the lake through the wooded park. A restaurant with a specialist chef is a popular feature. A 32-acre site with 38 touring pitches and 269 statics.

**Leisure:**

**Facilities:**

**Services:** →

**Notes:** No tents. Boat launching

### ►►►► 77% Park Cliffe Camping & Caravan Estate (SD391912)

GOLD

Birks Rd, Tower Wood LA23 3PG

☎ 01539 531344 Fax 01539 531971

**email:** info@parkcliffe.co.uk

**web:** www.parkcliffe.co.uk

**Dir:** *M6 junct 36 onto A590. Right at Newby Bridge onto A592. 4m right into site. (NB Due to difficult access from main road this is the only advised direction for approaching the site)*

★ £23 £23 £19-£23

Open Mar-14 Nov (Facilities open fully wknds/school hols) Booking advisable BH, Aug Last arrival 22.00hrs Last departure noon

A lovely hillside park set in 25 secluded acres of fell land. The camping area is sloping and uneven in places, but well drained and sheltered; some pitches have spectacular views of Lake Windermere and the Langdales. The park is very well equipped for families, and there is

*Park Cliffe Camping & Caravan Estate*

an attractive bar lounge. A 25-acre site with 250 touring pitches, 60 hardstandings and 55 statics.

**Leisure:**

**Facilities:**

**Services:** →

**Notes:** No noise 22.30hrs-07.30hrs. Off-licence

### ►►►► 90% Windermere Camping & Caravanning Club Site (SD479964)

Ashes Ln LA8 9JS

☎ 01539 821119

**web:** www.campingandcaravanningclub.co.uk/windermere

**Dir:** *Signed off A591, 0.75m from rdbt with B5284 towards Windermere*

★ £18.35-£23.25 £18.35-£23.25 £18.35-£23.25

Open 13 Mar-3 Nov Booking advisable BH & peak periods Last arrival 21.00hrs Last departure noon

A top Club site in a beautifully landscaped setting bordered by bluebell woods. Many mature trees and shrubs add to the natural beauty, and there are rocky outcrops and lovely views to be enjoyed. First class toilet facilities, good security, a large adventure playground, and a bar (The Whistling Pig) serving breakfasts, snacks and hot meals all add to the popularity of this very well-redeveloped site. A 24-acre site with 250 touring pitches, 88 hardstandings and 75 statics.

**Leisure:**

**Facilities:**

**Services:** →

**Notes:** Site gates closed 23.00hrs-07.00hrs

ENGLAND

►►► 83% **Hill of Oaks & Blakeholme** *(SD386899)*

GOLD

A12 8NR

☎ 015395 31578 015395 30431

**email:** enquiries@hillofoaks.co.uk

**web:** www.hillofoaks.co.uk

**Dir:** *M6 junct 36 onto A590 towards Barrow. At rdbt signed Bowness turn right onto A592. Site approx 3m on left*

£10-£27 £10-£27

Open Mar-14 Nov Booking advisable BH, school hols Last departure noon

A secluded, heavily wooded park on the shores of Lake Windermere. Pretty lakeside picnic areas, woodland walks and a play area make this a delightful park for families, with excellent serviced pitches, a licensed shop and a heated toilet block. Watersports include sailing and canoeing, with private jetties for boat launching. A 31-acre site with 43 touring pitches and 215 statics.

**Leisure:**

**Facilities:**

**Services:**

## DERBYSHIRE

### ASHBOURNE — MAP 10 SK14

*see also Fenny Bentley*

►► 87% **Carsington Fields Caravan Park** *(SK251493)*

Millfields Ln, Nr Carsington Water DE6 3JS

☎ 01335 372872

**web:** www.carsingtoncaravaning.co.uk

**Dir:** *From Belper towards Ashbourne on A517 turn right approx 0.25m past Hulland Ward into Dog Lane. 0.75m right at x-roads signed Carsington. Site on right after approx 0.75m*

£13-£16 £13-£16 £13-£16

Open end Mar-mid Oct Booking advisable Last arrival 21.00hrs Last departure 18.00hrs

A very well presented and spacious park with a good toilet block, open views and a large fenced pond that attracts plenty of wildlife. The popular tourist attraction of Carsington Water is a short stroll away, with its variety of leisure facilities including fishing, sailing, windsurfing and children's play area. The park is also a good base for walkers. A 6-acre site with 10 touring pitches, 10 hardstandings.

**Facilities:**

**Services:**

**Notes:** No large groups

►► 77% ***Peakland Caravan and Camping Park*** *(SK236467)*

Belper Rd, Bradley DE6 3EN

☎ 01335 370855

**email:** holidays@peaklandcaravanandcampingpark.co.uk

**web:** www.peaklandcaravanandcampingpark.co.uk

**Dir:** *Off A517, 0.5m from village of Bradley*

Open Feb-Nov Booking advisable Apr-Sep Last arrival 21.00hrs Last departure noon

A delightful little park which is ideal for adults visiting the many attractions of this popular area. The park, which is sheltered by hedging, is directly off the A517 with easy access to all pitches. The attractive market town of Ashbourne is a ten minute drive from the park, while the nearby Carsington Water offers a wide variety of leisure activities. A 5-acre site with 40 touring pitches, 20 hardstandings.

**Facilities:**

**Services:**

**Notes:** Adults only

### BAKEWELL — MAP 16 SK26

*see also Youlgreave*

►►► 77% **Greenhills Holiday Park** *(SK202693)*

Crowhill DE45 1PX

☎ 01629 813052 & 813467 01629 815760

**email:** info@greenhillsleisure.com

**web:** www.greenhillsleisure.com

**Dir:** *1m NW of Bakewell on A6. Signed before Ashford-in-the-Water, 50yds along unclass road on right*

★ fr £14 fr £13 fr £10.50

Open Feb-Nov (rs Oct, Mar & Apr bar & shop closed) Booking advisable Etr-Sep Last arrival 22.00hrs Last departure noon

A well-established park set in lovely countryside within the Peak District National Park. Many pitches enjoy uninterrupted views, and there is easy accessibility to all facilities. A clubhouse, shop and children's playground are popular features. An 8-acre site with 172 touring pitches, 21 hardstandings and 63 statics.

**Leisure:**

**Facilities:**

**Services:**

ENGLAND

## BUXTON MAP 16 SK07

### ►►►► 79% **Lime Tree Park** *(SK070725)*

Dukes Dr SK17 9RP

☎ 01298 22988 📠 01298 22988

**email:** info@limetreeparkbuxton.co.uk

**web:** www.limetreeparkbuxton.co.uk

**Dir:** *1m S of Buxton, between A515 & A6*

★ fr £17 fr £17 fr £13

Open Mar-Oct Booking advisable BH, Jul-Aug Last arrival 21.00hrs Last departure noon

A most attractive and well-designed site, set on the side of a narrow valley in an elevated location. Its backdrop of magnificent old railway viaduct and views over Buxton and the surrounding hills make this a sought-after destination. A 10.5-acre site with 99 touring pitches, 8 hardstandings and 43 statics.

**Leisure:**

**Facilities:**

**Services:** →

### ►►► 78% **Clover Fields Touring Caravan Park** *(SK075704)*

1 Heath View, Harpur Hill SK17 9PU

☎ 01298 78731

**email:** cloverfields@tiscali.co.uk

**web:** www.cloverfieldstouringpark.co.uk

**Dir:** *A515, B5053, then immediately right. Park 0.5m on left*

★ £14-£15 £14-£15 £10-£11

Open all year Booking advisable Last departure 18.00hrs

A developing, spacious park with very good facilities, just over a mile from the attractions of Buxton. All pitches are fully serviced including individual barbecues, and are set out on terraces, each with extensive views over the countryside. Children will enjoy the small animals which the enthusiastic owners rear in the surrounding meadows. A 12-acre site with 25 touring pitches, 25 hardstandings.

**Facilities:**

**Services:** →

**Notes:** No cars by tents

### ►► 78% **Cottage Farm Caravan Park** *(SK122720)*

Beech Croft, Blackwell in the Peak SK17 9TQ

☎ 01298 85330

**email:** mail@cottagefarmsite.co.uk

**web:** www.cottagefarmsite.co.uk

**Dir:** *Off A6 midway between Buxton and Bakewell. Site signed*

★ fr £12 fr £12 fr £10

Open mid Mar-Oct Booking advisable BH, school hols Last arrival 21.30hrs

A small terraced site in an attractive farm setting with lovely views. Hardstandings are provided for caravans, and there is a separate field for tents. An ideal site for those touring or walking in the Peak District. A 3-acre site with 30 touring pitches, 25 hardstandings.

**Facilities:**

**Services:**

**Notes:**

### ►► 71% **Thornheyes Farm Campsite** *(SK084761)*

Thornheyes Farm, Longridge Ln, Peak Dale SK17 8AD

☎ 01298 26421

**Dir:** *1.5m from Buxton on A6 turn E for Peak Dale. After 0.5m S at x-rds to site on right*

Open Etr-Oct Booking advisable BH, high season Last arrival 21.30hrs Last departure evenings

A pleasant mainly-sloping farm site run by a friendly family team in the central Peak District. Toilet and other facilities are very simple but extremely clean. A 2-acre site with 10 touring pitches.

**Facilities:**

**Services:** →

**Notes:** Adults only No ball games, no bicycles, unisex showers

## CROWDEN MAP 16 SK0

### ►► 70% **Crowden Camping & Caravanning Club Site** *(SK072992)*

Woodhead Rd SK13 1HZ

☎ 01457 866057

**web:** www.campingandcaravanningclub.co.uk/crowden

**Dir:** *A628 (Manchester to Barnsley road). At Crowden follow sign for car park/youth hostel & camp site. Site approx 300yds from main road*

★ £8.70-£13.60

Open 13 Mar-29 Sep Booking advisable BH & peak periods Last arrival 21.00hrs Last departure noon

A beautifully located moorland site, overlooking the reservoirs and surrounded by hills. Tents only, with backpackers' drying room. A 2.5-acre site with 45 touring pitches.

**Facilities:**

**Services:** →

**Notes:** Site gates closed 23.00hrs-07.00hrs

## EDALE MAP 16 SK18

### ►► 69% Coopers Camp & Caravan Park

*(SK121859)*

Newfold Farm, Edale Village S33 7ZD

☎ 01433 670372

**Dir:** *From A6187 at Hope take minor road for 4m to Edale. Right onto unclass road, site on left in 800yds opposite school*

Open all year Booking advisable BH Last arrival 23.30hrs Last departure 15.00hrs

Rising grassland behind a working farm, divided by a wall into two fields, culminating in the 2062ft Edale Moor. Facilities have been converted from original farm buildings, and include a café for backpackers, and a well-stocked shop. A 6-acre site with 135 touring pitches and 11 statics.

**Facilities:**

**Services:**

**Notes:**

## HAYFIELD MAP 16 SK08

### ►► 75% Hayfield Camping & Caravanning Club Site *(SK048868)*

Kinder Rd SK22 2LE

☎ 01663 745394

**web:** www.campingandcaravanningclub.co.uk/hayfield

**Dir:** *Off A624, Glossop to Chapel-en-le-Frith (Hayfield by-pass). Well signed into village, follow wood-carved signs to site*

★ £14.05-£18.85 £14.05-£18.85

Open 13 Mar-3 Nov Booking advisable BH & peak periods Last arrival 21.00hrs Last departure noon

On level ground along the River Sett valley, a peaceful location overlooked on three sides by mature woodland, with the hills of the North Derbyshire moors on the fourth side. The camping area is in two fields with central amenities. A 6-acre site with 90 touring pitches.

**Facilities:**

**Services:**

**Notes:** Site gates closed 23.00hrs-07.00hrs

## HOPE MAP 16 SK18

### ►► 75% Pindale Farm Outdoor Centre

*(SK163825)*

Pindale Rd S33 6RN

☎ 01433 620111 01433 620729

**email:** bookings@pindale.fsbusiness.co.uk

**web:** www.pindale.fsbusiness.co.uk

**Dir:** *From A625 in Hope turn into Pindale Lane between church & Woodroffe Arms. Pass cement works, over bridge, site in 400yds, well signed*

Open Mar-Oct Booking advisable Last departure 11.00hrs

An ideal base for walking, climbing and various outdoor pursuits, offering excellent facilities for campers and with a self-contained bunkhouse for up to 60 people. The heated toilet facilities are very good on this well-run campsite. A 1-acre site with 10 touring pitches.

**Facilities:**

**Services:**

**Notes:** Dogs must be kept on leads

## MATLOCK MAP 16 SK35

### ►►►► 74% Lickpenny Caravan Site *(SK339597)*

SILVER

Lickpenny Ln, Tansley DE4 5GF

☎ 01629 583040 01629 583040

**email:** lickpenny@btinternet.com

**web:** www.lickpennycaravanpark.co.uk

**Dir:** *From A615 between Alfreton & Matlock, approx 1m N of Tansley. Turn into Lickpenny Lane at x-rds*

★ £15-£19 £15-£21

Open all year Booking advisable Last arrival 20.00hrs Last departure noon

A picturesque site in the grounds of an old plant nursery with areas broken up and screened by a variety of shrubs, and spectacular views. Pitches, several fully serviced, are spacious and well marked, and facilities are to a very good standard. A bistro/coffee shop is popular with visitors. A 16-acre site with 80 touring pitches, 80 hardstandings.

**Leisure:**

**Facilities:**

**Services:**

**Notes:** Child bath available

## NEWHAVEN MAP 16 SK16

### ►►► 77% **Newhaven Holiday Camping & Caravan Park** *(SK167602)*

SK17 0DT

01298 84300 01332 726027

**web:** www.newhavencaravanpark.co.uk

**Dir:** *Between Ashbourne & Buxton at A515 & A5012 junct*

£10.25-£11.75 £10.25-£11.75 £10.25-£11.75

Open Mar-Oct Booking advisable BH & wknds Last arrival 23.00hrs Last departure anytime

Pleasantly situated within the Peak District National Park, with mature trees screening the three touring areas. Very good toilet facilities cater for touring vans and a large tent field, and there's a restaurant adjacent to the site. A 30-acre site with 125 touring pitches, 18 hardstandings and 73 statics.

**Leisure:**

**Facilities:**

**Services:** →

## RIPLEY MAP 16 SK35

### ►►►► 73% **Golden Valley Caravan & Camping Park** *(SK408513)*

GOLD

Coach Rd, Butterley Park DE55 4ES

01773 513881

**email:** enquiries@goldenvalleycaravanpark.co.uk

**web:** www.goldenvalleycaravanpark.co.uk

**Dir:** *M1 junct 26 onto A610 to Codnor. Right at lights, then right onto Alfreton Road, park 1m on left*

Open Mar-Sep Booking advisable Last arrival 18.00hrs Last departure noon

A park set within 30 acres of woodland in the Amber Valley. The fully-serviced pitches are set out in informal groups in clearings amongst the trees. The park has a cosy bar and bistro with outside patio, a fully stocked fishing lake, an on-site jacuzzi and fully equipped fitness suite. There is also a wildlife pond. A 26-acre site with 24 touring pitches, 24 hardstandings.

**Leisure:**

**Facilities:**

**Services:** →

**Notes:** No open fires or disposable BBQs

## ROSLISTON MAP 10 SK21

### ►► 82% **Beehive Woodland Lakes** *(SK249161)*

DE12 8HZ

01283 763981 01283 763981

**email:** info@beehivefarm-woodlandlakes.co.uk

**web:** www.beehivefarm-woodlandlakes.co.uk

**Dir:** *Turn S off A444 at Castle Gresley onto Mount Pleasant Road, follow Rosliston signs. Park on left at T-junct at end of Linton road*

★ fr £13

Open Mar-Nov Booking advisable Last arrival 20.00hrs Last departure 10.30hrs

A small, informal caravan area secluded from an extensive woodland park in the heart of The National Forest. Young children will enjoy the on-site animal farm and playground, whilst anglers will appreciate fishing the three lakes within the park. The Honey Pot tearoom provides snacks and is open most days. A 2.5-acre site with 25 touring pitches, 3 hardstandings.

**Leisure:**

**Facilities:**

**Services:** →

## ROWSLEY MAP 16 SK26

### ►►► 73% **Grouse & Claret** *(SK258660)*

Station Rd DE4 2EB

01629 733233 01629 735194

**email:** grouseandclaret.matlock@marstons.co.uk

**Dir:** *M1 junct 29. Site on A6, 5m from Matlock & 3m from Bakewell*

£15 £15 £10

Open all year Booking advisable BH, wknds & peak periods Last arrival 20.00hrs Last departure noon

A well-designed, purpose-built park at the rear of an eating house on the A6 between Bakewell and Chatsworth, and adjacent to the New Peak Shopping Village. The park comprises a level grassy area running down to the river, and all pitches have hardstandings and electric hook-ups. A 2.5-acre site with 26 touring pitches, 26 hardstandings.

**Leisure:**

**Facilities:**

**Services:** →

**Notes:** No cars by tents, dogs must be under strict control

## SHARDLOW MAP 11 SK43

### ►►► 68% Shardlow Marina Caravan Park

*(SK444303)*

London Rd DE72 2GL

☎ 01332 792832 📠 01332 792832

**Dir:** *M1 junct 24a, take A50 Derby. Exit junct 1 at rdbt signed Shardlow. Site 1m on right*

★ £10-£15 £10-£15

Open Mar-Jan Booking advisable all the time Last arrival 17.00hrs Last departure 14.00hrs

A large marina site with restaurant facilities, situated on the Trent/Merseyside Canal. Pitches are on grass surrounded by mature trees, and for the keen angler the site offers fishing within the marina. An attractive grass touring area overlooks the marina. A 25-acre site with 70 touring pitches and 73 statics.

**Facilities:**

**Services:**

**Notes:** Max 2 dogs per unit

## SWADLINCOTE MAP 10 SK21

### NEW U Conkers Camping & Caravanning Club Site *(SK305157)*

National Forest, Bath Ln, Moira DE12 6BD

☎ 0845 130 7631

**web:** www.campingandcaravanningclub.co.uk/conkers

**Dir:** *A444 towards Overseal. Left onto Moira Rd, 4th left into park.*

★ £11.25-£12.85 £11.25-£12.85 £11.25-£12.85

Open all year Booking advisable BH & peak periods Last arrival 21.00hrs Last departure noon

The rating for this site is not confirmed at the time of going to press. This new Club site is gently sloping and situated in the heart of the country's youngest forest, and within walking disance of Conkers, an award-winning Discovery Centre. The AA inspector was unable to assess all the facilities as the site will only become fully operational in 2008. A 4-acre site with 90 touring pitches, 90 hardstandings.

**Facilities:**

**Services:**

**Notes:** Site gates close 23.00hrs-07.00hrs

## YOULGREAVE MAP 16 SK26

### ► 72% Bakewell Camping & Caravanning Club Site *(SK206632)*

Hopping Farm DE45 1NA

☎ 01629 636555

**web:** www.campingandcaravanningclub.co.uk/bakewell

**Dir:** *A6/B5056, after 0.5m turn right to Youlgreave. Turn sharp left after church down Bradford Lane, opposite George Hotel. 0.5m to sign turn right*

★ £11.25-£12.85 £11.25-£12.85 £11.25-£12.85

Open 13 Mar-3 Nov Booking advisable BH & peak periods Last arrival 21.00hrs Last departure noon

Ideal for touring and walking in the Peak District National Park, this gently sloping grass site is accessed through narrow streets and along unadopted hardcore. Own sanitary facilities essential. A 14-acre site with 100 touring pitches, 6 hardstandings.

**Leisure:**

**Facilities:**

**Services:**

**Notes:** Site gates closed 23.00hrs-07.00hrs

# DEVON

## ASHBURTON MAP 03 SX77

### ►►►► 80% Parkers Farm Holidays

DAVID BELLAMY CONSERVATION AWARD SILVER

*(SX779713)*

Higher Mead Farm TQ13 7LJ

☎ 01364 654869 📠 01364 654004

**email:** parkersfarm@btconnect.com

**web:** www.parkersfarm.co.uk

**Dir:** *From Exeter on A38, take 2nd left after Plymouth 26m sign, at Alston, signed Woodland-Denbury. From Plymouth on A38 take A383 Newton Abbot exit, turn right across bridge and rejoin A38, then as above.*

£6.50-£18 £6.50-£18 £6.50-£18

Open Etr-end Oct Booking advisable Etr, Whitsun & school hols Last arrival 22.00hrs Last departure 10.00hrs

A well-developed site terraced into rising ground. Part of a working farm, this park offers beautifully maintained, quality facilities. Large family rooms with two shower cubicles, a large sink and a toilet are especially appreciated by families with small children. There are regular farm walks when all the family can meet and feed the various animals. An 8-acre site with 100 touring pitches, 5 hardstandings and 16 statics.

**Leisure:**

**Facilities:**

**Services:**

**Facilities:** Bath · Shower · Electric Shaver · Hairdryer · Ice Pack Facility · Disabled Facilities · Public Telephone · Shop on Site or within 200yds · Mobile Shop (calls at least 5 days a week) · BBQ Area · Picnic Area · Dog Exercise Area

ENGLAND

## ASHBURTON CONTINUED

### ►►►► 78% River Dart Country Park (SX734700)

Holne Park TQ13 7NP

☎ 01364 652511 🖷 01364 652020

**email:** info@riverdart.co.uk

**web:** www.riverdart.co.uk

**Dir:** *From M5 take A38 towards Plymouth, turn off at 2nd junct Ashburton following brown signs to River Dart Country Park. Site 1m on left*

★ £13.50-£22 £13.50-£22 £10.50-£19

Open Apr-Sep (rs low season café bar restricted opening hours) Booking advisable Spring BH & Jul-Aug Last arrival 21.00hrs Last departure 11.00hrs

Set in 90 acres of magnificent parkland that was once part of a Victorian estate, with many specimen and exotic trees, and in spring a blaze of colour from the many azaleas and rhododendrons. There are numerous outdoor activities for all ages including abseiling, caving and canoeing, plus high quality, well-maintained facilities. The open moorland of Dartmoor is only a few minutes away. A 90-acre site with 170 touring pitches, 12 hardstandings.

**Leisure:**

**Facilities:**

**Services:**

**Notes:** Wi-fi. Adventure playground

## AXMINSTER MAP 04 SY29

### ►►►► 76% Andrewshayes Caravan Park (ST248088)

Dalwood EX13 7DY

☎ 01404 831225 🖷 01404 831893

**email:** info@andrewshayes.co.uk

**web:** www.andrewshayes.co.uk

**Dir:** *On A35, 3m from Axminster. Turn N at Taunton Cross signed Stockland/Dalwood. Site 150mtrs on right*

£11-£22 £11-£22 £11-£22

Open Mar-Nov (rs Sep-Nov shop hrs limited, pool closed Sep-mid May) Booking advisable Spring BH & Jul-Aug Last arrival 22.00hrs Last departure noon

A lively park within easy reach of Lyme Regis, Seaton, Branscombe and Sidmouth in an ideal touring location. This popular park boasts an attractive bistro beside the swimming pool, a bar, laundry and shop. A 12-acre site with 150 touring pitches, 105 hardstandings and 80 statics.

**Leisure:**

**Facilities:**

**Services:**

**Notes:** Dogs must be kept on leads

## BARNSTAPLE MAP 03 SS53

### ►►► 80% Tarka Holiday Park (SS533346)

GOLD

Braunton Rd, Ashford EX31 4AU

☎ 01271 343691 🖷 01271 326355

**email:** info@tarkaholidaypark.co.uk

**web:** www.tarkaholidaypark.co.uk

**Dir:** *2m from Barnstaple on A361 towards Chivenor. (NB This is a fast dual-carriageway & care should be taken)*

Open 22 Jan-1 Jan Booking advisable at all times. Last arrival 22.00hrs Last departure noon

A gently-sloping grass park near the banks of the River Taw, and close to the Tarka cycle trail. It offers a licensed bar for food and drink with occasional entertainment, a putting green, a bouncy castle and children's playground. The site is about 5m from sandy beaches. A 10-acre site with 35 touring pitches, 16 hardstandings and 82 statics.

**Leisure:**

**Facilities:**

**Services:**

**Notes:** Eating area in clubhouse

## BERRYNARBOR MAP 03 SS54

### ►►► 76% Mill Park (SS559471)

Mill Ln EX34 9SH

☎ 01271 882647 🖷 01271 882667

**email:** millparkdevon@btconnect.com

**web:** www.millpark.co.uk

**Dir:** *M5 junct 27 onto A361 towards Barnstaple. Right onto A399 towards Combe Martin. At Sawmills Inn take turn opposite for Berrynarbor*

Open Mar-30 Oct Booking advisable Last arrival 22.00hrs Last departure 10.00hrs

This family owned and run park is set in an attractive wooded valley with a stream running into a lake where coarse fishing is available. There is a quiet bar/restaurant with a family room, and the park is just a stroll across the road from the small harbour at Watermouth. A 23-acre site with 160 touring pitches, 9 hardstandings.

**Leisure:**

**Facilities:**

**Services:**

## BICKINGTON (NEAR ASHBURTON) MAP 03 SX87

### ►►►► 80% Lemonford Caravan Park

*(SX793723)*

TQ12 6JR

☎ 01626 821242 & 821263 01626 821263

**email:** mark@lemonford.co.uk

**web:** www.lemonford.co.uk

**Dir:** *From Exeter A38 take A382, then 3rd exit on rdbt , follow Bickington signs*

★ £9-£14 £9-£14 £9-£14

Open Mar-Oct Booking advisable school hols Last arrival 22.00hrs Last departure 11.00hrs

Small, secluded and well-maintained park with a good mixture of attractively laid out pitches. The friendly owners pay a great deal of attention to detail, and the toilets in particular are kept spotlessly clean. This good touring base is only one mile from Dartmoor and ten miles from the seaside at Torbay. A 7-acre site with 85 touring pitches, 55 hardstandings and 28 statics.

**Leisure:**

**Facilities:**

**Services:**

**Notes:** Clothes drying area

*see advert on this page*



### ►►► 71% The Dartmoor Halfway Inn Caravan Park *(SX804719)*

TQ12 6JW

☎ 01626 821270 01626 821820

**email:** info@dartmoor-halfway-inn.co.uk

**web:** www.dartmoor-halfway-inn.co.uk

**Dir:** *Direct access from A383, 1m from A38 (Exeter-Plymouth road)*

Open all year Booking advisable BH & high season Last arrival 23.00hrs Last departure 10.00hrs

A well-developed park tucked away on the edge of Dartmoor, beside the River Lemon and adjacent to the Halfway Inn. The neat and compact park has a small toilet block with immaculate facilities, and pitches separated by mature shrubs. An extensive menu at the inn offers reasonably-priced food all day and in the evening. A 2-acre site with 22 touring pitches.

**Leisure:**

**Facilities:**

**Services:**

## BRATTON FLEMING MAP 03 SS63

### ►►► 76% Greenacres Farm Touring Caravan Park *(SS658414)*

EX31 4SG

☎ 01598 763334

**Dir:** *M5 junct 27 onto A361 towards Barnstaple. At 2nd rdbt near South Molton turn right onto A399 signed Blackmoor Gate/Combe Martin. Approx 10m turn left at Stowford Cross. Site signed on left. (NB Do not follow signs to Bratton Fleming)*

★ £5.50-£11 £5.50-£11

Open Apr-Oct Booking advisable all times Last arrival 23.00hrs Last departure 11.00hrs

Located on the edge of Exmoor National Park, this small park is sheltered behind mature hedges, and well landscaped with a mix of grass and hard pitches. There are extensive views, and very well maintained facilities. A 4-acre site with 30 touring pitches, 6 hardstandings.

**Leisure:**

**Facilities:**

**Services:**

**Notes:**

## BRAUNTON MAP 03 SS43

### ►►►► 84% Hidden Valley Park *(SS499408)*

GOLD

EX34 8NU

☎ 01271 813837 01271 814041

**email:** relax@hiddenvalleypark.com

**web:** www.hiddenvalleypark.com

**Dir:** *Direct access off A361, 8m from Barnstaple & 2m from Mullacott Cross*

Open all year (rs 15 Nov-15 Mar all weather pitches only) Booking advisable peak season Last arrival 21.30hrs Last departure 10.00hrs

A delightful, well-appointed family site set in a wooded valley, with superb facilities and a cafe. The park is set in a very rural, natural position not far from the beautiful coastline around Ilfracombe. A 25-acre site with 135 touring pitches, 74 hardstandings.

**Leisure:**

**Facilities:**

**Services:**

**Notes:** Gardens, woodland walks & lake

*see advert on page 135*

### ►►► 77% Lobb Fields Caravan & Camping Park *(SS475378)*

Saunton Rd EX33 1EB

☎ 01271 812090 01271 812090

**email:** info@lobbfields.com

**web:** www.lobbfields.com

**Dir:** *At x-rds in Braunton take B3231 to Croyde. Site signed on right leaving Braunton*

★ £8-£24 £8-£24 £6-£24

Open Mar-Oct Booking advisable Jul-Aug, BH Last arrival 22.00hrs Last departure 10.30hrs

A bright, tree-lined park with the gently-sloping grass pitches divided into two open areas and a camping field in August. Braunton is an easy walk away, and the golden beaches of Saunton Sands and Croyde are within easy reach. A 14-acre site with 181 touring pitches, 7 hardstandings.

**Leisure:** **Facilities:**

**Services:** →

**Notes:** No under 18s unless accompanied by an adult Baby changing facilities, surfing, boards & wet suits to hire, wet suit washing areas

## BRIDESTOWE MAP 03 SX58

### ►►► 75% Bridestowe Caravan Park *(SX519893)*

EX20 4ER

☎ 01837 861261

**email:** ali.young53@btinternet.com

**Dir:** *Leave A30 at A386/Sourton Cross junct, follow B3278 signed Bridestowe, turn left in 3m. In village centre, left down unclass road for 0.5m*

★ £10-£15 £10-£15 £8-£13

Open Mar-Dec Booking advisable summer Last arrival 22.30hrs Last departure noon

A small, well-established park in a rural setting close to Dartmoor National Park. This mainly static park has a small, peaceful touring space, and there are many activities to enjoy in the area including fishing and riding. Part of the National Cycle Route 27 (the Devon coast to coast) passes close to this park. A 1-acre site with 13 touring pitches, 3 hardstandings and 40 statics.

**Leisure:** **Facilities:**

**Services:** → **Notes:**

BRIDGERULE MAP 02 SS20

### ►►► 82% *Hedleywood Caravan & Camping Park* (*SS262013*)

EX22 7ED

☎ 01288 381404 ▤ 01288 382011

**email:** alan@hedleywood.co.uk

**web:** www.hedleywood.co.uk

**Dir:** *From B3254 take Widemouth road (unclass) at the Devon/ Cornwall border*

Open all year (Bar/restaurant open at main hols) Booking advisable public hols & Jul-Aug Last arrival anytime Last departure anytime

Set in a very rural location about 4 miles from Bude, this relaxed family-owned site has a peaceful, easy-going atmosphere. Pitches are in separate paddocks, some with extensive views, and this wooded park is quite sheltered in the lower areas. A 16.5-acre site with 120 touring pitches, 14 hardstandings and 16 statics.

**Leisure:**

**Facilities:**

**Services:**

**Notes:** Dog kennels, nature trail

*see advert on this page*

### ►► 88% Highfield House Camping & Caravanning (*SS279035*)

Holsworthy EX22 7EE

☎ 01288 381480

**email:** nikki@highfieldholidays.freeserve.co.uk

**Dir:** *Exit A3072 at Red Post x-rds onto B3254 towards Launceston. Direct access just over Devon border on right*

Open all year Booking advisable

Set in a quiet and peaceful rural location, this park has extensive views over the valley to the sea at Bude, five miles away. The friendly young owners, with small children of their own, offer a relaxing holiday for families, with the simple facilities carefully looked after. A 4-acre site with 20 touring pitches and 3 statics.

**Leisure:**

**Facilities:**

**Services:** →

**Notes:**

**Facilities:** Bath Shower Electric Shaver Hairdryer Ice Pack Facility Disabled Facilities Public Telephone Shop on Site or within 200yds Mobile Shop (calls at least 5 days a week) BBQ Area Picnic Area Dog Exercise Area

ENGLAND

## BRIXHAM MAP 03 SX95

### ►►► 77% Galmpton Touring Park

(SX885558)
Greenway Rd TQ5 0EP
☎ 01803 842066
**email:** galmptontouringpark@hotmail.com
**web:** www.galmptontouringpark.co.uk
**Dir:** *Signed from A3022 (Torbay to Brixham road) at Churston*
★ £9.10-£16.40 £9.10-£16.40 £9.10-£16.40

Open Etr-Sep Booking advisable BH & Jul-Aug Last arrival 21.00hrs Last departure 11.00hrs

An excellent location on high ground overlooking the River Dart, with outstanding views of the creek and anchorage. Pitches are set on level terraces, and facilities are bright and clean. A 10-acre site with 120 touring pitches, 7 hardstandings.

**Leisure:**

**Facilities:**

**Services:**

**Notes:** Families & couples only, no dogs during peak season. Bathroom for under 5s (charged)

## BRIXTON MAP 03 SX55

### ►► 72% *Brixton Caravan & Camping Park*

(SX550520)
Venn Farm PL8 2AX
☎ 01752 880378 01752 880378
**email:** info@vennfarm.co.uk
**web:** www.vennfarm.co.uk
**Dir:** *Leave A38 at Marsh Mills rdbt in Plymouth onto A379, signed Modbury and Kingsbridge. In approx 4m, turn right at mini-rdbt in centre of village, turn right into private road, site signed*

Open 15 Mar-14 Oct (rs 15 Mar-Jun & Sep-14 Oct no warden) Booking advisable Jul-Aug Last arrival 23.00hrs Last departure noon

A small park adjacent to a farm in the village, in a quiet rural area. The park is divided into two paddocks, and is just 100yds from the village services. A 2-acre site with 43 touring pitches.

**Facilities:**

**Services:**

## BROADWOODWIDGER MAP 03 SX48

### ►► 78% Roadford Lake (SX421900)

Lower Goodacre PL16 0JL
☎ 01409 211507 01566 778503
**email:** info@swlakestrust.org.uk
**web:** www.swlakestrust.org.uk
**Dir:** *Exit A30 between Okehampton & Launceston at Roadford Lake signs, follow road across dam wall, watersports centre is 0.25m on right.*
★ £10 £10

Open Apr-Oct Booking advisable

Located right at the edge of Devon's largest inland water, this popular rural park is well screened by mature trees and shrubs. It boasts an excellent watersports school with hire and day launch facilities, and is an ideal location for fly fishing for brown trout. A 1.5-acre site with 30 touring pitches, 4 hardstandings.

**Facilities:**

**Services:**

## BUCKFASTLEIGH MAP 03 SX76

### ► 84% Beara Farm Caravan & Camping Site

(SX751645)
Colston Rd TQ11 0LW
☎ 01364 642234
**Dir:** *From Exeter take Buckfastleigh exit at Dart Bridge, follow South Devon Steam Railway/Butterfly Farm signs. In 200mtrs take 1st left to Old Totnes Rd, 0.5m right at brick cottages signed Beara Farm*
★ fr £9 fr £9 fr £9

Open all year Booking advisable peak periods & Jul-Aug

A very good farm park with clean unisex facilities and very keen and friendly owners. A well-trimmed camping field offers peace and quiet. Close to the River Dart and the Dart Valley steam railway line, and within easy reach of sea and moors. The approach is narrow with passing places, and needs care. A 3.75-acre site with 30 touring pitches, 1 hardstanding.

**Facilities:**

**Services:**

**Notes:**

ENGLAND

► 84% **Churchill Farm Campsite** *(SX743664)*
TQ11 0EZ
☎ 01364 642844
**email:** apedrick@btinternet.com
**Dir:** *A38 Dart Bridge exit for Buckfastleigh/Totnes towards Buckfast Abbey. Pass Abbey entrance, proceed up hill, and then left at x-roads to site opposite Holy Trinity church*

★ £8-£12 £8-£12 £8-£12

Open Etr-Sep Booking advisable Jul & Aug Last arrival 22.30hrs

A working family farm in a relaxed and peaceful setting, with keen, friendly owners. Set on the hills above Buckfast Abbey, this attractive park is maintained to a good standard. The spacious pitches in the neatly trimmed paddock enjoy extensive country views, and the clean, simple toilet facilities have modern showers. A 3-acre site with 25 touring pitches.

**Facilities:**

**Services:**

**Notes:** Dogs must be kept on leads (working farm). Campsite within a Site of Special Scientific Interest

## BUDLEIGH SALTERTON — MAP 03 SY08

►► 78% **Pooh Cottage Holiday Park** *(SY053831)*
Bear Ln EX9 7AQ
☎ 01395 442354
**email:** info@poohcottage.co.uk
**web:** www.poohcottage.co.uk
**Dir:** *M5 junct 30 onto A376 towards Exmouth. Left onto B3179 towards Woodbury & Budleigh Salterton. Left into Knowle on B3178. Through village, at brow of hill take sharp left into Bear Lane (very narrow). Site 200yds*

£10-£15 £10-£15 £10-£15

Open Etr-Oct Booking advisable Jul-Aug Last arrival 23.00hrs Last departure 11.00hrs

A rural park with widespread views of the sea and surrounding peaceful countryside. Expect a friendly welcome to this attractive site, with its lovely play area, and easy access to plenty of walks, as well as the Buzzard Cycle Way. An 8-acre site with 52 touring pitches and 2 statics.

**Leisure:**

**Facilities:**

**Services:**

**Notes:**

## CHAPMANS WELL — MAP 03 SX39

►►► 84% **Chapmanswell Caravan Park** *(SX354931)*
PL15 9SG
☎ 01409 211382 01409 211154
**email:** george@chapmanswellcaravanpark.co.uk
**web:** www.chapmanswellcaravanpark.co.uk
**Dir:** *Off A388, midway between Launceston & Holsworthy*

★ £11.50-£16 £11.50-£16 £9.50-£14

Open all year Booking advisable Jul & Aug

Set on the borders of Devon and Cornwall in peaceful countryside, this park is just waiting to be discovered. It enjoys extensive views towards Dartmoor from level pitches, and is within easy driving distance of Launceston (7m) and the golden beaches at Bude (14m). A 10-acre site with 50 touring pitches, 35 hardstandings and 50 statics.

**Leisure:**

**Facilities:**

**Services:**

**Notes:** Wi-fi

## CHIVENOR — MAP 03 SS53

►►► 75% **Chivenor Caravan Park** *(SS501351)*
EX31 4BN

SILVER

☎ 01271 812217 01271 812644
**email:** chivenorcp@lineone.net
**web:** www.chivenorcaravanpark.co.uk
**Dir:** *On rdbt at Chivenor Cross take right exit to park.*

★ £9.50-£11.50 £9.50-£11.50 £9.50-£11.50

Open mid Mar-mid Jan Booking advisable Jun-Aug Last arrival 21.00hrs Last departure noon

A nicely maintained grassy park with some hard pitches, set in a good location for touring North Devon, and handy for the bus stop into Barnstaple. The site is about 5 miles from sandy beaches. A 3.5-acre site with 30 touring pitches, 5 hardstandings and 10 statics.

**Leisure:**

**Facilities:**

**Services:**

**Notes:** Off licence

ENGLAND

## CHUDLEIGH MAP 03 SX87

### ►►► 78% Holmans Wood Holiday Park *(SX881812)*

Harcombe Cross TQ13 0DZ

☎ 01626 853785 🖹 01626 853792

**email:** enquiries@holmanswood.co.uk

**web:** www.holmanswood.co.uk

**Dir:** *Follow M5 past Exeter onto A38 after racecourse at top of Haldon Hill. Left at BP petrol station signed Chudleigh, park entrance on left of slip road*

★ £12-£18 £12-£18 ▲ £12-£14

Open mid Mar-end Oct Booking advisable Last arrival 22.00hrs Last departure 11.00hrs

Delightful small park set back from the A38 in a secluded wooded area, handy for touring Dartmoor National Park, and the lanes and beaches of South Devon. The facilities are bright and clean, and the grounds are attractively landscaped. A 12-acre site with 85 touring pitches, 71 hardstandings and 34 statics.

**Leisure:**

**Facilities:**

**Services:** → 

**Notes:** Information room

## COLYTON MAP 04 SY29

### ►►► 90% Leacroft Touring Park *(SY217925)*

Colyton Hill EX24 6HY

☎ 01297 552823

**Dir:** *1m from Stafford Cross on A3052 towards Colyton*

★ £13-£17 £13-£17 ▲ £13-£17

Open Etr-mid Oct Booking advisable Jul-Aug & Spring BH Last arrival 21.00hrs Last departure 11.00hrs

Located outside the little village of Colyton in the east Devon countryside, the park has distant sea views across Lyme Bay from its slightly elevated position. A wooded area with walks is nearby, and the traffic-free seaside resort of Seaton is about 2.5 miles away. The park is slightly sloping with all pitches well spaced and level. A 10-acre site with 138 touring pitches, 10 hardstandings.

**Leisure:**

**Facilities:**

**Services:** →

**Notes:** Off licence

### ►► 80% Ashdown Caravan Park *(SY216922)*

Colyton Hill EX24 6HY

☎ 01297 20292 & 22052

**email:** ashdowncaravans@tiscali.co.uk

**web:** www.ashdowncaravanpark.co.uk

**Dir:** *From W take A3052 through Sidmouth towards Seaton, left at Stafford Cross, site 0.5m on left. From E exit A35 onto A358 signed Seaton, right onto A3052 signed Sidmouth. 4m at Stafford Cross turn right for site*

Open Apr-Oct Booking advisable public hols Last departure noon

Sheltered by mature trees and shrubs in quiet, unspoilt surroundings, this grassy park is divided into two spacious areas around the perimeter. Most pitches have electricity, and Seaton with its famous tramway is only 3 miles away. A 9-acre site with 90 touring pitches and 3 statics.

**Facilities:**

**Services:** →

**Notes:** Dogs must be kept on leads

## COMBE MARTIN MAP 03 SS54

*see also Berrynarbor*

### ►►►► 84% Stowford Farm Meadows *(SS560427)*

GOLD

Berry Down EX34 0PW

☎ 01271 882476 🖹 01271 883053

**email:** enquiries@stowford.co.uk

**web:** www.stowford.co.uk

**Dir:** *M5 junct 27 onto A361 to Barnstaple. Take A39 from town centre towards Lynton, in 1m turn left onto B3230. Right at garage at Lynton Cross onto A3123, site 1.5m on right*

★ £7.50-£20.25 £8.50-£21.25 ▲ £7.50-£24.25

Open all year (rs Winter pool & bars closed) Booking advisable BH & Jul-Aug Last arrival 20.00hrs Last departure 10.00hrs

Very gently sloping, grassy, sheltered and south-facing site approached down a wide, well-kept driveway. This large farm park is set in 500 acres, and offers many quality amenities, including a large swimming pool, horse riding and crazy golf. A 60-acre wooded nature trail is an added attraction, as is the mini zoo with its stock of friendly animals. A 100-acre site with 700 touring pitches, 70 hardstandings.

**Leisure:** **Facilities:**

**Services:** →

**Notes:** Cycle hire, caravan accessory shop

*see advert on opposite page*

### ►►► 76% Newberry Valley Park *(SS576473)*

Woodlands EX34 0AT

☎ 01271 882334

**email:** relax@newberryvalleypark.co.uk

**web:** www.newberryvalleypark.co.uk

**Dir:** *From M5 junct 27, take A361 to North Aller rdbt. Right onto A399, through Combe Martin to sea. Left into site*

★ £9-£25 ▲ £9-£25

Open Mar-Sep Booking advisable peak season & BH Last arrival 20.45hrs Last departure 10.00hrs

A family owned and run touring park on the edge of Combe Martin, with all its amenities just five minutes walk away. The park is set in a wooded valley with its own coarse fishing lake. The safe beaches of Newberry and Combe Martin are reached by a short footpath opposite the park entrance, where the South West coast path is located. A 20-acre site with 125 touring pitches.

**Leisure:** **Facilities:**

**Services:** →

**Notes:** No camp fires

*see advert on page 135*

## CROCKERNWELL MAP 03 SX79

### ►►► 84% Barley Meadow *(SX757925)*

EX6 6NR

☎ 01647 281629

**email:** welcome@barleymeadow.com

**web:** www.barleymeadow.com

**Dir:** *M5 junct 31 take A30 to 3rd exit signed Woodleigh. Through Cheriton Bishop, park signed just beyond Crockernwell. From Cornwall take A30 to Merrymead rdbt, then 1st exit to Cheriton Bishop, park 3m on right*

★ £10-£14 £10-£14 £6-£14

Open 15 Mar-1 Nov Booking advisable BH & Jul-Aug Last arrival 22.00hrs Last departure 11.00hrs

A small, very well maintained park set on high ground in the Dartmoor National Park in a quiet location. The grassy pitches are mostly level, and the park is well placed to explore Dartmoor. Special campfire equipment is available for hire at your own pitch. A 4-acre site with 60 touring pitches, 22 hardstandings.

**Leisure:**

**Facilities:**

**Services:**

**Notes:** Fire pits, croissants/baguettes baked daily

## CROYDE MAP 03 SS43

### ►►► 76% Bay View Farm Caravan & Camping Park *(SS443388)*

EX33 1PN

☎ 01271 890501

**web:** www.bayviewfarm.co.uk

**Dir:** *M5 junct 27 onto A361, through Barnstaple to Braunton, turn left onto B3231. Site at entry to Croyde village*

Open Mar-Oct Booking advisable high season Last arrival 21.30hrs Last departure 11.00hrs

A very busy and popular park close to surfing beaches and rock pools, with a public footpath leading directly to the sea. Set in a stunning location with views out over the Atlantic to Lundy Island, it is just a short stroll from Croyde. Facilities are clean and well maintained, and there is a fish and chip shop on site. No dogs allowed. A 10-acre site with 70 touring pitches, 38 hardstandings.

**Leisure:**

**Facilities:**

**Services:**

**Notes:**



**Facilities:** Bath Shower Electric Shaver Hairdryer Ice Pack Facility Disabled Facilities Public Telephone Shop on Site or within 200yds Mobile Shop (calls at least 5 days a week) BBQ Area Picnic Area Dog Exercise Area

ENGLAND

## CROYDE BAY

MAP 03 SS43

### 82% Ruda Holiday Park *(SS438397)*

EX33 1NY
☎ 01271 890671 & 0871 641 0199
01271 890656
**email:** enquiries@parkdeanholidays.co.uk
**web:** www.parkdeanholidays.co.uk
**Dir:** *M5 junct 27, A361 to Braunton. Left at main lights, follow Croyde signs*

★ £9-£30 £12-£34 £9-£30

Open mid Mar-Nov Booking advisable all times Last arrival 21.00hrs Last departure 10.00hrs

A spacious, well-managed park with its own glorious blue flag sandy beach, a surfers' paradise. Set in well-landscaped grounds, and with a full leisure programme plus daytime and evening entertainment for all the family. Cascades tropical adventure pool and a nightclub are very popular features. A 220-acre site with 312 touring pitches and 289 statics.

**Leisure:**
**Facilities:**
**Services:**
**Notes:** Family entertainment, children's club, Coast Bar

## CULLOMPTON

*see Kentisbeare*

## DARTMOUTH

MAP 03 SX85

### ►►►► 78% Little Cotton Caravan Park

*(SX858508)*
Little Cotton TQ6 0LB
☎ 01803 832558 01803 834887
**email:** enquiries@littlecotton.co.uk
**web:** www.littlecotton.co.uk
**Dir:** *Exit A38 at Buckfastleigh, A384 to Totnes, A381 to Halwell, then A3122 Dartmouth Rd, park on right at entrance to town*

★ £12.75-£17.25 £12.75-£17.25 £12.75-£17.25

Open 15 Mar-Oct Booking advisable Jul & Aug Last arrival 22.00hrs Last departure 11.00hrs

A very good grassy touring park set on high ground above Dartmouth, with quality facilities, and park and ride to the town from the gate. The toilet blocks are heated and superbly maintained. The friendly owners are happy to offer advice on touring in this pretty area. A 7.5-acre site with 95 touring pitches, 20 hardstandings.

**Facilities:**
**Services:**

### ►►►► 92% Woodlands Leisure Park

*(SX813522)*
Blackawton TQ9 7DQ
☎ 01803 712598 01803 712680
**email:** fun@woodlandspark.com
**web:** www.woodlandspark.com
**Dir:** *4m from Dartmouth on A3122. From A38 take turn for Totnes & follow brown tourist signs*

★ £12-£18.50 £12-£18.50 £12-£18.50

Open Etr-6 Nov Booking advisable at all times Last departure 11.00hrs

An extensive woodland park with a terraced grass camping area, and quality facilities which are maintained to a very high standard. The park caters for all the family in a relaxed atmosphere under the supervision of the owner's family, and boasts the UK's biggest indoor venture zone, several water-coasters and rides, and a wildlife park. A 16-acre site with 350 touring pitches, 47 hardstandings.

**Leisure:**
**Facilities:**
**Services:**
**Notes:** Watercoasters, toboggan run, gliders, falconry centre

*see advert on opposite page*

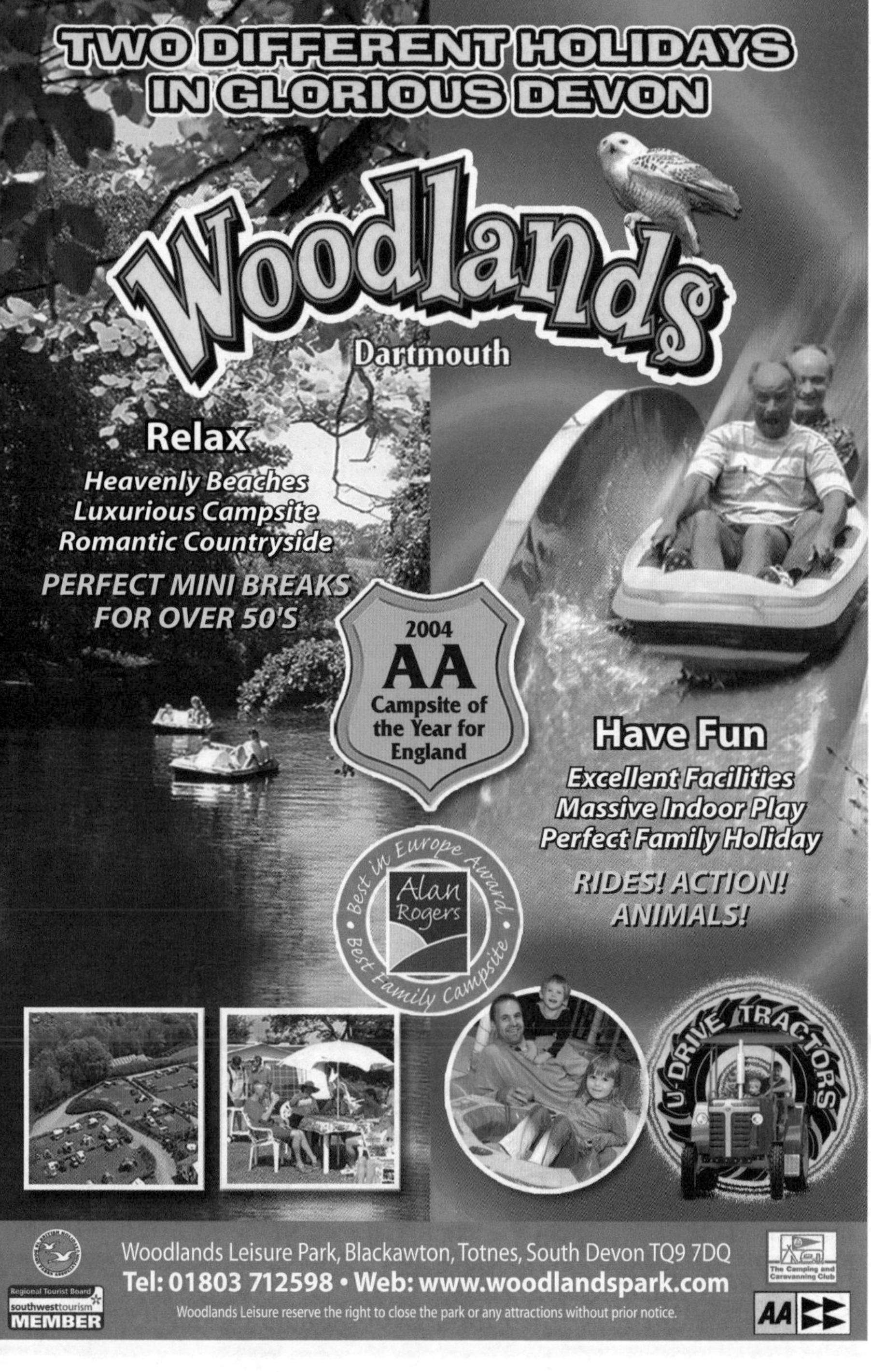
TWO DIFFERENT HOLIDAYS
IN GLORIOUS DEVON
Woodlands
Dartmouth
Relax
Heavenly Beaches
Luxurious Campsite
Romantic Countryside
PERFECT MINI BREAKS
FOR OVER 50'S
2004
AA
Campsite of
the Year for
England
Have Fun
Excellent Facilities
Massive Indoor Play
Perfect Family Holiday
RIDES! ACTION!
ANIMALS!
Best in Europe Award
Alan Rogers
Best Family Campsite
U-DRIVE TRACTORS
Woodlands Leisure Park, Blackawton, Totnes, South Devon TQ9 7DQ
Tel: 01803 712598 • Web: www.woodlandspark.com
Woodlands Leisure reserve the right to close the park or any attractions without prior notice.
Regional Tourist Board
southwesttourism
MEMBER
The Camping and Caravanning Club
AA

ENGLAND

## DARTMOUTH CONTINUED

### ►►► 73% Deer Park Touring and Camping (SX864493)

Dartmouth Rd, Stoke Fleming TQ6 0RF
☎ 01803 770253
**email:** info@deerparkinn.co.uk
**web:** www.deerparkinn.co.uk
**Dir:** *Direct access from A379 from Dartmouth before Stoke Fleming*

Open mid Mar-mid Nov Booking advisable BH & Jul-Aug Last arrival 21.00hrs Last departure 11.00hrs

Set on high ground with extensive sea views over Start Bay, this park is divided into three grassy paddocks. Good food is served next door at the Deer Park Inn, and there is a bus service to local beaches and Dartmouth. A 6-acre site with 160 touring pitches.

**Leisure:**
**Facilities:**
**Services:** →
**Notes:** Dogs must be kept on leads

## DAWLISH MAP 03 SX97

### 74% Golden Sands Holiday Park (SX968784)

Week Ln EX7 0LZ
☎ 01626 863099 01626 867149
**email:** info@goldensands.co.uk
**web:** www.goldensands.co.uk
**Dir:** *M5 junct 30 onto A379 signed Dawlish. After 6m pass small harbour at Cockwood, signed on left in 2m*

★ £11-£27 £11-£27 £11-£27

Open Etr-Oct Booking advisable May-Sep Last arrival 22.00hrs Last departure 10.00hrs

A holiday centre for all the family, offering a wide range of entertainment. The small touring area is surrounded by mature trees and hedges in a pleasant area, and visitors enjoy free use of the licensed club and heated swimming pools. Organised children's activities are a popular feature. A 12-acre site with 36 touring pitches and 200 statics.

**Leisure:**
**Facilities:**
**Services:** →
**Notes:** No pets

*see advert on this page*

## 78% **Lady's Mile Holiday Park** *(SX968784)*

EX7 0LX

01626 863411 01626 888689
**email:** info@ladysmile.co.uk
**web:** www.ladysmile.co.uk

**Dir:** *1m N of Dawlish on A379*

★ £11-£21 £11-£21 £11-£21

Open 17 Mar-27 Oct Booking advisable BH & Jul-Aug
Last arrival 20.00hrs Last departure 11.00hrs

A holiday site with all grass touring pitches, and plenty of activities for everyone. Two swimming pools with waterslides, a large adventure playground, 9-hole golf course, and a bar with entertainment in high season all add to the enjoyment of a stay here. Facilities are kept clean, and the surrounding beaches are easily accessed. A 16-acre site with 243 touring pitches and 43 statics.

**Leisure:**

**Facilities:**

**Services:**

*see advert on this page*

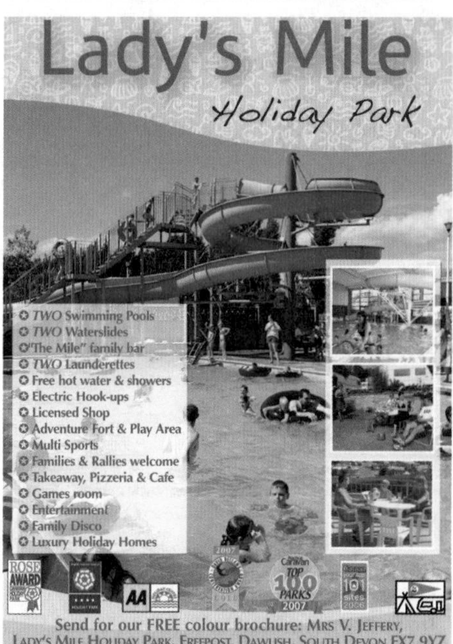

ENGLAND

## DAWLISH CONTINUED

### 78% Peppermint Park
*(SX978788)*

GOLD

Warren Rd EX7 0PQ

☎ 01626 863436 01626 866482

**email:** info@peppermintpark.co.uk

**web:** www.peppermintpark.co.uk

**Dir:** *From A379 at Dawlish follow signs for Dawlish Warren. Site 1m on left at bottom of hill*

★ £14-£24 £14-£24 £12-£20

Open Etr-Oct (rs early/late season shop, pool, club closed) Booking advisable Spring BH & Jul-Aug Last arrival 18.00hrs Last departure 11.00hrs

Well managed, attractive park close to the coast, with excellent facilities including club and bar which are well away from pitches. Nestling close to sandy beaches, the park offers individually marked pitches on level terraces in pleasant, sheltered grassland. The many amenities include a heated swimming pool and water chute, coarse fishing and launderette. A 26-acre site with 250 touring pitches, 24 hardstandings and 75 statics.

**Leisure:**

**Facilities:**

**Services:**

**Notes:** Wi-fi. Licensed club, entertainment

*see advert on page 129*

### ►►►► 77% Cofton Country Holidays
*(SX967801)*

GOLD

Starcross EX6 8RP

☎ 01626 890111 01626 891572

**email:** info@coftonholidays.co.uk

**web:** www.coftonholidays.co.uk

**Dir:** *On A379 (Exeter/Dawlish road) 3m from Dawlish*

★ £13-£25 £13-£25 £13-£23

Open Etr-Oct (rs Etr-Spring BH & mid Sep-Oct swimming pool closed) Booking advisable BH & Jul-Aug Last arrival 20.00hrs Last departure 11.00hrs

Set in a rural location surrounded by spacious open grassland, with plenty of well-kept flower beds throughout the park. Most pitches overlook either the swimming pool complex or the fishing lakes and woodlands. An on-site pub, with a family room, serves drinks, and meals or snacks and a mini-market caters for most shopping needs. A 16-acre site with 450 touring pitches, 20 hardstandings and 66 statics.

**Leisure:**

**Facilities:**

**Services:**

**Notes:** Families only. Wi-fi. Coarse fishing

*see advert on opposite page*

### ►►► 76% Leadstone Camping *(SX974782)*

Warren Rd EX7 0NG

☎ 01626 864411 01626 873833

**email:** info@leadstonecamping.co.uk

**web:** www.leadstonecamping.co.uk

**Dir:** *M5 junct 30, A379 to Dawlish. Before village turn left on brow of hill, signed Dawlish Warren. Site 0.5m on right*

★ £15.80-£18.90 £12-£14.50 £12-£14.50

Open 13 Jun-7 Sep Booking advisable 12 Jul-25 Aug Last arrival 22.00hrs Last departure noon

A traditional, mainly level grassy camping park approx 0.5m walk from sands and dunes at Dawlish Warren, an Area of Outstanding Natural Beauty. This mainly tented park has been run by the same friendly family for many years, and is an ideal base for touring south Devon. A regular bus service from outside the gate takes in a wide area. An 8-acre site with 137 touring pitches.

**Leisure:**

**Facilities:**

**Services:**

**Notes:** No noise after 23.00hrs

DREWSTEIGNTON MAP 03 SX79

### ►►► 76% Woodland Springs Adult Touring Park (SX695912)

Venton EX6 6PG

☎ 01647 231695

**email:** enquiries@woodlandsprings.co.uk

**web:** www.woodlandsprings.co.uk

**Dir:** *Exit A30 at Whiddon Down Junction, left onto A382 towards Moretonhampstead. Site 1.5m on left*

★ £12-£17.50 £12-£17.50 ▲ £9.50-£17.50

Open all year Booking advisable Jul-Aug, Xmas Last arrival 22.00hrs Last departure 11.00hrs

An attractive park in a rural area within Dartmoor National Park. This site is surrounded by woodland and neighbouring farmland, and is very peaceful. Children are not admitted. A 4-acre site with 85 touring pitches, 34 hardstandings.

**Facilities:**

**Services:**

**Notes:** Adults only No fires, no noise 23.00hrs-08.00hrs

EAST ALLINGTON MAP 03 SX74

### ►►► 73% Mounts Farm Touring Park (SX757488)

The Mounts TQ9 7QJ

☎ 01548 521591

**email:** mounts.farm@lineone.net

**web:** www.mountsfarm.co.uk

**Dir:** *A381 from Totnes towards Kingsbridge (NB ignore signs for East Allington). At The Mounts site is 0.5m on left*

★ £13-£17 £13-£17 ▲ £13-£17

Open 15 Mar-Oct Booking advisable BH & peak season Last arrival anytime Last departure at any time

A neat grassy park divided into four paddocks by mature natural hedges. Three of the paddocks house the tourers and campers, and the fourth is the children's play area. The laundry and well-stocked little shop are in converted farm buildings. A 7-acre site with 50 touring pitches.

**Leisure:**

**Facilities:**

**Services:**

**Notes:** Onsite provisions & camping accessories available



**Leisure:** Indoor swimming pool · Outdoor swimming pool · Tennis court · Games room · Children's playground · Stables · 9/18 hole golf course · Boats for hire · Cinema · Fishing · Mini golf · Watersports · Separate TV room

ENGLAND



## EAST ANSTEY — MAP 03 SS82

### ►►►► 84% **Zeacombe House Caravan Park**

*(SS860240)*

Blackerton Cross EX16 9JU

☎ 01398 341279

**email:** enquiries@zeacombeadultretreat.co.uk

**web:** www.zeacombeadultretreat.co.uk

**Dir:** *M5 junct 27 onto A361 signed Barnstaple, turn right at next rdbt onto A396 signed Dulverton/Minehead. In 5m at Exeter Inn turn left. 1.5m at Black Cat junct left onto B3227 towards South Molton, site in 7m on left*

★ £14-£18 £14-£18 £14-£18

Open 7 Mar-Oct Booking advisable BH & Jul-Aug Last arrival 21.00hrs Last departure noon

Set on the southern fringes of Exmoor National Park, this 'garden' park is nicely landscaped in a tranquil location, and enjoys panoramic views towards Exmoor. This adult-only park offers a choice of grass or hardstanding pitches, and a unique restaurant-style delivery service allows you to eat an evening meal in the comfort of your own unit. A 5-acre site with 50 touring pitches, 12 hardstandings.

**Facilities:**

**Services:** →

**Notes:** Adults only

## EAST WORLINGTON — MAP 03 SS71

### ►►►► 73% ***Yeatheridge Farm Caravan Park*** *(SS768110)*

EX17 4TN

☎ 01884 860330

**email:** yeatheridge@talk21.com

**web:** www.yeatheridge.co.uk

**Dir:** *M5 junct 27, A361, at 1st rdbt at Tiverton take B3137 for 9m towards Witheridge. Fork left 1m past Nomansland onto B3042. Site on left in 3.5m. (NB Do not go to East Worlington)*

Open Etr-Sep Booking advisable Etr, Spring BH & school hols Last arrival 22.00hrs Last departure 22.00hrs

Gently sloping grass site with mature trees, set in meadowland in rural Devon. There are good views of distant Dartmoor, and the site is of great appeal to families with its farm animals, horse riding, and two indoor swimming pools, one with a flume. There are many attractive villages in this area. A 9-acre site with 85 touring pitches.

**Leisure:**

**Facilities:**

**Services:** →

**Notes:** Fishing, pool table

*see advert on this page*

## EXETER

*see Kennford*

ENGLAND

## EXMOUTH MAP 03 SY08

*see also Woodbury Salterton*

### 90% Devon Cliffs Holiday Park *(SY036807)*

Sandy Bay EX8 5BT

☎ 01395 226226 Fax 01395 268677

**web:** www.devoncliffs-park.co.uk

**Dir:** *M5 junct 30/A376 towards Exmouth, follow brown signs to Sandy Bay*

★ £35-£55

Open mid Mar-Oct (rs mid Mar-May & Sep-Oct some facilities may be reduced) Booking advisable school hols Last arrival 19.00hrs Last departure 10.00hrs

A large and exciting holiday park on a hillside setting close to Exmouth, with spectacular views across Sandy Bay. The all-action park offers a superb entertainment programme for all ages throughout the day, with very modern sports and leisure facilities available for everyone. An internet café is just one of the quality amenities, and though some visitors may enjoy relaxing and watching others play, the temptation to join in is overpowering. A 163-acre site with 193 touring pitches, 43 hardstandings and 2000 statics.

**Leisure:**

**Facilities:**

**Services:**

**Notes:** Dogs must be on leads

### ►►►► 85% Webbers Farm Caravan & Camping Park *(SY018874)*

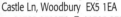

Castle Ln, Woodbury EX5 1EA

☎ 01395 232276 Fax 01395 233389

**email:** reception@webberspark.co.uk

**web:** www.webberspark.co.uk

**Dir:** *From M5 junct 30 take A376, then B3179 to Woodbury. Site 500yds E of village*

★ £11-£17

Open mid Mar-Oct Booking advisable peak season & BH Last arrival 20.00hrs Last departure 11.00hrs

An unspoilt family park set in three areas, offering a quiet and relaxing touring location. A high quality toilet block provides cubicled family rooms and plenty of smart private facilities. The park has good views towards the Haldon Hills, and plenty to explore including 3,000 acres of Woodbury Common and nearby beaches. An 8-acre site with 115 touring pitches and 4 statics.

**Leisure:**

**Facilities:**

**Services:**

**Notes:** Pets' corner, caravan storage facilities

### NEW ►► 74% Prattshayes Farm National Trust Campsite *(SY030810)*

Maer Ln EX8 5DB

☎ 01395 276626 Fax 01395 276626

**Dir:** *A376 Exmouth, follow signs towards Sandy Bay. At narrow bridge by Clinton Arms public house, turn right, site in 0.5m on right.*

£8-£12 £8-£12 £8-£12

Open Apr-Sep Booking advisable Jul-Aug Last arrival 21.00hrs Last departure 10.30hrs

Set in a quiet rural location, with grassy pitches surrounded by mature hedging. Converted farm buildings house the good toilet/shower facilities. An ideal spot for exploring the start of the Jurassic Coast. 30 touring pitches.

**Facilities:**

**Services:**

**Notes:** Dogs not to be exercised on site, no generators, no open fires or ground level BBQs

### ►► 76% St Johns Caravan & Camping Park *(SY027834)*

St Johns Rd EX8 5EG

☎ 01395 263170 Fax 01395 273004

**email:** stjohns.farm@virgin.net

**Dir:** *M5 junct 30 follow A376/Exmouth signs. Left through Woodbury towards Budleigh Salterton on B3179 & B3180. Turn right 1m after Exmouth exit*

★ £8-£12 £8-£12 £8-£12

Open mid Feb-Dec Booking advisable school summer hols Last arrival 22.00hrs Last departure noon

A quiet rural site with attractive country views, only 2 miles from Exmouth's sandy beaches, and half a mile from Woodbury Common. The owners offer a warm welcome to visitors. A 6-acre site with 45 touring pitches, 8 hardstandings.

**Leisure:**

**Facilities:**

**Services:**

**Notes:** Farm shop

ENGLAND

## HOLSWORTHY MAP 03 SS30

### ► 75% Noteworthy Caravan and Campsite

*(SS303052)*

Noteworthy, Bude Rd EX22 7JB

☎ 01409 253731

**email:** enquiries@noteworthy-devon.co.uk

**web:** www.noteworthy-devon.co.uk

**Dir:** *On A3072 between Holsworthy & Bude. 3m from Holsworthy on right*

Open all year Booking advisable Aug

This campsite is owned by a friendly young couple with their own small children. There are good views from the quiet rural location, and simple toilet facilities. A 5-acre site with 5 touring pitches and 1 static.

**Leisure:**

**Facilities:**

**Services:**

**Notes:** No open fires. Dog grooming available

### NEW ► 74% Tamarstone Farm *(SS286056)*

Bude Rd, Pancrasweek EX22 7JT

☎ 01288 381734

**email:** camping@tamarstone.co.uk

**web:** www.tamarstone.co.uk

**Dir:** *A30 to Launcestone then B3254 towards Bude approx 14m. Turn right towards Holsworthy on the A3072, site on left.*

£10-£12 £10-£12 £10-£12

Open Etr-end Oct Booking advisable Last departure noon

Four acres of river-bordered meadow and woodland providing a wildlife haven for those who enjoy peace and seclusion. The wide sandy beaches of Bude are just five miles away, and coarse fishing is provided free on site for visitors. A 1-acre site with 16 touring pitches and 1 static.

**Leisure:**

**Facilities:**

**Services:**

**Notes:** Dogs on lead at all times. Unisex facilities

## ILFRACOMBE MAP 03 SS54

*see also Berrynarbor*

### ►►►► 82% Hele Valley Holiday Park

*(SS533472)*

Hele Bay EX34 9RD

☎ 01271 862460 01271 867926

**email:** holidays@helevalley.co.uk

**web:** www.helevalley.co.uk

**Dir:** *M5 junct 27 onto A361. Through Barnstaple & Braunton to Ilfracombe. Then A399 towards Combe Martin. Follow brown Hele Valley signs. 400mtrs sharp right, then to T-junct. Reception on left.*

★ £11-£18 £11-£27

Open May-Sep Booking advisable at all times Last arrival 18.00hrs Last departure 11.00hrs

A deceptively spacious park set in a picturesque valley with glorious tree-lined hilly views from most pitches. High quality toilet facilities are provided, and the park is close to a lovely beach, with the harbour and other attractions of Ilfracombe just a mile away. A 17-acre site with 58 touring pitches, 8 hardstandings and 80 statics.

**Leisure:**

**Facilities:**

**Services:**

**Notes:** No groups. Post collection, internet access, info service

### ►►► 82% *Watermouth Cove Holiday Park*

*(SS558477)*

Berrynarbor EX34 9SJ

☎ 01271 862504

**email:** info@watermouthcoveholidays.co.uk

**web:** www.watermouthcoveholidays.co.uk

**Dir:** *From M5 junct 27, take A361 to 2nd rdbt at South Molton, then A399 through Coombe Martin. Turn left at seafront & site 2m on right*

Open Etr-Oct (rs Etr-Whit & Sep-Oct pool, takeaway, club & shop limited) Booking advisable Whit & Jul-Aug Last arrival 22.00hrs Last departure 11.00hrs

A popular site in very attractive surroundings, set amidst trees and bushes in meadowland with access to sea, beach and main road. This beautiful cove has a private sandy beach, and offers launching for boats and other water craft, as well as swimming. The site is two miles from both Combe Martin and Ilfracombe. A 6-acre site with 90 touring pitches, 10 hardstandings.

**Leisure:**

**Facilities:**

**Services:**

**Notes:** Coastal headland fishing

ENGLAND

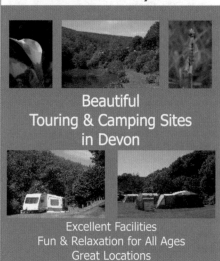



## KENTISBEARE

MAP 03 ST00

### ►►► 78% Forest Glade Holiday Park *(ST100075)*

Cullompton EX15 2DT

☎ 01404 841381 🖹 01404 841593

**email:** enquiries@forest-glade.co.uk

**web:** www.forest-glade.co.uk

**Dir:** *Tent traffic from A373, signed at Keepers Cottage Inn, 2.5m E of M5 junct 28. Touring caravans via Honiton/Dunkeswell road: phone for access details*

★ £12.50-£17 £12.50-£17 £10-£14

Open 2 wks before Etr-end Oct (rs low season limited shop hours) Booking advisable school hols Last arrival 21.00hrs

A quiet, attractive park in a forest clearing with well-kept gardens and beech hedge screening. One of the main attractions is the immediate proximity of the forest, which offers magnificent hillside walks with surprising views over the valleys. Please telephone for route details. A 15-acre site with 80 touring pitches, 40 hardstandings and 57 statics.

**Leisure:**

**Facilities:**

**Services:**

**Notes:** Families and couples only. Wi-fi. Adventure play area, paddling/ball pools

*see advert on this page*

## KENNFORD

MAP 03 SX98

### ►►►► 75% Kennford International Caravan Park *(SX912857)* EX6 7YN

☎ 01392 833046 🖹 01392 833046

**email:** ian@kennfordint.fsbusiness.co.uk

**web:** www.kennfordint.co.uk

**Dir:** *At end of M5, take A38, site signed at Kennford slip road*

Open all year Last arrival 21.00hrs Last departure 11.00hrs

Screened by trees and shrubs from the A38, this park offers many pitches divided by hedging for privacy. A high quality toilet block complements the park's facilities. A good, centrally-located base for touring the coast and countryside of Devon; Exeter is easily accessible by bus. A 15-acre site with 127 touring pitches and 15 statics. Booking advised.

**Leisure:** **Facilities:**

**Services:**



**Leisure:** Indoor swimming pool · Outdoor swimming pool · Tennis court · Games room · Children's playground · Stables · 9/18 hole golf course · Boats for hire · Cinema · Fishing · Mini golf · Watersports · Separate TV room

## LYDFORD MAP 03 SX58

### ►►► 72% Lydford Camping & Caravanning Club Site *(SX512853)*

EX20 4BE

☎ 01822 820275

**web:** www.campingandcaravanningclub.co.uk/lydford

**Dir:** *From A30 take A386 signed to Tavistock & Lydford. Past Fox & Hounds on left, right at Lydford sign. Right at war memorial, keep right to site in 200yds*

★ £15.45-£20.15 £15.45-£20.15 £15.45-£20.15

Open 13 Mar-3 Nov Booking advisable BH & peak periods Last arrival 21.00hrs Last departure noon

Site on mainly level ground looking towards the western slopes of Dartmoor at the edge of the village, near the spectacular gorge. This popular park is close to the Devon coast to coast cycle route, between Tavistock and Okehampton. A 7.75-acre site with 90 touring pitches, 27 hardstandings.

**Facilities:**

**Services:** →

**Notes:** Site gates closed 23.00hrs-07.00hrs

## LYNTON MAP 03 SS74

*see also Oare (Somerset)*

### ►►►► 70% Channel View Caravan and Camping Park

*(SS724482)*

GOLD

Manor Farm EX35 6LD

☎ 01598 753349 01598 752777

**email:** relax@channel-view.co.uk

**web:** www.channel-view.co.uk

**Dir:** *A39 E for 0.5m on left past Barbrook*

★ £10-£17 £10-£17 £3.50-£17

Open 15 Mar-15 Nov Booking advisable Jul-Aug Last arrival 22.00hrs Last departure noon

On the top of the cliffs overlooking the Bristol Channel, a well-maintained park on the edge of Exmoor, and close to both Lynton and Lynmouth. Pitches can be selected from a hidden hedged area, or with panoramic views over the coast. A 6-acre site with 76 touring pitches, 15 hardstandings and 31 statics.

**Leisure:**

**Facilities:**

**Services:** →

**Notes:** Groups by prior arrangement only. Parent & baby room

*see advert on this page*

### ►►► 73% Lynton Camping & Caravanning Club Site *(SS703481)*

Caffyns Cross EX35 6JS

☎ 01598 752379

**web:** www.campingandcaravanningclub.co.uk/lynton

**Dir:** *M5 junct 27 onto A361 to Barnstable. Turn right to Blackmoor Gate signed Lynmouth & Lynton. Approx 5m to Caffyns Cross, immediately right to site in 1m*

★ £14.05-£18.85 £14.05-£18.85 £14.05-£18.85

Open 13 Mar-29 Sep Booking advisable BH & peak periods Last arrival 21.00hrs Last departure noon

Set on high ground with excellent views over the Bristol Channel, and close to the twin resorts of Lynton & Lynmouth. This area is known as Little Switzerland because of its wooded hills, and the park is ideal for walking, and cycling on the nearby National Cycle Network. A 5.5-acre site with 105 touring pitches, 10 hardstandings.

**Leisure:**

**Facilities:**

**Services:** →

**Notes:** Site gates closed 23.00hrs-07.00hrs

### ►►► 76% Sunny Lyn Holiday Park

*(SS719486)*

Lynbridge EX35 6NS

☎ 01598 753384 🖹 01598 753273

**email:** info@caravandevon.co.uk

**web:** www.caravandevon.co.uk

**Dir:** *M5 junct 27, A361 to South Molton. Right onto A399 to Blackmoor Gate, right onto A39, left onto B3234 towards Lynmouth. Site 1m on right*

£13.50-£14.50 £13.50-£14.50 £11.50-£12.50

Open Mar-Oct Booking advisable Etr, Spring BH & mid Jul-Aug Last arrival 20.00hrs Last departure 11.00hrs

Set in a sheltered riverside location in a wooded combe within a mile of the sea, in Exmoor National Park. This family-run park offers good facilities including an excellent café. A 4.5-acre site with 9 touring pitches, 4 hardstandings and 7 statics.

**Facilities:**

**Services:**

**Notes:** No cars by tents. Table tennis & trout fishing

## MODBURY MAP 03 SX65

### ►►► 79% California Cross Camping & Caravanning Club Site *(SX705530)*

PL21 0SG

☎ 01548 821297

**web:** www.campingandcaravanningclub.co.uk/californiacross

**Dir:** *Leave A38 at Wrangton Cross onto A3121, continue to x-rds. Cross over onto B3196, left after California Cross sign before petrol station, site on right*

★ £14.05-£18.85 £14.05-£18.85 £14.05-£18.85

Open 13 Mar-3 Nov Booking advisable BH & peak periods Last arrival 21.00hrs Last departure noon

A gently sloping site with some terracing, set in a rural location midway between Ivybridge and Kingsbridge. This well ordered site is protected by high hedging, and is an ideal base for exploring the lovely South Devon countryside. A 3.75-acre site with 80 touring pitches, 7 hardstandings.

**Leisure:**

**Facilities:**

**Services:**

**Notes:** Site gates closed 23.00hrs-07.00hrs

### ►►► 89% Moor View Touring Park

*(SX705533)*

California Cross PL21 0SG

☎ 01548 821485

**email:** info@moorviewtouringpark.co.uk

**web:** www.moorviewtouringpark.co.uk

**Dir:** *Exit A38 at Wrangaton Cross, left at top of slip road onto B3121. Over x-rds for 4m past petrol station. Park 0.5m*

Open all year Booking advisable Last arrival 18.00hrs Last departure 11.00hrs

A compact terraced park in picturesque South Hams, with wide views of Dartmoor. Many pitches are divided by low mature hedging, and most are hardstandings with electricity, water and grey waste. The excellent facilities include a bright, modern toilet block, and a games room/TV lounge. The park is for adults only. A 5.5-acre site with 68 touring pitches, 65 hardstandings.

**Leisure:**

**Facilities:**

**Services:**

**Notes:** Adults only. Wi-fi

### ►►► 79% Pennymoor Camping & Caravan Park *(SX685516)*

PL21 0SB

☎ 01548 830542 & 830020 🖹 01548 830542

**email:** enquiries@pennymoor-camping.co.uk

**web:** www.pennymoor-camping.co.uk

**Dir:** *Exit A38 at Wrangaton Cross. Left & straight over x-roads. Then 4m, pass petrol station & 2nd left. Site 1.5m on right*

Open 15 Mar-15 Nov (rs 15 Mar-mid May one toilet & shower block only open) Booking advisable Jul-Aug Last arrival 20.00hrs Last departure 10.00hrs

A well-established rural park on part level, part gently sloping grass with good views over distant Dartmoor and the countryside in between. The park has been owned and run by the same family since 1935, and is very carefully tended, with a relaxing atmosphere.

**Leisure:**

**Facilities:**

**Services:**

**Notes:** No skateboards

*see advert on page 138*

ENGLAND



## MOLLAND — MAP 03 SS82

### ►►► 74% Yeo Valley Holiday Park

*(SS788265)*

SILVER

EX36 3NW

☎ 01769 550297 Fax 01769 550101

**email:** info@yeovalleyholidays.com

**web:** www.yeovalleyholidays.com

**Dir:** *From A361 onto B3227 towards Bampton. Follow brown signs for Blackcock Inn. Site opposite*

★ £13.50-£18 £10-£14.50

Open all year (rs Sep-Mar swimming pool closed) Booking advisable Jul-Aug Last arrival 22.30hrs Last departure 10.00hrs

Set in a beautiful secluded valley on the edge of Exmoor National Park, this family-run park has easy access to both the moors and the north Devon coastline. The park is adjacent to the Blackcock Inn (under the same ownership), and has a very good heated indoor pool. A 7-acre site with 65 touring pitches, 16 hardstandings and 5 statics.

**Leisure:**

**Facilities:**

**Services:**

**Notes:** Bike hire

## MORTEHOE — MAP 03 SS44

*see also Woolacombe*

### 82% Twitchen House Holiday Parc *(SS465447)*

Station Rd EX34 7ES

☎ 01271 870343 Fax 01271 870089

**email:** goodtimes@woolacombe.com

**web:** www.woolacombe.com

**Dir:** *From Mullacott Cross rdbt take B3343 (Woolacombe road) to Turnpike Cross junct. Take right fork, site 1.5m on left*

Open Mar-Oct Booking advisable Etr/Whit & Jul-Aug Last arrival mdnt Last departure 10.00hrs

A very attractive park with good leisure facilities. Visitors can use the amenities at all three of Woolacombe Bay holiday parks, and a bus service connects them all with the beach. The touring features pitches offering either sea views or a country and woodland outlook. A 45-acre site with 334 touring pitches, 110 hardstandings and 278 statics.

**Leisure:**

**Facilities:**

**Services:**

**Notes:** Table tennis, sauna, kids' club

### ►►► 74% Easewell Farm Holiday Parc & Golf Club *(SS465455)*

EX34 7EH

☎ 01271 870343 Fax 01271 870089

**email:** goodtimes@woolacombe.com

**web:** www.woolacombe.com

**Dir:** *Take B3343 to Mortehoe. Turn right at fork, site 2m on right*

Open Etr-Oct (rs Etr) Booking advisable Jul-Aug, Etr, Whitsun Last arrival 22.00hrs Last departure 10.00hrs

A peaceful clifftop park with full facility pitches for caravans and motorhomes, and superb views. The park offers a range of activities including indoor bowling and a golf course, and all the facilities of the three other nearby holiday centres within this group are open to everyone. A 17-acre site with 302 touring pitches, 50 hardstandings and 1 static.

**Leisure:**

**Facilities:**

**Services:**

**Notes:** 9-hole golf on site, indoor bowls, snooker

*see advert on page 152*

►►► 85% **North Morte Farm Caravan & Camping Park** *(SS462455)*
lorth Morte Rd EX34 7EG
01271 870381 01271 870115
**email:** info@northmortefarm.co.uk
**web:** www.northmortefarm.co.uk
**Dir:** *From B3343 into Mortehoe, right at post office. Park 500yds on left*

★ £15-£19 £12-£19 £12-£16

Open Apr-Sep Last arrival 22.30hrs Last departure noon

et in spectacular coastal countryside close to National Trust land nd 500yds from Rockham Beach. This attractive park is very well run nd maintained by friendly family owners, and the quaint village of lortehoe with its cafés, shops and pubs, is just a 5 minute walk away. A 2-acre site with 180 touring pitches, 18 hardstandings and 73 statics.

**eisure:**

**acilities:**

**ervices:**

**lotes:** No large groups, dogs on leads at all times

►►► 88% **Warcombe Farm Caravan & Camping Park** *(SS478445)*
tation Rd EX34 7EJ
01271 870690 & 07774 428770 01271 871070
**mail:** info@warcombefarm.co.uk
**veb:** www.warcombefarm.co.uk
**ir:** *N towards Mortehoe from Mullacot Cross rdbt at A361 junct vith B3343. Site 2m on right*

★ £13-£28 £13-£28 £13-£28

Open 15 Mar-Oct Booking advisable Jul-Aug Last arrival 2.00hrs Last departure noon

xtensive views over the Bristol Channel can be enjoyed from the pen areas of this attractive park, while other pitches are sheltered in addocks with maturing trees. The superb sandy beach with Blue Flag ward at Woolacombe Bay is only 1.5m away, and there is a fishing ke with direct access from some pitches. A 19-acre site with 250 ouring pitches, 10 hardstandings.

**eisure:**

**acilities:**

**ervices:**

**otes:** No groups unless booked in advance. Private fishing, internet ccess

## NEWTON ABBOT — MAP 03 SX87

*see also Bickington*

### PREMIER PARK

►►►►► 90% **Dornafield** *(SX838683)*
Dornafield Farm, Two Mile Oak
TQ12 6DD
01803 812732 01803 812032
**email:** enquiries@dornafield.com
**web:** www.dornafield.com
**Dir:** *Take A381 (Newton Abbot-Totnes) for 2m. At Two Mile Oak Inn turn right, then left at x-roads in 0.5m to site on right*

★ £12.50-£23 £12.50-£23 £12.50-£23

Open 15 Mar-4 Jan Booking advisable BH & Jul-Aug Last arrival 22.00hrs Last departure 11.00hrs

An immaculately kept park in a tranquil wooded valley between Dartmoor and Torbay, offering either de-luxe or fully-serviced pitches. A lovely 15th-century farmhouse sits at the entrance, and the park is divided into three separate areas, served by two superb, ultra-modern toilet blocks. The friendly family owners are always available. A 30-acre site with 135 touring pitches, 97 hardstandings.

**Leisure:**

**Facilities:**

**Services:**

**Notes:** Wi-fi. Caravan storage (all year)

ENGLAND

## NEWTON ABBOT CONTINUED

PREMIER PARK

### ►►►►► 95% Ross Park
(SX845671)
Park Hill Farm, Ipplepen TQ12 5TT
☎ 01803 812983 01803 812983
**email:** enquiries@rossparkcaravanpark.co.uk
**web:** www.rossparkcaravanpark.co.uk
**Dir:** *Off A381, 3m from Newton Abbot towards Totnes, signed opposite 'Power' garage towards 'Woodland'*

★ £11.50-£21 £11.50-£21  Å £10.50-£20

Open Mar-2 Jan (rs Nov-Feb & 1st 3wks of Mar restaurant/bar closed (ex Xmas/New Year)) Booking advisable Jul, Aug & BH Last arrival 21.00hrs Last departure 10.00hrs

A top-class park in every way, with large secluded pitches, high quality toilet facilities and lovely floral displays throughout the 26 acres. The beautiful tropical conservatory also offers a breathtaking show of colour. This very rural park enjoys superb views of Dartmoor, and good quality meals to suit all tastes and pockets are served in the restaurant. A 26-acre site with 110 touring pitches, 82 hardstandings.

**Leisure:**

**Facilities:**

**Services:** → 

**Notes:** Bikes, skateboards/scooters only allowed on leisure field. Wi-fi. Snooker, table tennis, badminton, croquet

### ►►► 78% Twelve Oaks Farm Caravan Park
(SX852737)
Teigngrace TQ12 6QT
☎ 01626 352769 01626 352769
**email:** info@twelveoaksfarm.co.uk
**web:** www.twelveoaksfarm.co.uk
**Dir:** *A38 from Exeter left signed Teigngrace (only), 0.25m before Drumbridges rdbt. 1.5m, through village, site on left. From Plymouth pass Drumbridges rdbt, take slip road for Chudleigh Knighton. Right over bridge, rejoin A38 towards Plymouth. Left for Teigngrace (only), then as above*

Å

*Twelve Oaks Farm Caravan Park*

Open all year Booking advisable Last arrival 21.00hrs Last departure 11.00hrs

An attractive small park on a working farm close to Dartmoor National Park, and bordered by the River Teign. The tidy pitches are located amongst trees and shrubs, and the modern facilities are very well maintained. Children will enjoy all the farm animals, and nearby is the Templar Way walking route. A 2-acre site with 35 touring pitches, 17 hardstandings.

**Leisure:**

**Facilities:**

**Services:** →

## PAIGNTON MAP 03 SX8

### 87% Beverley Parks Caravan & Camping Park (SX886582)
Goodrington Rd TQ4 7JE
☎ 01803 661979 01803 845427
**email:** info@beverley-holidays.co.uk
**web:** www.beverley-holidays.co.uk
**Dir:** *On A380/A3022, 2m S of Paignton turn left into Goodrington Road*

£14.50-£35 £14.50-£35 Å £11-£29

Open Feb-Dec Booking advisable Jun-Sep Last arrival 22.00hrs Last departure 10.00hrs

A high quality family-run park with extensive views of the bay, and plenty of on-site amenities. The park boasts indoor and outdoor heated swimming pools, and the toilet facilities are very modern and clean. The park complex is attractively laid out. A 12-acre site with 175 touring pitches, 36 hardstandings and 189 statics.

**Leisure:**

**Facilities:**

**Services:** →

**Notes:** No pets. Wi-fi. Table tennis, pool, spa bath, crazy golf, sauna, gym

*see advert on opposite page*

**Abbreviations:** BH-bank holiday/s Etr-Easter Whit-Whitsun dep-departure fr-from hrs-hours m-mile mdnt-midnight rdbt-roundabout rs-restricted service wk-week wknd-weekend no dogs No cards → following facilities within 3 miles of the site

ENGLAND

### ►►►► 78% *Widend Touring Park* *(SX852619)*

Berry Pomeroy Rd, Marldon TQ3 1RT
☎ 01803 550116 01803 550116
Dir: *Signed from Torbay ring road*

Open Apr-end Sep (rs Apr-mid May & mid Sep swimming pool & club house closed) Booking advisable Jul-Aug & Whit Last arrival 21.00hrs Last departure 10.00hrs

A terraced grass park paddocked and screened on high ground overlooking Torbay with views of Dartmoor. This attractive park is well laid out, divided up by mature trees and bushes but with plenty of open grassy areas. Facilities are of a high standard and offer a heated outdoor swimming pool with sunbathing area, a small lounge bar and a well-stocked shop. A 22-acre site with 207 touring pitches, 6 hardstandings.

**Leisure:**

**Facilities:**

**Services:**

**Notes:** No dogs mid Jul-Aug

### ►►► 85% **Byslades International Touring & Camping Park** *(SX853603)*

Totnes Rd TQ4 7PY
☎ 01803 555072 01803 555669
**email:** info@byslades.co.uk
**web:** www.byslades.co.uk
**Dir:** *on A385, halfway between Paignton & Totnes*

★ £6-£12.50 £6-£12.50 £6-£14.50

Open Whit-Aug BH (rs May bar & swimming pool closed) Booking advisable Jul-Aug Last arrival 18.00hrs Last departure 10.00hrs

A well-kept terraced park in beautiful countryside, only two miles from Paignton. It offers a good mix of amenities, including a lounge bar, a children's playground, and large heated outdoor swimming pool with special area for toddlers. A 23-acre site with 190 touring pitches, 40 hardstandings.

**Leisure:**

**Facilities:**

**Services:**

**Notes:** No commercial vehicles, no dogs mid Jul-Aug. Crazy golf

ENGLAND

## PAIGNTON CONTINUED

### ►►► 80% Whitehill Country Park *(SX857588)*

GOLD

Stoke Rd TQ4 7PF

☎ 01803 782338 01803 782722

**email:** info@whitehill-park.co.uk

**web:** www.whitehill-park.co.uk

**Dir:** *A385 through Totnes towards Paignton. Turn right by Parkers Arms onto Stoke Rd towards Stoke Gabriel. Site on left after approx 1.5m*

£12-£26 £12-£26 £11-£24

Open Etr-Sep Booking advisable Jul-Aug Last arrival 21.00hrs Last departure 10.00hrs

A family-owned and run park set in rolling countryside, with many scenic beaches just a short drive away. This extensive country park covers 40 acres with woodland walks, and plenty of flora and fauna. It offers ideal facilities for an excellent holiday. A 40-acre site with 260 touring pitches and 60 statics.

**Leisure:**

**Facilities:**

**Services:**

**Notes:** No Pets. Walking & cycling trails, craft room, table tennis

*see advert on this page*

## PLYMOUTH MAP 03 SX45

### ►►►► 79% *Riverside Caravan Park* *(SX515575)*

Longbridge Rd PL6 8LL

☎ 01752 344122 01752 344122

**email:** info@riversidecaravanpark.com

**web:** www.riversidecaravanpark.com

**Dir:** *A38 follow signs at Marsh Mills rdbt, take 3rd exit, then left. 400yds turn right (keep River Plym on right) to park*

Open all year (rs Oct-Etr bar, restaurant & take-away closed) Booking advisable Jun-Aug Last arrival 22.00hrs Last departure 10.00hrs

A well-groomed site on the outskirts of Plymouth on the banks of the River Plym, in a quiet location surrounded by woodland. The toilet

**Services:** Toilet Fluid · Café/ Restaurant · Fast Food/Takeaway · Baby Care · Electric Hook Up · Motorvan Service Point · Launderette · Licensed Bar · Calor Gas · Camping Gaz · Battery Charging

ENGLAND

acilities are to a very good standard, and include private cubicles. his park is an ideal stopover for the ferries to France and Spain, and nakes an excellent base for touring Dartmoor and the coast. An 11-cre site with 293 touring pitches.

**eisure:**

**acilities:**

**ervices:**

*see advert on this page*

RIVERSIDE
CARAVAN PARK
Longbridge Road, Marsh Mills, Plymouth
Telephone: Plymouth (01752) 344122
"The award-winning touring park that'll stop you touring!"
"Riverside" the conveniently situated, secluded, countryside park has all the amenities, scenery, and relaxed atmosphere that will make you want to stay for the rest of your holiday. Surrounded by woodlands, and bordered by the River Plym, this pleasant site has the luxury of permanent facilities without losing the country charm.
Within a short distance you can also reach the freedom of Dartmoor, the shops and history of Plymouth, and the fun of many beaches and coves. The numerous sports, activities and attractions of the whole area mean "Riverside" can be the centre of a complete holiday experience. Ring or write for details.
★ Bar, Restaurant and Takeaway ★ Heated swimming pool ★ Games room ★ TV room and play areas ★ Shop and Telephone ★ Coffee bar ★ Off licence ★ Level pitches ★ Electricity ★ Tarmac roads ★ Street lights ★ Toilet and shower blocks ★ Laundry and dishwashing facilities ★ Special over 50's rates.


## PRINCETOWN MAP 03 SX57

### ►► 76% The Plume of Feathers Inn

*(SX592734)*

Plymouth PL20 6QQ

☎ 01822 890240

**Dir:** *Site accessed directly from B3212 rdbt (beside Plume of Feathers Inn) in centre of Princetown*

Open all year Booking advisable all year Last arrival 23.30hrs Last departure 11.00hrs

Set amidst the rugged beauty of Dartmoor not far from the notorious prison, this campsite boasts good toilet facilities and all the amenities of the inn. The Plume of Feathers is Princetown's oldest building, and serves all day food in an atmospheric setting. The campsite is mainly for tents. A 3-acre site with 85 touring pitches.

**Leisure:**

**Facilities:**

**Services:**

**Notes:** No caravans

## SALCOMBE MAP 03 SX73

### ►► 72% *Bolberry House Farm Caravan & Camping Park* *(SX687395)*

Bolberry TQ7 3DY

☎ 01548 561251

**email:** bolberry.house@virgin.net

**web:** www.bolberryparks.co.uk

**Dir:** *At Malborough on A381 turn right signed Hope Cove/Bolberry. Take left fork after village signed Soar/Bolberry. 0.6m right again. Site signed in 0.5m*

Open Etr-Oct Booking advisable Jun-Sep Last arrival 20.00hrs Last departure 11.00hrs

A very popular park in a peaceful setting on a coastal farm with sea views, fine cliff walks and nearby beaches. Discount in low season for senior citizens. A 6-acre site with 70 touring pitches and 10 statics.

**Leisure:** **Facilities:**

**Services:**

**Notes:** Children's play area, play barn

### ►►► 75% *Higher Rew Caravan & Camping Park* *(SX714383)*

Higher Rew, Malborough TQ7 3BW

☎ 01548 842681 01548 843681

**email:** enquiries@higherrew.co.uk

**web:** www.higherrew.co.uk

**Dir:** *A381 to Malborough. Right at Townsend Cross, follow signs to Soar for 1m. Left at Rew Cross*

Open Etr-Oct Booking advisable Spring BH & mid Jul-Aug Last arrival 22.00hrs Last departure noon

A long-established park in a remote location in sight of the sea. The spacious, open touring field has some tiered pitches in the sloping grass, and there are lovely countryside or sea views from every pitch. Friendly family owners are continually improving the facilities. A 5-acre site with 85 touring pitches.

**Leisure:** **Facilities:**

**Services:**

**Notes:** Play barn

ENGLAND

SALCOMBE CONTINUED

### ►►► 79% Karrageen Caravan & Camping Park (SX686395)

Bolberry, Malborough TQ7 3EN

☎ 01548 561230 📠 01548 560192

**email:** phil@karrageen.co.uk

**web:** www.karrageen.co.uk

**Dir:** *At Malborough on A381, turn sharp right through village, after 0.6m right again, after 0.9m site on right.*

★ £10-£17 £10-£17 ▲ £6-£21

Open Etr-Sep Booking advisable BH & school hols Last arrival 21.00hrs Last departure 11.30hrs

A small friendly, family-run park with terraced grass pitches giving extensive sea and country views. There is a varied takeaway menu available every evening, and a well-stocked shop. This park is just one mile from the beach and pretty hamlet of Hope Cove. A 7.5-acre site with 70 touring pitches and 25 statics.

**Facilities:**

**Services:** →

**Notes:** Licensed shop, 2 play areas, family shower room

### ►► 69% Alston Farm Camping & Caravan Site (SX716406)

Malborough, Kingsbridge TQ7 3BJ

☎ 01548 561260 & 0780 803 0921 📠 01548 561260

**email:** alston.campsite@ukgateway.net

**web:** www.welcome.to/alstonfarm

**Dir:** *1.5m W of town off A381 towards Malborough*

★ £9-£13 £8-£13 ▲ £8-£11

Open 15 Mar-Oct Booking advisable Aug

An established farm site in a rural location adjacent to the Kingsbridge/Salcombe estuary. The site is well sheltered and screened and approached down a long well-surfaced narrow farm lane with passing places. The toilet facilities are basic. A 16-acre site with 90 touring pitches and 58 statics.

**Leisure:**

**Facilities:**

**Services:** →

**Notes:**

SAMPFORD PEVERELL MAP 03 ST0

### ►►►► 85% Minnows Touring Park (SS042148)

Holbrook Ln EX16 7EN

☎ 01884 821770 📠 01884 829199

**web:** www.ukparks.co.uk/minnows

**Dir:** *M5 junct 27 take A361 signed Tiverton & Barnstaple. In 600yds take 1st slip road, then right over bridge, site ahead*

★ £12.10-£22.90 £12.10-£22.90 ▲ £8.80-£14.80

Open 10 Mar-3 Nov Booking advisable BH & Jun-Sep Last arrival 20.00hrs Last departure 11.30hrs

A small, well-sheltered park, peacefully located amidst fields and mature trees. The toilet facilities are of a high quality in keeping with the rest of the park, and there is a good laundry. The park has direct gated access to the canal towpath. A 5.5-acre site with 45 touring pitches, 43 hardstandings and 1 static.

**Leisure:**

**Facilities:**

**Services:** →

**Notes:** No cycling, no groundsheets on grass. Tourist information centre

SEATON

*see Colyton*

ENGLAND

## SHALDON MAP 03 SX97

### NEW 74% Coast View Holiday Park *(SX935716)*

Torquay Rd TQ14 0BG

01626 872392

**Dir:** *M5 junct 31, A38 then A380 towards Torquay. Then A381 towards Teignmouth. Right in 4m at lights, over Shaldon Bridge. 0.75m, up hill, site on right*

Open mid Mar-mid Jan

This park has stunning coast and sea views from both its level terraced pitches and slightly sloping grass pitches. The park has a full entertainment programme every night plus outdoor and indoor activities for children, and will appeal to lively families. A 3-acre site with 186 touring pitches.

**Facilities:**

## SIDMOUTH MAP 03 SY18

### ►►►► 81% Oakdown Touring & Holiday Caravan Park

(SY167902)

Gatedown Ln, Weston EX10 0PD

01297 680387 01297 680541

**mail:** enquiries@oakdown.co.uk

**veb:** www.oakdown.co.uk

**Dir:** *Off A3052, 2.5m E of junct with A375*

★ £10.25-£24.95 £10.25-£24.95 £10.25-£24.95

Open Apr-Oct Booking advisable Spring BH & Jul-Aug Last arrival 22.00hrs Last departure 10.30hrs

riendly, well-maintained park with good landscaping and plenty of maturing trees. Pitches are grouped in paddocks surrounded by hrubs, and the park is well screened from the A3502. The park's onservation areas with their natural flora and fauna offer attractive valks, and there is a hide by the Victorian reed bed for both casual nd dedicated bird watchers. A 13-acre site with 100 touring pitches, 0 hardstandings and 62 statics.

**eisure:**

**acilities:**

**ervices:**

**lotes:** Dogs must be kept on leads & exercised off park, no bikes, no kateboards, no kite flying. Use of microwave, field trail to donkey sanctuary

### ►►► 75% Kings Down Tail Caravan & Camping Park *(SY173907)*

Salcombe Regis EX10 0PD

01297 680313 01297 680313

**email:** info@kingsdowntail.co.uk

**web:** www.kingsdowntail.co.uk

**Dir:** *Off A3052 3m E of junct with A375*

★ £10-£15.25 £10-£15.25 £10-£15.25

Open 15 Mar-15 Nov Booking advisable Whit, BH & mid Jul-Sep Last arrival 22.00hrs Last departure noon

A well-kept site on level ground in a tree-sheltered spot on the side of the Sid Valley. This neat family-run park makes a good base for exploring the east Devon coast. A 5-acre site with 100 touring pitches, 51 hardstandings.

**Leisure:**

**Facilities:**

**Services:**

**Notes:** Dogs on a lead at all times. Wet room for disabled or family use

*see advert on this page*

## SIDMOUTH CONTINUED

### ►►► 80% Salcombe Regis Caravan & Camping Park *(SY153892)*

Salcombe Regis EX10 0JH

☎ 01395 514303 01395 514314

**email:** contact@salcombe-regis.co.uk

**web:** www.salcombe-regis.co.uk

**Dir:** *Off A3052 1m E of junct with A375. From other direction turn left past Donkey Sanctuary*

★ £10-£18.20 £10-£18.20 £10-£18.20

Open Etr-Oct Booking advisable BH & Jul-Aug Last arrival 20.15hrs Last departure 10.30hrs

Set in quiet countryside with glorious views, this spacious park has well-maintained facilities, and a good mix of grass and hardstanding pitches. A footpath runs from the park to the coastal path and the beach. A 16-acre site with 100 touring pitches, 40 hardstandings and 10 statics.

**Leisure:**

**Facilities:**

**Services:**

**Notes:** Wi-fi. Putting

## SLAPTON MAP 03 SX84

### ►►► 77% Slapton Sands Camping & Caravanning Club Site *(SX825450)*

Middle Grounds TQ7 2QW

☎ 01548 580538

**web:** www.campingandcaravanningclub.co.uk/slaptonsands

**Dir:** *On A379 from Kingsbridge. Site entrance 0.25m from A379, beyond brow of hill approaching Slapton*

★ £15.45-£22.15 £15.45-£22.15 £15.45-£22.15

Open 13 Mar-3 Nov Booking advisable BH & peak periods Last arrival 21.00hrs Last departure noon

A very attractive location and well-run site overlooking Start Bay, with extensive views from some pitches, and glimpses of the sea from others. The shingle beach of Slapton Sands, and the Blue Flag beach at Blackpool Sands are among attractions, along with a nearby freshwater lake and nature reserve. A 5.5-acre site with 115 touring pitches, 10 hardstandings.

**Leisure:** **Facilities:**

**Services:**

**Notes:** Members' touring caravans only. Site gates closed 23.00hrs-07.00hrs

## SOURTON CROSS MAP 03 SX59

### ►►► 74% Bundu Camping & Caravan Park *(SX546916)*

EX20 4HT

☎ 01837 861611 01837 861611

**email:** frances@bunduplus.com

**web:** www.bundu.co.uk

**Dir:** *W on A30, past Okehampton. Take A386 to Tavistock. Take 1st left & left again*

★ £9.50-£12 £9.50-£12 £7-£9.50

Open all year Booking advisable Jul & Aug Last arrival 23.30hrs Last departure 14.00hrs

Welcoming, friendly owners set the tone for this well-maintained site, ideally positioned on the border of the Dartmoor National Park. Along with fine views and level grassy pitches, the Granite Way cycle track from Lydford to Okehampton along the old railway line, part of the Devon Coast to Coast cycle trail, passes the edge of the park. A 4.5-acre site with 38 touring pitches, 8 hardstandings.

**Facilities:**

**Services:**

**Notes:**

## SOUTH MOLTON MAP 03 SS72

### NEW ►►► 82% Riverside Caravan & Camping Park *(SS723274)*

Marsh Ln, North Molton Rd EX36 3HQ

☎ 01769 579269

**email:** relax@exmoorriverside.co.uk

**web:** www.exmoorriverside.co.uk

**Dir:** *M5 junct 27 onto A361 towards Barnstaple. Site signed 1m before South Molton on right*

★ £13-£15 £13-£15 £10-£14

Open all year Last arrival 22.00hrs Last departure 11.00hrs

A newly-developed family-run park, set alongside the River Mole, where supervised children can play, and fishing is available. This is an ideal base for exploring Exmoor, as well as North Devon's golden beaches. A 40-acre site with 42 touring pitches.

**Facilities:**

**Services:**

**Notes:** Pets must be on leads

## STARCROSS

*see Dawlish*

ENGLAND

## STOKE GABRIEL MAP 03 SX85

### ►►► 77% **Broadleigh Farm Park** *(SX851587)*

Coombe House Ln, Aish TQ9 6PU
☎ 01803 782309 & 782110
**email:** enquiries@broadleighfarm.co.uk
**web:** www.broadleighfarm.co.uk
**Dir:** *From Exeter on A38 then A380 towards Tor Bay. Right onto A385 for Totnes. After 0.5m at Parkers Arms left for Stoke Gabriel. Right after Whitehill Country Park to site*

Open Mar-Oct Booking advisable all times Last arrival 21.00hrs Last departure 11.30hrs

Set in a very rural location on a working farm which borders Paignton and Stoke Gabriel. The large sloping field with a timber-clad toilet block in the centre is sheltered and peaceful, surrounded by rolling countryside but handy for the beaches. A 3-acre site with 35 touring pitches.

**Facilities:**
**Services:**
**Notes:**

*see advert on this page*

### ►►► 82% **Higher Well Farm Holiday Park** *(SX857577)*

Waddeton Rd TQ9 6RN
☎ 01803 782289
**email:** higherwell@talk21.com
**web:** www.higherwellfarmholidaypark.co.uk
**Dir:** *From Exeter A380 to Torbay turn right onto A385 for Totnes, in 0.5m left for Stoke Gabriel, follow signs*

£8.50-£14 £8.50-£14 ▲ £8.50-£14

Open 31 Mar-2 Nov Booking advisable BH & mid Jul-Aug Last arrival 22.00hrs Last departure 10.00hrs

Set on a quiet farm yet only four miles from Paignton, this rural holiday park is on the outskirts of the picturesque village of Stoke Gabriel. A toilet block with some combined cubicled facilities is a considerable amenity, and tourers are housed in an open field with some very good views. A 10-acre site with 80 touring pitches, 3 hardstandings and 19 statics.

**Facilities:**
**Services:**
**Notes:** No commercial vehicles



## TAVISTOCK MAP 03 SX47

### ►►►► 88% **Higher Longford Caravan & Camping Park** *(SX520747)*

DAVID BELLAMY CONSERVATION AWARD GOLD

Moorshop PL19 9LQ
☎ 01822 613360 & 07717 507434 01822 618722
**email:** stay@higherlongford.co.uk
**web:** www.higherlongford.co.uk
**Dir:** *From A30 to Tavistock take B3357 towards Princetown. 2m on right before hill onto moors*

★ £13-£17 £13-£17 ▲ £11-£17

*Higher Longford Caravan & Camping Park*

Open all year Booking advisable Etr, Jun-Oct Last arrival 21.00hrs Last departure noon

A very pleasant park in Dartmoor National Park, with panoramic views of the moors. The mainly grassy pitches are sheltered, and some are secluded for extra peace and quiet. Higher Longford is surrounded by moorland parks, lanes and pretty rivers, yet Tavistock is only 2.5m away. The park is well served with a shop. A 7-acre site with 82 touring pitches, 20 hardstandings and 4 statics.

**Leisure:**
**Facilities:**
**Services:**
**Notes:** Dogs must be kept on leads. No bikes, skateboards or scooters. Pool table, campers lounge, off licence, breakfast takeaway, fresh bread

## *TAVISTOCK* CONTINUED

### ►►►► 81% **Woodovis Park**
*(SX431745)*
Gulworthy PL19 8NY
☎ 01822 832968 🖹 01822 832948
**email:** info@woodovis.com
**web:** www.woodovis.com

**Dir:** *A390 from Tavistock signed Callington & Gunnislake. At top of hill turn right at rdbt signed Lamerton & 'Chipshop'. Park 1m on left*

★ £15-£22.50 £15-£22.50 £15-£22.50

Open 15 Mar-1 Nov Booking advisable Jun-Aug Last arrival 22.00hrs Last departure noon

A well-kept park in a remote woodland setting on the edge of the Tamar Valley. This peacefully-located park is set at the end of a half-mile, private, tree-lined road, and has lots of on-site facilities. The toilets are excellent, and there is an indoor swimming pool, all in a friendly, purposeful atmosphere. A 14.5-acre site with 50 touring pitches, 18 hardstandings and 35 statics.

**Leisure:**

**Facilities:**

**Services:** → 

**Notes:** Dogs must be kept on leads. Mini golf, sauna, jacuzzi

### ►►► 80% **Harford Bridge Holiday Park** *(SX504767)*
Peter Tavy PL19 9LS
☎ 01822 810349 🖹 01822 810028
**email:** enquiry@harfordbridge.co.uk
**web:** www.harfordbridge.co.uk

**Dir:** *2m N of Tavistock, off A386 Okehampton Rd, take Peter Tavy turn, entrance 200yds on right*

Open all year (rs Nov-Mar statics only & 5 hardstanding pitches) Booking advisable Aug, Etr, BH Last arrival 21.00hrs Last departure noon

This beautiful spacious park is set beside the River Tavy in the Dartmoor National Park. Pitches are located beside the river and around the copses, and the park is very well equipped for the holidaymaker. An adventure playground and games room entertain children, and there is fly-fishing and a free tennis court. A 16-acre site with 120 touring pitches, 5 hardstandings and 80 statics.

**Leisure:**

**Facilities:**

**Services:** →

**Notes:** No large groups. Fly fishing

### ►►► 80% **Langstone Manor Camping & Caravan Park** *(SX524738)*
Moortown PL19 9JZ
☎ 01822 613371 🖹 01822 613371
**email:** jane@langstone-manor.co.uk
**web:** www.langstone-manor.co.uk

**Dir:** *Take B3357 from Tavistock to Princetown. Approx 1.5m turn right at x-rds, follow signs*

★ £10-£12 £10-£12 £10-£12

Open 15 Mar-Oct (rs week days in low season restricted hours in bar & restaurant) Bookieeng advisable BH & Jul-Aug Last arrival 22.00hrs Last departure 11.00hrs

A secluded site set in the well-maintained grounds of a manor house in Dartmoor National Park. Many attractive mature trees provide a screen within the park, and there is a popular lounge bar with a menu of reasonably priced evening meals. Plenty of activities and places of interest can be found within the surrounding moorland. A 5.5-acre site with 40 touring pitches, 5 hardstandings and 25 statics.

**Leisure:**

**Facilities:**

**Services:** →

**Notes:** No skateboards, scooters, cycles, ball games

ENGLAND

## TEDBURN ST MARY MAP 03 SX89

### ►►► 80% Springfield Holiday Park

*(SX788935)*
EX6 6EW
☎ 01647 24242 📠 01647 24131
**email:** enquiries@springfieldholidaypark.co.uk
**web:** www.springfieldholidaypark.co.uk
**Dir:** *M5 junct 31, A30 towards Okehampton, exit at 3rd junct, signed to Cheriton Bishop. Follow brown tourist signs to park*

★ £12-£18 £12-£18 £12-£18

Open 15 Mar-15 Nov Booking advisable Jul-Aug Last arrival 22.00hrs Last departure noon

Set in a quiet rural location with countryside views, this park continues to be upgraded to a smart standard. It has the advantage of being located close to Dartmoor National Park, with village pubs and stores just two miles away. A 9-acre site with 48 touring pitches, 38 hardstandings and 49 statics.

**Leisure:**
**Facilities:**
**Services:**
**Notes:** Dogs must be kept on leads Family shower rooms

## TIVERTON

*see East Worlington*

## TORQUAY MAP 03 SX96

*see also Newton Abbot*

### ►►►► 80% Widdicombe Farm Touring Park *(SX880650)*

Marldon TQ3 1ST
☎ 01803 558325
**email:** info@widdicombefarm.co.uk
**web:** www.widdicombefarm.co.uk
**Dir:** *On A380, midway between Torquay & Paignton ring road*

★ £6.50-£19 £6.50-£19 £6.50-£19

Open mid Mar-mid Oct Booking advisable Whit & Jul-Aug Last arrival 21.00hrs Last departure 10.00hrs

A friendly family-owned and run park on a working farm, with good quality facilities and extensive views. The level pitches are terraced to take advantage of the views towards the coast and Dartmoor. A quiet but happy atmosphere pervades this park, encouraged by a large children's play area. Other amenities include a well-stocked shop, a restaurant, and a lounge bar. There are adults-only areas. An 8-acre site with 196 touring pitches, 180 hardstandings and 3 statics.

**Leisure:**
**Facilities:**
**Services:**
**Notes:** Families & couples only, 1 family field, 3 adults only fields. Family bathrooms, BBQ patio, entertainment

## UMBERLEIGH MAP 03 SS62

### ►►► 75% Umberleigh Camping & Caravanning Club Site *(SS604241)*

Over Weir EX37 9DU
☎ 01769 560009
**web:** www.campingandcaravanningclub.co.uk/umberleigh
**Dir:** *On A377 from Barnstaple turn right at Umberleigh sign onto B3227. Site on right in 0.25m*

★ £15.45-£20.15 £15.45-£20.15 £15.45-£20.15

Open 13 Mar-29 Sep Booking advisable BH & peak periods Last arrival 21.00hrs Last departure noon

There are fine country views from this compact site set on high ground. The site has the advantage of a games room with table tennis and skittle alley, and two quality tennis courts, with an adjacent wooded area for walks, and a nearby fishing pond. A 3-acre site with 60 touring pitches, 12 hardstandings.

**Leisure:**
**Facilities:**
**Services:**
**Notes:** Site gates closed 23.00hrs-07.00hrs. Fishing

## WITHERIDGE MAP 03 SS81

### ►►► 73% West Middlewick Farm Caravan & Camping Site *(SS826136)*

Nomansland EX16 8NP
☎ 01884 861235 📠 01884 861235
**email:** stay@westmiddlewick.co.uk
**web:** www.westmiddlewick.co.uk
**Dir:** *From M5 junct 27, A361 to Tiverton. Then B3137, follow Witheridge signs. Site 1m past Nomansland on right (8m from Tiverton)*

Open all year Booking advisable Jul-Aug Last arrival 22.00hrs Last departure noon

A working dairy farm on a ridge west of the hamlet of Nomansland, with extensive rural views. This park offers campers a quiet and relaxing break, and is approximately one mile from the attractive and charming village of Witheridge which has a variety of amenities. A 3.5-acre site with 25 touring pitches, 16 hardstandings.

**Facilities:**
**Services:**
**Notes:** Dogs must be kept on leads, children must be supervised. Ball area

ENGLAND

## WOODBURY SALTERTON MAP 03 SY08

### ►►► 85% Browns Farm Caravan Park

*(SY016885)*

Browns Farm EX5 1PS

☎ 01395 232895

**Dir:** *M5 junct 30, A3052 for 3.7m. Right at White Horse Inn follow sign to Woodbury, at village road junct turn right, site on left*

★ £8-£12 £8-£12 £8-£11

Open all year Booking advisable all times

A small farm park adjoining a 14th-century thatched farmhouse, and located in a quiet village. Pitches back onto hedgerows, and friendly owners keep the facilities very clean. The tourist information and games room with table tennis, chess etc is housed in a purpose-built building. The park is just a mile from the historic heathland of Woodbury Common with its superb views. A 2.5-acre site with 20 touring pitches, 12 hardstandings.

**Leisure:**

**Facilities:**

**Services:**

**Notes:** No ground sheets in awnings, no music. Hardstandings for winter period, caravan storage

## WOOLACOMBE MAP 03 SS44

*see also Mortehoe*

### 76% Golden Coast Holiday Village *(SS482436)*

Station Rd EX34 7HW

☎ 01271 870343 01271 870089

**email:** goodtimes@woolacombe.com

**web:** www.woolacombe.com

**Dir:** *Follow road to Woolacombe Bay from Mullacott & site is 1.5m on left*

Open Feb-Dec (rs mid Sep-May Outdoor pools closed) Booking advisable BH & mid Jul-end Aug Last arrival 24.00hrs Last departure 10.00hrs

A holiday village offering excellent leisure facilities as well as the amenities of the other Woolacombe Bay holiday parks. There is a neat touring area with a unisex toilet block, maintained to a high standard. Bowling alleys, a number of bars and plenty of activities add to the holiday experience. A 10-acre site with 91 touring pitches, 53 hardstandings and 444 statics.

**Leisure:**

**Facilities:**

**Services:**

**Notes:** Only assist dogs allowed. Wi-fi. Sauna, solarium, golf, fishing, snooker, cinema

*see advert on opposite page*

### 80% Woolacombe Bay Holiday Village *(SS465442)*

Sandy Ln EX34 7AH

☎ 01271 870343 01271 870089

**email:** goodtimes@woolacombe.com

**web:** www.woolacombe.com

**Dir:** *From Mullacott Cross rdbt take B3343 (Woolacombe road) to Turnpike Cross junct. Right towards Mortehoe, site approx 1m on left*

Open Mar-Oct (rs Mar-mid May, mid Sep-Oct no camping) Booking advisable Whit & summer hols Last arrival mdnt Last departure 10.00hrs

A well-developed touring section in a holiday complex with a full entertainment and leisure programme. This park offers excellent facilities including a steam room and sauna. For a small charge a bus takes holidaymakers to the other Woolacombe Bay holiday centres where they can take part in any of the activities offered, and there is also a bus to the beach. An 8.5-acre site with 180 touring pitches and 237 statics.

**Leisure:**

**Facilities:**

**Services:**

**Notes:** Entertainment, kids' club, health suite

*see advert on opposite page*

### 75% *Woolacombe Sands Holiday Park* *(SS471434)*

Beach Rd EX34 7AF

☎ 01271 870569 01271 870606

**email:** lifesabeach@woolacombe-sands.co.uk

**web:** www.woolacombe-sands.co.uk

**Dir:** *M5 junct 27, A361 to Barnstaple. Follow Ilfracombe signs, until Mullacott Cross. Turn left onto B3343 to Woolacombe. Site on left*

Open Apr-Oct Booking advisable 24-31 May & 19 Jul-30 Aug Last arrival 22.00hrs Last departure 10.00hrs

Set in rolling countryside with grassy terraced pitches, most with spectacular views overlooking the sea at Woolacombe. The lovely blue flag beach can be accessed directly by footpath in 10-15 minutes, and there is a full entertainment programme for all the family in high season. A 20-acre site with 200 touring pitches and 80 statics.

**Leisure:**

**Facilities:**

**Services:**

**Notes:** Kids' club, heated indoor/outdoor swimming pools

*see advert on page 152*

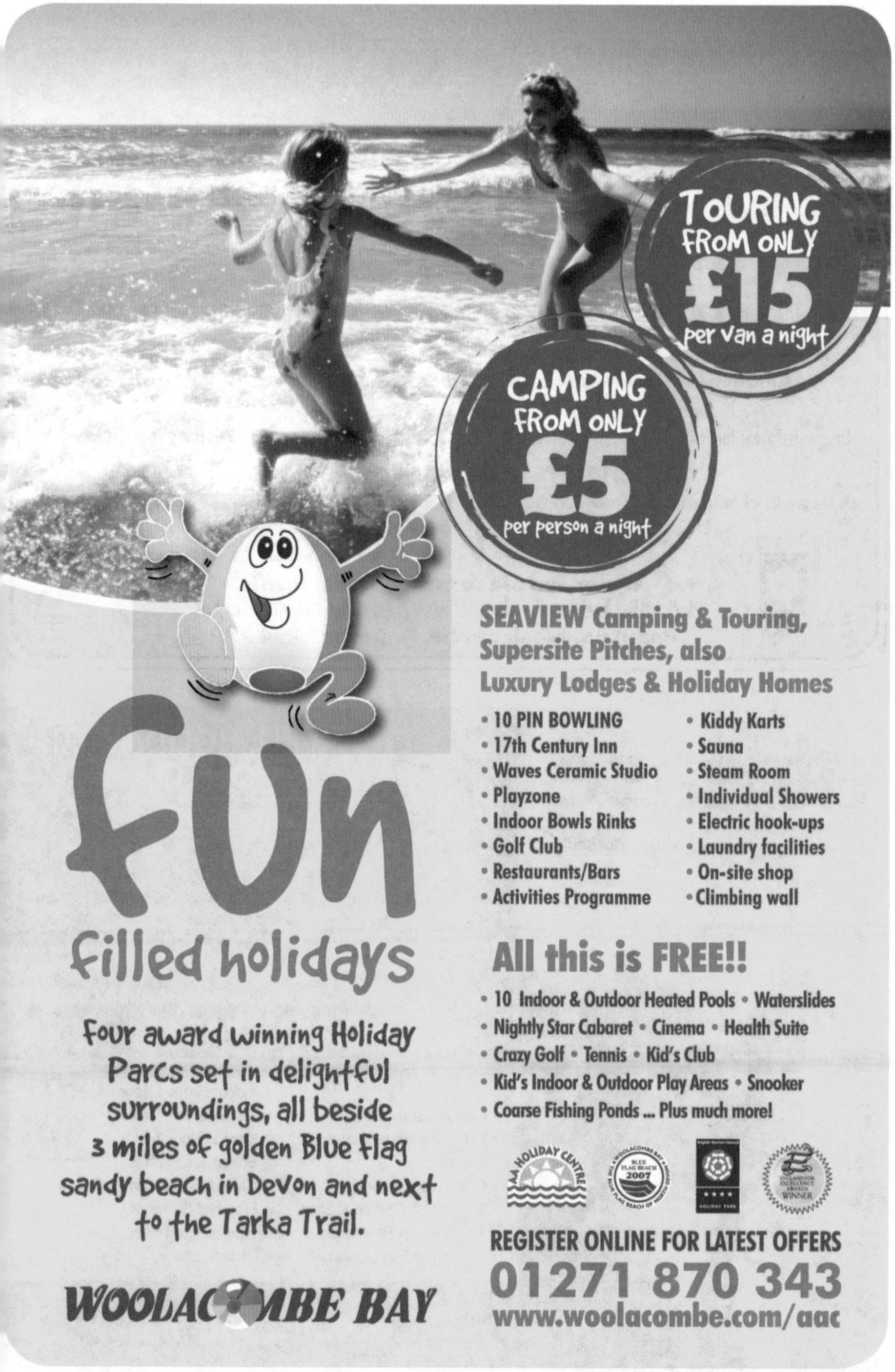
TOURING
FROM ONLY
£15
per van a night
CAMPING
FROM ONLY
£5
per person a night
SEAVIEW Camping & Touring,
Supersite Pitches, also
Luxury Lodges & Holiday Homes
• 10 PIN BOWLING
• 17th Century Inn
• Waves Ceramic Studio
• Playzone
• Indoor Bowls Rinks
• Golf Club
• Restaurants/Bars
• Activities Programme
• Kiddy Karts
• Sauna
• Steam Room
• Individual Showers
• Electric hook-ups
• Laundry facilities
• On-site shop
• Climbing wall
fun
filled holidays
All this is FREE!!
• 10 Indoor & Outdoor Heated Pools • Waterslides
• Nightly Star Cabaret • Cinema • Health Suite
• Crazy Golf • Tennis • Kid's Club
• Kid's Indoor & Outdoor Play Areas • Snooker
• Coarse Fishing Ponds ... Plus much more!
Four award winning Holiday Parcs set in delightful surroundings, all beside 3 miles of golden Blue Flag sandy beach in Devon and next to the Tarka Trail.
REGISTER ONLINE FOR LATEST OFFERS
01271 870 343
www.woolacombe.com/aac
WOOLACOMBE BAY

**Abbreviations:** BH-bank holiday/s Etr-Easter Whit-Whitsun dep-departure fr-from hrs-hours m-mile mdnt-midnight rdbt-roundabout rs-restricted service wk-week wknd-weekend no dogs No cards → following facilities within 3 miles of the site

WOOLACOMBE CONTINUED

**►►► 77% *Europa Park*** *(SS475435)*
Beach Rd EX34 7AN
☎ 01271 871425 📠 01271 871425
**email:** europaparkwoolacombe@yahoo.co.uk
**Dir:** *M5 junct 27, A361 through Barnstaple to Mullacott Cross. Left onto B3343 signed Woolacombe. Site on right at Spa shop/garage*
★ £14-£22 £14-£22 £14-£22

Open all year Booking advisable BH & high season Last arrival 23.00hrs

A very lively family-run site handy for the beach at Woolacombe, and catering well for surfers. Set in a stunning location high above the bay, it provides a wide range of accommodation including surf cabins, and generous touring pitches. Visitors can enjoy the indoor pool and sauna, games room, restaurant/café/bar and clubhouse. A 16-acre site with 200 touring pitches, 20 hardstandings and 22 statics.

**Leisure:**
**Facilities:**
**Services:**
**Notes:** Beer deck, off licence, pub, big screen TV

## DORSET

### ALDERHOLT MAP 05 SU11

**►►►► 81% Hill Cottage Farm Camping and Caravan Park** *(SU119133)*
Sandleheath Rd SP6 3EG
☎ 01425 650513 📠 01425 652339
**Dir:** *Take B3078 W of Fordingbridge. Turn off at Alderholt, site 0.25m on left after railway bridge*
★ £12-£16 £12-£16 £10-£16

Open Mar-Oct Booking advisable BH & Jul-Aug Last arrival 19.00hrs Last departure 11.00hrs

Set within extensive grounds this rural, beautifully landscaped park has mainly full facility pitches set in individual hardstanding bays with mature hedges between giving adequate pitch privacy. A modern toilet block is kept immaculately clean, and there's a good range of leisure facilities. In high season there is an area available for tenting. 34 touring pitches, 34 hardstandings.

**Leisure:** **Facilities:**
**Services:**
**Notes:**

### BERE REGIS MAP 04 SY89

**►►► 79% *Rowlands Wait Touring Park*** *(SY842933)*
Rye Hill BH20 7LP
☎ 01929 472727 📠 01929 472275
**email:** aa@rowlandswait.co.uk
**web:** www.rowlandswait.co.uk
**Dir:** *On approach to Bere Regis follow signs to Bovington Tank Museum. At top of Rye Hill, 0.75m from village turn right. 200yds to site*

Open mid Mar-Oct (winter by arrangement) Booking advisable BH & Jul-Aug Last arrival 21.30hrs Last departure noon

This park lies in a really attractive setting overlooking Bere and the Dorset countryside, set amongst undulating areas of trees and shrubs. Two family rooms have been added to the toilet facilities. Within a few miles of the Tank Museum with its mock battles. An 8-acre site with 71 touring pitches.

**Leisure:** **Facilities:**
**Services:**

ENGLAND

## BLANDFORD FORUM MAP 04 ST80

### ►►►► 76% **The Inside Park** *(ST869046)*

Down House Estate DT11 9AD

☎ 01258 453719 🖷 01258 459921

**email:** inspark@aol.com

**web:** http://members.aol.com/inspark/inspark

**Dir:** *From town, over River Stour, follow Winterborne Stickland signs. Site in 1.5m*

★ £11-£17.45 £11-£17.45 £11-£17.45

Open Etr-Oct Booking advisable BH & Jul-Aug Last arrival 22.00hrs Last departure noon

An attractive, well-sheltered and quiet park, 0.5m off a country lane in a wooded valley. Spacious pitches are divided by mature trees and shrubs, and amenities are housed in an 18th-century coach house and stables. There are some lovely woodland walks within the park. A 12-acre site with 125 touring pitches.

**Leisure:**

**Facilities:**

**Services:**

**Notes:** Farm trips (main season), kennels for hire

## BRIDPORT MAP 04 SY49

### 82% **Freshwater Beach Holiday Park** *(SY493892)*

Burton Bradstock DT6 4PT

☎ 01308 897317 🖷 01308 897336

**email:** enquiries@freshwaterbeach.co.uk

**web:** www.freshwaterbeach.co.uk

**Dir:** *Take B3157 from Bridport towards Burton Bradstock. Site 1.5m from Crown rdbt on right*

Open 15 Mar-10 Nov Booking advisable Jul-Aug Last arrival 22.00hrs Last departure 10.00hrs

A family holiday centre sheltered by a sandbank and enjoying its own private beach. The park offers a wide variety of leisure and entertainment programmes for all the family. It is well placed at one end of the Weymouth/Bridport coast with spectacular views of Chesil Beach. There are three immaculate toilet blocks. A 40-acre site with 500 touring pitches and 250 statics.

**Leisure:**

**Facilities:**

**Services:**

**Notes:** No unaccompanied minors. Large TV, internet, entertainment

*see advert on opposite page*

ENGLAND

## BRIDPORT *CONTINUED*

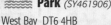

### 79% West Bay Holiday Park *(SY461906)*

West Bay DT6 4HB
01308 422424 & 0871 641 0199 01308 421371
**email:** enquiries@parkdeanholidays.co.uk
**web:** www.parkdeanholidays.co.uk
**Dir:** *From A35 (Dorchester road), W towards Bridport, take 1st exit at 1st rdbt, 2nd exit at 2nd rdbt into West Bay, park on right*
★ £10-£28 £13-£30 £10-£28

Open Mar-Oct Booking advisable peak season Last arrival 21.00hrs Last departure 10.00hrs

Overlooking the pretty little harbour at West Bay, and close to the shingle beach, this park offers a full entertainment programme for all ages. There are children's clubs and sports activities for all the family, and plenty of evening fun with talent shows and cabaret etc. The grassy touring area is terraced to enjoy the seaward views. A large adventure playground is very popular. A 6-acre site with 131 touring pitches and 307 statics.

**Leisure:**
**Facilities:**
**Services:** →
**Notes:** Family entertainment, kids' clubs

## PREMIER PARK

### ►►►►► 84% Highlands End Holiday Park *(SY454913)*

Eype DT6 6AR
01308 422139 01308 425672
**email:** holidays@wdlh.co.uk
**web:** www.wdlh.co.uk
**Dir:** *1m W of Bridport on A35, turn south for Eype. Park signed*
★ £12.50-£23 £12.50-£23 £9.75-£17.50

Open mid Mar-early Nov Booking advisable public hols & Jul-Aug Last arrival 22.00hrs Last departure 11.00hrs

A well-screened site with magnificent clifftop views over the Channel and Dorset coast, adjacent to National Trust land and overlooking Lyme Bay. Pitches are mostly sheltered by hedging and well spaced on hardstandings. There is a mixture of statics and tourers, but the tourers enjoy the best clifftop positions. A 9-acre site with 195 touring pitches, 45 hardstandings and 160 statics.

**Leisure:** **Facilities:**
**Services:** →
**Notes:** Gym, steam room, sauna, pitch & putt, tourist info

*see advert on opposite page*

## CERNE ABBAS MAP 04 ST60

### ►►► 81% Lyons Gate Caravan and Camping Park *(ST660062)*

Lyons Gate DT2 7AZ
01300 345260
**email:** info@lyons-gate.co.uk
**web:** www.lyons-gate.co.uk
**Dir:** *Signed with direct access from A352, 3m N of Cerne Abbas*

Open all year Booking advisable peak times Last arrival 20.00hrs Last departure 11.30hrs

A peaceful park with pitches set out around the four attractive coarse fishing lakes. It is surrounded by mature woodland, with many footpaths and bridleways. Other easily accessible attractions include the Cerne Giant carved into the hills, the old market town of Dorchester, and the superb sandy beach at Weymouth. A 10-acre site with 90 touring pitches, 14 hardstandings.

**Leisure:** **Facilities:**
**Services:** →
**Notes:**

### ►► 69% Giant's Head Caravan & Camping Park (ST675029)

Giants Head Farm, Old Sherborne Rd DT2 7TR
☎ 01300 341242
**email:** holidays@giantshead.co.uk
**web:** www.giantshead.co.uk
**Dir:** *From Dorchester into town avoiding by-pass, at Top O'Town rdbt take Sherborne road, 500yds right fork at Esso (Loder's garage) site signed.*

£8-£13 £8-£13 £8-£13

Open Etr-Oct (rs Etr shop & bar closed) Booking advisable Aug Last arrival anytime Last departure 13.00hrs

A pleasant though rather basic park set in Dorset downland near the Cerne Giant (the local landmark figure cut into the chalk) with stunning views. A good stopover site, ideal for tenters and backpackers on the Ridgeway route. A 4-acre site with 50 touring pitches.

**Facilities:** **Services:**
**Notes:**

## CHARMOUTH — MAP 04 SY39

**PREMIER PARK**

### ►►►►► 84% Wood Farm Caravan & Camping Park (SY356940)

The Best of British Touring and Holiday Parks

Axminster Rd DT6 6BT
☎ 01297 560697 01297 561243
**email:** holidays@woodfarm.co.uk
**web:** www.woodfarm.co.uk
**Dir:** *Park entered directly off A35 rdbt, on Axminster side of Charmouth*

Open Etr-Oct Booking advisable school hols Last arrival 19.00hrs Last departure noon

A pleasant, well-established and mature park overlooking Charmouth, the sea and the Dorset hills and valleys. It stands on a high spot, and the four camping fields are terraced, each with its own impressive toilet block. Convenient for Lyme Regis, Axminster, and the famous fossil coastline. A 13-acre site with 216 touring pitches, 175 hardstandings and 81 statics.

**Leisure:** **Facilities:**
**Services:**
**Notes:** No skateboards, scooters or roller skates. Coarse fishing lake

### ►►►► 80% Charmouth Camping & Caravanning Club Site (SY330965)

Monkton Wylde Farm DT6 6DB
☎ 01297 32965
**web:** www.campingandcaravanningclub.co.uk/charmouth
**Dir:** *From Dorchester on A35 turn right onto B3165 signed Hawkchurch, site on left in 0.25m*

★ £18.25-£22.15 £18.25-£22.15 £18.25-£22.15

Open 13 Mar-3 Mar Booking advisable BH & peak periods Last arrival 21.00hrs Last departure noon

Located in a rural setting almost on the Devon/Dorset border, this attractively terraced park with high quality toilet facilities is ideally placed for visiting the resorts of Charmouth, Lyme Regis and the Jurassic Coast. Friendly managers keep the whole park in tiptop condition. A 12-acre site with 125 touring pitches, 34 hardstandings.

**Leisure:**
**Facilities:**
**Services:**
**Notes:** Site gates closed 23.00hrs-07.00hrs

## CHARMOUTH CONTINUED

### ►►►► 80% Monkton Wyld Farm Caravan Park (SY336964)

DT6 6DB
☎ 01297 34525 & 631131 (May-Sep) 01297 33594
**email:** holidays@monktonwyld.co.uk
**web:** www.monktonwyld.co.uk
**Dir:** *From Charmouth on A35 towards Axminster, after approx 3m (ignore 1st sign to Monkton Wyld - road very steep) take next right signed Marshwood. Site 500mtrs on left*

★ £12.60-£16.50 £12.60-£16.50 £12.60-£16.50

Open Etr-Oct Booking advisable school hols Last arrival 22.00hrs Last departure 11.00hrs

An attractive family park in a secluded location yet central for Charmouth, Lyme and the coast. It has been tastefully designed in a maturing landscape, with perimeter trees providing a screen, and every pitch backed by hedges or shrubs. A 20-acre site with 150 touring pitches, 79 hardstandings.

**Leisure:**
**Facilities:**
**Services:**
**Notes:** Wi-fi. Two family shower rooms

### ►►►► 85% Newlands Caravan & Camping Park (SY374935)

DT6 6RB
☎ 01297 560259 01297 560787
**email:** enq@newlandsholidays.co.uk
**web:** www.newlandsholidays.co.uk
**Dir:** *4m W of Bridport on A35*

★ £13-£30 £13-£30 £10-£27

Open all year (rs Nov-Mar restaurant, bar & shop closed) Booking advisable school hols Last arrival 22.30hrs Last departure 10.00hrs

A very smart site with excellent touring facilities. The park offers a full cabaret and entertainment programme for all ages, and boasts an indoor swimming pool with spa and an outdoor pool with water slide. Set on gently sloping ground in hilly countryside near the sea. A 23-acre site with 240 touring pitches, 52 hardstandings and 86 statics.

**Leisure:**
**Facilities:**
**Services:**

*see advert on opposite page*

### ►►► 79% Manor Farm Holiday Centre (SY368937)

DT6 6QL
☎ 01297 560226
**email:** enq@manorfarmholidaycentre.co.uk
**web:** www.manorfarmholidaycentre.co.uk
**Dir:** *W on A35 to Charmouth, site 0.75m on right*

★ £11-£21 £11-£21 £11-£21

Open all year (rs End Oct-mid Mar statics only) Booking advisable high season Last arrival 20.00hrs Last departure 10.00hrs

Set just a short walk from the safe sand and shingle beach at Charmouth, this popular family park offers a good range of facilities. Children enjoy the activity area and outdoor swimming pool (so do their parents!), and the park also offers a lively programme in the extensive bar and entertainment complex. A 15-acre site with 250 touring pitches, 80 hardstandings and 29 statics.

**Leisure:**
**Facilities:**
**Services:**
**Notes:** No skateboards

## CHIDEOCK MAP 04 SY49

### ►►►► 83% Golden Cap Caravan Park (SY422919)

Seatown DT6 6JX
☎ 01308 422139 & 01297 489341 01308 425672
**email:** holidays@wdlh.co.uk
**web:** www.wdlh.co.uk
**Dir:** *On A35, in Chideock turn S for Seatown, park signed*

★ £12.50-£26.50 £12.50-£26.50 £12.50-£21

Open mid Mar-early Nov Booking advisable public hols & Jul-Aug Last arrival 22.00hrs Last departure 11.00hrs

A grassy site, overlooking sea and beach and surrounded by National Trust parkland. This uniquely placed park slopes down to the sea, although pitches are generally level. A slight dip hides the beach view from the back of the park, but this area benefits from having trees, scrub and meadows, unlike the barer areas closer to the sea. Ideal base for touring Dorset and Devon. An 11-acre site with 108 touring pitches, 24 hardstandings and 234 statics.

**Leisure:**

**Facilities:**

**Services:**

**Notes:** Fishing lake, tourist information

*see advert on page 152*

## CHRISTCHURCH — MAP 05 SZ19

### ►►►► 88% Grove Farm Meadow Holiday Caravan Park *(SZ136946)*

Stour Way BH23 2PQ

☎ 01202 483597 🖷 01202 483878

**email:** enquiries@meadowbank-holidays.co.uk

**web:** www.meadowbank-holidays.co.uk

**Dir:** *A31 onto A338 towards Bournemouth. Take 1st exit after 5m then left towards Christchurch on B3073. Right at 1st rdbt into St Catherine's Way/River Way. Stour Way 3rd right, site at end of road*

★ £8-£26 £8-£26

*Grove Farm Meadow Holiday Caravan Park*

Open Mar-Oct Booking advisable at all times Last arrival 21.00hrs Last departure noon

A very smart park on the banks of the River Stour, with a colourful display of hanging baskets and flower-filled tubs placed around the superb reception area. The toilet facilities are modern, and there is excellent play equipment for children. Visitors can choose between pitch sizes, including luxury fully-serviced ones. A 2-acre site with 41 touring pitches, 22 hardstandings and 180 statics.

**Leisure:**

**Facilities:**

**Services:**

**Notes:** No pets, no tents. Fishing on site

ENGLAND

## CORFE CASTLE MAP 04 SY98

### ►►► 80% **Woodland Caravan & Camping Park** *(SY953818)*

The Glebe, Bucknowle Farm, Bucknowle BH20 5PQ

☎ 01929 480280 🖹 01929 480280

**email:** hazel.parker@btconnect.com

**Dir:** *From Wareham A351 towards Swanage. In 4m turn right at foot of Corfe Castle signed Church Knowle. 0.75m right to site*

£12-£15 £12-£15

Open Mar-Oct Last departure 11.00hrs

A quiet family park set in a clearing within a wooded area, with touring pitches spread around the perimeter in secluded areas. The central grass area is kept free as a play space, and there are many walks from the park. A toilet and amenities block provides very good facilities. A 5-acre site with 80 touring pitches.

**Leisure:**

**Facilities:**

**Services:** →

**Notes:** Quiet after 22.30hrs. Baby changing area

## DORCHESTER

*see Cerne Abbas*

## EVERSHOT MAP 04 ST50

### ►►► 78% ***Clay Pigeon Caravan Park***

*(ST610077)*

Wardon Hill DT2 9PW

☎ 01935 83492

**Dir:** *Turn off A37 onto unclassified road signed Batcombe, site on right in 150yds*

Open all year Booking advisable Last arrival 21.00hrs

A level, close-mown park with mature trees in a rural area. The toilet block is well equipped, and adjacent to the site is a go-kart track and clay pigeon shooting range. A 3-acre site with 60 touring pitches, 12 hardstandings and 6 statics.

**Leisure:**

**Facilities:**

**Services:** →

**Notes:** Dogs must be kept on leads

## FERNDOWN MAP 05 SU00

### ►►► 74% **St Leonards Farm Caravan & Camping Park** *(SU093014)*

Ringwood Rd, West Moors BH22 0AQ

☎ 01202 872637 🖹 01202 855683

**web:** www.stleonardsfarm.biz

**Dir:** *From E (Ringwood): entrance directly off A31 after crossing rdbt, opposite Texaco garage. From W: u-turn at rdbt after Texaco garage, turn left into park*

Open Apr-Sep Booking advisable Jul-Aug Last departure 14.00hrs

The private road off A31 leads to this well-screened park divided into paddocks, with spacious pitches. This is one of the nearest parks to Bournemouth with its many holiday amenities. A 12-acre site with 151 touring pitches.

**Leisure:**

**Facilities:**

**Services:** →

**Notes:** Dogs on leads, no noise after 23.00hrs, no large groups, no disposable BBQ's

ENGLAND

## HOLTON HEATH MAP 04 SY99

### 82% Sandford Holiday Park (SY939916)

BH16 6JZ

☎ 0870 0667793 & 01202 622513 🖹 01202 625678

**email:** bookings@weststarholidays.co.uk

**web:** www.weststartouring.co.uk

**Dir:** *A35 from Poole towards Dorchester, at lights onto A351 towards Wareham. Right at Holton Heath. Park 100yds on left*

★ £12.75-£33.50 £12.75-£33.50 £12.75-£33.50

Open Mar-Nov Booking advisable BH & Jul-Aug Last arrival 22.00hrs Last departure 10.00hrs

With touring pitches set individually in 20 acres surrounded by woodland, this park offers a full range of leisure activities and entertainment for the whole family. The touring area is neat and well maintained, and there are children's clubs in the daytime and nightly entertainment. A reception area with lounge, bar, café and restaurant creates an excellent and attractive entrance, with a covered area outside with tables and chairs and well landscaped gardens. A 64-acre site with 500 touring pitches and 305 statics.

**Leisure:**

**Facilities:**

**Services:**

**Notes:** No unaccompanied minors. Wi-fi. Fun factory, bowling, entertainment, crazy golf

*see advert on page 164*

## HORTON MAP 05 SU00

### ►►► 75% Meadow View Caravan Park (SU045070)

Wigbeth BH21 7JH

☎ 01258 840040 🖹 01258 840040

**email:** mail@meadowviewcaravanpark.co.uk

**web:** www.meadowviewcaravanpark.co.uk

**Dir:** *Follow unclass road from Horton to site, 0.5m from Druscilla pub*

★ £8.50-£13 £8.50-£13 £8.50-£13

Open all year Booking advisable Jul-Aug Last arrival 21.00hrs Last departure 11.00hrs

A small family-owned park, part of a specialised commercial turf farm, and set in a very rural area with its own lake and nature reserve. This very good park is always neatly trimmed and clean. A 1.5-acre site with 15 touring pitches, 7 hardstandings.

**Facilities:**

**Services:**

**Notes:** Dogs must be kept on leads. Coarse fishing

## LYME REGIS MAP 04 SY39

*see also Charmouth*

### ►►►► 81% Shrubbery Touring Park (SY300914)

Rousdon DT7 3XW

☎ 01297 442227 🖹 01297 446086

**email:** enqshrubberypark@tiscali.co.uk

**web:** www.ukparks.co.uk/shrubbery

**Dir:** *3m W of Lyme Regis on A3052 (coast road)*

£9.25-£14.25 £8.75-£13.50 £8.75-£14.25

Open mid Mar-Oct Booking advisable BH & Jul-Aug Last arrival 23.00hrs Last departure 11.00hrs

Mature trees enclose this peaceful park which has distant views of the lovely surrounding countryside. The modern facilities are well kept, and there is plenty of space for children to play in the grounds. Located on the Devon/Dorset borders, just 3 miles from Lyme Regis. A 10-acre site with 120 touring pitches.

**Leisure:**

**Facilities:**

**Services:**

**Notes:** No motor scooters, roller skates, skateboards, no groups (except rallies). Crazy golf

### ►►► 82% Hook Farm Caravan & Camping Park (SY323930)

Gore Ln, Uplyme DT7 3UU

☎ 01297 442801 🖹 01297 442801

**email:** information@hookfarm-uplyme.co.uk

**web:** www.hookfarm-uplyme.co.uk

**Dir:** *From A35, take B3165 towards Lyme Regis & Uplyme at Hunters Lodge pub. 2m turn right into Gore Lane, site 400yds on right*

£12.50-£24.50 £10-£24

Open 15 Mar-Oct (rs shop closed in low season) Booking advisable Etr, May BH, Jul & Aug Last arrival 21.30hrs Last departure 11.00hrs

Set in a peaceful and very rural location with views of Lym Valley and just a mile from the seaside at Lyme Regis. There are modern toilet facilities and good on-site amenities. Most pitches are level due to excellent terracing. A 5.5-acre site with 100 touring pitches and 17 statics.

**Leisure:** **Facilities:**

**Services:**

**Notes:** No groups of 6 adults or more, no dangerous dog breeds

## LYTCHETT MATRAVERS — MAP 04 SY99

### ►►► 74% Huntick Farm Caravan Park

(SY955947)

Huntick Rd BH16 6BB

☎ 01202 622222

**Dir:** *Between Lytchett Minster & Lytchett Matravers*

★ £9.50-£16

Open Apr-Oct Booking advisable Last arrival 21.00hrs Last departure noon

A really attractive little park nestling in rural surroundings edged by woodland, a mile from the village amenities of Lytchett Matravers. This neat grassy park is divided into three paddocks offering a peaceful location and yet close to the attractions of Poole and Bournemouth. A 4-acre site with 24 touring pitches.

**Leisure:**

**Facilities:**

**Services:** →

## LYTCHETT MINSTER — MAP 04 SY99

### ►►►► 82% South Lytchett Manor

(SY954926)

Dorchester Rd BH16 6JB

☎ 01202 622577

**email:** info@southlytchettmanor.co.uk

**web:** www.southlytchettmanor.co.uk

**Dir:** *On B3067, off A35, 1m E of Lytchett Minster, 600yds on right after village*

Open Etr-14 Oct Booking advisable Last arrival 21.00hrs Last departure noon

A newly redeveloped park set along the tree-lined driveway of an old manor house with pitches enjoying rural views. All the amenities here have been completely renewed to a very high quality. The park is close to the popular resorts of Poole and Bournemouth. A 20-acre site with 150 touring pitches, 15 hardstandings.

**Leisure:**

**Facilities:**

**Services:** →

**Notes:** Internet access

## MORETON — MAP 04 SY88

### ►►► 79% Moreton Camping & Caravanning Club Site (SY782892)

Station Rd DT2 8BB

☎ 01305 853801

**web:** www.campingandcaravanningclub.co.uk/moreton

**Dir:** *From Poole on A35, past Bere Regis, left onto B3390 signed Alfpuddle. After approx 2m site on left before Moreton Station and next to public house*

★ £15.45-£22.15 £15.45-£22.15 £15.45-£22.15

Open 13 Mar-17 Nov Booking advisable BH & peak periods Last arrival 21.00hrs Last departure noon

Modern purpose-built site on level ground with good amenities. This tidy, well-maintained park offers electric hook-ups to most pitches, and there is a very good play area for children. A 7-acre site with 120 touring pitches, 10 hardstandings.

**Leisure:**

**Facilities:**

**Services:** →

**Notes:** Site gates closed 23.00hrs-07.00hrs

## ORGANFORD — MAP 04 SY99

### ►►►► 83% Pear Tree Touring Park

(SY938915)

Organford Rd, Holton Heath BH16 6LA

☎ 01202 622434

**email:** info@visitpeartree.co.uk

**web:** www.visitpeartree.co.uk

**Dir:** *From Poole take A35 towards Dorchester, onto A351 towards Wareham, at 1st lights turn right, park 300yds on left*

£11-£24 £11-£24 £10.50-£24

Open May-Sep Booking advisable Spring BH & end Jul-Aug Last arrival 21.00hrs Last departure 11.00hrs

A quiet, sheltered country park offering quality and comfort. The touring area is divided into terraces with mature hedges for screening, with a separate level tenting area on the edge of woodland. The friendly atmosphere at this attractive park, and the many colourful flower beds help to ensure a relaxing holiday. A bridle path leads into Wareham Forest. A 9-acre site with 125 touring pitches, 10 hardstandings and 40 statics.

**Leisure:**

**Facilities:**

**Services:** →

ENGLAND

## OSMINGTON MILLS MAP 04 SY78

### ►►► 76% **Osmington Mills Holidays**

*(SY736820)*
DT3 6HB
☎ 01305 832311 Fax 01305 835251
**email:** holidays@osmingtonmills.fsnet.co.uk
**web:** www.osmington-mills-holidays.co.uk
**Dir:** *Take A353 towards Weymouth. At Osmington Mills sign (opposite garage) turn left to site*

★ £10-£20

Open May-Oct (rs May & Oct pool closed) Booking advisable Last departure 10.00hrs

A large, slightly sloping field with hedging and natural screening providing bays, in a peaceful setting close to the Dorset coastline and footpaths. The facilities are of a very good quality. The park offers seasonal entertainment in a ranch-style bar, and an outdoor swimming pool with paddling pools. A 14-acre site with 225 touring pitches and 83 statics.

**Leisure:**

**Facilities:**

**Services:**

**Notes:** Families & couples only. Riding stables & coarse fishing

## OWERMOIGNE MAP 04 SY78

### ►►► 80% **Sandyholme Caravan Park** *(SY768863)*

GOLD

Moreton Rd DT2 8HZ
☎ 01305 852677 Fax 01305 854677
**email:** smeatons@sandyholme.co.uk
**web:** www.sandyholme.co.uk
**Dir:** *From A352 (Wareham to Dorchester road) turn right to Owermoigne for 1m. Site on left*

★ £11-£15.50 £11-£15.50 £11-£15.50

Open Apr-Oct (rs Etr) Booking advisable peak periods Last arrival 21.30hrs Last departure 10.30hrs

A quiet family-run site in a tree-lined rural setting within easy reach of the coast at Lulworth Cove, and handy for several seaside resorts. The facilities are very good, including a superb toilet block, and good food is available in the lounge/bar. A 6-acre site with 50 touring pitches and 30 statics.

**Leisure:**

**Facilities:**

**Services:**

**Notes:** Dogs must be kept on leads. Table tennis

## POOLE MAP 04 SZ09

*see also Lytchett Minster, Organford & Wimborne Minster*

### 78% **Rockley Park** *(SY982909)*

GOLD

Hamworthy BH15 4LZ
☎ 01202 679393 Fax 01202 683159
**web:** www.rockley-park.co.uk
**Dir:** *Take A31 off M27 to Poole centre, then follow signs to park*

★ £17-£84 £17-£84 £17-£84

Open mid Mar-Oct (rs mid Mar-May & Sep-Oct some facilities may be reduced) Booking advisable school hols Last departure 10.00hrs

A complete holiday experience including a wide range of day- and night-time entertainment, and plenty of sports and leisure activities. Water sports are comprehensively covered, and there is also mooring and launching from the park. The touring area provides good quality facilities. A 90-acre site with 71 touring pitches, 71 hardstandings and 1077 statics.

**Leisure:**

**Facilities:**

**Services:**

**Notes:** Dogs not allowed during peak periods or on touring pitches. Sailing school

*see advert on this page*

## POOLE CONTINUED

### ►►► 75% *Beacon Hill Touring Park* (SY977945)

Blandford Rd North BH16 6AB

☎ 01202 631631 📠 01202 625749

**email:** bookings@beaconhilltouringpark.co.uk

**web:** www.beaconhilltouringpark.co.uk

**Dir:** *On A350, 0.25m N of junct with A35, 4m N of Poole*

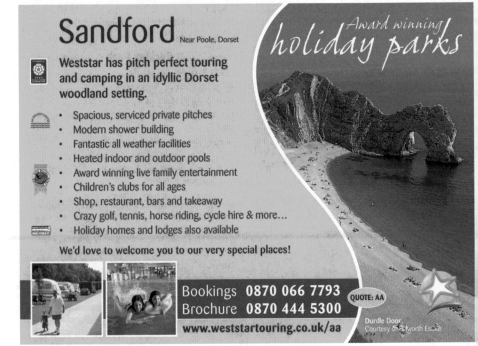

Open Etr-Sep (rs low & mid season some services closed/ restricted opening) Booking advisable Etr, Whit & Jul-Aug Last arrival 23.00hrs Last departure 11.00hrs

Set in attractive, wooded area with conservation very much in mind. Two large ponds for coarse fishing are within the grounds and the terraced pitches, informally sited so that visitors can choose their favourite spot, offer some fine views. A 30-acre site with 170 touring pitches, 10 hardstandings.

**Leisure:**

**Facilities:**

**Services:** →

**Notes:** Groups of young people only accepted at management's discretion

## PORTESHAM — MAP 04 SY68

### ►►►► 78% Portesham Dairy Farm Campsite (SY602854)

DT3 4HG

☎ 01305 871297

**email:** info@porteshamdairyfarm.co.uk

**web:** www.porteshamdairyfarm.co.uk

**Dir:** *From Dorchester on A35 towards Bridport. After 5m left at Winterbourne Abbas, follow Portesham signs. Through village, left at Kings Arms pub, site in 350yds on right*

★ £8-£20.50 £8-£20.50 £8-£20.50

Open mid Mar-Oct Booking advisable at busy times Last arrival 22.00hrs Last departure 16.00hrs

Located at the edge of the picturesque village of Portesham, this family run park is part of a small working farm in a quiet rural location. This level park has a local pub near the site entrance where meals are



**Abbreviations:** BH-bank holiday/s Etr-Easter Whit-Whitsun dep-departure fr-from hrs-hours m-mile mdnt-midnight rdbt-roundabout rs-restricted service wk-week wknd-weekend no dogs No cards → following facilities within 3 miles of the site

served, and with a garden for children. An 8-acre site with 90 touring pitches, 61 hardstandings.

**Leisure:**

**Facilities:**

**Services:**

**Notes:** Fully serviced pitches, seasonal pitches, caravan storage

## PUNCKNOWLE MAP 04 SY58

### 74% Home Farm Caravan and Campsite (SY535887)

Home Farm, Rectory Ln DT2 9BW

01308 897258

**Dir:** *From Dorchester on A35 towards Bridport, turn left at start of dual carriageway, at bottom of hill turn right to Litton Cheney. Through village, 2nd left to Puncknowle. Left at T-junct, left at phone box. Site 150mtrs on right*

Open Apr or Etr-Oct Booking advisable May Day BH & Jul-Aug Last arrival 21.00hrs Last departure noon

A quiet site hidden away on the edge of this little hamlet. It offers sweeping views of the Dorset countryside from most pitches, and is just 5 miles from Abbotsbury, and 1.5 miles from the South West Coastal Footpath. A 6.5-acre site with 47 touring pitches.

**Facilities:**

**Services:**

**Notes:** Dogs on leads, no cats, no wood burning fires

## ST LEONARDS MAP 05 SU10

### 80% Back of Beyond Touring Park (SU103034)

234 Ringwood Rd BH24 2SB

01202 876968 01202 876968

**email:** melandsuepike@aol.com

**web:** www.backofbeyondtouringpark.co.uk

**Dir:** *From E: on A31 over Little Chef rdbt, pass St Leonard's Hotel, at next rdbt u-turn into lane immediately left to site at end of lane. From W: on A31 pass Texaco garage & Woodsman Inn, immediatley left to site*

★ £13-£18 £13-£18 £13-£18

Open Mar-Oct Booking advisable summer Last arrival 19.00hrs Last departure noon

Set well off the beaten track in natural woodland surroundings, with its own river and lake yet close to many attractions. This tranquil park has been completely redeveloped by keen, friendly owners, and the quality facilities are for adults only. A 28-acre site with 80 touring pitches.

**Facilities:**

**Services:**

**Notes:** Adults only. No commercial vehicles. Lake & river fishing, 9-hole pitch & putt course, boule piste

### 91% Shamba Holidays (SU105029)

230 Ringwood Rd BH24 2SB

01202 873302 01202 873392

**email:** enquiries@shambaholidays.co.uk

**web:** www.shambaholidays.co.uk

**Dir:** *Off A31, from Poole turn left into Eastmoors Lane, 100yds past 2nd rdbt from Texaco garage. Park 0.25m on right*

★ £16-£26 £16-£26 £16-£26

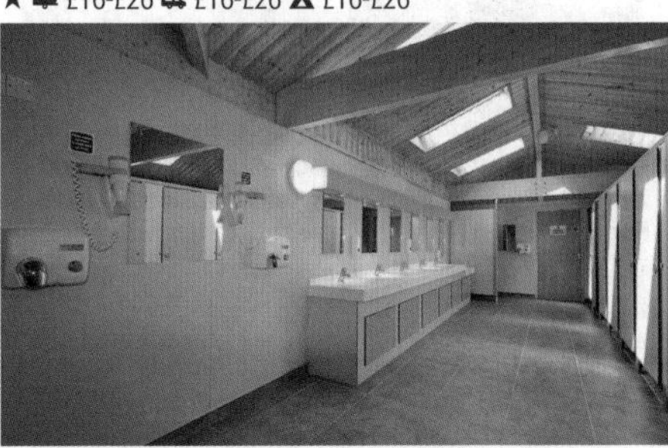

Open Mar-Oct (rs low season some facilities only open at wknds) Booking advisable BH & Jul-Aug Last arrival 22.00hrs Last departure 11.00hrs

A relaxed touring park in pleasant countryside between the New Forest and Bournemouth. The park is very well equipped for holidaymakers, with swimming pool, good playground, and bar, shop and takeaway. A 7-acre site with 150 touring pitches.

**Leisure:** **Facilities:**

**Services:**

**Notes:** No large groups, no commercial vehicles. Phone card top-up facility

*see advert on page 166*

### 78% Forest Edge Touring Park (SU104024)

229 Ringwood Rd BH24 2SD

01590 648331 01590 645610

**email:** holidays@shorefield.co.uk

**web:** www.shorefield.co.uk

**Dir:** *From E: on A31 over 1st rdbt (Little Chef), pass St Leonards Hotel & left at next rdbt into Boundary Lane, site 100yds on left. From W: on A31 pass Texaco garage & Woodsman Inn, right at rdbt into Boundary Lane*

★ £9.50-£28 £9.50-£28 £9.50-£28

Open Feb-Dec (pool/bar only open school & summer hols) Booking advisable at all times Last arrival 21.00hrs Last departure 10.00hrs

A tree-lined park set in grassland with plenty of excellent amenities for all the family, including an outdoor heated swimming pool and toddlers' pool, an adventure playground, and two launderettes. Visitors are invited to use the superb leisure club plus all amenities and entertainment at the sister site of Oakdene Forest Park less than a mile away. Some pitches may experience traffic noise from the nearby A31. A 9-acre site with 94 touring pitches and 28 statics.

**Leisure:** **Facilities:**

**Services:**

**Notes:** 1 dog & car per pitch

*see advert on page 183*

ENGLAND

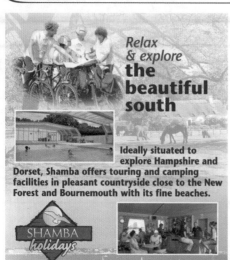



## SHAFTESBURY — MAP 04 ST82

### ►► 76% Blackmore Vale Caravan & Camping Park *(ST835233)*

Sherborne Causeway SP7 9PX

☎ 01747 851523 & 852573 🖷 01747 851671

**email:** bmvgroup@ukf.net

**web:** www.ukcampsite.co.uk

**Dir:** *From Shaftesbury's Ivy Cross rdbt take A30 signed Sherborne. Site 2m on right*

£9.50-£12 £9-£10 ▲ £8-£10

Open all year Booking advisable BH Last arrival 21.00hrs

A comfortable touring park with spacious pitches and well-maintained facilities. Set behind a caravan sales showground and dealership, and about two miles from Shaftesbury. A 3-acre site with 26 touring pitches, 6 hardstandings.

**Facilities:**

**Services:**

**Notes:** Caravan sales & accessories

## SIXPENNY HANDLEY — MAP 04 ST91

### ►►► 75% Church Farm Caravan & Camping Park *(ST994173)*

The Bungalow, Church Farm High St SP5 5ND

☎ 01725 552563 🖷 01725 552563

**email:** churchfarmcandcpark@yahoo.co.uk

**web:** www.churchfarmcandcpark.co.uk

**Dir:** *1m S of Handley Hill rdbt. Turn off for Sixpenny Handley, right by school, site 300yds by church*

£11-£13 £11-£13 ▲ £11-£13

Open all year Booking advisable BH in May & Aug Last arrival 21.00hrs Last departure anytime

A spacious, open park located within the Cranborne Chase in an Area of Outstanding Natural Beauty. There are good quality toilet facilities, and the pretty village of Sixpenny Handley with all its amenities is 200yds away. A 10-acre site with 35 touring pitches, 2 hardstandings and 2 statics.

**Leisure:**

**Facilities:**

**Services:**

**Notes:** Dogs must be kept on leads, quiet after 23.00hrs. Recycling facilities, caravan storage

## SWANAGE — MAP 05 SZ07

### ►►► 79% Herston Caravan & Camping Park *(SZ018785)*

Washpond Ln BH19 3DJ

☎ 01929 422932

**Dir:** *From Wareham on A351 towards Swanage. Washpond Lane on left just after 'Welcome to Swanage' sign.*

★ £13-£35 £13-£35 ▲ £13-£25

Open all year Booking advisable

Set in a rural area with extensive views of the Purbecks, this tree lined park has many full facility pitches and quality toilet facilities. Herston Halt is within walking distance, a stop for the famous Swanage steam railway between the town centre and Corfe Castle. A 10-acre site with 100 touring pitches, 71 hardstandings and 5 statics.

**Facilities:**

**Services:**

**Notes:** Wi-fi

## ►►► 75% **Swanage Coastal Park** *(SZ024797)*

Priestway BH19 2RS

☎ 01590 648331 Fax 01590 645610

**email:** holidays@shorefield.co.uk

**web:** www.shorefield.co.uk

**Dir:** *A351 from Wareham. 1m past 'Welcome to Swanage' sign, right into High St. 1st right into Bell Street Up hill, 1st left into Priests Road, 1st right into Priestway to site*

★ £7.50-£20 £7.50-£20 £7.50-£20

Open 24 Mar-Oct Booking advisable at all times Last arrival 22.00hrs Last departure 10.00hrs

A spacious site set in stunning countryside with views over Swanage Bay and the Purbeck Hills. The shops and beaches at Swanage are less than a mile away, and the adjacent holiday park offers day membership to its health and fitness club, including bar, indoor swimming pool, gym, sauna, solarium, shop and restaurant. A 15-acre site with 5 touring pitches, 5 hardstandings and 52 statics.

**Leisure:**

**Facilities:**

**Services:**

**Notes:** Dogs must be kept on leads

*see advert on page 183*

## ►►► 80% **Ulwell Cottage Caravan Park** *(SZ019809)*

GOLD

Ulwell Cottage, Ulwell BH19 3DG

☎ 01929 422823 Fax 01929 421500

**email:** enq@ulwellcottagepark.co.uk

**web:** www.ulwellcottagepark.co.uk

**Dir:** *From Swanage N for 2m on unclass road towards Studland*

★ £14-£38.50 £14-£38.50 £10.60-£36

Open Mar-7 Jan (rs Mar-Spring BH & mid Sep-early Jan takeaway closed, shop open variable hrs) Booking advisable BH & Jul-Aug Last arrival 22.00hrs Last departure 11.00hrs

Nestling under the Purbeck Hills surrounded by scenic walks and only 2 miles from the beach. This family-run park caters well for families and couples, offering high quality facilities including an indoor heated swimming pool and village inn. A 13-acre site with 77 touring pitches, 19 hardstandings and 140 statics.

**Leisure:**

**Facilities:**

**Services:**

**Notes:** Wi-fi

*see advert on this page*

## ► 72% **Acton Field Camping Site** *(SY991785)*

Acton Field, Langton Matravers BH19 3HS

☎ 01929 424184 & 439424 Fax 01929 424184

**email:** jojochisnoll@aol.com

**Dir:** *From A351 right after Corfe Castle onto B3069 to Langton Matravers, 2nd right after village sign (bridleway)*

£8-£12 £8-£12 £6-£12

Open mid Jul-early Sep Booking advisable Last arrival 22.00hrs Last departure noon

An informal campsite bordered by farmland on the outskirts of Langton Maltravers. There are superb views of the Purbeck Hills and towards the Isle of Wight, and a footpath leads to the coastal path. The site was once a stone quarry, and rock pegs are required. A 7-acre site with 50 touring pitches.

**Facilities:**

**Services:**

**Notes:** No open fires or noise after mdnt. Dogs on leads. Freezer for freezer packs

## THREE LEGGED CROSS MAP 05 SU00

### ►►► 75% Woolsbridge Manor Farm Caravan Park *(SU099052)*

BH21 6RA
☎ 01202 826369 01202 820603
**email:** woolsbridge@btconnect.com
**web:** www.woolsbridgemanorcaravanpark.co.uk
**Dir:** *2m off A31, 3m W of Ringwood. From Three Legged Cross continue S to Woolsbridge. Site 1.75m on left*

★ £15.50-£20.50 £15.50-£20.50 £15.50-£20.50
Open Mar-Oct Booking advisable BH & Aug Last arrival 20.00hrs Last departure 10.30hrs

A small farm site with spacious pitches on a level field. This quiet site is an excellent central base for touring the New Forest, Salisbury and the south coast, and is close to Moors Valley Country Park for outdoor family activities. A 6.75-acre site with 60 touring pitches.

**Leisure:**
**Facilities:**
**Services:** →

## VERWOOD MAP 05 SU00

### ►►► 75% Verwood Camping & Caravanning Club Site *(SU069098)*

Sutton Hill, Woodlands BH21 8NQ
☎ 01202 822763
**web:** www.campingandcaravanningclub.co.uk/verwood
**Dir:** *Turn left on A354, 13m from Salisbury onto B3081, site is 1.5m W of Verwood*

★ £15.45-£20.15 £15.45-£20.15 £15.45-£20.15
Open 13 Mar-3 Nov Booking advisable BH & peak periods Last arrival 21.00hrs Last departure noon

Set on rising ground between the woodland of the New Forest and the rolling downs of Cranborne Chase and Salisbury Plains. This comfortable site is well kept by very keen wardens. A 12.75-acre site with 150 touring pitches, 18 hardstandings.

**Leisure:**
**Facilities:**
**Services:** →
**Notes:** Sites gates closed 23.00hrs-07.00hrs

## WAREHAM MAP 04 SY98

### 77% East Creech Camping & Caravan Park *(SY928827)*

East Creech Farm, East Creech BH20 5AP
☎ 01929 480519 & 481312 01929 481312
**email:** east.creech@virgin.net
**web:** www.eastcreechfarm.co.uk
**Dir:** *From Wareham on A351 S towards Swanage. On bypass at 3rd rdbt take Furzebrook/Blue Pool Rd exit, approx 2m site on right*

Open Apr-Oct Booking advisable BH & peak season
A grassy park set in a peaceful location beneath the Purbeck Hills, with extensive views towards Poole and Brownsea Island. The park boasts a woodland play area, bright, clean toilet facilities, and a farm shop selling milk, eggs and bread. There are also three coarse fishing lakes teeming with fish. A 4-acre site with 80 touring pitches.

**Leisure:** **Facilities:**
**Services:** →
**Notes:**

### ►►►► 89% Wareham Forest Tourist Park *(SY894912)*

North Trigon BH20 7NZ
☎ 01929 551393 01929 558321
**email:** holiday@wareham-forest.co.uk
**web:** www.wareham-forest.co.uk
**Dir:** *Telephone for directions*

★ £14-£22.75 £14-£22.75 £11.50-£22.75

Open all year (rs off-peak season limited services) Booking advisable Spring BH & Jul-Aug Last arrival 21.00hrs Last departure 10.30hrs

A woodland park within the tranquil Wareham Forest, with its many walks and proximity to Poole, Dorchester and the Purbeck coast. Two luxury blocks, with combined washbasin/WCs for total privacy, maintain a high standard of cleanliness. A heated outdoor swimming pool, off licence, shop and games room add to the pleasure of a stay here. A 42-acre site with 200 touring pitches, 70 hardstandings.

**Leisure:** **Facilities:**
**Services:** →
**Notes:** Couples & families only, no group bookings

ENGLAND

### ►►► 82% *Birchwood Tourist Park*

*(SY896905)*
Bere Rd, North Trigon BH20 7PA
☎ 01929 554763 🖹 01929 556635
**web:** www.birchwoodtouristpark.co.uk
**Dir:** *From Poole (A351) or Dorchester (A352) on N side of railway line at Wareham, follow road signed Bere Regis (unclassified). 2nd tourist park after 2.25m*

Open Mar-Oct Booking advisable BH & Jul-Aug Last arrival 21.00hrs Last departure 11.30hrs

Set in 50 acres of parkland located within Wareham Forest, this site offers direct access into ideal areas for walking, mountain biking, and horse and pony riding. The modern facilities are centrally located and well organised. A 25-acre site with 175 touring pitches, 8 hardstandings.

**Leisure:**
**Facilities:**
**Services:** → U
**Notes:** No generators, no groups at Bank Holidays. Games field, bike hire, pitch & putt, paddling pool

*see advert on this page*

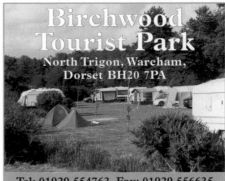

### ►►► 77% **Lookout Holiday Park** *(SY927858)*

Stoborough BH20 5AZ
☎ 01929 552546 🖹 01929 556662
**email:** enquiries@caravan-sites.co.uk
**web:** www.caravan-sites.co.uk
**Dir:** *Take A351 through Wareham, after crossing River Frome & through Stoborough, site signed on left*
£13-£26 £13-£26 £10-£19

Open all year Booking advisable BH & Jul-Aug Last arrival 22.00hrs Last departure noon

Divided into two paddocks and set well back from the Swanage road, this touring park is separated from the static part of the operation. A superb children's playground and plenty of other attractions make this an ideal centre for families. A 15-acre site with 150 touring pitches, 94 hardstandings and 89 statics.

**Leisure:**
**Facilities:**
**Services:** → U
**Notes:** No pets, family park

*see advert on this page*

ENGLAND

## WAREHAM CONTINUED

### ►►► 75% Ridge Farm Camping & Caravan Park (SY939868)

Barnhill Rd, Ridge BH20 5BG
☎ 01929 556444
**email:** info@ridgefarm.co.uk
**web:** www.ridgefarm.co.uk
**Dir:** *From Wareham take B3075 towards Corfe Castle, cross river to Stoborough, then left to Ridge and follow site signs for 1.5m*

Open Etr-Sep Booking advisable Jul & Aug Last arrival 21.00hrs Last departure noon

A quiet rural park, adjacent to a working farm and surrounded by trees and bushes. This away-from-it-all park is ideally located for touring this part of Dorset, and especially for bird watchers, or those who enjoy walking and cycling. A 3.5-acre site with 60 touring pitches, 2 hardstandings.

**Facilities:**

**Services:**

**Notes:** No dogs Jul-Aug

### ►►► 75% *Woodlands Camping Park* (SY867861)

Bindon Ln, East Stoke BH20 6AS
☎ 01929 462327 01929 462327
**email:** stay@woodlandscampingpark.co.uk
**web:** www.woodlandscampingpark.co.uk
**Dir:** *From Wool - at rail crossing turn off A352 onto B3071, at right bend turn left into Bindon Lane. Park 1.5m on right. From Wareham - A352 onto B3070 at junct for East Stoke, right into Bindon/Holme Lane. Park 1.5m on left*

Open Apr-Sep Booking advisable BH & May-Aug Last arrival 21.30hrs Last departure noon

A rural tents-only park set in an Area of Outstanding Natural Beauty surrounded by woodland. The park is divided into three areas by trees, and is appreciated by people looking for peace and quiet. Facilities are well kept, and security is good. Conversational French, German and Spanish are spoken. A 2.75-acre site with 50 touring pitches.

**Facilities:**

**Services:**

**Notes:** No camp fires, no loud radios, no groups except award schemes, no ball games. Fridge-freezer

## WEYMOUTH MAP 04 SY67

### 80% Littlesea (SY654783)

GOLD

Lynch Ln DT4 9DT
☎ 01305 774414 01305 760038
**email:** lisa.michalowicz@bourne-leisure.co.uk
**web:** www.littlesea-park.co.uk
**Dir:** *A35 onto A354 signed Weymouth. Right at 1st rdbt, 3rd exit at 2nd rdbt towards Chickerell. Left into Lynch Lane after lights. Park at far end of road*

★ £9-£61 £9-£61 £9-£47

Open end Mar-end Oct (rs mid Mar-May & Sep-Oct facilities may be reduced) Booking advisable school hols Last arrival anytime Last departure 10.00hrs

Just 3 miles from Weymouth with its lovely beaches and many attractions, Littlesea has a cheerful family atmosphere and fantastic facilities. Indoor and outdoor entertainment and activities are on offer for all the family, and the toilet facilities on the touring park are of a good quality. A 75-acre site with 120 touring pitches and 823 statics.

**Leisure:**

**Facilities:**

**Services:**

**Notes:** No commercial vehicles, no boats. Wi-fi

*see advert on opposite page*

### 75% Seaview Holiday Park (SY707830)

Preston DT3 6DZ
☎ 01305 833037 01305 833169
**email:** katie.watson@bourne-leisure.co.uk
**web:** www.seaview-park.com
**Dir:** *A354 to Weymouth, signs for Preston/Wareham onto A353. Park 3m on right just after Weymouth Bay Holiday Park*

Open mid Mar-Oct (rs mid Mar-May & Sep-Oct Facilities may be reduced) Booking advisable school hols Last arrival 22.00hrs Last departure noon

A fun-packed holiday centre for all the family, with plenty of activities and entertainment during the day and evening. Terraced pitches are provided for caravans, and there is a separate field for tents. The park is close to Weymouth and other coastal attractions. A 20-acre site with 96 touring pitches and 259 statics.

**Leisure:**

**Facilities:**

**Services:**

**Notes:** No groups bookings under 21yrs

ENGLAND

►►►► 91% **East Fleet Farm Touring Park** *(SY640797)*

Chickerell DT3 4DW

☎ 01305 785768

**email:** enquiries@eastfleet.co.uk

**web:** www.eastfleet.co.uk

**Dir:** *On B3157 (Weymouth-Bridport road), 3m from Weymouth*

★ £8-£18 £8-£18 £8-£18

Open 16 Mar-Oct Booking advisable peak season Last arrival 22.00hrs Last departure 10.30hrs

Set on a working organic farm overlooking Fleet Lagoon and Chesil Beach, with a wide range of amenities and quality toilet facilities in a Scandinavian log cabin. The friendly owners are welcoming and helpful, and their family bar serving meals and take-away food is open from Easter, with glorious views from the patio area. A 21-acre site with 400 touring pitches, 50 hardstandings.

**Leisure:**

**Facilities:**

**Services:**

►►► 76% **Bagwell Farm Touring Park** *(SY627816)*

Knights in the Bottom, Chickerell DT3 4EA

☎ 01305 782575 01305 780554

**email:** aa@bagwellfarm.co.uk

**web:** www.bagwellfarm.co.uk

**Dir:** *4m W of Weymouth on B3157 (Weymouth-Bridport), past Chickerell, turn left into park 500yds after Victoria Inn*

Open all year (rs winter bar closed) Booking advisable BH & school hols Last arrival 21.00hrs Last departure 11.00hrs

An idyllically-placed terraced site on a hillside and a valley overlooking Chesil Beach. The park is well equipped with mini-supermarket, children's play area and pets' corner, plus a bar and grill serving food in high season. A 14-acre site with 320 touring pitches, 10 hardstandings.

**Leisure:**

**Facilities:**

**Services:**

**Notes:** Families only, dogs must be kept on leads. Wet suit shower, campers' shelter

►►► 74% ***Pebble Bank Caravan Park*** *(SY659775)*

Camp Rd, Wyke Regis DT4 9HF

☎ 01305 774844

**email:** info@pebblebank.co.uk

**web:** www.pebblebank.co.uk

**Dir:** *From Weymouth take Portland road. At last rdbt turn right, then 1st left to Army Tent Camp. Site opposite*

Open Etr-mid Oct (bar open high season & wknds only) Booking advisable peak times Last arrival 21.00hrs Last departure 11.00hrs

Overlooking Lyme Bay and Chesil Beach, this gently sloping grass site is only 1.5m from Weymouth town centre. The tenting field shares the same wonderful views, and there is a friendly little bar. A 4-acre site with 40 touring pitches and 80 statics.

**Leisure:**

**Facilities:**

**Services:**

**Leisure:** Indoor swimming pool · Outdoor swimming pool · Tennis court · Games room · Children's playground · Stables · 9/18 hole golf course · Boats for hire · Cinema · Fishing · Mini golf · Watersports · Separate TV room

## WEYMOUTH CONTINUED

### ►►► 74% West Fleet Holiday Farm

*(SY625811)*

Fleet DT3 4EF

☎ 01305 782218 🖷 01305 775396

**email:** aa@westfleetholidays.co.uk

**web:** www.westfleetholidays.co.uk

**Dir:** *From Weymouth take B3157 towards Bridport for 3m. In Chickerell turn left at mini-rdbt to Fleet, 1m on right*

£10-£21 £10-£21

Open Etr-Sep Booking advisable BH & school hols Last arrival 22.00hrs Last departure noon

A spacious farm site with both level and sloping pitches divided into paddocks, and screened with hedging. Good views of the Dorset countryside, and a relaxing site for a family holiday with its heated outdoor pool and club house. A 12-acre site with 250 touring pitches.

**Leisure:**

**Facilities:**

**Services:** →

**Notes:** Non-family groups by arrangement only, dogs must be on leads at all times & restricted to certain areas

### ►► 72% Sea Barn Farm *(SY625807)*

Fleet DT3 4ED

☎ 01305 782218 🖷 01305 775396

**email:** aa@seabarnfarm.co.uk

**web:** www.seabarnfarm.co.uk

**Dir:** *From Weymouth take B3157 towards Bridport for 3m. In Chickerell turn left at mini-rdbt towards Fleet. Site 1m on left*

£10-£20 £10-£20

Open 15 Mar-Oct Booking advisable Spring & Aug BH & school hols Last arrival 22.00hrs Last departure noon

A quiet site bordering the Fleet nature reserve, and close to the Dorset coastal path. Optional use of the clubhouse and swimming pool at West Fleet Holiday Farm is available. Pitches are sheltered by hedging, and there is plenty of space for games. A 12-acre site with 250 touring pitches and 1 static.

**Leisure:**

**Facilities:**

**Services:** →

**Notes:** Non-family groups by arrangement, dogs must be kept on leads at all times. Café, pool & clubhouse available at next door site

## WIMBORNE MINSTER MAP 05 SZ09

PREMIER PARK

### ►►►►► 72% Merley Court

*(SZ008984)*

Merley BH21 3AA

☎ 01590 648331 🖷 01590 645610

**email:** holidays@shorefield.co.uk

**web:** www.shorefield.co.uk

**Dir:** *Site signed on A31, Wimborne by-pass & Poole junct rdbt*

★ £10-£33 £10-£29 £10-£23

Open Feb-7 Jan (rs low season pool closed & bar, shop open limited hrs) Booking advisable BH & Jun-Sep Last arrival 21.00hrs Last departure 11.00hrs

A quiet site in a rural position on the edge of Wimborne, with woodland on two sides and good access roads. The park is well landscaped, and offers generous individual pitches in sheltered grassland. There are plenty of amenities for all the family, including heated outdoor pool, tennis court and adventure playground. A 20-acre site with 160 touring pitches, 50 hardstandings.

**Leisure:**

**Facilities:**

**Services:** →

**Notes:** Couples & families only

*see advert on page 183*

ENGLAND

PREMIER PARK

**►►►►► 85% *Wilksworth Farm Caravan Park*** *(SU004018)*

GOLD

Cranborne Rd BH21 4HW

☎ 01202 885467 📠 01202 885467

**email:** rayandwendy@wilksworthfarmcaravanpark.co.uk

**web:** www.wilksworthfarmcaravanpark.co.uk

**Dir:** *1m N of Wimborne on B3078*

Open Apr-Oct (rs Apr & Oct no shop or coffee shop) Booking advisable Spring BH & Jul-Aug Last arrival 20.00hrs Last departure 11.00hrs

A popular and attractive park set in the grounds of a listed house, tranquilly placed in the heart of rural Dorset. The spacious site has much to offer visitors, including a heated swimming pool, take-away and café, plus games room. The ultra-modern toilet facilities contain family rooms. An 11-acre site with 85 touring pitches, 20 hardstandings and 77 statics.

**Leisure:**

**Facilities:**

**Services:**

**Notes:** Paddling pool, volley ball, mini football pitch

*see advert on opposite page*

**►►► 74% Charris Camping & Caravan Park**

*(SY992988)*

Candy's Ln, Corfe Mullen BH21 3EF

☎ 01202 885970 📠 01202 881281

**email:** bookings@charris.co.uk

**web:** www.charris.co.uk

**Dir:** *From E, exit Wimborne bypass (A31) W end. 300yds after Caravan Sales, follow brown sign. From W on A31, over A350 rdbt, take next turn after B3074, follow brown signs*

£9.75-£11.75 £9.75-£11.75 £8.75-£11.75

Open Mar-Jan Booking advisable at all times Last arrival 21.00hrs Last departure 11.00hrs

A sheltered park of grassland lined with trees, on the edge of the Stour Valley. The owners are friendly and welcoming, and they maintain the park facilities to a good standard. Barbecues are a popular occasional event. A 3.5-acre site with 45 touring pitches, 12 hardstandings.

**Facilities:** **Services:**

**Notes:** Earliest arrival time 11.00hrs

**►►► 77% Springfield Touring Park**

*(SY987989)*

Candys Ln, Corfe Mullen BH21 3EF

☎ 01202 881719

**Dir:** *Turn left off Wimborne by-pass (A31) western end, after Caravan Sales follow brown sign.*

£13-£15 £13-£15 £10-£15

Open Etr-Oct Booking advisable BH & Jul-Aug Last arrival 21.00hrs Last departure 11.00hrs

A small touring park with extensive views over the Stour Valley, with a quiet and friendly atmosphere. The park is maintained immaculately, and has a well-stocked shop. A 3.5-acre site with 45 touring pitches, 18 hardstandings.

**Leisure:**

**Facilities:**

**Services:**

**Notes:**

WOOL — MAP 04 SY88

**►►►► 79% Whitemead Caravan Park**

*(SY841869)*

East Burton Rd BH20 6HG

☎ 01929 462241 📠 01929 462241

**email:** whiteme adcp@aol.com

**web:** www.whitemeadcaravanpark.co.uk

**Dir:** *Signed from A352 at level crossing on Wareham side of Wool*

Open mid Mar-Oct Booking advisable public hols & mid Jul-Aug Last arrival 22.00hrs Last departure noon

A well laid-out site in the valley of the River Frome, close to the village and surrounded by woodland. A shop and games room enhance the facilities here, and the toilets are heated, providing an excellent amenity. A 5-acre site with 95 touring pitches.

**Leisure:**

**Facilities:**

**Services:**

**Notes:**

**Facilities:** Bath · Shower · Electric Shaver · Hairdryer · Ice Pack Facility · Disabled Facilities · Public Telephone · Shop on Site or within 200yds · Mobile Shop (calls at least 5 days a week) · BBQ Area · Picnic Area · Dog Exercise Area

ENGLAND

# CO DURHAM

## BARNARD CASTLE MAP 19 NZ01

### ►►►► 80% Barnard Castle Camping & Caravanning Club Site *(NZ025168)*

Dockenflatts Ln, Lartington DL12 9DG

☎ 01833 630228

**web:** www.campingandcaravanningclub.co.uk/barnardcastle

**Dir:** *From Barnard Castle take B6277 to Middleton-in-Teesdale. After 1m turn left signed Raygill Riding Stables. Site 500mtrs on left*

★ £15.45-£20.15 £15.45-£20.15 £15.45-£20.15

Open 13 Mar-3 Nov Booking advisable BH & peak periods Last arrival 21.00hrs Last departure noon

A peaceful site surrounded by mature woodland and meadowland, with first class facilities. This immaculately maintained park is set in the heart of the countryside. Pitches are well laid out and generous, on mainly level grass with some hardstandings. A 10-acre site with 90 touring pitches, 15 hardstandings.

**Leisure:**

**Facilities:**

**Services:**

**Notes:** Site gates closed 23.00hrs-07.00hrs

### ►►► 75% Pecknell Farm Caravan Park

*(NZ028178)*

Lartington DL12 9DF

☎ 01833 638357

**Dir:** *1.5m from Barnard Castle. From A66 take B6277. Site on right 1.5m from junct with A67*

★ £10-£12 £10-£12

Open Apr-Oct Booking advisable BH & Jul-Aug Last arrival 20.00hrs Last departure flexible

A small well laid out site on a working farm in beautiful rural meadowland, with spacious marked pitches on level ground. A 1.5-acre site with 15 touring pitches, 5 hardstandings.

**Facilities:**

**Services:**

**Notes:** Showers are unisex

## BEAMISH MAP 19 NZ25

### ►►► 74% *Bobby Shafto Caravan Park*

*(NZ232545)*

Cranberry Plantation DH9 0RY

☎ 0191 370 1776 0191 370 1783

**Dir:** *From A1693 signed Beamish to sign for Beamish Museum. Take approach road and turn right immediately before museum, left at pub to site 1m on right*

Open Mar-Oct Booking advisable school hols Last arrival 23.00hrs Last departure 11.00hrs

A tranquil rural park surrounded by trees, with very clean and well-organised facilities. The suntrap touring area has plenty of attractive hanging baskets, and there is a clubhouse with bar, TV and pool. The fully serviced pitches enhance the amenities. A 9-acre site with 83 touring pitches, 30 hardstandings and 54 statics.

**Leisure:**

**Facilities:**

**Services:**

## BLACKHALL COLLIERY MAP 19 NZ43

### NEW 79% Crimdon Dene

*(NZ477378)*

Coast Rd TS27 4BN

☎ 0871 664 9737

**email:** crimdon.dene@park-resorts.com

**web:** www.park-resorts.com

**Dir:** *From A19 just S of Peterlee, take B1281 signed Blackhall. Through Castle Eden, left in 0.5m signed Blackhall. Approx 3m right at T-junct onto A1086 towards Crimdon. Park in 1m signed on left, by Seagull pub*

£5-£22 £5-£22

Open 31 Mar-Oct Booking advisable

A large, popular coastal holiday park, handily placed for access to Teeside, Durham and Newcastle. The park contains a full range of holiday centre facilities for both children and their parents. Touring facilities are to a very good standard. 43 touring pitches and 586 statics.

**Leisure:**

**Facilities:**

**Services:**

## CONSETT MAP 19 NZ15

### 78% **Byreside Caravan Site** *(NZ122560)*

Hamsterley NE17 7RT

01207 560280 01207 560280

**Dir:** *From A694 onto B6310 & follow signs*

Open all year Booking advisable BH & Jul-Aug Last arrival 22.00hrs Last departure noon

A small, secluded family-run site on a working farm, with well-maintained facilities. It is immediately adjacent to the coast to coast cycle track so makes an ideal location for walkers and cyclists. Handy for Newcastle and Durham; the Roman Wall and Northumberland National Park are within an hour's drive. A 1.5-acre site with 31 touring pitches, 29 hardstandings.

**Facilities:**

**Services:** →

**Notes:** No ball games on site, dogs must be on leads. Caravan storage

## DURHAM MAP 19 NZ24

### 79% **Strawberry Hill Farm** *(NZ337399)*

Old Cassop DH6 4QA

0191 372 3457 & 372 2512 0191 372 2512

**email:** info@strawberryhf.co.uk

**web:** www.strawberry-hill-farm.co.uk

**Dir:** *Approx 4m from A1(M) junct 61. Site can only be accessed from eastbound carriageway of A181*

£13.50-£15.50 £13.50-£15.50 £13.50-£15.50

Open Mar-Dec Booking advisable BH & Jun-Aug Last arrival 21.00hrs Last departure noon

An attractive park, planted with many young trees and shrubs, and well screened from the road. The terraced pitches have superb panoramic views across lovely wooded countryside. Good toilet and laundry facilities, and a useful base for visiting Durham Castle and Cathedral, Beamish Museum and the coast. A 6.5-acre site with 45 touring pitches, 10 hardstandings and 3 statics.

**Facilities:**

**Services:** →

# ESSEX

## CANEWDON MAP 07 TQ99

### 76% **Riverside Village Holiday Park** *(TQ929951)*

Creeksea Ferry Rd, Wallasea Island SS4 2EY

01702 258297 01702 258555

**Dir:** *M25 junct 29, A127, towards Southend-on-Sea. Take B1013 towards Rochford. Follow signs for Wallsea Island & Baltic Wharf*

Open Mar-Oct Booking advisable at all times

Next to a nature reserve beside the River Crouch, this holiday park is surrounded by wetlands but only eight miles from Southend. A modern toilet block with disabled facilities has been provided for tourers. Several restaurants and pubs are within a short distance. A 25-acre site with 60 touring pitches and 162 statics.

**Leisure:**

**Facilities:**

**Services:** →

**Notes:** No dogs in tents

## CLACTON-ON-SEA MAP 07 TM11

### **NEW** 78% **Highfield Grange** *(TM173175)*

London Rd CO16 9QY

0871 664 9746

**email:** highfield.grange@park-resorts.com

**web:** www.park-resorts.com

**Dir:** *A12 to Colchester, then A120 (Harwich) then A133 to Clacton-on-Sea. Site on B1441 clearly signed on left*

£6-£32 £6-£32

Open 31 Mar-Oct Booking advisable

The modern leisure facilities at this attractively planned park make it an ideal base for a lively family holiday. The swimming complex with both indoor and outdoor pools and a huge water shoot is especially popular. There are 42 fully serviced touring pitches each with its own hard standing, located at the heart of the park. The nearby resorts of Walton-on-the-Naze, Frinton and Clacton all offer excellent beaches and a wide range of popular seaside attractions. 43 touring pitches and 509 statics.

**Leisure:**

**Facilities:**

**Services:** →

**Notes:** No pets

**Leisure:** Indoor swimming pool Outdoor swimming pool Tennis court Games room Children's playground Stables 9/18 hole golf course Boats for hire Cinema Fishing Mini golf Watersports Separate TV room

## CLACTON-ON-SEA *CONTINUED*

### 70% Martello Beach Holiday Park *(TM136128)*

Belsize Av, Jaywick CO15 2LF

☎ 0871 664 9782 & 01442 830100

**email:** martello.beach@park-resorts.com

**web:** www.park-resorts.com

**Dir:** *Telephone for directions*

★ £6-£29 £3-£26

Open Mar-Oct Booking advisable all times Last arrival 20.00hrs Last departure 10.00hrs

Direct access to a 7-mile long blue flag beach is an undoubted attraction at this holiday park. The touring area is next to the leisure complex, where an indoor and outdoor swimming pool, shops, cafés and bars and evening entertainment are all provided. A 40-acre site with 150 touring pitches and 294 statics.

**Leisure:** **Facilities:**

**Services:**

**Notes:** Kids' clubs, water sports, evening entertainment

## COLCHESTER MAP 13 TL92

### ►►►► 81% *Colchester Holiday Park* *(TL971252)*

Cymbeline Way, Lexden CO3 4AG

☎ 01206 545551 01206 710443

**email:** enquiries@colchestercamping.co.uk

**web:** www.colchestercamping.co.uk

**Dir:** *Follow tourist signs from A12, then A133 Colchester Central slip road*

Open all year Booking advisable BH & school hols Last arrival 20.30hrs Last departure noon

A well-designed campsite on level grassland, on the west side of Colchester near the town centre. Close to main routes to London (A12) and east coast. There is good provision for hardstandings, and the owner's attention to detail is reflected in the neatly trimmed grass and well-cut hedges. Toilet facilities are housed in three buildings, two of which are modern and well equipped. A 12-acre site with 168 touring pitches, 44 hardstandings.

**Leisure:** **Facilities:**

**Services:** → 

**Notes:** No commercial vehicles. Badminton court

## KELVEDON HATCH MAP 06 TQ59

### ►►► 74% Kelvedon Hatch Camping & Caravanning Club Site *(TQ577976)*

Warren Ln, Doddinghurst CM15 0JG

☎ 01277 372773

**web:** www.campingandcaravanningclub.co.uk/kelvedonhatch

**Dir:** *M25 junct 28. Brentwood 2m left on A128 signed Ongar. After 3m turn right. Site signed*

★ £14.05-£18.85 £14.05-£18.85 £14.05-£18.85

Open 13 Mar-3 Nov Booking advisable BH & peak periods Last arrival 21.00hrs Last departure noon

A very pretty rural site with many separate areas amongst the trees, and a secluded field for campers. This peaceful site has older-style toilet facilities which are kept very clean, and smart laundry equipment. A 12-acre site with 90 touring pitches, 23 hardstandings.

**Leisure:**

**Facilities:**

**Services:** → 

**Notes:** Site gates closed 23.00hrs-07.00hrs

## MERSEA ISLAND MAP 07 TM01

### 77% Waldegraves Holiday Park *(TM033133)*

GOLD

CO5 8SE

☎ 01206 382898 01206 385359

**email:** holidays@waldegraves.co.uk

**web:** www.waldegraves.co.uk

**Dir:** *B1025 to Mersea Island across the Strood. Left to East Mersea, 2nd turn on right, follow tourist signs to park*

★ £12-£25 £12-£25 £12-£25

Open Mar-Nov Booking advisable all times Last arrival 22.00hrs Last departure noon

A spacious and pleasant site, located between farmland and its own private beach on the Blackwater Estuary. Facilities include two freshwater fishing lakes, heated swimming pool, club, amusements, café and golf, and there is generally good provision for families. A 25-acre site with 60 touring pitches and 250 statics.

**Leisure:**

**Facilities:**

**Services:** → 

**Notes:** No large groups. Boating, fishing, golf

*see advert on opposite page*

## ST LAWRENCE — MAP 07 TL90

### NEW 79% Waterside St Lawrence Bay *(TL953056)*

Main Rd CM0 7LY

☎ 0871 664 9794

**email:** waterside@park-resorts.com

**web:** www.park-resorts.com

**Dir:** *A12 towards Chelmsford then A414 signed Maldon. Follow B1010 & signs to Latchingdon, then signs for Mayland/Steeple/St Lawrence. Left towards St Lawrence. Site on right*

£5-£23 £5-£23 £3-£20

Open 31 Mar-Oct Booking advisable

Waterside occupies a scenic location overlooking the Blackwater estuary. In addition to the range of onsite leisure facilities there are opportunities for beautiful coastal walks and visits to the attractions of Southend. Tents are welcome on this expansive site with 170 touring pitches (70 with electricity) and there are good toilet facilities. The park has its own boat storage and slipway onto the Blackwater. 170 touring pitches and 211 statics.

**Leisure:**

**Facilities:**

**Services:**

*see advert on this page*

## WALTON ON THE NAZE MAP 07 TM22

**NEW** 73% **Naze Marine** *(TM255226)*

Hall Ln CO14 8HL

☎ 0871 664 9755

**email:** naze.marine@park-resorts.com

**web:** www.park-resorts.com

**Dir:** *A12 to Colchester. Then A120 (Harwich road) then A133 to Weeley. Take B1033 to Walton seafront. Site on left*

£6-£24 £6-£24

Open 31 Mar-Oct Booking advisable

With its modern indoor swimming pool, show bar, bar/restaurant and amusements, this park offers a variety of on-site attractions. The park is within easy access of the beaches and attractions of Walton-on-Naze, Frinton and Clacton, and the more historic places of interest inland. This site does not cater for tents. 44 touring pitches and 485 statics.

**Leisure:**

**Facilities:**

**Services:** →

# GLOUCESTERSHIRE

## BERKELEY MAP 04 ST69

►►► 73% ***Hogsdown Farm Caravan & Camping Park*** *(ST710974)*

Hogsdown Farm, Lower Wick GL11 6DD

☎ 01453 810224

**Dir:** *M5 junct 14 (Falfield), take A38 towards Gloucester, turn right for site*

Open all year

A pleasant site with good toilet facilities, located between Bristol and Gloucester. It is well positioned for visiting Berkeley Castle and the Cotswold Edge country, and makes an excellent overnight stop when travelling to or from the West Country. A 5-acre site with 45 touring pitches.

**Leisure:**

**Facilities:**

**Services:** →

## CHELTENHAM MAP 10 SO92

►►► 77% **Briarfields** *(SO899215)*

Gloucester Rd GL51 0SX

☎ 01242 235324

**email:** briarfields@hotmail.co.uk

**web:** www.briarfields.net

**Dir:** *M5 junct 11, A40 towards Cheltenham. At 1st rdbt 1st left onto B4063. Park 200mtrs on left*

★ £13-£15 £13-£15 £10-£14

Open all year Booking advisable all year Last arrival 19.00hrs Last departure noon

A well designed level park with motel facilities adjacent. The park is well positioned between Cheltenham and Gloucester, with easy access to the Cotswolds. A 6-acre site with 72 touring pitches, 72 hardstandings.

**Facilities:**

**Services:** →

**Notes:** No cars by tents

## CIRENCESTER MAP 05 SP0(

►►►► 79% **Mayfield Touring Park** *(SP020055)*

Cheltenham Rd GL7 7BH

☎ 01285 831301

**email:** mayfield-park@cirencester.fsbusiness.co.uk

**web:** www.mayfieldpark.co.uk

**Dir:** *From Cirencester bypass take Burford rd/A429 junct exit towards Cirencester, then via A417 to A435, direct access onto site on left in 1.5m*

★ £10-£17 £10-£17 £8-£15

Open all year Booking advisable BH, Fairford Air Display & wknds Last arrival 20.00hrs Last departure noon

A gently sloping park on the edge of the Cotswolds, with level pitches and a warm welcome. Popular with couples and families, it offers a good licensed shop selling a wide selection of home-cooked takeaway food. Although some traffic noise can be heard at times, this lovely park makes an ideal base. A 12-acre site with 72 touring pitches, 31 hardstandings.

**Facilities:**

**Services:** →

**Notes:** Dogs only allowed if pre-booked. No cycles, skateboards. Off licence

## COLEFORD MAP 04 SO5]

►► 80% ***Woodlands View Camping & Caravan Park*** *(SO582085)*

Sling GL16 8JA

☎ 01594 835127 & 01989 750468

**email:** woodlandsview@tiscali.co.uk

**Dir:** *From Coleford take B4228 towards Chepstow. Approx 0.5m pass Puzzle Wood on right. 0.5m site signed on left*

Open Mar-Oct Booking advisable BH & Jul-Aug Last arrival 22.00hrs Last departure noon

A small peaceful park in the Forest of Dean, next to the charming village of Clearwell. The friendly owners provide a warm welcome, and maintain the park to a good standard. The four fully-serviced pitches are ideal for large motorhomes. A 1.5-acre site with 26 touring pitches

**Facilities:**

**Services:** →

**Notes:** Extra charge for very large tents

## GLOUCESTER MAP 10 SO81

### ►►► 71% Red Lion Camping & Caravan Park *(SO849258)*

Wainlode Hill, Norton GL2 9LW

☎ 01452 730251 🖷 01452 730251

**web:** www.redlioninn-caravancampingpark.co.uk

**Dir:** *Turn off A38 at Norton and follow road to river*

Open all year Booking advisable Spring BH Last arrival 22.00hrs Last departure 11.00hrs

An attractive meadowland park, adjacent to a traditional pub, with the River Severn just across a country lane. This is an ideal touring and fishing base. A 13-acre site with 60 touring pitches, 10 hardstandings and 20 statics.

**Leisure:**

**Facilities:**

**Services:**

**Notes:** Freshwater fishing & private lake

## NEWENT MAP 10 SO72

### ►►► 78% Pelerine Caravan and Camping *(SO645183)*

Ford House Rd GL18 1LQ

☎ 01531 822761

**email:** pelerine@hotmail.com

**web:** www.newent.biz

**Dir:** *1m from Newent*

£14-£16 £14-£16 £12-£16

Open Mar-Nov Booking advisable Last arrival 22.00hrs Last departure 16.00hrs

A pleasant site divided into two areas, one of which is for adults only, with hardstandings and electric hook ups in each area. It is close to several vineyards, and well positioned in the north of the Forest of Dean with Tewkesbury and Cheltenham within easy reach. A 5-acre site with 35 touring pitches.

**Facilities:**

**Services:**

**Notes:** Wi-fi

## SLIMBRIDGE MAP 04 SO70

### ►►► 80% Tudor Caravan & Camping *(SO728040)*

Shepherds Patch GL2 7BP

☎ 01453 890483

**email:** aa@tudorcaravanpark.co.uk

**web:** www.tudorcaravanpark.com

**Dir:** *From M5 junct 13 follow signs for WWT Wetlands Wildlife Centre-Slimbridge. Site at rear of Tudor Arms pub*

★ £11-£17.50 £11-£17.50 £7-£17.50

Open all year Booking advisable BH & school hols Last arrival 20.00hrs Last departure noon

An orchard-style park sheltered by mature trees and shrubs, set in an attractive meadow beside a canal. This tidy site offers both level grass and gravel pitches complete with electric hook-ups, and there is a separate area for adults only. Slimbridge Wetlands Centre is close by, and there is much scope locally for bird-watching. An 8-acre site with 75 touring pitches, 48 hardstandings.

**Facilities:**

**Services:** **Notes:**

## WINCHCOMBE MAP 10 SP02

### ►►► 83% Winchcombe Camping & Caravanning Club Site *(SP007324)*

Brooklands Farm, Alderton GL20 8NX

☎ 01242 620259

**web:** www.campingandcaravanningclub.co.uk/winchcombe

**Dir:** *M5 junct 9 onto A46, straight on at rdbt onto B4077 signed Stow-on-the-Wold. Site 3m on right*

★ £18.25-£20.15 £18.25-£20.15 £18.25-£20.15

Open 16 Mar-15 Jan Booking advisable BH & peak periods Last arrival 21.00hrs Last departure noon

A pleasant rural park with pitches spaced around two attractive lakes offering good fishing, and the benefit of a long season. This flower-filled park is in an area of historic buildings and picturesque villages between Cheltenham and Tewkesbury. A 20-acre site with 80 touring pitches, 63 hardstandings.

**Leisure:** **Facilities:**

**Services:**

**Notes:** Site gates closed 23.00hrs-07.00hrs Fishing, pool table, table tennis

ENGLAND

# GREATER MANCHESTER

## LITTLEBOROUGH MAP 16 SD91

### ►►► 70% Hollingworth Lake Caravan Park

*(SD943146)*

Round House Farm, Rakewood Rd, Rakewood OL15 0AT

☎ 01706 378661 & 373919

**Dir:** *From Littleborough or Milnrow (M62 junct 21), follow 'Hollingworth Lake Country Park' signs to Fishermans Inn. Take 'No Through Road' to Rakewood, then 2nd on right*

★ £10-£14 £10-£14 £8-£14

Open all year Booking advisable Apr-Sep Last arrival 20.00hrs Last departure 14.00hrs

A popular park adjacent to Hollingworth Lake, at the foot of the Pennines, within easy reach of many local attractions. Backpackers walking the Pennine Way are welcome at this family-run park, and there are also large rally fields. A 5-acre site with 50 touring pitches, 25 hardstandings and 53 statics.

**Facilities:**

**Services:** →

**Notes:** Dogs must be kept on leads, family groups only. Pony trekking

## ROCHDALE MAP 16 SD81

### ►►► 74% Gelder Wood Country Park *(SD852127)*

DAVID BELLAMY CONSERVATION AWARD GOLD

Ashworth Rd OL11 5UP

☎ 01706 364858 & 620300 01706 364858

**email:** gelderwood@aol.com

**web:** www.ukparks.co.uk/gelderwood

**Dir:** *Signed midway from B6222 Bury/Rochdale road. Turn into Ashworth Road, continue past the mill. Uphill for 800yds, site on right*

★ fr £14 fr £14

Open Mar-Oct Booking advisable Etr Last departure 11.00hrs

A very rural site in a peaceful private country park with excellent facilities. All pitches have extensive views of the moor, and this is a popular base for walkers and birdwatchers. The park is for adults only, and children are not allowed to visit. A 10-acre site with 34 touring pitches.

**Facilities:**

**Services:** →

**Notes:** Adults only

# HAMPSHIRE

## BRANSGORE MAP 05 SZ19

### ►►► 80% Harrow Wood Farm Caravan Park *(SZ194978)*

Harrow Wood Farm, Poplar Ln BH23 8JE

☎ 01425 672487 01425 672487

**email:** harrowwood@caravan-sites.co.uk

**web:** www.caravan-sites.co.uk

**Dir:** *Exit village from S, take last turn on left. Site at end of lane*

Open Mar-6 Jan Booking advisable BH & school hols Last arrival 22.00hrs Last departure noon

A well laid out site in a pleasant rural position adjoining onto woodland and fields. Free on-site coarse fishing is available at this peaceful park. A 6-acre site with 60 touring pitches.

**Facilities:**

**Services:** →

**Notes:**

*see advert on opposite page*

## CRAWLEY MAP 05 SU43

### ►► 77% Folly Farm Touring Caravan Park

*(SU415337)*

Crawley SO21 2PH

☎ 01962 776486

**Dir:** *Midway between Winchester & Stockbridge on B3049. Site 0.75m past Rack & Manger pub*

fr £13 fr £13 fr £13

Open all year Booking advisable all year Last arrival 22.00hrs

A small farm site set in rural mid-Hampshire between Stockbridge and Winchester, ideal for visiting the ancient capital of Wessex or the New Forest, and the south coast is only a short drive away. The clean facilities are located in farm outbuildings, and there is a small campers' kitchen. A 2.5-acre site with 30 touring pitches.

**Leisure:**

**Facilities:**

**Services:** →

**Notes:** No children in farm area, dogs must be on leads. Local info & local produce available

## FORDINGBRIDGE MAP 05 SU11

### 88% **Sandy Balls Holiday Centre**

*(SU167148)*

Sandy Balls Estate Ltd, Godshill SP6 2JY
☎ 01425 653042 🖷 01425 653067
**email:** post@sandy-balls.co.uk
**web:** www.sandy-balls.co.uk

**Dir:** *M27 junct 1 onto B3078/B3079, W 8m to Godshill. Park 0.25m after cattle grid*

£22-£30 £22-£30 ▲ £22-£30

Open all year (rs Nov-Feb pitches reduced, no activities) Booking advisable BH & school hols & wknds Last arrival 21.00hrs Last departure 11.00hrs

A large, mostly wooded New Forest holiday complex with good provision of touring facilities on terraced, well laid-out fields. Pitches are fully serviced with shingle bases, and groups can be sited beside the river and away from the main site. Excellent sport, leisure and entertainment facilities for the whole family, and eight ready-erected tents for hire. A 120-acre site with 230 touring pitches, 230 hardstandings and 267 statics.

**Leisure:**

**Facilities:**

**Services:**

**Notes:** Groups by arrangement, no gazebos. Jacuzzi, sauna, gym, horse riding, bike hire, spa

*see advert on this page*

## FRITHAM

*see Landford (Wiltshire)*

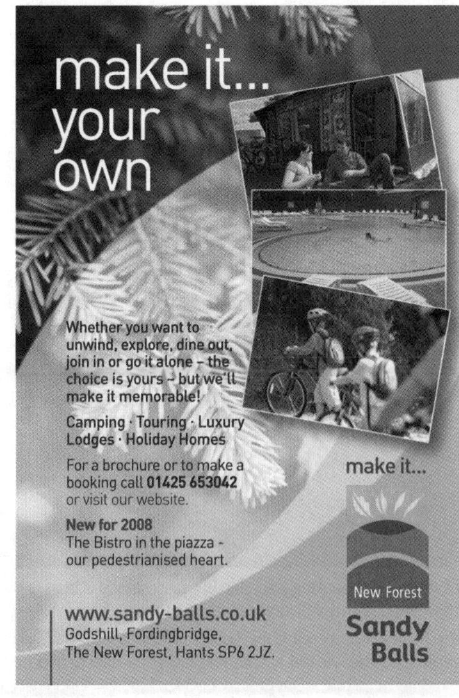

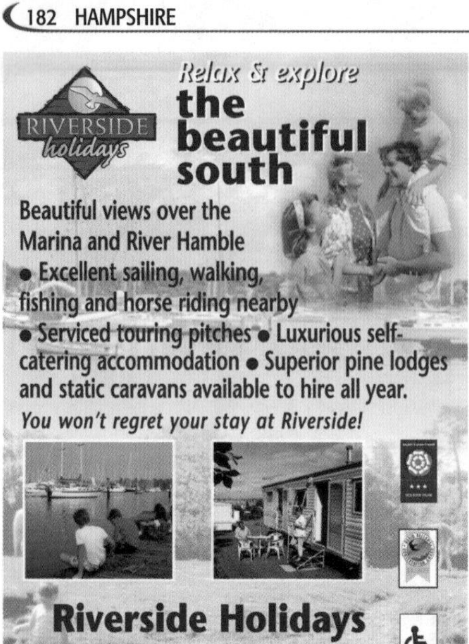

RIVERSIDE holidays
Relax & explore
the beautiful south
Beautiful views over the Marina and River Hamble
• Excellent sailing, walking, fishing and horse riding nearby
• Serviced touring pitches • Luxurious self-catering accommodation • Superior pine lodges and static caravans available to hire all year.
You won't regret your stay at Riverside!
Riverside Holidays
Satchell Lane, Hamble, Hampshire SO31 4HR
Please call: 02380 453220
for your free colour brochure or visit our website:
www.riversideholidays.co.uk
AA


## HAMBLE MAP 05 SU40

### ►►► 71% Riverside Holidays

BRONZE

*(SU481081)*
Satchell Ln SO31 4HR
☎ 023 8045 3220 🖹 023 8045 3611
**email:** enquiries@riversideholidays.co.uk
**web:** www.riversideholidays.co.uk
**Dir:** *M27 junct 8, follow signs to Hamble B3397. Turn left into Satchell Lane, 1m down lane on left*

★ £13.50-£29 £13.50-£29 £11.50-£24

Open Mar-Oct Booking advisable BH, peak season & boat show wk Last arrival 22.00hrs Last departure 11.00hrs

A small, peaceful park next to the marina, and close to the pretty village of Hamble. The park is neatly kept, though the toilet facilities are dated. A pub and restaurant are very close by. A 6-acre site with 77 touring pitches and 45 statics.

**Facilities:** **Services:**

**Notes:** Bike hire, baby changing facilities

*see advert on this page*

## LINWOOD MAP 05 SU10

### ►►► 79% Red Shoot Camping Park

*(SU187094)*
BH24 3QT
☎ 01425 473789 🖹 01425 471558
**email:** enquiries@redshoot-campingpark.com
**web:** www.redshoot-campingpark.com
**Dir:** *A31 onto A338 towards Fordingbridge & Salisbury. Right at brown signs for caravan park towards Linwood on unclassified roads, park signed*

★ £11.04-£16.80 £11.04-£16.80 £11.04-£16.80

Open Mar-Oct Booking advisable Last arrival 20.30hrs Last departure 13.00hrs

Sitting behind the Red Shoot Inn in one of the most attractive parts of the New Forest, this park is in an ideal spot for nature lovers, walkers and tourers. It is personally supervised by friendly owners, and offers many amenities including a children's play area. A 3.5-acre site with 130 touring pitches.

**Leisure:** **Facilities:**

**Services:**

**Notes:** Quiet after 22.30. Dogs must be kept on a lead Mountain bike hire

## MILFORD ON SEA MAP 05 SZ29

### ►►► 86% Lytton Lawn Touring Park *(SZ293937)*

BRONZE

Lymore Ln SO41 0TX
☎ 01590 648331 🖹 01590 645610
**email:** holidays@shorefield.co.uk
**web:** www.shorefield.co.uk
**Dir:** *From Lymington A337 to Christchurch for 2.5m to Everton. Left onto B3058 to Milford on Sea. After 0.25m left onto Lymore Lane*

★ £9.50-£31 £9.50-£31 £9.50-£28

Open Feb-2 Jan (rs Xmas/New Year no grass pitches available) Booking advisable at all times Last arrival 22.00hrs Last departure 10.00hrs

A pleasant well-run park with good facilities, located near the coast. The park is peaceful and quiet, but the facilities of a sister park 2.5 miles away are available to campers, including swimming pool, tennis courts, bistro and bar/carvery, and large club with family entertainment. Fully-serviced pitches provide good screening, and standard pitches are on gently-sloping grass. A 5-acre site with 136 touring pitches, 48 hardstandings.

**Leisure:** **Facilities:**

**Services:**

**Notes:** Family only park. Free use of Shorefield Leisure Club

*see advert on opposite page*

**Services:** Toilet Fluid · Café/ Restaurant · Fast Food/Takeaway · Baby Care · Electric Hook Up · Motorvan Service Point · Launderette · Licensed Bar · Calor Gas · Camping Gaz · Battery Charging

**Leisure:** Indoor swimming pool · Outdoor swimming pool · Tennis court · Games room · Children's playground · Stables · 9/18 hole golf course · Boats for hire · Cinema · Fishing · Mini golf · Watersports · Separate TV room

## OWER — MAP 05 SU31

### ►►► 79% **Green Pastures Farm** *(SU321158)*

SO51 6AJ

☎ 023 8081 4444

**email:** enquiries@greenpasturesfarm.com

**web:** www.greenpasturesfarm.com

**Dir:** *M27 junct 2. Follow Salisbury signs for 0.5m. Then follow brown tourist signs for Green Pastures. Also signed from A36 & A3090 at Ower*

★ £15 £15 £12-£20

Open 15 Mar-Oct Booking advisable BH & peak periods Last departure 11.00hrs

A pleasant site on a working farm, with good screening of trees and shrubs around the perimeter. The touring area is divided by a border of shrubs and, at times, colourful foxgloves. This peaceful location is close to the M27 and New Forest. A 5-acre site with 45 touring pitches, 2 hardstandings.

**Facilities:**

**Services:** →

**Notes:** Day kennels

## RINGWOOD

*see St Leonards (Dorset)*

## ROMSEY — MAP 05 SU32

### ►►►► 85% **Hill Farm Caravan Park** *(SU287238)*

Branches Ln, Sherfield English SO51 6FH

☎ 01794 340402 01794 342358

**email:** gjb@hillfarmpark.com

**web:** www.hillfarmpark.com

**Dir:** *Signed from A27 (Salisbury to Romsey road) in Sherfield English, 4m NW of Romsey & M27 junct 2*

★ £14-£26 £14-£26 £14-£26

Open Mar-Oct Booking advisable BH & school hols & wknds Last arrival 20.00hrs Last departure noon

A small, well-sheltered park peacefully located amidst mature trees and meadows. The two toilet blocks offer smart unisex showers as well as a fully en suite family/disabled room and plenty of privacy in the wash rooms. The owners are continuing to develop this attractive park, and with its proximity to Salisbury and the New Forest, it makes an appealing holiday location. A 10.5-acre site with 70 touring pitches, 16 hardstandings and 6 statics.

**Leisure:**

**Facilities:**

**Services:** →

**Notes:** Minimum noise at all times and no noise after 23.00hrs, one unit per pitch. Wi-fi. 9-hole pitch & putt, badminton

## WARSASH — MAP 05 SU40

### ►►► 79% **Dibles Park** *(SU505060)*

Dibles Rd SO31 9SA

☎ 01489 575232

**email:** diblespark@btconnect.com

**web:** www.diblespark.co.uk

**Dir:** *M27 junct 9, A27 signed Fareham. At St Margarets rdbt take 4th exit signed Warsash. 1st exit at next rdbt, after Tesco Express left onto Fleet End Rd. 2nd right into Dibles Road, park on right*

£12-£15 £12-£15

Open all year Booking advisable BH & Jul-Aug Last arrival 20.30hrs Last departure 11.00hrs

A small grassy touring area with hardstandings, adjacent to a private residential park. This site continues to improve, and there is always a warm welcome for visitors. Within easy reach of the River Hamble and the Solent. A 0.75-acre site with 14 touring pitches, 14 hardstandings and 46 statics.

**Facilities:**

**Services:** →

**Notes:** Tourist information office

# HEREFORDSHIRE

## HEREFORD MAP 10 SO53

### ► 68% Ridge Hill Caravan and Campsite

*(SO509355)*
HR1 1UN
☎ 01432 351293
**email:** ridgehill@fsmail.net
**web:** www.ridgehillcaravanandcampsite.co.uk
**Dir:** *From Hereford on A49, then B4399 signed Rotherwas. At 1st rdbt follow Dinedor/Little Dewchurch signs, in 1m signed Ridge Hill/Twyford, turn right, then right at phone box go 200yds, site on right.*

★ £6-£8 £6-£8 £5-£7

Open Mar-Oct Booking advisable Last departure noon

A simple, basic site set high on Ridge Hill 3 miles south of Hereford. This peaceful site offers outstanding views over the surrounding countryside. It does not have toilets or showers, and therefore own facilities are essential. A 1.5-acre site with 5 touring pitches.

**Services:**

**Notes:** Dogs must be kept on leads

## LITTLE TARRINGTON MAP 10 SO64

### ►►►► 81% *The Millpond*

*(SO625410)*
HR1 4JA
☎ 01432 890243 01432 890243
**email:** enquiries@millpond.co.uk
**web:** www.millpond.co.uk
**Dir:** *300yds off A438 on Ledbury side of Tarrington, entrance on right, 50yds before railway bridge*

Open Mar-Oct Booking advisable peak periods Last arrival 20.30hrs Last departure 11.00hrs

A spacious grassy park set beside a 3-acre coarse fishing lake in a peaceful location. Well-planted trees and shrubs help to divide and screen the park, and the modern toilet block provides good facilities. A 4.5-acre site with 55 touring pitches, 20 hardstandings.

**Facilities:**

**Services:**

**Notes:** Dogs must be kept on lead at all times

## PETERCHURCH MAP 09 SO33

**PREMIER PARK**

### ►►►►► 84% Poston Mill Caravan & Camping Park

*(SO355373)*
HR2 0SF
☎ 01981 550225 01981 550000
**email:** enquiries@poston-mill.co.uk
**web:** www.bestparks.co.uk
**Dir:** *11m SW of Hereford on B4348*

★ £14-£18 £14-£18 £14-£18

Open all year (rs Nov-Mar limited toilet facilities) Booking advisable BH & summer hols Last departure noon

Delightfully set in the Golden Valley and surrounded by hills, with beautiful views. This quality park has excellent facilities including sporting amenities which are to one side of the site. There is also an adjoining restaurant, The Mill, and a pleasant walk alongside the River Dore. A 33-acre site with 43 touring pitches, 33 hardstandings and 113 statics.

**Leisure:**

**Facilities:**

**Services:**

**Notes:** No gazebos, restricted use of scooters, bikes and skateboards. 9-hole pitch & putt

## STANFORD BISHOP MAP 10 SO65

### ►►► 79% Boyce Caravan Park *(SO692528)*

WR6 5UB
☎ 01886 884248 01886 884187
**email:** enquiries@boyceholidaypark.co.uk
**web:** www.boyceholidaypark.co.uk
**Dir:** *From B4220 (Malvern road) take sharp turn opposite Herefordshire House pub, then right after 0.25m. Signed Linley Green, then 1st drive on right*

£14 £14 £14

Open Feb-Dec Booking advisable BH, wknds & Jun-Aug Last arrival 18.00hrs Last departure noon

A friendly and peaceful park with access allowed onto the 100 acres of farmland. Coarse fishing is also available in the grounds, and there are extensive views over the Malvern and Suckley Hills. Many walks available. A 10-acre site with 15 touring pitches and 150 statics.

**Leisure:**

**Facilities:**

**Services:**

**Notes:** No dangerous dog breeds

### SYMONDS YAT (WEST) MAP 10 SO51

**►►► 79% Doward Park Camp Site** *(SO539167)*

Great Doward HR9 6BP

☎ 01600 890438

**email:** enquiries@dowardpark.co.uk

**web:** www.dowardpark.co.uk

**Dir:** *2m from A40 between Ross-on-Wye & Monmouth. Take Symonds Yat (West) turn, then Crockers Ash, follow signs to site*

Open Mar-Oct Booking advisable wknds, BH & Jul-Aug Last arrival 20.00hrs Last departure 11.30hrs

This delightful little park is set in peaceful woodlands on the hillside above the Wye Valley. It is ideal for campers and motor homes but not caravans due to the narrow approach roads. A warm welcome awaits and the facilities are kept spotless. A 1.5-acre site with 24 touring pitches.

**Leisure:**

**Facilities:**

**Services:**

**Notes:** No caravans or fires, quiet after 22.00hrs, dogs must be on leads

**►► 68% Symonds Yat Caravan & Camping Park** *(SO554174)*

HR9 6BY

☎ 01600 890883 & 891069

**email:** enquiries@campingandcaravan.com

**web:** www.campingandcaravan.com

**Dir:** *On A40 between Ross-on-Wye & Monmouth, take Symonds Yat (West) exit. Follow signs*

Open Mar-Oct Booking advisable BH & wknds Last departure noon

A popular little park next to the River Wye, with its own canoe hire and launching ramp. Some noise can be heard at times from the leisure park next door, but this park is well suited to young tenters who enjoy canoeing. A 1.25-acre site with 35 touring pitches, 10 hardstandings.

**Facilities:**

**Services:**

**Notes:** No cycling or ball games on site. Fishing on site (permits sold), canoe hire

## HERTFORDSHIRE

### HERTFORD MAP 06 TL31

**►►►► 77% Hertford Camping & Caravanning Club Site** *(TL334113)*

Mangrove Rd SG13 8QF

☎ 01992 586696

**web:** www.campingandcaravanningclub.co.uk/hertford

**Dir:** *From A10 follow A414/Hertford signs to next rdbt (Foxholes), straight over. In 200yds left signed Balls Park & Hertford University. Left at T-junct into Mangrove Road. Site on left*

★ £18.25-£20.15 £18.25-£20.15 £18.25-£20.15

Open all year Booking advisable BHs & peak periods Last arrival 21.00hrs Last departure noon

A spacious, well-landscaped club site in a rural setting one mile south of Hertford, with immaculate modern toilet facilities. There are several hedged areas with good provision of hardstandings, and a cosy camping section in an old orchard. All kinds of wildlife flourish around the lake. A 32-acre site with 250 touring pitches, 54 hardstandings.

**Leisure:**

**Facilities:**

**Services:**

**Notes:** Site gates closed 23.00hrs-07.00hrs

### WALTHAM CROSS MAP 06 TL30

**►► 70% Theobalds Park Camping & Caravanning Club Site** *(TL344005)*

Theobalds Park, Bulls Cross Ride EN7 5HS

☎ 01992 620604

**web:** www.campingandcaravanningclub.co.uk/theobaldspark

**Dir:** *M25 junct 25. A10 towards London keep in right lane. Right at 1st lights. Right at T-junct, right behind dog kennels. Site towards top of lane on right*

★ £12.75-£16.75 £12.75-£16.75 £12.75-£16.75

Open 13 Mar-3 Nov Booking advisable BH & peak periods Last arrival 21.00hrs Last departure noon

A lovely open site surrounded by mature trees, and set in parkland at Theobalds Hall. The portacabin toilet facilities are freshly painted and extremely clean, and there are two separate glades for tents. A 14-acre site with 90 touring pitches.

**Leisure:**

**Facilities:**

**Services:**

**Notes:** Site gates closed 23.00hrs-07.00hrs

## KENT

### ASHFORD MAP 07 TR04

**►►►► 86% Broad Hembury Caravan & Camping Park** *(TR009387)*

The Best of British Touring and Holiday Parks

Steeds Ln, Kingsnorth TN26 1NQ

☎ 01233 620859 🖷 01233 620918

**email:** holidaypark@broadhembury.co.uk

**web:** www.broadhembury.co.uk

**Dir:** *From M20 junct 10 take A2070. Left at 2nd rdbt signed Kingsnorth, then left at 2nd x-roads in village*

Open all year Booking advisable BH & Jul-Aug Last arrival 23.00hrs Last departure noon

Well-run and maintained small family park surrounded by open pasture and neatly landscaped, with pitches sheltered by mature hedges. Some super pitches have proved a popular addition, and there is a well-equipped campers' kitchen. A 10-acre site with 60 touring pitches, 24 hardstandings and 25 statics.

**Leisure:**

**Facilities:**

**Services:**

**Notes:** Sports field

### BIDDENDEN MAP 07 TQ83

**►►► 66% Woodlands Park** *(TQ867372)*

Tenterden Rd TN27 8BT

☎ 01580 291216 🖷 01580 291216

**email:** woodlandsp@aol.com **web:** www.campingsite.co.uk

**Dir:** *From A28 onto A262. Site 1.5m on right*

★ £12-£16.50 £12-£16.50 £5-£16.50

Open Mar-Oct (rs Mar-Apr weather permitting) Booking advisable BH & Jul-Aug

A site of level grassland bordered by hedges and trees, with two ponds and a smart and well-maintained modern toilet block. Ideal centre for Kent, Sussex and Channel ports. A 9-acre site with 200 touring pitches and 205 statics.

**Facilities:** **Services:**

**Notes:** Camping accessory sales & small site shop

ENGLAND

## BIRCHINGTON — MAP 07 TR36

### ►►► 77% Quex Caravan Park *(TR321685)*

Park Rd CT7 0BL
☎ 01843 841273
**email:** info@keatfarm.co.uk
**web:** www.keatfarm.co.uk
**Dir:** *From Birchington (A28) turn SE into Park Road to site in 1m*

Open Mar-Nov Booking advisable BH Last arrival anytime Last departure noon

A small parkland site in a quiet and secluded woodland glade, with a very clean toilet block housed in a log cabin. This picturesque site is just one mile from the village of Birchington, while Ramsgate, Margate and Broadstairs are all within easy reach. An 11-acre site with 48 touring pitches and 145 statics.

**Leisure:**
**Facilities:**
**Services:** →

*see advert on this page*

### ►►► 79% Two Chimneys Caravan Park

*(TR320684)*
Shottendane Rd CT7 0HD
☎ 01843 841068 & 843157 01843 848099
**email:** info@twochimneys.co.uk
**web:** www.twochimneys.co.uk
**Dir:** *From A28 to Birchington Sq, right into Park Lane (B2048). Left at Manston Road (B2050) then 1st left*

★ £13-£27 £13-£27 £13-£25

Open Mar-Oct (rs Mar-May & Sep-Oct shop, bar, pool & takeaway restricted) Booking advisable BH & school hols Last arrival 22.00hrs Last departure noon

An impressive entrance leads into this well-managed site, which boasts two swimming pools and a fully-licensed clubhouse. Other attractions include a tennis court and children's play area, and the immaculately clean toilet facilities fully meet the needs of this busy family park. A 30-acre site with 200 touring pitches, 5 hardstandings and 200 statics.

**Leisure:**
**Facilities:**
**Services:** →
**Notes:** Amusement arcade

## CANTERBURY — MAP 07 TR15

### ►►► 85% Canterbury Camping & Caravanning Club Site *(TR172577)*

Bekesbourne Ln CT3 4AB
☎ 01227 463216
**web:** www.campingandcaravanningclub.co.uk/canterbury
**Dir:** *From Canterbury follow A257 signs (Sandwich), turn right opposite golf course*

★ £15.45-£20.15 £15.45-£20.15 £15.45-£20.15

Open all year Booking advisable BH & peak periods Last arrival 21.00hrs Last departure noon

An attractive tree-screened site in pleasant rural surroundings yet within walking distance of the city centre. The park is well landscaped, and offers very smart toilet facilities in one block, with another older but well-kept building housing further facilities. A 20-acre site with 200 touring pitches, 21 hardstandings.

**Leisure:**
**Facilities:**
**Services:** →

ENGLAND

►► 78% **Ashfield Farm** *(TR138508)*
Waddenhall, Petham CT4 5PX
☎ 01227 700624
**email:** mpatterson@ashfieldfarm.freeserve.co.uk
**Dir:** *7m S of Canterbury on B2068*
★ £11-£14 £11-£14 £11-£14
Open Apr-Oct Booking advisable Jul & Aug Last arrival anytime Last departure noon
Small rural site with simple facilities and well-drained pitches, set in beautiful countryside and enjoying lovely open views. Located south of Canterbury, and with very security-conscious owners. A 4.5-acre site with 30 touring pitches and 1 static.
**Facilities:**
**Services:**
**Notes:** Mini golf, short term kennelling

## DOVER MAP 07 TR34

►►►► 74% **Hawthorn Farm Caravan Park** *(TR342464)*
Station Rd, Martin Mill CT15 5LA
☎ 01304 852658 & 852914 01304 853417
**email:** info@keatfarm.co.uk
**web:** www.keatfarm.co.uk
**Dir:** *Signed from A258*

Open Mar-Nov (rs winter water turned off if weather cold) Booking advisable BH & Jul-Aug Last arrival anytime Last departure noon
This pleasant rural park set in 28 acres of beautifully-landscaped gardens is screened by young trees and hedgerows, in grounds which include woods and a rose garden. The decent facilities include a shop and laundry. A 28-acre site with 147 touring pitches, 5 hardstandings and 176 statics.
**Facilities:**
**Services:**
*see advert on opposite page*

## EASTCHURCH MAP 07 TQ97

74% ***Warden Springs Caravan Park*** *(TR019722)*
Warden Point ME12 4HF
☎ 01795 880216 01795 880218
Panoramic views from the scenic clifftop setting can be enjoyed at their best from the touring area of this holiday park. All of the many and varied leisure activities provided by the park are included in the pitch tariff, including a heated outdoor swimming pool, an adventure playground and family entertainment. There's a good choice of food outlets. 48 touring pitches and 198 statics.

## FOLKESTONE MAP 07 TR23

►►► 83% **Folkestone Camping & Caravanning Club Site** *(TR246376)*
The Warren CT19 6NQ
☎ 01303 255093
**web:** www.campingandcaravanningclub.co.uk/folkestone
**Dir:** *From A2 or A20 onto A260, left at island into Folkstone. Continue straight over x-rds into Wear Bay Road, 2nd left past Martello Tower, site 0.5m on right*
★ £15.45-£22.15 £15.45-£22.15
Open 13 Mar-3 Nov Booking advisable BH & peak periods Last arrival 21.00hrs Last departure noon
This site commands marvellous views across the Strait of Dover, and is well located for the Channel ports. It nestles on the side of the cliff, and is tiered in some areas. The toilet facilities are modern and tasteful, with cubicled wash basins in both blocks. No caravans accepted. A 4-acre site with 80 touring pitches, 9 hardstandings.
**Facilities:**
**Services:**
**Notes:** Site gates closed 23.00hrs-07.00hrs

►►► 80% **Little Satmar Holiday Park** *(TR260390)*
Winehouse Ln, Capel Le Ferne CT18 7JF
☎ 01303 251188 01303 251188
**email:** info@keatfarm.co.uk
**web:** www.keatfarm.co.uk
**Dir:** *Signed off B2011*
Open Mar-Nov Booking advisable BH & Jul-Aug Last arrival 23.00hrs Last departure 14.00hrs
A quiet, well-screened site well away from the road and statics, with clean and tidy facilities. A useful base for visiting Dover and Folkestone, and just a short walk from cliff paths with their views of the Channel, and sandy beaches below. A 5-acre site with 60 touring pitches and 80 statics.
**Leisure:** **Facilities:**
**Services:**
*see advert on opposite page*

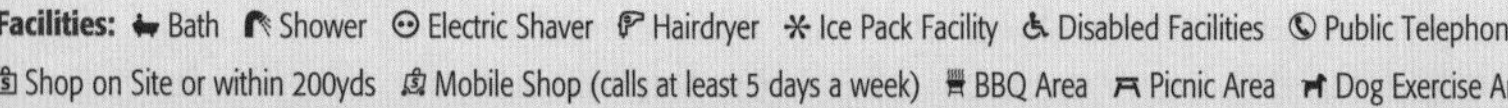

ENGLAND

## FOLKESTONE CONTINUED

### ►► 74% Little Switzerland Camping & Caravan Site *(TR248380)*

Wear Bay Rd CT19 6PS

☎ 01303 252168

**email:** btony328@aol.com

**web:** www.caravancampingsites.co.uk/kent/littleswitzerland.htm

**Dir:** *Signed from A20 E of Folkestone. Approaching from A259 or B2011 on E outskirts of Folkestone follow signs for Wear Bay/Martello Tower, then tourist sign to site, follow signs to country park*

★ £10-£18 £10-£18 £3.50-£7

Open Mar-Oct Booking advisable at all times Last arrival mdnt Last departure noon

Set on a narrow plateau below the white cliffs, this unusual site enjoys fine views across Wear Bay and the Strait of Dover. The licensed café with an alfresco area is popular; the basic toilet facilities are unsuitable for the disabled. A 3-acre site with 32 touring pitches and 13 statics.

**Facilities:**

**Services:**

**Notes:** No open fires

## LEYSDOWN-ON-SEA MAP 07 TR07

### ►►► 71% Priory Hill *(TR038704)*

Wing Rd ME12 4QT

☎ 01795 510267 01795 511503

**email:** info@prioryhill.co.uk

**web:** www.prioryhill.co.uk

**Dir:** *Take A249 signed to Sheerness then B2231 to Leysdown, follow brown tourist signs.*

£13-£25 £13-£25 £13-£25

Open Mar-Oct (rs low season shorter opening times for pool & club) Booking advisable BH, wknds & Jul-Aug Last arrival 20.00hrs Last departure noon

A small well-maintained touring area on an established family-run holiday park close to the sea, with views of the north Kent coast. Amenities include a clubhouse and a swimming pool. The pitch price includes membership of clubhouse with live entertainment, and use of indoor swimming pool. A 1.5-acre site with 40 touring pitches.

**Leisure:**

**Facilities:**

**Services:** →

## SANDWICH MAP 07 TR35

### ►►►► 81% *Sandwich Leisure Park* *(TR326581)*

SILVER

Woodnesborough Rd CT13 0AA

☎ 01304 612681 01304 615252

**email:** info@sandwichleisurepark.co.uk

**web:** www.sandwichleisurepark.co.uk

**Dir:** *From Sandwich town centre, then follow brown tourist signs*

Open Mar-Oct Booking advisable Etr, Spring BH & Jul-Aug Last arrival 20.00hrs Last departure 11.00hrs

A large site with impressive toilet facilities, including a suite of family rooms, and 18 fully-serviced pitches. Visitors can choose between pitches with hook-ups or those in a separate field with a more natural ambience. The park backs onto open farmland on the edge of Sandwich, and is well planted with mature and newer trees. A 15-acre site with 187 touring pitches, 34 hardstandings and 103 statics.

**Leisure:**

**Facilities:**

**Services:** →

**Notes:** No unaccompanied minors, no commercial vehicles

## SEVENOAKS MAP 06 TQ55

### ►►► 72% Oldbury Hill Camping & Caravanning Club Site *(TQ577564)*

Styants Bottom, Seal TN15 0ET

☎ 01732 762728

**web:** www.campingandcaravanningclub.co.uk/oldburyhill

**Dir:** *Take A25 from Sevenoaks towards Borough Green. Left just after Crown Point Inn, on right, down narrow lane to Styants Bottom. Site on left*

★ £14.05-£18.85 £14.05-£18.85 £14.05-£18.85

Open 13 Mar-3 Nov Booking advisable BH & peak periods Last arrival 21.00hrs Last departure noon

A remarkably tranquil site in the centre of National Trust woodland, with buildings blending well into the surroundings. Expect the usual high standard of customer care found at all Club sites. A 6-acre site with 60 touring pitches.

**Leisure:**

**Facilities:**

**Services:** →

**Notes:** Site gates closed 23.00hrs-07.00hrs

ENGLAND

## ST NICHOLAS AT WADE — MAP 07 TR26

### 72% St Nicholas Camping Site *(TR254672)*

Court Rd CT7 0NH

01843 847245

**Dir:** *Signed off A299 and A28, at W end of village near church*

★ £12-£15 £11-£14 £9-£13

Open Etr-Oct Booking advisable Jul-Aug Last arrival 22.00hrs Last departure 14.00hrs

A gently-sloping field with mature hedging, on the edge of the village close to the shop. This rustic site offers simple facilities, and is conveniently located close to primary routes. A 3-acre site with 75 touring pitches.

**Leisure:**

**Facilities:**

**Services:**

**Notes:** No music after 22.30hrs

## WHITSTABLE — MAP 07 TR16

### 82% Homing Park

SILVER

*(TR095645)*

Church Ln, Seasalter CT5 4BU

01227 771777 01227 273512

**email:** info@homingpark.co.uk

**web:** www.homingpark.co.uk

**Dir:** *Exit A299 for Whitstable & Canterbury, left at brown camping/caravan sign into Church Lane. Park entrance has 2 large flag poles*

£9.50-£20 £9.50-£20 £9.50-£20

Open Mar-Oct Booking advisable Etr, BH & Aug Last arrival 20.00hrs Last departure 11.00hrs

A small touring park close to Seasalter Beach and Whitstable, which is famous for its oysters. All pitches are generously sized and fully serviced, and most are separated by hedging and shrubs. A clubhouse and swimming pool are available on the adjacent residential park at a small cost. A 12.75-acre site with 43 touring pitches and 195 statics.

**Leisure:**

**Facilities:**

**Services:**

**Notes:** No commercial vehicles, no tents greater than 8 berth, no unaccompanied minors. Fitness centre

### 75% Seaview Holiday Village

SILVER

*(TR145675)*

St John's Rd CT5 2RY

01227 792246 01227 792247

**email:** info@parkholidaysuk.com

**web:** www.parkholidaysuk.com

**Dir:** *From A299 take A2990 then B2205 to Swalecliffe, site between Herne Bay & Whitstable*

Open Mar-Oct Booking advisable all times Last arrival 21.30hrs Last departure noon

A pleasant open site on the edge of Whitstable, set well away from the static area, with a smart, modern toilet block and both super and hardstanding pitches. A 12-acre site with 171 touring pitches, 41 hardstandings and 452 statics.

**Leisure:**

**Facilities:**

**Services:**

**Notes:** Amusements in games room & adventure trail

*see advert on page 187*

## WROTHAM HEATH — MAP 06 TQ65

### 76% Gate House Wood Touring Park

*(TQ635585)*

Ford Ln TN15 7SD

01732 843062

**email:** gatehousewood@btinternet.com

**web:** www.gatehousewoodtouringpark.co.uk

**Dir:** *From M26 junct 2a take A20 S towards Maidstone, through lights at Wrotham Heath. 1st left signed Trottiscliffe, left at next junct into Ford Lane. Park 100yds on left*

★ £11-£14.50 £11-£14.50 £6.50-£14.50

Open Mar-Oct Booking advisable BH Last arrival 22.00hrs Last departure noon

A well-sheltered and mature site in a former quarry surrounded by tall deciduous trees and gorse banks. The well-designed facilities include reception, shop and smart toilets, and there is good entrance security. A 3.5-acre site with 55 touring pitches.

**Leisure:**

**Facilities:**

**Services:**

**Notes:** No commercial vehicles. No pets

ENGLAND

# LANCASHIRE

*see also sites under Greater Manchester & Merseyside*

## BLACKPOOL MAP 18 SD33

*see also Lytham St Annes & Thornton*

### 75% Marton Mere Holiday Village *(SD347349)*

GOLD

Mythop Rd FY4 4XN

☎ 01253 767544 01253 791544

**web:** www.havenholidays.com

**Dir:** *M55 junct 4, A583 towards Blackpool. Right at Clifton Arms lights, onto Mythop Road. Park 150yds on left*

★ £12-£70 £12-£70

Open mid Mar-Oct Booking advisable school hols Last departure 10.00hrs

A very attractive holiday centre in an unusual setting on the edge of the mere, with plenty of birdlife to be spotted. The on-site entertainment is directed at all ages, and includes a superb show bar. There's a regular bus service into Blackpool for those who want to explore further afield. The separate touring area is well equipped with hardstandings and electric pitches, and there are good quality facilities. A 30-acre site with 197 touring pitches, 197 hardstandings and 218 statics.

**Leisure:**

**Facilities:**

**Services:** →

**Notes:** No more than 2 dogs per group, no adult only groups

## BOLTON-LE-SANDS MAP 18 SD46

### ►►► 83% Sandside Caravan & Camping Park *(SD472681)*

The Shore LA5 8JS

☎ 01524 822311 01524 822311

**web:** www.sandside.co.uk

**Dir:** *M6 junct 35 follow A6 through Carnforth, turn right after far Pavillion in Bolton-le-Sands, and over level crossing to site*

Open Mar-Oct Booking advisable BH & Jul-Aug Last arrival 20.00hrs Last departure 13.00hrs

A well-kept park located in a pleasant spot overlooking Morecambe Bay, with distant views of the Lake District. The site is next to a busy main West Coast railway line with a level crossing. A shop and reception are an asset to this welcoming park. A 9-acre site with 70 touring pitches, 42 hardstandings and 33 statics.

**Facilities:**

**Services:** →

**Notes:**

### ►► 76% Detron Gate Farm *(SD478683)*

LA5 9TN

☎ 01524 733617

**Dir:** *W of A6, 1m N of Bolton-le-Sands*

Open Mar-Oct (rs Mar-May shop hours restricted) Booking advisable BH Last arrival 22.00hrs Last departure 18.00hrs

A rural grassy site with lovely views out over Morecambe Bay to the Lakeland hills, on slightly sloping ground close to a small farm. An attractive barn houses the shop, paperback library and table tennis. A 10-acre site with 100 touring pitches and 42 statics.

**Leisure:**

**Facilities:**

**Services:** →

**Notes:**

### ►► 72% Red Bank Farm *(SD472681)*

LA5 8JR

☎ 01524 823196 01524 824981

**email:** archer_mark@lycos.co.uk

**web:** www.redbankfarm.co.uk

**Dir:** *Take A5105 (Morecambe road), after 200mtrs right on Shore Lane. At rail bridge, turn right to site*

Open Mar-Oct Booking advisable BH

A gently sloping grassy field with mature hedges, close to the sea shore and a RSPB reserve. This farm site has superb views across Morecambe Bay to the distant Lake District hills, and is popular with tenters. The basic toilet facilities are clean and bright. A 3-acre site with 60 touring pitches.

**Facilities:**

**Services:** →

**Notes:** Dogs must be kept on leads. Pets' corner

## CAPERNWRAY MAP 18 SD57

### ►►► 92% Old Hall Caravan Park *(SD533716)*

SILVER

LA6 1AD

☎ 01524 733276 01524 734488

**email:** info@oldhallcaravanpark.co.uk

**web:** www.oldhallcaravanpark.co.uk

**Dir:** *M6 junct 35 follow signs to Over Kellet, left onto B6254, left at village green signed Capernwray. Site 1.5m on right*

★ £16.50-£18.50 £16.50-£18.50

Open Mar-Oct Booking advisable BH, wknds & Jul-Aug

A lovely secluded park set in a clearing amongst trees at the end of a half-mile long drive. This peaceful park is home to a wide variety of wildlife, and there are marked walks in the woods. Facilities are well maintained by friendly owners. A 3-acre site with 38 touring pitches, 38 hardstandings and 220 statics.

**Leisure:** **Facilities:**

**Services:** →

ENGLAND

## CLITHEROE MAP 18 SD74

### ►►► 77% Clitheroe Camping & Caravanning Club Site (SD727413)

Edisford Rd BB7 3LA

☎ 01200 425294

**web:** www.campingandcaravanningclub.co.uk/clitheroe

**Dir:** *From W follow A671 to Clitheroe. Follow sign for left turn to Longridge/Sports Centre. Into Greenacre Rd approx 25mtrs after pelican crossing. To T-junct. (Sports Centre on right). Site 50mtrs on left*

★ £15.45-£20.15 £15.45-£20.15 Å £15.45-£20.15

Open Mar-Oct Booking advisable BH & peak periods Last arrival 21.00hrs Last departure noon

Set on the banks of the River Ribble, this park is attractively landscaped with mature trees and shrubs. An ideal spot for walking and fishing, and the site is also adjacent to a park with a café, pitch and putt, leisure centre, swimming pool and miniature steam railway. The Ribble Country Way is nearby. A 6-acre site with 80 touring pitches, 30 hardstandings.

**Facilities:**

**Services:** → 

## COCKERHAM MAP 18 SD45

### ►►►► 80% *Mosswood Caravan Park* (SD456497)

GOLD

Crimbles Ln LA2 0ES

☎ 01524 791041 01524 792444

**email:** info@mosswood.co.uk

**web:** www.mosswood.co.uk

**Dir:** *Approx 4m from A6/M6 junct 33, 1m W of Cockerham on A588*

Å

Open Mar-Oct Booking advisable BH & Jul-Sep Last arrival 20.00hrs Last departure 16.00hrs

A tree-lined grassy park with sheltered, level pitches, located on peaceful Cockerham Moss. The modern toilet block is attractively clad in stained wood, and the facilities include cubicled washing facilities and a launderette. A 25-acre site with 25 touring pitches, 25 hardstandings and 143 statics.

**Leisure:**

**Facilities:**

**Services:** → 

**Notes:** Woodland walks

## CROSTON MAP 18 SO51

### ►►► 78% *Royal Umpire Caravan Park* (SD504190)

Southport Rd PR26 9JB

☎ 01772 600257 01772 600662

**web:** www.royalumpire.co.uk

**Dir:** *From Chorley take A581, 3.5m towards Croston, park on right*

A pleasant level site set in open countryside, with an attractive sunken garden and seating area. Plenty of leisure opportunities include an interesting children's playground, and a large playing field. The toilets, laundry and dishwashing area are of a very good quality. A restaurant and a pub are within walking distance.

**Leisure:**

**Facilities:**

**Services:** → 

**Notes:** Assault course, five-a-side football pitch

*see advert on this page*

ENGLAND

GARSTANG MAP 18 SD44

**►►►► 80% Claylands Caravan Park**

*(SD496485)*

Cabus PR3 1AJ

☎ 01524 791242 📠 01524 792406

**email:** alan@claylands.com

**web:** www.claylands.com

**Dir:** *From M6 junct 33 S to Garstang, approx 6m pass Little Chef, signed off A6 into private road on Lancaster side of Garstang*

★ £9-£11 £9-£11 £9-£11

Open Mar-4 Jan (rs Jan & Feb holiday park only) Booking advisable BH & Jul-Aug Last arrival 23.00hrs Last departure 14.00hrs

A well-maintained site with lovely river and woodland walks and good views over the River Wyre towards the village of Scorton. This friendly park is set in delightful countryside. Guests can enjoy fishing, and the atmosphere is very relaxed. The quality facilities and amenities are of a high standard, and everything is immaculately maintained. A 14-acre site with 30 touring pitches, 30 hardstandings and 68 statics.

**Leisure:**

**Facilities:**

**Services:** →

**Notes:** Pets must be kept on leads, no roller blades or skateboards

**►►► 74% Bridge House Marina & Caravan Park** *(SD483457)*

Nateby Crossing Ln, Nateby PR3 0JJ

☎ 01995 603207 📠 01995 601612

**email:** edwin@bridgehousemarina.co.uk

**web:** www.bridgehousemarina.co.uk

**Dir:** *Off A6 at pub and sign for Knott End, immediately right into Nateby Crossing Lane, over canal bridge to site on left*

Open Mar-4 Jan Booking advisable BH Last arrival 22.00hrs Last departure 13.00hrs

A well-maintained site in attractive countryside by the Lancaster Canal, with good views towards the Trough of Bowland. The boatyard atmosphere is interesting, and there is a super children's playground. A 4-acre site with 50 touring pitches, 45 hardstandings and 20 statics.

**Leisure:**

**Facilities:**

**Services:** →

GISBURN MAP 18 SD84

**►►► 82% Rimington Caravan Park**

*(SD825469)*

Hardacre Ln, Rimington BB7 4EE

☎ 01200 445355

**email:** rimingtoncaravanpark@btinternet.com

**web:** www.rimingtoncaravanpark.co.uk

**Dir:** *Off A682 1m S of Gisburn, site on right in 1m*

★ £16 £16

Open Mar-Oct (rs Mar hardstanding available only) Booking advisable BH & Jul-3 Sep Last arrival 18.00hrs Last departure noon

A very well-cared for park set in an attractive rural valley close to the Pendle Hills. The high quality facilities are kept very clean, and the family owners pay a great deal of attention to customer needs. An 11-acre site with 4 touring pitches, 4 hardstandings and 150 statics.

**Facilities:**

**Services:** →

**Notes:** Adults only No cars by caravans

HEYSHAM MAP 18 SD46

**74% Ocean Edge Leisure Park** *(SD407591)*

Moneyclose Ln LA3 2XA

☎ 01524 855657 📠 01524 855884

**email:** enquiries@southlakelandparks.co.uk

**web:** www.southlakelandparks.co.uk

**Dir:** *From M6 junct 34 follow A683 to Heysham. In Heysham site signed before ferry port*

Open mid Feb-Jan Booking advisable BH & school hols Last arrival 22.00hrs Last departure 10.00hrs

An open touring area of a large holiday complex adjacent to the sea, and with good sea views. Facilities include a large bar and café, and nightly entertainment including bingo, quizzes, cabaret and singsongs. A 10-acre site with 94 touring pitches and 600 statics.

**Leisure:**

**Facilities:**

**Services:** →

LANCASTER MAP 18 SD46

**►► 86% New Parkside Farm Caravan Park**

*(SD507633)*

Denny Beck, Caton Rd LA2 9HH

☎ 01524 770723

**web:** www.ukparks.co.uk/newparkside

**Dir:** *M6 junct 34, take A683 towards Caton/Kirkby Lonsdale. Park 1m on right*

Open Mar-Oct Booking advisable BH & Jul-Aug Last arrival 20.00hrs Last departure 16.00hrs

Peaceful, friendly grassy park on a working farm with extensive views of Lune Valley and Ingleborough. A 3-acre site with 40 touring pitches and 10 statics.

**Facilities:**

**Services:** →

**Notes:** Dogs must be kept on leads. Dishwashing sink

ENGLAND

## LYTHAM ST ANNES MAP 18 SD32

### ►►► 73% *Eastham Hall Caravan Site* *(SD379291)*

SILVER

Saltcotes Rd FY8 4LS

01253 737907 01253 732559

**email:** info@easthamhall.co.uk

**web:** www.easthamhall.co.uk

**Dir:** *Leave M55 junct 3. Straight over 3 rdbts onto B5259. Through Wrea Green & Moss Side, park 1m after level crossing*

Open Mar-Oct Booking advisable BH, Jul-Aug & Oct Last arrival 21.00hrs Last departure noon

Secluded park with trees and hedgerows in a rural setting. The helpful owners ensure that facilities are maintained to a high standard. A 15-acre site with 200 touring pitches, 30 hardstandings and 200 statics.

**Leisure:**

**Facilities:**

**Services:**

**Notes:** No tents, breathable groundsheets only in awnings

## MIDDLETON (NEAR MORECAMBE) MAP 18 SD45

### ►►► 66% **Melbreak Caravan Park** *(SD415584)*

Carr Ln LA3 3LH

01524 852430

**Dir:** *M6 junct 34 onto A683. After 6m turn left at rdbt, pass Middleton & turn right into village. Site in 0.5m*

Open Mar-Oct Booking advisable Jul-Aug Last arrival 22.00hrs Last departure noon

A small rural park run by friendly owners, in open countryside south of Morecambe. It offers simple but clean facilities and ample hardstands. Good access to historic Sunderland Point, Heysham Port for Isle of Man ferries, and the seaside attractions of Morecambe. A 2-acre site with 10 touring pitches and 32 statics.

**Facilities:**

**Services:**

**Notes:**

## MORECAMBE MAP 18 SD46

### ►►► 69% *Riverside Caravan Park* *(SD448615)*

Lancaster Rd, Snatchems LA3 3ER

01524 844193

**email:** info@riverside-morecambe.co.uk

**web:** www.riverside-morecambe.co.uk

**Dir:** *On unclass road off B5273 near Heaton*

Open Mar-Oct Booking advisable public hols & high season Last arrival 20.00hrs Last departure noon

A grassy site with views over the River Lune and Morecambe Bay. The sanitary facilities in a modern toilet block are clean and fresh. Road access is subject to tidal river flooding, and it is advisable to check tide times before crossing. A 7-acre site with 50 touring pitches and 52 statics.

**Leisure:**

**Facilities:**

**Services:**

### ►►► 76% **Venture Caravan Park** *(SD436633)*

Langridge Way, Westgate LA4 4TQ

01524 412986 01524 422029

**email:** mark@venturecaravanpark.co.uk

**web:** www.venturecaravanpark.co.uk

**Dir:** *From M6 junct 34 follow Morecambe signs. At rdbt take road towards Westgate & follow park signs. 1st right after fire station*

Open all year (rs 6 Jan-22 Feb touring vans only, one toilet block open) Booking advisable BH & peak periods Last arrival 22.00hrs Last departure noon

A large park with good modern facilities, including a small indoor heated pool, a licensed clubhouse and a family room with children's entertainment. The site has many statics, and is close to the town centre. A 17.5-acre site with 56 touring pitches, 40 hardstandings and 304 statics.

**Leisure:**

**Facilities:**

**Services:**

**Notes:** Amusement arcade, off licence

ENGLAND

## ORMSKIRK MAP 15 SD40

### ►►►► 78% Abbey Farm Caravan Park

(SD434098)
Dark Ln L40 5TX
☎ 01695 572686 📠 01695 572686
**email:** abbeyfarm@yahoo.com
**web:** www.abbeyfarmcaravanpark.co.uk
**Dir:** *M6 junct 27 onto A5209 to Burscough. 4m left onto B5240. Immediate right into Hobcross Ln. Park 1.5m on right*

★ £14.20-£17.30 £14.20-£17.30 ▲ £10.50-£16.60

Open all year Booking advisable BH & Jul-Aug Last arrival 21.00hrs Last departure 13.00hrs

Delightful hanging baskets and flower beds brighten this garden-like rural park which is sheltered by hedging and mature trees. Modern, very clean facilities include a family bathroom, and there are special pitches for the disabled near the toilets. A superb recreation field caters for children of all ages, and there is an indoor games room, large library, fishing lake and dog walk. Tents have their own area with BBQ and picnic tables. A 6-acre site with 56 touring pitches and 44 statics.

**Leisure:**
**Facilities:**
**Services:** → 
**Notes:** Off-licence, farm walk

### ►►► 77% Shaw Hall Caravan Park

(SD397119)
Smithy Ln, Scarisbrick L40 8HJ
☎ 01704 840298 📠 01704 840539
**email:** shawhall@btconnect.com
**web:** www.shawhall.co.uk
**Dir:** *200yds S of canal bridge at Scarisbrick, 0.25m off A570 at Smithy Lane*

★ £21-£24 £21-£24

Open Mar-7 Jan Booking advisable BH & peak periods Last arrival 20.30hrs

A large, pleasant park with 20 super pitches and good toilets. The clubhouse and bar offer cabaret and discos which are popular with families. The park also boasts canal walks from its direct access to the Leeds-Liverpool Canal, a football field, and putting and bowling greens. A 26-acre site with 37 touring pitches, 37 hardstandings and 300 statics.

**Leisure:**
**Facilities:**
**Services:** → 
**Notes:** Fishing

## SILVERDALE MAP 18 SD47

PREMIER PARK

### ►►►►► 95% Holgate's Caravan Park (SD455762)

DAVID BELLAMY CONSERVATION AWARD GOLD

Middlebarrow Plain, Cove Rd LA5 0SH
☎ 01524 701508 📠 01524 701580
**email:** caravan@holgates.co.uk
**web:** www.holgates.co.uk
**Dir:** *M6 junct 35. 5m NW of Carnforth. From Carnforth centre take unclass Silverdale road & follow tourist signs after Warton*

★ £32.50 £32.50 ▲ £29.50

Open 22 Dec-6 Nov Booking advisable school hols, BH & wknds Last arrival 22.00hrs Last departure noon

A superb family holiday park set in wooded countryside next to the sea. This park demonstrates high quality in all areas, and offers a wide range of leisure amenities. Its relaxing position overlooking Morecambe Bay combined with the excellent touring facilities mark this park out as special. A 10-acre site with 70 touring pitches, 70 hardstandings and 339 statics.

**Leisure:**
**Facilities:**
**Services:** → 
**Notes:** No unaccompanied children. Sauna, spa bath, steam room, mini-golf, gym

## THORNTON MAP 18 SD34

### ►►►► 79% Kneps Farm Holiday Park

*(SD353429)*

River Rd, Stanah FY5 5LR

☎ 01253 823632 01253 863967

**email:** enquiries@knepsfarm.co.uk

**web:** www.knepsfarm.co.uk

**Dir:** *Leave A585 at rdbt onto B5412 to Little Thornton. Right at mini-rdbt after school onto Stanah Rd, over 2nd mini-rdbt, leading to River Road*

★ £16-£17.50 £16-£17.50 £13-£17.50

Open Mar-mid Nov Booking advisable at all times Last arrival 20.00hrs Last departure noon

A quality park adjacent to the River Wyre and the Wyre Estuary Country Park, handily placed for the attractions of Blackpool and the Fylde coast. This family-run park offers an excellent toilet block with immaculate facilities, and a mixture of hard and grass pitches. The park is quietly located, but there is some noise from a nearby plastics plant. A 10-acre site with 60 touring pitches, 40 hardstandings and 68 statics.

**Leisure:**

**Facilities:**

**Services:**

**Notes:** Max 2 dogs per group, dogs must be kept on leads and a charge is made. No commercial vehicles

## WEETON MAP 18 SD33

### ►► 82% Little Orchard Caravan Park

*(SD399355)*

Shorrocks Barn, Back Ln PR4 3HN

☎ 01253 836658

**web:** www.littleorchardcaravanpark.com

**Dir:** *M55 junct 3 onto A585 signed Fleetwood. Left in 0.5m at Blue Anchor pub into Greenhalgh Lane, right at T-junct in 0.75m, site 1st left.*

£14-£15 £14-£15

Open 14 Feb-1 Jan Booking advisable Last arrival 20.00hrs Last departure 13.00hrs

Set in a quiet rural location in an orchard, this attractive park welcomes the mature visitor. The new toilet facilities are to a very high standard. Two excellent fisheries are within easy walking distance. A 4-acre site with 30 touring pitches, 30 hardstandings.

**Facilities:**

**Services:**

**Notes:** No ball games & skateboards

# LEICESTERSHIRE

*See also Wolvey, Warwickshire*

## BURBAGE MAP 11 SP49

### ►► 72% *Crossways Farm Caravan Site*

*(SP450912)*

Lutterworth Rd LE10 3AH

☎ 01455 239261

**email:** user@burbage60.fsnet.co.uk

**web:** www.crossways-holidays.com

**Dir:** *M69 junct 1 onto A5 towards Lutterworth, 1m, onto B578 to Burbage. Site 0.75m up hill on right*

Open Mar-Oct Booking advisable at all times Last arrival 22.00hrs

A small rural site with modern unisex toilet facilities and excellent security. Pubs and shops will be found in the nearby village, and there are many opportunities for walking across farmland, fishing, golf and tennis. A 1-acre site with 36 touring pitches, 3 hardstandings and 2 statics.

**Facilities:**

**Services:**

**Notes:** Dogs must be kept on leads, charge of £1 per night per dog

ENGLAND

## CASTLE DONINGTON MAP 11 SK42

### ►►► 71% Donington Park Farmhouse Hotel *(SK414254)*

Melbourne Rd, Isley Walton DE74 2RN
☎ 01332 862409 01332 862364
**email:** info@parkfarmhouse.co.uk
**web:** www.parkfarmhouse.co.uk
**Dir:** *M1 junct 24, pass airport to Isley Walton, right towards Melbourne. Park 0.5m on right*

★ £18-£25 £21-£28 £12-£20

Open Jan-23 Dec (rs winter months hardstanding only) Booking advisable summer Last arrival 21.00hrs Last departure noon

A secluded touring site at the rear of a hotel beside Donington Park motor racing circuit, which is very popular on race days when booking is essential. Both daytime and night flights from nearby East Midlands Airport may cause disturbance. A 7-acre site with 60 touring pitches, 10 hardstandings.

**Leisure:**

**Facilities:**

**Services:**

**Notes:** Dogs must be kept on leads. Bread & milk sold, hotel on site for bar/dining

## ULLESTHORPE MAP 11 SP58

### ► 72% *Ullesthorpe Garden Centre*

*(SP515872)*
Lutterworth Rd LE17 5DR
☎ 01455 202144 01455 202585
**email:** enquiries@ullesthorpegardencentre.co.uk
**web:** www.ullesthorpegardencentre.co.uk
**Dir:** *From M1 junct 20 take A4303 through Lutterworth, then B577 for 2m. Site just SE of Ullesthorpe*

Open Mar-Oct Booking advisable at all times Last arrival 18.00hrs Last departure sunset

A pleasant site next to the garden centre, ideal for the self-contained caravanner, with nature walk and fishing on site. A 7-acre site with 150 touring pitches.

**Facilities:**

**Services:**

**Notes:** Tents only allowed with a caravan

# LINCOLNSHIRE

## ANCASTER MAP 11 SK94

### ►►► 76% Woodland Waters *(SK979435)*

Willoughby Rd NG32 3RT
☎ 01400 230888 01400 230888
**email:** info@woodlandwaters.co.uk
**web:** www.woodlandwaters.co.uk
**Dir:** *On A153 W of x-roads with B6403*

★ £14.50-£16 £14.50-£16 £12-£16

Open all year Booking advisable BH Last arrival 21.00hrs Last departure noon

Peacefully set around five impressive fishing lakes, with a few log cabins in a separate area, a pleasant open park. The access road is through mature woodland, and there is a very good heated toilet block, and a pub/club house with restaurant. A 5-acre site with 62 touring pitches.

**Leisure:**

**Facilities:**

**Services:**

**Notes:** Dogs must be kept on leads at all times

## BOSTON MAP 12 TF34

### ►►►► 77% *Orchard Park*

*(TF274432)*
Frampton Ln, Hubbert's Bridge PE20 3QU
☎ 01205 290328 01205 290247
**web:** www.orchardpark.co.uk
**Dir:** *On B1192, between A52 (Boston-Grantham) & A1121 (Boston-Sleaford)*

GOLD

Open Mar-Nov Booking advisable BH Last arrival 22.30hrs Last departure 11.00hrs

Ideally located for exploring the unique fenlands, this rapidly-improving park has two lakes - one for fishing and the other set aside for conservation. A very attractive restaurant and bar are popular with visitors. A 36-acre site with 87 touring pitches, 3 hardstandings and 164 statics.

**Leisure:**

**Facilities:**

**Services:**

**Notes:** Adults only

ENGLAND

## CLEETHORPES MAP 17 TA30

### 75% Thorpe Park Holiday Centre *(TA321035)*

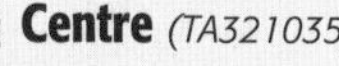

DN35 0PW

01472 813395 01472 812146

**web:** www.thorpepark.park.co.uk

**Dir:** *Take unclass road off A180 at Cleethorpes, signed Humberstone & Holiday Park*

★ £10-£74 £10-£74 £10-£52

Open mid Mar-Oct (rs mid Mar-May & Sep-Oct some facilities may be reduced) Booking advisable BH & school hols Last arrival anytime Last departure 10.00hrs

A large static site with touring facilities, including fully-serviced pitches, adjacent to the beach. This holiday centre offers excellent recreational and leisure activities, including an indoor pool with bar, bowling greens, crazy golf, tennis courts, and a games area. Parts of the site overlook the sea. A 300-acre site with 110 touring pitches, 64 hardstandings and 281 statics.

**Leisure:**

**Facilities:**

**Services:**

**Notes:** Max 2 dogs per group. Pitch and putt, roller ring, fishing lakes

*see advert on this page*

## MABLETHORPE MAP 17 TF58

### 73% Golden Sands Holiday Park *(TF501861)*

GOLD

Quebec Rd LN12 1QJ

01507 477871 01507 472066

**web:** www.goldensands-park.co.uk

**Dir:** *From centre of Mablethorpe turn left on seafront road towards north end. Park on left*

★ £6-£49 £6-£49 £6-£33

Open mid Mar-Oct Booking advisable school hols Last arrival 22.00hrs Last departure 10.00hrs

A large, well-equipped seaside holiday park with separate touring facilities on two sites, including fully modernised toilets. The first floor entertainment rooms are only accessible via stairs (no lifts). A 23-acre site with 195 touring pitches and 1300 statics.

**Leisure:**

**Facilities:**

**Services:**

**Notes:** Maximum of 2 dogs per group. Mini bowling alley, snooker/pool, indoor fun palace.



### ►►► 77% Kirkstead Holiday Park

*(TF509835)*

North Rd, Trusthorpe LN12 2QD

01507 441483

**email:** mark@kirkstead.co.uk

**web:** www.kirkstead.co.uk

**Dir:** *From Mablethorpe town centre take A52 S towards Sutton-on-Sea. 1m turn sharp right by phone box into North Rd. Site signed in 300yds*

★ £14-£18.50 £14-£18.50 £10-£18

Open Mar-Nov Booking advisable BH & Jul-Aug Last arrival 22.00hrs Last departure 17.00hrs

Controlled entry is a welcome security feature of this pleasant family-run site. The touring area and good quality toilets are centrally located, and the grounds are particularly well maintained. A 10-acre site with 80 touring pitches and 75 statics.

**Leisure:**

**Facilities:**

**Services:**

**Notes:** No pets. Snooker, volleyball, football pitch, basketball

ENGLAND

## MABLETHORPE CONTINUED

### ►►► 75% Mablethorpe Camping & Caravanning Club Site *(TF499839)*

Highfield, 120 Church Ln LN12 2NU
☎ 01507 472374
**web:** www.campingandcaravanningclub.co.uk/mablethorpe
**Dir:** *On outskirts of Mablethorpe, on A1104, just after the 'Welcome to Mablethorpe' sign turn right into Church Lane. 800yds to end of lane. Site on right*

★ £14.05-£18.85 £14.05-£18.85 £14.05-£18.85

Open Mar-Oct Booking advisable BH & peak periods Last arrival 21.00hrs Last departure noon

Located next to flat agricultural land one mile from the sea, and well away from the road. The camping area is in two hedged fields with rural views, and the modern toilet facilities and laundry are centrally sited. A 6-acre site with 105 touring pitches, 1 hardstanding.

**Leisure:**

**Facilities:**

**Services:** →

**Notes:** Site gates closed 23.00hrs-07.00hrs

## OLD LEAKE MAP 17 TF45

### ►►► 71% White Cat Caravan & Camping Park *(TF415498)*

Shaw Ln PE22 9LQ
☎ 01205 870121 01205 870121
**email:** kevin@klannen.freeserve.co.uk
**web:** www.whitecatpark.com
**Dir:** *Just off A52, 7m NE of Boston, opposite B1184*

★ £11-£15 £11-£15 £11-£15

Open Apr-Oct Booking advisable BH Last arrival 20.00hrs Last departure noon

A pleasant, well-maintained small touring park set down a rural lane just off the A52, surrounded by the tranquillity of the Fenlands. It makes a peaceful base for exploring Boston and the Lincolnshire coast. A 2.5-acre site with 30 touring pitches, 4 hardstandings and 10 statics.

**Leisure:**

**Facilities:**

**Services:** →

**Notes:**

## ORBY MAP 17 TF46

### ►►► 85% Heron's Mead Fishing Lake & Touring Park *(TF508673)*

Marsh Ln PE24 5JA
☎ 01754 811340
**email:** mail@heronsmeadtouringpark.co.uk
**web:** www.heronsmeadtouringpark.co.uk
**Dir:** *From A158 Lincoln to Skegness road turn left at rdbt, through Orby for 0.5m*

£14.50-£17.50 £14.50-£17.50 fr £14.50

Open Mar-1 Nov Booking advisable BH & school hols Last arrival 21.00hrs Last departure noon

A pleasant fishing and touring park with coarse fishing and an 8-acre woodland walk. The owners have made many improvements to the facilities, which are particularly appealing to quiet couples and elderly visitors. A 16-acre site with 30 touring pitches, 30 hardstandings.

**Facilities:**

**Services:** →

**Notes:** No cars by caravans or tents. No ball games, no motorbikes. 2 disabled pegs for fishing, carp lake

## SALTFLEET MAP 17 TF49

### NEW 78% Sunnydale *(TF455941)*

BRONZE

Sea Ln LN11 7RP
☎ 0871 664 9776
**email:** sunnydale@park-resorts.com
**web:** www.park-resorts.com
**Dir:** *From A16 towards Louth take B1200 through Manby & Saltfleetby. Left into Saltfleet. Sea Lane on right. Site in approx 400mtrs*

£5-£24 £5-£24

Open 31 Mar-Oct Booking advisable

Set in a peaceful and tranquil location in the village of Saltfleet between the seaside resorts of Cleethorpes and Mablethorpe. This park offers modern leisure facilities including an indoor pool, the bar with entertainment, amusements and a coarse fishing pond. There is also direct access to the huge Saltfleet beach. The touring facilities are incorporated into the leisure complex, and are modern and well cared for. 38 touring pitches and 260 statics.

**Leisure:** **Facilities:**

**Services:** →

## SALTFLEETBY ST PETER MAP 17 TF48

### ►►► 80% **Saltfleetby Fisheries** *(TF425892)*

Main Rd LN11 7SS
☎ 01507 338272
**email:** saltfleetbyfish@btinternet.com
**web:** www.saltfleetbyfisheries.co.uk
**Dir:** *On B1200, 6m E of junct with A16; 3m W of A103*
★ £10-£12 £10-£12 £10-£12

Open Mar-Nov Booking advisable BH Last arrival 18.00hrs Last departure noon

A pretty little site beside three well-stocked fishing lakes by the owner's house. An excellent toilet block offers quality facilities, and there are electric hook ups and spacious hardstandings. A 12-acre site with 18 touring pitches, 12 hardstandings and 1 static.

**Facilities:**
**Services:** → 
**Notes:** Adults only

## SUTTON ST JAMES MAP 12 TF31

### ►►► 80% **Foremans Bridge Caravan Park** *(TF409197)*

GOLD

Sutton Rd PE12 0HU
☎ 01945 440346
**email:** foremansbridge@btconnect.com
**web:** www.foremans-bridge.co.uk
**Dir:** *2m from A17 on B1390*
£14 £14 £10-£14

Open Mar-Jan Booking advisable BH Last arrival 21.00hrs Last departure 10.00hrs

A small site set beside the South Holland Main Drain which flows past, and offers good fishing. This quiet park is mainly used by adults. A 2.5-acre site with 40 touring pitches, 22 hardstandings and 15 statics.

**Facilities:**
**Services:** → 
**Notes:** No cycling or ball games, dogs must be kept on a lead. Cycle hire centre, fishing

## WADDINGHAM MAP 17 SK99

### ►►► 73% **Brandy Wharf Leisure Park** *(TF014968)*

Brandy Wharf DN21 4RT
☎ 01673 818010 01673 818010
**email:** brandywharflp@freenetname.co.uk
**web:** www.brandywharfleisurepark.co.uk
**Dir:** *From A15 onto B1205 through Waddingham. Site 3m from Waddingham*
fr £12.50 fr £12.50 fr £11

Open Etr-Oct Booking advisable Etr-Sep Last arrival dusk Last departure 17.00hrs

A delightfully refurbished site in a very rural area on the banks of the River Ancholme, where fishing is available. The unisex facilities offer combined toilet, washbasin and shower, and there is a new laundry. All of the grassy pitches have electricity, and there's a playing/picnic area. The site attracts a lively clientele at weekends, and music is allowed until 1am. Advance booking is necessary for weekend pitches. A 5-acre site with 30 touring pitches.

**Leisure:** **Facilities:**
**Services:** → 
**Notes:** No disposable BBQs on grass, no music after 01.00hrs. Fishing/boat mooring, canoe hire, pets' corner

## WOODHALL SPA MAP 17 TF16

### ►►► 79% **Woodhall Spa Camping & Caravanning Club Site** *(TF225633)*

Wellsyke Ln, Kirkby-on-Bain LN10 6YU
☎ 01526 352911
**web:** www.campingandcaravanningclub.co.uk/woodhallspa
**Dir:** *From Sleaford or Horncastle take A153 to Haltham. At garage turn onto side road. Over bridge, left towards Kirkby-on-Bain. 1st turn right, signed.*
★ £15.45-£20.15 £15.45-£20.15 £15.45-£20.15

Open 13 Mar-3 Oct Booking advisable BH & peak periods Last arrival 21.00hrs Last departure noon

A pleasant site in silver birch wood and moorland, with pitches laid out around a central lake (no fishing). Facilities include a family room, and a unisex room with en suite facilities. A 6-acre site with 90 touring pitches.

**Facilities:**
**Services:** → 
**Notes:** Site gates closed 23.00hrs-07.00hrs

ENGLAND

# LONDON

## E4 CHINGFORD MAP 06 TQ39

### ►►► 81% Lee Valley Campsite *(TQ381970)*

Sewardstone Rd E4 7RA

☎ 020 8529 5689 🖷 020 8559 4070

**email:** scs@leevalleypark.org.uk

**Dir:** *M25 junct 26, A112. Site signed*

★ £12.90 £12.90 ▲ £12.90

Open Apr-Oct Booking advisable BH & Jul-Aug Last arrival 21.00hrs Last departure noon

Overlooking King George's Reservoir and close to Epping Forest, this park has excellent modern facilities and a very peaceful atmosphere. A bus calls at the site hourly to take passengers to the nearest tube station, and Enfield is easily accessible. This impressive park is maintained to a high standard. A 12-acre site with 100 touring pitches, 20 hardstandings and 43 statics.

**Leisure:**

**Facilities:**

**Services:**

**Notes:** Under 18s must be accompanied by an adult

## N9 EDMONTON MAP 06 TQ39

### ►►► 84% Lee Valley Camping & Caravan Park *(TQ360945)*

Meridian Way N9 0AS

☎ 020 8803 6900 🖷 020 8884 4975

**email:** leisurecomplex@leevalleypark.org.uk

**Dir:** *From M25 junct 25, A10 S, 1st left on A1055, approx 5m to Leisure Centre. From A406 (North Circular), N on A1010, left after 0.25m, right (Pickets Lock Lane)*

★ £12.80-£15.50 £12.80-£15.50 ▲ £12.80-£15.50

Open all year Booking advisable Jul-Aug Last arrival 21.00hrs Last departure noon

A pleasant, open site within easy reach of London yet peacefully located close to two large reservoirs. The very good toilet facilities are beautifully kept by dedicated wardens, and the site has the advantage of being adjacent to a restaurant and bar, and a multi-screen cinema. A 4.5-acre site with 160 touring pitches, 41 hardstandings.

**Leisure:**

**Facilities:**

**Services:**

**Notes:** No commercial vehicles. Kitchen, cinema

# MERSEYSIDE

## SOUTHPORT MAP 15 SD31

### 82% Riverside Holiday Park *(SD405192)*

BRONZE

Southport New Rd PR9 8DF

☎ 01704 228886 🖷 01704 505886

**web:** www.riversideleisurecentre.co.uk

**Dir:** *M6 junct 27, A5209 towards Parbold/Burscough, right onto A59. Left onto A565 at lights in Tarleton. Continue to dual carriageway. At rdbt straight across, park 1m on left*

★ £13-£18 £13-£18 ▲ £12-£25

Open Mar-6 Jan Booking advisable BH & school hols Last arrival 17.00hrs Last departure 11.00hrs

A large, spacious park with a lively family entertainment complex for cabaret, dancing and theme nights. Children have their own club and entertainer with food and games. A superb health and leisure centre next door is available at an extra charge. An 100-acre site with 260 touring pitches, 130 hardstandings and 355 statics.

**Leisure:**

**Facilities:**

**Services:**

**Notes:** Dogs must be kept on leads, one car per pitch

*see advert on opposite page*

### ►►► 76% Hurlston Hall Country Caravan Park *(SD398107)*

Southport Rd L40 8HB

☎ 01704 841064 🖷 01704 841700

**Dir:** *On A570, 3m from Ormskirk towards Southport*

★ £12.50-£15 £12.50-£15

Open Etr-Oct Booking advisable BH Last arrival 21.00hrs Last departure 17.00hrs

A peaceful tree-lined touring park next to a static site in attractive countryside about 10 minutes' drive from Southport. The park is maturing well, with growing trees and a coarse fishing lake. No dogs permitted. A 5-acre site with 60 touring pitches and 68 statics.

**Leisure:**

**Facilities:**

**Services:**

**Notes:** No tents. Coarse fishing, golf facilities

### ►►► 83% Willowbank Holiday Home Touring Park *(SD305110)*

GOLD

Coastal Rd, Ainsdale PR8 3ST
☎ 01704 571566 📠 01704 571576
**email:** info@willowbankcp.co.uk
**web:** www.willowbankcp.co.uk
**Dir:** *From A565, between Formby and Ainsdale, turn at the Woodvale lights onto coastal road, site 150mtrs on left*

Open Mar-10 Jan Booking advisable BH & special events Last arrival 21.00hrs Last departure noon

Set in a wooded clearing on a nature reserve next to the beautiful sand dunes, this attractive park is just off the coastal road to Southport. The immaculate toilet facilities are well equipped. A 6-acre site with 54 touring pitches, 30 hardstandings and 228 statics.

**Leisure:** **Facilities:**
**Services:**
**Notes:** Baby changing facility

## NORFOLK

**BARNEY** **MAP 13 TF93**

### ►►►► 91% The Old Brick Kilns *(TG007328)*

GOLD

Little Barney Ln NR21 0NL
☎ 01328 878305 📠 01328 878948
**email:** enquiries@old-brick-kilns.co.uk
**web:** www.old-brick-kilns.co.uk
**Dir:** *From A148 (Fakenham-Cromer) follow brown tourist signs to Barney, then left into Little Barney Lane. Site at end of lane*

Open Mar-6 Jan (rs low season bar food/takeaway selected nights only) Booking advisable BH & Jul-Aug Last arrival 22.00hrs Last departure noon

A secluded and peaceful park approached via a quiet leafy country lane. The park is on two levels with its own boating and fishing pool and many mature trees. Excellent, well-planned toilet facilities can be found in two blocks, and there is a short dog walk. Due to a narrow access road there can be no arrivals before 1pm. A 12.75-acre site with 65 touring pitches, 65 hardstandings.

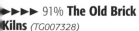

**Leisure:**
**Facilities:**
**Services:**
**Notes:** Outdoor draughts, chess, family games

ENGLAND



## BELTON MAP 13 TG40

### 67% Wild Duck Holiday Park (*TG475028*)

GOLD

Howards Common NR31 9NE

☎ 01493 780268 01493 782308

**web:** www.wildduck-park.co.uk

**Dir:** *From A47 towards Gt Yarmouth take A143 towards Beccles. Turn right at Burgh Castle, right at T-junct, left at next T-junct, park 200mtrs on right*

★ £9-£60 £9-£60 £9-£44

Open mid Mar-Oct (rs mid Mar-May & Sep-Oct some facilities may be reduced) Booking advisable school hols Last arrival 22.30hrs Last departure 10.00hrs

This a large holiday complex with plenty to do for all ages both indoors and out. This level grassy site is set in a forest with small cleared areas for tourers and well laid out facilities. Clubs for children and teenagers, sporting activities and evening shows all add to the fun of a stay here. A 97-acre site with 130 touring pitches and 365 statics.

**Leisure:**

**Facilities:**

**Services:** →

*see advert on page 208*

### ►►►► 87% Rose Farm Touring & Camping Park (*TG488033*)

Stepshort NR31 9JS

☎ 01493 780896 01493 780896

**web:** www.rosefarmtouringpark.co.uk

**Dir:** *Follow signs to Belton off A143, right at lane signed Stepshort, site 1st on right*

Open all year Booking advisable Jul-Aug

A former railway line is the setting for this very peaceful site which enjoys rural views and is beautifully presented throughout. The ever-improving toilet facilities are spotlessly clean and inviting to use, and the park is brightened with many flower and herb beds. Customer care is truly exceptional. A 10-acre site with 80 touring pitches, 15 hardstandings.

**Leisure:** **Facilities:**

**Services:** →

**Notes:**

## BURGH CASTLE MAP 13 TG40

### NEW 77% Breydon Water (*TG479042*)

Butt Ln NR31 9QB

☎ 0871 664 9710

**email:** breydon.water@park-resorts.com

**web:** www.park-resorts.com

**Dir:** *From Gt Yarmouth on A12 towards Lowestoft over 2 rdbts. Follow Burgh Castle sign. Right at lights signed Diss & Beccles. 1.5m, right signed Burgh Castle & Belton. At mini rdbt right onto Stepshort. Site on right*

£5-£28 £5-£28 £3-£25

Open 31 Mar-Oct Booking advisable

This large park has two village areas just a short walk apart. Choose Yare village for family fun and superb entertainment, and Bure village for a quieter base. Although the villages are separated, guests are more than welcome to use facilities at both. Both villages have touring areas with modern, well maintained toilets, and tents are welcome. They are just a short drive from the bright lights of Yarmouth and the unique Norfolk Broads. 176 touring pitches and 327 statics.

**Leisure:**

**Facilities:**

**Services:** →

*see advert on this page*

ENGLAND

## CLIPPESBY MAP 13 TG41

### PREMIER PARK

**►►►►► 82% Clippesby Hall**

(TG423147)
Clippesby Hall NR29 3BL
☎ 01493 367800 📠 01493 367809
**email:** holidays@clippesby.com
**web:** www.clippesby.com
**Dir:** *From A47 follow tourist signs for The Broads. At Acle rdbt take A1064, after 2m left onto B1152, 0.5m turn left opposite village sign, 400yds on right*

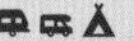

Open end Mar-end Oct (rs Etr-23 May no swimming/tennis. Pub/café BH wknds) Booking advisable school hols Last arrival 17.30hrs Last departure 11.00hrs

A lovely country house estate with secluded pitches hidden among the trees or in sheltered sunny glades. The toilet facilities are appointed to a very good standard, providing a wide choice of cubicle. Amenities include a café, clubhouse and family crazy-golf. A 30-acre site with 120 touring pitches, 9 hardstandings.

**Leisure:**
**Facilities:**
**Services:**
**Notes:** Dogs must be kept on leads. Bicycle hire & mini golf

*see advert on this page*

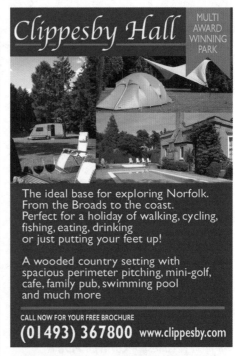

## CROMER MAP 13 TG24

**►►► 73% Forest Park** (TG233405)

Northrepps Rd NR27 0JR
☎ 01263 513290 📠 01263 511992
**email:** info@forest-park.co.uk
**web:** www.forest-park.co.uk
**Dir:** *A140 from Norwich, left at T-junct signed Cromer, right signed Northrepps, right then immediate left, left at T-junct, site on right*

Open 15 Mar-15 Jan Booking advisable Etr, Spring BH & Jul-Aug Last arrival 21.00hrs Last departure 11.00hrs

*Forest Park*

Surrounded by forest, this gently sloping park offers a wide choice of pitches. Visitors have the use of a heated indoor swimming pool, and a large clubhouse with entertainment. A 100-acre site with 344 touring pitches and 372 statics.

**Leisure:**
**Facilities:**
**Services:**
**Notes:** Wi-fi, BMX track, hair salon

ENGLAND

## CROMER CONTINUED

### ►►► 73% Manor Farm Caravan & Campsite (TG198416)

East Runton NR27 9PR
☎ 01263 512858
**email:** manor-farm@ukf.net
**web:** www.manorfarmcaravansite.co.uk
**Dir:** *1m W of Cromer, turn off A148 or A149 at Manor Farm sign*

Open Etr-Sep Booking advisable BH & all season for EHU points Last arrival 20.30hrs Last departure noon

A well-established family-run site on a working farm enjoying panoramic sea views. There are good modern facilities across the site, which is elevated above Cromer. A 17-acre site with 250 touring pitches.

**Leisure:**

**Facilities:**

**Services:**

**Notes:** 2 dog-free fields

## DISS

*see Scole*

## DOWNHAM MARKET MAP 12 TF60

### ►►► 82% *Lakeside Caravan Park & Fisheries* (TF608013)

Sluice Rd, Denver PE38 0DZ
☎ 01366 387074 & 07770 663237 🖷 01366 387074
**email:** richesflorido@aol.com
**web:** www.west-hall-farm-holidays.co.uk
**Dir:** *Off A10 towards Denver, follow signs to Denver Windmill*

Open all year (rs Oct-Mar) Booking advisable Last arrival 22.00hrs Last departure noon

A peaceful, rapidly improving park set around four pretty fishing lakes. Several grassy touring areas are sheltered by mature hedging and trees. There is a function room, shop and laundry. A 10-acre site with 100 touring pitches and 1 static.

**Leisure:**

**Facilities:**

**Services:**

**Notes:** Dogs must be kept on leads. Pool table

## FAKENHAM MAP 13 TF92

### ►►► 77% Caravan Club M.V.C. Site (TF926288)

Fakenham Racecourse NR21 7NY
☎ 01328 862388 🖷 01328 855908
**email:** caravan@fakenhamracecourse.co.uk
**web:** www.fakenhamracecourse.co.uk
**Dir:** *Towards Fakenham follow brown signs for 'racecourse' with tent & caravan symbols, directly to site entrance*

Open all year (rs race days) Booking advisable Jun-Sep Last arrival 21.00hrs Last departure noon

A very well laid out site set around the racecourse, with a grandstand offering smart modern toilet facilities. Tourers move to the centre of the course on race days, and enjoy free racing, and there's a wide range of sporting activities in the club house. An 11.5-acre site with 120 touring pitches, 25 hardstandings.

**Facilities:**

**Services:**

**Notes:** TV aerial hook-ups

### ►► 70% Crossways Caravan & Camping Park (TF961321)

Crossways, Holt Rd, Little Snoring NR21 0AX
☎ 01328 878335
**email:** hollands@mannasolutions.com
**web:** www.crosswayscaravan.co.uk
**Dir:** *From Fakenham take A148 towards Cromer. After 3m pass exit for Little Snoring. Site on A148 on left behind Post Office*

★ £4.50-£10 £4.50-£10 £4.50-£10

Open all year Booking advisable high season, BH & school hols Last arrival 22.00hrs Last departure noon

Set on the edge of the peaceful hamlet of Little Snoring, this level site enjoys views across the fields towards the North Norfolk coast some seven miles away. Visitors can use the health suite for a small charge, and there is a shop on site, and a good village pub. A 2-acre site with 26 touring pitches, 10 hardstandings and 1 static.

**Facilities:**

**Services:**

**Notes:** Dogs must be kept on leads. Health suite, sauna, sunbed, hot spa bath

### ►► 81% *Fakenham Camp Site* (TF907310)

Burnham Market Rd, Sculthorpe NR21 9SA
☎ 01328 856614
**email:** desmondfrench@btconnect.com
**Dir:** *Just off A148 (King's Lynn road), 0.75m from Fakenham*

Open all year Booking advisable Last arrival 22.00hrs Last departure 11.00hrs

A peaceful site surrounded by tranquil countryside, part of a 9-hole golf complex and driving range. The toilet facilities are of a good quality, and there is a golf shop and licensed bar. A 1.75-acre site with 32 touring pitches.

**Facilities:**

**Services:**

**Notes:** Adults only. Par 3 golf course & driving range

## GREAT HOCKHAM MAP 13 TL99

### NEW ►►► 75% Thetford Forest Camping & Caravanning Club Site *(TL941926)*

Puddledock Farm IP24 1PA

☎ 01953 498455

**web:** www.campingandcaravanningclub.co.uk/thetfordforest

**Dir:** *Off A1075 between Norwich & Cambridge*

★ £18.15-£20.15 £18.15-£20.15 £18.15-£20.15

Open all year Booking advisable BH & peak periods Last arrival 21.00hrs Last departure noon

This expansive site on the edge of Thetford Forest occupies a central location in East Anglia, providing a multitude of touring options. The 88 pitches are generously proportioned and well sheltered. There is a small fishing lake on site. 60 touring pitches, 60 hardstandings.

**Leisure:** **Facilities:**

**Services:**

**Notes:** Site gates closed 23.00hrs-07.00hrs. Fishing

## GREAT YARMOUTH MAP 13 TG50

### 82% Vauxhall Holiday Park *(TG520083)*

SILVER

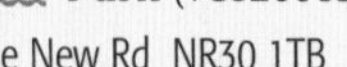

4 Acle New Rd NR30 1TB

☎ 01493 857231 01493 331122

**email:** info@vauxhallholidays.co.uk

**web:** www.vauxhall-holiday-park.co.uk

**Dir:** *On A47 approaching Great Yarmouth*

Open Etr, mid May-Sep & Oct half term Booking advisable mid Jul-Aug Last arrival 21.00hrs Last departure 10.00hrs

A very large holiday complex with plenty of entertainment and access to beach, river, estuary, lake and the A47. The touring pitches are laid out in four separate areas, each with its own amenity block, and all arranged around the main entertainment. A 40-acre site with 220 touring pitches and 421 statics.

**Leisure:**

**Facilities:**

**Services:**

**Notes:** No pets. Children's pool, sauna, solarium, fitness centre

*see advert on this page*

## NEW ►►► 73% The Grange Touring Park

*(TG510142)*

Yarmouth Rd, Ormesby St Margaret NR29 3QG

☎ 01493 730306 01493 730188

**email:** info@grangetouring.co.uk

**web:** www.grangetouring.co.uk

**Dir:** *From A419, 3m N of Great Yarmouth. Site at junct of A419 & B1159. Signed*

★ £8-£13.50 £8-£13.50 £7-£13.50

Open Etr-Sep Booking advisable school hols Last arrival 22.00hrs Last departure 10.00hrs

A mature site with plenty of trees, located just one mile from the sea, within easy reach of both coastal attractions and the Norfolk Broads. The level grassy pitches have electric hook-ups, and there are clean, modern toilets. There is Wi-fi access to all pitches. A 3.5-acre site with 70 touring pitches.

**Leisure:**

**Facilities:**

**Services:** →



## HUNSTANTON MAP 12 TF64

## 80% Searles Leisure Resort *(TF671400)*

AA HOLIDAY CENTRE · DAVID BELLAMY CONSERVATION AWARD GOLD

South Beach Rd PE36 5BB

☎ 01485 534211 01485 533815

**email:** bookings@searles.co.uk

**web:** www.searles.co.uk

**Dir:** *A149 from King's Lynn to Hunstanton. At rdbt follow signs for South Beach. Straight on at 2nd rdbt. Site on left*

Open all year (rs 25 Dec & Feb-May limited entertainment & restaurant) Booking advisable BH & Jul-Aug Last arrival 20.45hrs Last departure 11.00hrs

A large seaside holiday complex with well-managed facilities, adjacent to sea and beach. The tourers have their own areas, including two excellent toilet blocks, and pitches are individually marked by small maturing shrubs for privacy. The bars and entertainment, restaurant, bistro and takeaway, heated indoor and outdoor pools, golf, fishing and bowling green make this park popular throughout the year. A 50-acre site with 332 touring pitches, 100 hardstandings and 460 statics.

**Leisure:**

**Facilities:**

**Services:** →

**Notes:** Hire shop, beauty salon

*see advert on opposite page*

## KING'S LYNN

*see Stanhoe*

## MUNDESLEY MAP 13 TG33

### ►► 70% Links Camping & Caravan Site

*(TG305365)*

Links Rd NR11 8AT

☎ 01263 720665

**Dir:** *From B1159 at Mundesley into Church Road, then right into Links Road. From B1145 to village centre. Left up hill to Links Road & follow signs to golf course.*

Open Etr-last wk Oct Booking advisable BH & peak season Last arrival 21.00hrs Last departure noon

A pleasant site on a south-facing slope with level pitches, with distant rural views. The site is popular with those who enjoy peace and simplicity, and there is a golf course adjacent. A 2-acre site with 32 touring pitches.

**Leisure:**

**Facilities:**

**Services:**

**Notes:**

## NORTH WALSHAM MAP 13 TG23

### ►►►► 90% Two Mills Touring Park *(TG291286)*

Yarmouth Rd NR28 9NA

☎ 01692 405829 📠 01692 405829

**email:** enquiries@twomills.co.uk

**web:** www.twomills.co.uk

**Dir:** *1m S of North Walsham on Old Yarmouth road past police station & hospital on left*

★ £13-£19 £13-£19 £13-£19

Open Mar-3 Jan Booking advisable Jul & Aug Last arrival 20.30hrs Last departure noon

Set in superb countryside in a peaceful spot which is also convenient for touring. Some fully-serviced pitches offer panoramic views over the site, and the layout of pitches and facilities is excellent. The very friendly and helpful owners keep the park in immaculate condition. This park does not accept children. A 5-acre site with 50 touring pitches, 50 hardstandings.

**Leisure:**

**Facilities:**

**Services:**

**Notes:** Adults only. 2 dogs max per pitch. Tourist information room & library

ENGLAND

## NORWICH MAP 13 TG20

### ►►► 72% Norwich Camping & Caravanning Club Site *(TG237063)*

Martineau Ln NR1 2HX

☎ 01603 620060

**web:** www.campingandcaravanningclub.co.uk/norwich

**Dir:** *From A47 onto A146 towards city centre. Left at lights to next lights, under low bridge to Cock pub, turn left. Site 150yds on right*

★ £15.45-£20.15 £15.45-£20.15 £15.45-£20.15

Open 13 Mar-3 Nov Booking advisable BH & peak periods Last arrival 21.00hrs Last departure noon

A very pretty small site on the outskirts of the city, close to the River Yare. The park is built on two levels, with the lower meadow enjoying good rural views, and there is plenty of screening from nearby houses. The older-style toilet block is kept immaculately clean. A 2.5-acre site with 50 touring pitches.

**Facilities:**

**Services:** →

**Notes:** Site gates closed 23.00hrs-07.00hrs. Fishing

## ST JOHN'S FEN END MAP 12 TF51

### ►►►► 73% Virginia Lake Caravan Park *(TF538113)*

Smeeth Rd PE14 8JF

☎ 01945 430332 & 430585

**email:** louise@virginialake.co.uk

**web:** www.virginialake.co.uk

**Dir:** *From A47 E of Wisbech follow tourist signs to Terrington St John. Park on left*

Open all year Booking advisable BH Last arrival 23.00hrs Last departure noon

A well-established park beside a 2-acre fishing lake with good facilities for both anglers and tourers. The toilet facilities are very good, and security is carefully observed throughout the park. A clubhouse serves a selection of meals. A 5-acre site with 100 touring pitches, 20 hardstandings.

**Leisure:**

**Facilities:**

**Services:** →

**Notes:** Pool tables, large screen TV

## SANDRINGHAM MAP 12 TF62

### ►►►► 87% Sandringham Camping & Caravanning Club Site *(TF683274)*

The Sandringham Estate, Double Lodges PE35 6EA

☎ 01485 542555

**web:** www.campingandcaravanningclub.co.uk/sandringham

**Dir:** *From A148 onto B1440 signed West Newton. Follow signs to site. From A149 turn left & follow site signs*

★ £18.25-£22.15 £18.25-£22.15 £18.25-£22.15

Open 14 Feb-24 Nov Booking advisable BH & peak periods Last arrival 21.00hrs Last departure noon

A prestige park, very well landscaped and laid out in mature woodland, with toilets and other buildings blending in with the scenery. There are plenty of walks from the site, and this is a good touring base for the rest of Norfolk. A 28-acre site with 275 touring pitches, 2 hardstandings.

**Leisure:**

**Facilities:**

**Services:** →

**Notes:** Site gates closed 23.00hrs-07.00hrs

## SCOLE MAP 13 TM17

### ►► 70% *Willows Camping & Caravan Park* *(TM146789)*

Diss Rd IP21 4DH

☎ 01379 740271 01379 740271

**Dir:** *At Scole rdbt on A140 turn onto A1066, site 150yds on left*

Open Etr-Oct Booking advisable BH & school hols Last arrival 23.00hrs Last departure noon

A quiet garden site on the banks of the River Waveney, bordered by willow trees. The park is well placed on the Norfolk/Suffolk border, and ideal for touring both counties. A 4-acre site with 32 touring pitches, 12 hardstandings.

**Leisure:**

**Facilities:**

**Services:** →

**Notes:** Fishing

ENGLAND

## SCRATBY MAP 13 TG51

### ►►► 82% *Scratby Hall Caravan Park*

*(TG501155)*

NR29 3PH

☎ 01493 730283

**Dir:** *5m N of Great Yarmouth. Exit A149 onto B1159, site signed*

Open Spring BH-mid Sep Booking advisable Spring BH wk & Jul-Aug Last arrival 22.00hrs Last departure noon

A neatly-maintained site with a popular children's play area, well-equipped shop and outdoor swimming pool with sun terrace. The toilets have been completely refurbished and are kept very clean. The beach and the Norfolk Broads are close by. A 5-acre site with 108 touring pitches.

**Leisure:**

**Facilities:**

**Services:** → 

**Notes:** No commercial vehicles. Food preparation room

## SEA PALLING MAP 13 TG42

### NEW ►►► 75% Golden Beach Holiday Centre *(TG429271)*

Beach Rd NR12 0AL

☎ 01692 598269

**email:** goldenbeach@keme.co.uk

**web:** www.goldenbeachpark.co.uk

**Dir:** *From A149 at Stalham follow signs to Sea Palling. From Stalham Road take Beach Road, park on left*

★ £11.50-£13.50 £11.50-£13.50 £11.50-£13.50

Open 20 Mar-26 Oct Booking advisable BH & school hols Last arrival 20.00hrs Last departure 10.00hrs

Just a few yards from the sea, Golden Beach is ideally located for family holidays. The touring field is well grassed, and served by its own toilet block offering standard facilities. There is a small friendly bar, plus café, pool room and shop, all housed in modern buildings. Sea Palling is a quiet village situated away from, but close to, seaside attractions. A 6-acre site with 37 touring pitches and 111 statics.

**Leisure:**

**Facilities:**

**Services:** →

**Notes:** No boats/jet skis

## STANHOE MAP 13 TF83

### ►►► 78% The Rickels Caravan & Camping Park *(TF794355)*

Bircham Rd PE31 8PU

☎ 01485 518671

**Dir:** *A148 from King's Lynn to Hillington. B1153 to Great Bircham. B1155 to x-rds, straight over, site on left*

Open Mar-Oct Booking advisable BH Last arrival 21.00hrs Last departure 11.00hrs

Set in three acres of grassland, with sweeping country views and a pleasant, relaxing atmosphere fostered by being for adults only. The meticulously maintained grounds and facilities are part of the attraction, and the slightly sloping land has some level areas and sheltering for tents. A 3-acre site with 30 touring pitches.

**Leisure:**

**Facilities:**

**Services:** →

**Notes:** Adults only Dogs must be on leads, no ground sheets. Field available to hire for rallies

## SWAFFHAM MAP 13 TF80

### ►►► 80% Breckland Meadows Touring Park *(TF809094)*

Lynn Rd PE37 7PT

☎ 01760 721246

**email:** info@brecklandmeadows.co.uk

**web:** www.brecklandmeadows.co.uk

**Dir:** *1m W of Swaffham on old A47*

★ £11.75-£16 £11.75-£16 £8-£16

Open all year Booking advisable BH Last arrival 21.00hrs Last departure 14.00hrs

An immaculate, well-landscaped little park on the edge of Swaffham. The impressive toilet block is well equipped, and there are hardstandings, full electricity and laundry equipment. Plenty of planting is resulting in attractive screening. A 3-acre site with 45 touring pitches, 29 hardstandings.

**Facilities:**

**Services:** →

**Notes:** Adults only Tourist information centre

## SYDERSTONE MAP 13 TF83

### ►►► 76% The Garden Caravan Site

*(TF812337)*

Barmer Hall Farm PE31 8SR

☎ 01485 578220 & 578178 📠 01485 578178

**email:** nigel@gardencaravansite.co.uk

**web:** www.gardencaravansite.co.uk

**Dir:** *Signed from B1454 at Barmer between A148 & Docking, 1m W of Syderstone*

★ £13-£16 £13-£16 £13-£16

Open Mar-Nov Booking advisable at all times Last departure noon

In the tranquil setting of a former walled garden beside a large farmhouse, with mature trees and shrubs, a secluded site surrounded by woodland. The site is run mainly on trust, with a daily notice indicating which pitches are available, and an honesty box for basic foods. An ideal site for the discerning camper, and well placed for touring north Norfolk. A 3.5-acre site with 30 touring pitches.

**Facilities:**

**Services:** →

**Notes:** Max 2 dogs per pitch

## TRIMINGHAM MAP 13 TG23

### ►►► 70% *Woodlands Leisure Park*

*(TG274388)*

NR11 8AL

☎ 01263 579208 📠 01263 576477

**email:** info@woodland-park.co.uk

**web:** www.woodland-park.co.uk

**Dir:** *4m SE on B1159 coast road*

Open Mar-Dec Booking advisable public hols & Jul-Aug Last arrival 23.00hrs Last departure noon

A secluded woodland site in an open enclosure, close to the sea but well sheltered from the winds by tall trees. Facilities include two bars, a restaurant, an indoor swimming pool, bowling green and sauna, and entertainment is provided in the clubhouse. A 55-acre site with 55 touring pitches and 230 statics.

**Leisure:**

**Facilities:**

**Services:** →

## WEST RUNTON MAP 13 TG14

### ►►►► 85% West Runton Camping & Caravanning Club Site *(TG189419)*

Holgate Ln NR27 9NW

☎ 01263 837544

**web:** www.campingandcaravanningclub.co.uk/westrunton

**Dir:** *From King's Lynn on A148 towards West Runton. Left at Roman Camp Inn. Site track on right at crest of hill, 0.5m to site opposite National Trust sign*

★ £18.25-£22.15 £18.25-£22.15 £18.25-£22.15

Open 13 Mar-3 Nov Booking advisable BH & peak periods Last arrival 21.00hrs Last departure noon

A lovely, well-kept site with some gently sloping pitches on pleasantly undulating ground. This peaceful park is surrounded on three sides by woodland, with the fourth side open to fields and the coast beyond. The very well equipped family rooms and toilet blocks are excellent. A 15-acre site with 200 touring pitches, 3 hardstandings.

**Leisure:**

**Facilities:**

**Services:** →

**Notes:** Site gates closed 23.00hrs-07.00hrs

## WORTWELL MAP 13 TM28

### ►►►► 81% Little Lakeland Caravan Park *(TM279849)*

COUNTRYSIDE DISCOVERY

IP20 0EL

☎ 01986 788646 📠 01986 788646

**email:** information@littlelakeland.co.uk

**web:** www.littlelakeland.co.uk

**Dir:** *From W: exit A143 at sign for Wortwell. In village turn right 300yds past garage. From E: on A143, left onto B1062, then right. After 800yds turn left*

★ £10.80-£15.80 £10.80-£15.80 £10.80-£15.80

Open 15 Mar-Oct (rs Mar-Etr restricted laundry facilities) Booking advisable BH & peak periods Last arrival 22.00hrs Last departure noon

A well-kept and pretty site built round a fishing lake, and accessed by a lake-lined drive. The individual pitches are sited in hedged enclosures for complete privacy, and the purpose-built toilet facilities are excellent. A 4.5-acre site with 38 touring pitches, 6 hardstandings and 21 statics.

**Leisure:**

**Facilities:**

**Services:** →

**Notes:** Library

ENGLAND

# NORTHUMBERLAND

## BAMBURGH MAP 21 NU13

### ►►►► 74% Waren Caravan Park (NU155343)

GOLD

Waren Mill NE70 7EE
☎ 01668 214366 📠 01668 214224
**email:** waren@meadowhead.co.uk
**web:** www.meadowhead.co.uk

**Dir:** *2m E of town. From A1 onto B1342 signed Bamburgh. Take unclass road past Waren Mill, signed Budle*

★ £11-£19.50 £11-£19.50 £11-£16.50

Open Apr-Oct Booking advisable Spring BH & Jul-Aug Last arrival 20.00hrs Last departure noon

Attractive seaside site with footpath access to the beach, surrounded by a slightly sloping grassy embankment giving shelter to caravans. The park offers excellent facilities including several family bathrooms. There is also a wigwam 'village'. A 4-acre site with 180 touring pitches, 24 hardstandings and 300 statics.

**Leisure:**

**Facilities:**

**Services:**

**Notes:** 100 acres of private heathland

### ►►► 71% Glororum Caravan Park (NU166334)

Glororum Farm NE69 7AW
☎ 01668 214457 📠 01688 214622
**email:** info@glororum-caravanpark.co.uk
**web:** www.glororum-caravanpark.co.uk

**Dir:** *Exit A1 at junct with B1341 (Purdy's Lodge). In 3.5m left onto unclass road. Site 300yds on left*

★ £17-£19 £17-£19

Open Apr-Oct Booking advisable BH & school hols Last arrival 22.00hrs Last departure noon

A pleasantly situated site where tourers have their own well-established facilities. The open countryside setting affords good views of Bamburgh Castle and surrounding farmland. A 6-acre site with 100 touring pitches and 150 statics.

**Leisure:**

**Facilities:**

**Services:**

**Notes:** No tents. Information centre

## BEADNELL MAP 21 NU22

### ►► 71% Beadnell Bay Camping & Caravanning Club Site (NU231297)

NE67 5BX
☎ 01665 720586
**web:** www.campingandcaravanningclub.co.uk/beadnellbay

**Dir:** *A1 onto B1430 signed Seahouses. At Beadnell ignore signs for Beadnell village. Site on left after village, just after left bend*

★ £14.05-£18.85 £14.05-£18.85

Open 28 Apr-29 Sep Booking advisable BH & peak periods Last arrival 21.00hrs Last departure noon

A level grassy site in a coastal area just across the road from the sea and sandy beach. Popular with divers, anglers, surfboarders and canoeists, and ideal for visiting many tourist attractions. Motorvans and tents only. A 6-acre site with 150 touring pitches.

**Facilities:**

**Services:**

**Notes:** Site gates closed 23.00hrs-07.00hrs

## BELLINGHAM MAP 21 NY88

### ►►►► 82% Bellingham Brown Rigg Camping & Caravanning Club Site (NY835826)

Brown Rigg NE48 2JY
☎ 01434 220175
**web:** www.campingandcaravanningclub.co.uk/bellingham

**Dir:** *From A69 take A68 N. Then B6318 to Chollerford & B6320 to Bellingham. Pass Forestry Commission land, site 0.5m S of Bellingham*

★ £18.15-£20.05 £18.15-£20.05 £18.15-£20.05

Open 17 Mar-Oct Booking advisable BH & peak periods Last arrival 21.00hrs Last departure noon

Set in a pleasant rural location, this quiet park is surrounded by trees on one side and extensive views on the other. The camping area is flat and grassy, with marked pitches for caravans. There are spacious showers and toilets of a very good standard. The park is handy for the various attractions of Northumberland. A 5-acre site with 64 touring pitches, 64 hardstandings.

**Leisure:**

**Facilities:**

**Services:**

**Notes:** Site gates closed 23.00hrs-07.00hrs. Wi-fi. Bike hire, fishing, rock climbing, horse riding

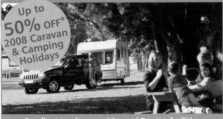

**BERWICK-UPON-TWEED** **MAP 21 NT95**

74% **Haggerston Castle** *(NU041435)*

Beal TD15 2PA

01289 381333 01289 381433

**web:** www.havenholidays.com

**Dir:** *On A1, 7m S of Berwick-upon-Tweed, site signed*

★ £12-£66 £12-£66

Open mid Mar-Oct (rs mid Mar-May & Sep-Oct some facilities may be reduced) Booking advisable school hols Last arrival anytime Last departure 10.00hrs

A large holiday centre with a very well equipped touring park, offering comprehensive holiday activities. The entertainment complex contains amusements for the whole family, and there are several bars, an adventure playground, boating on the lake, a children's club, a 9-hole golf course, tennis courts, and various eating outlets. A 7-acre site with 150 touring pitches, 150 hardstandings and 1200 statics.

**Leisure:**

**Facilities:**

**Services:**

*see advert on this page*

## PREMIER PARK

►►►►► 80% **Ord House Country Park** *(NT982515)*

East Ord TD15 2NS

01289 305288 01289 330832

**email:** enquiries@ordhouse.co.uk

**web:** www.ordhouse.co.uk

**Dir:** *On A1, Berwick bypass, turn off at 2nd rdbt at East Ord, follow 'Caravan' signs*

Open all year Booking advisable BH & Jul-Aug Last arrival 23.00hrs Last departure noon

A very well run park set in the pleasant grounds of an 18th-century country house. Touring pitches are marked and well spaced, some of them fully-serviced. The very modern toilet facilities include family bath and shower suites, and first class disabled rooms. There is a six-hole golf course and an outdoor leisure shop with a good range of camping and caravanning spares, as well as clothing and equipment. A 42-acre site with 79 touring pitches, 46 hardstandings and 255 statics.

**Leisure:**

**Facilities:**

**Services:**

**Notes:** Crazy golf, table tennis, giant draughts

►► 76% **Old Mill Caravan Site** *(NU055401)*

West Kyloe Farm, Fenwick TD15 2PG

01289 381279 & 07971 411625 01289 381279

**email:** treasasmalley@westkyloe.demon.co.uk

**web:** www.westkyloe.co.uk

**Dir:** *Take B6353 off A1, 9m S of Berwick-upon-Tweed. Road signed to Lowick/Fenwick. Site 0.5m*

★ £10-£20 £10-£15 fr £10

Open Etr-Oct Booking advisable at all times Last arrival 19.00hrs Last departure 11.00hrs

Small, secluded site accessed through a farm complex, and overlooking a mill pond complete with resident ducks. Some pitches are in a walled garden, and the amenity block is simple but well kept. Delightful walks can be enjoyed on the 600-acre farm. A 2.5-acre site with 12 touring pitches.

**Facilities:**

**Services:**

**Notes:** Dogs must be kept on lead when on site

## CRASTER MAP 21 NU21

### ►►► 77% **Dunstan Hill Camping & Caravanning Club Site** *(NU236214)*

Dunstan Hill, Dunstan NE66 3TQ

☎ 01665 576310

**web:** www.campingandcaravanningclub.co.uk/dunstanhill

**Dir:** *From A1, just N of Alnwick, take B1340 signed Seahouses. Continue to T-junct at Criston Bank, turn right. 2nd right signed Embleton. Right at x-rds then 1st left signed Craster*

★ £15.45-£20.15 £15.45-£20.15 £15.45-£20.15

Open 13 Mar-3 Nov Booking advisable BH & peak periods Last arrival 21.00hrs Last departure noon

An immaculately maintained site with pleasant landscaping, close to the beach and Craster harbour. The historic town of Alnwick is nearby, as is the ruined Dunstanburgh Castle. A 14-acre site with 150 touring pitches, 20 hardstandings.

**Leisure:**

**Facilities:**

**Services:**

**Notes:** Site gates closed 23.00hrs-07.00hrs

## HALTWHISTLE MAP 21 NY76

### ►►► 73% **Haltwhistle Camping & Caravanning Club Site** *(NY685621)*

Burnfoot Park Village NE49 0JP

☎ 01434 320106

**web:** www.campingandcaravanningclub.co.uk/haltwhistle

**Dir:** *From A69 Haltwhistle bypass (NB do not enter town) take Alston Road S signed A689, then right signed Kellan*

★ £12.75-£16.75 £12.75-£16.75 £12.75-£16.75

Open 13 Mar-3 Nov Booking advisable BH & peak periods Last arrival 21.00hrs Last departure noon

An attractive site on the banks of the River South Tyne amidst mature trees, on the Bellister Castle estate. This peaceful, relaxing site is a good cross-country transit stop in excellent walking country. A 3.5-acre site with 50 touring pitches, 15 hardstandings.

**Facilities:**

**Services:**

**Notes:** Site gates closed 23.00hrs-07.00hrs. Fishing

## HEXHAM MAP 21 NY96

### ►►► 65% **Hexham Racecourse Caravan Site** *(NY919623)*

Hexham Racecourse NE46 3NN

☎ 01434 606847 & 606881 01434 605814

**email:** hexrace@aol.com

**Dir:** *From Hexham take B6305 signed Allendale/Alston. Left in 3m signed to racecourse. Site 1.5m on right*

★ £12-£15 £12-£15 fr £8

Open May-Sep Booking advisable wknds & BH for electric hook-up Last arrival 20.00hrs Last departure noon

A part-level and part-sloping grassy site situated on a racecourse overlooking Hexhamshire Moors. A 4-acre site with 40 touring pitches.

**Leisure:**

**Facilities:**

**Services:**

**Notes:**

## NORTH SEATON MAP 21 NZ28

### **NEW** 71% **Sandy Bay** *(NZ302858)*

BRONZE

NE63 9YD

☎ 0871 664 9764

**email:** sandy.bay@park-resorts.com

**web:** www.park-resorts.com

**Dir:** *From A1 at Seaton Burn take A19 signed Tyne Tunnel. Then A189 signed Ashington, Approx 8m, at rdbt right onto B1334 towards Newbiggin-by-the-Sea. Site on right*

£5-£23 £5-£23

Open 31 Mar-Oct Booking advisable

A beach-side holiday park on the outskirts of the small village of North Seaton, within easy reach of Newcastle. The site is handily placed for exploring the magnificent coastline and countryside of Northumberland, but for those who do not wish to travel it offers the full range of holiday centre attractions, both for parents and children. 48 touring pitches and 396 statics.

**Leisure:**

**Facilities:**

**Services:**

## ROTHBURY MAP 21 NU00

### ►►► 76% **Coquetdale Caravan Park** *(NU055007)*

Whitton NE65 7RU

☎ 01669 620549

**email:** enquiries@coquetdalecaravanpark.co.uk

**web:** www.coquetdalecaravanpark.co.uk

**Dir:** *0.5m SW of Rothbury towards Newtown*

★ £12-£16 £12-£16

Open Etr-Oct Booking advisable at all times Last arrival 21.00hrs Last departure 14.00hrs

A very pleasant mainly static site in a lovely location beside the River Coquet, with good open views of moorland and the Simonside Hills. Tourers are on the site's upper area with their own purpose-built toilet facilities. An ideal place for relaxing and touring. A 13-acre site with 30 touring pitches and 160 statics.

**Leisure:**

**Facilities:**

**Services:**

**Notes:** Adventure playground for older children/adults

ENGLAND

# NOTTINGHAMSHIRE

## CHURCH LANEHAM MAP 17 SK87

### ►►► 73% Trentfield Farm *(SK815774)*

DN22 0NJ

☎ 01777 228651 📠 01777 228178

**email:** post@trentfield.co.uk

**web:** www.trentfield.co.uk

**Dir:** *From A1 take A57 towards Lincoln for 6m. Turn left to Laneham, 1.5m through Laneham & Church Laneham (pass Ferryboat pub on left). Site 300yds on right*

Open Etr-Nov Booking advisable Last arrival 21.00hrs Last departure 11.00hrs

A delightfully rural, level grass park tucked away on the banks of the River Trent. The park has its own river frontage with free coarse fishing available to park residents. The cosy village pub which serves food is a 5-minute walk from the park. A 30-acre site with 25 touring pitches.

**Facilities:**

**Services:** →

**Notes:** Wi-fi. Nature reserve

## NEWARK

*see Southwell*

## RADCLIFFE ON TRENT MAP 11 SK63

### ►►► 71% Thornton's Holt Camping Park

*(SK638377)*

Stragglethorpe Rd, Stragglethorpe NG12 2JZ

☎ 0115 933 2125 & 933 4204 📠 0115 933 3318

**email:** camping@thorntons-holt.co.uk

**web:** www.thorntons-holt.co.uk

**Dir:** *Take A52, 3m E of Nottingham. Turn S at lights towards Cropwell Bishop. Park 0.5m on left. Or A46 SE of Nottingham. N at lights. Park 2.5m on right*

★ £10-£15 £10-£15 £10-£15

Open all year (rs 2 Nov-24 Mar no pool, shop or games room) Booking advisable BH & wknds mid May-Oct Last arrival 21.00hrs Last departure 13.00hrs

A well-run family site in former meadowland, with pitches located among young trees and bushes for a rural atmosphere and outlook. The toilets are housed in converted farm buildings, and an indoor swimming pool is a popular attraction. A 13-acre site with 155 touring pitches, 35 hardstandings.

**Leisure:**

**Facilities:**

**Services:** →

**Notes:** Noise curfew at 22.00hrs. Pub & restaurant in 100mtrs

*see advert on opposite page*

## SOUTHWELL MAP 17 SK65

### ►►► 75% New Hall Farm Touring Park

*(SK660550)*

New Hall Farm, New Hall Ln NG22 8BS

☎ 01623 883041 📠 01623 883041

**email:** enquiries@newhallfarm.co.uk

**web:** www.newhallfarm.co.uk

**Dir:** *From A614 at White Post Modern Farm Centre, turn E signed Southwell. Immediately after Edingley turn S into New Hall Lane to park (0.5m)*

Open Mar-Oct Booking advisable Last arrival 21.00hrs Last departure 13.00hrs

A park on a working stock farm with the elevated pitching area enjoying outstanding panoramic views. It is within a short drive of medieval Newark and Sherwood Forest. A log cabin viewing gantry offers a place to relax and take in the spectacular views. A 2.5-acre site with 25 touring pitches, 5 hardstandings.

**Facilities:**

**Services:** →

**Notes:** Adults only Dogs must be on leads

## TEVERSAL

MAP 16 SK46

### ►►►► 92% Teversal Camping & Caravanning Club Site *(SK472615)*

SILVER

Silverhill Ln NG17 3JJ

☎ 01623 551838

**web:** www.campingandcaravanningclub.co.uk/teversal

**Dir:** *M1 junct 28 onto A38 towards Mansfield. Left at lights onto B6027. At top of hill straight over at lights & left at Peacock Hotel. Right onto B6014, left at Craven Arms, site on left*

★ £18.25-£20.15 £18.25-£20.15 £18.25-£20.15

Open all year Booking advisable BH Last arrival 21.00hrs Last departure noon

A top notch park with excellent purpose-built facilities, set in a rural former mining area. Each pitch is spacious, and there are views of and access to the countryside and nearby Silverhill Community Woods. The attention to detail and all-round quality are truly exceptional. A 6-acre site with 126 touring pitches, 58 hardstandings and 1 static.

**Leisure:**

**Facilities:**

**Services:**

**Notes:** Site gates closed 23.00hrs-07.00hrs

## TUXFORD

MAP 17 SK77

### ►►► 80% Orchard Park Touring Caravan & Camping Park *(SK754708)*

Marnham Rd NG22 0PY

☎ 01777 870228 01777 870320

**email:** info@orchardcaravanpark.co.uk

**web:** www.orchardcaravanpark.co.uk

**Dir:** *Exit A1 at Tuxford onto A6075 towards Lincoln. 0.5m, right into Marnham Rd. Site 0.75m on right*

★ £15-£17 £15-£17 £15-£17

Open mid Mar-Oct Booking advisable BH & Jul-Aug Last arrival mdnt Last departure 18.00hrs

A rural site set in an old fruit orchard with spacious pitches arranged in small groups separated by shrubs. Many of them are served with water and electricity. There is a network of grass pathways and picnic clearings in a woodland area, plus a superb adventure playground. A 7-acre site with 60 touring pitches, 30 hardstandings.

**Leisure:**

**Facilities:**

**Services:**

**Notes:** Wi-fi. Family shower room

## WORKSOP

MAP 16 SK57

### ►►► 78% Riverside Caravan Park *(SK582790)*

Central Av S80 1ER

☎ 01909 474118

**Dir:** *From A57 E of town follow international camping sign to site.*

★ fr £14 fr £14 fr £14

Open all year Booking advisable BH & wknds Last arrival 20.00hrs Last departure 14.00hrs

A very well maintained park within the attractive market town of Worksop and next door to the cricket/bowls club where Riverside customers are made welcome. This is an ideal park for those wishing to be within walking distance of all amenities yet within a 10 minute car journey of the extensive Clumber Park and numerous good garden centres. The towpath of the adjacent Chesterfield Canal provides excellent walking opportunities. A 4-acre site with 60 touring pitches, 59 hardstandings.

**Facilities:** **Services:**

**Notes:** Dogs must be kept on leads

ENGLAND

# OXFORDSHIRE

## BANBURY MAP 11 SP44

### ►►►► 80% Barnstones Caravan & Camping Site *(SP455454)*

Great Bourton OX17 1QU

01295 750289

**Dir:** *Take A423 from Banbury signed Southam. In 3m turn right signed Gt Bourton/Cropredy, site 100yds on right*

Open all year Booking advisable public hols

Popular, neatly laid-out site with plenty of hardstandings, some fully serviced pitches, and a smart up-to-date toilet block. Well run by personable owner. A 3-acre site with 49 touring pitches, 44 hardstandings.

**Leisure:**

**Facilities:**

**Services:**

**Notes:**

### ►►►► 80% Bo Peep Farm Caravan Park

*(SP481348)*

Bo Peep Farm, Aynho Rd, Adderbury OX17 3NP

01295 810605 01295 810605

**email:** warden@bo-peep.co.uk

**web:** www.bo-peep.co.uk

**Dir:** *1m E of Adderbury & A4260, on B4100 (Aynho road)*

£15-£18 £15-£18 £13-£15

Open Mar-Oct Booking advisable BH, British Grand Prix Last arrival 20.00hrs Last departure noon

A delightful park with good views and a spacious feel. Four well laid out camping areas including two with hardstandings and a separate tent field are all planted with maturing shrubs and trees. The two facility blocks are in attractive Cotswold stone. Unusually there is a bay in which you can clean your caravan or motorhome. A 13-acre site with 98 touring pitches.

**Facilities:**

**Services:**

**Notes:**

### ►►► 80% Anita's Touring Caravan Park

*(SP443477)*

The Yews, Mollington OX17 1AZ

01295 750731 & 07966 171959 01295 750731

**email:** anitagail@btopenworld.com

**Dir:** *M40 junct 11 onto A422 signed Banbury. Take A423 signed Southam, site 3.5m on left. (NB Do not enter village, site on main road just past village entrance)*

★ £11.50-£12.50 £11.50-£12.50 £6-£10

Open all year Booking advisable BH & wknds Last arrival 20.00hrs Last departure noon

A neat, well-run small farm site with brick-built toilet facilities. On the edge of the village, adjacent to A423, the farm is a centre for rearing pedigree Suffolk sheep and Welsh mountain ponies. There is a large area for ball games. A 2-acre site with 36 touring pitches, 24 hardstandings.

**Facilities:**

**Services:**

**Notes:** Field play area, rally area

## BLETCHINGDON MAP 11 SP51

### ►►► 84% Diamond Farm Caravan & Camping Park *(SP513170)*

Islip Rd OX5 3DR

01869 350909

**email:** warden@diamondpark.co.uk

**web:** www.diamondpark.co.uk

**Dir:** *From M40 junct 9 onto A34 S for 3m, then B4027 to Bletchingdon. Site 1m on left*

Open Mar-Nov Booking advisable BH & Jul-Sep Last arrival dusk Last departure 11.00hrs

A well-run, quiet rural site in good level surroundings, and ideal for touring the Cotswolds. Situated seven miles north of Oxford in the heart of the Thames Valley. This popular park has excellent facilities, and offers a heated outdoor swimming pool and a games room for children. A 3-acre site with 37 touring pitches, 13 hardstandings.

**Leisure:**

**Facilities:**

**Services:**

**Notes:**

**►►► 78% Greenhill Leisure Park** *(SP488178)*
Greenhill Farm, Station Rd OX5 3BQ
☎ 01869 351600 01869 350918
**email:** info@greenhill-leisure-park.co.uk
**web:** www.greenhill-leisure-park.co.uk
**Dir:** *M40 junct 9, A34 south for 3m. Take B4027 to Bletchingdon. Site 0.5m after village on left*
fr £10 fr £10 ▲ fr £10

Open all year (rs Oct-Mar shop & games room closed) Booking advisable BH & Jul-Aug Last arrival 22.00hrs Last departure noon

An all-year round park set in open countryside near the village of Bletchingdon. Fishing is available in the nearby river, and the park has its own farm shop. It makes an ideal base for touring the Cotswolds and Oxford. A 7-acre site with 36 touring pitches, 25 hardstandings.

**Leisure:**
**Facilities:**
**Services:** →
**Notes:** Pets' corner

## CHARLBURY MAP 11 SP31

**►►►► 81% Cotswold View Touring Park** *(SP365210)*
Enstone Rd OX7 3JH
☎ 01608 810314 01608 811891
**email:** bookings@gfwiddows.co.uk
**web:** www.cotswoldview.co.uk
**Dir:** *Signed from A44 on to B4022*
£15-£19.50 £15-£19.50 ▲ £15-£19.50

Open Etr or Apr-Oct Booking advisable BH & summer wknds Last arrival 21.00hrs Last departure noon

A good Cotswold site, well screened and with attractive views across the countryside. The toilet facilities include fully-equipped family rooms and bathrooms, and there are spacious, sheltered pitches, some with hardstandings. Breakfast and take-away food available from the shop. A 10-acre site with 125 touring pitches.

**Leisure:**
**Facilities:**
**Services:** →
**Notes:** Off licence, skittle alley, chess, boules

## CHIPPING NORTON MAP 10 SP32

**►►► 80% Chipping Norton Camping & Caravanning Club Site** *(SP315244)*
Chipping Norton Rd, Chadlington OX7 3PE
☎ 01608 641993
**web:** www.campingandcaravanningclub.co.uk/chippingnorton
**Dir:** *Take A44 to Chipping Norton onto A361 Burford road. After 1.5m bear left at fork signed Chadlington*
★ £15.45-£20.15 £15.45-£20.15 ▲ £15.45-£20.15

Open 13 Mar-3 Nov Booking advisable BH & peak periods Last arrival 21.00hrs Last departure noon

A hilltop site surrounded by trees but close to a busy main road. The toilets are very clean and visitors are given the usual warm Club welcome. A 4-acre site with 105 touring pitches.

**Leisure:** **Facilities:**
**Services:** →
**Notes:** Site gates closed 23.00hrs-07.00hrs

## HENLEY-ON-THAMES MAP 05 SU78

**►►► 80% Swiss Farm International Camping** *(SU759837)*
Marlow Rd RG9 2HY
☎ 01491 573419
**email:** enquiries@swissfarmcamping.co.uk
**web:** www.swissfarmcamping.co.uk
**Dir:** *On A4155, N of Henley, next left after rugby club, towards Marlow*
★ £12-£18 £12-£18 ▲ £10-£16

Open Mar-Oct Booking advisable all year Last arrival 21.00hrs Last departure noon

CONTINUED

**Leisure:** Indoor swimming pool Outdoor swimming pool Tennis court Games room Children's playground Stables 9/18 hole golf course Boats for hire Cinema Fishing Mini golf Watersports Separate TV room

## HENLEY-ON-THAMES CONTINUED

A conveniently-located site within a few minutes walk of Henley. Visitors are invited to fish in the park's well-stocked lake, which is set in a secluded wooded area. A 6-acre site with 165 touring pitches, 12 hardstandings and 6 statics.

**Leisure:**

**Facilities:**

**Services:** →

**Notes:** No groups, max 1 dog per booking, no dangerous breeds. Wi-fi

## OXFORD — MAP 05 SP50

### ►►► 70% Oxford Camping & Caravanning Club Site (SP519039)

426 Abingdon Rd OX1 4XG

☎ 01865 244088

**web:** www.campingandcaravanningclub.co.uk/oxford

**Dir:** *From M40 onto A34, exit at A423 for Oxford. Turn left immediately after junct into Abingdon Road, site on left behind Touchwood Sports*

★ £15.45-£20.15 £15.45-£20.15 £15.45-£20.15

Open all year Booking advisable BH & peak periods Last arrival 21.00hrs Last departure noon

A very busy town site with handy park-and-ride into Oxford. All pitches are on grass, and most offer electric hook-ups. A 5-acre site with 85 touring pitches.

**Facilities:** **Services:** →

**Notes:** Site gates closed 23.00hrs-07.00hrs

## STANDLAKE — MAP 05 SP30

### PREMIER PARK

### ►►►►► 93% Lincoln Farm Park Oxfordshire (SP395028)

The Best of British Touring and Holiday Parks

High St OX29 7RH

☎ 01865 300239 01865 300127

**email:** lincolnfarmpark@btconnect.com

**web:** www.lincolnfarmpark.co.uk

**Dir:** *In village off A415 between Abingdon & Witney, 5m SE of Witney*

£14.95-£24.95 £14.95-£24.95 £13.95-£19.95

Open Feb-Nov Booking advisable BH, Jul-Aug & most wknds Last arrival 21.00hrs Last departure noon

An attractively landscaped park in a quiet village setting, with superb facilities and a high standard of maintenance. Family rooms, fully-serviced pitches, two indoor swimming pools and a fully-equipped gym are part of the comprehensive amenities. A 9-acre site with 90 touring pitches, 75 hardstandings and 19 statics.

**Leisure:** **Facilities:**

**Services:** →

**Notes:** No gazebos. Wi-fi. Indoor leisure centre, putting green, outdoor chess

# RUTLAND

## GREETHAM — MAP 11 SK91

### ►►► 86% Rutland Caravan & Camping

*(SK925148)*

Park Ln LE15 7NX

☎ 01572 813520 01572 812616

**email:** info@rutlandcaravanandcamping.co.uk

**web:** www.rutlandcaravanandcamping.co.uk

**Dir:** *From A1 onto B668 towards Greetham. Before Greetham turn right at x-rds, then 2nd left to site*

Open all year Booking advisable BH

A pretty caravan park built to a high specification, and surrounded by well-planted banks which will provide good screening. The spacious grassy site is close to the Viking Way and other footpath networks, and well sited for visiting Rutland Water and the many picturesque villages in the area. A 5-acre site with 67 touring pitches, 67 hardstandings.

**Leisure:**

**Facilities:**

**Services:** →

**Notes:** Wi-fi

**Abbreviations:** BH-bank holiday/s Etr-Easter Whit-Whitsun dep-departure fr-from hrs-hours m-mile mdnt-midnight rdbt-roundabout rs-restricted service wk-week wknd-weekend no dogs No cards → following facilities within 3 miles of the site

# SHROPSHIRE

## BRIDGNORTH MAP 10 SO79

**Regional Winner – AA Heart of England Campsite of the Year 2008**

►►►► 91% **Stanmore Hall Touring Park** *(SO742923)*

Stourbridge Rd WV15 6DT

☎ 01746 761761 📠 01746 768069

**email:** stanmore@morris-leisure

**web:** www.morris-leisure.co.uk

**Dir:** *2m E of Bridgnorth on A458*

★ £16.10-£19.50 £16.10-£19.50 Å £16.10-£19.50

Open all year Booking advisable BH, school hols & Jul-Aug Last arrival 20.00hrs Last departure noon

An excellent park in peaceful surroundings offering outstanding facilities. The pitches, many of them fully serviced, are arranged around the lake in Stanmore Hall, home of the Midland Motor Museum. Handy for touring Ironbridge and the Severn Valley Railway, while Bridgnorth itself is an attractive old market town. A 12.5-acre site with 131 touring pitches, 44 hardstandings.

**Leisure:**

**Facilities:**

**Services:** →

**Notes:** Max of 2 dogs

## BROOME MAP 09 SO48

►► 71% **Engine & Tender Inn** *(SO399812)*

SY7 0NT

☎ 01588 660275

**Dir:** *W from Craven Arms on B4368, fork left to B4367, site in village, 2m on right*

Å

Open all year Booking advisable BH Last arrival 21.00hrs Last departure 14.00hrs

A rural site in a pleasant setting adjacent to the country pub, and accessible through the pub car park. The site has clean but fairly basic facilities. A 1-acre site with 20 touring pitches and 2 statics.

**Leisure:**

**Facilities:**

**Services:** →

## CRAVEN ARMS MAP 09 SO48

►► 74% **Wayside Camping and Caravan Park** *(SO399816)*

Aston on Clun SY7 8EF

☎ 01588 660218

**email:** waysidecamping@hotmail.com

**web:** www.waysidecamping.co.uk

**Dir:** *A49 Craven Arms, turn W on B4368 towards Clun Valley. Site 2m on right, just before Aston on Clun*

★ £10-£12 £10-£12 Å fr £10

Open Apr-Oct Booking advisable BH

A peaceful park with lovely views, close to many places of interest. The modern toilet facilities provide a good level of comfort, and there are several electric hook-ups. A 2.5-acre site with 20 touring pitches and 2 statics.

**Facilities:**

**Services:** →

**Notes:** Adults only on BH, only one dog per unit. Seasonal organic vegetables for sale

## ELLESMERE

*see Lyneal*

## HAUGHTON MAP 10 SJ51

► 87% **Ebury Hill Camping & Caravanning Club Site** *(SJ546164)*

Ebury Hill, Ring Bank SY4 4GB

☎ 01743 709334

**web:** www.campingandcaravanningclub.co.uk/eburyhill

**Dir:** *2.5m through Shrewsbury on A53. Turn right signed Haughton & Upton Magna. Continue 1.5m site on right*

★ £11.25-£12.85 £11.25-£12.85 Å £11.25-£12.85

Open 13 Mar-3 Nov Booking advisable BH & peak periods Last arrival 21.00hrs Last departure noon

A wooded hill fort with a central lake overlooking the countryside. The site is well screened by mature trees, and there is good fishing in a disused quarry. Although there are no toilet or shower facilities, this lovely park is very popular with discerning visitors. An 18-acre site with 100 touring pitches, 21 hardstandings.

**Leisure:**

**Facilities:**

**Services:** →

**Notes:** Site gates closed 23.00hrs-07.00hrs. Fishing

ENGLAND

## HUGHLEY MAP 10 SO59

### ►►► 75% *Mill Farm Holiday Park* *(SO564979)*

SY5 6NT

☎ 01746 785208

**email:** mail@millfarmcaravanpark.co.uk

**web:** www.millfarmcaravanpark.co.uk

**Dir:** *On unclass road off B4371 through village of Hughley, 3m SW of Much Wenlock, 11m SW of Church Stretton*

Open Mar-Jan Booking advisable peak periods Last arrival 20.00hrs Last departure noon

A well-established farm site set in meadowland adjacent to river, with mature trees and bushes providing screening, situated below Wenlock Edge. A 20-acre site with 20 touring pitches and 90 statics.

**Facilities:**

**Services:** →

**Notes:** Site best suited for adults. Fishing, horse riding

## KINNERLEY MAP 15 SJ32

### NEW ►►► 84% **Oswestry Camping & Caravanning Club Site** *(SJ366211)*

SY10 8DY

☎ 01743 741118

**web:** www.campingandcaravanningclubsite.co.uk/oswestry

**Dir:** *Turn off A5 at rdbt at N end of dual carriageway signed B4396 Knockin.*

★ £18.15-£20.05 £18.15-£20.05 £18.15-£20.05

Open all year Booking advisable BH & peak periods Last arrival 21.00hrs Last departure noon

This developing park is well positioned for visiting nearby Oswestry or Shrewsbury, and is very much the gateway to Wales. The park has excellent access from the A5. It provides excellent, well cared for facilities. A 4-acre site with 65 touring pitches, 65 hardstandings.

**Facilities:**

**Services:**

**Notes:** Site gates closed 23.00hrs-07.00hrs

## LYNEAL (NEAR ELLESMERE) MAP 15 SJ43

### ►►►► 78% **Fernwood Caravan Park** *(SJ445346)*

GOLD

SY12 0QF

☎ 01948 710221 01948 710324

**email:** enquiries@fernwoodpark.co.uk

**web:** www.fernwoodpark.co.uk

**Dir:** *From A495 in Welshampton take B5063, over canal bridge, turn right as signed*

★ £16.50-£21 £16.50-£21

Open Mar-Nov Booking advisable all peak periods Last arrival 21.00hrs Last departure 17.00hrs

A peaceful park set in wooded countryside, with a screened, tree-lined touring area and coarse fishing lake. The approach is past flower beds, and the static area which is tastefully arranged around an attractive children's playing area. There is a small child-free touring area for those wanting complete relaxation, and the park has 20 acres of woodland walks. A 26-acre site with 60 touring pitches, 8 hardstandings and 165 statics.

**Leisure:**

**Facilities:**

**Services:** →

## MINSTERLEY MAP 15 SJ30

### ►► 92% **The Old School Caravan Park** *(SO322977)*

Shelve SY5 0JQ

☎ 01588 650410 01588 650410

**Dir:** *6.5m SW of Minsterley on A488*

£13 £13 £13

Open Mar-Jan Booking advisable BH Last arrival 21.00hrs Last departure 10.30hrs

A very well designed park in a beautiful setting, with impressive facilities housed in an attractive brick and stone building. Self-contained cubicles with shower, wash basin and toilet are an added bonus of this small park, and the grounds are immaculate. A 1.5-acre site with 22 touring pitches, 6 hardstandings.

**Facilities:**

**Services:** →

**Notes:** No ball games. TV aerial connection

ENGLAND

## SHREWSBURY MAP 15 SJ41

### PREMIER PARK

**►►►►► 84% Beaconsfield Farm Caravan Park** *(SJ522189)*

Battlefield SY4 4AA

☎ 01939 210370 & 210399 🖷 01939 210349

**email:** mail@beaconsfield-farm.co.uk

**web:** www.beaconsfield-farm.co.uk

**Dir:** *At Hadnall, 1.5m NE of Shrewsbury. Follow sign for Astley off A49*

Open all year Booking advisable BH Last arrival 19.00hrs Last departure noon

A purpose-built, family-run park on farmland in open countryside. This pleasant park offers quality in every area, including superior toilets, heated indoor swimming pool, and attractive landscaping. Fly and coarse fishing are available from the park's own fishing lake. The Bothy restaurant is relaxed and welcoming, and offers a menu using freshly prepared local produce. Only adults over 21 years are accepted. Car hire is now available direct from the site, and there's a new steam room, plus a free internet wireless network. A 16-acre site with 60 touring pitches, 50 hardstandings and 35 statics.

**Leisure:**

**Facilities:**

**Services:**

**Notes:** Adults only

**►►►► 91% Oxon Hall Touring Park** *(SJ455138)*

Welshpool Rd SY3 5FB

☎ 01743 340868 🖷 01743 340869

**email:** oxon@morris-leisure.co.uk

**web:** www.morris-leisure.co.uk

**Dir:** *Leave A5 ring road at junct with A458. Park shares entrance with 'Oxon Park & Ride'*

★ £16.10-£19.50 £16.10-£19.50 £16.10-£19.50

Open all year Booking advisable high season Last arrival 21.00hrs

A delightful park with quality facilities, and a choice of grass and fully-serviced pitches. An adults-only section is very popular with those wanting a peaceful holiday, and there is an inviting patio area next to reception and the shop, overlooking a small lake. This site is ideally located for visiting Shrewsbury and the surrounding countryside, and there is always a warm welcome here. A 15-acre site with 124 touring pitches, 72 hardstandings and 42 statics.

**Leisure:**

**Facilities:**

**Services:**

## TELFORD MAP 10 SJ60

**►►► 90% *Severn Gorge Park*** *(SJ705051)*

Bridgnorth Rd, Tweedale TF7 4JB

☎ 01952 684789

**email:** info@severngorgepark.co.uk

**web:** www.severngorgepark.co.uk

**Dir:** *Signed off A442, 1m S of Telford*

Open all year Booking advisable BH & wknds summer months Last arrival 23.00hrs Last departure noon

A very pleasant wooded site in the heart of Telford, well-screened and maintained. The sanitary facilities are fresh and immaculate, and landscaping of the grounds is carefully managed. An upgrade makes it a really delightful park to stay on, and it is also well positioned for visiting nearby Ironbridge. A 6-acre site with 40 touring pitches, 40 hardstandings.

**Leisure:**

**Facilities:**

**Services:**

ENGLAND

## WEM MAP 15 SJ52

### ►►► 77% Lower Lacon Caravan Park

*(SJ534304)*

SY4 5RP

01939 232376 01939 233606

**email:** info@llcp.co.uk

**web:** www.llcp.co.uk

**Dir:** *Take A49 to B5065. Site 3m on the right*

★ £15.50-£22.50 £15.50-£22.50 £15.50-£22.50

Open all year (rs Nov-Mar club wknds only, toilets closed if frost occurs) Booking advisable public hols & Jul-Aug Last arrival 20.00hrs Last departure 16.00hrs

A large, spacious park with lively club facilities and an entertainments barn, set safely away from the main road. The park is particularly suitable for families, with an outdoor swimming pool and farm animals. A 48-acre site with 270 touring pitches, 30 hardstandings and 50 statics.

**Leisure:**

**Facilities:**

**Services:**

**Notes:** No skateboards, no commercial vehicles. Crazy golf

## WENTNOR MAP 15 SO39

### ►►► 76% The Green Caravan Park *(SO380932)*

SY9 5EF

01588 650605

**email:** info@greencaravanpark.co.uk

**web:** www.greencaravanpark.co.uk

**Dir:** *1m NE of Bishop's Castle on A489. Turn right at brown tourist sign*

★ fr £10 fr £10 fr £10

Open Etr-Oct Booking advisable BH & wknds Last arrival 21.00hrs Last departure 13.00hrs

A pleasant site in a peaceful setting convenient for visiting Ludlow or Shrewsbury. The grassy pitches are mainly level. A 15-acre site with 140 touring pitches, 4 hardstandings and 20 statics.

**Leisure:**

**Facilities:**

**Services:**

**Notes:** Dogs must be kept on leads at all times

# SOMERSET

## BATH MAP 04 ST76

### ►►►► 86% Newton Mill Caravan and Camping Park *(ST715649)*

Newton Rd BA2 9JF

01225 333909

**email:** newtonmill@hotmail.com

**web:** www.campinginbath.co.uk

**Dir:** *From Bath W on A4 to A39 rdbt, immediate left, site 1m on left*

Open all year Booking advisable public hols & Jul-Aug Last arrival 21.00hrs Last departure noon

An attractive, high quality park set in a sheltered valley and surrounded by woodland, with a stream running through. It offers excellent toilet facilities with private cubicles and rooms, and there is an appealing restaurant and bar offering a wide choice of menus throughout the year. The city is easily accessible by bus or via the Bristol to Bath cycle path. A 42-acre site with 195 touring pitches, 85 hardstandings.

**Leisure:**

**Facilities:**

**Services:**

**Notes:** Fishing, satellite TV hook ups

**Abbreviations:** BH-bank holiday/s Etr-Easter Whit-Whitsun dep-departure fr-from hrs-hours m-mile mdnt-midnight rdbt-roundabout rs-restricted service wk-week wknd-weekend no dogs No cards → following facilities within 3 miles of the site

ENGLAND

## BAWDRIP MAP 04 ST33

### ▶▶▶ 71% The Fairways International Touring Caravan & Camping Park *(ST349402)*

SILVER

Bath Rd TA7 8PP

☎ 01278 685569 01278 685569

**email:** holiday@fairwaysinternational.co.uk

**web:** www.fairwaysinternational.co.uk

**Dir:** *A39 onto B3141, site 100yds on right*

★ £9-£16.50 £9-£16.50 fr £4

Open Mar-mid Nov Booking advisable Etr, Mayday, Whitsun, summer hols Last arrival 22.00hrs Last departure 22.00hrs

This family orientated site is well positioned for visiting the many attractions in the area including Burnham-on-Sea, Weston-Super-Mare and Glastonbury. The park also makes a convenient overnight stop off the M5. A 5.75-acre site with 200 touring pitches.

**Leisure:**

**Facilities:**

**Services:**

**Notes:** Wi-fi. Accessory centre, Euros accepted

## BREAN MAP 04 ST25

### 84% Warren Farm Holiday Centre *(ST297564)*

Brean Sands TA8 2RP

☎ 01278 751227

**email:** enquiries@warren-farm.co.uk

**web:** www.warren-farm.co.uk

**Dir:** *M5 junct 22 onto B3140 through Burnham-on-Sea to Berrow and Brean. Centre 1.5m past Brean Leisure Park*

★ £6.50-£14 £6.50-£14 £6.50-£14

Open Apr-Oct Booking advisable BH & school hols Last arrival 20.00hrs Last departure noon

A large family-run holiday park close to the beach, divided into several fields each with its own designated facilities. Pitches are spacious and level, and enjoy panoramic views of the Mendip Hills and Brean Down. A bar and restaurant are part of the complex, which provide entertainment for all the family, and there is also separate entertainment for children. A 100-acre site with 575 touring pitches and 800 statics.

**Leisure:**

**Facilities:**

**Services:**

**Notes:** No commerical vehicles. Wi-fi, fishing lake & ponds, indoor play area

*see advert on this page*

**Facilities:** Bath · Shower · Electric Shaver · Hairdryer · Ice Pack Facility · Disabled Facilities · Public Telephone · Shop on Site or within 200yds · Mobile Shop (calls at least 5 days a week) · BBQ Area · Picnic Area · Dog Exercise Area

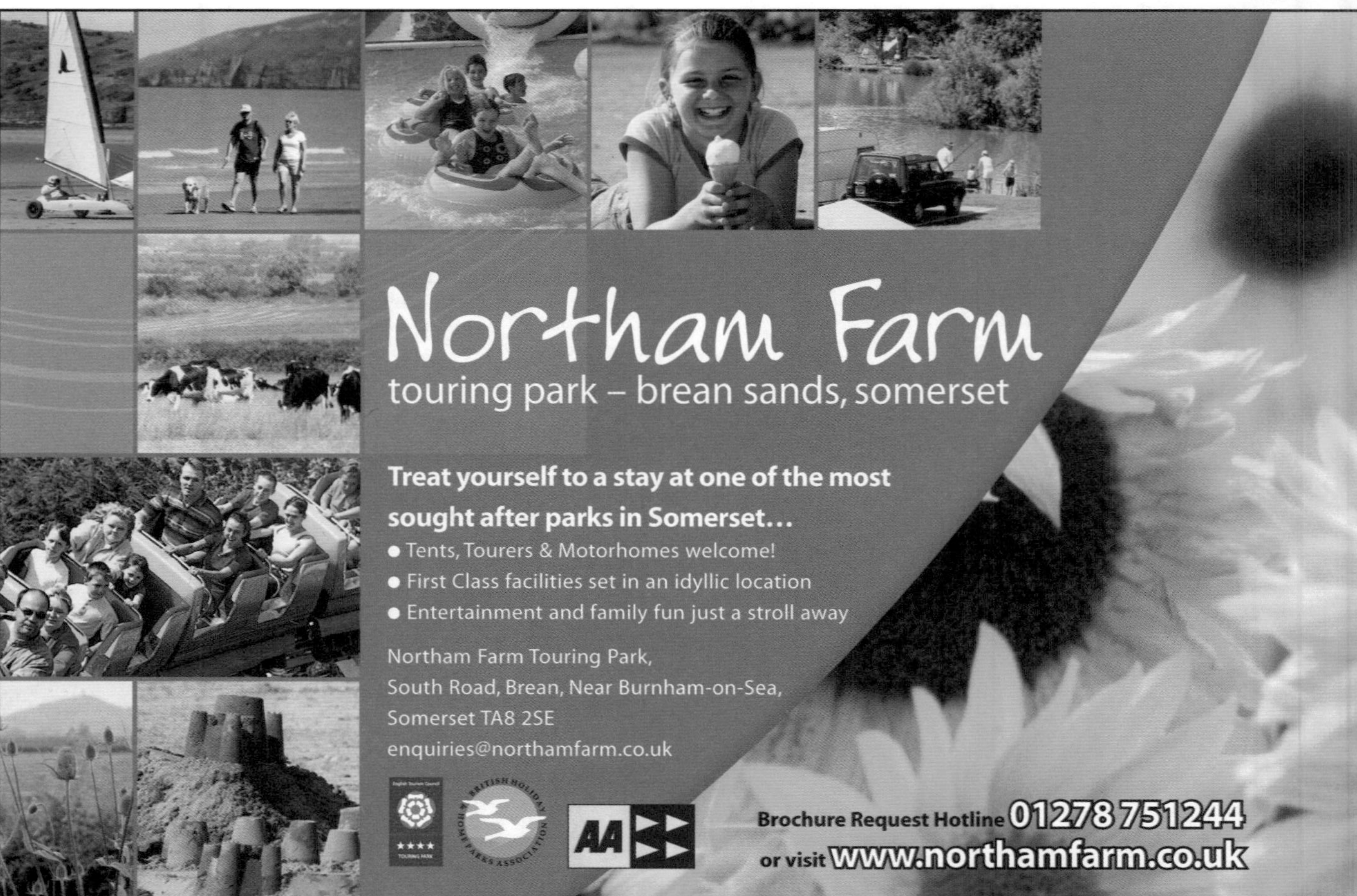

Northam Farm
touring park – brean sands, somerset
Treat yourself to a stay at one of the most sought after parks in Somerset...
• Tents, Tourers & Motorhomes welcome!
• First Class facilities set in an idyllic location
• Entertainment and family fun just a stroll away
Northam Farm Touring Park,
South Road, Brean, Near Burnham-on-Sea,
Somerset TA8 2SE
enquiries@northamfarm.co.uk
BRITISH HOLIDAY & HOME PARKS ASSOCIATION
AA
Brochure Request Hotline 01278 751244
or visit www.northamfarm.co.uk

## BREAN *CONTINUED*

### ►►►► 79% Northam Farm Caravan & Touring Park *(ST299556)*

TA8 2SE

☎ 01278 751244 01278 751150

**email:** enquiries@northamfarm.co.uk

**web:** www.northamfarm.co.uk

**Dir:** *From M5 junct 22 to Burnham-on-Sea. In Brean, Northam Farm on right 0.5m past Brean leisure park*

★ £6.25-£20 £6.25-£20 Å £6.25-£17

Open Mar-Oct (rs Mar & Oct shop/café/takeaway open limited hours) Booking advisable BH & school hols Last arrival 21.00hrs Last departure 10.30hrs

An attractive site a short walk from the sea with game, coarse fishing and sea fishing close by. The quality park has lots of children's play areas, and is near a long sandy beach. It also runs the Seagull Inn about 600yds away, which includes a restaurant and entertainment. A 30-acre site with 350 touring pitches, 156 hardstandings and 112 statics.

**Leisure:**

**Facilities:**

**Services:** →

**Notes:** Families & couples only, no motorcycles or commercial vans. Wi-fi. Fishing lake

*see advert on opposite page*

## BRIDGETOWN MAP 03 SS93

### ►►► 86% Exe Valley Caravan Site *(SS923333)*

Mill House TA22 9JR

☎ 01643 851432

**email:** paul@paulmatt.fsnet.co.uk

**web:** www.exevalleycamping.co.uk

**Dir:** *Take A396 (Tiverton to Minehead road). Turn W in centre of Bridgetown, site 40yds on right*

★ £8-£13 £8-£13 Å £8-£13

Open 14 Mar-13 Oct Booking advisable at all times Last arrival 22.00hrs

Set in the Exmoor National Park, this 'adults only' park occupies an enchanting, peaceful spot in a wooded valley alongside the River Exe. There is free fly fishing, and an abundance of wildlife, with excellent walks directly from the park. The inn opposite serves lunchtime and evening meals. A 4-acre site with 50 touring pitches, 10 hardstandings.

**Facilities:**

**Services:** →

**Notes:** Adults only 17th-century mill, cycle hire

## BRIDGWATER MAP 04 ST23

### ►►► 72% Mill Farm Caravan & Camping Park *(ST219410)*

Fiddington TA5 1JQ

☎ 01278 732286 01278 732281

**web:** www.millfarm.biz

**Dir:** *From Bridgwater take A39 W, turn left at Cannington rdbt for 2m, then right just beyond Apple Inn towards Fiddington and follow camping signs*

★ £13-£22 £13-£22 Å £13-£22

Open all year Booking advisable peak periods Last arrival 23.00hrs Last departure 10.00hrs

A mature site with plenty to interest all the family. A waterfall, stream and safe boating pool are popular features, and there are heated indoor and outdoor swimming pools, a games room, and riding school. The park is divided into three caravan areas and a large space for tents, each with its own facilities and play equipment. A 6-acre site with 125 touring pitches.

**Leisure:**

**Facilities:**

**Services:** →

**Notes:** Canoeing, pool table, trampolines, entertainment

*see advert on page 228*

## BURNHAM-ON-SEA MAP 04 ST34

### 78% Burnham-on-Sea Holiday Village *(ST305485)*

Marine Dr TA8 1LA

☎ 01278 783391 01278 793776

**email:** elaine.organ@bourne-leisure.co.uk

**web:** www.burnhamonsea-park.co.uk

**Dir:** *On A38 to Highbridge, cross rail bridge, turn right to Burnham-on-Sea. 1m turn left into Marine Parade, follow signs to site on left*

★ £12-£84 £12-£84 Å £12-£60

Open mid Mar-Oct (rs mid Mar-May & Sep-Oct Facilities may be reduced) Booking advisable Jul-Aug Last arrival anytime Last departure 10.00hrs

A large family-orientated holiday village complex with a separate touring park containing 43 super pitches. There is a wide range of activities including excellent indoor and outdoor pools, plus bars, restaurants and entertainment for all the family. The coarse fishing lake is very popular, and the seafront at Burnham is only half a mile away. A 76-acre site with 74 touring pitches and 770 statics.

**Leisure:**

**Facilities:**

**Services:** →

**Notes:**

*see advert on page 228*

ENGLAND



## BURTLE MAP 04 ST34

### ► 72% Orchard Camping *(ST397434)*

Ye Olde Burtle Inn, Catcott Rd TA7 8NG
☎ 01278 722269 & 722123 📠 01278 722269
**email:** food@theinn.eu
**web:** www.theinn.eu
**Dir:** *From M5 junct 23 onto A39, approx 4m turn left onto unclass road to Burtle, site by pub in village centre*

★ Ă £11-£14

Open all year Booking advisable BH & peak season Last arrival anytime

A simple campsite set in an orchard at the rear of a lovely 17th-century family inn in the heart of the Somerset Levels. The restaurant offers a wide range of meals, and breakfast can be pre-ordered by campers. A shower and disabled toilet are available to campers outside pub opening hours. A 0.75-acre site with 30 touring pitches.

**Leisure:**

**Facilities:**

**Services:**

**Notes:** No cars by tents. Bicycle & tent hire, sleeping bags & equipment

ENGLAND

## CHARD MAP 04 ST30

### ►►► 84% Alpine Grove Touring Park (ST342071)

DAVID BELLAMY CONSERVATION AWARD SILVER

Forton TA20 4HD
☎ 01460 63479 📠 01460 63479
**email:** stay@alpinegrovetouringpark.com
**web:** www.alpinegrovetouringpark.com
**Dir:** *Turn off A30 between Chard & Crewkerne towards Cricket St Thomas, follow signs. Park 2m on right*

Open 1 wk before Etr-Sep Booking advisable BH & Jul-Aug Last arrival 21.00hrs Last departure 11.00hrs

A warm welcome awaits at this attractive, quiet wooded park with both hardstandings and grass pitches, close to Cricket St Thomas Wildlife Park. The facilities are kept spotlessly clean. Families particularly enjoy the small swimming pool and terrace in summer. Log cabins are also available for hire on this park. An 8.5-acre site with 40 touring pitches, 15 hardstandings.

**Leisure:**
**Facilities:**
**Services:**
**Notes:** Dogs must be kept on leads, dog-sitting service, no open fires

## CHEDDAR MAP 04 ST45

PREMIER PARK

### ►►►►► 74% Broadway House Holiday Caravan & Camping Park (ST448547)

DAVID BELLAMY CONSERVATION AWARD GOLD

Axbridge Rd BS27 3DB
☎ 01934 742610 📠 01934 744950
**email:** info@broadwayhouse.uk.com
**web:** www.broadwayhouse.uk.com
**Dir:** *From M5 junct 22 follow signs to Cheddar Gorge & Caves (8m). Park midway between Cheddar & Axbridge on A371*

★ £13-£24 £11-£19 £13-£22

Open Mar-mid Nov (rs Mar-end May & Oct-Nov bar & pool closed, limited shop hours) Booking advisable BH & end Jul-Aug Last arrival 23.00hrs Last departure noon

A well-equipped family park on the slopes of the Mendips with an exceptional range of activities for all ages. This is a busy and lively park in the main holiday periods, but can be quiet and peaceful off-peak. Broadway has its own activity centre based on the site, providing archery, shooting, climbing, caving, ballooning and much more. The slightly-terraced pitches face south, and are backed by the Mendips. A 30-acre site with 200 touring pitches, 60 hardstandings and 37 statics.

**Leisure:**
**Facilities:**
**Services:**
**Notes:** Children to be supervised at all times. Wi-fi, table tennis, bike hire, BMX track, skate park

### ►►►► 79% Cheddar Bridge Touring Park (ST459529)

Draycott Rd BS27 3RJ
☎ 01934 743048 📠 01934 743048
**email:** enquiries@cheddarbridge.co.uk
**web:** www.cheddarbridge.co.uk
**Dir:** *From M5 junct 22 (Burnham-on-Sea) take A38 towards Cheddar & Bristol, for approx 5m. Right onto A371 at Cross, follow Cheddar signs. Through Cheddar village towards Wells, site on right just before Caravan Club site*

Open Mar-Oct Booking advisable Last arrival 22.00hrs Last departure 11.00hrs

A peaceful adults-only park on the edge of the village of Cheddar, with the River Yeo passing attractively through its grounds. It is handy for exploring the Cheddar Gorge and Wookey Hole, Wells and Bath. The toilet facilities are very good. A 4-acre site with 45 touring pitches, 10 hardstandings and 3 statics.

**Facilities:**
**Services:**
**Notes:** Adults only. Table tennis

## COWSLIP GREEN MAP 04 ST46

### ►►► 78% Brook Lodge Farm Camping & Caravan Park *(ST486620)*

Cowslip Green BS40 5RB

☎ 01934 862311 🖷 01934 862311

**email:** brooklodgefarm@aol.com

**web:** www.brooklodgefarm.com

**Dir:** *M5 junct 18/22 follow signs for Bristol Airport. Park 3m on left of A38 at bottom of hill after Darlington Arms*

Open Mar-Oct Booking advisable 22 May-4 Sep Last arrival 22.30hrs Last departure noon

A naturally sheltered country touring park nestling in a valley of the Mendip Hills, surrounded by trees and a historic walled garden.

Country walks can be enjoyed from the park, and there is trout fishing nearby. A 3.5-acre site with 29 touring pitches, 3 hardstandings.

**Leisure:**

**Facilities:**

**Services:**

**Notes:** Dogs only by prior arrangement. Bicycle hire & walking maps provided

## CROWCOMBE MAP 03 ST13

### ►►►► 79% Quantock Orchard Caravan Park *(ST138357)*

TA4 4AW

☎ 01984 618618 🖷 01984 618618

**email:** qocp@flaxpool.freeserve.co.uk

**web:** www.flaxpool.freeserve.co.uk

**Dir:** *Site set back from A358*

Open all year Booking advisable BH & Jul-Aug Last arrival 22.00hrs Last departure noon

An attractive, quiet site with wonderful views, sitting at the western foot of the Quantocks midway between Taunton and Minehead. The park is laid out in an old orchard with plenty of colourful flower beds, and the quality facilities are very well maintained. A fitness complex next to the swimming pool offers jacuzzi, sauna and exercise machines. Ideal for visiting Exmoor National Park, and the nearby West Somerset Steam Railway. A 3.5-acre site with 75 touring pitches.

**Leisure:**

**Facilities:**

**Services:**

**Notes:** Gym & leisure suite, off-licence on site

*see advert on this page*

**Services:** Toilet Fluid · Café/ Restaurant · Fast Food/Takeaway · Baby Care · Electric Hook Up · Motorvan Service Point · Launderette · Licensed Bar · Calor Gas · Camping Gaz · Battery Charging

## DULVERTON — MAP 03 SS92

*see also East Anstey (Devon)*

### ►►► 74% Wimbleball Lake *(SS960300)*

TA22 9NU

☎ 01398 371257

**email:** cvallance@swlakestrust.org.uk

**web:** www.swlakestrust.org.uk

**Dir:** *From A396 (Tiverton-Minehead road) take B3222 signed Dulverton Services, follow signs to Wimbleball Lake. Ignore 1st entry (fishing) & take 2nd entry for tea-room & camping. (NB care needed - narrow roads)*

★ £10

Open Apr-1 Nov Booking advisable high season Last departure 14.00hrs

A grassy site overlooking Wimbleball Lake, set high up on Exmoor National Park. The camping area is in its own paddock with toilet facilities, and surrounded by farmland in a quiet setting. The lake is nationally renowned for its trout fishing, and boats can be hired with advance notice. A 1.25-acre site with 30 touring pitches, 4 hardstandings.

**Leisure:** **Facilities:**

**Services:** →

**Notes:** Dogs must be kept on leads. Watersports centre, lakeside walks

## EMBOROUGH — MAP 04 ST65

### ►►► 81% Old Down Touring Park

*(ST628513)*

Old Down House BA3 4SA

☎ 01761 232355 01761 232355

**email:** jsmallparkhomes@aol.com

**web:** www.olddowntouringpark.co.uk

**Dir:** *A37 from Farrington Gurney through Ston Easton. In 2m left onto B3139 to Radstock. Site opposite Old Down Inn*

Open Mar-Nov Booking advisable BH & Jul-Aug Last arrival 20.00hrs Last departure noon

A small family-run site set in open parkland, surrounded by well-established trees. The toilet facilities are excellent, and well maintained along with every other aspect of the park. Children are welcome. A 4-acre site with 30 touring pitches, 15 hardstandings.

**Facilities:**

**Services:** →

**Notes:** Dogs must be kept on leads at all times

## EXFORD — MAP 03 SS83

### ►► 83% Westermill Farm

*(SS825398)*

TA24 7NJ

☎ 01643 831238 01643 831216

**email:** aa@westermill.com

**web:** www.westermill.com

**Dir:** *Leave Exford on Porlock road. After 0.25m fork left, continue along valley until 'Westermill' sign on tree. Take left fork*

★ £10-£11

Open all year (rs Nov-May larger toilet block & shop closed) Booking advisable Spring BH & Jul-Aug

An idyllic site for peace and quiet, in a sheltered valley in the heart of Exmoor, which has won awards for conservation. There are four waymarked walks over the 500-acre working farm. The site should only be approached from Exford (other approaches are difficult). A 6-acre site with 60 touring pitches.

**Facilities:**

**Services:** →

**Notes:** Shallow river for fishing/bathing

## FROME — MAP 04 ST74

### ►►► 82% Seven Acres Caravan & Camping Site *(ST777444)*

Seven Acres, West Woodlands BA11 5EQ

☎ 01373 464222

**Dir:** *On B3092 approx 0.75m from rdbt with A361, Frome bypass*

★ fr £11 fr £11 fr £7.50

Open Mar-Oct Booking advisable

A level meadowland site beside the shallow River Frome, with a bridge across to an adjacent field, and plenty of scope for families (though no laundry, but launderette 0.5m away). Set on the edge of the Longleat Estate with its stately home, wildlife safari park, and many other attractions. A 3-acre site with 16 touring pitches, 16 hardstandings.

**Leisure:**

**Facilities:**

**Services:** →

**Notes:** Dogs must be kept on leads

**Leisure:** Indoor swimming pool · Outdoor swimming pool · Tennis court · Games room · Children's playground · Stables · 9/18 hole golf course · Boats for hire · Cinema · Fishing · Mini golf · Watersports · Separate TV room

ENGLAND

## GLASTONBURY MAP 04 ST53

PREMIER PARK

### ►►►►► 91% Old Oaks Touring Park *(ST521394)*

Wick Farm, Wick BA6 8JS
☎ 01458 831437
**email:** info@theoldoaks.co.uk
**web:** www.theoldoaks.co.uk
**Dir:** *On A361 from Glastonbury towards Shepton Mallet. In 1.75m turn left at Wick sign, site on left in 1m*

Open Mar-20 Nov (rs low season reduced shop & reception hours) Booking advisable BH & main season Last arrival 20.00hrs Last departure noon

An idyllic park on a working farm with panoramic views towards the Mendip Hills. Old Oaks offers sophisticated services whilst retaining a farming atmosphere, and there are some 'super' pitches as well as en suite toilet facilities. Glastonbury's two famous 1,000-year-old oak trees, Gog and Magog, are on site. This is an adult-only park. A 10-acre site with 100 touring pitches, 29 hardstandings.

**Facilities:**
**Services:** →
**Notes:** Adults only. Group or block bookings only at owners' discretion. Fishing, bicycle hire, off licence

### ►►►► 74% Isle of Avalon Touring Caravan Park *(ST494397)*

Godney Rd BA6 9AF
☎ 01458 833618 01458 833618
**Dir:** *M5 junct 23, A39 to outskirts of Glastonbury, 2nd exit signed Wells at B&Q rdbt, straight over next rdbt, 1st exit at 3rd rdbt (B3151), site 200yds right*

Open all year Booking advisable mid Jul-mid Aug Last arrival 21.00hrs Last departure 11.00hrs

A popular site on the south side of this historic town and within easy walking distance of the town centre. This level park offers a quiet environment in which to stay and explore the many local attractions including the Tor, Wells, Wookey Hole and Clark's Village. An 8-acre site with 120 touring pitches, 70 hardstandings.

**Leisure:**
**Facilities:**
**Services:** →
**Notes:** Cycle hire, Wi-fi

### ►► 92% Greenacres Camping *(ST553416)*

Barrow Ln, North Wootton BA4 4HL
☎ 01749 890497
**Dir:** *A361 to Glastonbury. Turn at Steanbow Farm, from A39 turn at Browns Garden Centre. Follow campsite signs & sign for North Wootton*

★ £12 £12

Open Apr-Sep Booking advisable school hols, Glastonbury Festival Last arrival 21.00hrs Last departure noon

An immaculately maintained site peacefully set within sight of Glastonbury Tor. Mainly family orientated with many thoughtful extra facilities provided. A 4.5-acre site with 30 touring pitches.

**Leisure:**
**Facilities:**
**Services:** →
**Notes:** No caravans. Free use of fridges & freezers

## LANGPORT MAP 04 ST42

### ►►► 84% *Bowdens Crest Caravan & Camping Park* *(ST414288)*

Bowdens TA10 0DD
☎ 01458 250553 01458 253360
**email:** bowcrest@btconnect.com
**web:** www.bowdenscrest.co.uk
**Dir:** *Off A372 (Langport to Bridgwater road), signed*

Open all year Booking advisable BH & Aug Last arrival 22.00hrs Last departure noon

A tranquil park with spectacular panoramic views over the Somerset Levels and the distant Blackdown Hills. The tasteful restaurant with adjoining patio help to make this quiet park appealing to both couples and families. An excellent new toilet block and games room have considerably enhanced the facilities, and there is now an internet station and Wi-fi. A 16.5-acre site with 30 touring pitches, 2 hardstandings and 13 statics.

**Leisure:**
**Facilities:**
**Services:** →
**Notes:** Special diets catered for

**Abbreviations:** BH-bank holiday/s Etr-Easter Whit-Whitsun dep-departure fr-from hrs-hours m-mile mdnt-midnight rdbt-roundabout rs-restricted service wk-week wknd-weekend no dogs No cards → following facilities within 3 miles of the site

►►► 71% **Thorney Lakes Caravan Park** *(ST430237)*

GOLD

Thorney Lakes, Muchelney TA10 0DW

☎ 01458 250811

**web:** www.thorneylakes.co.uk

**Dir:** *From A303 at Podimore rdbt take A372 to Langport. At Huish Episcopi Church turn left for Muchelney. In 100yds left (signed Muchelney & Crewkerne). Site 300yds after John Leach Pottery*

★ £10-£15 £10-£15 £10-£15

Open Apr-Oct Booking advisable

A small, basic but very attractive park set in a cider apple orchard, with coarse fishing in the three well-stocked on-site lakes. The famous John Leach pottery shop is nearby. A 6-acre site with 36 touring pitches.

**Facilities:**

**Services:** →

**Notes:**

## MARTOCK MAP 04 ST41

►►►► 81% **Southfork Caravan Park** *(ST448188)*

Parrett Works TA12 6AE

☎ 01935 825661 01935 825122

**email:** southforkcaravans@btconnect.com

**web:** www.southforkcaravans.co.uk

**Dir:** *8m NW of Yeovil, 2m off A303. From E, take exit after Cartgate rdbt. From W, 1st exit off rdbt signed South Petherton, follow camping signs*

★ £9-£13 £9-£13 £9-£13

Open all year Booking advisable BH & Jul-Aug Last arrival 22.30hrs Last departure noon

A neat grass park in a quiet rural area, offering spotless facilities to those who enjoy the countryside. Located on the outskirts of a pretty village, with good amenities. A 2-acre site with 27 touring pitches, 2 hardstandings and 3 statics.

**Leisure:**

**Facilities:**

**Services:** →

**Notes:** Caravan service/repair centre, accessories shop

## MINEHEAD MAP 03 SS94

►►► 70% **Minehead & Exmoor Caravan & Camping Site** *(SS950457)*

Porlock Rd TA24 8SW

☎ 01643 703074

**Dir:** *1m W of Minehead centre, close to A39*

£10-£16 £10-£16 £10-£16

Open all year (rs Nov-Feb reduced no. of pitches) Booking advisable BH & Jul-Aug Last arrival 22.00hrs Last departure noon

A small terraced park on the edge of Exmoor, spread over five paddocks and screened by the mature trees that surround it. The level pitches provide a comfortable space for each unit on this family-run park. There is a laundrette in nearby Minehead. A 3-acre site with 50 touring pitches, 8 hardstandings.

**Leisure:**

**Facilities:**

**Services:** →

**Notes:**

►►► 79% **Minehead Camping & Caravanning Club Site** *(SS958471)*

Hill Rd, North Hill TA24 5LB

☎ 01643 704138

**web:** www.campingandcaravanningclub.co.uk/minehead

**Dir:** *From A39 towards town centre. In main street turn opposite W H Smith to Blenheim Rd. Left in 50yds (by pub) into Martlet Rd. Up hill, site on right*

★ £8.70-£13.60 £8.70-£13.60

Open 28 Apr-29 Sep Booking advisable BH & peak periods Last arrival 21.00hrs Last departure noon

A secluded site on a hilltop with glorious views of the Bristol Channel and the Quantocks. Good clean facilities plus a laundry and information room make this a popular choice for those seeking an isolated holiday. A 3.75-acre site with 60 touring pitches, 10 hardstandings.

**Facilities:**

**Services:** →

**Notes:** Site gates closed 23.00hrs-07.00hrs

## MUCHELNEY — MAP 04 ST42

### ►►► 73% Muchelney Caravan & Camping Site *(ST429249)*

Abbey Farm TA10 0DQ

01458 250112 & 07881 524426 01458 250112

**Dir:** *From A303 at Podimore rdbt take A372 towards Langport. At church in Huish Episcopi follow Muchelney Abbey sign. In Muchelney left at village cross. Site in 50mtrs*

★ £8-£10 £8-£10 £8-£10

Open all year Booking advisable BH & school hols

This small site is situated opposite Muchelney Abbey, an English Heritage property. This quiet and peaceful site will appeal to all lovers of the countryside, and is well positioned for visiting the Somerset Levels. A 3-acre site with 40 touring pitches, 5 hardstandings.

**Facilities:**

**Services:**

**Notes:** Dogs & cats must be kept on leads. Coarse fishing, canoeing

## OARE — MAP 03 SS74

### ►►► 75% Cloud Farm *(SS795468)*

EX35 6NU

01598 741234 01598 741154

**email:** doonevalleyholidays@hotmail.com

**web:** www.doonevalleyholidays.co.uk/pages/camping.html

**Dir:** *Exit A39 between Lynton & Porlock at Doone Valley/Oare/Oareford sign. To T-junct, turn right. Site signed in 0.75m on left (NB do not pass site due to narrow bridge & no-turning area)*

★ £11-£15 £11-£15 £11-£15

Open all year Booking advisable high season

Set in the heart of Exmoor's Doone Valley, this quiet, sheltered park is arranged over four riverside fields, with modern toilet facilities. It offers a good café and a little shop, with a large garden for outdoor eating. A 110-acre site with 70 touring pitches.

**Facilities:**

**Services:**

**Notes:** Off licence

## PORLOCK — MAP 03 SS84

### ►►►► 80% Porlock Caravan Park *(SS882469)*

DAVID BELLAMY CONSERVATION AWARD GOLD

TA24 8ND

01643 862269 01643 862269

**email:** info@porlockcaravanpark.co.uk

**web:** www.porlockcaravanpark.co.uk

**Dir:** *Through village fork right signed Porlock Weir, site on right*

★ fr £11 fr £12 fr £11

Open 15 Mar-Oct Booking advisable Etr, Whit & Jul-Aug Last arrival 22.00hrs Last departure noon

A sheltered touring park in the centre of lovely countryside on the edge of the village, with Exmoor right on the doorstep. The toilet facilities are superb, and there's a popular kitchen area with microwave and freezer. A 3-acre site with 40 touring pitches, 14 hardstandings and 56 statics.

**Facilities:**

**Services:**

**Notes:** No fires

### ►►► 89% Burrowhayes Farm Caravan & Camping Site *(SS897460)*

West Luccombe TA24 8HT

01643 862463

**email:** info@burrowhayes.co.uk

**web:** www.burrowhayes.co.uk

**Dir:** *A39 from Minehead towards Porlock for 5m. Left at Red Post to Horner & West Lucombe, site 0.25m on right, immediately before humpback bridge*

Open 15 Mar-Oct (rs shop closed until Sat before Etr) Booking advisable Etr, Spring BH & Jul-Aug Last arrival 22.00hrs Last departure noon

A delightful site on the edge of Exmoor, sloping gently down to Horner Water. The farm buildings have been converted into riding stables which offers escorted rides on the moors, and the excellent toilet facilities are housed in timber-clad buildings. There are many walks directly into the countryside. An 8-acre site with 120 touring pitches, 3 hardstandings and 20 statics.

**Facilities:**

**Services:**

## PRIDDY — MAP 04 ST55

### ►►►► 80% Cheddar, Mendip Heights Camping & Caravanning Club Site *(ST522519)*

Townsend BA5 3BP

01749 870241

**web:** www.campingandcaravanningclub.co.uk/cheddar

**Dir:** *From A39 take B3135 to Cheddar. After 4.5m turn left. Site 200yds on right*

★ £18.35-£23.25 £18.35-£23.25 £18.35-£23.25

Open 6 Mar-15 Nov Booking advisable BH Last arrival 21.00hrs Last departure noon

A gently sloping site set high on the Mendip Hills and surrounded by trees. This excellent site offers good self-catered facilities especially

**Services:** Toilet Fluid Café/ Restaurant Fast Food/Takeaway Baby Care Electric Hook Up Motorvan Service Point Launderette Licensed Bar Calor Gas Camping Gaz Battery Charging

for families, and fresh bread is baked daily. The site is well positioned for visiting local attractions like Cheddar, Wookey Hole, Wells and Glastonbury, and is popular with walkers. A 3.5-acre site with 90 touring pitches, 30 hardstandings and 2 statics.

**Leisure:**

**Facilities:**

**Services:**

**Notes:** Site gates closed 23.00hrs-07.00hrs. Licensed shop

## SPARKFORD MAP 04 ST62

### ►►► 79% Long Hazel Park *(ST602262)*

High St BA22 7JH

☎ 01963 440002 01963 440002

**email:** longhazelpark@hotmail.com

**web:** www.sparkford.f9.co.uk/lhi.htm

**Dir:** *Turn off A303 at Hazlegrove rdbt, follow signs for Sparkford. Park 400yds on left*

Open 16 Feb-16 Jan Booking advisable BH & Jul-Sep Last arrival 22.00hrs Last departure 11.00hrs

A very neat, adults only park next to the Sparkford Inn in the village high street. This attractive park is run by a friendly owner to a good standard. There are luxury lodges on site. A 3.5-acre site with 75 touring pitches, 40 hardstandings and 4 statics.

**Facilities:**

**Services:**

**Notes:** Adults only Dogs must be kept on leads & exercised off site

## TAUNTON MAP 04 ST22

### ►►►► 83% Cornish Farm Touring Park *(ST235217)*

Shoreditch TA3 7BS

☎ 01823 327746 01823 354946

**email:** info@cornishfarm.com

**web:** www.cornishfarm.com

**Dir:** *M5 junct 25 towards Taunton. Left at lights. 3rd left into Ilminster Road (follow Corfe signs). Right at rdbt, left at next. Right at T-junct, left into Killams Drive, 2nd left into Killams Ave. Follow road over motorway bridge. Site on left, take 2nd entrance*

Open all year Booking advisable BH & race days Last arrival anytime Last departure noon

This smart park provides quality facilities throughout. Although only two miles from Taunton, the park is set in open countryside and is a very convenient base for visiting the many attractions of the area such as Clarks Village, Glastonbury and Cheddar Gorge. A 3.5-acre site with 50 touring pitches, 25 hardstandings.

**Facilities:**

**Services:**

### ►►► 77% Ashe Farm Camping & Caravan Site *(ST279229)*

Thornfalcon TA3 5NW

☎ 01823 442567

**email:** camping@ashe-farm.fsnet.co.uk

**Dir:** *From M5 junct 25 take A358 E for 2.5m. Turn right at Nags Head pub. Site 0.25m on right*

★ £10-£12.50 £10-£12.50 £10

Open Apr-Oct Booking advisable Jul-Aug Last arrival 22.00hrs

A well-screened site surrounded by mature trees and shrubs, with two large touring fields. A facilities block includes smart toilets and a separate laundry room, while the old portaloos remain very clean and well-maintained. Not far from the bustling market town of Taunton, and handy for both coasts. A 7-acre site with 30 touring pitches, 8 hardstandings.

**Leisure:**

**Facilities:**

**Services:**

**Notes:** Baby changing facilities

**Leisure:** Indoor swimming pool Outdoor swimming pool Tennis court Games room Children's playground Stables 9/18 hole golf course Boats for hire Cinema Fishing Mini golf Watersports Separate TV room

## TAUNTON CONTINUED

### ►►► 79% **Holly Bush Park** *(ST220162)*

Culmhead TA3 7EA

☎ 01823 421515

**email:** info@hollybushpark.com

**web:** www.hollybushpark.com

**Dir:** *M5 junct 25 towards Taunton. At 1st lights turn left signed Corfe/Taunton Racecourse. 3.5m past Corfe on B3170 turn right at x-rds at top of hill on unclass road towards Wellington. Right at next junct, site 150yds on left*

Open all year Booking advisable BH & high season Last arrival 21.00hrs Last departure 11.00hrs

An immaculate little park set in an orchard in attractive countryside, with easy access to Wellington and Taunton. The friendly owners are welcoming and keen to help, and keep the facilities in good order. A 2-acre site with 40 touring pitches, 5 hardstandings.

**Facilities:**

**Services:** → 

## WATCHET MAP 03 ST04

### ►►► 83% **Home Farm Holiday Centre** *(ST106432)*

St Audries Bay TA4 4DP

☎ 01984 632487 01984 634687

**email:** dib@homefarmholidaycentre.co.uk

**web:** www.homefarmholidaycentre.co.uk

**Dir:** *Follow A39 towards Minehead, fork right onto B3191 at West Quantoxhead after St Audries garage, then right after 0.25m*

Open all year (rs mid Nov-Etr shop & bar closed) Booking advisable all year Last arrival dusk Last departure noon

In a hidden valley beneath the Quantock Hills, this park overlooks its own private beach. The atmosphere is friendly and quiet, and there are lovely sea views from the level pitches. Flower beds, woodland walks, and a koi carp pond all enhance this very attractive site, along with a lovely indoor swimming pool and a beer garden. A 45-acre site with 40 touring pitches, 35 hardstandings and 230 statics.

**Leisure:**

**Facilities:**

**Services:** →

**Notes:** No cars by caravans or tents

## WELLINGTON MAP 03 ST12

### ►►► 72% **Gamlins Farm Caravan Park** *(ST083195)*

Gamlins Farm House, Greenham TA21 0LZ

☎ 01823 672859 & 07986 832516 01823 673391

**Dir:** *M5 junct 26, A38 towards Tiverton. 4m turn right for Greenham, site 1m on right*

£8-£10 £8-£10 £6-£10

Open Etr-Sep Booking advisable BH Last arrival 20.00hrs

A well-planned site in a secluded position with panoramic views. The friendly owners keep the toilet facilities to a good standard of cleanliness. A 3-acre site with 25 touring pitches, 3 hardstandings and 1 static.

**Leisure:**

**Facilities:**

**Services:** →

**Notes:** Dogs must be kept on leads, no loud noise after 22.00. Free coarse fishing on site

## WELLS MAP 04 ST54

### ►► 80% **Homestead Park** *(ST532474)*

Wookey Hole BA5 1BW

☎ 01749 673022 01749 673022

**email:** enquiries@homesteadpark.co.uk

**web:** www.homesteadpark.co.uk

**Dir:** *0.5m NW off A371 (Wells to Cheddar road) (NB weight limit on bridge into touring area now 1 tonne)*

★ £13

Open Etr-Sep Booking advisable BH Last arrival 20.00hrs Last departure noon

This attractive, small site for tents only is by a stream and has mature trees. Set in hilly woods and meadowland with access to the river and Wookey Hole. This park is for adults only. A 2-acre site with 30 touring pitches and 28 statics.

**Facilities:**

**Services:** →

**Notes:** Adults only Tents only

ENGLAND

## WESTON-SUPER-MARE MAP 04 ST36

### ►►► 80% Country View Holiday Park

*(ST335647)*
Sand Rd, Sand Bay BS22 9UJ
☎ 01934 627595
**web:** www.cvhp.co.uk
**Dir:** *M5 junct 21, A370 towards Weston-Super-Mare. Immediately take left lane, follow Kewstoke/Sand Bay signs. Straight over 3 rdbts onto Lower Norton Ln. At Sand Bay right into Sand Rd, site on right*

£12-£22 £12-£22 £12-£22

Open Mar-Jan Booking advisable BH, wknds & peak periods Last arrival 20.00hrs Last departure noon

A pleasant open site in a rural area a few hundred yards from Sandy Bay and beach. The park is also well placed for energetic walks along the coast at either end of the beach. The facilities are excellent and well maintained. An 8-acre site with 120 touring pitches, 90 hardstandings and 65 statics.

**Leisure:**
**Facilities:**
**Services:**
**Notes:**

*see advert on this page*

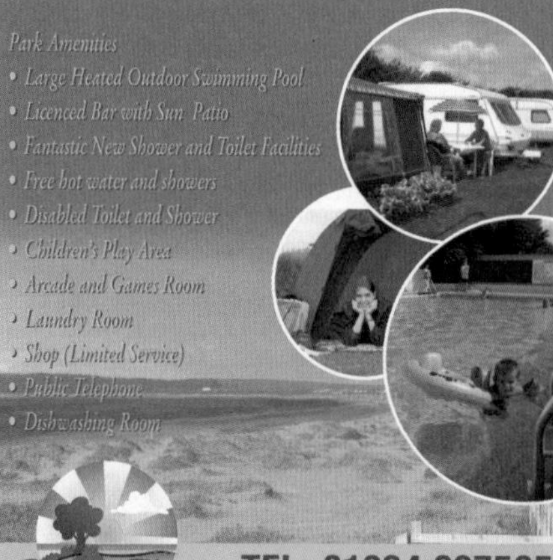


### ►►► 81% *West End Farm Caravan & Camping Park* *(ST354600)*

Locking BS24 8RH
☎ 01934 822529 01934 822529
**Dir:** *From M5 junct 21 onto A370. Follow International Helicopter Museum signs. Right at rdbt, follow signs to site*

Open all year Booking advisable peak periods Last arrival 18.00hrs Last departure noon

A delightful park bordered by hedges, with good landscaping and well-kept facilities. It is handily located next to a helicopter museum, and offers good access to Weston-Super-Mare and the Mendips. A 10-acre site with 75 touring pitches and 20 statics.

**Leisure:**
**Facilities:**
**Services:**
**Notes:**

## WINSFORD MAP 03 SS93

### ►►► 77% Halse Farm Caravan & Camping Park

COUNTRYSIDE DISCOVERY
DAVID BELLAMY CONSERVATION AWARD GOLD

*(SS894344)*
TA24 7JL
☎ 01643 851259 01643 851592
**email:** enquiries@halsefarm.co.uk
**web:** www.halsefarm.co.uk
**Dir:** *Signed from A396 at Bridgetown. In Winsford turn left and bear left past pub. 1m up hill, entrance on left immediately after cattle grid*

£10-£12 £10-£12 £10-£12

*Halse Farm Caravan & Camping Park*

Open 22 Mar-Oct Booking advisable BH & mid Jul-Aug Last arrival 22.00hrs Last departure noon

A peaceful little site on Exmoor overlooking a wooded valley with glorious views. This moorland site is quite remote, but it provides good modern toilet facilities which are kept immaculately clean. A 3-acre site with 44 touring pitches, 11 hardstandings.

**Leisure:**
**Facilities:**
**Services:**

### WIVELISCOMBE MAP 03 ST02

**►►►► 89% Waterrow Touring Park** *(ST053251)*

TA4 2AZ

☎ 01984 623464 📠 01984 624280

**web:** www.waterrowpark.co.uk

**Dir:** *From M5 junct 25 take A358 (signed Minehead) around Taunton, then B3227 through Wiveliscombe. Site after 3m at Waterrow, 0.25m past Rock Inn*

★ £13-£18 £13-£18 £13-£18

Open all year Booking advisable BH & Jun-Sep Last arrival 19.00hrs Last departure 11.30hrs

A pretty park for adults only with individual pitches and plenty of hardstandings. The River Tone runs along a valley beneath the park, accessed by steps to a nature area created by the owners, where fly fishing is permitted. Painting workshops and other activities are available, and the local pub is a short walk away. A 6-acre site with 45 touring pitches, 38 hardstandings and 1 static.

**Facilities:**

**Services:**

**Notes:** Adults only. Wi-fi, watercolour painting

### YEOVIL MAP 04 ST51

**►► 73% Halfway Caravan & Camping Park** *(ST530195)*

Ilchester Rd BA22 8RE

☎ 01935 840342

**email:** halfwaycaravanpark@earthlink.net

**web:** www.halfwaycaravanpark.com

**Dir:** *On A37 between Ilchester & Yeovil*

★ £10-£12.50 £7-£10

Open all year Booking advisable

An attractive little park near the Somerset and Dorset border, and next to the Halfway House pub and restaurant. It overlooks a fishing lake and is surrounded by attractive countryside, with free fishing for people staying at the park. A 2-acre site with 20 touring pitches, 10 hardstandings.

**Services:**

**Notes:** 1 unisex shower

## STAFFORDSHIRE

### CANNOCK MAP 10 SJ91

**►►► 80% Cannock Chase Camping & Caravanning Club Site** *(SK039145)*

Old Youth Hostel, Wandon WS15 1QW

☎ 01889 582166

**web:** www.campingandcaravanningclub.co.uk/cannockchase

**Dir:** *on A460 to Hednesford, right at Rawnsley/Hazelslade sign, then 1st left. Site 0.5m past golf club*

★ £15.45-£20.15 £15.45-£20.15 £15.45-£20.15

Open 13 Mar-3 Nov Booking advisable BH & Jul-Aug Last arrival 21.00hrs Last departure noon

Very popular and attractive site in an excellent location in the heart of the Chase, with gently sloping ground and timber-built facilities. Walks from the site into this Area of Outstanding Natural Beauty are a pleasant feature of this park, just 2.5 miles from Rugeley. A 5-acre site with 60 touring pitches, 6 hardstandings.

**Facilities:**

**Services:**

**Notes:** Site gates closed 23.00hrs-07.00hrs

### CHEADLE MAP 10 SK04

**►►► 80% Quarry Walk Park** *(SK045405)*

Coppice Ln, Croxden Common, Freehay ST10 1RQ

☎ 01538 723412 📠 01538 724093

**email:** quarry@quarrywalkpark.co.uk

**web:** www.quarrywalkpark.co.uk

**Dir:** *From A522 (Uttoxeter-Cheadle road) turn at Crown Inn at Mabberley signed Freehay. In 1m at rdbt by Queen pub turn to Great Gate. Site signed on right in 1.25m*

★ £17-£19 £17-£19 £12-£14

Open all year Booking advisable BH Last arrival 21.00hrs Last departure noon

A pleasant park in an old quarry with well-screened pitches, all with water and electricity. Mature trees and shrubs enhance the peaceful ambience. Facilities include a small shop and information area, and family toilets. For children, there is a well equipped play area, and Alton Towers is nearby. A 14-acre site with 40 touring pitches, 40 hardstandings.

**Leisure:**

**Facilities:**

**Services:**

## LEEK

MAP 16 SJ95

### ►►► 82% Leek Camping & Caravanning Club Site *(SK004591)*

Blackshaw Grange, Blackshaw Moor ST13 8TL

☎ 01538 300285

**web:** www.campingandcaravanningclub.co.uk/leek

**Dir:** *2m from Leek on A53 Leek to Buxton road. Site 200yds past sign for 'Blackshaw Moor' on left*

★ £15.45-£20.15 £15.45-£20.15 Ʌ £15.45-£20.15

Open all year Booking advisable BH & peak periods Last arrival 21.00hrs Last departure noon

A beautifully located club site with well-screened pitches. The very good facilities are kept in pristine condition, and children will enjoy the enclosed play area. A 6-acre site with 70 touring pitches, 39 hardstandings.

**Leisure:**

**Facilities:**

**Services:**

**Notes:** Site gates closed 23.00hrs-07.00hrs. Play equipment

## LONGNOR

MAP 16 SK06

### ►►►► 74% Longnor Wood Caravan & Camping Park *(SK072640)*

DAVID BELLAMY CONSERVATION AWARD GOLD

SK17 0NG

☎ 01298 83648 01298 83648

**email:** info@longnorwood.co.uk

**web:** www.longnorwood.co.uk

**Dir:** *1.25m from Longnor (off Longnor to Leek road), signed from village*

★ £15.50-£17 £15.50-£17 Ʌ £13.50-£15.50

Open Mar-10 Jan Booking advisable BH, wknds & Jun-Aug Last arrival 21.00hrs Last departure noon

This spacious adult only park enjoys a secluded setting in the Peak National Park, an Area of Outstanding Natural Beauty. It is surrounded by beautiful rolling countryside and sheltered by woodland, with wildlife encouraged. The nearby village of Longnor offers pub food, restaurants and shops. A 10.5-acre site with 47 touring pitches, 26 hardstandings and 14 statics.

**Facilities:**

**Services:**

**Notes:** Adults only. Pitch & putt, badminton, boule

# SUFFOLK



## BECCLES

MAP 13 TM48

### ►► 79% Beulah Hall Caravan Park

*(TM478892)*

Dairy Ln, Mutford NR34 7QJ

☎ 01502 476609

**email:** beulah.hall@btinternet.com

**Dir:** *0.5m from A146, midway between Beccles & Lowestoft. At Barnby exit A146 into New Road, right at T-junct, park 2nd on right (300yds)*

★ £10-£12 £10-£12 Ʌ £10-£12

Open Apr-Oct Booking advisable Jul-Aug Last arrival 22.00hrs Last departure noon

Small secluded site in well kept grounds with mature trees and hedging. The neat pitches and pleasant tent area are beneath large trees opposite the swimming pool, and there are clean and well maintained portaloo toilets. This park is for adults only. A 2.5-acre site with 30 touring pitches.

**Facilities:**

**Services:**

**Notes:** Adults only

## BUCKLESHAM

MAP 13 TM24

### NEW ►►►► 84% Westwood Caravan Park

*(TM253411)*

Old Felixstowe Rd IP10 0BN

☎ 01279 739477

**Dir:** *From A14 junct 58 (SE of Ipswich) follow signs for Bucklesham. Site SE of Bucklesham near Kembroke Hall*

This new site is in the heart of rural Suffolk in an idyllic, peaceful setting. All buildings are of traditional Suffolk style, and the toilet facilities are of outstanding quality. There is also a spacious room for the disabled, and plenty of space for children to play. 100 touring pitches.

ENGLAND

## BUNGAY — MAP 13 TM38

### ►►► 68% Outney Meadow Caravan Park
*(TM333905)*

Outney Meadow NR35 1HG

☎ 01986 892338 🖷 01986 896627

**email:** c.r.hancy@ukgateway.net

**web:** www.outneymeadow.co.uk

**Dir:** *At Bungay park signed from rdbt junction of A143 & A144*

★ £12-£16 £12-£16 Å £12-£16

Open Mar-Oct Booking advisable public hols Last arrival 21.00hrs Last departure 16.00hrs

Three pleasant grassy areas beside the River Waveney, with screened pitches. The central toilet block offers good modern facilities, especially in the ladies, and is open at all times. The views from the site across the wide flood plain could be straight out of a Constable painting. Canoeing and boating, coarse fishing and cycling are all available here. A 6-acre site with 45 touring pitches, 5 hardstandings and 30 statics.

**Facilities:**

**Services:** →

**Notes:** Dogs must be kept on leads. Boat, canoe & bike hire

## BURY ST EDMUNDS — MAP 13 TL86

### ►►►► 85% The Dell Touring & Caravan Park
*(TL928640)*

Beyton Rd, Thurston IP31 3RB

☎ 01359 270121

**email:** thedellcaravanpark@btinternet.com

**Dir:** *Signed from A14 at Beyton/Thurston (4m E of Bury St Edmunds) & from A143 at Barton/Thurston*

★ £11-£13 £11-£13 Å £11-£24

Open all year Booking advisable BH Last arrival 21.00hrs Last departure noon

A small site with enthusiastic owners that has been developed to a high specification with more improvements planned. Set in a quiet spot with lots of mature trees, the quality purpose-built toilet facilities include family rooms, dishwashing and laundry. An ideal base for exploring this picturesque area. A 6-acre site with 60 touring pitches, 12 hardstandings.

**Facilities:**

**Services:** →

**Notes:** No footballs

## BUTLEY — MAP 13 TM35

### ►►► 69% *Forest Camping* *(TM355485)*

Rendlesham Forest IP12 3NF

☎ 01394 450707

**email:** admin@forestcamping.co.uk

**web:** www.forestcamping.co.uk

**Dir:** *From A12 & A1152 junct follow tourist signs to Rendlesham Forest Centre on B1084*

Å

Open Apr-Oct Booking advisable at all times Last arrival 22.00hrs Last departure noon

Set off the beaten track deep in Rendlesham Forest, this peaceful park with adequate toilet facilities is in an open grassy area surrounded by pine trees. Deer can often be seen in the vicinity. A 7-acre site with 90 touring pitches.

**Leisure:**

**Facilities:**

**Services:** →

**Notes:** No fires, dogs must be kept on leads

## DUNWICH — MAP 13 TM47

### ►► 68% *Haw Wood Farm Caravan Park*
*(TM421717)*

Hinton IP17 3QT

☎ 01986 784248

**Dir:** *Turn right off A12, 1.5m N of Darsham level crossing at Little Chef. Park 0.5m on right*

Å

Open Mar-Oct Booking advisable BH & Jul-Aug Last arrival 21.00hrs Last departure noon

An unpretentious family-orientated park set in two large fields surrounded by low hedges. The toilets are clean and functional, and there is plenty of space for children to play. An 8-acre site with 65 touring pitches and 25 statics.

**Leisure:**

**Facilities:**

**Services:** →

**Notes:**

**Abbreviations:** BH-bank holiday/s Etr-Easter Whit-Whitsun dep-departure fr-from hrs-hours m-mile mdnt-midnight rdbt-roundabout rs-restricted service wk-week wknd-weekend no dogs No cards → following facilities within 3 miles of the site

## FELIXSTOWE MAP 13 TM33

### ►►► 71% Peewit Caravan Park *(TM290338)*

Walton Av IP11 2HB

☎ 01394 284511

**web:** www.peewitcaravanpark.co.uk

**Dir:** *Signed from A14 in Felixstowe, 100mtrs past dock gate 1, 1st on left*

★ £14.50-£20 £14.50-£20 £10-£20

Open Apr or Etr-Oct Booking advisable BH & school hols Last arrival 21.00hrs Last departure 11.00hrs

A grass touring area fringed by trees, with well-maintained grounds and a colourful floral display. This handy urban site is not overlooked by houses, and the toilet facilities are clean and well cared for. A function room contains a TV and library. The beach is a few minutes away by car. A 13-acre site with 45 touring pitches, 4 hardstandings and 200 statics.

**Leisure:**

**Facilities:**

**Services:**

**Notes:** Only foam footballs. Boules area, bowling green, adventure trail

## HOLLESLEY MAP 13 TM34

### NEW ►►► 85% Run Cottage Touring Park *(TM350440)*

Alderton Rd IP12 3RQ

☎ 01394 411309

**email:** info@run-cottage.co.uk

**web:** www.run-cottage.co.uk

£12-£14 £12-£14 £12-£14

Open all year Booking advisable Last arrival 20.00hrs Last departure 11.00hrs

Located in the peaceful village of Hollesley on the Suffolk coast, this landscaped park is set behind the owners' home. The generously-sized pitches are serviced by a well-appointed and immaculately maintained toilet block. Handy for Sutton Hoo and the bird reserves at Dunwich and Minsmere. A 2.5-acre site with 20 touring pitches, 6 hardstandings.

**Facilities:**

**Services:**

**Notes:** No groundsheets

## IPSWICH MAP 13 TM14

### ►►►► 87% Priory Park *(TM198409)*

IP10 0JT

☎ 01473 727393 & 726373 01473 278372

**email:** jwl@priory-park.com

**web:** www.priory-park.com

**Dir:** *Exit A14 at Ipswich southern by-pass towards town centre. 300mtrs left towards Priory Park. Follow single track road into park*

★ £16-£24 £16-£24 £16-£24

Open Apr-Oct (rs Apr-Jun & Sep-Oct limited pitches, club & pool closed) Booking advisable at all times Last arrival 18.00hrs Last departure 14.00hrs

A well-screened and very peaceful south-facing park set close to the banks of the tidal River Orwell, and with panoramic views out over the water. The park is attractively landscaped, and offers superb toilet facilities with smartly-tiled, fully-serviced cubicles. A 100-acre site with 75 touring pitches, 59 hardstandings and 260 statics.

**Leisure:**

**Facilities:**

**Services:**

**Notes:** No commercial vehicles, pup tents or group bookings. 9-hole golf, small boat launching, table tennis

*see advert on page 242*

### ►►► 77% Low House Touring Caravan Centre *(TM227425)*

Bucklesham Rd, Foxhall IP10 0AU

☎ 01473 659437 & 07710 378029 01473 659880

**email:** low.house@btopenworld.com

**Dir:** *From A14 south ring road take slip road to A1156 signed East Ipswich. Right in 1m, right again in 0.5m. Site on left*

Open all year Booking advisable Last arrival anytime Last departure 14.00hrs

A secluded site surrounded by hundreds of mature trees. Buildings have been hand-crafted by the owner in stained timber, and there is a children's play area, and a collection of caged rabbits, bantams and guinea fowl. Tents accepted only if space available. A 3.5-acre site with 30 touring pitches.

**Leisure:**

**Facilities:**

**Services:**

**Notes:** Dogs must be kept on leads

## KESSINGLAND — MAP 13 TM58

### 65% Kessingland Beach Holiday Park *(TM535852)*

Beach Rd NR33 7RN

01502 740636 01502 740907

**email:** holidaysales.kessinglandbeach@park-resorts.com

**web:** www.park-resorts.com

★ £6-£28 £6-£28 £3-£25

Open Etr-2 Nov Booking advisable Jul-Aug Last arrival mdnt Last departure 10.00hrs

A large holiday centre with direct access onto the beach, and a variety of leisure facilities. The touring area is tucked away from the statics, and served by a clean and functional toilet block. A fish and chip shop and Boat House Restaurant are popular features. A 69-acre site with 90 touring pitches.

**Leisure:**

**Facilities:**

**Services:**

**Notes:** Kid's clubs, entertainment, mini ten pin bowling

*see advert on this page*

## ►►►► 86% Heathland Beach Caravan Park *(TM533877)*

GOLD

London Rd NR33 7PJ
☎ 01502 740337 🖷 01502 742355
**email:** heathlandbeach@btinternet.com
**web:** www.heathlandbeach.co.uk
**Dir:** *1m N of Kessingland off A12 onto B1437*

★ £17-£21 £17-£21 £8-£21

Open Apr-Oct Booking advisable peak periods Last arrival 21.00hrs Last departure 11.00hrs

A well-run and maintained park offering superb toilet facilities. The park is set in meadowland, with level grass pitches, and mature trees and bushes. There is direct access to the sea and beach, and good provisions for families on site with a heated swimming pool and three play areas. A 5-acre site with 63 touring pitches and 200 statics.

**Leisure:**

**Facilities:**

**Services:** →

**Notes:** One dog only per unit. Freshwater & sea fishing

## ►►►► 84% Kessingland Camping & Caravanning Club Site *(TM520860)*

Suffolk Wildlife Park, Whites Ln NR33 7TF
☎ 01502 742040
**web:** www.campingandcaravanningclub.co.uk/kessingland
**Dir:** *On A12 from Lowestoft at Kessingland rdbt, follow Wildlife Park signs, turn right through park entrance*

★ £15.45-£22.15 £15.45-£22.15 £15.45-£22.15

Open 13 Mar-3 Nov Booking advisable BH & peak periods Last arrival 21.00hrs Last departure noon

A well screened open site next to Suffolk Wildlife Park, where concessions are available for visitors. An extensive renovation has created superb facilities, including three family rooms, a disabled unit, and smart reception. A well-equipped laundry and covered dishwashing sinks add to the quality amenities. A 5-acre site with 90 touring pitches.

**Leisure:**

**Facilities:**

**Services:** →

**Notes:** Site gates closed 23.00hrs-7.00hrs. Play equipment

### LEISTON MAP 13 TM46

## ►►► 77% Cakes & Ale *(TM432637)*

Abbey Ln, Theberton IP16 4TE
☎ 01728 831655 🖷 01728 831998
**email:** info@cakesandale.f2s.com
**web:** www.cakesandale.net
**Dir:** *From Saxmundham E on B1119. 3m follow minor road over level crossing, turn right, in 0.5m straight on at x-rds, entrance 0.5m on left*

★ £16-£22 £16-£22 £16-£22

Open Apr-Oct (rs low season club, shop & reception limited hours) Booking advisable public & school hols Last arrival 20.00hrs Last departure 13.00hrs

A large, well spread out site with many trees and bushes on a former Second World War airfield. The spacious touring area includes plenty of hardstandings and super pitches, and there is a good bar and a well-maintained toilet block. Wi-fi is available on site. A 5-acre site with 50 touring pitches, 50 hardstandings and 200 statics.

**Leisure:** **Facilities:**

**Services:** →

**Notes:** No group bookings, no noise between 21.00hrs-08.00hrs. Wi-fi. 5-acre recreation ground, driving range/net

### LOWESTOFT
*see Kessingland*

### SAXMUNDHAM MAP 13 TM36

## ►►► 74% Whitearch Touring Caravan Park *(TM379610)*

Main Rd, Benhall IP17 1NA
☎ 01728 604646 & 603773
**Dir:** *At junct of A12 & B1121*

★ fr £13.50

Open Apr-Oct Booking advisable BH Last arrival 20.45hrs

A small, maturing park set around an attractive coarse-fishing lake, with decent toilet facilities and secluded pitches tucked away among trees and shrubs. The park is popular with anglers; there is some traffic noise from the adjacent A12. A 14.5-acre site with 50 touring pitches, 50 hardstandings.

**Leisure:** **Facilities:**

**Services:** →

**Notes:** No cars by caravans. No bicycles

**Leisure:** Indoor swimming pool Outdoor swimming pool Tennis court Games room Children's playground Stables 9/18 hole golf course Boats for hire Cinema Fishing Mini golf Watersports Separate TV room

ENGLAND

## SAXMUNDHAM )A?N5?P,+

### ►► 78% Marsh Farm Caravan Site

*(TM385608)*

Sternfield IP17 1HW

☎ 01728 602168

**Dir:** *From A12 take A1094 Aldeburgh road, at Snape x-roads turn left signed Sternfield, follow signs to farm*

Open all year Booking advisable Jun-Aug Last arrival 21.00hrs Last departure 17.00hrs

A very pretty site overlooking reed-fringed lakes which offer excellent coarse fishing. The facilities are very well maintained, and the park is a truly peaceful haven. A 30-acre site with 45 touring pitches.

**Facilities:**

**Services:** →

**Notes:** Dogs must be kept on leads

## SUDBURY MAP 13 TL84

### ►►► 75% Willowmere Caravan Park

*(TL886388)*

Bures Rd, Little Cornard CO10 0NN

☎ 01787 375559 01787 375559

**Dir:** *1.5m S of Sudbury on B1508 (Bures road)*

fr £11 fr £11 fr £8

Open Etr-Sep Booking advisable BH Last arrival any time Last departure noon

A pleasant little site in a quiet location tucked away beyond a tiny residential static area, offering spotless facilities. A 3-acre site with 40 touring pitches and 9 statics.

**Facilities:**

**Services:** →

**Notes:** Fishing

ENGLAND

## WOODBRIDGE MAP 13 TM24

### PREMIER PARK

►►►►► 92% **Moon & Sixpence**
*(TM263454)*
Newbourn Rd, Waldringfield IP12 4PP
☎ 01473 736650 🖷 01473 736270
**email:** info@moonandsixpence.eu
**web:** www.moonandsixpence.eu
**Dir:** *Follow caravan & Moon & Sixpence signs from A12 Ipswich (East bypass). Turn left at x-roads 1.5m from A12*

★ £18-£26 £18-£26 Å £18-£26

Open Apr-Oct (rs low season club, shop, reception open limited hours) Booking advisable BH & school hols Last arrival 20.00hrs Last departure noon

A well-planned site, with tourers occupying a sheltered valley position around an attractive boating lake with a sandy beach. Toilet facilities are housed in a smart Norwegian cabin, and there is a laundry and dishwashing area. Leisure facilities include two tennis courts, a bowling green, fishing, boating and a games room. There is an adult-only area, and a strict no groups and no noise after 9pm policy. A 5-acre site with 65 touring pitches and 225 statics.

**Leisure:**

**Facilities:**

**Services:**

**Notes:** No group bookings or commercial vehicles. Quiet 21.00hrs-08.00hrs. Wi-fi. Lake, cycle trail, 10-acre sports area/9-hole golf

*see advert on opposite page*

►► 83% **Moat Barn Touring Caravan Park**
*(TM269530)*
Dallinghoo Rd, Bredfield IP13 6BD
☎ 01473 737520
**web:** www.moatbarn.co.uk
**Dir:** *Exit A12 at Bredfield, take 1st right at village pump. Through village, 1m site on left*

★ £13 £13 Å £13

Open Mar-15 Jan Booking advisable BH Last arrival 22.00hrs Last departure noon

An attractive small park set in idyllic Suffolk countryside, ideally located for touring the heritage coastline and Sutton Hoo. The modern toilet block is well equipped and maintained. Bed and breakfast and cycle hire are available, but there are no facilities for children. A 2-acre site with 25 touring pitches.

**Facilities:**

**Services:**

**Notes:** No ball games, breathable groundsheets only, dogs on leads

# SURREY

## CHERTSEY MAP 06 TQ06

►►►► 83% **Chertsey Camping & Caravanning Club Site** *(TQ052667)*
Bridge Rd KT16 8JX
☎ 01932 562405
**web:** www.campingandcaravanningclub.co.uk/chertsey
**Dir:** *M25 junct 11, follow A317 to Chertsey. At rdbt take 1st exit to lights. Straight over at next lights. Turn right 400yds, turn left into site*

GOLD

★ £18.35-£23.25 £18.35-£23.25 Å £18.35-£23.25

Open all year Booking advisable BH & peak periods Last arrival 21.00hrs Last departure noon

A pretty Thames-side site set amongst trees and shrubs in well-tended grounds, ideally placed for the M3/M25 and for visiting London. Some attractive riverside pitches are very popular, and fishing and boating is allowed from the site on the river. The toilet facilities are very good. A 12-acre site with 150 touring pitches, 50 hardstandings.

**Leisure:**

**Facilities:**

**Services:**

**Notes:** Site gates closed 23.00hrs-7.00hrs

## EAST HORSLEY MAP 06 TQ05

►►► 80% **Horsley Camping & Caravanning Club Site** *(TQ083552)*
Ockham Rd North KT24 6PE
☎ 01483 283273
**web:** www.campingandcaravanningclub.co.uk/horsley
**Dir:** *M25 junct 10. S & take 1st major turn signed Ockham/ Southend/Ripley. Left & site 2.5m on right. From S take A3 past Guildford & take B2215 towards Ripley*

★ £15.45-£22.15 £15.45-£22.15 Å £15.45-£22.15

Open 13 Mar-3 Nov Booking advisable BH & peak periods Last arrival 21.00hrs Last departure noon

A beautiful lakeside site with plenty of trees and shrubs and separate camping fields, providing a tranquil base within easy reach of London. Toilet facilities are well maintained and clean. A 9.5-acre site with 130 touring pitches, 41 hardstandings.

**Leisure:**

**Facilities:**

**Services:**

**Notes:** Site gates closed 23.00hrs-7.00hrs. Fishing

ENGLAND

# SUSSEX, EAST

## BATTLE MAP 07 TQ71

►►► 74% **Brakes Coppice Park** *(TQ765134)*

Forewood Ln TN33 9AB

☎ 01424 830322

**email:** brakesco@btinternet.com

**web:** www.brakescoppicepark.co.uk

**Dir:** *From Battle on A2100 towards Hastings. After 2m turn right for Crowhurst. Site 1m on left*

★ £14-£16 £12-£16 £12-£16

Open Mar-Oct Booking advisable public hols & Jul-Aug Last arrival 21.00hrs Last departure noon

Secluded farm site in meadow surrounded by woodland with small stream and fishing lake, and a raised garden in the centre. Pitches are neatly laid out on a terrace, and tents are pitched on grass edged by woodland. A 3-acre site with 30 touring pitches, 10 hardstandings.

**Leisure:** **Facilities:**

**Services:**

**Notes:** No fires, footballs or kite flying, dogs must be kept on leads, small coarse fishing lake

## CAMBER MAP 07 TQ91

**NEW** 66% **Camber Sands** *(TQ972184)*

New Lydd Rd TN31 7RT

☎ 0871 664 9719

**email:** camber.sands@park-resorts.com

**web:** www.park-resorts.com

**Dir:** *From M20 junct 10 (Ashford International Station) onto A2070 signed Brenzett. Follow Hastings & Rye signs, on A259. 1m before Rye, left signed Camber. Site in 3m*

£6-£30 £6-£30

Open 31 Mar-Oct Booking advisable

Located opposite Camber's vast sandy beach, this large holiday centre offers a good range of leisure and entertainment facilities. The touring area is positioned close to the reception and entrance, and is served by a clean and functional toilet block. 40 touring pitches and 921 statics.

**Leisure:**

**Facilities:**

**Services:**

## CROWBOROUGH MAP 06 TQ53

►►► 79% **Crowborough Camping & Caravanning Club Site** *(TQ520315)*

Goldsmith Recreation Ground TN6 2TN

☎ 01892 664827

**web:** www.campingandcaravanningclub.co.uk/crowborough

**Dir:** *Turn off A26 into entrance to 'Goldsmiths Ground', signed Leisure Centre. At top of road right onto site lane*

★ £15.45-£20.15 £15.45-£20.15 £15.45-£20.15

Open Mar-Dec Booking advisable BH & peak periods Last arrival 21.00hrs Last departure noon

A spacious terraced site with stunning views across the Weald to the North Downs in Kent. This good quality site has clean, modern toilets, a kitchen and eating area for campers, a recreation room, and good provision of hardstandings. An excellent leisure centre is adjacent to the park. A 13-acre site with 90 touring pitches, 26 hardstandings.

**Leisure:**

**Facilities:**

**Services:**

**Notes:** Site gates closed 23.00hrs-7.00hrs

## FURNER'S GREEN MAP 06 TQ42

►► 81% **Heaven Farm** *(TQ403264)*

TN22 3RG

☎ 01825 790226 01825 790881

**web:** www.heavenfarm.co.uk

**Dir:** *On A275 between Lewes & East Grinstead, 1m N of Sheffield Park Gardens*

Open Apr-Oct Booking advisable Last arrival 21.00hrs Last departure noon

Delightful small rural site on a popular farm complex incorporating a farm museum, craft shop, tea room and nature trail. Good clean facilities in well-converted outbuildings. A 1.5-acre site with 25 touring pitches.

**Facilities:**

**Services:**

**Notes:** Prefer no children between 6-18yrs. Fishing

ENGLAND

## HEATHFIELD MAP 06 TQ52

### ►► 74% *Greenviews Caravan Park*

*(TQ605223)*
Burwash Rd, Broad Oak TN21 8RT
☎ 01435 863531 📠 01435 863531
**Dir:** *Through Heathfield on A265 for 1m. Site on left after Broad Oak sign*

Open Apr-Oct (rs early & late season bookings only, subject to weather) Booking advisable Jul-Aug Last arrival 22.00hrs Last departure 10.30hrs

A small touring area adjoining a residential park, with a smart clubhouse. The facility block includes a room for disabled visitors. The owners always offer a friendly welcome, and they take pride in the lovely flower beds which adorn the park. A 3-acre site with 10 touring pitches and 51 statics.

**Facilities:**
**Services:**
**Notes:**

## HORAM MAP 06 TQ51

### ►►► 78% Horam Manor Touring Park

*(TQ579170)*
TN21 0YD
☎ 01435 813662
**email:** camp@horam-manor.co.uk
**web:** www.horam-manor.co.uk
**Dir:** *On A267, 3m S of Heathfield and 10m N of Eastbourne*

★ £14.50 £14.50 £14.50

Open Mar-Oct Booking advisable peak periods Last arrival 22.00hrs Last departure 18.00hrs

A well landscaped park in a peaceful location on former estate land, set in gently-sloping grassland surrounded by woods and fishing lakes. There is free entry to nearby nature trails and a farm museum for site visitors. A 7-acre site with 90 touring pitches.

**Leisure:**
**Facilities:**
**Services:**
**Notes:** Parent and toddler room

## NORMAN'S BAY MAP 06 TQ60

### ►►► 77% Norman's Bay Camping & Caravanning Club Site *(TQ682055)*

BN24 6PR
☎ 01323 761190
**web:** www.campingandcaravanningclub.co.uk/normansbay
**Dir:** *From rdbt junct of A27/A259 follow A259 signed Eastbourne. In Pevensey Bay village take 1st left signed Beachlands only. 1.25m site on left*

★ £15.45-£22.15 £15.45-£22.15 £15.45-£22.15

Open 13 Mar-3 Nov Booking advisable BH & peak periods Last arrival 21.00hrs Last departure noon

A well kept site with immaculate toilet block, right beside the sea. This popular family park enjoys good rural views towards Rye and Pevensey. A 13-acre site with 200 touring pitches, 5 hardstandings.

**Leisure:**
**Facilities:**
**Services:**
**Notes:** Site gates closed 23.00hrs-7.00hrs

## PEVENSEY BAY MAP 06 TQ60

### ►►► 80% Bay View Park *(TQ648028)*

Old Martello Rd BN24 6DX
☎ 01323 768688 📠 01323 769637
**email:** holidays@bay-view.co.uk
**web:** www.bay-view.co.uk
**Dir:** *Signed from A259 W of Pevensey Bay. On sea side of A259 along private road towards beach*

★ £13.50-£18.50 £13.50-£18.50 fr £13.50

GOLD

Open Mar-Oct Booking advisable BH & school hols Last arrival 20.00hrs Last departure noon

A pleasant well-run site just yards from the beach, in an area east of the town centre known as 'The Crumbles'. The level grassy site is very well maintained. A 6-acre site with 94 touring pitches, 4 hardstandings.

**Leisure:**
**Facilities:**
**Services:**
**Notes:** Couples & families only, no commercial vehicles

# SUSSEX, WEST

## ARUNDEL MAP 06 TQ00

### ►► 76% Ship & Anchor Marina

GOLD

*(TQ002040)*

Station Rd, Ford BN18 0BJ

☎ 01243 551262 📠 01243 555256

**email:** ysm36@dial.pipex.com

**Dir:** *From A27 at Arundel take road S signed Ford. Site 2m from Arundel on left after level crossing*

★ £11.50-£16.50 £11.50-£16.50 £11.50-£16.50

Open Mar-Oct Booking advisable during Goodwood Motor Festival Last arrival 21.00hrs Last departure noon

A neat and tidy site in a pleasant position beside the Ship & Anchor pub and the tidal River Arun. There are good walks from the site both to Arundel and to the coast. A 12-acre site with 120 touring pitches, 11 hardstandings and 40 statics.

**Leisure:**

**Facilities:**

**Services:** →

**Notes:** River fishing from site

## BARNS GREEN MAP 06 TQ12

### ►►► 84% Sumners Ponds Fishery & Campsite *(TQ125268)*

GOLD

Chapel Rd RH13 0PR

☎ 01403 732539

**email:** sumnersponds@dsl.co.uk

**web:** www.sumnersponds.co.uk

**Dir:** *From A272 at Coolham x-rds, N towards Barns Green. In 1.5m take 1st left at small x-rds. 1m, over level crossing. Site on left just after right bend*

Open all year Booking advisable all year Last arrival 20.00hrs Last departure 17.00hrs

A touring area on a working farm on the edge of the quiet village of Barnes Green, with purpose built facilities of a high standard. There are three well-stocked fishing lakes set in attractive surroundings, and a woodland walk with direct access to miles of footpaths. Horsham and Brighton are within easy reach. A 40-acre site with 61 touring pitches, 31 hardstandings.

**Leisure:**

**Facilities:**

**Services:** →

**Notes:** Only one car per pitch. Cycling paths, cycle racks

## BILLINGSHURST MAP 06 TQ02

### ►► 72% Limeburners Arms Camp Site

*(TQ072255)*

Lordings Rd, Newbridge RH14 9JA

☎ 01403 782311

**email:** chippy.sawyer@virgin.net

**Dir:** *From A29 turn W onto A272 for 1m, then left onto B2133. Site 300yds on left*

★ fr £10 fr £10 fr £10

Open Apr-Oct Booking advisable BH & Jul-Aug Last arrival 22.00hrs Last departure 14.00hrs

A secluded site in rural West Sussex, at the rear of the Limeburners Arms public house, and surrounded by fields. It makes a pleasant base for touring the South Downs and the Arun Valley. The toilets are basic but very clean. A 2.75-acre site with 40 touring pitches.

**Leisure:**

**Facilities:**

**Services:** →

## BIRDHAM MAP 05 SU80

### NEW ► 71% Tawny Touring Park *(SZ818991)*

Tawny Nurseries, Bell Ln PO20 7HY

☎ 01243 512168

**email:** tawny@pobox.co.uk

**web:** www.tawnytouringpark.co.uk

**Dir:** *From A27 at Stockbridge rdbt take A286 towards The Witterings. 5m to mini rdbt in Birdham. 1st exit onto B2198. Park 300mtrs on left*

★ £11 £11

Open all year Booking advisable BH Last arrival 21.00hrs Last departure 21.00hrs

A small site for the self-contained tourer only, on a landscaped field adjacent to the owners' nurseries. There are no toilet facilities, so tents are only allowed with caravans. The beach is just one mile away. A 4.5-acre site with 30 touring pitches, 5 hardstandings.

**Services:** →

**Notes:** Dogs must be kept on leads

ENGLAND

## CHICHESTER

MAP 05 SU80

### ►►► 76% Ellscott Park *(SU829995)*

Sidlesham Ln, Birdham PO20 7QL

☎ 01243 512003 📠 01243 512003

**email:** camping@ellscottpark.co.uk

**web:** www.ellscottpark.co.uk

**Dir:** *Take A286 (Chichester/Wittering road) for approx 4m, left at Butterfly Farm sign, site 500yds right*

★ £12-£15 £12-£15 £10-£13

Open Mar-Oct Booking advisable BH & Aug

A well-kept park set in meadowland behind the owners' nursery and van storage area. The park attracts a peace-loving clientele, and is handy for the beach and other local attractions. Home-grown produce and eggs are for sale. A 2.5-acre site with 50 touring pitches.

**Leisure:**

**Facilities:**

**Services:**

**Notes:**

## DIAL POST

MAP 06 TQ11

### ►►►► 86% *Honeybridge Park*

*(TQ152183)*

Honeybridge Ln RH13 8NX

☎ 01403 710923 📠 01403 712815

**email:** enquiries@honeybridgepark.co.uk

**web:** www.honeybridgepark.co.uk

**Dir:** *10m S of Horsham on A24. Turn left 1m past Dial Post sign at Old Barn Nurseries, park 300yds on right*

Open all year Booking advisable BH & high season Last arrival 20.00hrs Last departure noon

An attractive and very popular park on gently-sloping ground surrounded by hedgerows and mature trees. A comprehensive amenities building houses upmarket toilet facilities including luxury family and disabled rooms, as well as a laundry, shop and off-licence. There are plenty of hardstandings and electric hook-ups, and an excellent children's play area. Performance kites are sold, and instruction in flying them is given. A 15-acre site with 150 touring pitches, 68 hardstandings.

**Leisure:**

**Facilities:**

**Services:**

**Notes:** No groups of unaccompanied minors. Licensed shop

## GRAFFHAM

MAP 06 SU91

### ►►► 78% Graffham Camping & Caravanning Club Site *(SU941187)*

Great Bury GU28 0QJ

☎ 01798 867476

**web:** www.campingandcaravanningclub.co.uk/graffham

**Dir:** *From Petworth on A285 pass Badgers pub on left & BP garage on right. Next right signed Selham Graffham. Follow sign to site*

★ £15.45-£20.15 £15.45-£20.15 £15.45-£20.15

Open 13 Mar-3 Nov Booking advisable BH & peak periods Last arrival 21.00hrs Last departure noon

A superb woodland site with some pitches occupying their own private, naturally-screened areas. A peaceful retreat, or base for touring the South Downs, Chichester and the south coast. A 20-acre site with 90 touring pitches.

**Facilities:**

**Services:**

**Notes:** Site gates closed 23.00hrs-07.00hrs

## HORSHAM

*see Barns Green & Dial Post*

## LITTLEHAMPTON

MAP 06 TQ00

### ►►► 78% White Rose Touring Park

*(TQ029039)*

Mill Ln, Wick BN17 7PH

☎ 01903 716176 📠 01903 732671

**email:** snowdondavid@hotmail.com

**web:** www.whiterosetouringpark.co.uk

**Dir:** *From A27 take A284, turn left into Mill Lane, after approx 1.5m site just after Six Bells Pub*

Open 15 Mar-14 Dec Booking advisable BH & Jul-Aug Last arrival 22.00hrs Last departure noon

Farmland surrounds this carefully maintained site located on well-drained ground close to Arundel and Littlehampton. The family-run site offers a choice of super pitches and mini pitches for tents, and there is good hedging and landscaping. A 7-acre site with 127 touring pitches and 13 statics.

**Leisure:**

**Facilities:**

**Services:**

## SELSEY — MAP 05 SZ89

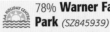

### 78% **Warner Farm Touring Park** *(SZ845939)*

Warner Ln, Selsey PO20 9EL

☎ 01243 608440 & 604499 📠 01243 604095

**email:** touring@bunnleisure.co.uk

**web:** www.bunnleisure.co.uk

**Dir:** *Turn right onto School Lane & follow signs*

£18.50-£32 £18.50-£32 £16.50-£30

Open Mar-Oct Booking advisable 4 wks prior to arrival Last arrival 17.30hrs Last departure 10.00hrs

A well-screened touring site adjoining the three static parks under the same ownership. A courtesy bus runs around the complex to entertainment areas and supermarkets. The park backs onto open grassland, and the leisure facilities with bar, amusements and bowling alley, and swimming pool/sauna complex are also accessible to tourers. A 10-acre site with 250 touring pitches, 60 hardstandings and 1500 statics.

**Leisure:**

**Facilities:**

**Services:** →

*see advert on this page*

## SLINDON — MAP 06 SU90

### ► 80% **Slindon Camping & Caravanning Club Site** *(SU958084)*

Slindon Park BN18 0RG

☎ 01243 814387

**web:** www.campingandcaravanningclub.co.uk/slindon

**Dir:** *From A27 Fontwell to Chichester turn right at sign for Brittons Lane & 2nd right to Slindon. Site on this road*

★ £11.25-£12.85 £11.25-£12.85 £11.25-£12.85

Open 13 Mar-29 Sep Booking advisable BH & peak periods Last arrival 21.00hrs Last departure noon

A beautiful former orchard, completely screened by National Trust trees, and very quiet. It is ideal for the self-contained camper, and own sanitary facilities are essential. The entrance gate is narrow and on a bend, and touring units are advised to take a wide sweep on approach from private gravel roadway. A 2-acre site with 40 touring pitches.

**Facilities:**

**Services:** →

**Notes:** Site gates closed 23.00hrs-07.00hrs

## SOUTHBOURNE — MAP 05 SU70

### ►►► 78% **Chichester Camping & Caravanning Club Site** *(SU774056)*

Main Rd PO10 8JH

☎ 01243 373202

**web:** www.campingandcaravanningclub.co.uk/chichester

**Dir:** *From Chichester take A259 to Southbourne, site on right past Inlands Road*

★ £18.25-£22.15 £18.25-£22.15 £18.25-£22.15

Open 7 Feb-17 Nov Booking advisable BH & peak periods Last arrival 21.00hrs Last departure noon

Situated in open meadow and orchard, a very pleasant, popular site with well looked after, clean facilities. Well placed for Chichester, South Downs and the ferry ports. A 3-acre site with 58 touring pitches, 42 hardstandings.

**Facilities:**

**Services:** →

**Notes:** Site gates closed 23.00hrs-07.00hrs

### WEST WITTERING MAP 05 SZ79

**►►► 78% Wicks Farm Camping Park** *(SZ796995)*

GOLD

Redlands Ln PO20 8QE

☎ 01243 513116

**web:** www.wicksfarm.co.uk

**Dir:** *From A27 Chichester take A286/B2179 to West Wittering. Follow for 6m and 2nd right after Lamb Inn*

Open 14 Mar-Oct Booking advisable peak periods Last arrival 21.00hrs Last departure noon

A pleasant rural site, well screened by trees and with good clean toilet facilities. The park has a spacious recreation field, and good local walks, with the beach just two miles away. No caravans, only motorhomes and tents. A 14-acre site with 40 touring pitches.

**Leisure:**

**Facilities:**

**Services:** →

## WARWICKSHIRE

### ASTON CANTLOW MAP 10 SP16

**►►► 77% Island Meadow Caravan Park** *(SP137596)*

GOLD

The Mill House B95 6JP

☎ 01789 488273 01789 488273

**email:** holiday@islandmeadowcaravanpark.co.uk

**web:** www.islandmeadowcaravanpark.co.uk

**Dir:** *From A46 or A3400 for Aston Cantlow. Park 0.25m W off Mill Lane*

★ £16 £16 £12.50-£18

Open Mar-Oct Booking advisable Jun-Aug Last arrival 21.00hrs Last departure noon

A small well-kept site bordered by the River Alne on one side and its mill stream on the other. Mature willows line the banks, and this is a very pleasant place to relax and unwind. A 7-acre site with 24 touring pitches, 14 hardstandings and 56 statics.

**Facilities:**

**Services:** →

**Notes:** Free fishing for guests

### HARBURY MAP 11 SP35

**NEW ►►► 80% Harbury Fields** *(SP352604)*

Harbury Fields Farm CV33 9JN

☎ 01926 612457

**email:** rdavis@harburyfields.co.uk

**web:** www.harburyfields.co.uk

**Dir:** *M40 junct 12 onto B4451 (signed Kenton/Gaydon). 0.75m turn right signed Lightborne. 4m turn right at rdbt onto B4455 (signed Harbury). 3rd right by petrol station, site entrance in 700yds (by two cottages)*

★ £11-£14

Open 2 Jan-19 Dec Booking advisable at all times Last arrival 22.00hrs Last departure 14.00hrs

This developing park is in a peaceful farm setting with lovely countryside views. All pitches have hardstandings with electricity, and the facilities are spotless. It is well positioned for visiting Warwick and Leamington Spa as well as the exhibition centres at NEC Birmingham, NAC Stoneleigh or Warwick. A 3-acre site with 30 touring pitches, 25 hardstandings.

**Facilities:**

**Services:** →

**Notes:** Wi-fi

### KINGSBURY MAP 10 SP29

**►►►► 86% Kingsbury Water Park Camping & Caravanning Club Site** *(SP202968)*

Kingsbury Water Park, Bodymoor, Heath Ln B76 0DY

☎ 01827 874101

**web:** www.campingandcaravanningclub.co.uk/kingsburywaterpark

**Dir:** *From M42 junct 9 take B4097 Kingsbury road. Left at rdbt, past main entrance to water park, over motorway, take next right. Follow lane for 0.5m to site*

★ £18.25-£20.15 £18.25-£20.15 £18.25-£20.15

Open all year Booking advisable BH & peak periods Last arrival 21.00hrs Last departure noon

A very upmarket site providing high standards in every area. Along with private washing facilities in the quality toilets, there is good security on this attractive former gravel pit, with its complex of lakes, canals, woods and marshland, with good access roads. An 18-acre site with 150 touring pitches, 75 hardstandings.

**Leisure:**

**Facilities:**

**Services:** →

**Notes:** Site gates closed 23.00hrs-07.00hrs

ENGLAND

## KINGSBURY *CONTINUED*

### ► 70% Tame View Caravan Site *(SP209979)*

Cliff B78 2DR

☎ 01827 873853

**Dir:** *400yds off A51 (Tamworth-Kingsbury road), 1m N of Kingsbury opp pub. Signed Cliff Hall Lane*

Open all year Booking advisable 1 month in advance Last arrival 23.00hrs Last departure 23.00hrs

A secluded spot overlooking the Tame Valley and river, sheltered by high hedges. Sanitary facilities are minimal, but the site is popular with many return visitors. A 5-acre site with 5 touring pitches.

**Facilities:** **Services:** →

**Notes:** Fishing

## RUGBY — MAP 11 SP57

### ►► 68% Lodge Farm Campsite *(SP476748)*

Bilton Ln, Long Lawford CV23 9DU

☎ 01788 560193 01788 550603

**email:** alec@lodgefarm.com

**web:** www.lodgefarm.com

**Dir:** *From Rugby take A428 (Lawford Road) 1.5m towards Coventry. At Sheaf & Sickle pub left into Bilton Lane, site 500yds*

£12-£20 £12-£20 £10-£15

Open Etr-Nov Booking advisable BH Last arrival 22.00hrs

A small, simple farm site set behind the friendly owner's home and self-catering cottages, with converted stables housing the toilet facilities. Rugby is only a short drive away, and the site is tucked well away from the main road. A 2.5-acre site with 35 touring pitches, 3 hardstandings and 10 statics.

**Facilities:**

**Services:** →

**Notes:** Wi-fi

## WOLVEY — MAP 11 SP48

### ►►► 75% Wolvey Villa Farm Caravan & Camping Site *(SP428869)*

LE10 3HF

☎ 01455 220493 & 220630

**web:** www.wolveycaravanpark.itgo.com

**Dir:** *From M6 junct 2 take B4065 follow Wolvey signs. Or M69 junct 1 & follow Wolvey signs*

★ £12 £12 £12

Open all year Booking advisable Spring BH-mid Aug Last arrival 22.00hrs Last departure noon

A level grass site surrounded by trees and shrubs, on the borders of Warwickshire and Leicestershire. This quiet country site has its own popular fishing lake, and is convenient for visiting the major cities of Coventry and Leicester. A 7-acre site with 110 touring pitches, 24 hardstandings.

**Leisure:** **Facilities:**

**Services:** →

**Notes:** No twin axles. Putting green, off licence

# WEST MIDLANDS

## MERIDEN — MAP 10 SP28

### ►►►► 80% Somers Wood Caravan Park *(SP225824)*

Somers Rd CV7 7PL

☎ 01676 522978 01676 522978

**email:** somerswoodcpk@aol.com

**web:** www.somerswood.co.uk

**Dir:** *M42 junct 6, A45 signed Coventry. Keep left (do not take flyover). Then right onto A452 signed Meriden/Leamington. At next rdbt left onto B4102, Hampton Lane. Site in 0.5m on left*

Open Feb-12 Dec Booking advisable NEC exhibitions & BH

A peaceful adults-only park set in the heart of England with spotless facilities. The park is well positioned for visiting the National Exhibition Centre (NEC) or the NEC Arena and National Indoor Arena (NIA), and Birminghan is only 12 miles away. The park also makes and ideal touring base for Warwick, Coventry and Stratford-upon-Avon just 22 miles away. A 4-acre site with 48 touring pitches, 48 hardstandings.

**Facilities:**

**Services:** →

**Notes:** Adults only. No tents

# WIGHT, ISLE OF

## BEMBRIDGE

*see Whitecliff Bay*

## COWES — MAP 05 SZ49

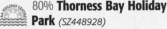

### 80% Thorness Bay Holiday Park *(SZ448928)*

GOLD

Thorness PO31 8NJ

☎ 01983 523109 01983 822213

**email:** holidaysales.thornessbay@park-resorts.com

**web:** www.park-resorts.com

**Dir:** *On A3054 towards Yarmouth, 1st right after BMW garage, signed Thorness Bay*

★ £6-£30 £6-£30 £3-£27

Open Apr-1 Nov Booking advisable Jul-Aug Last arrival anytime Last departure 10.00hrs

Splendid views of the Solent can be enjoyed from this rural park located just outside Cowes. A footpath leads directly to the coast, while on site there is an all-weather sports court, entertainment clubs for children, and cabaret, shows and a bar for all the family. There are 23 serviced pitches with TV boosters. A 148-acre site with 80 touring pitches, 20 hardstandings and 560 statics.

**Leisure:**

**Facilities:**

**Services:** →

**Notes:** Kids' clubs, evening entertainment, water slide

*see advert on opposite page*

**Abbreviations:** BH-bank holiday/s Etr-Easter Whit-Whitsun dep-departure fr-from hrs-hours m-mile mdnt-midnight rdbt-roundabout rs-restricted service wk-week wknd-weekend no dogs No cards → following facilities within 3 miles of the site

ENGLAND

FRESHWATER MAP 05 SZ38

## ►►► 82% **Heathfield Farm Camping** *(SZ335879)*

Heathfield Rd PO40 9SH

☎ 01983 756756

**email:** web@heathfieldcamping.co.uk

**web:** www.heathfieldcamping.co.uk

**Dir:** *2m W from Yarmouth ferry port on A3054, left to Heathfield Rd, entrance 200yds on right*

★ £10-£15 £10-£15 £8.75-£13.50

Open May-Sep Booking advisable BH & Jul-Aug Last arrival 22.00hrs Last departure 22.00hrs

A good quality park with friendly owners and lovely views across the Solent to Hurst Castle. The toilet facilities, amenities and grounds are very well maintained, and this park is constantly improving to meet the needs of campers and caravanners. A 10-acre site with 60 touring pitches.

**Facilities:**

**Services:**

**Notes:** Family camping only. Separate playing field for ball games etc

**Facilities:** Bath Shower Electric Shaver Hairdryer Ice Pack Facility Disabled Facilities Public Telephone Shop on Site or within 200yds Mobile Shop (calls at least 5 days a week) BBQ Area Picnic Area Dog Exercise Area

ENGLAND

## NEWBRIDGE MAP 05 SZ48

PREMIER PARK

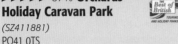

### 87% Orchards Holiday Caravan Park

*(SZ411881)*

PO41 0TS

01983 531331 & 531350 01983 531666

**email:** info@orchards-holiday-park.co.uk

**web:** www.orchards-holiday-park.co.uk

**Dir:** *4m E of Yarmouth; 6m W of Newport on B3401*

★ £13-£20 £13-£20 £13-£20

Open 11 Feb-2 Jan (rs Nov-Jan & Feb-mid Mar shop/ takeaway closed, pool closed Sep-May) Booking advisable Etr, Spring BH, Jun-Aug, Oct half term Last arrival 23.00hrs Last departure 11.00hrs

A really excellent, well-managed park set in a peaceful village location amid downs and meadowland, with glorious downland views. Pitches are terraced, and offer a good provision of hardstandings, including super pitches. The toilet facilities are immaculate, and the park has indoor and outdoor swimming pools, a shop, takeaway and licensed coffee shop. There is excellent provision for families, and disabled access to all facilities on site, plus disabled toilets. A 15-acre site with 171 touring pitches, 74 hardstandings and 65 statics.

**Leisure:**

**Facilities:**

**Services:**

**Notes:** Coarse fishing, petanque

## NEWCHURCH MAP 05 SZ58

Regional Winner – AA South East of England Campsite of the Year 2008

PREMIER PARK

### 89% Southland Camping Park *(SZ557847)*

PO36 0LZ

01983 865385 01983 867663

**email:** info@southland.co.uk

**web:** www.southland.co.uk

**Dir:** *A3056 towards Sandown. 2nd left after Fighting Cocks pub towards Newchurch. Site 1m on left*

★ £10.80-£16.20 £10.80-£16.20 £10.80-£16.20

Open Apr-Sep Booking advisable Jun-Aug Last arrival 21.30hrs Last departure 11.00hrs

Beautifully maintained site, peacefully located and impressively laid out on the outskirts of the village in the Arreton Valley. Good quality sanitary facilities including spacious family rooms enhance the park. Pitches are well screened by lovely trees and shrubs. A 9-acre site with 120 touring pitches.

**Leisure:** **Facilities:**

**Services:** **Notes:** Wi-fi

## PONDWELL MAP 05 SZ69

### 75% Pondwell Camp Site *(SZ622911)*

PO34 5AQ

01983 612330 01983 613511

**Dir:** *From Ryde take A3055 then left on B3330 to Seaview. Site next to Wishing Well pub*

Open May-26 Sep Booking advisable Aug Last arrival 23.00hrs Last departure 11.00hrs

A secluded site in quiet rural surroundings close to the sea, on slightly sloping ground with some level areas. The village is within easy walking distance. A 9-acre site with 150 touring pitches.

**Leisure:**

**Facilities:**

**Services:**

**Notes:** No pets, no unaccompanied children

## RYDE MAP 05 SZ59

### ►►►► 86% **Whitefield Forest Touring Park** *(SZ604893)*

Brading Rd PO33 1QL

☎ 01983 617069

**email:** pat&louise@whitefieldforest.co.uk

**web:** www.whitefieldforest.co.uk

**Dir:** *From Ryde follow A3055 towards Brading, after Tesco rdbt site 0.5m on left.*

£10.60-£16 £10.60-£16 £10.60-£16

Open Etr-Oct Booking advisable Last arrival 21.00hrs Last departure 11.00hrs

This newly developed park is beautifully laid out in Whitefield Forest, and offers a wide variety of pitches, all of which have electricity. It offers excellent modern facilities which are spotlessly clean. The park takes great care in retaining the natural beauty of the forest, and is a haven for wildlife, including the red squirrel. A 23-acre site with 80 touring pitches, 20 hardstandings.

**Leisure:**

**Facilities:**

**Services:**

### ►► 79% ***Roebeck Camping and Caravan Park*** *(SZ581903)*

Gatehouse Rd, Upton Cross PO33 4BP

☎ 01983 611475 & 07930 992080

**Dir:** *Turn right from Fishbourne ferry terminal (west of Ryde). At lights turn left onto A3054 towards Ryde. In outskirts straight on at 'All Through Traffic' sign. At end of Pellhurst Rd right in Upton Rd. Site 50yds beyond mini-rdbt in Upton*

Open Apr-Nov

A quiet park in a country setting on the outskirts of Ryde. There is coarse fishing on site, and ready-erected tepees for hire. A 3-acre site with 37 touring pitches.

**Facilities:**

## ST HELENS MAP 05 SZ68

### 79% **Nodes Point Holiday Park** *(SZ636897)*

GOLD

Nodes Rd PO33 1YA

☎ 01983 872401 01983 874696

**email:** gm.nodespoint@park-resorts.com

**web:** www.park-resorts.com

**Dir:** *From Ryde take B3330 signed Seaview/Puckpool. At junct for Puckpool bear right. 1m past Road Side Inn in Nettlestone, site on left*

★ £6-£32 £6-£32 £3-£29

Open Apr-Oct (rs Mar park open, no facilities) Booking advisable May-Aug Last arrival 21.00hrs Last departure 10.00hrs

A well-equipped holiday centre on an elevated position overlooking Bembridge Bay with direct access to the beach. The touring area is mostly sloping with some terraces. A major upgrading programme has created new super pitches, an excellent toilet block, and a multi-sports facility. Activities are organised for youngsters, and there is entertainment for the whole family. Buses pass the main entrance road. A 16-acre site with 145 touring pitches and 195 statics.

**Leisure:**

**Facilities:**

**Services:**

**Notes:** Family park

*see advert on page 253*

## SANDOWN MAP 05 SZ58

### ►►►► 79% **Adgestone Camping & Caravanning Club Site** *(SZ590855)*

Lower Adgestone Rd PO36 0HL

☎ 01983 403432

**web:** www.campingandcaravanningclub.co.uk/adgestone

**Dir:** *Turn off A3055 (Sandown/Shanklin road) at Manor House pub, in Lake. Past school & golf course on left, turn right at T-junct, park 200yds on right*

★ £17.75-£22.45 £17.75-£22.45 £17.75-£22.45

Open 13 Mar-3 Nov Booking advisable BH & peak periods Last arrival 21.00hrs Last departure noon

A popular, well-managed park in a quiet, rural location not far from Sandown. The level pitches are imaginatively laid out, and surrounded by beautiful flower beds and trees set close to a small river. This planting offers good screening as well as enhancing the appearance of the park. There is excellent provision for families in general. A 22-acre site with 270 touring pitches.

**Leisure:**

**Facilities:**

**Services:**

**Notes:** Site gates closed 23.00hrs-07.00hrs. Fishing

ENGLAND

## SANDOWN CONTINUED

### ►►►► 78% **Old Barn Touring Park**
*(SZ573833)*

GOLD

Cheverton Farm, Newport Rd, Apse Heath
PO36 9PJ
☎ 01983 866414 01983 865988
**email:** oldbarn@weltinet.com
**web:** www.oldbarntouring.co.uk
**Dir:** *On A3056 from Newport, site on left after Apse Heath*

£12-£17 £12-£17 £12-£17

Open May-Sep Booking advisable BH & peak periods Last arrival 21.00hrs Last departure noon

A terraced site with good quality facilities, bordering on open farmland. The spacious pitches are secluded and fully serviced, and there is a good modern toilet block. A 5-acre site with 60 touring pitches, 9 hardstandings.

**Leisure:**

**Facilities:**

**Services:** →

### ► 78% **Queen Bower Dairy Caravan Park**
*(SZ567846)*

Alverstone Rd, Queen Bower PO36 0NZ
☎ 01983 403840 & 407392 01983 409671
**email:** qbdcaravanpark@aol.com
**web:** www.queenbowerdairy.co.uk
**Dir:** *3m N of Sandown off A3056 turn right towards Alverstone, site 1m on left*

★ £4.50-£7 £4.50-£7 £4.50-£7

Open May-Oct Booking advisable Jul-Aug

A small site with basic amenities that will appeal to campers keen to escape the crowds and the busy larger sites. The enthusiastic owners keep the facilities clean. A 2.5-acre site with 20 touring pitches.

**Facilities:**

**Services:** →

**Notes:** Dogs must be kept on leads & exercised off site

## SHANKLIN MAP 05 SZ58

### 83% **Lower Hyde Holiday Park** *(SZ575819)*

Landguard Rd PO37 7LL
☎ 01983 866131 01983 862532
**email:** holidaysales.lowerhyde@park-resorts.com
**web:** www.park-resorts.com
**Dir:** *From Fishbourne ferry terminal follow A3055 to Shanklin. Park signed just past lake*

★ £6-£32 £6-£32 £3-£29

Open 17 Apr-1 Nov Booking advisable all year Last arrival anytime Last departure 10.00hrs

A popular holiday park on the outskirts of Shanklin, close to the sandy beaches. There is an outdoor swimming pool and plenty of organised activities for youngsters of all ages. In the evening there is a choice of family entertainment. The touring facilities are located in a quiet area away from the main complex, with good views over the downs. A 65-acre site with 82 touring pitches and 313 statics.

**Leisure:**

**Facilities:**

**Services:** →

**Notes:** Water flume, evening entertainment, kids' club

*see advert on page 253*

### ►►► 79% **Landguard Camping Park** *(SZ577825)*

GOLD

Landguard Manor Rd PO37 7PH
☎ 01983 867028 01983 865988
**email:** landguard@weltinet.com
**web:** www.landguard-camping.co.uk
**Dir:** *A3056 to Sandown, right after passing Morrisons at Lake into Whitecross Lane. Follow site signs*

★ £12.50-£16 £12.50-£16 £12.50-£16

Open May-Sep Booking advisable school hols Last arrival 20.00hrs Last departure noon

Surrounded by trees in a rural setting, this peaceful and secluded touring park is within walking distance of Shanklin. Facilities are clean and tidy, and the park benefits from a very good outdoor pool. A 7-acre site with 150 touring pitches, 6 hardstandings.

**Leisure:** **Facilities:**

**Services:** →

**Notes:** Families only Wi-fi

**Abbreviations:** BH-bank holiday/s Etr-Easter Whit-Whitsun dep-departure fr-from hrs-hours m-mile mdnt-midnight rdbt-roundabout rs-restricted service wk-week wknd-weekend no dogs No cards → following facilities within 3 miles of the site

## TOTLAND BAY MAP 05 SZ38

### ►► 78% Stoats Farm Caravan & Camping *(SZ324865)*

PO39 0HE

☎ 01983 755258 & 753416 📠 01983 755258

**email:** david@stoats-farm.co.uk

**web:** www.stoats-farm.co.uk

**Dir:** *On Alum Bay road, 1.5m from Freshwater & 0.75m from Totland*

★ £10-£12 £9-£12 £7.50-£11

Open Mar-Oct Booking advisable Aug

A friendly, personally run site in a quiet country setting close to Alum Bay, Tennyson Down and The Needles. It has good laundry and shower facilities, and the shop, though small, is well stocked. Popular with families, walkers and cyclists. A 10-acre site with 100 touring pitches.

**Facilities:**

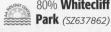

**Services:**

## WHITECLIFF BAY MAP 05 SZ68

### 80% Whitecliff Bay Holiday Park *(SZ637862)*

GOLD

Hillway Rd, Bembridge PO35 5PL

☎ 01983 872671 📠 01983 872941

**email:** holiday@whitecliff-bay.com

**web:** www.whitecliff-bay.com

**Dir:** *1m S of Bembridge, signed off B3395 in village*

★ £9.85-£17.35 £9.85-£17.35 £9.85-£17.35

Open Mar-Oct Booking advisable Jul-Aug Last arrival 21.00hrs Last departure 10.30hrs

A large seaside complex on two sites, with tourers and tents on one, and tourers and statics on the other. There is an indoor and outdoor swimming pool, a leisure centre, and plenty of traditional on-site entertainment, plus easy access to a lovely sandy beach. A 49-acre site with 400 touring pitches, 50 hardstandings and 227 statics.

**Leisure:**

**Facilities:**

**Services:**

**Notes:** Adults & families only, no dogs during high season. Leisure centre with fun pool, spa bath & sauna

*see advert on this page*

**Facilities:** Bath · Shower · Electric Shaver · Hairdryer · Ice Pack Facility · Disabled Facilities · Public Telephone · Shop on Site or within 200yds · Mobile Shop (calls at least 5 days a week) · BBQ Area · Picnic Area · Dog Exercise Area

ENGLAND

## WOOTTON BRIDGE MAP 05 SZ59

### ►►► 77% Kite Hill Farm Caravan Park

*(SZ549906)*

Firestone Copse Rd PO33 4LE

☎ 01983 882543 & 883261 🖷 01983 883883

**email:** barry@kitehillfarm.freeserve.co.uk

**web:** www.campingparkisleofwight.com

**Dir:** *Signed off A3054 at Wootton Bridge, between Ryde & Newport*

★ £9-£10 £9-£10 Å £9-£10

Open all year Booking advisable Jun-Aug

The park, on a gently sloping field, is tucked away behind the owners' farm, just a short walk from the village and attractive river estuary. Facilities are well maintained and the atmosphere pleasantly relaxing. A 12.5-acre site with 50 touring pitches, 10 hardstandings.

**Leisure:** **Facilities:**

**Services:**

## YARMOUTH

*see Newbridge*

# WILTSHIRE

## CALNE MAP 04 ST97

### ►►► 73% Blackland Lakes Holiday & Leisure Centre *(ST973687)*

Stockley Ln SN11 0NQ

☎ 01249 813672 🖷 01249 811346

**email:** info@blacklandlakes.co.uk

**web:** www.blacklandlakes.co.uk

**Dir:** *From Calne take A4 E for 1.5m, right at camp sign. Site 1m on left*

★ £15-£20 £15-£20 Å £10-£15

Open all year (rs Nov-mid Mar pre-paid bookings only) Booking advisable all year Last arrival 22.00hrs Last departure noon

A rural site surrounded by the North and West Downs. The park is divided into several paddocks separated by hedges, trees and fences, and there are two well-stocked carp fisheries for the angling enthusiast. Some excellent walks close by, and the interesting market town of Devizes is a few miles away. A 15-acre site with 180 touring pitches, 25 hardstandings.

**Leisure:** **Facilities:**

**Services:**

**Notes:** Wildfowl sanctuary, fishing facilities, bike trail

## DEVIZES MAP 04 SU06

### ►►►► 84% Devizes Camping & Caravanning Club Site *(ST951619)*

DAVID BELLAMY CONSERVATION AWARD GOLD

Spout Ln, Nr Seend, Melksham SN12 6RN

☎ 01380 828839

**web:** www.campingandcaravanningclub.co.uk/devizes

**Dir:** *From Devizes on A361 turn right onto A365, over canal, next left down lane beside 3 Magpies pub. Site on right*

★ £13.95-£20.15 £13.95-£20.15 Å £13.95-£20.15

Open all year Booking advisable BH & peak periods Last arrival 21.00hrs Last departure noon

An excellent club site with well designed, quality facilities and a high level of staff commitment. This popular park is set beside the Kennet and Avon Canal, with a gate to the towpath for walking and cycling, and with fishing available in the canal. Well situated for exploring Salisbury Plain and the Marlborough Downs. A 13.5-acre site with 90 touring pitches, 70 hardstandings.

**Leisure:**

**Facilities:**

**Services:**

**Notes:** Site gates closed 23.00hrs-07.00hrs

## LACOCK MAP 04 ST96

### ►►► 85% Piccadilly Caravan Park Ltd

*(ST913683)*

Folly Ln West SN15 2LP

☎ 01249 730260 🖷 01249 730260

**email:** piccadillylacock@aol.com

**Dir:** *4m S of Chippenham just past Lacock. Turn right off A350 signed Gastard. Site 300yds on left*

£12.50-£14.50 £12.50-£14.50 Å £12.50-£14.50

Open Etr-Oct Booking advisable BH & school hols Last arrival 21.00hrs Last departure noon

A peaceful, pleasant site, well established and beautifully laid out, close to the village of Lacock. Facilities and grounds are immaculately kept, and there is very good screening. A 2.5-acre site with 41 touring pitches, 12 hardstandings.

**Leisure:**

**Facilities:**

**Services:**

**Notes:**

ENGLAND

## LANDFORD MAP 05 SU21

### ►►► 72% Greenhill Farm Camping & Caravan Park *(SU266183)*

Greenhill Farm, New Rd SP5 2AZ

☎ 01794 324117 & 023 8081 1506 🖷 023 8081 3209

**email:** greenhillcamping@btconnect.com

**web:** www.newforest-uk.com/greenhill.htm

**Dir:** *M27 junct 2, A36 towards Salisbury, approx 3m after Hants/Wilts border, (Shoe Inn pub on right, BP garage on left) take next left into New Rd, signed Nomansland, 2nd site on left*

£10-£15 £10-£15 £10-£15

Open 16 Jan-21 Dec Booking advisable BH & Jul-Aug Last arrival 21.30hrs Last departure 10.30hrs

A tranquil, well-landscaped park hidden away in unspoilt countryside on the edge of the New Forest. Pitches overlooking the fishing lake include hardstandings. Facilities are housed in portable type buildings. This park is for adults only. A 13-acre site with 80 touring pitches, 30 hardstandings.

**Facilities:**

**Services:**

**Notes:** Adults only. Dogs must be on leads, no kites/flags. Fishing, disposable BBQs

## MARSTON MEYSEY MAP 05 SU19

### ►► 67% Second Chance Touring Park

*(SU140960)*

SN6 6SZ

☎ 01285 810675 & 810939

**Dir:** *A419 from Cirencester towards Swindon, leave at Latton junct. Through Latton, left at next mini-rdbt, towards Fairford. Follow signs to park. From M4 junct 15, take A419 towards Fairford, turn right after Marston Meysey*

Open Mar-Nov Booking advisable BH & peak periods Last arrival 21.00hrs Last departure 13.30hrs

An attractive, quiet site located near the source of the Thames, and well positioned for those wishing to visit the nearby Cotswold Water Park. The facilities are a bit dated but clean. A 1.75-acre site with 22 touring pitches, 10 hardstandings and 4 statics.

**Facilities:**

**Services:**

**Notes:** No loud music or parties. Fishing, access for canoes

## ORCHESTON MAP 05 SU04

### ►►► 75% Stonehenge Touring Park

*(SU061456)*

SP3 4SH

☎ 01980 620304

**email:** stay@stonehengetouringpark.com

**web:** www.stonehengetouringpark.com

**Dir:** *Off A360*

★ £7-£12 £7-£12 £7-£12

Open all year Booking advisable BH & Jul-Aug Last arrival 21.00hrs Last departure 11.00hrs

A quiet site adjacent to the small village of Orcheston near the centre of Salisbury Plain and four miles from Stonehenge. A 2-acre site with 30 touring pitches, 12 hardstandings.

**Leisure:**

**Facilities:**

**Services:**

**Notes:** Wi-fi

## SALISBURY MAP 05 SU12

### ►►►► 78% Coombe Touring Park

*(SU099282)*

Race Plain, Netherhampton SP2 8PN

☎ 01722 328451 🖷 01722 328451

**Dir:** *Turn off A36 onto A3094, then 2m SW, adjacent to Salisbury racecourse*

£11-£13 £11-£13 £11-£13

Open 3 Jan-20 Dec (rs Oct-May shop closed) Booking advisable BH (by letter only) Last arrival 21.00hrs Last departure noon

A very neat and attractive site adjacent to the racecourse with views over the downs. The park is well landscaped with shrubs and maturing trees, and the very colourful beds are stocked from the owner's greenhouse. A comfortable park with a superb luxury toilet block. A 3-acre site with 50 touring pitches.

**Facilities:**

**Services:**

**Notes:** No disposable BBQs or fires, no mini motorbikes. Children's bathroom

ENGLAND

## SALISBURY CONTINUED

### ►►►► 80% Salisbury Camping & Caravanning Club Site (SU140320)

Hudsons Field, Castle Rd SP1 3RR

☎ 01722 320713

**web:** www.campingandcaravanningclub.co.uk/salisbury

**Dir:** *1.5m from Salisbury on A345. (Large open field next to Old Sarum)*

★ £15.45-£20.15 £15.45-£20.15 £15.45-£20.15

Open 13 Mar-3 Nov Booking advisable BH & peak periods Last arrival 21.00hrs Last departure noon

Well placed within walking distance of Salisbury, this tidy site has friendly and helpful wardens, and immaculate toilet facilities with cubicled wash basins. A 4.5-acre site with 150 touring pitches, 16 hardstandings.

**Facilities:**

**Services:** →

**Notes:** Site gates closed 23.00hrs-07.00hrs

### ►►► 71% Alderbury Caravan & Camping Park (SU197259)

Southampton Rd, Whaddon SP5 3HB

☎ 01722 710125

**email:** alderbury@aol.com

**Dir:** *Just off A36, 3m from Salisbury, opposite The Three Crowns*

★ £11-£12 £11-£12 £11-£12

Open all year Booking advisable at all times Last arrival 21.00hrs Last departure 12.30hrs

A pleasant, attractive park set in the village of Whaddon not far from Salisbury. The small site is well maintained by friendly owners, and is ideally positioned near the A36 for overnight stops for Southampton ferry ports. A 1.5-acre site with 39 touring pitches, 12 hardstandings and 1 static.

**Facilities:**

**Services:** →

**Notes:** Microwave, electric kettle, small fridge

## TROWBRIDGE MAP 04 ST85

### ►► 73% Stowford Manor Farm (ST810577)

Stowford, Wingfield BA14 9LH

☎ 01225 752253

**email:** stowford1@supanet.com

**web:** www.stowfordmanorfarm.co.uk

**Dir:** *From Trowbridge take A366 W towards Radstock. Site on left in 3m*

★ £10-£12 £10-£12 £8-£12

Open Etr-Oct Booking advisable BH & school hols

A very simple farm site set on the banks of the River Frome behind the farm courtyard. The owners are friendly and relaxed, and the park enjoys a similarly comfortable ambience. A 1.5-acre site with 15 touring pitches.

**Facilities:**

**Services:** →

**Notes:** No open fires. Fishing, boating, swimming in river

## WESTBURY MAP 04 ST85

### ►►►► 77% Brokerswood Country Park (ST836523)

GOLD

Brokerswood BA13 4EH

☎ 01373 822238 01373 858474

**email:** woodland.park@virgin.net

**web:** www.brokerswood.co.uk

**Dir:** *From M4 junct 17 south on A350. Right at Yarnbrook to Rising Sun pub at North Bradley, then left at rdbt. Left on bend approaching Southwick, follow lane for 2.5m, site on right*

£10-£28 £10-£28 £10-£28

Open all year Booking advisable BH & peak season Last arrival 21.30hrs Last departure 11.00hrs

A popular park on the edge of an 80-acre woodland park with nature trails and fishing lakes. An adventure playground offers plenty of fun for all ages, and there is a miniature railway, an indoor play centre, and a café. A new toilet block offers high quality facilities. A 5-acre site with 69 touring pitches, 21 hardstandings.

**Leisure:**

**Facilities:**

**Services:** →

**Notes:** Families only, no cycling, no disposable BBQs

# WORCESTERSHIRE

## CLENT HILLS

*see Romsley*

## HANLEY SWAN — MAP 10 SO84

**►►►► 80% Blackmore Camping & Caravanning Club Site** *(SO812440)*

Blackmore Camp Site No 2 WR8 0EE

☎ 01684 310280

**web:** www.campingandcaravanningclub.co.uk/blackmore

**Dir:** *A38 to Upton on Severn. Turn N over river bridge. 2nd left, then 1st left signed Hanley Swan. Site 1m on right*

★ £18.25-£20.15 £18.25-£20.15 Ă £18.25-£20.15

Open all year Booking advisable BH & peak periods Last arrival 21.00hrs Last departure noon

Blackmore is a well-established, level wooded park, ideally located for exploring the Malvern Hills and Worcester. The excellent toilet facilities are spotlessly maintained. A 17-acre site with 200 touring pitches, 66 hardstandings.

**Leisure:**

**Facilities:**

**Services:**

**Notes:** Site gates closed 23.00hrs-07.00hrs

## HONEYBOURNE — MAP 10 SP14

**►►►► 84% Ranch Caravan Park** *(SP113444)*

GOLD

Station Rd WR11 7PR

☎ 01386 830744 01386 833503

**email:** enquiries@ranch.co.uk

**web:** www.ranch.co.uk

**Dir:** *Through village x-rds towards Bidford, site 400mtrs on left*

★ £16.50-£21

Open Mar-Nov (rs Mar-May & Sep-Nov swimming pool closed, shorter club hours) Booking advisable school hols Last arrival 20.00hrs Last departure noon

An attractive and well-run park set amidst farmland in the Vale of Evesham and landscaped with trees and bushes. Tourers have their own excellent facilities in two locations, and the use of an outdoor heated swimming pool in peak season. There is also a licensed club serving meals. A 12-acre site with 120 touring pitches, 30 hardstandings and 195 statics.

**Leisure:**

**Facilities:**

**Services:**

**Notes:** No unaccompanied minors, no tents. Gym & sauna (chargable)

*see advert on this page*

## ROMSLEY — MAP 10 SO98

**►►►► 78% Clent Hills Camping & Caravanning Club Site** *(SO955795)*

Fieldhouse Ln B62 0NH

☎ 01562 710015

**web:** www.campingandcaravanningclub.co.uk/clenthills

**Dir:** *From M5 junct 3 take A456. Left on B4551 to Romsley. Turn right past Sun Hotel, take 5th left, then next left. Site 330yds on left*

★ £15.45-£20.15 £15.45-£20.15 Ă £15.45-£20.15

Open 13 Mar-3 Nov Booking advisable BH & peak periods Last arrival 21.00hrs Last departure noon

A very pretty, well tended park surrounded by wooded hills. The site offers excellent facilities, including hardstandings to provide flat pitches for motorhomes. Lovely views of the Clent Hills can be enjoyed from this park, and there are plenty of local scenic walks. A 7.5-acre site with 95 touring pitches, 27 hardstandings.

**Leisure:**

**Facilities:**

**Services:**

**Notes:** Site gates closed 23.00hrs-07.00hrs

ENGLAND

### WOLVERLEY MAP 10 SO87

**►►► 76% Wolverley Camping & Caravanning Club Site** *(SO833792)*
Brown Westhead Park DY10 3PX
☎ 01562 850909
**web:** www.campingandcaravanningclub.co.uk/wolverley
**Dir:** *From Kidderminster A449 to Wolverhampton, turn left at lights onto B4189 signed Wolverley. Follow brown camping signs, turn right. Site on left*

★ £15.45-£20.15 £15.45-£20.15 £15.45-£20.15

Open 13 Mar-3 Nov Booking advisable BH & peak periods Last arrival 21.00hrs Last departure noon

A very pleasant grassy site on the edge of the village, with the canal lock and towpath close to the entrance, and a pub overlooking the water. The site has good access to and from nearby motorways. A 12-acre site with 120 touring pitches.

**Leisure:**
**Facilities:**
**Services:** →
**Notes:** Site gates closed 23.00hrs-07.00hrs

## YORKSHIRE, EAST RIDING OF

### BEVERLEY
*see Little Weighton*

### BRANDESBURTON MAP 17 TA14

**►►► 76% *Dacre Lakeside Park*** *(TA118468)*
YO25 8RT
☎ 0800 1804556 01964 544040
**email:** dacrepark@btconnect.com
**web:** www.dacrepark.co.uk
**Dir:** *Off A165 bypass, midway between Beverley & Hornsea*

Open Mar-Oct Booking advisable BH Last arrival 21.00hrs Last departure noon

A large lake popular with watersports enthusiasts is the focal point of this grassy site. The clubhouse offers plenty of indoor activities; there's a fish and chip shop, pub and Chinese takeaway in the village, which is within walking distance. The 6-acre lake is used for windsurfing, sailing, kayaking, canoeing and fishing. An 8-acre site with 120 touring pitches.

**Leisure:**
**Facilities:**
**Services:** →
**Notes:** Bowling

### BRIDLINGTON MAP 17 TA16
*see also Rudston*

**►►► 80% Fir Tree Caravan Park** *(TA195702)*
Jewison Ln, Sewerby YO16 6YG
☎ 01262 676442 01262 676442
**email:** info@flowerofmay.com
**web:** www.flowerofmay.com
**Dir:** *1.5m from centre of Bridlington. Turn left off B1255 at Marton Corner. Site 600yds on left*

Open Mar-Oct (rs early & late season bar & entertainment restrictions) Last arrival 21.00hrs Last departure noon

Fir Tree Park has a well laid out touring area with its own facilities within a large, mainly static park. It has an excellent swimming pool complex, and the adjacent bar-cum-conservatory serves meals. There is also a family bar, games room and outdoor children's play area. A 22-acre site with 45 touring pitches, 45 hardstandings and 400 statics.

**Leisure:**
**Facilities:**
**Services:** →
**Notes:** Dogs by arrangement only

**►► 88% Poplars Touring Park** *(TA194701)*
45 Jewison Ln, Sewerby YO15 1DX
☎ 01262 677251
**web:** www.the-poplars.co.uk
**Dir:** *B1255 towards Flamborough, at 2nd bend off Z-bend, 1st left after Marton Hall, site 0.33m on left*

Open Mar-Oct Booking advisable BH & school summer hols Last arrival 21.00hrs Last departure noon

A small, peaceful and mainly adult park with immaculate facilities including a well-appointed toilet block. The friendly owners also run a B&B next door, and there is a good pub close by. A 1.25-acre site with 30 touring pitches, 10 hardstandings.

**Facilities:**
**Services:** →
**Notes:** No large groups

### KINGSTON UPON HULL
*see Sproatley*

ENGLAND

## LITTLE WEIGHTON MAP 17 SE93

### ►►►► 83% *Croft Park* (SE982333)

55 Rowley Rd HU20 3XJ

☎ 01482 840600 01482 840600

**email:** info@croftpark.net

**web:** www.croftpark.net

**Dir:** *Turn W off A164 approx 4m S of Beverley signed Skidby. In Little Weighton turn S along Rowley Road. Site approx 100mtrs on left.*

Open mid Mar-end Oct Booking advisable Last arrival 21.00hrs Last departure noon

A tranquil and up-market park exclusively for adults on the edge of the village of Little Weighton. The spacious gravel pitches are thoughtfully laid out in what was the owner's garden, and are fully serviced including TV connection. The park has a tasteful restaurant and deli, and a very comfortable TV lounge/reading room. A 3-acre site with 10 touring pitches.

**Leisure:**

**Facilities:**

**Services:**

**Notes:** Adults only. Dogs must be kept on leads. Patio sets at each pitch

## RUDSTON MAP 17 TA06

### ►►► 78% Thorpe Hall Caravan & Camping Site (TA108677)

GOLD

Thorpe Hall YO25 4JE

☎ 01262 420393 & 420574 01262 420588

**email:** caravansite@thorpehall.co.uk

**web:** www.thorpehall.co.uk

**Dir:** *5m from Bridlington on B1253*

★ £12-£24 £12-£24 £8-£20

Open Mar-Oct (rs reception & shop limited opening hours) Booking advisable BH & peak periods Last arrival 22.00hrs Last departure noon

A delightful, peaceful small park within the walled gardens of Thorpe Hall yet within a few miles of the bustling seaside resort of Bridlington. The site offers a games field, its own coarse fishery, pitch & putt, and a games and TV lounge, and there are numerous walks locally. A 4.5-acre site with 90 touring pitches.

**Leisure:**

**Facilities:**

**Services:**

**Notes:** Golf practice area (4.5 acres)

*see advert on this page*

*Thorpe Hall Caravan & Camping Site*

## SKIPSEA — MAP 17 TA15

### 84% Low Skirlington Leisure Park *(TA188528)*

YO25 8SY

01262 468213 & 468466 01262 468105

**email:** info@skirlington.com

**web:** www.skirlington.com

**Dir:** *From M62 towards Beverley then Hornsea. Between Skipsea & Hornsea on B1242*

Open Mar-Oct Booking advisable at all times

A large well-run seaside park set close to the beach in partly-sloping meadowland with young trees and shrubs. The site has five toilet blocks, a supermarket and an amusement arcade, with occasional entertainment in the clubhouse. The wide range of family amenities include an indoor heated swimming pool complex with sauna, jacuzzi and sunbeds. A 10-pin bowling alley and indoor play area for children are added attractions. A 24-acre site with 285 touring pitches, 9 hardstandings and 450 statics.

**Leisure:**

**Facilities:**

**Services:**

**Notes:** Putting green

## SPROATLEY — MAP 17 TA13

### ►►► 80% Burton Constable Holiday Park *(TA186357)*

Old Lodges HU11 4LN

01964 562508 01964 563420

**email:** info@burtonconstable.co.uk

**web:** www.burtonconstable.co.uk

**Dir:** *Off A165 onto B1238 to Sproatley. Follow signs to park*

★ £13-£24 £13-£24 £13-£25

Open Mar-Jan Booking advisable BH & wknds Last arrival 22.00hrs Last departure 14.00hrs

A very attractive parkland site overlooking the fishing lakes, in the grounds of Burton Constable Hall. The toilet facilities are kept very clean, and the Lakeside Club provides a focus for relaxing in the evening. Children will enjoy the extensive adventure playground. A 50-acre site with 180 touring pitches, 14 hardstandings and 260 statics.

**Leisure:**

**Facilities:**

**Services:** → 

**Notes:** Dogs must be kept on leads, no skateboards/rollerblades. Two 10-acre fishing lakes, snooker table

## WITHERNSEA — MAP 17 TA32

### NEW 72% Withernsea Sands *(TA335289)*

North Rd HU19 2BS

0871 664 9803

**email:** withernsea.sands@park-resorts.com

**web:** www.park-resorts.com

**Dir:** *From M62 junct 38 take A63 through Hull. At end of dual carriageway, turn right onto A1033, follow Withernsea signs. Through village, left at mini rdbt onto B1242. Next right at lighthouse. Site 0.5m on left*

£5-£22 £5-£22

Open 31 Mar-Oct Booking advisable

Touring is very much at the heart of this holiday park's operation, with 100 all electric pitches and additional space for tents. Park Resorts are in the process of upgrading the facilities and attractions, and the new leisure complex with its futuristic design is especially impressive. 40 touring pitches and 350 statics.

**Leisure:** **Facilities:**

**Services:** →

# YORKSHIRE, NORTH

## ACASTER MALBIS — MAP 16 SE54

### ►► 76% *Moor End Farm* *(SE589457)*

YO23 2UQ

01904 706727 & 07860 405872

**email:** moorendfarm@acaster99.fsnet.co.uk

**web:** www.ukparks.co.uk/moorend

**Dir:** *Follow signs to Acaster Malbis from A64/A1237 junct at Copmanthorpe*

Open Etr or Apr-Oct Booking advisable BH & end Jul-Aug Last arrival 22.00hrs Last departure 14.00hrs

A very pleasant farm site with modernised facilities including a heated family/disabled shower room. A riverboat pickup to York is 150yds from the site entrance, and the village inn and restaurant are a short stroll away. A good place to hire a boat or simply watch them go by. A 1-acre site with 10 touring pitches and 7 statics.

**Leisure:** **Facilities:**

**Services:** →

**Notes:** Use of fridge/freezer & microwave

## ALLERSTON — MAP 19 SE88

### ►►►► 79% Vale of Pickering Caravan Park *(SE879808)*

SILVER

Carr House Farm YO18 7PQ
☎ 01723 859280 Fax 01723 850060
**email:** tony@valeofpickering.co.uk
**web:** www.valeofpickering.co.uk
**Dir:** *On B1415, 1.75m off A170 (Pickering-Scarborough road)*

Open Mar-6 Jan (rs Mar) Booking advisable BH Last arrival 21.00hrs Last departure noon

A well-maintained, spacious family park with excellent facilities including a well-stocked shop. Younger children will enjoy the attractive play area, while the large ball sports area will attract older ones. The park is set in open countryside bounded by hedges, and is handy for the North Yorkshire Moors and the attractions of Scarborough. A 13-acre site with 120 touring pitches, 80 hardstandings.

**Leisure:**
**Facilities:**
**Services:**
**Notes:** Microwave

## ALNE — MAP 19 SE46

### ►►►► 76% Alders Caravan Park *(SE497654)*

Home Farm YO61 1RY
☎ 01347 838722 Fax 01347 838722
**email:** enquiries@homefarmalne.co.uk
**web:** www.alderscaravanpark.co.uk
**Dir:** *From A19 exit at Alne sign, in 1.5m turn left at T-junct, 0.5m park on left in village centre*

★ £11.50-£13 £11.50-£13 £11-£11.50

Open Mar-Oct Booking advisable BH Last arrival 21.00hrs Last departure 14.00hrs

A tastefully developed park on a working farm with screened pitches laid out in horseshoe-shaped areas. This well designed park offers excellent toilet facilities including a bathroom and fully-serviced washing and toilet cubicles. A woodland and a water meadow are pleasant places to walk. A further field with its own amenity block is planned for 2008. A 6-acre site with 40 touring pitches, 4 hardstandings.

**Facilities:**
**Services:**
**Notes:** Summer house

## BISHOP MONKTON — MAP 19 SE36

### ►►► 69% Church Farm Caravan Park *(SE328660)*

Knaresborough Rd HG3 3QQ
☎ 01765 677668 & 07932 158924 Fax 01765 677668
**email:** churchfarmcaravans@uwclub.net
**Dir:** *Left at Boroughbridge off A1, or right off A61. Park opposite church.*

Open Mar-Oct Booking advisable BH Last arrival 22.30hrs Last departure 15.30hrs

A very pleasant rural site on a working farm, on the edge of the attractive village of Bishop Monkton with its well-stocked shop and pubs. Whilst very much a place to relax, there are many attractions close by including Fountains Abbey, Newby Hall, Ripon and Harrogate. A 4-acre site with 45 touring pitches and 3 statics.

**Facilities:**
**Services:**
**Notes:** No ball games, pets must be kept on leads

## BOLTON ABBEY — MAP 19 SE05

### ►►► 81% Howgill Lodge *(SD065593)*

GOLD

Barden BD23 6DJ
☎ 01756 720655
**email:** info@howgill-lodge.co.uk
**web:** www.howgill-lodge.co.uk
**Dir:** *From Bolton Abbey take B6160 signed Burnsall. In 3m at Barden Tower turn right signed Appletreewick. 1.5m at phone box turn right into lane to site*

★ £14 £14 £14

Open mid Mar-Oct Booking advisable Last arrival 21.00hrs

A beautifully-maintained and secluded site offering panoramic views of Wharfedale. The spacious hardstanding pitches are mainly terraced, and there is a separate tenting area with numerous picnic tables. There are three toilet facilities spread throughout the site, and a well-stocked shop. A 4-acre site with 40 touring pitches, 20 hardstandings.

**Facilities:**
**Services:**

**Facilities:** Bath, Shower, Electric Shaver, Hairdryer, Ice Pack Facility, Disabled Facilities, Public Telephone, Shop on Site or within 200yds, Mobile Shop (calls at least 5 days a week), BBQ Area, Picnic Area, Dog Exercise Area

ENGLAND

## BOROUGHBRIDGE MAP 19 SE36

### 77% Boroughbridge Camping & Caravanning Club Site (SE384662)

Bar Ln, Roecliffe YO51 9LS
01423 322683
**web:** www.campingandcaravanningclub.co.uk/boroughbridge
**Dir:** *From A1(M) junct 48 follow signs for Bar Lane Ind Est & Roecliffe. Site 0.25m from rdbt*

★ £18.25-£20.15 £18.25-£20.15 £18.25-£20.15

Open all year Booking advisable BH & peak periods Last arrival 21.00hrs Last departure noon

A quiet riverside site with direct access onto the River Ure, with fishing and boating available. Close enough to the A1(M) but far enough away to hear little traffic noise, this site is a perfect stopover for longer journeys. Ripon, Knaresborough, Harrogate and York are within easy reach, and Boroughbridge offers plenty of facilities just a short walk away. A 5-acre site with 85 touring pitches, 13 hardstandings.

**Leisure:**
**Facilities:**
**Services:**
**Notes:** Site gates closed 23.00hrs-07.00hrs. Fishing

## CAWOOD MAP 16 SE53

### 74% *Cawood Park* (SE563385)

Ryther Rd YO8 3TT
01757 268450
**email:** cawoodpark@aol.com
**web:** www.cawoodpark.com
**Dir:** *From A1(M) take B1222, turn at Cawood lights signed Tadcaster onto B1223 for 1m, park on left*

Booking advisable BH & Jul-Aug Last arrival 19.00hrs Last departure 11.00hrs

An attractive park in a rural area with its own fishing lake, overlooked by the camping area. The site is bordered by hedges and mature trees, and is well away from the road, with modern amenities. The lakeside club house provides regular entertainment, and coarse fishing is available. A 12-acre site with 60 touring pitches, 3 hardstandings and 10 statics.

**Leisure:**
**Facilities:**
**Services:**

## CONSTABLE BURTON MAP 19 SE19

### 81% Constable Burton Hall Caravan Park (SE158907)

DL8 5LJ
01677 450428
**Dir:** *Off A684*

★ £14-£17 £14-£17

Open Apr-Oct Booking advisable public hols Last arrival 20.00hrs Last departure noon

A pretty site in the former deer park of the adjoining Constable Burton Hall, screened from the road by the deer park walls and surrounded by mature trees in a quiet rural location. The laundry is housed in a converted 18th-century deer barn, and there is a pub and restaurant opposite. A 10-acre site with 120 touring pitches.

**Facilities:**
**Services:**
**Notes:** Dogs on leads, no commercial vehicles, no games, no tents

## EASINGWOLD MAP 19 SE56

### 67% *Folly Garth* (SE543687)

Green Ln YO61 3ES
01347 821150
**Dir:** *From Easingwold take Stillington road for 1.5m, site on right*

Open Feb-Dec

A small country site tucked away at the end of a lane, just 1.5 miles from the Georgian market town of Easingwold. Facilities include a well-equipped kitchen and a fully-carpeted lounge with table and chairs, opening onto a decking area. The toilets are to a good standard. A 3-acre site with 20 touring pitches.

**Facilities:**
**Services:**

## FILEY MAP 17 TA18

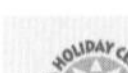

### 73% Blue Dolphin Holiday Park (TA095829)

Gristhorpe Bay YO14 9PU
01723 515155 01723 512059
**web:** www.bluedolphin-park.com
**Dir:** *Park off A165, 2m N of Filey*

★ £6-£53 £6-£53 £6-£53

Open mid Mar-Oct (rs mid Mar-May & Sep-Oct some facilities may be reduced) Booking advisable school hols Last arrival mdnt Last departure 10.00hrs

There are great clifftop views to be enjoyed from this fun-filled holiday centre with an extensive and separate touring area. The emphasis is on non-stop entertainment, with organised sports and clubs, all-weather leisure facilities, heated swimming pools and plenty of well-planned amusements. Pitches are mainly on level or gently-sloping grass plus some fully-serviced hardstandings, and the beach is just 2 miles away. An 85-acre site with 370 touring pitches, 10 hardstandings and 210 statics.

**Leisure:**
**Facilities:**
**Services:**
**Notes:** Dogs must be on leads, maximum of 2 dogs per group. Multi-sports court

*see advert on opposite page*

## 88% **Flower of May Holiday Park** *(TA085835)*

Lebberston Cliff YO11 3NU

☎ 01723 584311 01723 581361

**email:** info@flowerofmay.com

**web:** www.flowerofmay.com

**Dir:** *Signed off A165 on Scarborough side of Filey*

Open Etr-Oct (rs early & late season restricted opening in cafe, shop & bars) Booking advisable spring BH wk, Jul-Aug & BH Last arrival 21.00hrs Last departure noon

A well-run, high quality family holiday park with top class facilities. This large landscaped park offers a full range of recreational activities, with plenty to occupy everyone. Grass or hard pitches are available, all on level ground, and arranged in avenues screened by shrubs. A 13-acre site with 270 touring pitches, 100 hardstandings and 193 statics.

**Leisure:**

**Facilities:**

**Services:**

**Notes:** 1 dog by arrangement only. Squash, bowling, 9-hole golf & basketball court, skate park

*see advert on page 279*

## 80% **Primrose Valley Holiday Park** *(TA123778)*

YO14 9RF

☎ 01723 513771 & 0870 405 0126

01723 513777

**web:** www.primrosevalley-park.com

**Dir:** *Signed off A165 (Scarborough-Bridlington road), 3m S of Filey*

★ £15-£74 £15-£74

Open mid Mar-Oct Booking advisable at all times Last arrival anytime Last departure 10.00hrs

A large all-action holiday centre with a wide range of sports and leisure activities to suit everyone from morning until late in the evening. The touring area is completely separate from the main park with its own high quality amenity block. All touring pitches are fully-serviced hardstandings with grassed awning strips. A 160-acre site with 49 touring pitches and 1800 statics.

**Leisure:**

**Facilities:**

**Services:**

**Notes:** Maximum of 2 dogs per group

ENGLAND

*FILEY* CONTINUED

### 68% **Reighton Sands Holiday Park** *(TA142769)*

Reighton Gap YO14 9SH
☎ 01723 890476 🖷 01723 891043
**web:** www.reightonsands-park.com
**Dir:** *On A165 5m S of Filey at Reighton Gap, signed*
★ £6-£33 £6-£49 £6-£49

Open mid Mar-Oct (rs mid Mar-May & Sep-Oct some facilities may be reduced) Booking advisable school hols Last arrival 22.00hrs Last departure noon

A large, lively holiday centre with a wide range of entertainment and all-weather leisure facilities, located just a 10-minute walk from a long sandy beach. Each of the three touring areas has its own facilities block, and the site is particularly geared towards families with young children. A 229-acre site with 160 touring pitches, 160 hardstandings and 800 statics.

**Leisure:**
**Facilities:**
**Services:** →
**Notes:** Wi-fi. Indoor play area

*see advert on this page*

### ►►►► 84% **Lebberston Touring Park** *(TA077824)*

Filey Rd YO11 3PE
☎ 01723 585723
**email:** info@lebberstontouring.co.uk
**web:** www.lebberstontouring.co.uk
**Dir:** *Off A165 (Filey to Scarborough road). Site signed*
£13-£21 £13-£21

Open Mar-Oct Booking advisable BH & school hols Last arrival 21.00hrs Last departure noon

A peaceful family park in a gently-sloping rural area, where the quality facilities are maintained to a high standard of cleanliness. The keen owners are friendly and helpful, and create a relaxing atmosphere. A natural area offers views of the surrounding countryside through the shrubbery. A 7.5-acre site with 125 touring pitches, 25 hardstandings.

**Facilities:**
**Services:** →
**Notes:** No tents, dogs must be kept on leads

### ►►► 76% **Centenary Way Camping & Caravan Park** *(TA115798)*

Muston Grange YO14 0HU
☎ 01723 516415 & 512313
**Dir:** *Just off A1039 near A165 junct towards Bridlington*

Open Mar-Oct Booking advisable BH & Jul-Aug Last arrival 21.00hrs Last departure noon

A well set-out family-owned park, with footpath access to nearby beach. Close to the seaside resort of Filey, and caravan pitches enjoy views over open countryside. A 3-acre site with 75 touring pitches, 25 hardstandings.

**Leisure:** **Facilities:**
**Services:** →
**Notes:** No group bookings in peak period, no 9-12 berth tents

ENGLAND

**►►► 74% Crows Nest Caravan Park**
*TA094826)*
Gristhorpe YO14 9PS
01723 582206 01723 582206
**email:** enquires@crowsnestcaravanpark.com
**web:** www.crowsnestcaravanpark.com
**Dir:** *5m S of Scarborough & 2m N of Filey. On seaward side of 165, signed off rdbt, near petrol station*
fr £15 fr £15 fr £15
Open Mar-Oct Booking advisable school hols Last departure noon

A beautifully situated park on the coast between Scarborough and Filey, with excellent panoramic views. This large and mainly static park offers lively entertainment, and two bars. The touring caravan area is near the entertainment complex, whilst the tenting pitches are at the top of the site. A 20-acre site with 49 touring pitches, 49 hardstandings and 217 statics.

**Leisure:**
**Facilities:**
**Services:** → 
**Notes:** Entertainment in bar - no charge

## GRASSINGTON
*See Threshfield*

## HARROGATE MAP 19 SE35

### PREMIER PARK

**►►►►► 72% Ripley Caravan Park** *(SE289610)*
Knaresborough Rd, Ripley HG3 3AU
01423 770050 01423 770050
**email:** ripleycaravanpark@talk21.com
**web:** www.ripleycaravanpark.com
**Dir:** *3m N of Harrogate on A61. Right at rdbt onto B6165 signed Knaresborough. Park 300yds left*
★ £13-£15 £13-£15 £13-£15
Open Etr-Oct Booking advisable BH Last arrival 21.00hrs Last departure noon

A well-run rural site in attractive meadowland which has been landscaped with mature tree plantings. The resident owners lovingly maintain their facilities, and there is a heated swimming pool and sauna, a games room, and a covered play room for small children. An 18-acre site with 100 touring pitches, 35 hardstandings and 50 statics.

**Leisure:**
**Facilities:**
**Services:** →
**Notes:** Family camping only, dogs on leads, BBQs must be off the ground. Nursery playroom, football, TV (games room), sauna

### PREMIER PARK

**►►►►► 80% Rudding Holiday Park** *(SE333531)*
Follifoot HG3 1JH
01423 870439 01423 870859
**email:** holiday-park@ruddingpark.com
**web:** www.ruddingpark.com
**Dir:** *From A1 take A59 to A658, then S signed Bradford. 4.5m then right, follow signs*
★ £15.50-£30 £15.50-£30 £15.50-£30

Open Mar-Jan (rs Nov-Jan shop & Deer House pub - limited opening) Booking advisable BH, school hols & wknds Last arrival 22.30hrs Last departure 14.00hrs

A spacious park set in the stunning 200-acres of mature parkland and walled gardens of Rudding Park. The setting has been tastefully enhanced with terraced pitches and dry-stone walls. A separate area houses super pitches where all services are supplied including a picnic table and TV connection, and there are excellent toilets. An 18-hole golf course, heated outdoor swimming pool, the Deer House bar and restaurant, and a children's play area complete the amenities. A 55-acre site with 141 touring pitches, 60 hardstandings and 95 statics.

**Leisure:**
**Facilities:**
**Services:** →
**Notes:** Under 18s must be accompanied by adult. Wi-fi. 18-hole golf course, driving range

*see advert on page 270*

**acilities:** Bath Shower Electric Shaver Hairdryer Ice Pack Facility Disabled Facilities Public Telephone
Shop on Site or within 200yds Mobile Shop (calls at least 5 days a week) BBQ Area Picnic Area Dog Exercise Area

*HARROGATE* CONTINUED

### ►►►► 77% High Moor Farm Park
*(SE242560)*

Skipton Rd HG3 2LT

01423 563637 & 564955 01423 529449

**Dir:** *On A59 (Harrogate-Skipton road)*

Open Etr or Apr-Oct Booking advisable public hols Last arrival 23.30hrs Last departure 15.00hrs

An excellent site with very good facilities, set beside a small wood and surrounded by thorn hedges. The numerous touring pitches are located in meadowland fields, each area with its own toilet block. A large heated indoor swimming pool, games room, golf course, full-sized crown bowling green, and a bar serving meals and snacks are all popular. A 15-acre site with 320 touring pitches, 51 hardstandings and 158 statics.

**Leisure:**

**Facilities:**

**Services:** →

**Notes:** Coarse fishing, 9-hole golf course, bowling green

### ►►► 64% Shaws Trailer Park *(SE325557)*

Knaresborough Rd HG2 7NE

01423 884432 01423 883622

**Dir:** *On A59, 1m from town centre. 0.5m SW of Starbeck railway crossing, by Johnsons dry cleaners*

Open all year Booking advisable public hols Last arrival 20.00hrs Last departure 14.00hrs

A long-established site just a mile from the centre of Harrogate. The all-weather pitches are arranged around a carefully kept grass area, and the toilets are basic but functional and clean. The entrance is on the bus route to Harrogate. An 11-acre site with 60 touring pitches, 24 hardstandings and 146 statics.

**Facilities:**

**Services:** →

**Notes:** Adults only

### ►► 78% Bilton Park *(SE317577)*

Village Farm, Bilton Ln HG1 4DH

01423 863121

**Dir:** *Turn E off A59 at Skipton Inn into Bilton Lane. Site approx 1m*

★ fr £13.50 fr £13.50

Open Apr-Oct Booking advisable

An established family-owned park in open countryside yet only two miles from the shops and tearooms of Harrogate. The spacious grass pitches are complemented by a well appointed toilet block with private facilities. The Nidd Gorge right on the doorstep. A 4-acre site with 50 touring pitches.

**Leisure:**

**Facilities:**

**Services:** →

**Notes:**

ENGLAND

## HAWES MAP 18 SD88

### ►►► 78% Honeycott Caravan Park

(SD865897)
Ingleton Rd DL8 3LH
☎ 01969 667310
**email:** info@honeycott.co.uk
**web:** www.honeycott.co.uk
**Dir:** *On B6255, 0.25m from A684 on SW side of Hawes*

£13-£15 £13-£15

Open Mar-Oct Booking advisable at all times Last arrival 21.30hrs Last departure noon

Set on the edge of the upper Wensleydale village of Hawes, with fully serviced touring pitches enjoying splendid views over the dale to the hills beyond. The centrally heated amenity block is immaculate, though laundry facilities will be found a few minutes away in Hawes. A visit to Wensleydale Cheese visitor's centre is a must for cheese lovers. A 3.5-acre site with 18 touring pitches, 7 hardstandings and 28 statics.

**Facilities:**
**Services:**
**Notes:** Dogs must be kept on leads

### ►► 86% Bainbridge Ings Caravan & Camping Site (SD879895)

DL8 3NU
☎ 01969 667354
**email:** janet@bainbridge-ings.co.uk
**web:** www.bainbridge-ings.co.uk
**Dir:** *Approaching Hawes from Bainbridge on A684, left at Gayle sign, site 300yds on left*

fr £11 fr £10.50 fr £10.50

Open Apr-Oct Booking advisable school hols Last arrival 22.00hrs Last departure noon

A quiet, well-organised site in open countryside close to Hawes in the heart of Upper Wensleydale, popular with ramblers. Pitches are sited around the perimeter of several fields, each bounded by traditional stone walls. A 5-acre site with 70 touring pitches, 4 hardstandings and 15 statics.

**Facilities:**
**Services:**
**Notes:** No noise after 23.00hrs

## HELMSLEY MAP 19 SE68

### ►►►► 80% *Golden Square Touring Caravan Park* (SE604797)

DAVID BELLAMY CONSERVATION AWARD GOLD

Oswaldkirk YO62 5YQ
☎ 01439 788269 01439 788236
**email:** barbara@goldensquarecaravanpark.freeserve.co.uk
**web:** www.goldensquarecaravanpark.com
**Dir:** *1m from Ampleforth towards Helmsley on caravan route. Turn off B1257 to Ampleforth, 0.5m on right*

Open Mar-Oct Booking advisable BH Last arrival 21.00hrs Last departure noon

An excellent, popular spacious site with very good facilities. This friendly park is set in a quiet rural situation with lovely views over the North Yorks Moors. Terraced on three levels and surrounded by trees, it caters particularly for families. Country walks and mountain bike trails start here. Caravans are prohibited on the A170 at Sutton Bank between Thirsk and Helmsley. A 12-acre site with 129 touring pitches, 10 hardstandings and 1 static.

**Leisure:**
**Facilities:**
**Services:**
**Notes:** Microwave

### ►►► 75% Foxholme Caravan Park

(SE658828)
Harome YO62 5JG
☎ 01439 771241 01439 771744
**Dir:** *A170 from Helmsley towards Scarborough, right signed Harome, left at church, through village, follow signs*

£15 £15 £15

Open Etr-Oct Booking advisable BH & school hols Last arrival 23.00hrs Last departure noon

A quiet park set in secluded wooded countryside, with well-shaded pitches in individual clearings divided by mature trees. The facilities are well maintained, and the site is ideal as a touring base or a place to relax. Caravans are prohibited on the A170 at Sutton Bank between Thirsk and Helmsley. A 6-acre site with 60 touring pitches.

**Facilities:**
**Services:**
**Notes:** Adults only 1 unisex bath available

## HIGH BENTHAM MAP 18 SD66

**Regional winner – AA North East of England Campsite of the Year 2008**

### ►►►► 82% **Riverside Caravan Park** *(SD665688)*

GOLD

LA2 7FJ

☎ 015242 61272 🖷 015242 62835

**email:** info@riversidecaravanpark.co.uk

**web:** www.riversidecaravanpark.co.uk

**Dir:** *Off B6480, signed from High Bentham town centre*

★ fr £15 fr £15

Open Mar-Nov Booking advisable BH & school hols Last arrival 20.00hrs Last departure noon

A well-managed riverside park developed to a high standard, with level grass pitches set in avenues separated by trees. It has a well-equipped amenities block including excellent facilities for family tenters. The games room and adventure playground are popular with families, and the market town of High Bentham is close by. A 12-acre site with 61 touring pitches, 12 hardstandings and 206 statics.

**Leisure:** **Facilities:**

**Services:** →

**Notes:** Wi-fi. Permits for private fishing (chargeable)

### ► 79% **Lowther Hill Caravan Park** *(SD696695)*

LA2 7AN

☎ 015242 61657

**web:** www.caravancampingsites.co.uk/northyorkshire/lowtherhill

**Dir:** *From A65 at Clapham onto B6480 signed Bentham. 3m to site on right*

£12.50-£15 £12.50-£15 fr £10

Open Mar-Nov Booking advisable Last arrival 21.00hrs Last departure 14.00hrs

A simple site with stunning panoramic views from every pitch. Peace reigns on this little park, though the tourist villages of Ingleton, Clapham and Settle are not far away. All pitches have electricity, and there is a heated toilet/washroom. A 1-acre site with 9 touring pitches, 4 hardstandings and 1 static.

**Services:** →

**Notes:** Toilet, washbasin, shower are unisex

## HINDERWELL MAP 19 NZ71

### ►►► 76% **Serenity Touring and Camping Park** *(NZ792167)*

26A High St TS13 5JH

☎ 01947 841122

**email:** patandni@aol.com

**web:** www.serenitycaravanpark.co.uk

**Dir:** *Off A174 in village of Hinderwell*

Open Mar-Oct Booking advisable peak periods Last arrival 21.00hrs Last departure noon

A charming park mainly for adults that has been developed by enthusiastic owners. It lies behind the village of Hinderwell with its two pubs and store, and is handy for backpackers on the Cleveland Way. The sandy Runswick Bay and old fishing port of Staithes are close by, whilst Whitby is a short drive away. A 5.5-acre site with 20 touring pitches, 2 hardstandings.

**Facilities:**

**Services:** →

**Notes:** Mainly adult site, no ball games, kites or frisbees

## HUNMANBY MAP 17 TA07

### ►►► 79% **Orchard Farm Holiday Village** *(TA105779)*

Stonegate YO14 0PU

☎ 01723 891582 🖷 01723 891582

**email:** sharon.dugdale@virgin.net

**web:** www.orchardfarmholidayvillage.co.uk

**Dir:** *A165 from Scarborough towards Bridlington. Turn right signed Hunmanby, park on right just after rail bridge*

★ £10-£16 £10-£16 £10-£16

Open Mar-Oct Booking advisable BH & peak season Last arrival 23.00hrs Last departure 11.00hrs

Pitches are arranged around a large coarse fishing lake at this grassy park. The young owners are keen and friendly, and offer a wide range of amenities including an indoor heated swimming pool and a licensed bar. A 14-acre site with 91 touring pitches, 34 hardstandings and 46 statics.

**Leisure:**

**Facilities:**

**Services:** →

**Notes:** Fishing lake, minature railway

## HUTTON-LE-HOLE MAP 19 SE79

### ►►►► 76% Hutton-le-Hole Caravan Park

*(SE705895)*

Westfield Lodge YO62 6UG

☎ 01751 417261 🖷 01751 417876

**email:** rwstrickland@farmersweekly.net

**web:** www.westfieldlodge.co.uk

**Dir:** *From A170 onto Hutton-le-Hole road, N for approx 2m, over cattle grid, 500yds left into Park Drive, signed into site*

£11.50-£15 £11.50-£15 £9.50-£12.50

Open Etr-Oct Booking advisable BH Last arrival 22.00hrs Last departure noon

A small high quality park on a working farm in the North York Moors National Park. The purpose-built toilet block offers en suite family rooms, and there is a choice of hard-standing or grass pitches within a well-tended area surrounded by hedges and shrubs. The village facilities are a 10-minute walk away. Caravans are prohibited on the A170 at Sutton Bank between Thirsk and Helmsley. A 2.5-acre site with 22 touring pitches.

**Facilities:**

**Services:**

**Notes:** Farm walks

## KNARESBOROUGH MAP 19 SE35

### ►►► 74% Kingfisher Caravan Park

*(SE343603)*

Low Moor Ln, Farnham HG5 9JB

☎ 01423 869411 🖷 01423 869411

**Dir:** *From Knaresborough take A6055. After 1m turn left towards Farnham & left again in village signed Scotton. Site 1m on left*

★ £11-£15 £11-£15 £11-£15

Open Mar-Oct Booking advisable BH & 15 Jul-1 Sep Last arrival 23.00hrs Last departure 16.00hrs

A large grassy site with open spaces set in a wooded area in rural countryside. Whilst Harrogate, Fountains Abbey and York are within easy reach, anglers will want to take advantage of on-site coarse and fly fishing lakes. The park has a separate flat tenting field with electric hookups available. A 4-acre site with 35 touring pitches and 30 statics.

**Leisure:**

**Facilities:**

**Services:**

**Notes:** Pets on leads under strict adult control

## LONG PRESTON MAP 18 SD85

### ►►►► 77% Gallaber Park *(SD840570)*

BD23 4QF

☎ 01729 851397 🖷 01729 851398

**email:** info@gallaberpark.co.uk

**web:** www.gallaberpark.com

**Dir:** *On A682 between Long Preston & Gisburn*

★ £16.50-£23.50 £16.50-£23.50 £16.50-£20.50

Open mid Mar-Oct Booking advisable BH Last arrival 20.00hrs Last departure 13.00hrs

Set in the picturesque Ribble Valley, this park enjoys lovely views across the Dales. A stone barn houses excellent toilets and a family bathroom, and there are various types of pitches including some fully serviced ones. The emphasis is on quiet relaxation, and the spacious grounds and plentiful young shrubs and trees support this impression. 63 touring pitches, 27 hardstandings and 21 statics.

**Leisure:**

**Facilities:**

**Services:**

**Notes:** Family bathroom

## MARKINGTON MAP 19 SE26

### ►►► 76% Yorkshire Hussar Inn Holiday Caravan Park *(SE288650)*

High St HG3 3NR

☎ 01765 677327

**email:** yorkshirehussar@yahoo.co.uk

**web:** www.yorkshire-hussar-inn.co.uk

**Dir:** *Between Harrogate & Ripon (A61) turn W at Wormald Green, 1m into Markington, turn left past Post Office into the High Street*

Open Etr-Oct Booking advisable BH & school hols Last arrival 21.00hrs Last departure noon

A terraced site behind the village inn with well-kept grass. This pleasant site offers spacious pitches with some hardstandings and electricity. A 5-acre site with 20 touring pitches, 2 hardstandings and 73 statics.

**Leisure:**

**Facilities:**

**Services:**

**Notes:** Dogs must be kept on leads. Paddling pool

ENGLAND

## MASHAM MAP 19 SE28

### ►►► 76% Old Station Caravan Park

*(SE232812)*

Old Station Yard, Low Burton HG4 4DF

☎ 01765 689569 🖷 01765 689569

**email:** oldstation@tiscali.co.uk

**web:** www.oldstation-masham.co.uk

**Dir:** *Exit A1 onto B6267 signed Masham & Thirsk. In 8m left onto A6108. In 100yds turn left into site*

£12-£16.50 £12-£16.50 ▲ £11-£14

Open Mar-Nov Booking advisable Last arrival 20.00hrs Last departure noon

An interesting site on a former station. The enthusiastic and caring family owners have maintained the railway theme in creating a park with high quality facilities. The small town of Masham with its Theakston and Black Sheep breweries is within easy walking distance of the park. The reception/café is in a carefully restored wagon shed. A 3.75-acre site with 50 touring pitches and 12 statics.

**Facilities:**

**Services:**

**Notes:** No fast cycling around site, no campfires

## NABURN MAP 16 SE54

### ►►► 79% Naburn Lock Caravan Park

*(SE596446)*

YO19 4RU

☎ 01904 728697 🖷 01904 728697

**email:** wilks@naburnlock.co.uk

**web:** www.naburnlock.co.uk

**Dir:** *From A64 (McArthur Glen designer outlet) take on A19 N, turn left signed Naburn on B1222, site on right 0.5m past village*

★ fr £14 fr £14 ▲ fr £12

Open Mar-6 Nov Booking advisable at all times Last arrival 20.00hrs Last departure 14.00hrs

A family park whose enthusiastic owners are steadily improving its quality. The mainly grass pitches are arranged in small groups separated by mature hedges. The park is close to the River Ouse, and the river towpath provides excellent walking and cycling opportunities. The river bus to nearby York leaves from a jetty beside the park. A 7-acre site with 100 touring pitches, 12 hardstandings.

**Facilities:**

**Services:**

**Notes:** Adult only section. River fishing

## NETHERBY MAP 16 SE34

### ►►►► 79% *Maustin Caravan Park*

David Bellamy Conservation Award GOLD

*(SE332470)*

Kearby with Netherby LS22 4DA

☎ 0113 288 6234

**email:** info@maustin.co.uk

**web:** www.maustin.co.uk

**Dir:** *From A61 follow signs for Kirkby Overblow. Down lane turn right for Kearby, pass farm buildings to x-rds. Right to site*

▲

A secluded park for adults only, with pitches set around a well-tended grassed area. Adjacent to the pitching area, the amenity block offers a high standard of facilities. The charming Stables Restaurant with its cosy bar and patio is open at weekends and bank holidays, and the park's own flat bowling green where competitions are held throughout the season. An 8-acre site with 25 touring pitches and 70 statics.

## NORTHALLERTON MAP 19 SE39

### ►►►► 77% Otterington Park *(SE378882)*

David Bellamy Conservation Award GOLD

Station Park, South Otterington DL7 9JB

☎ 01609 780656 & 780263

**Dir:** *Turn W off A168 midway between Northallerton & Thirsk, signed South Otterington. Site on right just before South Otterington*

Open Mar-Oct

A high quality park on a working farm with open outlooks across the Vale of York. A peaceful location with a lovely nature walk and on-site fishing which is popular. Young children will enjoy the play area. Toilet facilities are very good. The attractions of Northallerton and Thirsk are a few minutes drive away. A 5-acre site with 40 touring pitches, 40 hardstandings.

**Leisure:**

**Facilities:**

**Services:**

**Notes:** Hot tub

ENGLAND

## NORTH STAINLEY MAP 19 SE27

### ►►► 78% **Sleningford Watermill Caravan Camping Park** *(SE280783)*

HG4 3HQ
☎ 01765 635201
**email:** sleningford@hotmail.co.uk
**web:** www.ukparks.co.uk/sleningford
**Dir:** *Adjacent to A6108. 5m N of Ripon & 1m N of North Stainley*
★ £10-£16.50 £10-£16.50 £8.50-£14.50

Open Etr & Apr-Oct Booking advisable BH, school hols & wknds Last arrival 21.00hrs Last departure 12.30hrs

The old watermill and the River Ure make an attractive setting for this touring park which is laid out in two areas. Pitches are placed in meadowland and close to mature woodland, and the park has two enthusiastic managers. Popular place with canoeists. A 14-acre site with 80 touring pitches.

**Leisure:** **Facilities:**

**Services:**

**Notes:** Youth groups by prior arrangement only. Off-licence, canoe access, fly fishing

## OSMOTHERLEY MAP 19 SE49

### ►►►► 76% **Cote Ghyll Caravan & Camping Park** *(SE459979)*

DL6 3AH
☎ 01609 883425
**email:** hills@coteghyll.com
**web:** www.coteghyll.com
**Dir:** *Exit A19 dual carriageway at A684 (Northallerton junct). Follow signs to Osmotherley. Left in village centre. Site entrance 0.5m on right*
★ £13-£16 £13-£16 £13-£16

Open Mar-Oct Booking advisable BH & school hols Last arrival 23.00hrs Last departure noon

Quiet, peaceful site in a pleasant valley on the edge of moors, close to the village. The park is divided into terraces bordered by woodland, and the well-appointed amenity block is a welcome addition to this attractive park. There are pubs and shops nearby. A 7-acre site with 77 touring pitches, 12 hardstandings and 18 statics.

**Leisure:** **Facilities:**

**Services:**

**Notes:** Family park, dogs must be kept on leads at all times. Tourist information, packed lunch service

## PICKERING MAP 19 SE78

### ►►► 80% ***Upper Carr Touring Park*** *(SE804816)*

Upper Carr Ln, Malton Rd YO18 7JP
☎ 01751 473115 01751 473115
**email:** harker@uppercarr.demon.co.uk
**Dir:** *Off A169 (Malton-Pickering road), approx 1.5m from Pickering. Signed opposite Black Bull pub*

Open Mar-Oct Booking advisable Last arrival 21.00hrs Last departure noon

Attractive and well-maintained rural touring park set amongst mature trees and hedges, with an animal corner and adjacent 9-hole golf course. A nature trail leads to the quaint village of Thornton-le-Dale, which has streams running through the centre. There is a family pub directly opposite the park. A 6.25-acre site with 80 touring pitches.

**Leisure:**

**Facilities:**

**Services:**

**Notes:** Off licence, rare breed hens & owls

### ►►► 77% **Wayside Caravan Park** *(SE764859)*

Wrelton YO18 8PG
☎ 01751 472608 01751 472608
**email:** waysideparks@freenet.co.uk
**web:** www.waysideparks.co.uk
**Dir:** *2.5m W of Pickering off A170, follow signs at Wrelton*
£15 £14.50 £12

Open Etr-early Oct Booking advisable Etr, Spring BH & Jul-Aug Last arrival 23.00hrs Last departure noon

Located in the village of Wrelton, this well-maintained park is divided into small paddocks by mature hedging. The village pub and restaurant are within a few minutes walk of the park. Caravans are prohibited on the A170 at Sutton Bank between Thirsk and Helmsley. A 10-acre site with 50 touring pitches, 4 hardstandings and 96 statics.

**Leisure:**

**Facilities:**

**Services:**

**Notes:** Dogs must be on leads

RICHMOND MAP 19 NZ10

## ►►►► 76% Brompton Caravan Park

*(NZ199002)*

Brompton-on-Swale DL10 7EZ

☎ 01748 824629 01748 826383

**email:** brompton.caravanpark@btinternet.com

**web:** www.bromptoncaravanpark.co.uk

**Dir:** *Exit A1 signed Catterick, continue on B6271 to Brampton-on-Swale, site 1m on left*

★ £18-£23 £18-£23 fr £15

Open Mar-Oct Booking advisable summer & wknds Last arrival 20.00hrs Last departure noon

A family riverside park run by enthusiastic young owners with local connections. Fishing is available on the River Swale which flows through the park, and there is a good children's playground. A 14.5-acre site with 177 touring pitches, 6 hardstandings and 22 statics.

**Leisure:**

**Facilities:**

**Services:** →

**Notes:** Family park

## ►►► 76% Swale View Caravan Park

*(NZ134013)*

Reeth Rd DL10 4SF

☎ 01748 823106 01748 823106

**email:** swaleview@teesdaleonline.co.uk

**web:** www.swaleviewcaravanpark.co.uk

**Dir:** *3m W of Richmond on A6108 (Reeth to Leyburn road)*

★ £20-£25 £10-£20

Open Mar-Oct Booking advisable BH & summer hols Last arrival 21.00hrs Last departure noon

Shaded by trees and overlooking the River Swale is this attractive, mainly grassy site. The facilities were extensively upgraded by enthusiastic owners in recent years. This park is a short distance from Richmond, and well situated for exploring Swaledale and Wensleydale. A 13-acre site with 50 touring pitches, 50 hardstandings and 130 statics.

*Swale View Caravan Park*

**Leisure:**

**Facilities:**

**Services:** →

**Notes:** 1 dog per pitch

RIPON MAP 19 SE37

*see also North Stainley*

## ►►► 80% Riverside Meadows Country Caravan Park *(SE317726)*

Ure Bank Top HG4 1JD

☎ 01765 602964 01765 604045

**email:** info@flowerofmay.com

**web:** www.flowerofmay.com

**Dir:** *On A61 at N end of bridge out of Ripon, W along river (NB do not cross river). Site 400yds, signed*

Open Etr-Oct (rs Mar-Apr bar open wknds only) Booking advisable BH & high season Last arrival 21.00hrs Last departure noon

This pleasant, well-maintained site stands on high ground overlooking the River Ure, one mile from the town centre. The site has an excellent club with family room and quiet lounge. There is no access to the river from the site. A 28-acre site with 131 touring pitches and 269 statics.

**Leisure:**

**Facilities:**

**Services:** →

**Notes:** Dogs by arrangement only

*see advert on page 279*

## ROBIN HOOD'S BAY MAP 19 NZ90
*see also Whitby*

### ►►►► 75% Middlewood Farm Holiday Park *(NZ945045)*

Middlewood Ln, Fylingthorpe YO22 4UF
☎ 01947 880414 🖹 01947 880871
**email:** info@middlewoodfarm.com
**web:** www.middlewoodfarm.com
**Dir:** *From A171 towards Robin Hood's Bay & into Fylingthorpe. Park signed from A171*

Open Mar-4 Jan Booking advisable BH & school hols for electric hook ups Last arrival 21.00hrs Last departure noon

A peaceful, friendly family park enjoying panoramic views of Robin Hood's Bay in a picturesque fishing village. The park has two toilet blocks with private facilities. The village pub is a 5-minute walk away, and the beach is a 10 minute walk. A 7-acre site with 100 touring pitches, 16 hardstandings and 30 statics.

**Leisure:** **Facilities:**

**Services:**

**Notes:** Dogs on lead at all times, dangerous breeds not accepted, no radios/noise after 22.00hrs

*see advert on this page*

### ►►► 78% Grouse Hill Caravan & Camping Park *(NZ928002)*

Flask Bungalow Farm, Fylingdales YO22 4QH
☎ 01947 880543 & 880560 🖹 01947 880543
**web:** www.grouse-hill.co.uk
**Dir:** *Off A171 (Whitby-Scarborough road), entered via loop road at Flask Inn*

£12-£18 £12-£18 £9-£16

Open Mar-Oct (rs Etr-May shop & reception restricted) Booking advisable public hols Last arrival 22.00hrs Last departure noon

A spacious family park on a south-facing slope, with many terraced pitches overlooking the North Yorkshire Moors National Park. The owners are constantly improving the park, and it is an ideal base for walking and touring. A 14-acre site with 175 touring pitches, 30 hardstandings.

**Leisure:** **Facilities:**

**Services:**

**Notes:** Dogs on leads at all times

*see advert on this page*

**Facilities:** Bath Shower Electric Shaver Hairdryer Ice Pack Facility Disabled Facilities Public Telephone Shop on Site or within 200yds Mobile Shop (calls at least 5 days a week) BBQ Area Picnic Area Dog Exercise Area

## ROSEDALE ABBEY MAP 19 SE79

### ►►►► 73% Rosedale Caravan & Camping Park *(SE725958)*

YO18 8SA

☎ 01751 417272

**email:** info@flowerofmay.com

**web:** www.flowerofmay.com

**Dir:** *From Pickering take A170 towards Sinnington for 2.25m. At Wrelton turn right onto unclass road signed Cropton & Rosedale, 7m. Park on left in village*

Open Mar-Oct Booking advisable BH & high season Last arrival 21.00hrs Last departure noon

Set in a sheltered valley in the centre of the North Yorkshire Moors National Park, and divided into separate areas for tents, tourers and statics. A very popular park, with well-tended grounds, and close to the pretty village of Rosedale Abbey. Two toilet blocks offer private, combined facilities. A 10-acre site with 100 touring pitches and 35 statics.

**Leisure:**

**Facilities:**

**Services:**

**Notes:** Dogs by arrangement only

*see advert on opposite page*

## SCARBOROUGH MAP 17 TA08

*see also Filey & Wykeham*

**PREMIER PARK**

### ►►►►► 75% Jacobs Mount Caravan Park *(TA021868)*

Jacobs Mount, Stepney Rd YO12 5NL

☎ 01723 361178 🖷 01723 361178

**email:** jacobsmount@yahoo.co.uk

**web:** www.jacobsmount.co.uk

**Dir:** *Direct access from A170*

★ £11.50-£17.50 £11.50-£17.50 £11.50-£17.50

Open Mar-Nov (rs Mar-May & Oct limited hours at shop/bar) Booking advisable BH & late Jun-early Sep Last arrival 22.00hrs Last departure noon

An elevated family-run park surrounded by woodland and open countryside, yet only two miles from the beach. Touring pitches are terraced gravel stands with individual services. A licensed bar and family room provide meals and snacks, and there is a separate well-equipped games room for teenagers. An 18-acre site with 156 touring pitches, 131 hardstandings and 60 statics.

**Leisure:** **Facilities:**

**Services:**

**Notes:** Pets must be kept on leads. Food preparation area

### ►►►► 77% Scarborough Camping & Caravanning Club Site *(TA025911)*

Field Ln, Burniston Rd YO13 0DA

☎ 01723 366212

**web:** www.campingandcaravanningclub.co.uk/scarborough

**Dir:** *On W side of A165, 1m N of Scarborough*

★ £18.35-£23.25 £18.35-£23.25 £18.35-£23.25

Open Apr-3 Nov Booking advisable BH & peak periods Last arrival 21.00hrs Last departure noon

This spacious site offers high standard facilities. The majority of pitches are hardstandings of plastic webbing which allow the grass to grow through naturally. This is an excellent family-orientated park with its own shop and takeaway, within easy reach of the resort of Scarborough. A 20-acre site with 300 touring pitches, 100 hardstandings.

**Leisure:** **Facilities:**

**Services:**

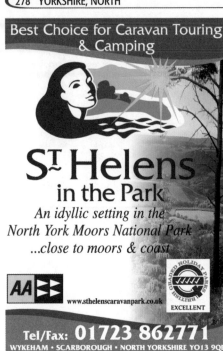

ENGLAND

## SCARBOROUGH CONTINUED

### ►►► 77% Killerby Old Hall *(TA063829)*

Killerby YO11 3TW
☎ 01723 583799 🖹 01723 581608
**email:** graham.white3@tesco.net
**web:** www.killerbyoldhall.com
**Dir:** *Direct access via B1261 at Killerby, near Cayton*

★ £14.50-£18.50 £14.50-£18.50

Open Mar-Oct Booking advisable BH & school hols Last departure noon

A small secluded park, well sheltered by mature trees and shrubs, located at the rear of the old hall. Use of the small indoor swimming pool is shared by visitors to the hall's holiday accommodation. A children's play area is a recent addition to the facilities. A 2-acre site with 20 touring pitches, 20 hardstandings.

**Leisure:**

**Facilities:**

**Services:** →

### ►►► 78% Scalby Close Park

DAVID BELLAMY CONSERVATION AWARD GOLD

*(TA020925)*
Burniston Rd YO13 0DA
☎ 01723 365908
**email:** info@scalbyclosepark.co.uk
**web:** www.scalbyclosepark.co.uk
**Dir:** *2m N of Scarborough on A615 coast road, 1m from junct with A171*

★ £13-£21 £13-£21 £13-£21

Open Mar-Oct Booking advisable BH & high season Last arrival 22.00hrs Last departure noon

An attractive park with enthusiastic owners who have carried out many improvements. The site has a shower block, a laundry and fully-serviced pitches, and the landscaping is also very good. An ideal base from which to explore the nearby coast and countryside. A 3-acre site with 42 touring pitches, 40 hardstandings and 5 statics.

**Facilities:**

**Services:** →

**Notes:**

## SCOTCH CORNER MAP 19 NZ20

### ►►► 73% Scotch Corner Caravan Park

*(NZ210054)*
DL10 6NS
☎ 01748 822530 🖹 01748 822530
**email:** marshallleisure@aol.com
**web:** www.scotchcornercaravanpark.co.uk
**Dir:** *From Scotch Corner junct of A1 & A66 take A6108 towards Richmond. 250mtrs then cross central reservation, return 200mtrs to site entrance*

Open Etr-Oct Booking advisable public hols & Jul-Aug Last arrival 22.30hrs Last departure noon

A well-maintained site with good facilities, ideally situated as a stopover, and an equally good location for touring. The Vintage Hotel which serves food can be accessed from the rear of the site. A 7-acre site with 96 touring pitches, 4 hardstandings.

**Facilities:**

**Services:** →

**Notes:** Recreation area for children

## SELBY MAP 16 SE63

### ►►► 79% The Ranch Caravan Park

*(SE664337)*
Cliffe Common YO8 6EF
☎ 01757 638984 🖹 01757 630089
**email:** contact@theranchcaravanpark.co.uk
**web:** www.theranchcaravanpark.co.uk
**Dir:** *Exit A63 at Cliffe signed Skipwith. Site 1m N on left*

Open all year Booking advisable BH Last arrival 22.00hrs Last departure noon

**Abbreviations:** BH-bank holiday/s Etr-Easter Whit-Whitsun dep-departure fr-from hrs-hours m-mile mdnt-midnight rdbt-roundabout rs-restricted service wk-week wknd-weekend no dogs No cards → following facilities within 3 miles of the site

compact, sheltered park in open countryside offering excellent menities. The enthusiastic and welcoming family owners have reated a country club feel, with a tasteful bar, plus a sauna and icuzzi in a wooden chalet. A 7-acre site with 50 touring pitches, 50 ardstandings.

**eisure:**

**acilities:**

**ervices:**

## HERIFF HUTTON MAP 19 SE66

### ►►► 81% Sheriff Hutton Camping & Caravanning Club Site *(SE638652)*

racken Hill YO60 6QG

01347 878660

**veb:** www.campingandcaravanningclub.co.uk/ heriffhutton

**ir:** *From York follow 'Earswick Strensall' signs. Keep left at filling tation & Ship Inn. Follow signs for Sheriff Hutton. Turn left in illage of Strensall, site 2nd on right*

£14.85-£20.15 £14.85-£20.15 £14.85-£20.15

Open 13 Mar-3 Nov Booking advisable BH & peak periods ast arrival 21.00hrs Last departure noon

quiet rural site in open meadowland within easy reach of York. This vell-established park is friendly and welcoming, and the landscaping attractive and mature. A 10-acre site with 90 touring pitches, 16 ardstandings.

**eisure:**

**acilities:**

**ervices:**

## LINGSBY MAP 19 SE67

### ►►► 74% Robin Hood Caravan & Camping Park *(SE701748)*

Green Dyke Ln YO62 4AP

01653 628391 01653 628392

**mail:** info@robinhoodcaravanpark.co.uk

**veb:** www.robinhoodcaravanpark.co.uk

**ir:** *On edge of Slingsby. Access off B1257 (Malton-Helmsley oad)*

£12-£20 £12-£20 £12-£20

pen Mar-Oct Booking advisable BH & 15 Jul-1 Sep Last rrival 18.00hrs Last departure noon

pleasant, well-maintained grassy park, in a good position for touring orth Yorkshire. Situated on the edge of the village of Slingsby, the ark has hardstandings and electricity for every pitch. A 2-acre site ith 32 touring pitches, 22 hardstandings and 35 statics.

**eisure:**

**acilities:**

**ervices:**

**otes:** Caravan hire, off-licence

### ►►► 82% Slingsby Camping & Caravanning Club Site *(SE699755)*

Railway St YO62 4AA

01653 628335

**web:** www.campingandcaravanningclub.co.uk/slingsby

**Dir:** *0.25m N of Slingsby. Also signed from Helmsley/Malton on B1257*

★ £15.45-£20.15 £15.45-£20.15 £15.45-£20.15

Open 13 Mar-3 Nov Booking advisable BH & peak periods Last arrival 21.00hrs Last departure noon

A well cared for park in a traditional North Yorkshire village. Pitches are a mixture of grass and hardstanding, and there is a well-appointed toilet block with cubicled facilities. The village pub serving food is a few minutes walk away. Caravans are prohibited on the A170 at Sutton Bank between Thirsk and Helmsley. A 3-acre site with 60 touring pitches, 16 hardstandings.

**Facilities:**

**Services:**

**Notes:** Site gates closed 23.00hrs-07.00hrs

## SNAINTON MAP 17 SE98

### ►►►► 81% Jasmine Caravan Park *(SE928813)*

GOLD

Cross Ln YO13 9BE

01723 859240 01723 859240

**email:** info@jasminepark.co.uk

**web:** www.jasminepark.co.uk

**Dir:** *Turn S off A170 in Snainton, then follow signs*

fr £15 fr £15 fr £15

Open Mar-Oct Booking advisable 5 wks in advance for BH Last arrival 22.00hrs Last departure noon

A peaceful and beautifully-presented park on the edge of a pretty village, and sheltered by high hedges. The toilet block with individual wash cubicles is maintained to a very high standard. This picturesque park lies midway between Pickering and Scarborough on the southern edge of the North Yorkshire Moors. A 5-acre site with 94 touring pitches, 1 hardstanding and 11 statics.

**Facilities:**

**Services:**

**Notes:** Dogs must be on leads. Baby changing unit

**acilities:** Bath Shower Electric Shaver Hairdryer Ice Pack Facility Disabled Facilities Public Telephone Shop on Site or within 200yds Mobile Shop (calls at least 5 days a week) BBQ Area Picnic Area Dog Exercise Area

## STAINFORTH MAP 18 SD86

### 75% Knight Stainforth Hall Caravan & Campsite *(SD816672)*

BD24 0DP

01729 822200 01729 823387

**email:** info@knightstainforth.co.uk

**web:** www.knightstainforth.co.uk

**Dir:** *From W, on A65 take B6480 for Settle, left before swimming pool signed Little Stainforth. From E, through Settle on B6480, over bridge to swimming pool, then turn right*

★ £14 £14 £12-£14

Open May-Oct Booking advisable BH & Jul-Aug Last arrival 22.00hrs Last departure noon

Located near Settle and the River Ribble in the Yorkshire Dales National Park, this well-maintained family site is sheltered by mature woodland. It is an ideal base for walking or touring in the beautiful surrounding areas. The toilet block is appointed to a very high standard. A 6-acre site with 100 touring pitches and 60 statics.

**Leisure:**

**Facilities:**

**Services:**

**Notes:** No groups of unaccompanied minors. Wi-fi. Fishing

## STAXTON MAP 17 TA07

### 72% Spring Willows *(TA026794)*

Main Rd, Staxton Roundabout YO12 4SB

01723 891505 01723 892123

**email:** enquires@springwillows.co.uk

**web:** www.blackshawleisure.co.uk

**Dir:** *A64 to Scarborough, then take A1039 to Filey. Entrance on right*

Open Mar-Jan (rs Mar & Oct bar, pool, take-away, restaurant restricted) Booking advisable BH, Etr, Jul & Aug Last arrival 18.00hrs Last departure 11.00hrs

A lively, popular family park, with a spacious club providing free evening entertainment during weekends and in high season. At these times, food is served throughout the day, together with a popular take-away service. The swimming pool and games room with its many video games are popular with older children. The attractions of Scarborough and Filey are a short drive away. A 26-acre site with 181 touring pitches.

**Leisure:**

**Facilities:**

**Services:**

**Notes:** No gazebos

## STILLINGFLEET MAP 16 SE54

### 69% Home Farm Caravan & Camping *(SE595427)*

Moreby YO19 6HN

01904 728263 01904 720059

**email:** home_farm@hotmail.co.uk

**Dir:** *6m from York on B1222, 1.5m N of Stillingfleet*

★ fr £8 fr £8 fr £7

Open Feb-Dec Booking advisable BH Last arrival 22.00hrs

A traditional meadowland site on a working farm bordered by parkland on one side and the River Ouse on another. Facilities are in converted farm buildings, and the family owners extend a friendly welcome to tourers. An excellent site for relaxing and unwinding, yet only a short distance from the attractions of York. A 5-acre site with 25 touring pitches and 2 statics.

**Facilities:**

**Services:**

**Notes:** Dogs must be kept on leads

## SUTTON-ON-THE-FOREST MAP 19 SE56

### 83% Goosewood Caravan Park *(SE595636)*

YO61 1ET

01347 810829 01347 811498

**email:** edward@goosewood.co.uk

**web:** www.goosewood.co.uk

**Dir:** *From A1237 take B1363. After 5m turn right. Take right turn after 0.5m & site on right*

★ £15.50-£20 £15.50-£20

Open Feb-14 Jan Booking advisable BH, Jul & Aug Last arrival 20.00hrs Last departure noon

An immaculately maintained park with its own lake and seasonal fishing, set in attractive woodland just six miles north of York. The generous patio pitches are randomly spaced throughout the site, and there's a good play area for younger children, with a recreation barn for teenagers, plus a health spa. A 20-acre site with 75 touring pitches, 75 hardstandings and 35 statics.

**Leisure:**

**Facilities:**

**Services:**

ENGLAND

## 'HIRSK MAP 19 SE48

### IEW ►►►► 78% Hillside Caravan Park
*SE447889)*

anvas Farm, Knayton YO7 4BR

01845 537349

**mail:** info@hillsidecaravanpark.co.uk

**ir:** *From Thirsk take A19 north. Turn left at Knayton sign. In 25m turn right (crossing bridge over A19), through village. Site n left in approx 1.5m*

newly developed, high quality, spacious park with first-class facilities, t in open countryside. It is an excellent base for walkers and for ose wishing to explore the Thirsk area. The park does not take tents. 5 touring pitches.

### ►► 64% Sowerby Caravan ark *(SE437801)*

owerby YO7 3AG

01845 522753 01845 574520

**mail:** sowervanpark@tiscali.co.uk

**eb:** www.ukparks.co.uk/sowerby

**ir:** *From A19 approx 3m S of Thirsk, turn W for Sowerby. Turn ght at junct. Site 1m on left*

£9.40-£10.75 £9.40-£10.75

pen Mar-Oct Booking advisable BH Last arrival 22.00hrs

grassy site beside a tree-lined river bank, with basic but functional ilet facilities. Tourers enjoy a separate grassed area with an open itlook, away from the statics. A 1-acre site with 25 touring pitches, 5 rdstandings and 85 statics.

**isure:** **Facilities:**

**rvices:**

**otes:**

### ► 72% Thirkleby Hall Caravan Park
*E472794)*

irkleby YO7 3AR

01845 501360 & 07799 641815

**mail:** greenwood.parks@virgin.net

**eb:** www.greenwoodparks.com

**ir:** *3m S of Thirsk on A19. Turn E through arched gatehouse to park*

Open Mar-Oct Booking advisable BH & Aug wknds Last arrival 20.00hrs Last departure 16.30hrs

A long-established site in the grounds of the old hall, with statics in wooded areas around a fishing lake and tourers based on slightly sloping grassy pitches. Toilet facilities are basic but clean and functional, and this well-screened park has superb views of the Hambledon Hills. A 53-acre site with 50 touring pitches and 185 statics.

**Leisure:**

**Facilities:**

**Services:**

**Notes:** Dogs must be kept on leads

## THRESHFIELD MAP 18 SD96

### ►►► 81% Wood Nook Caravan Park *(SD974641)*

DAVID BELLAMY CONSERVATION AWARD GOLD

Skirethorns BD23 5NU

01756 752412 01756 752946

**email:** info@woodnook.net

**web:** www.woodnook.net

**Dir:** *From Skipton take B6265 to Threshfield, then B6160 for 50yds. Left into Skirethorns Lane, follow signs to park*

★ £14-£16 fr £14 fr £13.50

Open Mar-Oct Booking advisable BH & peak periods Last arrival 20.00hrs Last departure noon

Gently-sloping site in a rural setting, completely hidden by natural features of surrounding hills and woodland. Toilet facilities are housed in converted farm buildings within the farmhouse courtyard, and pitches are all on firm, well-drained ground or hardstandings. The park is well situated for ramblers, while the market town of Skipton is only nine miles away. A 2-acre site with 48 touring pitches, 27 hardstandings and 11 statics.

**Leisure:**

**Facilities:**

**Services:**

**Notes:** No groups, no gazebos. Wi-fi

## TOLLERTON MAP 19 SE56

### ►►► 69% Tollerton Holiday Park *(SE513643)*

Station Rd YO61 1RD

☎ 01347 838313 🖷 01347 838313

**email:** greenwood.parks@virgin.net

**web:** www.greenwoodparks.com

**Dir:** *From York take A19 towards Thirsk. At Cross Lanes left towards Tollerton. 1m to Chinese restaurant just before rail bridge. Site entrance through restaurant car park*

★ £14-£15 £ fr £12

Open Mar-Oct Booking advisable BH Last arrival 20.00hrs Last departure 16.00hrs

A small park within a few minutes walk of Tollerton village. It is set in open countryside a short drive from the Park & Ride for York. There is little disturbance from the East Coast mainline which passes near to the park. A 5-acre site with 50 touring pitches and 75 statics.

**Leisure:**

**Facilities:**

**Services:** →

**Notes:** No groups

## TOWTHORPE MAP 19 SE65

### ►►►► 76% York Touring Caravan Site *(SE648584)*

Greystones Farm, Towthorpe Moor Ln YO32 9ST

☎ 01904 499275 🖷 01904 499271

**email:** info@yorkcaravansite.co.uk

**web:** www.yorkcaravansite.co.uk

**Dir:** *Leave A64 at exit for Strensall/Haxby, site 1.5m on left*

£11.50-£18.50 £11.50-£18.50 £10-£18.50

Open all year Booking advisable BH Last arrival 20.00hrs Last departure noon

A purpose-built, high quality site with a select 'country club' feel. It is part of a leisure complex with a golf driving range and a 9-hole putting course, as well as an intimate bar and tasteful bistro. The generous pitches are set within well-manicured grassland with a backdrop of trees and shrubs. A 6-acre site with 44 touring pitches, 12 hardstandings.

**Leisure:**

**Facilities:**

**Services:** →

## WEST KNAPTON MAP 19 SE87

### ►►► 77% Wolds Way Caravan and Camping *(SE896743)*

West Farm YO17 8JE

☎ 01944 728463 & 728180

**email:** knapton.wold.farms@farming.co.uk

**web:** www.rydalesbest.co.uk

**Dir:** *Signed between Rillington & West Heslerton on A64 (Malton to Scarborough road). Site 1.5m*

★ £10.50-£16 £10.50-£16 £10-£15

Open Mar-Oct Booking advisable Last arrival 22.30hrs Last departure 19.00hrs

A park on a working farm in a peaceful, high position on the Yorkshire Wolds, with magnificent views over the Vale of Pickering. This is an excellent walking area, with the Wolds Way passing the entrance to the park. A pleasant 1.5 mile path leads to a lavender farm, with its first-class coffee shop. A 7.5-acre site with 70 touring pitches, 30 hardstandings.

**Leisure:**

**Facilities:**

**Services:** →

**Notes:**

**Abbreviations:** BH-bank holiday/s Etr-Easter Whit-Whitsun dep-departure fr-from hrs-hours m-mile mdnt-midnight rdbt-roundabout rs-restricted service wk-week wknd-weekend no dogs No cards → following facilities within 3 miles of the site

ENGLAND

## WHITBY MAP 19 NZ81

*see also Robin Hood's Bay*

### ►►► 78% Ladycross Plantation Caravan Park *(NZ821080)*

GOLD

Egton YO21 1UA

☎ 01947 895502

**email:** enquiries@ladycrossplantation.co.uk

**web:** www.ladycrossplantation.co.uk

**Dir:** *On unclassified road (signed) off A171 (Whitby-Teeside road)*

★ £14-£17 £14-£17

Open end Mar-Oct Booking advisable BH & Aug Last arrival 20.30hrs Last departure noon

A delightful woodland setting with pitches sited in small groups in clearings around an amenities block. An additional amenity block has now been completed. The site is well placed for Whitby and the Moors. Children will enjoy exploring the woodland around the site. A 12-acre site with 130 touring pitches, 18 hardstandings.

**Facilities:**

**Services:**

### ►►► 75% Rigg Farm Caravan Park *(NZ915061)*

Stainsacre YO22 4LP

☎ 01947 880430

**Dir:** *From A171 Scarborough road left onto B1416 signed Ruswarp. Right in 3.25m onto unclass road signed Hawsker. Left in 1.25m. Site in 0.5m*

£12-£17 £12-£17 £10-£14

Open Mar-Oct Booking advisable BH & Jul-Aug Last arrival 22.00hrs Last departure noon

A neat rural site with distant views of the coast and Whitby Abbey, set in peaceful surroundings. The former farm buildings are used to house reception and a small games room. A 3-acre site with 14 touring pitches, 14 hardstandings and 15 statics.

**Leisure:**

**Facilities:**

**Services:**

**Notes:** No ball games, cycling, skateboards, roller skating or kite flying

## WYKEHAM MAP 17 SE98

### ►►►► 83% St Helens Caravan Park *(SE967836)*

GOLD

St Helens in the Park YO13 9QD

☎ 01723 862771 01723 866613

**email:** caravans@wykeham.co.uk

**web:** www.sthelenscaravanpark.co.uk

**Dir:** *On A170 in village, 150yds on left beyond Downe Arms Hotel towards Scarborough*

★ £13.80-£16.50 £13.80-£16.50 £10-£13

Open all year (rs Nov-Jan shop/laundry closed) Booking advisable BH & Jul-Aug Last arrival 22.00hrs Last departure 17.00hrs

Set on the edge of the North York Moors National Park, this delightfully landscaped park is well-maintained and thoughtfully laid out with top quality facilities. The site is divided into terraces with tree-screening creating smaller areas, including an adults' zone. A cycle route leads through the surrounding Wykeham Estate, and there is a short pathway to the adjoining Downe Arms country pub. A 25-acre site with 250 touring pitches, 10 hardstandings.

**Leisure:**

**Facilities:**

**Services:**

**Notes:** Wi-fi. Caravan storage

*see advert on page 278*

## YORK MAP 16 SE65

### ►►► 63% Riverside Caravan & Camping Park *(SE598477)*

Ferry Ln, Bishopthorpe YO23 2SB

☎ 01904 705812 & 704442 01904 705824

**email:** info@yorkmarine.co.uk

**web:** www.yorkmarine.co.uk

**Dir:** *From A64 take A1036. Right at lights signed Bishopthorpe, left into main street at T-junct. At end of road right into Ancaster Lane, left in 150yds*

★ £14-£18 £14-£18 £8-£13

Open Apr-Oct Booking advisable BH & Jul-Sep Last arrival 22.00hrs Last departure noon

A small level grassy park in a hedged field on the banks of the River Ouse, on the outskirts of York. This is a popular site with those who enjoy messing about on the river. A 1-acre site with 25 touring pitches.

**Leisure:**

**Facilities:**

**Services:**

**Notes:** Dogs must be kept on leads. Wi-fi. Boat hire, slipway, fishing

ENGLAND

# YORKSHIRE, SOUTH

## WORSBROUGH MAP 16 SE30

### ►► 74% Greensprings Touring Park (SE330020)

Rockley Abbey Farm, Rockley Ln S75 3DS

☎ 01226 288298 📠 01226 288298

**Dir:** *M1 junct 36, A61 to Barnsley. Turn left after 0.25m onto road signed Pilley. Site 1m at bottom of hill*

★ fr £11 fr £11 fr £4.50

Open Apr-Oct Booking advisable for hook ups Last arrival 21.00hrs Last departure noon

A secluded and attractive farm site set amidst woods and farmland, with access to the river and several good local walks. There are two touring areas, one gently sloping. A new well-appointed toilet block was under construction at the time of the last inspection. Although not far from the M1, there is almost no traffic noise, and this site is convenient for exploring the area's industrial heritage, as well as the Peak District. A 4-acre site with 65 touring pitches, 13 hardstandings.

**Facilities:** **Services:**

**Notes:** TV hook up

# YORKSHIRE, WEST

## BARDSEY MAP 16 SE34

### ►►► 81% Glenfield Caravan Park (SE351421)

120 Blackmoor Ln LS17 9DZ

☎ 01937 574657 📠 01937 579529

**email:** glenfieldcp@aol.com

**web:** www.ukparks.co.uk/glenfieldcp

**Dir:** *From A58 at Bardsey turn into Church Lane, past church, up hill. Continue 0.5m, site on right*

Open all year Booking advisable Last arrival 23.00hrs Last departure noon

A quiet family-owned rural site in a well-screened, tree-lined meadow. The site has an excellent toilet block complete with family room. A convenient touring base for Leeds and the surrounding area. Discounted golf, and food are both available at the local golf club. A 4-acre site with 30 touring pitches, 30 hardstandings and 1 static.

**Facilities:**

**Services:**

**Notes:**

### ►►► 74% Moor Lodge Park (SE352423)

Blackmoor Ln LS17 9DZ

☎ 01937 572424 📠 01937 572424

**email:** rodatmlcp@aol.com

**web:** www.ukparks.co.uk/moorlodge

**Dir:** *Turn right after Bracken Fox pub (Ling Lane) then right at x-roads, site 0.5m on right*

£12.50 £12.50

Open all year Booking advisable BH Last arrival 23.00hrs Last departure 23.00hrs

A neat, well-kept site in a peaceful and pleasant rural location convenient to surrounding areas of interest as well as Leeds. The touring area is for adults only. A 7-acre site with 12 touring pitches and 60 statics.

**Facilities:**

**Services:**

**Notes:** Adults only

## HORSFORTH MAP 19 SE23

### ►►► 78% St Helena's Caravan Park (SE240421)

DAVID BELLAMY CONSERVATION AWARD GOLD

Otley Old Rd LS18 5HZ

☎ 0113 284 1142

**Dir:** *From A658 follow signs for Leeds/Bradford Airport. Then follow site signs*

Open Apr-Oct Booking advisable Last arrival 19.30hrs Last departure 14.00hrs

A well-maintained parkland setting surrounded by woodland yet within easy reach of Leeds with its excellent shopping and cultural opportunities, Ilkley, and the attractive Wharfedale town of Otley. Some visitors may just want to relax in this adults-only park's spacious and pleasant surroundings. A 12-acre site with 60 touring pitches and 40 statics.

**Facilities:**

**Services:**

**Notes:** Adults only

ENGLAND

# CHANNEL ISLANDS

## Guernsey

### CASTEL MAP 24

**►►► 81% Fauxquets Valley Farm**
GY5 7QA
☎ 01481 236951 🖷 01481 251797
**email:** info@fauxquets.co.uk
**web:** www.fauxquets.co.uk
**Dir:** *Off pier. 2nd exit off rdbt. Top of hill left onto Queens Rd. Continue for 2m. Turn right onto Candie Rd. Opposite sign for German Occupation Museum*

★ Ⱥ £11-£13.60

Open mid Jun-Aug (rs Etr-mid Jun Haybarn restaurant & bar closed) Booking advisable last 2 wks Jul-1st 3 wks Aug

A beautiful, quiet farm site in a hidden valley close to the sea. Friendly helpful owners, who understand campers' needs, offer good quality facilities and amenities, including an outdoor swimming pool, bar/restaurant, nature trail and sports areas. A 3-acre site with 100 touring pitches.

**Leisure:** **Facilities:**

**Services:** → 

**Notes:** Bird watching

### ST SAMPSON MAP 24

**►►► 80% Le Vaugrat Camp Site**
Route de Vaugrat GY2 4TA
☎ 01481 257468 🖷 01481 251841
**email:** enquiries@vaugratcampsite.com
**web:** www.vaugratcampsite.com
**Dir:** *From main coast road on NW of island, site is signed at Port Grat Bay into Route de Vaugrat, near Peninsula Hotel*

Open May-mid Sep Booking advisable at all times

Overlooking the sea and set within the grounds of a lovely 17th-century house, this level grassy park is backed by woodland, and close to lovely sandy beaches of Port Grat and Grand Havre. It is run by a warm and welcoming family who pride themselves on their magnificent floral displays. A 6-acre site with 150 touring pitches.

**Leisure:** **Facilities:**

**Services:** →

**Notes:** No animals

### VALE MAP 24

**►►► 79% La Bailloterie Camping & Leisure**
Bailloterie Ln GY3 5HA
☎ 01481 243636 & 07781 103420 🖷 01481 243225
**email:** info@campinginguernsey.com
**web:** www.campinginguernsey.com
**Dir:** *3m N of St Peter Port, take Vale road to Crossways, turn right into Rue du Braye. Site 1st left at sign*

Open 15 May-15 Sep Booking advisable at all times Last arrival 23.00hrs

A pretty rural site with one large touring field and a few small, well-screened paddocks. This delightful site has been in the same family ownership for over 30 years, and offers super facilities in converted outbuildings. A 12-acre site with 100 touring pitches.

**Leisure:**

**Facilities:**

**Services:** →

**Notes:** Dogs by arrangement. Volleyball net, boules pitch

## Herm

### HERM MAP 24

**►►► 79% Seagull Campsite**
GY1 3HR
☎ 01481 722377 🖷 01481 700334
**email:** camping@herm-island.com
**web:** www.herm-island.com

Open May-Sep Last arrival 17.00hrs Last departure 17.30hrs

An away-from-it-all location on the idyllic tiny island of Herm. The well-maintained grassy site offers stunning views over the sea and surrounding islands, and all pitches are level, with some in individually-terraced bays. Herm is traffic free, so parking must be arranged with Trident Travel at St Peter Port, Guernsey, on 01481 721379, or ask when booking. Campers should check in at the information office on the quay. 50 touring pitches.

**Facilities:** →

**Notes:** Groceries can be delivered

ENGLAND

# Jersey

## ST MARTIN MAP 24

### PREMIER PARK

**►►►►► 80% Beuvelande Camp Site**

Beuvelande JE3 6EZ

☎ 01534 853575 01534 857788

**email:** info@campingjersey.com

**web:** www.campingjersey.com

**Dir:** *Take A6 from St Helier to St Martin & follow signs to campsite before St Martins Church*

Open Apr-Sep (rs Apr-May & Sep restaurant closed, shop hours limited) Booking advisable

A well-established site with excellent toilet facilities, accessed via narrow lanes in peaceful countryside close to St Martin. An attractive bar/restaurant is the focal point of the park, especially in the evenings, and there is a small swimming pool and playground. Motorhomes and towed caravans will be met at the ferry and escorted to the site if requested when booking. A 6-acre site with 150 touring pitches and 75 statics.

**Leisure:**

**Facilities:**

**Services:** →

**►►►► 78% *Rozel Camping Park***

Summerville Farm JE3 6AX

☎ 01534 855200 01534 856127

**email:** rozelcampingpark@jerseymail.co.uk

**web:** www.rozelcamping.co.uk

**Dir:** *Take A6 from St Helier through Five Oaks to St Martins Church, turn right onto A38 towards Rozel, site on right*

Open May-mid Sep Booking advisable Jul-Aug Last departure noon

An attractive and secluded holiday site offering excellent amenities in a lovely farm location. The site is divided into paddocks, with hedges for screening and shelter, and there are ready-erected tents for hire. It is only a short walk from the beautiful sandy beach and harbour at Rozel Bay. Motorhomes and towed caravans will be met at the ferry and escorted to the park by arrangement when booking. A 4-acre site with 100 touring pitches and 20 statics.

**Leisure:**

**Facilities:**

**Services:** →

**Notes:** Dogs only during low season. Mini golf

## ST OUEN MAP 24

### ►►► 74% Bleu Soleil Campsite

La Route de Vinchelez, Leoville JE3 2DB

☎ 01534 481007 🖹 01534 481525

**email:** info@bleusoleilcamping.com

**web:** www.bleusoleilcamping.com

**Dir:** *From St Helier ferry port take A2 towards St Aubin then turn right onto A12 passing airport to Leoville. Site on right of La Route de Vinchelez*

Å £4-£30

Open 28 Apr-Sep Booking advisable Jul-Aug Last arrival 23.00hrs Last departure 10.00hrs

A compact tent park set in the NW corner of the island and surrounded by beautiful countryside. Greve-de-Lacq beach is close by, and the golden beaches at St Ouen's Bay and St Brelade's Bay are only a short drive away. There are 45 ready-erected tents for hire. A 1.5-acre site with 55 touring pitches, 8 hardstandings and 45 statics.

**Leisure:**

**Facilities:**

**Services:** → 

**Notes:** No noise after 22.00hrs, owners must clean up after dogs. Wi-fi

# ISLE OF MAN

## KIRK MICHAEL MAP 24 SC39

### ►►► 76% *Glen Wyllin Campsite* *(SC302901)*

IM6 1AL

☎ 01624 878231 & 878836 🖹 01624 878836

**email:** michaelcommissioners@manx.net

**web:** www.michaelcommissioners.com

**Dir:** *From Douglas take A1 to Ballacraine, right at lights onto A3 to Kirk Michael. Left onto A4 signed Peel. Site 100yds on right*

Open Apr-mid Sep Booking advisable end May-mid Jun & Aug Last departure noon

Set in a beautiful wooded glen with bridges over a pretty stream dividing the camping areas. A gently-sloping tarmac road gives direct access to a good beach. Hire tents available. A 9-acre site with 90 touring pitches.

**Leisure:**

**Facilities:**

**Services:** →

**Notes:** No excess noise after mdnt, dogs must be kept under control

## LAXEY MAP 24 SC48

### ►► 70% Laxey Commissioners Campsite

*(SC438841)*

Quarry Rd, Minorca Hill IM7 4BG

☎ 01624 862623 🖹 01624 862623

**email:** laxeycommissioners@manx.net

**web:** www.laxey.org

**Dir:** *Off main road at Fairy Cottage filling station. Down Old Laxey Hill, over bridge, up Minorca Hill, left before tram bridge, past school*

Open May-Sep Booking advisable

A level grass park with open views over Laxey Glen, with easy foot access to the village and trams to Douglas and Ramsey. A large kitchen is well equipped with a communal dining table and microwave ovens, and there's a good range of local tourist information. A 2-acre site with 20 touring pitches.

**Facilities:**

**Services:** →

**Notes:** No unaccompanied minors

**Facilities:** Bath · Shower · Electric Shaver · Hairdryer · Ice Pack Facility · Disabled Facilities · Public Telephone · Shop on Site or within 200yds · Mobile Shop (calls at least 5 days a week) · BBQ Area · Picnic Area · Dog Exercise Area

# Scotland

Loch Katrine, Stirling

# ABERDEENSHIRE

## ABOYNE MAP 23 NO59

### ►►► 68% Aboyne Loch Caravan Park *(NO538998)*

AB34 5BR T

☎ 013398 86244 & 01330 811351 📠 013398 86244

**Dir:** *On A93, 1m E of Aboyne*

★ fr £15 fr £15 fr £10

Open 31 Mar-Oct Booking advisable Jul-Aug Last arrival 20.00hrs Last departure 11.00hrs

Attractively-sited caravan park set amidst woodland on the shores of the lovely Aboyne Loch in scenic Deeside. The facilities are modern and immaculately maintained, and amenities include boat-launching, boating and fishing. An ideally-situated park for touring Royal Deeside and the Aberdeenshire uplands. A 6-acre site with 35 touring pitches, 25 hardstandings and 80 statics.

**Leisure:**

**Facilities:**

**Services:**

**Notes:** Coarse & pike fishing, boats for hire

## FORDOUN MAP 23 NO77

### ►►► 73% Brownmuir Caravan Park *(NO740772)*

AB30 1SJ

☎ 01561 320786 📠 01561 320786

**email:** brownmuircaravanpark@talk21.com

**web:** www.brownmuircaravanpark.co.uk

**Dir:** *From N on A90 take B966 signed Fettercairn & site 1.5m on left. From S take A90, turn off 4m N of Laurencekirk signed Fordoun, site 1m on right*

★ £10-£11.50 £10-£11.50 £7-£10

Open Apr-Oct Booking advisable Last arrival 23.00hrs Last departure noon

A mainly static site set in a rural location with level pitches and good touring facilities. The area is ideal for cyclists, walkers and golfers, as well as those wanting to visit Aberdeen, Banchory, Ballater, Balmoral, Glamis and Dundee. A 7-acre site with 11 touring pitches, 4 hardstandings and 49 statics.

**Leisure:**

**Facilities:**

**Services:** **Notes:**

## HUNTLY MAP 23 NJ53

**AA Campsite of the Year for Scotland 2008**

### ►►►► 85% *Huntly Castle Caravan Park* *(NJ525405)*

The Best of British Touring and Holiday Parks

The Meadow AB54 4UJ

☎ 01466 794999

**email:** enquiries@huntlycastle.co.uk

**web:** www.huntlycastle.co.uk

**Dir:** *From Aberdeen on A96 to Huntly. 0.75m after rdbt on outskirts of Huntly turn right towards town centre, left into Riverside Drive*

Open Apr-Oct Booking advisable Last arrival 20.00hrs Last departure noon

A quality parkland site within striking distance of the Speyside Malt Whisky Trail, the beautiful Moray coast, and the Cairngorm Mountains. The park provides exceptional toilet facilities, and there are some fully serviced pitches. The Indoor Activity Centre provides a wide range of games, and the attractive town of Huntly with its ruined castle is only 5 minutes walk away, with a wide variety of restaurants and shops. A 15-acre site with 90 touring pitches, 46 hardstandings and 40 statics.

**Leisure:**

**Facilities:**

**Services:**

**Notes:** Indoor activity centre, badminton, table tennis

## KINTORE MAP 23 NJ71

### ►►► 77% Hillhead Caravan Park *(NJ777163)*

AB51 0YX

☎ 01467 632809 & 08704 130870 📠 01467 633173

**email:** enquiries@hillheadcaravan.co.uk

**web:** www.hillheadcaravan.co.uk

**Dir:** *1m from village & A96 (Aberdeen-Inverness road). From A96 follow signs to park on B994, then unclass road*

Open all year Booking advisable at all times Last arrival 22.00hrs Last departure 13.00hrs

A peaceful site in the River Don Valley, with pitches well screened by shrubs and trees, and laid out around a small central area containing a children's play space. Enthusiastic owners are constantly improving the facilities, and the park is very well maintained. A 1.5-acre site with 24 touring pitches, 8 hardstandings and 4 statics.

**Leisure:**

**Facilities:**

**Services:**

**Notes:** Caravan storage, accessories shop

## MACDUFF MAP 23 NJ76

### ►► 68% **Wester Bonnyton Farm Site**
*(NJ741638)*
Gamrie AB45 3EP
☎ 01261 832470 01261 831853
**email:** taylor@westerbonnyton.freeserve.co.uk
**web:** www.westerbonnyton.co.uk
**Dir:** *From A98 (1m S of Macduff) take B9031 signed Rosehearty. Site 1.25m on right*

★ fr £10 fr £10 £7-£10

Open Mar-Oct Booking advisable Jul-Aug

A spacious farm site in a screened meadow, with level touring pitches enjoying views across Moray Firth. The site is continually improving, and offers some electric hook-ups and a laundry. A 4-acre site with 10 touring pitches, 5 hardstandings and 50 statics.

**Leisure:** **Facilities:**

**Services:**

**Notes:** Children's playbarn

## NORTH WATER BRIDGE MAP 23 NO66

### ►►► 74% **Dovecot Caravan Park** *(NO648663)*
SILVER
AB30 1QL
☎ 01674 840630 01674 840630
**email:** dovecotcaravanpark@tinyworld.co.uk
**Dir:** *Take A90, 5m S of Laurencekirk. At Edzell Woods sign turn left. Site 500yds on left*

★ £10-£11 £10-£11 £7-£10

Open Apr-Oct Booking advisable Jul & Aug for hook ups Last arrival 20.00hrs Last departure noon

A level grassy site in a country area close to the A90, with mature trees screening one side and the River North Esk on the other. The immaculate toilet facilities make this a handy overnight stop in a good touring area. A 6-acre site with 25 touring pitches, 8 hardstandings and 44 statics.

**Leisure:** **Facilities:**

**Services:**

**Notes:**

## ST CYRUS MAP 23 NO76

### ►►►► 79% **East Bowstrips Caravan Park** *(NO745654)*
DD10 0DE
☎ 01674 850328 01674 850328
**email:** tully@bowstrips.freeserve.co.uk
**web:** www.caravancampingsites.co.uk/aberdeenshire/eastbowstrips.htm
**Dir:** *From S on A92 (coast road) into St Cyrus. Pass hotel on left. 1st left then 2nd right signed*

★ £12-£13 £12-£13 £9-£11

Open Etr or Apr-Oct Booking advisable Jun-Aug Last arrival 22.00hrs Last departure noon

A quiet, rural site close to a seaside village, with modernised facilities and a particular welcome for the disabled. The park is surrounded by farmland on the edge of a village, with extensive views. Touring pitches are sited on rising ground amongst attractive landscaping. A 4-acre site with 32 touring pitches, 22 hardstandings and 18 statics.

**Leisure:** **Facilities:**

**Services:**

**Notes:** If camping - no dogs allowed, if touring - dogs must be kept on short lead at all times. Separate garden with boule pitch

## TARLAND MAP 23 NJ40

### ►►► 77% **Tarland Camping & Caravanning Club Site** *(NJ477044)*
AB34 4UP
☎ 01339 881388
**web:** www.campingandcaravanningclub.co.uk/tarland
**Dir:** *A93 from Aberdeen turn right in Aboyne at Struan Hotel onto B9094. After 6m take next right, then fork left before bridge, 600yds site on left*

★ £14.05-£18.05 £14.05-£18.05 £14.05-£18.05

Open 13 Mar-3 Nov Booking advisable BH & peak periods Last arrival 21.00hrs Last departure noon

A pretty park on the edge of the village, laid out on two levels. The upper area has hardstandings and electric hook-ups, and views over hills and moorland, while the lower level is well screened with mature trees and is grassy. An 8-acre site with 90 touring pitches, 32 hardstandings and 40 statics.

**Leisure:** **Facilities:**

**Services:**

# ANGUS

## KIRRIEMUIR MAP 23 NO35

### ►►►► 77% **Drumshademuir Caravan Park**
*(NO381509)*
Roundyhill DD8 1QT
☎ 01575 573284 01575 570130
**email:** info@drumshademuir.com
**web:** www.drumshademuir.com
**Dir:** *Take A928 from A90 or A94 to Kirriemuir. Park 3m N of Glamis Castle*

★ £13-£15 £13-£15 £10-£12

Open all year Booking advisable public hols & Jun-Aug Last arrival 22.00hrs Last departure 16.00hrs

Set amidst farmland with lovely views across the Strathmore Valley. The park offers excellent toilet facilities with heating in winter. All pitches have wheel runs or hardstandings so that caravans are always level on the slightly sloping site. Some separately sited larger pitches are also available. A 15-acre site with 60 touring pitches, 22 hardstandings and 47 statics.

**Leisure:** **Facilities:**

**Services:**

**Notes:** Adults only in tents. Bar food, putting, woodland walk, caravan storage

SCOTLAND

SCOTLAND

### MONIFIETH — MAP 21 NO43

**►►►► 78% Riverview Caravan Park** *(NO502322)*

Best of British Touring and Holiday Parks — David Bellamy Conservation Award SILVER

Marine Dr DD5 4NN

☎ 01382 535471

**email:** info@riverview.co.uk

**web:** www.riverview.co.uk

**Dir:** *From Dundee follow signs to Monifieth on A930, continue past supermarket and turn right signed for golf course and right under railway bridge. Site is signed on left.*

★ £13-£15 £13-£15

Open Apr-Oct Booking advisable Jul-Aug Last arrival 22.00hrs Last departure 12.30hrs

A well-landscaped seaside site with individual hedged pitches, and direct access to the beach. The modernised toilet block has excellent facilities which are immaculately maintained. Amenities include a multi-gym, sauna and steam rooms. A 5.5-acre site with 40 touring pitches, 40 hardstandings and 46 statics.

**Leisure:**

**Facilities:**

**Services:** →

## ARGYLL & BUTE

### BARCALDINE — MAP 20 NM94

**►►► 78% Oban Camping & Caravanning Club Site** *(NM966420)*

PA37 1SG

☎ 01631 720348

**web:** www.campingandcaravanningclub.co.uk/oban

**Dir:** *N on A828, 7m from Connel Bridge, turn into site at Club sign on right (opposite Marine Resource Centre)*

★ £14.05-£18.85 £14.05-£18.85 £14.05-£18.85

Open 13 Mar-3 Nov Booking advisable BH & peak periods Last arrival 21.00hrs Last departure noon

A sheltered site within a walled garden, bordered by Barcaldine Forest, close to Loch Creran. Tourers are arranged against the old garden walls. There are pleasant woodland walks from the park, including the Sutherland memorial woods close by. A 4.5-acre site with 75 touring pitches, 24 hardstandings and 18 statics.

**Leisure:**

**Facilities:**

**Services:** →

**Notes:** Site gates closed 23.00hrs-07.00hrs

### CARRADALE — MAP 20 NR83

**►►► 79% Carradale Bay Caravan Park** *(NR815385)*

PA28 6QG

☎ 01583 431665

**email:** info@carradalebay.com

**web:** www.carradalebay.com

**Dir:** *A83 from Tarbert towards Campbeltown, left onto B842 (Carradale road), right onto B879. Site 0.5m*

Open Apr-Sep Booking advisable BH & Jul-Aug Last arrival 22.00hrs Last departure noon

A beautiful, natural site on the sea's edge with superb views over Kilbrannan Sound to the Isle of Arran. Pitches are landscaped into small bays broken up by shrubs and bushes, and backed by dunes close to the long sandy beach. An 8-acre site with 75 touring pitches and 12 statics.

**Facilities:**

**Services:** →

### GLENDARUEL — MAP 20 NR98

**►►► 77% Glendaruel Caravan Park**

*(NR005865)*

PA22 3AB

☎ 01369 820267 Fax 01369 820367

**email:** mail@glendaruelcaravanpark.co.uk

**web:** www.glendaruelcaravanpark.co.uk

**Dir:** *From A83 take A815 to Strachur, then 13m to park on A886. By ferry from Gourock to Dunoon then B836, then A886 for approx 4m N. (NB this route not recommended for towing vehicles - 1:5 uphill gradient on B836)*

★ fr £15 fr £15 £15-£18

Open Apr-Oct Booking advisable Spring BH & mid Jul-Aug Last arrival 22.00hrs Last departure noon

A very pleasant, well-established site in the beautiful Victorian gardens of Glendaruel House. The level grass and hardstanding pitches are set in 23 acres of wooded parkland in a valley surrounded by mountains, with many rare specimen trees. The owners are hospitable and friendly. A 3-acre site with 35 touring pitches, 24 hardstandings and 30 statics.

**Leisure:**

**Facilities:**

**Services:** →

**Notes:** Dogs must be kept on lead at all times. Sea trout & salmon fishing

## INVERUGLAS MAP 20 NN30

### ►►► 79% Loch Lomond Holiday Park

*(NN320092)*
G83 7DW
☎ 01301 704224 🖷 01301 704206
**email:** enquiries@lochlomond-caravans.co.uk
**web:** www.lochlomond-lodges.co.uk
**Dir:** *On A82 3.5m N of Tarbet*

★ £17-£19 £17-£19

Open Mar-Oct Booking advisable May-Aug Last arrival 20.00hrs Last departure 11.45hrs

A lovely setting on the shores of Loch Lomond with views of forests and mountains, and boat hire available. The small touring area is beautifully situated overlooking the loch, and handily placed for the toilets and residents' lounge. A 13-acre site with 19 touring pitches, 19 hardstandings and 72 statics.

**Leisure:**

**Facilities:**

**Services:**

**Notes:** No jet skis. Satellite TV, pool tables

## LUSS MAP 20 NS39

### ►►► 78% Luss Camping & Caravanning Club Site *(NS360936)*

G83 8NT
☎ 01436 860658
**web:** www.campingandcaravanningclub.co.uk/luss
**Dir:** *From Erskine bridge take A82 N towards Tarbet. (NB ignore 1st sign for Luss). After workshops take next right at Lodge of Loch Lomond & International Camping sign. Site 200yds*

★ £15.45-£20.15 £15.45-£20.15 £15.45-£20.15

Open 13 Mar-3 Nov Booking advisable BH & peak periods Last arrival 21.00hrs Last departure noon

A lovely tenting site on the grassy western shore of Loch Lomond. The site has two well equipped toilet blocks, including a parent and child facility, and a good laundry. Club members' caravans and motorvans only permitted. A 12-acre site with 90 touring pitches, 30 hardstandings.

**Leisure:**

**Facilities:**

**Services:**

**Notes:** Caravan pitches for members only, site gates closed 23.00hrs-07.00hrs

## OBAN MAP 20 NM82

*see also Barcaldine*

### ►►► 78% *Oban Caravan & Camping Park*

*(NM831277)*
Gallanachmore Farm, Gallanach Rd PA34 4QH
☎ 01631 562425 🖷 01631 566624
**email:** info@obancaravanpark.com
**web:** www.obancaravanpark.co.uk
**Dir:** *From Oban centre follow signs for Mull Ferry. Take turn past terminal signed Gallanach. 2m to site*

Open Etr/Apr-Oct Booking advisable Last arrival 23.00hrs Last departure noon

A tourist park in an attractive location close to sea and ferries. This family park is a popular base for walking, sea based activities and for those who just want to enjoy the peace and tranquillity. A 15-acre site with 150 touring pitches, 35 hardstandings and 12 statics.

**Leisure:**

**Facilities:**

**Services:**

**Notes:** Indoor kitchen for tent campers

# DUMFRIES & GALLOWAY

## ANNAN MAP 21 NY16

### ► 68% Galabank Caravan & Camping Group *(NY192676)*

North St DG12 5DQ
☎ 01461 203539 & 204108
**Dir:** *Enter site via North Street*

Open Apr-early Sep Booking advisable Last departure noon

A tidy, well-maintained grassy little park close to the centre of town but with pleasant rural views, and skirted by River Annan. A 1-acre site with 30 touring pitches.

**Facilities:**

**Services:**

**Notes:** Dogs must be on leads. Adjacent social club

SCOTLAND

SCOTLAND

## BALMINNOCH MAP 20 NX26

### ►►►► 80% Three Lochs Holiday Park *(NX272655)*

GOLD

DG8 0EP

☎ 01671 830304 🖷 01671 830335

**email:** info@3lochs.co.uk

**web:** www.3lochs.co.uk

**Dir:** *Follow A75 W towards Stranraer. Approx 10m from Newton Stewart rdbt turn right at small x-roads, follow signs to site, park 4m on right*

Open Mar-Oct Booking advisable BH & Jul-Aug Last arrival 22.00hrs Last departure 11.00hrs

A remote and very peaceful park set in beautiful moorland on the banks of Loch Heron, with further lochs and woodland nearby. This spacious grass park offers some fully-serviced pitches in a stunning location, and as well as being an ideal holiday spot for walkers and anglers, it provides a heated indoor swimming pool and well-equipped games room. A 22.5-acre site with 45 touring pitches, 20 hardstandings and 90 statics.

**Leisure:**

**Facilities:**

**Services:**

**Notes:** Snooker

## BARGRENNAN MAP 20 NX37

### ►►► 77% Glentrool Holiday Park *(NX350769)*

DG8 6RN

☎ 01671 840280 🖷 01671 840342

**email:** enquiries@glentroolholidaypark.co.uk

**web:** www.glentroolholidaypark.co.uk

**Dir:** *Leave Newton Stewart on A714 towards Girvan, right at Bargrennan towards Glentrool. Park on left before village*

★ £9.50-£10.50 £9.50-£10.50 £9.50-£10.50

Open Mar-Oct Booking advisable Jul-Aug & BH Last arrival 21.00hrs Last departure noon

A small park close to the village of Glentrool, and bordered by the Galloway National Park. The keen owners are experienced caravanners, and keep their site neat, clean and freshly painted. The on-site shop is well stocked. A 6.75-acre site with 14 touring pitches, 12 hardstandings and 26 statics.

**Leisure:**

**Facilities:**

**Services:**

**Notes:** No cars by tents

## BEATTOCK MAP 21 NT00

### ►►► 77% Craigielands Country Park *(NY079023)*

DG10 9RE

☎ 01683 300591 🖷 01683 300105

**email:** admin@craigielandsleisure.com

**web:** www.craigielands.co.uk

**Dir:** *A74(M) junct 15 follow Beattock. Site in 350yds*

★ £15-£19 £15-£19 £11-£15

Open Mar-6 Jan (pub open wknds only) Booking advisable Last arrival 23.00hrs Last departure 14.00hrs

A relaxed park in part of a former country estate on the edge of the village of Beattock. A very large coarse fishing lake is available free to campers, stocked with trout, tench and carp. A bar and restaurant serve home cooking, and there is some entertainment at weekends during the high season. A 56-acre site with 125 touring pitches, 6 hardstandings and 104 statics.

**Leisure:**

**Facilities:**

**Services:**

**Notes:** Dogs must be kept on leads

## BRIGHOUSE BAY MAP 20 NX64

PREMIER PARK

### ►►►►► 93% *Brighouse Bay Holiday Park* *(NX628453)*

DG6 4TS

☎ 01557 870267 🖷 01557 870319

**email:** aa@brighouse-bay.co.uk

**web:** www.gillespie-leisure.co.uk

**Dir:** *Off B727 (Kirkcudbright to Borgue) or take A755 (Kirkcudbright) off A75 2m W of Twynholm. Site signed*

Open all year (rs Nov-Mar leisure club closed 2 days each week) Booking advisable Etr, Spring BH & Jul-Aug Last arrival 21.30hrs Last departure 11.30hrs

This grassy site enjoys a marvellous coastal setting adjacent to the beach and with superb sea views. Pitches have been imaginatively sculpted into the meadowland, with stone walls and hedges blending in with the site's mature trees. These features together with the large range of leisure activities make this an excellent holiday centre. Many of the facilities are available at an extra charge. A 30-acre site with 190 touring pitches and 120 statics.

**Leisure:**

**Facilities:**

**Services:**

**Notes:** Mini golf, 18-hole golf, riding, fishing, quad bikes

**Services:** Toilet Fluid · Café/ Restaurant · Fast Food/Takeaway · Baby Care · Electric Hook Up · Motorvan Service Point · Launderette · Licensed Bar · Calor Gas · Camping Gaz · Battery Charging

## CASTLE DOUGLAS MAP 21 NX76

### ▶▶▶ 78% Lochside Caravan & Camping Site (NX766618)

Lochside Park DG7 1EZ
☎ 01556 502949 & 503806 📠 01556 503806
**email:** scottg2@dumgal.gov.uk
**web:** www.dumgal.gov.uk/lochsidecs
**Dir:** *Off A75 towards Castle Douglas by Carlingwark Loch*
★ £10.50-£15.10 £10.50-£15.10 £10.50-£15.10
Open Etr-Oct Booking advisable from Mar Last arrival 19.30hrs Last departure noon

Well-managed municipal touring site in a pleasant location adjacent to Carlingwark Loch and parkland but close to the town. A 5.5-acre site with 161 touring pitches, 74 hardstandings.

**Leisure:**
**Facilities:**
**Services:**
**Notes:** Height restriction barrier. Putting & pedalo boats (weekends & high season)

## CREETOWN MAP 20 NX46

**PREMIER PARK**

### ▶▶▶▶▶ 84% Castle Cary Holiday Park (NX475576)

DG8 7DQ
☎ 01671 820264 📠 01671 820670
**email:** enquiries@castlecarypark.f9.co.uk
**web:** www.castlecary-caravans.com
**Dir:** *Signed with direct access off A75, 0.5m S of village*

Open all year (rs Oct-Mar reception/shop, no heated outdoor pool) Booking advisable BH & Jul-Aug Last arrival anytime Last departure noon

This attractive site in the grounds of Cassencarie House is sheltered by woodlands, and faces south towards Wigtown Bay. The park is in a secluded location with beautiful landscaping and excellent facilities. The bar/restaurant is housed in part of an old castle, and enjoys extensive views over the River Cree estuary. A 12-acre site with 50 touring pitches, 50 hardstandings and 26 statics.

**Leisure:**
**Facilities:**
**Services:**
**Notes:** Dogs must be kept on leads at all times. Bike hire, crazy golf, fishing, football pitch

*see advert on page 30*



### ▶▶▶ 79% Creetown Caravan Park (NX474586)

Silver St DG8 7HU
☎ 01671 820377 📠 01671 820377
**email:** creetowncaravan@btconnect.com
**web:** www.creetown-caravans.co.uk
**Dir:** *Off A75 into Creetown, turn between clock tower & hotel, then left along Silver Street*
★ fr £12 fr £12 fr £12
Open Mar-Oct Booking advisable Jul-Aug Last arrival 22.30hrs Last departure 14.00hrs

A neat and well-maintained park set in the village centre with views across the estuary on the coast of Wigtown Bay. Its attractive setting is beside the Moneypool Burn on the River Cree. Plenty of good amenities, including a heated outdoor swimming pool. A 3-acre site with 20 touring pitches and 54 statics.

**Leisure:**
**Facilities:**
**Services:**
**Notes:** Games room

## CROCKETFORD MAP 21 NX87

### ►►►► 84% Park of Brandedleys

(NX830725)
DG2 8RG
☎ 0845 456 1760 01556 690681
**email:** brandedleys@holgates.com
**web:** www.holgates.com

**Dir:** *In village on A75, from Dumfries towards Stranraer site on left up minor road, entrance 200yds on right*

★ £14-£19.50 £14-£19.50 £14-£19.50

Open all year (rs Nov-Mar bar/restaurant open Fri-Sun afternoon) Booking advisable public hols & Jul-Aug Last arrival 22.00hrs Last departure noon

A well-maintained site in an elevated position off the A75, with fine views of Auchenreoch Loch and beyond. This comfortable park offers a wide range of amenities, including a fine games room and a tastefully-designed bar with adjoining bistro. Well placed for enjoying walking, fishing, sailing and golf. A 24-acre site with 80 touring pitches, 40 hardstandings and 63 statics.

**Leisure:**

**Facilities:**

**Services:** → 

**Notes:** Guidelines issued on arrival. Badminton court

*see advert on page 297*

## DALBEATTIE MAP 21 NX86

### ►►►► 75% Glenearly Caravan Park

(NX838628)
DG5 4NE
☎ 01556 611393 01556 612058
**email:** glenearlycaravan@btconnect.com

**Dir:** *From Dumfries A711 towards Dalbeattie. Park entrance is past Edingham Farm on right, 200yds before boundary sign*

Open all year Booking advisable Jun-Aug Last arrival 19.00hrs Last departure noon

An excellent small park set in open countryside with panoramic views of Long Fell, Maidenpap and Dalbeattie Forest. The park is located in 84 beautiful acres of farmland which visitors are invited to enjoy. Luxury extras are provided in the laundry and toilets, including washing powder and conditioner, sachets of shampoo and shower gel, pegs and washing lines, washing up liquid, brushes and cloths in the dish washing area. A 10-acre site with 39 touring pitches, 33 hardstandings and 57 statics.

**Leisure:**

**Facilities:**

**Services:** →

**Notes:** No commercial vehicles, dogs must be kept on leads

## DUMFRIES

*see Shawhead*

## ECCLEFECHAN MAP 21 NY17

**PREMIER PARK**

### ►►►►► 77% Hoddom Castle Caravan Park (NY154729)

Hoddom DG11 1AS
☎ 01576 300251 01576 300757
**email:** hoddomcastle@aol.com
**web:** www.hoddomcastle.co.uk

**Dir:** *M74 junct 19, follow signs to site. From A75 W of Annan take B723 for 5m, follow signs to site*

★ £7.50-£17 £7.50-£17 £6.50-£14

Open Etr or Apr-Oct (rs early season cafeteria closed) Booking advisable BH & Jul-Aug Last arrival 21.00hrs Last departure 14.00hrs

The peaceful, well-equipped park can be found on the banks of the River Annan, and offers a good mix of grassy and hard pitches, beautifully landscaped and blending into the surroundings. There are signed nature trails, maintained by the park's countryside ranger, a 9-hole golf course, trout and salmon fishing, and plenty of activity ideas for children. A 28-acre site with 200 touring pitches, 150 hardstandings and 54 statics.

**Leisure:**

**Facilities:**

**Services:** →

**Notes:** Visitors' centre

**Abbreviations:** BH-bank holiday/s Etr-Easter Whit-Whitsun dep-departure fr-from hrs-hours m-mile mdnt-midnight rdbt-roundabout rs-restricted service wk-week wknd-weekend no dogs No cards → following facilities within 3 miles of the site

## GATEHOUSE OF FLEET MAP 20 NX55

### 79% Auchenlarie Holiday Park (NX536522)

DG7 2EX

☎ 01557 840251 01557 840333

**email:** enquiries@auchenlarie.co.uk

**web:** www.auchenlarie.co.uk

**Dir:** *Direct access off A75, 5m W of Gatehouse of Fleet*

Open Mar-Oct Booking advisable all year Last arrival 20.00hrs Last departure noon

A well-organised family park set on cliffs overlooking Wigtown Bay, with its own sandy beach. The tenting area, in sloping grass surrounded by mature trees, has its own sanitary facilities, while the marked caravan pitches are in paddocks with open views, and enjoy high quality toilets. The leisure centre includes swimming pool, gym, solarium and sports hall. A 32-acre site with 49 touring pitches, 49 hardstandings and 350 statics.

**Leisure:**

**Facilities:**

**Services:** →

**Notes:** Baby changing facilities

### ►►► 81% Anwoth Caravan Site (NX595563)

DG7 2JU

☎ 01557 814333 & 840251 01557 814333

**email:** enquiries@auchenlarie.co.uk

**web:** www.ukparks.co.uk/anworth

**Dir:** *From A75 into Gatehouse of Fleet, park on right towards Stranraer. Signed from town centre*

Open Mar-Oct Booking advisable Jul-Aug Last arrival 20.00hrs Last departure noon

A peaceful sheltered park within easy walking distance of the village, ideally placed for exploring the scenic hills, valleys and coastline. Guests may use the leisure facilities at the sister park, Auchenlarie Holiday Park. A 2-acre site with 28 touring pitches and 44 statics.

**Facilities:**

**Services:** →

### ►►► 80% Mossyard Caravan & Camping Park (NX546518)

Mossyard DG7 2ET

☎ 01557 840226 01557 840226

**email:** enquiry@mossyard.co.uk

**web:** www.mossyard.co.uk

**Dir:** *0.75m off A75 on private tarmaced farm road, 4.5m W of Gatehouse of Fleet*

★ £11-£16 £11-£15 £10-£12

Open Etr/Apr-Oct Booking advisable Spring BH, Jul-Aug, wknds Last departure noon

A grassy park with its own beach, located on a working farm, and offering an air of peace and tranquillity. Stunning sea and coastal views from touring pitches, and the tenting field is almost on the beach. A 6.5-acre site with 35 touring pitches and 33 statics.

**Facilities:**

**Services:** →

**Notes:** Wi-fi

## GLENLUCE MAP 20 NX15

### ►►► 77% Glenluce Holiday Park (NX198574)

DG8 0QR

☎ 01581 300412 01581 300434

**email:** enquiries@glenlucecaravans.co.uk

**web:** www.glenlucecaravans.co.uk

**Dir:** *in middle of village*

★ £12-£17 £12-£17 £12-£17

Open all year Booking advisable

Set in the grounds of a former mansion, in the village of Glenluce with its shops and eating places. Pitches are in the park or walled garden, there is a heated indoor pool and spa. A 5-acre site with 20 touring pitches, 4 hardstandings and 30 statics.

**Leisure:**

**Facilities:**

**Services:** →

### ►►► 74% Whitecairn Holiday Park (NX300434)

DG8 0NZ

☎ 01581 300267 01581 300434

**email:** enquiries@whitecairncaravans.co.uk

**web:** www.whitecairncaravans.co.uk

**Dir:** *Turn off A75 at Glenluce. Park signed from main street onto unclassified road to Glassnock Bridge. Park 1.5m N*

£12-£20 £12-£20 £12-£20

Open all year Booking advisable Last arrival 22.00hrs Last departure 11.00hrs

A well-maintained farmland site, in open countryside with extensive views of Luce Bay. The park is next to the owner's working farm along a quiet country road. The toilets are centrally heated, and the laundry is well equipped. A 12-acre site with 10 touring pitches and 40 statics.

**Leisure:**

**Facilities:**

**Services:** →

SCOTLAND

**Facilities:** Bath Shower Electric Shaver Hairdryer Ice Pack Facility Disabled Facilities Public Telephone Shop on Site or within 200yds Mobile Shop (calls at least 5 days a week) BBQ Area Picnic Area Dog Exercise Area

SCOTLAND

## GRETNA — MAP 21 NY36

### ►►►► 73% Braids Caravan Park *(NY313674)*

Annan Rd DG16 5DQ

☎ 01461 337409

**email:** enquiries@thebraidscaravanpark.co.uk

**web:** www.thebraidscaravanpark.co.uk

**Dir:** *On B721, 0.5m from village on right, towards Annan*

£14-£16 £14-£16

Open all year Booking advisable May-Sep Last arrival 21.00hrs Last departure noon

A well-maintained grassy site in the centre of the village just inside Scotland. A good toilet block provides a high standard of facilities, and several hard pitches further enhance this busy and popular park. A 6-acre site with 93 touring pitches, 29 hardstandings.

**Facilities:**

**Services:**

**Notes:** No skateboards, dogs must be kept on leads at all times

### ►►► 81% Bruce's Cave Caravan & Camping Park *(NY266705)*

Cove Estate, Kirkpatrick Fleming DG11 3AT

☎ 01461 800285 01461 800269

**email:** enquiries@brucescave.co.uk

**web:** www.brucescave.co.uk

**Dir:** *Exit A74(M) junct 21 for Kirkpatrick Fleming follow N through village, pass Station Inn, at Bruce's Court turn left. Over rail crossing to site entrance.*

★ £10-£14 £10-£14 £8.50-£16

Open all year (rs Nov-Mar shop closed, water restriction) Booking advisable Last arrival 23.00hrs Last departure 19.00hrs

The lovely wooded grounds of an old castle and mansion are the setting for this pleasant park. The mature woodland is a haven for wildlife, and there is a riverside walk to Robert the Bruce's Cave. A toilet block with en suite facilities is of special appeal to families. An 80-acre site with 75 touring pitches, 60 hardstandings and 35 statics.

**Leisure:**

**Facilities:**

**Services:**

**Notes:** Dogs must be kept on leads. BMX bike hire, coarse fishing, first aid available

## KIPPFORD — MAP 21 NX85

### ►►► 79% Kippford Holiday Park

*(NX844564)*

DG5 4LF

DAVID BELLAMY CONSERVATION AWARD GOLD

☎ 01556 620636 01556 620607

**email:** info@kippfordholidaypark.co.uk

**web:** www.kippfordholidaypark.co.uk

**Dir:** *From Dalbeattie S on A710, site 3.5m on right, 300yds past junct for Kippford*

£14.50-£23 £14.50-£23 £11-£23

Open all year Booking advisable Last arrival 21.30hrs Last departure noon

An attractively landscaped park set in hilly countryside close to the Urr Water estuary and a sand/shingle beach, and with spectacular views. The level touring pitches are on grassed hardstands with private garden areas, and many are fully serviced. The Doon Hill and woodland walks separate the park from the lovely Kippford village. An 18-acre site with 45 touring pitches, 22 hardstandings and 119 statics.

**Leisure:**

**Facilities:**

**Services:**

**Notes:** Golf, fly fishing, nature walk, cycle hire

## KIRKCUDBRIGHT — MAP 20 NX65

### ►►►► 82% Seaward Caravan Park

*(NX662494)*

Dhoon Bay DG6 4TJ

☎ 01557 870267 & 331079 01557 870319

**email:** aa@seaward-park.co.uk

**web:** www.gillespie-leisure.co.uk

**Dir:** *2m SW off B727 (Borgue road)*

★ £14.35-£20.45 £14.35-£20.45 £10.75-£15.35

Open Mar-Oct (rs Mar-mid May & mid Sep-Oct swimming pool closed) Booking advisable Spring BH & Jul-Aug Last arrival 21.30hrs Last departure 11.30hrs

A very attractive elevated park with outstanding views over Kirkcudbright Bay which forms part of the Dee Estuary. Access to a sandy cove with rock pools is just across the road. Facilities are well organised and neatly kept, and the park offers a very peaceful atmosphere. The leisure facilities of the other Gillespie parks are available to guests. An 8-acre site with 26 touring pitches and 30 statics.

**Leisure:**

**Facilities:**

**Services:**

**Notes:** No motorised scooters or bikes (except disabled vehicles). Pitch & putt

►►► 78% **Silvercraigs Caravan & Camping Site** *(NX686508)*
Silvercraigs Rd DG6 4BT
☎ 01557 330123 & 01556 503806 01557 330123
email: scottg2@dumgal.gov.uk
web: www.dumgal.gov.uk/silvercraigscs
Dir: *In Kirkcudbright off Silvercraigs Rd. Access via A711, follow signs to site*

★ £10.50-£15.10 £10.50-£15.10 £10.50-£15.10

Open Etr-Oct Booking advisable at all times Last departure noon

A well-maintained municipal park in an elevated position with extensive views overlooking the picturesque, unspoilt town and harbour to the countryside beyond. Toilet facilities are of a very good standard, and the town centre is just a short stroll away. A 6-acre site with 50 touring pitches.

**Leisure:**

**Facilities:**

**Services:**

**Notes:** Dogs must be on leads

## KIRKGUNZEON MAP 21 NX86

►►► 69% ***Mossband Caravan Park***
*(NX872665)*
DG2 8JP
☎ 01387 760208 01387 760628
Dir: *Adjacent to A711 to Dalbeattie, 1.5m E of Kirkgunzeon*

Open Etr-Oct Booking advisable mid Jul-mid Aug

A level park on the site of an old railway station, set in a peaceful rural location. This family-run park has good views of the countryside, and functional, dated facilities. A 3-acre site with 25 touring pitches and 12 statics.

**Leisure:**

**Facilities:**

**Services:**

## LANGHOLM MAP 21 NY38

►►► 75% **Ewes Water Caravan & Camping Park** *(NY365855)*
Milntown DG13 0DH
☎ 013873 80386 013873 81670
email: aeneasmn@aol.com
Dir: *Directly off A7 approx 0.5m N of Langholm. Site in Langholm Rugby Club*

Open Apr-Sep Booking advisable last week in Jul Last departure noon

On the banks of the River Esk, this is a very attractive park in a sheltered wooded valley close to an unspoilt Borders town. A 2-acre site with 24 touring pitches.

**Facilities:**

**Services:**

**Notes:** Large playing area

## LOCHMABEN MAP 21 NY08

►► 80% **Kirk Loch Caravan & Camping Site**
*(NY082825)*
DG11 1PZ
☎ 01556 503806 & 07746 123783 01556 503806
email: scottg2@dumgal.gov.uk
web: www.dumgal.gov.uk/kirklochcs
Dir: *In Lochmaben enter via Kirkloch Brae*

★ £8.50-£12.50 £8.50-£12.50 £8.50-£12.50

Open Etr-Oct Last departure noon

A grassy lochside site with superb views and well-maintained facilities. Some hard pitches are available at this municipal park, which is adjacent to a golf club, and close to three lochs. A 1.5-acre site with 30 touring pitches, 14 hardstandings.

**Leisure:**

**Facilities:**

**Services:**

**Notes:** Dogs must be kept on leads

## LOCKERBIE
*see Ecclefechan*

SCOTLAND

SCOTLAND

## MOFFAT — MAP 21 NT00

### ►►► 78% Moffat Camping & Caravanning Club Site (NT085050)

Hammerlands Farm DG10 9QL

☎ 01683 220436

**web:** www.campingandcaravanningclub.co.uk/moffat

**Dir:** *From A74 follow Moffat sign. After 1m turn right by Bank of Scotland, right again in 200yds. Sign for site on right*

★ £15.45-£20.15 £15.45-£20.15 £15.45-£20.15

Open 13 Mar-3 Nov Booking advisable BH & peak periods Last arrival 21.00hrs Last departure noon

Well-maintained level grass touring site, with extensive views of the surrounding hilly countryside from many parts of the park. This busy stopover site is always well maintained, and looks bright and cheerful thanks to meticulous wardens. A 10-acre site with 180 touring pitches, 42 hardstandings.

**Leisure:**

**Facilities:**

**Services:** →

**Notes:** Site gates closed 23.00hrs-07.00hrs

## NEWTON STEWART — MAP 20 NX46

### ►►► 67% *Creebridge Caravan Park*

(NX415656)

Minnigaff DG8 6AJ

☎ 01671 402324 & 402432 01671 402324

**email:** johnsharples1@btopenworld.co.uk

**web:** www.creebridgecaravanpark.com

**Dir:** *0.25m E of Newton Stewart at Minnigaff on bypass, signed off A75*

Open all year (rs Mar only one toilet block open) Booking advisable Jul-Aug Last arrival 20.00hrs Last departure 10.00hrs

A small family-owned site a short walk from the town's amenities. The site is surrounded by mature trees, and the toilet facilities are clean and functional. A 5.5-acre site with 36 touring pitches, 12 hardstandings and 50 statics.

**Leisure:**

**Facilities:**

**Services:** →

**Notes:** Security street lighting

## PALNACKIE — MAP 21 NX85

### ►►► 77% *Barlochan Caravan Park*

(NX819572)

DG7 1PF

☎ 01556 600256 & 01557 870267 01557 870319

**email:** aa@barlochan.co.uk

**web:** www.gillespie-leisure.co.uk

**Dir:** *On A711, N of Palnackie, signed*

Open Apr-Oct Booking advisable Spring BH & Jul-Aug Last arrival 21.30hrs Last departure 11.30hrs

A small terraced park with quiet landscaped pitches in a level area backed by rhododendron bushes. There are spectacular views over the River Urr estuary, and the park has its own coarse fishing loch nearby. A 9-acre site with 20 touring pitches and 40 statics.

**Leisure:**

**Facilities:**

**Services:** →

**Notes:** Pitch & putt

## PARTON — MAP 20 NX67

### ►►► 69% Loch Ken Holiday Park

(NX687702)

DAVID BELLAMY CONSERVATION AWARD GOLD

DG7 3NE

☎ 01644 470282 01644 470297

**email:** penny@lochkenholidaypark.co.uk

**web:** www.lochkenholidaypark.co.uk

**Dir:** *On A713, N of Parton*

£16-£18 £16-£18 £12-£16

Open Mar-mid Nov (rs Mar/Apr (ex Etr) & late Sep-Nov restricted shop hours) Booking advisable Etr, Spring BH & Jun-Aug Last departure noon

A busy and popular park with a natural emphasis on water activities, set on the eastern shores of Loch Ken, with superb views. Family owned and run, it is in a peaceful and beautiful spot opposite the RSPB reserve, with direct access to the loch for boat launching. The park offers a variety of water sports, as well as farm visits and nature trails. A 7-acre site with 52 touring pitches, 4 hardstandings and 35 statics.

**Leisure:**

**Facilities:**

**Services:** →

**Notes:** Bike, boat & canoe hire, fishing on loch

## PORT WILLIAM MAP 20 NX34

### ►►► 75% Kings Green Caravan Site

*(NX340430)*
South St DG8 9SG
☎ 01988 700489
**web:** www.portwilliam.com
**Dir:** *Direct access from A747 at junct with B7085, towards Whithorn*

Open Etr-Oct Booking advisable Last departure noon

Set beside the unspoilt village with all its amenities and the attractive harbour, this level grassy park is community owned and run. Approached via the coast road, the park has views reaching as far as the Isle of Man. A 3-acre site with 30 touring pitches.

**Facilities:**

**Services:**

**Notes:** No golf on site

## ROCKCLIFFE MAP 21 NX85

### ►►► 76% Castle Point Caravan Park

*(NX851539)*
DG5 4QL
☎ 01556 630248
**email:** rosalind.bigham@btinternet.com
**web:** www.caravancampingsites.co.uk/dumfriesandgalloway/castlepoint.htm
**Dir:** *From Dalbeattie take A710. After approx 5m take road signed to Rockcliffe. On entering the village site is signed*

Open Etr-mid Oct Booking advisable Whit wk & Jul-Aug Last arrival 23.00hrs Last departure 11.00hrs

Set in an Area of Outstanding Natural Beauty, this level grass park is adjacent to a rocky shore, and has stunning views across the estuary and the surrounding hilly countryside. The park is noted for its flora and fauna, and has direct access to coastal walks and the attractive sandy beach. A 7-acre site with 22 touring pitches and 33 statics.

**Facilities:**

**Services:**

**Notes:**

## SANDHEAD MAP 20 NX04

### ►►►► 74% *Sands of Luce Holiday Park*

*(NX103510)*
Sands of Luce DG9 9JN
☎ 01776 830456 🖷 01776 830477
**email:** info@sandsofluceholidaypark.co.uk
**web:** www.sandsofluceholidaypark.co.uk
**Dir:** *From S & E - left off A75 onto B7084 signed Drummore. Site signed at junct with A716. From N - A77 through Stranraer towards Portpatrick, 2m & follow A716 signed Drummore, site signed in 5m*

Open Mar-Oct Booking advisable Jul-Aug Last arrival 20.00hrs Last departure noon

A friendly site on the grassy banks on the edge of a beautiful sandy beach, with lovely views across Luce Bay. Facilities are well-maintained and clean, and the area around the park is protected by the Nature Conservancy Council. A 30-acre site with 100 touring pitches and 190 statics.

**Leisure:**

**Facilities:**

**Services:**

**Notes:** Boat launching

SCOTLAND

## SANDYHILLS MAP 21 NX85

### ►►► 78% ***Sandyhills Bay Leisure Park*** *(NX892552)*

DG5 4NY

☎ 01557 870267 & 01387 780257 🖹 01557 870319

**email:** info@sandyhills-bay.co.uk

**web:** www.gillespie-leisure.co.uk

**Dir:** *On A710, 7m from Dalbeattie, 6.5m from Kirkbean*

Open Apr-Oct Booking advisable Spring BH & Jun-Aug Last arrival 21.30hrs Last departure 11.30hrs

A well-maintained park in a superb location beside a 'blue-flag' beach, and close to many attractive villages. The level, grassy site is sheltered by woodland, and the south-facing Sandyhills Bay and beach are a treasure trove for all the family, with their caves and rock pools. A 6-acre site with 26 touring pitches and 34 statics.

**Leisure:**

**Facilities:**

**Services:**

## SHAWHEAD MAP 21 NX87

### ►►► 79% **Barnsoul Farm** *(NX876778)*

DG2 9SQ

☎ 01387 730249 & 730453 🖹 01387 730453

**email:** barnsouldg@aol.com

**web:** www.barnsoulfarm.co.uk

**Dir:** *Exit A75 between Dumfries & Crocketford at site sign onto unclass road signed Shawhead. At T-junct turn right & immediate left. Site 1m on left, follow Barnsoul signs*

Open Apr-Oct Booking advisable Jul & Aug Last arrival 23.00hrs Last departure noon

A very spacious, peaceful and scenic farm site with views across open countryside in all directions. Set in 250 acres of woodland, parkland and farmland, and an ideal centre for touring the surrounding unspoilt countryside. It offers excellent kitchen facilities and a dining area for lightweight campers. A 100-acre site with 30 touring pitches, 12 hardstandings and 6 statics.

**Leisure:**

**Facilities:**

**Services:**

**Notes:** No groups unless by prior arrangement, 2-axled caravans by prior arrangement, no loud noise after 23.00hrs

## SOUTHERNESS MAP 21 NX95

### 79% **Southerness Holiday Village** *(NX976545)*

DG2 8AZ

☎ 01387 880256 & 0871 641 0199 🖹 01387 880429

**email:** enquiries@parkdeanholidays.co.uk

**web:** www.parkdeanholidays.co.uk

**Dir:** *From S take A75 from Gretna to Dumfries. From N take A74, exit at A701 to Dumfries. Take A710 coast road. Approx 16m, site easily seen*

★ £8-£22 £10-£26 £8-£22

Open Mar-Oct Booking advisable high season Last arrival 21.00hrs Last departure 10.00hrs

There are stunning views across the Solway Firth from this holiday centre at the foot of the Galloway Hills. A sandy beach on the Solway Firth is accessible directly from the park. The emphasis is on family entertainment, and facilities include all-weather pitches, a supermarket, large laundry and a leisure centre. A 50-acre site with 100 touring pitches, 45 hardstandings and 72 statics.

**Leisure:**

**Facilities:**

**Services:**

**Notes:** Amusement centre, live entertainment, kids' clubs

## STRANRAER MAP 20 NX06

### ►►►► 77% **Aird Donald Caravan Park** *(NX075605)*

London Rd DG9 8RN

☎ 01776 702025

**email:** enquiries@aird-donald.co.uk

**web:** www.aird-donald.co.uk

**Dir:** *Turn left off A75 on entering Stranraer, (signed). Opposite school, site 300yds*

★ £15.50 £15.50 £13

Open all year Booking advisable Last departure 16.00hrs

A spacious touring site, mainly grass but with tarmac hardstanding area, with pitches large enough to accommodate a car and caravan overnight without unhitching. On the fringe of town screened by mature shrubs and trees. Ideal stopover en route to Northern Irish ferry ports. A 12-acre site with 100 touring pitches, 30 hardstandings.

**Leisure:**

**Facilities:**

**Services:** **Notes:**

**Services:** Toilet Fluid · Café/ Restaurant · Fast Food/Takeaway · Baby Care · Electric Hook Up · Motorvan Service Point · Launderette · Licensed Bar · Calor Gas · Camping Gaz · Battery Charging

### WIGTOWN MAP 20 NX45

**►►► 85% Drumroamin Farm Camping & Touring Site** *(NX445507)*
1 South Balfern DG8 9DB
☎ 01988 840613
**email:** enquiry@drumroamin.co.uk
**web:** www.drumroamin.co.uk
**Dir:** *A75 towards Newton Stewart, turn onto A714 for Wigtown. Left on B7005 through Bladnock, A746 through Kirkinner. Take B7004 Garlieston, 2nd left opposite Kilsture Forest, site 0.75m at end of lane*

★ £12.50 £12.50 £11

Open all year Booking advisable Last arrival 21.00hrs Last departure noon

An open, spacious park in a quiet spot a mile from the main road, and close to Wigtown Bay. A superb toilet block offers spacious showers, and there's a lounge/games room and plenty of room for children to play. A 5-acre site with 48 touring pitches and 3 statics.

**Leisure:**
**Facilities:**
**Services:**
**Notes:** No fires. Ball games area

## EAST LOTHIAN

### ABERLADY MAP 21 NT47

**►► 67% Aberlady Caravan Park** *(NT482797)*
Haddington Rd EH32 0PZ
☎ 01875 870666 01875 870666
**Dir:** *Off A6137*

£15-£20 fr £15 £10-£25

Open Mar-Oct Booking advisable Last arrival 22.00hrs Last departure noon

A small, simple campsite in pleasantly wooded surroundings, with a delightful outlook towards the Lammermuir Hills. It offers level pitches in a well-maintained meadow with electric hook-ups, and is within easy reach of Edinburgh and the East Lothian coast. A 4.5-acre site with 15 touring pitches, 4 hardstandings.

**Leisure:**
**Facilities:**
**Services:**
**Notes:** No ball games, no loud music. Licensed shop



### DUNBAR MAP 21 NT67

## PREMIER PARK

**►►►►► 84% Thurston Manor Holiday Home Park** *(NT712745)*
Innerwick EH42 1SA
☎ 01368 840643 01368 840261
**email:** mail@thurstonmanor.co.uk
**web:** www.thurstonmanor.co.uk
**Dir:** *4m S of Dunbar, signed off A1*

★ £15-£25 £15-£25 £15-£20

Open Mar-8 Jan Booking advisable BH, Etr & high season Last arrival 23.00hrs Last departure noon

A pleasant park set in 250 acres of unspoilt countryside. The touring and static areas of this large park are in separate areas. The main touring area occupies an open, level position, and the toilet facilities are modern and exceptionally well maintained. The park boasts a well-stocked fishing loch, a heated indoor swimming pool, steam room, sauna, jacuzzi, mini-gym and fitness room and seasonal entertainment. A 250-acre site with 100 touring pitches, 45 hardstandings and 420 statics.

**Leisure:**
**Facilities:**
**Services:**

*see advert on this page*

SCOTLAND

## DUNBAR CONTINUED

### ►►► 68% Barns Ness Camping & Caravanning Club Site (NT723773)

Barns Ness EH42 1QP

☎ 01368 863536

**web:** www.campingandcaravanningclub.co.uk/barnsness

**Dir:** *On A1, 6m S of Dunbar (near power station). Sign for Barns Ness & Skateraw 1m down road. Turn right at site sign towards lighthouse*

★ £12.75-£16.75 £12.75-£16.75 £12.75-£16.75

Open 13 Mar-3 Nov Booking advisable BH & peak periods Last arrival 21.00hrs Last departure noon

A grassy, landscaped site close to the foreshore and lighthouse on a coastline noted for its natural and geological history. A 10-acre site with 80 touring pitches.

**Leisure:**

**Facilities:**

**Services:** →

**Notes:** Site gates closed 23.00hrs-07.00hrs

### ►►► 71% Belhaven Bay Caravan & Camping Park (NT661781)

GOLD

Belhaven Bay EH42 1TS

☎ 01368 865956 01368 865022

**email:** belhaven@meadowhead.co.uk

**web:** www.meadowhead.co.uk

**Dir:** *From A1 onto A1087 towards Dunbar. Site (1m) in John Muir Park*

£12-£21 £12-£21

Open Mar-30 Oct (rs 31 Oct-7 Jan) Booking advisable Last arrival 20.00hrs Last departure noon

Small, well-maintained park in a sheltered location and within walking distance of the beach. This is an excellent spot for seabird watching, and there is a good rail connection with Edinburgh from Dunbar. A 40-acre site with 52 touring pitches, 11 hardstandings and 64 statics.

**Leisure:**

**Facilities:**

**Services:** →

**Notes:** Dogs on leads at all times. Internet café

## LONGNIDDRY MAP 21 NT47

### 66% Seton Sands Holiday Village (NT420759)

EH32 0QF

☎ 01875 813333 01875 813531

**email:** lee.mckay@bourne-leisure.co.uk

**web:** www.havenholidays.com

**Dir:** *Take A1 to A198 exit, then B6371 to Cockenzie. Right onto B1348. Park 1m on right*

★ £9-£60 £9-£60 £9-£44

Open mid Mar-Oct (rs mid Mar-May & Sep-Oct some facilities may be reduced) Booking advisable school hols Last arrival 23.00hrs Last departure 10.00hrs

A well-equipped holiday centre with plenty of organised entertainment, clubs and bars, restaurants, and sports and leisure facilities. A multi-sports court, heated swimming pool, and various play areas ensure that there is plenty to do, and there is lots to see and do in and around nearby Edinburgh. The good touring facilities are separate from the large static areas. A 1.75-acre site with 38 touring pitches and 500 statics.

**Leisure:**

**Facilities:**

**Services:** →

**Notes:** Dogs not allowed at peak periods, max 2 dogs per pitch

## MUSSELBURGH MAP 21 NT37

►►►► 78% **Drum Mohr Caravan Park** *(NT373734)*
Levenhall EH21 8JS
☎ 0131 665 6867 0131 653 6859
**email:** bookings@drummohr.org
**web:** www.drummohr.org
**Dir:** *Leave A1 at junct with A199 towards Musselburgh, at rdbt turn right onto B1361 signed Prestonpans, take 1st left & site 400yds*

★ £14-£17 £14-£17 £14-£17
Open Mar-Oct Booking advisable Jul-Aug Last arrival 20.00hrs Last departure noon

This attractive park is sheltered by mature trees on all sides, and carefully landscaped within. The park is divided into separate areas by mature hedging and planting of trees and ornamental shrubs. Pitches are generous in size, and there are a number of fully serviced pitches plus first-class amenities. A 9-acre site with 120 touring pitches, 50 hardstandings and 12 statics.

**Leisure:**
**Facilities:**
**Services:**
**Notes:** Max of 2 dogs per pitch

*see advert on opposite page*

# FIFE

## LUNDIN LINKS MAP 21 NO40

►►► 81% **Woodland Gardens Caravan & Camping Site** *(NO418031)*
Blindwell Rd KY8 5QG
☎ 01333 360319
**email:** enquiries@woodland-gardens.co.uk
**web:** www.woodland-gardens.co.uk
**Dir:** *Off A915 (coast road) at Largo. At E end of Lundin Links, turn N off A915, 0.5m signed*

£10-£15 £10-£15 £8-£12
Open Apr-Oct Booking advisable Jul-Aug Last arrival 21.00hrs Last departure noon

A secluded and sheltered 'little jewel' of a site in a small orchard under the hill called Largo Law. This very attractive site is family owned and run to an immaculate standard, and pitches are grouped in twos and threes by low hedging and gorse. A 1-acre site with 20 touring pitches, 3 hardstandings and 4 statics.

**Leisure:**
**Facilities:**
**Services:**
**Notes:** Children over 14yrs only

## ST ANDREWS MAP 21 NO51

### PREMIER PARK

►►►►► 90% **Craigtoun Meadows Holiday Park** *(NO482150)*
Mount Melville KY16 8PQ
☎ 01334 475959 01334 476424
**email:** craigtoun@aol.com
**web:** www.craigtounmeadows.co.uk
**Dir:** *From M90 junct 8 onto A91 to St Andrews. Just after Guardbridge turn right for Strathkinness. At 2nd x-rds after Strathkinness turn left for Craigtoun*

★ £18-£24.50 £18-£24.50 £18
Open 15 Mar-15 Nov (rs Mar-Etr & Sep-Nov shops & restaurant open shorter hours) Booking advisable BH & Jun-Aug Last arrival 21.00hrs Last departure 11.00hrs

An attractive site set unobtrusively in mature woodlands, with large pitches in hedged paddocks. All pitches are fully serviced, and there are also some patio pitches and a summerhouse containing picnic tables and chairs. The modern toilet block provides cubicled en suite facilities as well as spacious showers, baths, disabled facilities and baby changing areas. A licensed restaurant and coffee shop are popular, and there is a takeaway, a launderette and shop, and indoor and outdoor games areas. Located near the sea and sandy beaches. A 32-acre site with 58 touring pitches, 58 hardstandings and 163 statics.

**Leisure:**
**Facilities:**
**Services:**
**Notes:** No groups of unaccompanied minors, no pets

*see advert on page 308*

# HIGHLAND

## ARISAIG MAP 22 NM68

►►►► 77% **Camusdarach Campsite** *(NM664916)*
Camusdarach PH39 4NT
☎ 01687 450221 01687 450394
**email:** camdarach@aol.com
**web:** www.camusdarach.com
**Dir:** *On B8008, 4m N of Arisaig. Turn off A830 at Arisaig, follow coast road*

★ £16 £16 £12-£14
Open 15 Mar-15 Oct Booking advisable school hols Last arrival 21.00hrs Last departure 18.00hrs

A very attractive, quiet and secluded park with direct access to a silver beach. The striking scenery and coastal setting are part of the appeal here, and the superbly designed and equipped toilet block is a pleasure to use. The site is four miles from the Arisaig ferry, and six miles from the Mallaig ferry to the Isle of Skye. A 2.75-acre site with 42 touring pitches, 2 hardstandings.

**Facilities:**
**Services:** **Notes:** Baby changing facilities

SCOTLAND

## BALMACARA — MAP 22 NG82

►►► 76% **Reraig Caravan Site** *(NG815272)*

IV40 8DH

☎ 01599 566215

**email:** warden@reraig.com

**web:** www.reraig.com

**Dir:** *On A87 3.5m E of Kyle, 2m W of junct with A890*

★ £10.30-£11 £10.30-£11 £10.30-£11

Open May-Sep Booking advisable (no phone bookings, post only) Last arrival 22.00hrs Last departure noon

Set on level, grassy ground surrounded by trees, the site is located on the saltwater Sound of Sleet, and looks south towards Loch Alsh and Skye. Very nicely organised with a high standard of maintenance, and handy for the bridge crossing to the Isle of Skye. A 2-acre site with 45 touring pitches, 26 hardstandings.

**Facilities:**

**Services:**

**Notes:** Awning restrictions, no large trailer or tents. Ramp access to block

## BOAT OF GARTEN — MAP 23 NH91

►►► 76% ***Campgrounds of Scotland***

*(NH939191)*

PH24 3BN

☎ 01479 831652 01479 831450

**email:** briangillies@totalise.co.uk

**web:** www.campgroundsofscotland.com

**Dir:** *From A9 take A95 to Grantown-on-Spey, then follow signs for Boat of Garten. Park in village centre.*

Open all year Booking advisable 26 Dec-2 Jan & 25 Jul-7 Aug Last arrival 22.00hrs Last departure 11.00hrs

A very attractive site in a beautiful location with outstanding views. Young trees and bushes enhance the park, which is set in mountainous woodland near the River Spey and Loch Garten. A 3.5-acre site with 37 touring pitches, 20 hardstandings and 60 statics.

**Leisure:**

**Facilities:**

**Services:**

## CANNICH — MAP 22 NH33

►►► 72% **Cannich Caravan and Camping Park** *(NH345317)*

IV4 7LN

☎ 01456 415364 01456 415364

**email:** enquiries@highlandcamping.co.uk

**web:** www.highlandcamping.co.uk

**Dir:** *On A831, 200yds SE of Cannich Bridge*

★ £10-£13 £10-£13 fr £10

Open Mar-Oct (rs Dec-Feb winter opening by arrangement) Booking advisable Jul & Aug Last arrival 23.00hrs Last departure noon

Quietly situated in Strath Glass, close to the River Glass and Cannich village. This family-run park has attractive mountain views, and is set in ideal walking and naturalist country. A 6-acre site with 43 touring pitches, 15 hardstandings and 15 statics.

**Leisure:**

**Facilities:**

**Services:**

**Notes:** Dogs must be kept on leads. Wi-fi. Mountain bike hire

## CORPACH — MAP 22 NN07

**PREMIER PARK**

### ►►►►► 83% Linnhe Lochside Holidays *(NN074771)*

PH33 7NL

☎ 01397 772376 Fax 01397 772007

**email:** relax@linnhe-lochside-holidays.co.uk

**web:** www.linnhe-lochside-holidays.co.uk

**Dir:** *On A830, 1m W of Corpach, 5m from Fort William*

Open Etr-Oct Booking advisable school hols & peak periods Last arrival 21.00hrs Last departure 11.00hrs

An excellently maintained site in a beautiful setting on the shores of Loch Eil, with Ben Nevis to the east and the mountains and Sunart to the west. The owners have worked in harmony with nature to produce an idyllic environment, where they offer the highest standards of design and maintenance. A 5.5-acre site with 85 touring pitches, 63 hardstandings and 20 statics.

**Leisure:**

**Facilities:**

**Services:**

**Notes:** No cars by tents. Launching slipway, free fishing

## DAVIOT — MAP 23 NH73

### ►►► 76% Auchnahillin Caravan and Camping Centre *(NH742386)*

IV2 5XQ

☎ 01463 772286

**email:** info@auchnahillin.co.uk

**web:** www.auchnahillin.co.uk

**Dir:** *7m S of Inverness, just off A9 on B9154 towards Moy/Daviot (E)*

★ £11-£15 £11-£15 £8-£10

Open 15 Mar-Oct Booking advisable Jul-Aug Last arrival 21.00hrs Last departure 17.00hrs

Surrounded by hills and forests, this level, grassy site offers clean and spacious facilities. The owner lives in a bungalow on the site. A 10-acre site with 75 touring pitches, 4 hardstandings and 35 statics.

**Leisure:** **Facilities:**

**Services:**

**Notes:** No noise after 23.00hrs, limited facilities for disabled visitors. Indoor dishwashing/food prep area available

## DINGWALL — MAP 23 NH55

### ►►► 76% Dingwall Camping & Caravanning Club Site *(NH555588)*

Jubilee Park Rd IV15 9QZ

☎ 01349 862236

**web:** www.campingandcaravanningclub.co.uk/dingwall

**Dir:** *A862 to Dingwall, right onto Hill Street, past filling station. Right onto High Street, 1st left after railway bridge. Site ahead*

★ £15.45-£20.15 £15.45-£20.15 £15.45-£20.15

Open 13 Mar-3 Nov Booking advisable BH & peak periods Last arrival 21.00hrs Last departure noon

A quiet park with attractive landscaping and very good facilities maintained to a high standard. A convenient touring centre, close to the historic market town of Dingwall. A 6.5-acre site with 83 touring pitches.

**Facilities:**

**Services:**

**Notes:** Site gates closed 23.00hrs-07.00hrs

## DORNOCH — MAP 23 NH78

### 76% Grannie's Heilan Hame Holiday Park *(NH818924)*

Embo IV25 3QD

☎ 01862 810383 & 0871 641 0199 Fax 01862 810368

**email:** enquiries@parkdeanholidays.co.uk

**web:** www.parkdeanholidays.co.uk

**Dir:** *A949 to Dornoch, left in square. Follow Embo signs*

★ £10-£26 £12-£28 £8-£22

Open Mar-Oct Booking advisable high season Last arrival 21.00hrs Last departure 10.00hrs

A holiday centre on the Highland coast, with a wide range of leisure facilities, including indoor swimming pool with sauna and solarium, separate play areas for under and over fives, putting green, tennis courts and very much more. The sanitary facilities are clean and well maintained, and there is a family pub and entertainment. A 60-acre site with 190 touring pitches and 186 statics.

**Leisure:**

**Facilities:**

**Services:**

**Notes:** Spa bath, sauna, solarium, family entertainment

SCOTLAND

## DORNOCH CONTINUED

### ►►►► 78% *Pitgrudy Caravan Park*

(NH795911)
Poles Rd IV25 3HY
☎ 01862 810001 01862 821382
**Dir:** *On B9168, between A9 and A949*

Open May-Sep Booking advisable Jul-Aug Last arrival 20.00hrs Last departure noon

An immaculate park in a lovely environment. Many of the pitches are fully serviced, and all have their own water supply. This very quiet park is close to the historic town of Dornoch in rural surroundings, and convenient for beaches, mountains and lochs. A 3.5-acre site with 50 touring pitches, 10 hardstandings and 38 statics.

**Facilities:**
**Services:** →

## FORT WILLIAM — MAP 22 NN17

*see also Corpach*

### ►►►► 85% Glen Nevis Caravan & Camping Park (NN124722)

GOLD

Glen Nevis PH33 6SX
☎ 01397 702191 01397 703904
**email:** holidays@glen-nevis.co.uk
**web:** www.glen-nevis.co.uk
**Dir:** *In northern outskirts of Fort William follow A82 to mini-rdbt. Exit for Glen Nevis. Site 2.5m on right*

Open 15 Mar-Oct (rs Mar & mid-end Oct limited shop & restaurant facilities) Booking advisable Jul-Aug Last arrival 22.00hrs Last departure noon

A tasteful site with well-screened enclosures, at the foot of Ben Nevis in the midst of some of the Highlands' most spectacular scenery; an ideal area for walking and touring. The park boasts a restaurant which offers a high standard of cooking and provides good value for money. A 30-acre site with 380 touring pitches, 150 hardstandings and 30 statics.

**Leisure:**
**Facilities:**
**Services:** →
**Notes:** Closed to vehicle entry at 23.00hrs, quiet 23.00hrs-08.00hrs

*see advert on opposite page*

## GAIRLOCH — MAP 22 NG87

### ►►► 77% Sands Holiday Centre (NG758784)

IV21 2DL
☎ 01445 712152 01445 712518
**email:** litsands@aol.co.uk
**web:** www.highlandcaravancamping.co.uk
**Dir:** *3m W of Gairloch on B8021*

★ £11-£13 £10-£12 £11-£13

Open 20 May-10 Sep Booking advisable Jul-Aug Last arrival 22.00hrs Last departure noon

Close to a sandy beach with a panoramic outlook towards Skye, a well-maintained park with very good facilities. A large laundry and good toilets make this an ideal family site. A 51-acre site with 360 touring pitches and 20 statics.

**Leisure:**
**Facilities:**
**Services:** →
**Notes:** Boat slipway

## GLENCOE — MAP 22 NN15

### ►►►► 78% Invercoe Caravan & Camping Park (NN098594)

PH49 4HP
☎ 01855 811210 01855 811210
**email:** holidays@invercoe.co.uk
**web:** www.invercoe.co.uk
**Dir:** *Exit A82 at Glencoe Hotel onto B863 for 0.25m*

Open all year Booking advisable Jul-Aug for electric hook ups Last departure noon

Level grass site set on the shore of Loch Leven, with excellent mountain views. The area is ideal for both walking and climbing, and also offers a choice of several freshwater and saltwater lochs. Convenient for the good shopping at Fort William. A 5-acre site with 60 touring pitches and 4 statics.

**Leisure:**
**Facilities:**
**Services:** →
**Notes:** No large group bookings

**►►► 78% Glencoe Camping & Caravanning Club Site** *(NN111578)*
PH49 4LA
☎ 01855 811397
**web:** www.campingandcaravanningclub.co.uk/glencoe
**Dir:** *1m SE from Glencoe village on A82, follow Glencoe visitors' centre sign*

★ £15.45-£20.15 £15.45-£20.15 £15.45-£20.15

Open 13 Mar-3-Nov Booking advisable BH & peak periods Last arrival 21.00hrs Last departure noon

A partly sloping site with separate areas of grass and gravel hardstands. Set in mountainous woodland one mile from the village, and adjacent to the visitors' centre. A 40-acre site with 120 touring pitches, 55 hardstandings.

**Facilities:**

**Services:**

**Notes:** Site gates closed 23.00hrs-07.00hrs

GRANTOWN-ON-SPEY MAP 23 NJ02

**►►►► 84% Grantown on Spey Caravan Park** *(NJ028283)*
Seafield Av PH26 3JQ
☎ 01479 872474 01479 873696
**email:** warden@caravanscotland.com
**web:** www.caravanscotland.com
**Dir:** *From town turn N at Bank of Scotland, park in 0.25m*

★ £14.50-£23 £14.50-£23 £9.50-£17.50

Open 15 Dec-30 Oct Booking advisable Etr, May Day, Spring BH & Jul-Aug Last arrival 22.00hrs Last departure noon

A scenic park in a mature setting near the river, surrounded by hills, mountains, moors and woodland. The park is very well landscaped, and is in a good location for golf, fishing, mountaineering, walking, sailing and canoeing. Fully-serviced pitches are much sought after, and there is a luxury toilet block. A 29-acre site with 120 touring pitches, 60 hardstandings and 45 statics.

**Leisure:**

**Facilities:**

**Services:**

**Notes:** Wi-fi. Freezer facility



INVERGARRY MAP 22 NH30

**►►► 77% Faichemard Farm Camping & Caravan Site** *(NH288016)*
Faichemard Farm PH35 4HG
☎ 01809 501314
**email:** dgrant@fsbdial.co.uk
**web:** www.faichemard-caravancamping.co.uk
**Dir:** *1m W of Invergarry off A87*

★ £5-£10 £5-£10 £5-£10

Open Apr-Oct Booking advisable Jul-Aug Last arrival 22.00hrs Last departure 11.30hrs

A beautiful location in mountainous country with outstanding views. The park has units spread widely in individual pitches amongst bracken-clad hills, but all pitches are level. A 10-acre site with 35 touring pitches, 10 hardstandings.

**Facilities:**

**Services:**

**Notes:** Adults only Every pitch has own picnic table

SCOTLAND

## JOHN O'GROATS MAP 23 ND37

### ►►► 74% John O'Groats Caravan Site

*(ND382733)*

KW1 4YR

☎ 01955 611329 & 07762 336359

**email:** info@johnogroatscampsite.co.uk

**web:** www.johnogroatscampsite.co.uk

**Dir:** *At end of A99*

fr £11 fr £11 fr £11

Open Apr-Sep Booking advisable Last arrival 22.00hrs Last departure noon

An attractive site in an open position above the seashore and looking out towards the Orkney Islands. The passenger ferry which runs day trips to the Orkneys is nearby; there are grey seals to watch, and sea angling can be organised by the site owners. A 4-acre site with 90 touring pitches, 20 hardstandings.

**Facilities:**

**Services:**

**Notes:**

## LAIRG MAP 23 NC50

### ►►► 69% *Dunroamin Caravan Park*

*(NC585062)*

Main St IV27 4AR

☎ 01549 402447 01549 402784

**email:** enquiries@lairgcaravanpark.co.uk

**web:** www.lairgcaravanpark.co.uk

**Dir:** *300mtrs from centre of Lairg on S side of A839*

Open Apr-Oct Booking advisable Last arrival 21.00hrs Last departure noon

An attractive little park with clean and functional facilities; adjacent to a licensed restaurant. The park is close to the lower end of Loch Shin, and a short distance from the town. A 4-acre site with 40 touring pitches, 8 hardstandings and 9 statics.

**Facilities:**

**Services:**

**Notes:** No vehicles to be driven on site 21.00hrs-07.00hrs

### ►►► 63% Woodend Caravan & Camping Site *(NC551127)*

Achnairn IV27 4DN

☎ 01549 402248 01549 402248

**Dir:** *4m N of Lairg off A836 onto A838, signed at Achnairn*

Open Apr-Sep Booking advisable Last arrival 23.00hrs

A clean, fresh site set in hilly moors and woodland with access to Loch Shin. The area is popular with fishing and boating enthusiasts, and there is a choice of golf courses within 30 miles. A spacious campers' kitchen is a useful amenity. A 4-acre site with 55 touring pitches.

**Leisure:**

**Facilities:**

**Services:**

**Notes:**

## NAIRN MAP 23 NH85

### 73% Nairn Lochloy Holiday Park *(NH895574)*

East Beach IV12 5DE

☎ 01667 453764 & 0871 641 0199 01667 454721

**email:** enquiries@parkdeanholidays.com

**web:** www.parkdeanholidays.com

**Dir:** *In Nairn, just off East Beach*

★ £12-£23 £12-£23

Open Mar-Oct Booking advisable high season Last arrival 21.00hrs Last departure 11.00hrs

A small touring site situated within a popular holiday centre with a wide range of leisure facilities including heated pool, sauna, children's play area and club, crazy golf, games arcade, bars, restaurant and shops. A small, well-maintained toilet block exclusively serves the touring area, on which all pitches have electricity available. Handily placed in the centre of Nairn, only minutes from the beach and within striking distance of Inverness and the Highlands. 13 touring pitches and 72 statics.

**Leisure:**

**Facilities:**

**Services:**

**Notes:** No cars by tents

### ►►► 75% Nairn Camping & Caravanning Club Site (NH847551)

Delnies Wood IV12 5NX

☎ 01667 455281

**web:** www.campingandcaravanningclub.co.uk/nairn

**Dir:** *Off A96 (Inverness to Aberdeen road). 2m W of Nairn*

★ £12.75-£16.75 £12.75-£16.75 £12.75-£16.75

Open 13 Mar-3-Nov Booking advisable BH & peak periods Last arrival 21.00hrs Last departure noon

An attractive site set amongst pine trees, with facilities maintained to a good standard. The park is close to Nairn with its beaches, shopping, golf and leisure activities. A 14-acre site with 75 touring pitches.

**Leisure:**

**Facilities:**

**Services:**

**Notes:** Site gates closed 23.00hrs-07.00hrs. Fishing

## POOLEWE MAP 22 NG88

### ►►► 77% Inverewe Camping & Caravanning Club Site (NG862812)

Inverewe Gardens IV22 2LF

☎ 01445 781249

**web:** www.campingandcaravanningclub.co.uk/inverewe

**Dir:** *On A832, N of Poolewe village*

★ £15.45-£20.15 £15.45-£20.15 £15.45-£20.15

Open 13 Mar-3 Nov Booking advisable BH & peak period Last arrival 21.00hrs Last departure noon

A well-run site located in Loch Ewe Bay, not far from Inverewe Gardens. The Club has improved this site in the past few years, and continues to upgrade the facilities. The warm waters of the Gulf Stream attract otters and seals. A 3-acre site with 55 touring pitches, 8 hardstandings.

**Facilities:**

**Services:**

**Notes:** Site gates closed 23.00hrs-07.00hrs

## RESIPOLE (LOCH SUNART) MAP 22 NM76

### ►►►► 77% Resipole Farm (NM725639)

PH36 4HX

☎ 01967 431235 01967 431777

**email:** info@resipole.co.uk

**web:** www.resipole.co.uk

**Dir:** *From Corran Ferry take A861. Park 8m W of Strontian*

★ £12-£13 £12-£13 £11-£13

Open Apr-Oct Booking advisable for electric hook ups Last arrival 22.00hrs Last departure 11.00hrs

A quiet, relaxing park in beautiful surroundings, with deer frequently sighted, and of great interest to naturalists. Situated on the saltwater Loch Sunart in the Ardnamurchan Peninsula, and offering a great deal of space and privacy. An 8-acre site with 85 touring pitches, 30 hardstandings and 9 statics.

**Facilities:**

**Services:**

**Notes:** Dogs must be kept on leads. Private slipway, art gallery

## ROSEMARKIE MAP 23 NH75

### ►►► 77% Rosemarkie Camping & Caravanning Club Site (NH739569)

Ness Rd East IV10 8SE

☎ 01381 621117

**web:** www.campingandcaravanningclub.co.uk/rosemarkie

**Dir:** *Take A832. A9 at Tore rdbt. Through Avoch, Fortrose then right at police house. Down Ness Rd. 1st left, small turn signed Golf & Caravan site*

★ £18.25-£20.15 £18.25-£20.15 £18.25-£20.15

Open 13 Mar-3 Nov Booking advisable BH & peak period Last arrival 21.00hrs Last departure noon

A superb Club site set along the water's edge, with beautiful views over the bay where resident dolphins swim. Two excellent toilet blocks, including a disabled room, and a family room with combined facilities, have greatly enhanced the facilities here. A smart reception area sets the standard for this very clean and well-maintained site. A 4-acre site with 60 touring pitches.

**Facilities:**

**Services:**

**Notes:** Site gates closed 23.00hrs-07.00hrs

## TAIN MAP 23 NH78

### ►►► 73% Dornoch Firth Caravan Park (NH749843)

Meikle Ferry South IV19 1JX

☎ 01862 892292 01862 892292

**email:** will@dornochfirth.co.uk

**web:** www.dornochfirth.co.uk

**Dir:** *Follow A9 N past Tain to Meikle ferry rdbt, straight across onto A836 then immediate 1st right*

★ £10.50-£16 £10.50-£16 £7.50-£9.50

Open Mar-Oct Booking advisable Jul-Aug Last arrival 22.00hrs Last departure noon

A pleasant family site with open views of Dornoch Firth and the lovely coastal and country scenery. The immaculately maintained facilities and pretty flower beds make this a delightful base for touring the immediate vicinity with its many places of interest. A 3.5-acre site with 20 touring pitches, 10 hardstandings and 30 statics.

**Leisure:**

**Facilities:**

**Services:**

**Notes:** Bar & restaurant adjacent to site

SCOTLAND

SCOTLAND

## ULLAPOOL MAP 22 NH19

### ►►► 69% Broomfield Holiday Park

*(NH123939)*

West Shore St IV26 2UT

☎ 01854 612020 & 612664 01854 613151

**email:** sross@broomfieldhp.com

**web:** www.broomfieldhp.com

**Dir:** *Take 2nd right past harbour*

★ fr £13 fr £12 £9-£13

Open Etr/Apr-Sep Booking advisable for group bookings only Last departure noon

Set right on the water's edge of Loch Broom and the open sea, with lovely views of the Summer Isles. The park is close to the harbour and town centre which have restaurants, bars and shops. A 12-acre site with 140 touring pitches.

**Leisure:**

**Facilities:**

**Services:** →

**Notes:** Pets must be kept on leads, no noise at night

# MORAY

## ABERLOUR MAP 23 NJ24

### NEW ►►► 77% Aberlour Gardens Caravan Park *(NJ282434)*

GOLD

AB38 9LD

☎ 01340 871586

**email:** aberlourgardens@aol.com

**Dir:** *Midway between Aberlour & Craigellachie on A95. Turn onto unclass road. Site signed. NB vehicles over 10'6" take A941 to Dufftown*

This attractive parkland site is set in the 5 acre walled garden of the Victorian Aberlour House, surrounded by the full range of spectacular scenery from the Cairngorm National Park, through pine clad glens, to the famous Moray coastline; the park is also well placed for the world renowned Speyside Malt Whiskey Trail. It offers a small, well appointed toilet block, laundry and small licensed shop. 34 touring pitches and 31 statics.

## ALVES MAP 23 NJ16

### ►►► 67% *North Alves Caravan Park*

*(NJ122633)*

IV30 8XD

☎ 01343 850223

**Dir:** *1m W of A96, halfway between Elgin & Forres. Site signed on right*

Open Apr-Oct Booking advisable peak periods Last arrival 23.00hrs Last departure noon

A quiet rural site in attractive rolling countryside within three miles of a good beach. The site is on a former farm, and the stone buildings are quite unspoilt. A 10-acre site with 45 touring pitches and 45 statics.

**Leisure:**

**Facilities:**

**Services:** →

## CRAIGELLACHIE MAP 23 NJ24

### ►►► 77% Speyside Camping & Caravanning Club Site *(NJ257449)*

AB38 9SL

☎ 01340 810414

**web:** www.campingandcaravanningclub.co.uk/speyside

**Dir:** *From S exit A9 at Carrbridge, A95 to Grantown-on-Spey, leave Aberlour on A941. Take next left onto B9102 signed Archiestown. Site 3m on left*

★ £15.45-£20.15 £15.45-£20.15 £15.45-£20.15

Open 13 Mar-3 Nov Booking advisable BH & peak periods Last arrival 21.00hrs Last departure noon

A very nice rural site with views across meadowland towards Speyside, and the usual high Club standards. Hardstandings are well screened on an upper level, and grass pitches with more open views are sited lower down. A 7-acre site with 75 touring pitches, 13 hardstandings.

**Leisure:**

**Facilities:**

**Services:** →

**Notes:** Site gates closed 23.00hrs-07.00hrs. Play equipment

## CULLEN MAP 23 NJ56

### ►►► 82% *Cullen Bay Holiday Park*

*(NJ516674)*
Logie Head AB56 4TW
01542 840766
**email:** enquiries@cullenbay.co.uk
**web:** www.cullenbayholidaypark.co.uk
**Dir:** *From Portsoy on A98 into Cullen, 1st right into Seafield Street, site at end of road*

Open Apr-Oct Booking advisable Last arrival 21.30hrs Last departure noon

A cliff top site with fine views over the small Scottish fishing port of Cullen. The site is well maintained, and offers a modern and well appointed toilet block with full disabled facilities and a good laundry. It is well placed for accessing the north-east coastline with its small, picturesque fishing ports and dolphin colonies offshore; it is but a short distance from the Speyside Malt Whisky Trail. A 4-acre site with 22 touring pitches, 7 hardstandings and 35 statics.

**Facilities:**
**Services:**
**Notes:**

## FINDHORN MAP 23 NJ06

### ►►► 68% Findhorn Bay Holiday Park

*(NJ058623)*
Findhorn IV36 3TY
01309 690203 01309 690933
**email:** info@findhornbayholidaypark.com
**web:** www.findhornbayholidaypark.com
**Dir:** *Turn off A96, follow Findhorn signs. Site 1m from Findhorn*
★ £14.50-£17.50 £14.50-£17.50 £10.50-£12.50

Open Apr-Oct Last arrival 21.00hrs Last departure noon

A meadowland site owned by and next to the Findhorn Foundation in the stunningly attractive bay, popular with watersports enthusiasts and nature lovers. Facilities include a café serving snacks in landscaped gardens, and a well-stocked shop. A 5-acre site with 45 touring pitches, 5 hardstandings and 19 statics.

**Leisure:**
**Facilities:**
**Services:**
**Notes:** Dogs allowed by prior agreement. Organic food shop, arts centre

## FOCHABERS MAP 23 NJ35

### ►►► 75% Burnside Caravan Park

*(NJ350580)*
IV32 7ET
01343 820511 01343 820511
**Dir:** *0.5m E of town off A96*
★ fr £15 fr £15 £8.50-£15

Open Apr-Oct Booking advisable Jul-Aug Last departure noon

Attractive site in a tree-lined, sheltered valley with a footpath to the village. Owned by the garden centre on the opposite side of the A96. A 5-acre site with 51 touring pitches, 30 hardstandings and 101 statics.

**Leisure:**
**Facilities:**
**Services:**
**Notes:** Jacuzzi & sauna

## LOSSIEMOUTH MAP 23 NJ27

### ►►►► 73% *Silver Sands Leisure Park*

*(NJ205710)*
Covesea, West Beach IV31 6SP
01343 813262 01343 815205
**email:** holidays@silversands.freeserve.co.uk
**web:** www.travel.to/silversands
**Dir:** *From Lossiemouth follow B9040, 2m W to site*

Open Apr-Oct (rs Apr, May & Oct shops & entertainment restricted) Booking advisable Jul-Aug Last arrival 22.00hrs Last departure noon

A large holiday park with entertainment during the peak season, set on the links beside the shore of the Moray Firth. Touring campers and caravans are catered for in three areas: one offers de-luxe fully-serviced facilities, while the others are either unserviced or include electric hook-ups and water. There's a well-stocked shop, a clubroom and bar, and takeaway food outlet. A 7-acre site with 140 touring pitches and 200 statics.

**Leisure:**
**Facilities:**
**Services:**
**Notes:** Over 14yrs only in bar. Children's entertainment

# NORTH AYRSHIRE

## SALTCOATS — MAP 20 NS24

**NEW** 73% **Sandylands**
*(NS258412)*

SILVER

James Miller Crescent, Auchenharvie Park KA21 5JN
☎ 0871 664 9767
**email:** sandylands@park-resorts.com
**web:** www.park-resorts.com
**Dir:** *From Glasgow take M77 & A77 to Kilmarnock, then A71 towards Irvine. Then follow signs for Ardrossan. Take A78, follow Stevenston signs. Through Stevenson, past Auchenharvie Leisure Centre, 1st left, follow Park signs to site on left*

£6-£28 £6-£28 £3-£25

Open 31 Mar-Oct Booking advisable

Sandylands is an all action holiday centre with plenty of on-site leisure and recreational activities for the whole family. Off park, there is a links golf course adjacent, and trips to the Isle of Arran from the nearby Ardrossan. The beaches of the east coast are close by, and the mountains are just a short drive away. 20 touring pitches and 438 statics.

**Leisure:**

**Facilities:**

**Services:**

# NORTH LANARKSHIRE

## MOTHERWELL — MAP 21 NS75

►►► 76% **Strathclyde Country Park Caravan Site** *(NS717585)*

366 Hamilton Rd ML1 3ED
☎ 01698 266155 & 402060 01698 252925
**email:** strathclydepark@northlan.gov.uk
**Dir:** *From M74 junct 5, direct access to park*

★ fr £13 fr £13 £4.50-£8.20

Open Apr-Oct Booking advisable Jun-Aug Last arrival 22.30hrs Last departure noon

An attractive landscaped site situated in a country park amidst woodland and meadowland with lots of attractions. A large grass area caters for 150 tents, while 100 well-screened pitches, with electrics and some hardstandings, are also available. 250 touring pitches.

**Leisure:**

**Facilities:**

**Services:**

**Notes:** Site rules available on request by post

*see advert on this page*

# PERTH & KINROSS

## ABERFELDY — MAP 23 NN84

►►► 73% ***Aberfeldy Caravan Park*** *(NN858495)*

Dunkeld Rd PH15 2AQ
☎ 01887 820662 & 01738 475211 01738 475210
**Dir:** *Off A827, on E edge of town*

Open late Mar-late Oct Booking advisable Jun-Aug Last arrival 20.00hrs Last departure noon

A very well-run and well-maintained site, with good facilities and some landscaping, at the eastern end of the town and lying between main road and banks of the River Tay. Good views from site of surrounding hills. A 5-acre site with 92 touring pitches.

**Leisure:**

**Facilities:**

**Services:**

## BLAIR ATHOLL MAP 23 NN86

### PREMIER PARK

**►►►►► 80% Blair Castle Caravan Park**

*(NN874656)*

PH18 5SR

☎ 01796 481263 🖹 01796 481587

**email:** mail@blaircastlecaravanpark.co.uk

**web:** www.blaircastlecaravanpark.co.uk

**Dir:** *From A9 junct with B8079 at Aldclune, then NE to Blair Atholl. Park on right after crossing bridge in village*

★ £13.50-£16.50 £13.50-£16.50 £13.50-£16.50

Open Mar-Nov Booking advisable BH & Jul-Aug Last arrival 21.30hrs Last departure noon

Attractive site set in impressive seclusion within the Atholl estate, surrounded by mature woodland and the River Tilt. Although a large park, the various groups of pitches are located throughout the extensive parkland, and each has its own sanitary block with all-cubicled facilities of a very high standard. There is a choice of grass pitches, hardstandings, or fully-serviced pitches. This park is particularly suitable for the larger type of motorhome. A 32-acre site with 280 touring pitches and 101 statics.

**Leisure:**

**Facilities:**

**Services:** → 

**Notes:** Internet gallery with broadband access

*see advert on this page*



### PREMIER PARK

**►►►►► 80% River Tilt Caravan Park**

*(NN875653)*

PH18 5TE

☎ 01796 481467 🖹 01796 481511

**email:** stuart@rivertilt.co.uk

**web:** www.rivertilt.co.uk

**Dir:** *7m N of Pitlochry on A9, take B8079 to Blair Atholl & site at rear of Tilt Hotel*

Open 16 Mar-12 Nov Booking advisable Jul-Aug Last arrival 21.00hrs Last departure noon

An attractive park with magnificent views of the surrounding mountains, idyllically set in hilly woodland country on the banks of the River Tilt, next to the golf course. Fully-serviced pitches are available, and the park boasts its own bistro and restaurant. There is also a leisure complex with heated indoor swimming pool, sun lounge area, spa pool and multi-gym, all available for an extra charge. Outdoors there is a short tennis court. The toilet facilities are very good. A 2-acre site with 37 touring pitches and 55 statics.

**Leisure:**

**Facilities:**

**Services:** → 

**Notes:** Sauna, solarium, steam room

## DUNKELD MAP 21 NO04

**►►► 77% Inver Mill Farm Caravan Park**

*(NO015422)*

Inver PH8 0JR

☎ 01350 727477 🖹 01350 727477

**email:** invermill@talk21.com

**web:** www.visitdunkeld.com/perthshire-caravan-park.htm

**Dir:** *Turn off A9 onto A822 then immediately right to Inver*

£14-£15 £14-£15 £12-£13

Open end Mar-Oct Booking advisable Jul-Aug & wknds Last arrival 22.00hrs Last departure noon

A peaceful park on level former farmland, located on the banks of the River Braan and surrounded by mature trees and hills. The active resident owners keep the park in very good condition. A 5-acre site with 65 touring pitches.

**Facilities:**

**Services:** → 

**Notes:**

SCOTLAND



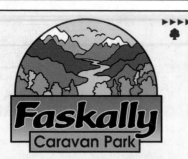

## KINLOCH RANNOCH — MAP 23 NN65

### ► 67% Kilvrecht Campsite *(NN623567)*

PH16 5QA
☎ 01350 727284 Fax 01350 727811
**email:** hamish.murray@forestry.gsi.gov.uk
**Dir:** *3m along S shore of Loch Rannoch. Approach via unclass road along Loch, with Forestry Commission signs*

★ £6 £6 £3-£6

Open Etr-Oct Last arrival 22.00hrs Last departure 10.00hrs

Set in a remote and beautiful spot in a large forest clearing, about 0.75m from Loch Rannoch shore. This small and basic campsite has no hot water, but the few facilities are very well maintained. A 17-acre site with 60 touring pitches.

**Facilities:**

**Services:** →

**Notes:** No fires

## PITLOCHRY — MAP 23 NN95

### ►►►► 73% *Faskally Caravan Park*

*(NN916603)*
PH16 5LA
☎ 01796 472007 Fax 01796 473896
**email:** info@faskally.co.uk
**web:** www.faskally.co.uk
**Dir:** *1.5m N of Pitlochry on B8019*

Open 15 Mar-Oct Booking advisable Jul-Aug Last arrival 23.00hrs

A large park attractively divided into sections by mature trees, set in gently-sloping meadowland beside the tree-lined River Garry. The excellent amenities include a leisure complex with heated indoor swimming pool, spa, sauna and steam room, bar, restaurant and indoor amusements. The park is close to, but unaffected by, the A9. A 27-acre site with 300 touring pitches and 130 statics.

**Leisure:**

**Facilities:**

**Services:** →

**Notes:** Dogs must be kept on leads

*see advert on this page*

### ►►►► 77% Milton of Fonab Caravan Site

*(NN945573)*
Bridge Rd PH16 5NA
☎ 01796 472882 Fax 01796 474363
**email:** info@fonab.co.uk
**web:** www.fonab.co.uk
**Dir:** *0.5m S of town off A924*

★ £14-£16 £14-£16 £14-£16

Open Apr-Oct Booking advisable BH & Jul-Aug Last arrival 21.00hrs Last departure 13.00hrs

Set on the banks of the River Tummel, with extensive views down the river valley to the mountains, this park is close to the centre of Pitlochry, adjacent to the Pitlochry Festival Theatre. The sanitary facilities are exceptionally good, with most contained in combined shower/wash basin and toilet cubicles. A 15-acre site with 154 touring pitches and 36 statics.

**Facilities:**

**Services:** →

**Notes:** Couples & families only, no motor cycles. Mountain bike hire, free trout fishing

## SCONE MAP 21 NO12

►►► 69% **Scone Camping & Caravanning Club Site** *(NO108274)*

Scone Palace PH2 6BB

☎ 01738 552323

**web:** www.campingandcaravanningclub.co.uk/scone

**Dir:** *Follow signs for Scone Palace, once through Perth continue for 2m. Turn left, follow site signs. 1m left onto Racecourse Road. Site entrance from car park*

★ £14.05-£19.85 £14.05-£19.85 £14.05-£19.85

Open 13 Mar-3 Nov Booking advisable BH & peak periods Last arrival 21.00hrs Last departure noon

A delightful woodland site, sheltered and well screened from the adjacent Scone racecourse. The two amenity blocks are built of timber and blend in well with the surroundings of mature trees. Super pitches add to the park's appeal. A 16-acre site with 150 touring pitches, 40 hardstandings.

**Leisure:**

**Facilities:**

**Services:**

**Notes:** Site gates closed 23.00hrs-07.00hrs

## TUMMEL BRIDGE MAP 23 NN75

71% **Tummel Valley Holiday Park** *(NN764592)*

PH16 5SA

☎ 01882 634221 & 0871 641 0199 01882 634302

**email:** enquiries@parkdeanholidays.co.uk

**web:** www.parkdeanholidays.co.uk

**Dir:** *From Perth take A9 N to bypass Pitlochry. 3m after Pitlochry turn onto B8019 signed Tummel Bridge. Park 11m on left*

★ £10-£26 £10-£26

Open Mar-Oct Booking advisable at all times Last arrival 21.00hrs Last departure 10.00hrs

A well-developed site amongst mature forest in an attractive valley, beside the famous bridge on the banks of the River Tummel. Play areas and the bar are sited alongside the river, and there is an indoor pool, children's clubs and live family entertainment. This is an ideal place in which to relax. A 55-acre site with 34 touring pitches and 159 statics.

**Leisure:** **Facilities:**

**Services:** **Notes:** Cycle hire, fishing rod hire

# SCOTTISH BORDERS

## COLDINGHAM MAP 21 NT96

►►►► 79% **Scoutscroft Holiday Centre** *(NT906662)*

St Abbs Rd TD14 5NB

☎ 018907 71338 018907 71746

**email:** holidays@scoutscroft.co.uk

**web:** www.scoutscroft.co.uk

**Dir:** *From A1 take B6438 signed Coldingham & Scoutscroft on right; on Coldingham outskirts*

★ £16-£23 £16-£23

Open Mar-Nov (rs Mar-May, Sep-Oct Crofters Bar only, arcade wknds only) Booking advisable BH, Jul-Aug & wknds Last arrival mdnt Last departure noon

A large family-run site with good facilities and plenty of amenities including bars, restaurant, and children's games rooms. Set on the edge of the village and close to the sea, with separate areas and toilet blocks for tourers. A 16-acre site with 60 touring pitches, 32 hardstandings and 120 statics.

**Leisure:**

**Facilities:**

**Services:**

**Notes:** Dive centre, cash machine

## EYEMOUTH MAP 21 NT96

**NEW** 72% **Eyemouth** *(NT941646)*

Fort Rd TD14 5BE

☎ 0871 664 9740

**email:** eyemouth@park-resorts.com

**web:** www.park-resorts.com

**Dir:** *From A1, approx 6m N of Berwick-upon-Tweed follow A1107 to Eyemouth. On entering town, site is signed. Right after petrol station, left at bottom of hill into Fort Rd*

£6-£20 £6-£20

Open 31 Mar-Oct Booking advisable

A cliff top holiday park on the outskirts of the small fishing village of Eyemouth, within easy reach of Edinburgh and Newcastle. The site is handily placed for exploring the beautiful Scottish Borders, and the magnificent coastline and countryside of north Northumberland. 17 touring pitches and 242 statics.

**Leisure:**

**Facilities:**

**Services:**

SCOTLAND

SCOTLAND

## JEDBURGH MAP 21 NT62

### ►►► 75% Jedburgh Camping & Caravanning Club Site *(NT658219)*

Elliot Park, Edinburgh Rd TD8 6EF

☎ 01835 863393

**web:** www.campingandcaravanningclub.co.uk/jedburgh

**Dir:** *Site opposite Edinburgh & Jedburgh Woollen Mills. N of Jedburgh on A68 (Newcastle-Edinburgh road)*

★ £14.05-£18.85 £14.05-£18.85 Å £14.05-£18.85

Open 28 Apr-3 Nov Booking advisable BH & peak periods Last arrival 21.00hrs Last departure noon

A touring site on the northern edge of town, nestling at the foot of cliffs close to Jed Water. Hardstandings are a welcome feature for caravans. A 3-acre site with 60 touring pitches, 13 hardstandings.

**Facilities:**

**Services:**

**Notes:** Site gates closed 23.00hrs-07.00hrs

### ►►► 75% Jedwater Caravan Park

*(NT665160)*

TD8 6PJ

☎ 01835 840219 & 07050 219219 01835 840219

**email:** jedwater@clara.co.uk

**web:** www.jedwater.co.uk

**Dir:** *3.5m S of Jedburgh on A68*

Å

Open Etr-Oct Booking advisable high season Last arrival mdnt Last departure noon

A quiet riverside site in a beautiful valley, run by resident owners as a peaceful retreat. The touring area is separate from statics, and this site is an ideal touring base. A 10-acre site with 30 touring pitches and 75 statics.

**Leisure:**

**Facilities:**

**Services:**

**Notes:** Bike hire, trampoline, football field

## KELSO MAP 21 NT73

### ►►►► 78% Springwood Caravan Park *(NT720334)*

GOLD

TD5 8LS

☎ 01573 224596 01573 224033

**email:** admin@springwood.biz

**web:** www.springwood.biz

**Dir:** *On A699, signed Newton St Boswells*

★ £17 £17

Open 21 Mar-13 Oct Booking advisable BH & Jul-Aug Last arrival 23.00hrs

Set in a secluded position on the banks of the tree-lined River Teviot, this well-maintained site enjoys a pleasant and spacious spot in which to relax. It offers a high standard of modern toilet facilities which are mainly contained in cubicled units. Floors Castle and the historic town of Kelso are close by. A 2-acre site with 20 touring pitches, 20 hardstandings and 212 statics.

**Leisure:**

**Facilities:**

**Services:**

**Notes:** Dogs must be kept on leads

## LAUDER MAP 21 NT54

### ►►► 77% Lauder Camping & Caravanning Club Site *(NT509535)*

Carfraemill, Oxton TD2 6RA

☎ 01578 750697

**web:** www.campingandcaravanningclub.co.uk/lauder

**Dir:** *From Lauder, right at rdbt onto A697, then left at Lodge Hotel (signed). Site on right behind Carfraemill Hotel*

★ £14.05-£18.85 £14.05-£18.85 Å £14.05-£18.85

Open 13 Mar-3 Nov Booking advisable BH & peak periods Last arrival 21.00hrs Last departure noon

A meadowland site with good facilities housed in pine lodge buildings, and pleasant surroundings. Ideal either as a touring base or transit site, it is extremely well maintained. There are four wooden chalets for hire. A 5-acre site with 60 touring pitches, 9 hardstandings.

**Facilities:**

**Services:**

**Notes:** Site gates closed 23.00hrs-07.00hrs

### ►►► 73% Thirlestane Castle Caravan & Camping Site *(NT536473)*

Thirlestane Castle TD2 6RU
☎ 01578 718884 & 07976 231032
**email:** thirlestanepark@btconnect.com
**web:** www.thirlestanecastlepark.co.uk
**Dir:** *Signed off A68 & A697, just S of Lauder*

£12-£13 £12-£13 fr £12

Open Apr-1 Oct Booking advisable Jul-Aug Last arrival 22.00hrs Last departure noon

Set in the grounds of the impressive Thirlestane Castle, with mainly level grassy pitches. The park and facilities are kept in sparkling condition. A 5-acre site with 60 touring pitches and 15 statics.

**Facilities:**

**Services:**

**Notes:**

## PEEBLES — MAP 21 NT24

### ►►►► 77% Crossburn Caravan Park *(NT248417)*

Edinburgh Rd EH45 8ED
☎ 01721 720501 01721 720501
**email:** enquiries@crossburncaravans.co.uk
**web:** www.crossburncaravans.co.uk
**Dir:** *0.5m N of Peebles on A703*

★ £16-£18 £16-£18 £14-£16

Open Apr-Oct Booking advisable Jul-Aug Last arrival 21.00hrs Last departure 14.00hrs

A peaceful site in a relatively quiet location, despite the proximity of the main road which partly borders the site, as does the Eddleston Water. There are lovely views, and the park is well stocked with trees, flowers and shrubs. Facilities are maintained to a high standard, and fully-serviced pitches are available. A large caravan dealership is on the same site. A 6-acre site with 45 touring pitches, 15 hardstandings and 85 statics.

**Leisure:**

**Facilities:**

**Services:**

**Notes:** Dogs must be kept on leads

## SELKIRK — MAP 21 NT42

### ►►► 69% Victoria Park Caravan & Camping Park *(NT465287)*

Victoria Park, Buccleuch Rd TD7 5DN
☎ 01750 20897 01750 20897
**web:** www.bstt.org.uk
**Dir:** *From A707/A708 N of town, cross river bridge & take 1st left, then left again*

Open all year (rs mid-late Jun) Booking advisable Jul-Aug Last arrival 20.00hrs Last departure 14.00hrs

A consistently well-maintained site with good basic facilities forming part of public park and swimming pool complex close to River Ettrick. A 3-acre site with 60 touring pitches, 9 hardstandings.

**Leisure:** **Facilities:**

**Services:**

**Notes:** Fitness room, sauna, small soft play area

# SOUTH AYRSHIRE

## AYR — MAP 20 NS32

### 75% Craig Tara *(NS300184)*

KA7 4LB

GOLD

☎ 01292 265141 01292 445206
**email:** karen-mcdermot@bourne-leisure.co.uk
**web:** www.craigtara-park.co.uk
**Dir:** *Take A77 towards Stranraer, then 2nd right after Bankfield rdbt. Follow signs for A719 and to site*

★ £12-£61 £12-£61

Open mid Mar-Oct (rs mid Mar-May & Sep-Oct some facilities may be limited) Booking advisable school hols Last arrival anytime Last departure 11.00hrs

A large, well-maintained holiday centre with on-site entertainment and sporting facilities to suit all ages. The touring area is set apart from the main complex at the entrance to the park, and campers can use all the facilities, including water world, soft play areas, sports zone, show bars, and a supermarket with in-house bakery. There is a bus service to Ayr. A 213-acre site with 39 touring pitches, 10 hardstandings and 900 statics.

**Leisure:** **Facilities:**

**Services:**

**Notes:** Max 2 dogs per pitch. Access to beach from park

SCOTLAND

## BARRHILL MAP 20 NX28

### ►►►► 77% Barrhill Holiday Park

*(NX216835)*

KA26 0PZ

01465 821355 01465 821355

**email:** barrhill@surfree.co.uk

**web:** www.barrhillholidaypark.com

**Dir:** *On A714 (Newton Stewart to Girvan road). 1m N of Barrhill*

Open Mar-Jan Booking advisable

A small, friendly park in a tranquil rural location, screened from the A714 by trees. The park is terraced and well landscaped, and a high quality amenity block includes disabled facilities. A 6-acre site with 30 touring pitches, 9 hardstandings and 29 statics.

**Leisure:**

**Facilities:**

**Services:** →

**Notes:**

## COYLTON MAP 20 NS41

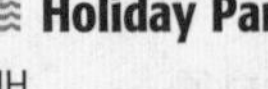

### 74% Sundrum Castle Holiday Park *(NS405208)*

BRONZE

KA6 5JH

01292 570057 & 0871 641 0199 01292 570065

**email:** enquiries@parkdeanholidays.co.uk

**web:** www.parkdeanholidays.co.uk

**Dir:** *Just off A70, 4m E of Ayr near Coylton*

★ £10-£23 £12-£27 £10-£23

Open Mar-Oct Booking advisable all times Last arrival 21.00hrs Last departure 10.00hrs

A large family holiday centre in rolling countryside, with plenty of on-site entertainment, and just a 10-minute drive from the centre of Ayr. Leisure facilities include an indoor swimming pool complex with flume, crazy golf, clubs for young children and teenagers, and the touring area is adequate and clean. A 30-acre site with 42 touring pitches and 67 statics.

**Leisure:**

**Facilities:**

**Services:** →

**Notes:** No cars by tents. Amusement arcade, live family entertainment

## MAYBOLE MAP 20 NS20

### ►►► 75% Culzean Castle Camping & Caravanning Club Site *(NS247103)*

Culzean Castle KA19 8JX

01655 760627

**web:** www.campingandcaravanningclub.co.uk/culzeancastle

**Dir:** *From N on A77 in Maybole turn right onto B7023 (signed Culzean & Maidens), left in 100yds. Site 4m on right*

★ £15.45-£20.15 £15.45-£20.15 £15.45-£20.15

Open 13 Mar-3 Nov Booking advisable BH & peak periods Last arrival 21.00hrs Last departure noon

A mainly level grass park with some gently sloping pitches and hard stands along the bed of an old railway, situated at the entrance to the castle and country park. The park is surrounded by trees on three sides and has lovely views over Culzean Bay. A 10-acre site with 90 touring pitches, 27 hardstandings.

**Leisure:**

**Facilities:**

**Services:** →

**Notes:** Site gates closed 23.00hrs-07.00hrs

# SOUTH LANARKSHIRE

## ABINGTON MAP 21 NS92

### ►►► 78% Mount View Caravan Park *(NS935235)*

BRONZE

ML12 6RW

01864 502808 01864 502808

**email:** info@mountviewcaravanpark.co.uk

**web:** www.mountviewcaravanpark.co.uk

**Dir:** *M74 junct 13 onto A702 S into Abington. Left into Station Road, over river & railway. Park on right*

★ fr £14 fr £14 £5-£14

Open Mar-Oct Booking advisable

A developing park, surrounded by the Southern Uplands and handily located between Carlisle and Glasgow. It is an excellent stopover site

*Mount View Caravan Park*

for those travelling between Scotland and the south. The West Coast railway passes beside the park. A 5.5-acre site with 51 touring pitches, 51 hardstandings and 20 statics.

**Leisure:** **Facilities:**

**Services:**

**Notes:** Dogs must be kept on leads. Emergency phone

## STIRLING

### ABERFOYLE MAP 20 NN50

**►►►► 78% Trossachs Holiday Park** *(NS544976)*

FK8 3SA

☎ 01877 382614 01877 382732

**email:** info@trossachshsolidays.co.uk

**web:** www.trossachsholidays.co.uk

**Dir:** *Access on E side of A81, 1m S of junct A821 & 3m S of Aberfoyle*

★ £14-£20 £14-£20 £12-£18

Open Mar-Oct Booking advisable anytime Last arrival 21.00hrs Last departure noon

An imaginatively designed terraced site offering a high degree of quality all round, with fine views across Flanders Moss. All touring pitches are fully serviced with water, waste, electricity and TV aerial, and customer care is a main priority. Set in 20 acres of ground within the Queen Elizabeth Forest Park, with plenty of opportunities for cycling off-road on mountain bikes, which can be hired or bought on site. A 40-acre site with 66 touring pitches, 46 hardstandings and 84 statics.

**Leisure:** **Facilities:**

**Services:**

*see advert on this page*

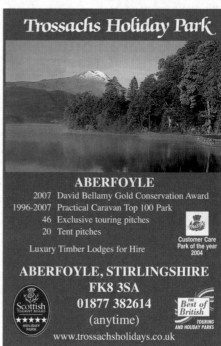



### AUCHENBOWIE MAP 21 NS78

**►►► 69% *Auchenbowie Caravan & Camping Site*** *(NS795880)*

FK7 8HE

☎ 01324 823999 01324 822950

**Dir:** *0.5m S of M9/M80 junct 9. Turn right off A872 for 0.5m, signed*

Open Apr-Oct Booking advisable mid Jul-mid Aug Last departure noon

A pleasant little site in a rural location, with mainly level grassy pitches. The friendly warden creates a relaxed atmosphere, and given its position close to the junction of the M9 and M80 motorways, this is a handy stopover spot for tourers. A 3.5-acre site with 60 touring pitches and 12 statics.

**Leisure:**

**Facilities:**

**Services:**

*see advert on page 324*

## BALMAHA — MAP 20 NS49

### ►►►► 79% Milarrochy Bay Camping & Caravanning Club Site *(NN407927)*

Milarrochy Bay G63 0AL

☎ 01360 870236

**web:** www.campingandcaravanningclub.co.uk/milarrockybay

**Dir:** *A811 (Balloch to Stirling road) take Drymen turn. In Drymen take B837 for Balmaha. In 5m road turns sharp right up steep hill. Site in 1.5m*

★ £15.45-£20.15 £15.45-£20.15 Å £15.45-£20.15

Open 13 Mar-3 Nov Booking advisable BH & peak periods Last arrival 21.00hrs Last departure noon

On the quieter side of Loch Lomond next to the 75,000-acre Queen Elizabeth Forest, this attractive site offers very good facilities. Disabled toilets and family rooms are appointed to a high standard. Towing vehicles should engage low gear immediately at steep hill warning sign in Balmaha. A 12-acre site with 150 touring pitches, 23 hardstandings.

**Leisure:**

**Facilities:**

**Services:**

**Notes:** Site gates closed 23.00hrs-07.00hrs. Fishing, Boat launching

## BLAIRLOGIE — MAP 21 NS89

### ►►►► 84% Witches Craig Caravan & Camping Park *(NS821968)*

FK9 5PX

☎ 01786 474947 01786 447286

**email:** info@witchescraig.co.uk

**web:** www.witchescraig.co.uk

**Dir:** *3m NE of Stirling on A91 (Hillfoots-St Andrews road)*

★ £12.50-£16.50 £12.50-£16.50 Å £12.50-£16.50

Open Apr-Oct Booking advisable Jul-Aug Last arrival 21.00hrs Last departure 13.00hrs

In an attractive setting with direct access to the lower slopes of the dramatic Ochil Hills, this is a well-maintained family-run park. It is in the centre of 'Braveheart' country, with easy access to historical sites and many popular attractions. A 5-acre site with 60 touring pitches, 26 hardstandings.

**Leisure:**

**Facilities:**

**Services:**

**Notes:** Food preparation, baby bath & changing area

## CALLANDER — MAP 20 NN60

### ►►► 86% Gart Caravan Park *(NN643070)*

The Gart FK17 8LE

☎ 01877 330002 01877 330002

**email:** enquiries@theholidaypark.co.uk

**web:** www.theholidaypark.co.uk

**Dir:** *1m E of Callander on A84*

★ £18

Open Etr or Apr-15 Oct Booking advisable BH & Jul-Aug Last arrival 22.00hrs Last departure 11.30hrs

A very well maintained spacious parkland site within easy walking distance of Callander. The on-site play area for children is excellent, whilst free fishing is available on a private stretch of the River Teith. A wide range of leisure activities is available within the locality. A 26-acre site with 128 touring pitches and 66 statics.

**Leisure:** **Facilities:**

**Services:**

**Notes:** No commercial vehicles

## LUIB — MAP 20 NN42

### ►►►► 79% *Glendochart Holiday Park* *(NN477278)*

FK20 8QT

☎ 01567 820637 01567 820024

**email:** info@glendochart-caravanpark.co.uk

**web:** www.glendochart-caravanpark.co.uk

**Dir:** *On A85 (Oban to Stirling road), midway between Killin & Crainlarich*

Open Mar-Oct Booking advisable Jul-Aug Last arrival 22.00hrs Last departure noon

**Services:** Toilet Fluid · Café/ Restaurant · Fast Food/Takeaway · Baby Care · Electric Hook Up · Motorvan Service Point · Launderette · Licensed Bar · Calor Gas · Camping Gaz · Battery Charging

A small, well maintained park on a hillside in Glendochart, with imaginative landscaping and glorious mountain and hill views. The site is well located for trout and salmon fishing, and ideal for walking. A 15-acre site with 35 touring pitches, 28 hardstandings and 60 statics.

**Facilities:**

**Services:**

## STIRLING

*see Auchenbowie & Blairlogie*

## STRATHYRE — MAP 20 NN51

### ►►► 71% ***Immervoulin Caravan and Camping Park*** *(NN560164)*

FK18 8NJ

☎ 01877 384285

**Dir:** *Off A84, approx 1m S of Strathyre*

Open Mar-Oct Booking advisable BH & Jul-Aug Last arrival 22.00hrs

A family run park on open meadowland next to the River Balvaig, where fishing, canoeing and other water sports can be enjoyed. A riverside walk leads to Loch Lubnaig, and the village of Strathyre offers restaurants. A relaxed park with lovely scenery. A 5-acre site with 50 touring pitches.

**Facilities:**

**Services:**

# WEST DUNBARTONSHIRE

## BALLOCH — MAP 20 NS38

### ►►►► 80% **Lomond Woods Holiday Park** *(NS383816)*

Old Luss Rd G83 8QP

☎ 01389 755000 Fax 01389 755563

**email:** lomondwoods@holiday-parks.co.uk

**web:** www.holiday-parks.co.uk

**Dir:** *From A82, 17m N of Glasgow, take A811(Stirling to Balloch road). Left at 1st rdbt, follow holiday park signs, 150yds on left*

★ £15-£20 £15-£20

Open all year Booking advisable all year Last arrival 21.00hrs Last departure noon

A mature park with well-laid out pitches screened by trees and shrubs, surrounded by woodland and hills. The park is within walking distance of 'Loch Lomond Shores', a complex of leisure and retailing experiences which is the main gateway to Scotland's first National Park. Amenities include the Loch Lomond Aquarium, an Interactive Exhibition, and loch cruises. A 13-acre site with 110 touring pitches, 110 hardstandings and 35 statics.

**Leisure:**

**Facilities:**

**Services:**

**Notes:** No tents, no jet skis

# WEST LOTHIAN

## EAST CALDER — MAP 21 NT06

### ►►► 83% **Linwater Caravan Park**

*(NT104696)*

West Clifton EH53 0HT

☎ 0131 333 3326 Fax 0131 333 1952

**email:** linwater@supanet.com

**web:** www.linwater.co.uk

**Dir:** *M9 junct 1, signed from B7030 or from Wilkieston on A71*

£12-£15 £12-£15 £10-£13

Open late Mar-late Oct Booking advisable BH & Aug Last arrival 21.00hrs Last departure noon

A farmland park in a peaceful rural area within easy reach of Edinburgh. The very good facilities are housed in a Scandinavian-style building, and are well maintained by resident owners. Nearby are plenty of pleasant woodland walks. A 5-acre site with 60 touring pitches, 14 hardstandings.

**Leisure:**

**Facilities:**

**Services:**

## LINLITHGOW — MAP 21 NS97

### ►►►► 79% **Beecraigs Caravan & Camping Site** *(NT006746)*

Beecraigs Country Park, The Park Centre EH49 6PL

☎ 01506 844516 Fax 01506 846256

**email:** mail@beecraigs.com

**web:** www.beecraigs.com

**Dir:** *From Linlithgow on A803 or from Bathgate on B792, follow signs to country park. Reception either at restaurant or park centre*

★ £11.90-£15 £11.90-£15 £7.25-£18.60

Open all year (rs 25-26 Dec, 1-2 Jan no new arrivals) Booking advisable all year Last arrival 22.00hrs Last departure noon

A wildlife enthusiast's paradise where even the timber facility buildings are in keeping with the environment. Beecraigs is situated peacefully in the open countryside of the Bathgate Hills. Small bays with natural shading offer intimate pitches, and there's a restaurant serving lunch and evening meals. The smart toilet block includes en suite facilities. A 6-acre site with 36 touring pitches, 36 hardstandings.

**Leisure:**

**Facilities:**

**Services:**

**Notes:** No cars by tents. No ball games near caravans, no noise after 22.00hrs. Children's bath, country park facilities

SCOTLAND

# SCOTTISH ISLANDS

## Isle of Arran

### LOCHRANZA MAP 20 NR95

►►► 78% **Lochranza Caravan & Camping Site** *(NR942500)*
KA27 8HL
☎ 01770 830273
**email:** office@lochgolf.demon.co.uk
**web:** www.lochranzagolf.com
**Dir:** *On A841 at N of island, beside Kintyre ferry & 14m N of Brodick for ferry to Ardrossan*

★ £15-£17 £13-£17 ▲ £10-£17

Open Mar-30 Oct Booking advisable Whit & Aug Last arrival 22.00hrs Last departure 13.00hrs

Attractive park in a beautiful location, run by friendly family owners. The park is adjacent to an 18-hole golf course, opposite the famous Arran Distillery, between tree-lined hills on the edge of the village. Golf and ferry packages can be arranged. A 2.5-acre site with 60 touring pitches, 10 hardstandings.

**Facilities:**
**Services:** →
**Notes:** No fires. Putting green

## Isle of Mull

### CRAIGNURE MAP 20 NM73

►►► 81% **Shieling Holidays** *(NM724369)*
PA65 6AY
☎ 01680 812496
**email:** info@shielingholidays.co.uk
**web:** www.shielingholidays.co.uk
**Dir:** *From ferry left onto A849 to Iona. 400mtrs left at church, follow site signs towards sea*

fr £14.50 fr £14.50 ▲ fr £14

Open Apr-Oct Booking advisable Spring BH & Jul-Aug Last arrival 22.00hrs Last departure noon

A lovely site on the water's edge with spectacular views, and less than one mile from ferry landing. Hardstandings and service points are provided for motorhomes, and there are astro-turf pitches for tents. The park offers bunkhouse accommodation for families. A 6-acre site with 90 touring pitches, 30 hardstandings and 15 statics.

**Leisure:**
**Facilities:**
**Services:** →
**Notes:** Adventure playground, bikes

## Isle of Skye

### EDINBANE MAP 22 NG35

►►► 76% **Loch Greshornish Caravan Site** *(NG343524)*
Borve, Arnisort IV51 9PS
☎ 01470 582230
**email:** info@skyecamp.com
**web:** www.skyecamp.com
**Dir:** *Approx 12m from Portree on A850 (Dunvegan road). By loch shore.*

★ £9-£11 £9-£11 ▲ £8.50-£9

Open Apr-Oct Booking advisable Jul-Aug Last arrival 22.00hrs Last departure noon

A pleasant open site, mostly level and with a high standard of maintenance. There is a campers' shelter in a disused byre which is popular in poor weather, and a licensed shop. A 5-acre site with 130 touring pitches, 6 hardstandings.

**Facilities:**
**Services:** →
**Notes:** Dogs must be kept under control & exercised off site. Bike hire, canoe hire

### STAFFIN MAP 22 NG46

►► 72% **Staffin Camping & Caravanning** *(NG492670)*
IV51 9JX
☎ 01470 562213 01470 562213
**email:** staffincampsite@btinternet.com
**web:** www.staffincampsite.co.uk
**Dir:** *On A855, 16m N of Portree. Turn right before 40mph signs*

fr £12 fr £12 ▲ fr £11

Open Apr-Oct Booking advisable Jul-Aug Last arrival 22.00hrs Last departure 11.00hrs

A large sloping grassy site with level hardstandings for motor homes and caravans, close to the village of Staffin. The toilet block is appointed to a very good standard. A 2.5-acre site with 50 touring pitches, 18 hardstandings.

**Facilities:**
**Services:** →
**Notes:** No music after 23.00hrs. Picnic tables, kitchen area

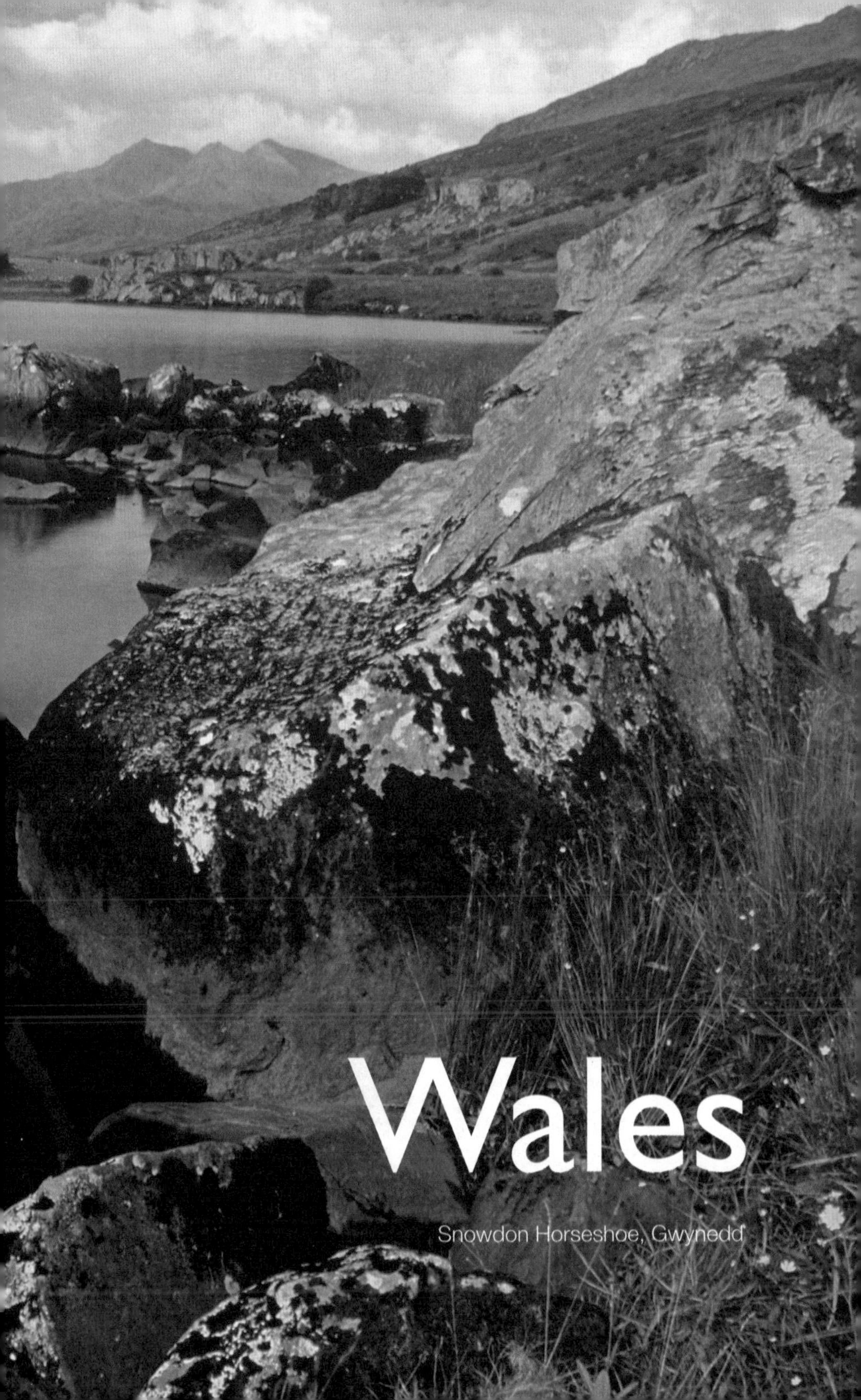

# Wales

Snowdon Horseshoe, Gwynedd

# ANGLESEY, ISLE OF

## DULAS — MAP 14 SH48

### ►►►► 77% Tyddyn Isaf Caravan Park (SH486873)

Lligwy Bay LL70 9PQ

☎ 01248 410203 🖷 01248 410667

**email:** enquiries@tyddynisaf.demon.co.uk

**web:** www.tyddynisaf.demon.co.uk

**Dir:** *Take A5025 through Benllech to Moelfre rdbt, left towards Amlwch to Brynrefail village. Turn right opposite craft shop. Park 0.5m down lane on right*

★ £16.50-£25.50 £16.50-£25.50 £16.50-£25.50

Open Mar-Oct (rs Mar-Jul & Sep-Oct bar & shop opening times limited) Booking advisable May BH & Jun-Aug Last arrival 21.30hrs Last departure 11.00hrs

A beautifully situated, very spacious family park on rising ground adjacent to a sandy beach, with magnificent views overlooking Lligwy Bay. Access to the beach is by private footpath (lengthy from some pitches), or by car for the less energetic. The park has very good toilet facilities, a well-stocked shop, and a clubhouse serving meals and takeaway food. A 16-acre site with 80 touring pitches, 36 hardstandings and 56 statics.

**Leisure:**

**Facilities:**

**Services:**

**Notes:** Dogs must be kept on leads, no groups. Baby changing unit

## LLANBEDRGOCH — MAP 14 SH58

### ►►► 76% Ty Newydd Leisure Park (SH508813)

LL76 8TZ

☎ 01248 450677 🖷 01248 450711

**email:** mike@tynewydd.com

**web:** www.tynewydd.com

**Dir:** *A5025 from Brittania Bridge. Through Pentraeth, bear left at layby. Site 0.75m on right*

★ £14-£28 £14-£28 £14-£28

Open Mar-Oct (rs Mar-Whit & mid Sep-Oct club/shop wknds only, outdoor pool closed) Booking advisable Etr, Whit & Jul-Aug Last arrival 23.30hrs Last departure 10.00hrs

A low-density park with many facilities including a heated outdoor pool, a club with restaurant, and a good playground. A 4-acre site with 48 touring pitches, 15 hardstandings and 62 statics.

**Leisure:** **Facilities:**

**Services:**

**Notes:** Wi-fi. Sauna, jacuzzi

*see advert on opposite page*

## MARIAN-GLAS — MAP 14 SH58

### ►►►► 92% Home Farm Caravan Park (SH498850)

LL73 8PH

☎ 01248 410614 🖷 01248 410900

**email:** enq@homefarm-anglesey.co.uk

**web:** www.homefarm-anglesey.co.uk

**Dir:** *on A5025, 2m N of Benllech. Park 300mtrs beyond church*

★ £11.50-£25 £15.50-£25 £11.50-£20.50

**Services:** Toilet Fluid · Café/ Restaurant · Fast Food/Takeaway · Baby Care · Electric Hook Up · Motorvan Service Point · Launderette · Licensed Bar · Calor Gas · Camping Gaz · Battery Charging

Open Apr-Oct Booking advisable BH Last arrival 21.00hrs Last departure noon

A first class park in an elevated and secluded position sheltered by trees. The peaceful rural setting affords views of farmland, the sea, and the mountains of Snowdonia. The modern toilet block has helped to win numerous awards, and there are excellent play facilities for children both indoors and out. The area is blessed with sandy beaches, and local pubs and shops cater for everyday needs. A 6-acre site with 98 touring pitches, 21 hardstandings and 84 statics.

**Leisure:**

**Facilities:**

**Services:**

**Notes:** No roller blades, skateboards or scooters. Indoor adventure playground

## PENTRAETH MAP 14 SH57

### ►►► 77% **Rhos Caravan Park** *(SH517794)*

Rhos Farm LL75 8DZ

☎ 01248 450214 01248 450214

**email:** rhosfarm@googlemail.com

**web:** www.rhoscaravanpark.co.uk

**Dir:** *Site on left of A5025, 1m N of Pentraeth*

★ £11-£13 £11-£13 £11-£13

Open Etr-Oct (rs Mar shop restricted) Booking advisable Spring BH & Jul-Aug Last arrival 22.00hrs Last departure 16.00hrs

A warm welcome awaits families at this spacious park on level, grassy ground with easy access to the main road to Amlwch. This 200-acre working farm has a games room, two play areas and farm animals to keep children amused, with good beaches, pubs, restaurants and shops nearby. The two toilet blocks are kept to a good standard by enthusiastic owners, who are constantly improving the facilities. A 15-acre site with 98 touring pitches and 66 statics.

**Leisure:**

**Facilities:**

**Services:**



## RHOS LLIGWY MAP 14 SH48

### ►►► 73% **Ty'n Rhos Caravan Park**

*(SH495867)*

LL72 8NL

☎ 01248 852417 01248 853417

**email:** robert@bodafonpark.co.uk

**web:** www.bodafonpark.co.uk

**Dir:** *Take A5025 from Benllech to Moelfre rdbt, turn right to T-junct in Moelfre. Left, then approx 2m to site on right*

★ £15-£21 £15-£21 fr £10

Open Mar-Oct Booking advisable BH & Aug Last arrival 21.00hrs Last departure noon

A well-established family park set in quiet countryside, close to the beautiful beach at Lligwy Bay, and cliff walks along the Heritage Coast. It makes a popular base for visiting historic Din Lligwy, and the shops at picturesque Moelfre, with sea and offshore fishing, boating and village inns all adding to its attractions. A 10-acre site with 50 touring pitches, 50 hardstandings and 80 statics.

**Facilities:**

**Services:**

WALES

### RHOSNEIGR MAP 14 SH37

**►►► 77% Ty Hen** *(SH323737)*

Station Rd LL64 5QZ

☎ 01407 810331 🖹 01407 810331

**email:** bernardtyhen@hotmail.com

**web:** www.tyhen.com

**Dir:** *A55 across Anglesey. At exit 5 follow signs to Rhosneigr, at clock turn right. Entrance 50mtrs before Rhosneigr railway station*

Open mid Mar-Oct Booking advisable at all times Last arrival 21.00hrs Last departure noon

Attractive seaside position near a large fishing lake and riding stables, in lovely countryside. A smart toilet block offers a welcome amenity at this popular family park, where friendly owners are always on hand. A 7.5-acre site with 38 touring pitches, 5 hardstandings and 42 statics.

**Leisure:**

**Facilities:**

**Services:** →

**Notes:** 1 motor vehicle per pitch, dogs on leads, children in tents/tourers/statics by 22.00hrs. Fishing, family room, walks

## BRIDGEND

### PORTHCAWL MAP 09 SS87

**►►► 69% Brodawel Camping & Caravan Park** *(SS816789)*

Moor Ln, Nottage CF36 3EJ

☎ 01656 783231

**Dir:** *M4 junct 37, A4229 towards Porthcawl. Site on right off A4229*

£13-£16 ▲ £13-£16

Open Apr-Sep Booking advisable Last arrival 19.00hrs Last departure 11.00hrs

A family run park catering mainly for families, on the edge of the village of Nottage. It is very convenient for Porthcawl and the Glamorgan Heritage Coast, both a 5-minute drive away. A 4-acre site with 100 touring pitches.

**Leisure:**

**Facilities:**

**Services:** →

**Notes:**

## CARMARTHENSHIRE

### CROSS HANDS MAP 08 SN51

**►►► 89% Black Lion Caravan & Camping Park** *(SN572129)*

78 Black Lion Rd, Gorslas SA14 6RU

☎ 01269 845365

**email:** blacklionsite@aol.com

**web:** www.caravansite.com

**Dir:** *M4 junct 49 onto A48 to Cross Hands rdbt, right onto A476 (Llandeilo). 0.5m at Gorslas sharp right into Black Lion Rd. Site 0.5m on right, (follow brown tourist signs from Cross Hands rdbt)*

Open Apr-Oct Booking advisable at all times Last arrival 22.00hrs Last departure 11.00hrs

Cheerful and friendly owners keep this improving park clean and well maintained. The very good toilet and shower facilities include a separate room for disabled guests, and this is a popular overnight stop for people travelling on the Irish ferries. The National Botanic Garden of Wales is about 10 minutes' drive away. A 12-acre site with 45 touring pitches, 10 hardstandings.

**Leisure:**

**Facilities:**

**Services:** →

**Notes:** Wi-fi. Caravan storage, hot tub, aviary, classic cars

### HARFORD MAP 08 SN64

**►►► 79% Springwater Lakes** *(SN637430)*

SA19 8DT

☎ 01558 650788 🖹 01558 650788

**web:** www.springwaterlakes.com

**Dir:** *4m E of Lampeter on A482, entrance well signed on right*

★ £13 £13 ▲ £13

Open Mar-Oct Booking advisable Jun-Aug Last arrival 20.00hrs Last departure 11.00hrs

In a rural setting overlooked by the Cambrian Mountains, this park is adjoined on each side by four spring-fed and well-stocked fishing lakes. All pitches have hardstandings, electricity and TV hook-ups, and there is a small and very clean toilet block and a shop. A 20-acre site with 20 touring pitches, 12 hardstandings.

**Facilities:**

**Services:** →

**Notes:** Dogs must be kept on leads at all times, children must be supervised around lakes

**Abbreviations:** BH-bank holiday/s Etr-Easter Whit-Whitsun dep-departure fr-from hrs-hours m-mile mdnt-midnight rdbt-roundabout rs-restricted service wk-week wknd-weekend no dogs No cards → following facilities within 3 miles of the site

WALES

## LLANDOVERY MAP 09 SN73

### ►►► 82% Erwlon Caravan & Camping Park *(SN776343)*

GOLD

Brecon Rd SA20 0RD

☎ 01550 721021

**email:** peter@erwlon.fsnet.co.uk

**Dir:** *0.5m E of Llandovery on A40*

★ £11-£12 £11-£12 £4-£12

Open all year Booking advisable BH Last arrival anytime Last departure noon

Long-established family-run site set beside a brook in the Brecon Beacons foothills. The town of Llandovery and the hills overlooking the Towy Valley are a short walk away. There is a superb facilities block with cubicled washrooms, and family and disabled rooms. Improvements continue at this park. An 8-acre site with 75 touring pitches, 15 hardstandings.

**Leisure:**

**Facilities:**

**Services:**

**Notes:** Quiet after 22.30hrs. Wi-fi. Fishing, bicycle storage & hire

## LLANGADOG MAP 09 SN72

### ►►► 76% Abermarlais Caravan Park

*(SN695298)*

SA19 9NG

☎ 01550 777868 & 777797

**web:** www.abermarlaiscaravanpark.co.uk

**Dir:** *On A40 midway between Llandovery & Llandeilo, 1.5m NW of Llangadog*

★ £9-£11 £9-£11 £9-£11

Open 15 Mar-15 Nov (rs Nov & Mar 1 toilet block, water point no hot water) Booking advisable BH & 15 Jul-Aug Last arrival 23.00hrs Last departure noon

An attractive, well-run site with a welcoming atmosphere. This part-level, part-sloping park is in a wooded valley on the edge of the Brecon Beacons National Park, beside the River Marlais. A 17-acre site with 88 touring pitches, 2 hardstandings.

**Leisure:**

**Facilities:**

**Services:**

**Notes:** Dogs must be kept on leads, no open fires, quiet from 23.00hrs-08.00hrs. Volleyball, badminton court, softball tennis net

## LLANWRDA

*see Harford*

## NEWCASTLE EMLYN MAP 08 SN34

**PREMIER PARK**

### ►►►►► 79% Cenarth Falls Holiday Park *(SN265421)*

Cenarth SA38 9JS

☎ 01239 710345 01239 710344

**email:** enquiries@cenarth-holipark.co.uk

**web:** www.cenarth-holipark.co.uk

**Dir:** *Off A484 on outskirts of Cenarth towards Cardigan*

Open Mar-16 Dec Booking advisable BH & Jul-Aug Last arrival 20.00hrs Last departure 11.00hrs

A high quality park with excellent facilities, close to the village of Cenarth where the famous salmon and sea trout River Teifi cascades through the Cenarth Falls Gorge. A well-landscaped park with an indoor heated swimming pool and fitness suite, and a restaurant and bar. A 2-acre site with 30 touring pitches, 30 hardstandings and 89 statics.

**Leisure:**

**Facilities:**

**Services:**

**Notes:** No dogs 15 Jul-2 Sep. Pool table, health & leisure complex

WALES

NEWCASTLE EMLYN CONTINUED

## ►►► 74% Afon Teifi Caravan & Camping Park *(SN338405)*

Pentrecagal SA38 9HT

01559 370532

**email:** afonteifi@btinternet.com

**web:** www.afonteifi.co.uk

**Dir:** *Signed off A484, 2m E of Newcastle Emlyn*

Open Apr-Oct Booking advisable peak periods Last arrival 23.00hrs

Set on the banks of the River Teifi, a famous salmon and sea trout river, this park is secluded with good views. Family owned and run, and only 2 miles from the market town of Newcastle Emlyn. A 6-acre site with 110 touring pitches, 22 hardstandings and 10 statics.

**Leisure:**

**Facilities:**

**Services:** →

**Notes:** 15 acres of woodland, fields & walks, ball area

## ►►► 82% Argoed Meadow Caravan and Camping Site *(SN268415)*

Argoed Farm SA38 9JL

01239 710690

**web:** www.cenarthcamping.co.uk

**Dir:** *From Newcastle Emlyn on A484 towards Cenarth, take B4332. Site 300yds on right.*

Open all year Booking advisable Last arrival anytime Last departure noon

Pleasant open meadowland on the banks of the River Teifi, very close to Cenarth Falls gorge. A modern toilet block adds to the general appeal. A 3-acre site with 30 touring pitches, 5 hardstandings.

**Facilities:**

**Services:** →

**Notes:** Dogs must be kept on leads, no bikes/skateboards

## ►►► 78% Dolbryn Camping & Caravanning *(SN296386)*

Capel Iwan Rd SA38 9LP

01239 710683

**email:** dolbryn@btinternet.com

**web:** www.dolbryn.co.uk

**Dir:** *A484 (Carmarthan to Cardigan road). At Newcastle Emlyn (signed) turn to Capel Iwan. Follow signs. NB larger vehicles should follow route via Newcastle Emlyn.*

Open Mar-Nov Booking advisable Last arrival 22.30hrs Last departure 13.00hrs

A secluded park, run by enthusiastic owners, set in a peaceful valley with a stream, ponds, mature trees and an abundance of wildlife in over 13 acres, that include a vineyard and plenty of nature walks. The tastefully appointed toilets and showers are located in rustic farm outbuildings. The cosy bar offers a chance to get together with fellow campers, or take part in family activities. A 13.5-acre site with 60 touring pitches, 2 hardstandings.

**Leisure:**

**Facilities:**

**Services:** →

**Notes:** Dogs must be kept on leads, quiet after 23.30hrs. Fishing, children's activities

## ►►► 74% Moelfryn Caravan & Camping Site *(SN321370)*

Ty-Cefn, Pant-y-Bwlch SA38 9JE

01559 371231

**email:** moelfryn@moelfryncaravanpark.co.uk

**web:** www.moelfryncaravanpark.co.uk

**Dir:** *A484 from Carmarthen towards Cynwyl Elfed. Pass Blue Bell Inn on right, 200yds take left fork onto B4333 towards Hermon. In 7m brown sign on left. Turn left, site on right*

★ £8-£12.50 £8-£12.50 £7-£11.50

Open Mar-10 Jan Booking advisable May-Aug Last arrival 22.00hrs Last departure noon

A small family-run park in an elevated location overlooking the valley of the River Teifi. Pitches are level and spacious, and well screened by hedging and mature trees. Facilities are well maintained, clean and tidy, and the playing field is well away from the touring area. A 3-acre site with 25 touring pitches, 13 hardstandings.

**Leisure:**

**Facilities:**

**Services:** →

**Notes:** Wi-fi. Caravan storage

### RHANDIRMWYN MAP 09 SN74

**79% Rhandirmwyn Camping & Caravanning Club Site** *(SN779435)*

SA20 0NT

01550 760257

**web:** www.campingandcaravanningclub.co.uk/rhandirmwyn

**Dir:** *From Llandovery take A483, turn left signed Rhandirmwyn for 7m, left at post office, site on left before river*

£15.45-£20.15 £15.45-£20.15 £15.45-£20.15

Open 13 Mar-3 Nov Booking advisable BH & peak periods Last arrival 21.00hrs Last departure noon

On the banks of the Afon Tywi near Towy Forest and the Llyn Brianne reservoir, this secluded park has superb views from all pitches. The park is divided into paddocks by mature hedging, and facilities and grounds are very well tended. An 11-acre site with 90 touring pitches, 17 hardstandings.

**Leisure:**

**Facilities:**

**Services:**

**Notes:** Site gates closed 23.00hrs-07.00hrs

## CEREDIGION

### ABERAERON MAP 08 SN46

**78% Aeron Coast Caravan Park**

*(SN460631)*

North Rd SA46 0JF

01545 570349 01545 571289

**email:** enquiries@aeroncoast.co.uk

**web:** www.aeroncoast.co.uk

**Dir:** *On A487 (coast road) on N edge of Aberaeron, signed. Filling station at entrance*

£14-£23 £14-£23 £14-£23

Open Mar-Oct Booking advisable BH & school hols Last arrival 23.00hrs Last departure 11.00hrs

A well-managed family holiday park on the edge of the attractive resort of Aberaeron, with direct access to the beach. The spacious pitches are all level. On-site facilities include an extensive outdoor pool complex, a multi-activity outdoor sports area, an indoor children's play area, a small lounge bar which serves food, a games room and an entertainment suite. A 22-acre site with 100 touring pitches, 23 hardstandings and 200 statics.

**Leisure:**

**Facilities:**

**Services:**

**Notes:** Families only, no motorcycles. Indoor leisure rooms, entertainment rooms

### ABERYSTWYTH MAP 08 SN58

**76% Ocean View Caravan Park**

*(SN592842)*

North Beach, Clarach Bay SY23 3DT

01970 828425 & 623361

**email:** alan@grover10.freeserve.co.uk

**web:** www.oceanviewholidays.com

**Dir:** *Turn off A487 in Bow Street. Straight on at next x-roads. Site 2nd on right*

£12.50-£16 £12.50-£16

Open Mar-Oct Booking advisable BH & high season Last arrival 20.00hrs Last departure noon

In a sheltered valley on gently sloping ground, with wonderful views of both the sea and the countryside. The beach of Clarach Bay is just 200 yards away, and this welcoming park is ideal for all the family. A 9-acre site with 24 touring pitches, 15 hardstandings and 56 statics.

**Facilities:**

**Services:**

**Notes:**

### BETTWS EVAN MAP 08 SN34

**72% Pilbach Holiday Park** *(SN306476)*

SA44 5RT

0845 050 8176 01970 828901

**email:** info@barkersleisure.com

**web:** www.barkersleisure.com

**Dir:** *S on A487, turn left onto B4333*

Open Mar-Oct (rs Mar-Spring BH & Oct swimming pool closed) Booking advisable Spring BH & Jul-Aug Last arrival 22.00hrs Last departure noon

Set in secluded countryside, with two separate paddocks and pitches clearly marked in the grass, close to nearby seaside resorts. It has a heated outdoor swimming pool, and entertainment in the club two or three times a week in high season. A 15-acre site with 65 touring pitches, 10 hardstandings and 70 statics.

**Leisure:**

**Facilities:**

**Services:**

**Notes:** Bike/skateboard parks

## BORTH MAP 14 SN69

### 69% Brynowen Holiday Park *(SN608893)*

GOLD

SY24 5LS

☎ 01970 871366 & 871125

**email:** brynowen@park-resorts.com

**web:** www.park-resorts.com

**Dir:** *Signed off B4353, S of Borth*

★ £5-£28 £5-£28

Open Etr-1 Nov Booking advisable Jul-Aug Last arrival 19.00hrs Last departure 10.00hrs

Enjoying spectacular views across Cardigan Bay and the Cambrian Mountains, a small touring park in a large and well-equipped holiday centre. The well-run park offers a wide range of organised activities and entertainment for all the family from morning until late in the evening. A long sandy beach is a few minutes drive away. A 52-acre site with 13 touring pitches and 480 statics.

**Leisure:**

**Facilities:**

**Services:** →

**Notes:** No cars by caravans. Kids' clubs, mini ten-pin bowling

WALES

## CROSS INN MAP 08 SN35

### ►►► 77% Cardigan Bay Camping & Caravanning Club Site *(SN383566)*

Llwynhelyg SA44 6LW

☎ 01545 560029

**web:** www.campingandcaravanningclub.co.uk/cardiganbay

**Dir:** *Left from A487 (Cardigan-Aberystwyth) at Synod Inn. Take A486 signed New Quay. In village of Cross Inn, left after Penrhiwgaled Arms Pub. Site 0.75m on right*

★ £14.05-£18.85 £14.05-£18.85 £14.05-£18.85

Open 13 Mar-29 Sep Booking advisable BH & peak periods Last arrival 21.00hrs Last departure noon

An excellent, attractive touring site in an elevated rural position with extensive country views. A footpath from the site joins the coastal walk, and the pretty village of New Quay is only a short drive away. A 14-acre site with 90 touring pitches, 6 hardstandings.

**Leisure:**

**Facilities:**

**Services:** →

**Notes:** Site gates closed 23.00hrs-07.00hrs

## LLANON MAP 08 SN56

### ►►► 74% Woodlands Caravan Park *(SN509668)*

SY23 5LX

☎ 01974 202342 & 202454 01974 202342

**Dir:** *Through Llanon, exit A487 at international sign, park 280yds on right*

★ fr £13 fr £13 fr £13

Open Apr-Oct Booking advisable school hols Last arrival 21.30hrs Last departure noon

A well maintained, mainly grass site surrounded by mature trees and shrubs near woods and meadowland, adjacent to the sea and a stony beach. The park is half a mile from the village. A 4-acre site with 40 touring pitches, 10 hardstandings and 54 statics.

**Facilities:**

**Services:** →

**Notes:**

## YSTRAD AERON MAP 08 SN55

### ►►► 71% Hafod Brynog *(SN525563)*

SA48 8AE

☎ 01570 470084

**email:** hafod@brynog.wanadoo.co.uk

**Dir:** *On A482 (Lampeter to Aberaeron road) in village of Ystrad Aeron, entrance next to Brynog Arms pub, opposite church*

★ £8-£11 £8-£11 £5-£11

Open Apr-Oct Booking advisable BH Last arrival 21.00hrs Last departure noon

This mainly adult, peaceful park with fine open views over the countryside is a perfect place to unwind, yet it is within easy reach of the coastal resort of Aberaeron. The village pubs which serve meals are a few minutes walk from the park. A 7-acre site with 30 touring pitches, 2 hardstandings and 40 statics.

**Facilities:**

**Services:** →

**Notes:**

# CONWY

## ABERGELE MAP 14 SH97

*see also Betws-Yn-Rhos*

►►► 83% **Roberts Caravan Park** *(SH937740)*
Waterloo Service Station, Penrefail Crossroads LL22 8PN
☎ 01745 833265
**email:** gailyroberts@btinternet.com
**Dir:** *From Abergele take A548 for 2m, turn left onto B5381 signed St Asaph, park entrance at filling station*

★ fr £12 fr £12

Open Mar-Oct Booking advisable BH & Jul-Aug

A pretty hillside park with countryside views towards the coast. The spacious serviced pitches and excellent toilet facilities enhance this beautifully landscaped park, and will appeal to those seeking peace and relaxation. The friendly owners are always on hand. A filling station and shop are handily placed at the entrance. A 3-acre site with 60 touring pitches.

**Facilities:**

**Services:** →

## BETWS-YN-RHOS MAP 14 SH97

►►►► 77% **Hunters Hamlet Caravan Park**
*(SH928736)*
Sirior Goch Farm LL22 8PL
☎ 01745 832237 & 07721 552106
**email:** huntershamlet@aol.com
**web:** www.huntershamlet.co.uk
**Dir:** *From A55 W'bound, A547 into Abergele. At 2nd lights turn left by George & Dragon pub, onto A548. In 2.75m right at x-rds onto B5381. Site 0.5m on left*

£15-£18 £15-£18

Open 21 Mar-Oct Booking advisable BH & Jul-Aug Last arrival 22.00hrs Last departure noon

A quiet working farm park next to the owners' Georgian farmhouse. Pitches are in two grassy paddocks with pleasant views, and the beach is 3 miles away. The very good toilets, including unisex bathrooms, are kept spotless. A 2-acre site with 23 touring pitches, 23 hardstandings.

**Leisure:**

**Facilities:**

**Services:** →

**Notes:** No tents, no football, dogs must not be left unattended. Baby bath & changing facilities

## CERRIGYDRUDION MAP 14 SH94

►►► 79% **Glan Ceirw** *(SH963461)*
Ty Nant LL21 0RF
☎ 01490 420346 01490 420346
**email:** glanceirwcaravanpark@yahoo.co.uk
**web:** www.ukparks.co.uk/glanceirw
**Dir:** *From A5 Betws-y-Coed onto unclass road 1m after Cerrig-y-Drudion. Park 0.25m on left. From Corwen for 8m, then 2nd left onto unclass road after Country Cooks*

Open Mar-Oct Booking advisable BH & Jul-Sep Last arrival 22.00hrs Last departure noon

A small riverside site in a rural location, with pleasant owners. Guests can enjoy the use of two games rooms, a bar lounge, a jacuzzi, and an amenity block. An ideal touring point for Snowdonia and North Wales. A 4.5-acre site with 15 touring pitches, 9 hardstandings and 29 statics.

**Leisure:**

**Facilities:**

**Services:** →

**Notes:** No cars by caravans or tents

## LLANDDULAS MAP 14 SH97

►►►► 84% **Bron-Y-Wendon Caravan Park**
*(SH903785)*
Wern Rd LL22 8HG
☎ 01492 512903 01492 512903
**email:** stay@northwales-holidays.co.uk
**web:** www.northwales-holidays.co.uk
**Dir:** *Take A55 W. Turn right at sign for Llanddulas A547 junct 23, then sharp right. 200yds, under A55 bridge. Park on left*

★ £16-£20 £16-£20

Open all year Booking advisable BH Last arrival anytime Last departure 11.00hrs

A good quality site with sea views from every pitch, and excellent purpose-built toilet facilities. Staff are helpful and friendly, and everything from landscaping to maintenance has a stamp of excellence. An ideal seaside base for touring Snowdonia, with lots of activities available nearby. An 8-acre site with 130 touring pitches, 85 hardstandings.

**Leisure:**

**Facilities:**

**Services:** →

**Notes:** Wi-fi, tourist info, heated shower blocks

WALES

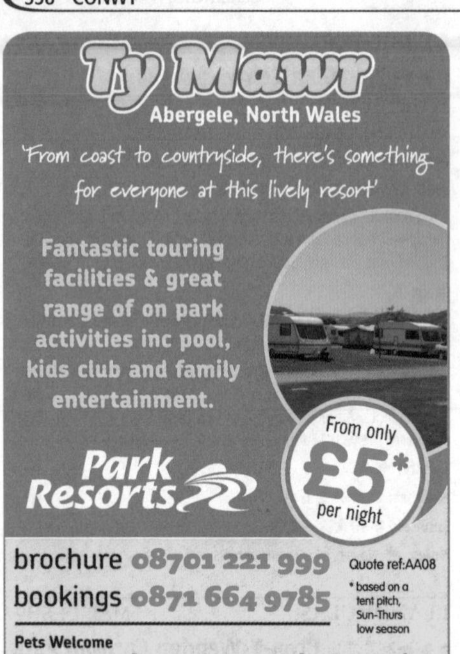


## LLANRWST — MAP 14 SH86

### ►►► 80% Bodnant Caravan Park *(SH805609)*

Nebo Rd LL26 0SD

☎ 01492 640248

**email:** ermin@bodnant-caravan-park.co.uk

**web:** www.bodnant-caravan-park.co.uk

**Dir:** *S in Llanrwst, turn off A470 opposite Birmingham garage onto B5427 signed Nebo. Site 300yds on right, opposite leisure centre*

★ £10-£15 £10-£15 Å £10-£13

Open Mar-end Oct (rs Mar only 1 toilet block open if weather is bad) Booking advisable Etr, May Day, Spring BH & Jul-Aug Last arrival 21.00hrs Last departure 11.00hrs

This stunningly attractive park is filled with flower beds, and the landscape includes shrubberies and trees. The statics are unobtrusively sited, and the toilet blocks are very well kept. There is a separate playing field and rally field. A 5-acre site with 54 touring pitches, 10 hardstandings and 2 statics.

**Leisure:**

**Facilities:**

**Services:** →

**Notes:** Main gates locked 23.00hrs-08.00hrs, no noise after 23.00hrs. 17 multi-service caravan pitches, TV hook up

### NEW ►►► 85% Bron Derw Touring Caravan Park *(SH798628)*

LL26 0YT

☎ 01492 640494 01492 640494

**email:** bronderw@aol.com

**web:** www.bronderw-wales.co.uk

**Dir:** *From A55 take A470 for Betwys-Y-Coed & Llanrwst. In Llanwrst left into Parry Rd signed Llanddoged. Left at T-junct, site signed at 1st farm entrance on right*

★ £13-£15 £13-£15

Open Mar-Oct Booking advisable Last arrival 22.00hrs Last departure noon

Attractively landscaped Bron Derw has been built to a very high standard. All pitches are fully serviced, and there is a new, heated, stone built toilet block with excellent facilities. The tiled utility room, set in a modern conservatory alongside the facility block, houses a washing machine, tumbler dryer and sinks for washing up and vegetable preparation. CCTV security covers the whole park. A 2-acre site with 15 touring pitches, 15 hardstandings.

**Facilities:**

**Services:** →

**Notes:**

## TAL-Y-BONT (NEAR CONWY) — MAP 14 SH76

### ► 88% Tynterfyn Touring Caravan Park *(SH768692)*

LL32 8YX

☎ 01492 660525

**Dir:** *5m S of Conwy on B5106, road sign Tal-y-Bont, 1st on left*

★ £8 £8.50 Å £2

Open Mar-Oct (tent pitches only for 28 days in year) Booking advisable BH & Jul-Aug Last arrival 22.00hrs Last departure noon

A quiet, secluded little park set in the beautiful Conwy Valley, and run by family owners. The grounds are tended with care, and the older-style toilet facilities sparkle. There is lots of room for children and dogs to run around. A 2-acre site with 15 touring pitches, 4 hardstandings.

**Leisure:**

**Facilities:**

**Services:** →

**Notes:**

WALES

## TOWYN (NEAR ABERGELE) MAP 14 SH97

### 72% **Ty Mawr Holiday Park** *(SH965792)*

Towyn Rd LL22 9HG

01745 832079 01745 827454

**email:** admin.tymawr@parkresorts.com

**web:** www.park-resorts.com

**Dir:** *On A548, 0.25m W of Towyn*

★ £8-£36 £8-£36 £5-£33

Open Etr-Oct (rs Apr excluding Etr) Booking advisable at all times Last arrival mdnt Last departure 10.00hrs

A very large coastal holiday park with extensive leisure facilities including sports and recreational amenities, and club and eating outlets. The touring facilities are rather dated but clean. An 18-acre site with 400 touring pitches and 464 statics.

**Leisure:**

**Facilities:**

**Services:**

**Notes:** Free evening entertainment, kids' club

*see advert on opposite page*

# DENBIGHSHIRE

## CORWEN MAP 15 SJ04

*see also Llandrillo*

### ►► 70% **Llawr-Betws Farm Caravan Park** *(SJ016424)*

LL21 0HD

01490 460224 & 460296

**web:** www.ukparks.co.uk/llawrbetws

**Dir:** *3m W of Corwen off A494 (Bala road)*

fr £8 fr £8 £6-£8

Open Mar-Oct Booking advisable BH & Jul-Aug Last arrival 23.00hrs Last departure noon

A quiet grassy park with mature trees and gently sloping pitches. The friendly owners keep the facilities in good condition. A 12.5-acre site with 35 touring pitches and 68 statics.

**Leisure:**

**Facilities:**

**Services:**

**Notes:** Fishing

## LLANDRILLO MAP 15 SJ03

### ►►► 75% ***Hendwr Country Park*** *(SJ042386)*

LL21 0SN

01490 440210 01490 440730

**web:** www.hendwrcaravanpark.freeserve.co.uk

**Dir:** *From Corwen (A5) take B4401 for 4m. Turn right at Hendwr sign. Site 0.5m on right down wooded driveway*

Open all year (rs Nov-Mar no toilet facilities) Booking advisable wknds, BH & school hols Last arrival 22.00hrs Last departure 16.00hrs

Set in parkland at the end of a tree-lined lane, Hendwr (meaning 'old tower') has a stream meandering through its grounds. All around is the stunning mountain range of Snowdonia, and the toilet facilities are good. A 10-acre site with 40 touring pitches, 2 hardstandings and 80 statics.

**Facilities:**

**Services:**

**Notes:** Dogs must be kept on leads at all times. Wet weather camping facilities

## LLANGOLLEN MAP 15 SJ24

### ►► 78% **Penddol Caravan Park** *(SJ209427)*

Abbey Rd LL20 8SS

01978 861851

**Dir:** *From Llangollen on A542, Abbey Rd, turn into Eisteddfodd Pavilion, then over humpback bridge. Site on left*

£12-£14 £12-£14 £12-£14

Open Mar-Oct Booking advisable BH Last arrival 22.00hrs Last departure 16.00hrs

An elevated adults-only park enjoying panoramic views across the beautiful Vale of Llangollen. The Llangollen canal runs alongside this tidy park, offering scenic walks and horse drawn barge trips. Nearby is the Eisteddfod Pavilion, and the Llangollen steam railway. A 2.25-acre site with 30 touring pitches.

**Facilities:** **Services:**

**Notes:** Adults only

### ►► 75% **Ty-Ucha Caravan Park** *(SJ232415)*

Maesmawr Rd LL20 7PP

01978 860677

**Dir:** *1m E of Llangollen. Signed 250yds off A5*

£10-£13 £9-£12

Open Etr-Oct (rs Mar toilet block closed) Booking advisable BH Last arrival 22.00hrs Last departure 13.00hrs

A very spacious site in beautiful surroundings, with a small stream on site, and superb views. Ideal for country and mountain walking, and handily placed near the A5. There is a games room with table tennis. A 4-acre site with 40 touring pitches.

**Leisure:**

**Facilities:**

**Services:**

**Notes:** No tents

WALES

## PRESTATYN — MAP 15 SJ08

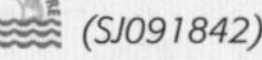

77% **Presthaven Sands** *(SJ091842)*

GOLD

Gronant LL19 9TT

☎ 01745 856471 🖷 01745 886646

**web:** www.presthaven-park.co.uk

**Dir:** *A548 from Prestatyn towards Gronant. Park signed*

Open mid Mar-Oct (rs mid Mar-May & Sep-Oct facilities may be reduced) Booking advisable school hols Last arrival 22.00hrs Last departure noon

Set beside two miles of superb sandy beaches and dunes, this large holiday centre offers extensive leisure and sports facilities and lively entertainment for all the family. The leisure complex houses clubs, swimming pools, restaurants, shops, launderette and pub, and the touring area is separate from the much larger static section. A 130-acre site with 34 touring pitches and 1052 statics.

**Leisure:**

**Facilities:**

**Services:** →

*see advert on this page*

## RHUALLT — MAP 15 SJ07

►►► 86% **Penisar Mynydd Caravan Park** *(SJ093770)*

Caerwys Rd LL17 0TY

☎ 01745 582227 🖷 01745 582227

**email:** penisarmynydd@btinternet.com

**Dir:** *From Llandudno take 1st left at top of Rhuallt Hill (junct 29). From Chester take junct 29, follow signs for Dyserth, park 500yds on right*

★ £12-£16 £12-£16 fr £10

Open Mar-15 Jan Booking advisable BH Last arrival 22.00hrs

A very tranquil, attractively laid-out park set in three grassy paddocks with superb facilities block including a disabled room and dishwashing area. The majority of pitches are super pitches. Everything is immaculately maintained, and the amenities of the seaside resort of Rhyll are close by. A 6.75-acre site with 75 touring pitches, 75 hardstandings.

**Facilities:**

**Services:** →

**Notes:**

## RUABON — MAP 15 SJ34

►►► 72% **James' Caravan Park** *(SJ300434)*

LL14 6DW

☎ 01978 820148 🖷 01978 820148

**email:** ray@carastay.demon.co.uk

**Dir:** *0.5m W of the A483/A539 junct to Llangollen*

★ fr £12 fr £12

Open all year Booking advisable BH Last arrival 21.00hrs Last departure 11.00hrs

A well-landscaped park on a former farm, with modern heated toilet facilities. Old farm buildings house a collection of restored original farm machinery, and the village shop, four pubs, take away and launderette are a ten-minute walk away. A 6-acre site with 40 touring pitches, 4 hardstandings.

**Facilities:**

**Services:** →

**Notes:** Chest freezer

WALES

# GWYNEDD

## ABERSOCH MAP 14 SH32

### ►►► 80% Beach View Caravan Park

*(SH316262)*
Bwlchtocyn LL53 7BT
☎ 01758 712956
**Dir:** *Through Abersoch & Sarn Bach. Over x-rds then next left signed Porthtocyn Hotel. Continue past chapel to another Porthocyn Hotel sign. Turn left, park on left*

Open mid Mar-mid Oct Booking advisable Jul, Aug & BH Last arrival 21.00hrs Last departure 11.00hrs

A compact family park with very enthusiastic owners who make continual improvements. Immaculately maintained grounds and excellent facilities are matched by great sea and country views. Six minutes walk from the beach. A 4-acre site with 47 touring pitches.

**Facilities:**

**Services:**

**Notes:**

### ►►► 78% Bryn Bach Caravan & Camping Site *(SH315258)*

Tyddyn Talgoch Uchaf, Bwlchtocyn LL53 7BT
☎ 01758 712285
**email:** brynbach@abersochcamping.co.uk
**web:** www.abersochcamping.co.uk
**Dir:** *From Abersoch take Sarn Bach road for approx 1m, left at sign for Bwlchtocyn. Site approx 1m on left*

★ £14-£17 £14-£17 £8-£15

Open Mar-Oct Booking advisable at all times Last arrival 22.00hrs Last departure 11.00hrs

This well-run, elevated park overlooks Abersoch Bay, with lovely sea views towards the Snowdonia mountain range. Pitches are well laid out in sheltered paddocks, with well-placed modern facilities. Fishing, watersports, golf and beach access are all nearby. A 4-acre site with 30 touring pitches, 1 hardstanding and 2 statics.

**Leisure:**

**Facilities:**

**Services:**

**Notes:** Families & couples only. Private shortcut to beach, boat storage

### ►►► 74% Deucoch Touring & Camping Park *(SH301269)*

Sarn Bach LL53 7LD
☎ 01758 713293
**Dir:** *From Abersoch take Sarn Bach road, at x-rds turn right, site on right in 800yds*

Open Mar-Oct Booking advisable school hols Last arrival 22.00hrs Last departure 11.00hrs

A sheltered site with sweeping views of Cardigan Bay and the mountains, just a mile from Abersoch and a long sandy beach. The facilities block is well maintained, and this site is of special interest to watersports enthusiasts and those touring the Llyn Peninsula. A 5-acre site with 68 touring pitches, 10 hardstandings.

**Leisure:**

**Facilities:**

**Services:**

**Notes:** Families only

### ►►► 68% Rhydolion *(SH284275)*

Rhydolion, LLangian LL53 7LR
☎ 01758 712342
**email:** enquiries@rhydolion.co.uk
**web:** www.rhydolion.co.uk/caravan_camping.htm
**Dir:** *From A499 take unclassified road to Llangian for 1m, turn left into & through Llangian. Site 1.5m after road fork towards Hell's Mouth/Porth Neigwl*

★ £10-£16 £10-£16

Open Mar-Oct Booking advisable BH wknds & Jul-Aug Last arrival 22.00hrs Last departure noon

A peaceful park with good views, on a working farm close to the long sandy surfers beach at Hell's Mouth. The toilet block is maintained to a high standard by the friendly owners, and nearby Abersoch is a mecca for boat owners and water sports enthusiasts. A 1.5-acre site with 28 touring pitches.

**Leisure:**

**Facilities:**

**Services:**

**Notes:** Families and couples only, dogs by arrangement only. 3 fridge freezers

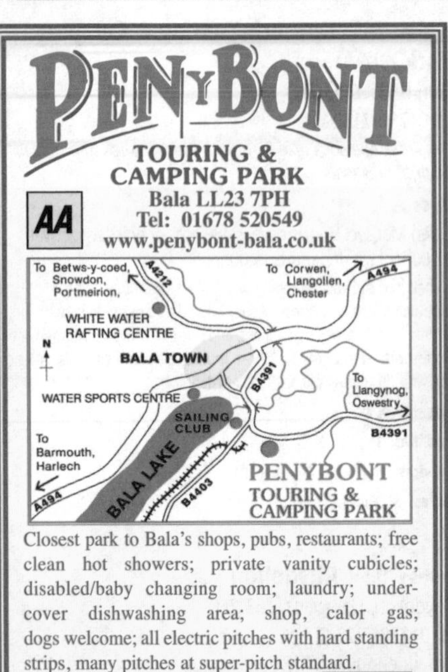

PENYBONT
TOURING & CAMPING PARK
Bala LL23 7PH
Tel: 01678 520549
www.penybont-bala.co.uk
AA
To Betws-y-coed, Snowdon, Portmeirion,
A4212
To Corwen, Llangollen, Chester
A494
WHITE WATER RAFTING CENTRE
N
BALA TOWN
B4391
To Llangynog, Oswestry
WATER SPORTS CENTRE
SAILING CLUB
B4391
To Barmouth, Harlech
BALA LAKE
A494
B4403
PENYBONT TOURING & CAMPING PARK
Closest park to Bala's shops, pubs, restaurants; free clean hot showers; private vanity cubicles; disabled/baby changing room; laundry; under-cover dishwashing area; shop, calor gas; dogs welcome; all electric pitches with hard standing strips, many pitches at super-pitch standard.
An Excellent Four Star Graded Park ★★★★


## BALA — MAP 14 SH93

### ►►►► 77% Pen-y-Bont *(SH932350)*

Llangynog Rd LL23 7PH

☎ 01678 520549 📠 01678 520006

**email:** penybont-bala@btconnect.com

**web:** www.penybont-bala.co.uk

**Dir:** *From A494 take B4391. Site 0.75m on right*

Open Mar-Oct Booking advisable BH & school hols Last arrival 21.00hrs Last departure noon

A very attractively landscaped park in a woodland country setting, very close to the River Dee and Bala Lake. The park offers excellent facilities, and most pitches have water and electricity. Lake Bala is famous for its water sports, with the River Tryweryn catering for enthusiasts of canoe slalom and white-water rafting. A 7-acre site with 95 touring pitches, 59 hardstandings.

**Facilities:**

**Services:**

**Notes:** No camp fires, quiet after 22.30hrs

*see advert on this page*

### ►►► 73% Bala Camping & Caravanning Club Site *(SH962391)*

Crynierth Caravan Park, Cefn-Ddwysarn LL23 7LN

☎ 01678 530324

**web:** www.campingandcaravanningclub.co.uk/bala

**Dir:** *A5 onto A494 to Bala. Through Bethal & Sarnau. Right at sign onto unclassified road, site 400yds on left*

★ £15.45-£19.65 £15.45-£19.65 £15.45-£19.65

Open 13 Mar-3 Nov Booking advisable BH & peak periods Last arrival 21.00hrs Last departure noon

A quiet pleasant park with interesting views and high class facilities, set back from the main road in a very secluded position. Lake Bala offers great appeal for the water sports enthusiast, as does the nearby River Tryweryn, a leading slalom course in white-water rafting. A 4-acre site with 50 touring pitches, 8 hardstandings.

**Leisure:**

**Facilities:**

**Services:**

**Notes:** Site gates closed 23.00hrs-07.00hrs

### ►►► 84% Tyn Cornel Camping & Caravan Park *(SH895400)*

Frongoch LL23 7NU

☎ 01678 520759 📠 01678 520759

**email:** peter.tooth@talk21.com

**web:** www.tyncornel.co.uk

**Dir:** *From Bala take A4212 (Porthmadog road) for 4m. Site on left before National Whitewater Centre*

★ £12-£15 £12-£15 £12-£15

Open Mar-Oct Booking advisable at all times Last arrival 21.00hrs Last departure noon

A delightful riverside park with mountain views, popular with those seeking a base for river kayaks and canoes, with access to the nearby White Water Centre and riverside walk with tearoom. The helpful, resident owners keep the modern facilities, including a laundry and dishwashing room, very clean. A 10-acre site with 37 touring pitches.

**Facilities:**

**Services:**

**Notes:** Quiet after 23.00hrs, silence after mdnt, no cycling & no fires. Fridge & freezer

## BANGOR MAP 14 SH57

### ►►► 73% Treborth Hall Farm Caravan Park *(SH553708)*

The Old Barn, Treborth Hall Farm LL57 2RX

☎ 01248 364399 📠 01248 364333

**email:** enquiries@treborthleisure.co.uk

**web:** www.treborthleisure.co.uk

**Dir:** *Off A487*

★ £13-£20 £13-£20 fr £8

Open Etr-end Oct Booking advisable BH Last arrival 22.30hrs Last departure 10.30hrs

Set in beautiful parkland with its own trout fishing lake and golf course, this well-run park offers serviced pitches in a sheltered, walled orchard. Tents have a separate grass area, and there is a good clean toilet block. An excellent base for families with easy access for the Menai Straits, Anglesey beaches, Snowdon and the Lleyn peninsula. An 8-acre site with 34 touring pitches, 34 hardstandings.

**Leisure:**

**Facilities:**

**Services:**

**Notes:** Dogs must be kept on leads

## BARMOUTH MAP 14 SH61

### ►►►► 79% Hendre Mynach Touring Caravan & Camping Park *(SH605170)*

Llanaber Rd LL42 1YR

☎ 01341 280262 📠 01341 280586

**email:** mynach@lineone.net

**web:** www.hendremynach.co.uk

**Dir:** *0.75m N of Barmouth on A496*

£10-£28 £10-£25 £8-£22

Open Mar-9 Jan (rs Nov-Etr shop closed) Booking advisable BH & Jul-Aug Last arrival 22.00hrs Last departure noon

A lovely site with immaculate facilities, just off the A496 and near the railway, with almost direct access to promenade and beach. Caravanners should not be put off by the steep descent, as park staff are always on hand if needed. Pitches have TV and satellite hook-up as well as water and electricity. A small café serves light meals and takeaways. A 10-acre site with 240 touring pitches, 50 hardstandings.

**Leisure:**

**Facilities:**

**Services:**

**Notes:** 50 TV hook ups

### ►►► 83% Trawsdir Touring Caravans & Camping Park *(SH596198)*

Caerddaniel Caravan Park, Llanaber LL42 1RR

☎ 01341 280999 & 280611 📠 01341 280740

**email:** enquiries@barmouthholidays.co.uk

**web:** www.barmouthholidays.co.uk

**Dir:** *3m N of Barmouth on A496, just past Wayside pub on right*

★ £23-£30 £23-£30 £15-£25

Open Mar-Oct Booking advisable Etr, Whit & Jul-Aug Last arrival 20.00hrs Last departure noon

A good quality park with spectacular views to the sea and hills, and very accessible to motor traffic. The facilities have been completely redeveloped to a very high standard, though were not completed at the time of inspection. Tents and caravans have their own designated areas divided by dry-stone walls, and the site is very convenient for large recreational vehicles. A 15-acre site with 70 touring pitches, 40 hardstandings.

**Leisure:** **Facilities:**

**Services:**

**Notes:** Families & couples only. Milk/bread etc available from reception

WALES

## BETWS GARMON MAP 14 SH55

### ►►►► 78% Bryn Gloch Caravan & Camping Park *(SH534574)*

LL54 7YY

☎ 01286 650216 📠 01286 650591

**email:** eurig@bryngloch.co.uk

**web:** www.bryngloch.co.uk

**Dir:** *On A4085, 5m SE of Caernarfon*

★ £18-£22 £18-£22

Open all year Booking advisable BH & school hols Last arrival 23.00hrs Last departure 17.00hrs

An excellent family-run site with immaculate modern facilities, and all level pitches in beautiful surroundings. The park offers the best of two worlds, with its bustling holiday atmosphere and the peaceful natural surroundings. The level fields are separated by mature hedges and trees, guaranteeing sufficient space for families wishing to spread themselves out. There are plenty of walks in the area, and a constant source of interest is the babbling stream, Gwyrfai. A 28-acre site with 160 touring pitches, 60 hardstandings and 40 statics.

**Leisure:** **Facilities:**

**Services:**

**Notes:** Family bathroom, mother & baby room

*see advert on page 344*

## CAERNARFON MAP 14 SH46

*see also Dinas Dinlle & Llandwrog*

### ►►► 77% Plas Gwyn Caravan Park

*(SH520633)*

Llanrug LL55 2AQ

☎ 01286 672619

**email:** info@plasgwyn.co.uk

**web:** www.plasgwyn.co.uk

**Dir:** *A4086, 3m E of Caernarfon*

★ £11.50-£15.50 £11.50-£15.50 Å £6.50-£13.50

Open Mar-Oct Booking advisable BH Last arrival 22.00hrs Last departure 11.30hrs

A secluded park handy for the beaches, historic Caernarfon, and for walking. The site is set within the grounds of Plas Gwyn House, a Georgian property with colonial additions, and the friendly owners are constantly improving the facilities. A 1.5-acre site with 27 touring pitches, 4 hardstandings and 18 statics.

**Facilities:**

**Services:** →

### ►►► 80% Riverside Camping *(SH505630)*

Seiont Nurseries, Pont Rug LL55 2BB

☎ 01286 678781 01286 677223

**email:** brenda@riversidecamping.co.uk

**web:** www.riversidecamping.co.uk

**Dir:** *2m from Caernarfon on right of A4086 towards Llanberis, also signed Seiont Nurseries*

★ £12-£18 £12-£18 Å £12-£14

Open Etr-end Oct Booking advisable BH & May-Aug Last arrival anytime Last departure noon

Set in the grounds of a large garden centre beside the small River Seiont, this park is approached by an impressive tree-lined drive. Facilities are very good, and include a café/restaurant and laundry. A 4.5-acre site with 60 touring pitches, 8 hardstandings.

**Leisure:**

**Facilities:**

**Services:** →

**Notes:** No fires, no loud music, dogs must be kept on leads. Family shower room & baby changing facilities

### ►►► 71% Ty'n yr Onnen Mountain Farm Caravan & Camping *(SH534588)*

Waunfawr LL55 4AX

☎ 01286 650281 01286 650043

**email:** tynronnen.farm@btconnect.com

**Dir:** *At Waunfawr on A4085, onto unclass road opposite church. Site signed*

Å

Open Etr-Oct (rs Etr & May Day BH open if weather permitting) Booking advisable Spring BH & Jul-Aug Last arrival 21.00hrs Last departure 10.00hrs

A gently-sloping site on a 200-acre sheep farm, set in magnificent surroundings with mountain views. This secluded park is well equipped, with quality toilet facilities. Access is by a single track unclassified road. A 4-acre site with 20 touring pitches and 4 statics.

**Leisure:**

**Facilities:**

**Services:** →

**Notes:** No music after 22.00hrs. Fishing & nature park

## ►► 81% Cwm Cadnant Valley *(SH487628)*

:wm Cadnant Valley, Llanberis Rd LL55 2DF

01286 673196 01286 675941

:mail: aa@cwmcadnant.co.uk

veb: www.cwmcadnant.co.uk

)ir: *On outskirts of Caernarfon on A4086 towards Llanberis, next ɔ fire station*

★ £11.50-£16.50 £11.50-£16.50 £8.50-£16.50

)pen 14 Mar-3 Nov Booking advisable BH & Jul-Aug Last ırrival 22.00hrs Last departure 11.00hrs

et in an attractive wooded valley with a stream is this terraced site vith secluded pitches. It is located on the outskirts of Caernarfon, lose to the main Caernarfon-Llanberis road. A 4.5-acre site with 60 ɔuring pitches.

**eisure:**

**acilities:**

**ervices:**

**lotes:** Family room with baby changing facilities

## :RICCIETH MAP 14 SH43

## ►►►► 80% Eisteddfa *(SH518394)*

isteddfa Lodge, Pentrefelin LL52 0PT

01766 522696

**mail:** eisteddfa@criccieth.co.uk

**veb:** www.eisteddfapark.co.uk

**)ir:** *From Porthmadog take A497 towards Criccieth. After approx :.5m, through Pentrefelin, park signed 1st right after Plas Gwyn ʼursing Home*

★ £10.60-£17 £10.60-£17 £10.60-£17

)pen Mar-Oct Booking advisable BH & school hols Last rrival 22.30hrs Last departure 11.00hrs

. quiet, secluded park on elevated ground, sheltered by the nowdonia Mountains and with lovely views of Cardigan Bay. The wners are carefully improving the park whilst preserving its unspoilt eauty, and are keen to welcome families, who will appreciate the ubicled facilities. There's a field and play area, and woodland walks, ith Criccieth nearby. An 11-acre site with 100 touring pitches, 17 ardstandings.

**eisure:**

**acilities:**

**ervices:**

**otes:** Football pitch, baby bath

## ►► 81% Llwyn-Bugeilydd Caravan & Camping Site *(SH498398)*

LL52 0PN

01766 522235 & 07854 063192

**Dir:** *From Porthmadog on A497, 1m N of Criccieth on B4411. Site 1st on right. From A55 take A487 through Caernarfon. After Bryncir right onto B4411, site on left in 3.5m*

★ £10-£14 £10-£14 £8-£14

Open Mar-Oct Booking advisable Etr, Whit & Jul-Aug Last arrival anytime Last departure 11.00hrs

A quiet rural site with sea and Snowdon mountain views, and well-tended grass pitches. The toilets are kept very clean, and the resident owners are always on hand. A 6-acre site with 45 touring pitches.

**Leisure:**

**Facilities:**

**Services:**

**Notes:**

WALES

## ► 64% Tyddyn Morthwyl Camping & Caravan Site *(SH491399)*

LL52 0NF

01766 522115

**email:** trumper@henstabl147freeserve.co.uk

**Dir:** *1.5m N of Criccieth on B4411*

★ fr £8 fr £8 fr £8

Open Etr-Oct (rs Mar & Oct) Booking advisable Spring BH & Jul-Aug Last departure 14.00hrs

A quiet sheltered site with level grass pitches in three fields. The simple facilities include some electric hook-ups, and the sea is close by. A 10-acre site with 60 touring pitches and 22 statics.

**Facilities:**

**Services:**

**Notes:** Dogs must be kept on leads at all times

## DINAS DINLLE MAP 14 SH45

### ►►►► 80% *Dinlle Caravan Park* (*SH438568*)

BRONZE

LL54 5TW
☎ 01286 830324 01286 831526
**email:** enq@thornleyleisure.co.uk
**web:** www.thornleyleisure.co.uk
**Dir:** *Turn right off A499 at sign for Caernarfon Airport. 2m W of Dinas Dinlle coast*

Open May-Aug Booking advisable Spring BH & Jul-Aug Last arrival 23.00hrs Last departure noon

A very accessible, well-kept grassy site, adjacent to sandy beach, with good views to Snowdonia. The park is situated in acres of flat grassland, with plenty of room for even the largest groups. A lounge bar and family room are comfortable places in which to relax, and children are well provided for with an exciting adventure playground. The beach road gives access to the golf club, a nature reserve, and to Air World at Caernarfon Airport. A 20-acre site with 175 touring pitches, 20 hardstandings and 167 statics.

**Leisure:**
**Facilities:**
**Services:**

*see advert on this page*

## DYFFRYN ARDUDWY MAP 14 SH52

### ►►► 77% **Murmur-yr-Afon Touring Park**

(*SH586236*)
LL44 2BE
☎ 01341 247353 01341 247353
**email:** mills@murmuryrafon25.freeserve.co.uk
**web:** www.murmuryrafon.co.uk
**Dir:** *On A496 N of village*

Open Mar-Oct Booking advisable BH Last arrival 22.00hrs Last departure 11.30hrs

A pleasant family-run park alongside a wooded stream on the edge of the village, and handy for large sandy beaches. Expect good, clean facilities, and lovely views of rolling hills and mountains. A 4-acre site with 67 touring pitches, 30 hardstandings.

**Leisure:**
**Facilities:**
**Services:**
**Notes:**

## LLANDWROG MAP 14 SH45

### ►►►► 75% White Tower Caravan Park

*(SH453582)*

LL54 5UH

☎ 01286 830649 & 07802 562785 01286 830649

**email:** whitetower@supanet.com

**web:** www.whitetower.supanet.com

**Dir:** *1.5m from village along Tai'r Eglwys road. From Caernarfon take A487 (Porthmadog road). Cross rdbt, take 1st right. Park 3m on right*

£16-£24 £16-£24 £16-£24

Open Mar-10 Jan (rs Mar-mid May & Sep-Oct bar open wknds only) Booking advisable BH & Jul-Aug Last arrival 23.00hrs Last departure noon

There are lovely views of Snowdonia from this park located just 2 miles from the nearest beach at Dinas Dinlle. A well-maintained toilet block has key access, and the hard pitches have water and electricity. Popular amenities include an outdoor heated swimming pool, a lounge bar with family room, and a games and TV room. A 6-acre site with 104 touring pitches, 80 hardstandings and 54 statics.

**Leisure:**

**Facilities:**

**Services:**

## LLANRUG MAP 14 SH56

### ►►► 79% Llys Derwen Caravan & Camping Site *(SH539629)*

Ffordd Bryngwyn LL55 4RD

☎ 01286 673322

**email:** llysderwen@aol.com

**web:** www.llysderwen.co.uk

**Dir:** *From A55 junct 13 (Caernarfon) take A4086 to Llanberis, through Llanrug, turn right at pub, site 60yds on right*

£10-£15 £10-£15 fr £10

Open Mar-Oct Booking advisable Last arrival 22.30hrs Last departure noon

A pleasant site set in woodland within easy reach of Caernarfon, Snowdon, Anglesey and the Lleyn Peninsula. The keen owners continue to plan improvements to the site. A 5-acre site with 30 touring pitches and 2 statics.

**Facilities:**

**Services:**

**Notes:** No open fires

## LLANYSTUMDWY MAP 14 SH43

### ►►► 76% Llanystumdwy Camping & Caravanning Club Site *(SH469384)*

Tyddyn Sianel LL52 0LS

☎ 01766 522855

**web:** www.campingandcaravanningclub.co.uk/llanystumdwy

**Dir:** *From Criccieth take A497 W, 2nd right to Llanystumdwy, site on right*

★ £15.45-£18.85 £15.45-£18.85 £15.45-£18.85

Open 13 Mar-3 Nov Booking advisable BH & peak period Last arrival 21.00hrs Last departure noon

An attractive site close to one of many beaches in the area, and with lovely mountain and sea views. There is a good range of well-maintained facilities, and the mainly sloping site is handy for walking in the Snowdonia National Park or on the local network of quiet country lanes. A 4-acre site with 70 touring pitches, 4 hardstandings.

**Facilities:**

**Services:**

**Notes:** Site gates closed 23.00hrs-07.00hrs

## PONTLLYFNI MAP 14 SH45

### ►► 71% Llyn-y-Gele Farm & Caravan Park

*(SH432523)*

LL54 5EG

☎ 01286 660289 & 660283

**Dir:** *Off A499, 7m S of Caernarfon. Right in Pontllyfni by garage*

Open Etr-Oct Booking advisable Jul-Aug Last arrival 22.00hrs Last departure 13.00hrs

A quiet, well-kept farm site with its own path to the beach 5-7 minutes walk away. This small park is in the centre of the village, and is well located for touring the Lleyn Peninsula, Anglesey and Snowdonia. A 4-acre site with 6 touring pitches and 24 statics.

**Leisure:**

**Facilities:**

**Services:**

**Notes:**

## PONT-RUG

*see Caernarfon*

WALES

## PORTHMADOG MAP 14 SH53

79% **Greenacres** *(SH539374)*

Black Rock Sands, Morfa Bychan LL49 9YF

01766 512781 01766 512084

**web:** www.greenacres-park.co.uk

**Dir:** *After high street, turn between Woolworths & post office towards Black Rock Sands. 2m park entrance on left*

★ £15-£84 £15-£84

Open mid Mar-Oct (rs mid Mar-May & Sep-Oct some facilities may be reduced) Booking advisable school hols Last arrival 18.00hrs Last departure 10.00hrs

A quality holiday park on level ground just a short walk from Black Rock Sands, and set against a backdrop of Snowdonia National Park. All touring pitches are on hardstandings surrounded by closely-mown grass, and near the entertainment complex. A full programme of entertainment, organised clubs, indoor and outdoor sports and leisure, pubs, shows and cabarets all add to a holiday here. A bowling alley and a large shop/bakery are useful amenities. A 121-acre site with 48 touring pitches and 370 statics.

**Leisure:** **Facilities:**

**Services:** →

**Notes:** Dogs not allowed during school holidays

WALES

## PWLLHELI MAP 14 SH33

74% **Abererch Sands Holiday Centre**

*(SH403359)* LL53 6PJ

01758 612327 01758 701556

**email:** enquiries@abererch-sands.co.uk

**web:** www.abererch-sands.co.uk

**Dir:** *On A497 (Porthmadog-Pwllheli road), site 1m from Pwllheli*

Open Mar-Oct Booking advisable BH & school hols Last arrival 21.00hrs Last departure 21.00hrs

Glorious views of Snowdonia and Cardigan Bay can be enjoyed from this very secure, family-run site adjacent to a railway station and a 4-mile stretch of sandy beach. A large heated indoor swimming pool, snooker room, pool room, fitness centre and children's play area make this an ideal holiday venue. An 85-acre site with 70 touring pitches, 70 hardstandings and 90 statics.

**Leisure:** **Facilities:**

**Services:** →

## TALSARNAU MAP 14 SH63

78% **Barcdy Touring Caravan & Camping Park** *(SH620375)*

LL47 6YG

01766 770736

**email:** anwen@barcdy.co.uk

**web:** www.barcdy.co.uk

**Dir:** *From Maentwrog turn left for Harlech, on A496. Site 4m on left*

fr £14 fr £14 fr £14

Open May-Sep (NB 2nd facility building only open Spring BH week & mid July-end Aug) Booking advisable at all times Last arrival 21.00hrs Last departure noon

A quiet picturesque park on the edge of the Vale of Ffestiniog near the Dwryd estuary. Two touring areas serve the park, one near the park entrance, and the other with more secluded terraced pitches beside a narrow valley. Footpaths through adjacent woodland lead to small lakes and an established nature trail. A 12-acre site with 80 touring pitches, 20 hardstandings and 30 statics.

**Facilities:**

**Services:** →

**Notes:** No noisy parties

## TYWYN MAP 14 SH50

80% **Ynysymaengwyn Caravan Park**

*(SH602021)*

LL36 9RY

01654 710684 01654 710684

**email:** rita@ynysy.co.uk

**web:** www.ynysy.co.uk

**Dir:** *On A493, 1m N of Tywyn, towards Dolgellau*

Open Etr or Apr-Oct Booking advisable Jul-Aug Last arrival 23.00hrs Last departure noon

A lovely park set in the wooded grounds of a former manor house, with woodland and river walks, fishing and a sandy beach nearby. The attractive stone amenity block is clean and well kept, and this smart municipal park is ideal for families. A 4-acre site with 80 touring pitches and 115 statics.

**Leisure:** **Facilities:**

**Services:** →

**Notes:** Dogs must be kept on leads at all times

# MONMOUTHSHIRE

## ABERGAVENNY — MAP 09 SO21

### 72% **Pyscodlyn Farm Caravan & Camping Site** *(SO266155)*

Llanwenarth Citra NP7 7ER

01873 853271 01873 853271

**email:** pyscodlyn.farm@virgin.net

**web:** www.pyscodlyncaravanpark.com

**Dir:** *From Abergavenny take A40 (Brecon road), site 1.5m from entrance of Nevill Hall Hospital, on left 50yds past phone box*

Open Apr-Oct Booking advisable BH

With its outstanding views of the mountains, this quiet park in the Brecon Beacons National Park makes a pleasant venue for country lovers. The Sugarloaf Mountain and the River Usk are within easy walking distance, and despite being a working farm, dogs are welcome. A 4.5-acre site with 60 touring pitches and 6 statics.

**Facilities:**

**Services:** →

**Notes:**

## DINGESTOW — MAP 09 SO41

### 80% **Bridge Caravan Park & Camping Site** *(SO459104)*

Bridge Farm NP25 4DY

01600 740241 01600 740241

**email:** info@bridgecaravanpark.co.uk

**Dir:** *Signed from Raglan. Off A449 (S Wales-Midlands road)*

£13-£15 £13-£15 £13-£14.50

Open Etr-Oct Booking advisable BH Last arrival 22.00hrs Last departure 16.00hrs

The River Trothy runs along the edge of this quiet village park, which has been owned by the same family for many years. Touring pitches are both grass and hardstanding, and there is a backdrop of woodland. The facilities are enhanced by good laundry equipment. A 4-acre site with 94 touring pitches, 15 hardstandings.

**Facilities:**

**Services:** →

**Notes:** Fishing

## MITCHEL TROY — MAP 09 SO41

### 71% ***Glen Trothy Caravan & Camping Park*** *(SO496105)*

NP25 4BD

01600 712295

**email:** enquiries@glentrothy.co.uk

**web:** www.glentrothy.co.uk

**Dir:** *Approx midway between Monmouth & Raglan, signed off B4293. Site at entrance to village*

Open Mar-Oct Booking advisable BH & high season Last arrival 21.00hrs Last departure noon

A very pretty park in a well-wooded area beside the River Trothy, where free fishing by licence is available. Three large fields are neatly cut, and the friendly owners keep the facilities to a good standard. A 6.5-acre site with 84 touring pitches, 64 hardstandings.

**Leisure:**

**Facilities:**

**Services:** →

**Notes:** No camp fires, BBQs must be purpose built & 18in off ground

## USK — MAP 09 SO30

### 83% **Pont Kemys Caravan & Camping Park** *(SO348058)*

Chainbridge NP7 9DS

01873 880688 01873 880270

**email:** info@pontkemys.com

**web:** www.pontkemys.com

**Dir:** *On B4598 (Usk-Abergavenny road), 300yds N of Chainbridge, 4m from Usk*

£14-£18 £14-£18 £14-£18

Open Mar-Oct Booking advisable BH & Jul-Aug Last arrival 21.00hrs Last departure noon

A peaceful park next to the River Usk, offering a good standard of facilities, including fully serviced pitches. The park is in a rural area with mature trees and country views, and attracts quiet visitors who enjoy the many attractions of this area. An 8-acre site with 65 touring pitches, 29 hardstandings.

**Leisure:**

**Facilities:**

**Services:** →

**Notes:** Dogs must be kept on leads at all times. Mother & baby room, kitchen facilities for groups



**Facilities:** Bath Shower Electric Shaver Hairdryer Ice Pack Facility Disabled Facilities Public Telephone Shop on Site or within 200yds Mobile Shop (calls at least 5 days a week) BBQ Area Picnic Area Dog Exercise Area

# PEMBROKESHIRE

## BROAD HAVEN MAP 08 SM81

### ►►► 83% Creampots Touring Caravan & Camping Park *(SM882131)*

Broadway SA62 3TU

☎ 01437 781776

**web:** www.creampots.co.uk

**Dir:** *From Haverfordwest take B4341 to Broadway. Turn left signed Milford Haven. Park 2nd entrance, 500yds on right*

Open Mar-Jan Booking advisable BH & Jul-Aug Last arrival 21.00hrs Last departure noon

Set just outside the Pembrokeshire National Park, this quiet site is just 1.5m from a safe sandy beach at Broad Haven, and the coastal footpath. The park is well laid out and carefully maintained, and the toilet block offers a good standard of facilities. The owners welcome families. An 8-acre site with 71 touring pitches, 9 hardstandings and 1 static.

**Facilities:**

**Services:**

WALES

### ►►► 74% South Cockett Caravan & Camping Park *(SM878136)*

South Cockett SA62 3TU

☎ 01437 781296 & 781760 01437 781296

**email:** esmejames@hotmail.co.uk

**web:** www.southcockett.co.uk

**Dir:** *From Haverfordwest take B4341 to Broadhaven, at Broadway turn left, site in 300yds*

★ £12-£14 £12-£14 £10-£12

Open Etr-Oct Booking advisable Jul-Aug Last arrival 22.30hrs

A small park on a working farm, with touring areas divided into neat paddocks by high, well-trimmed hedges. Good toilet facilities, and in a convenient location for the lovely beach at nearby Broad Haven. A 6-acre site with 73 touring pitches.

**Facilities:**

**Services:**

**Notes:**

## FISHGUARD MAP 08 SM93

### ►►► 79% Fishguard Bay Caravan & Camping Park *(SM984383)*

Garn Gelli SA65 9ET

☎ 01348 811415 01348 811425

**email:** enquiries@fishguardbay.com

**web:** www.fishguardbay.com

**Dir:** *Take A487 (Fishguard-Cardigan road). Park (signed) 3m from Fishguard, on left*

★ £13-£15 £13-£15 £12-£14

Open Mar-9 Jan Booking advisable Jul-Aug Last arrival after noon Last departure noon

Set high up on cliffs with outstanding views of Fishguard Bay, and the Pembrokeshire Coastal Path running right through the centre. The park is extremely well kept, with three good toilet blocks, a common room with TV, a lounge/library, decent laundry, and well-stocked shop. A 5-acre site with 50 touring pitches, 4 hardstandings and 50 statics.

**Leisure:**

**Facilities:**

**Services:**

### ►►► 74% Gwaun Vale Touring Park *(SM977356)*

Llanychaer SA65 9TA

☎ 01348 874698

**email:** margaret.harries@talk21.com

**web:** www.gwaunvale.co.uk

**Dir:** *From Fishguard take B4313. Site 1.5m on right*

★ £13-£14 £13-£14 £10-£13

Open Apr-Oct Booking advisable Jul-Aug Last arrival anytime Last departure 11.00hrs

Located at the opening of the beautiful Gwaun Valley, this well-kept park is set on the hillside with pitches tiered on two levels. There are lovely views of the countryside, and good facilities. A 1.75-acre site with 29 touring pitches, 5 hardstandings and 1 static.

**Leisure:**

**Facilities:**

**Services:**

**Notes:** Dogs must be kept on leads, no skateboards. Guidebooks available

## HASGUARD CROSS MAP 08 SM80

### ►►► 79% Hasguard Cross Caravan Park

*(SM850108)*
SA62 3SL
☎ 01437 781443 01437 781443
**email:** hasguard@aol.com
**web:** www.hasguardcross.co.uk
**Dir:** *From Haverfordwest take B4327 towards Dale. After 7m turn right at x-rds & site is 1st entrance on right*

★ £20-£22 £20-£22 £18-£20

Open all year (rs Aug tent field for 28 days) Booking advisable Spring BH & Jun-Aug Last arrival 21.00hrs Last departure 10.00hrs

A very clean, efficient and well-run site in Pembrokeshire National Park with views of surrounding hills and just 1.5m from sea and beach at Little Haven. The toilet and shower facilities are immaculately clean, and there is a licensed bar (evenings only) serving a good choice of food. A 4.5-acre site with 12 touring pitches and 42 statics.

**Facilities:**

**Services:** → U

**Notes:** Football field

### ►►► 81% Redlands Touring Caravan & Camping Park *(SM853109)*

SA62 3SJ
☎ 01437 781300
**email:** info@redlandscamping.co.uk
**web:** www.redlandstouring.co.uk
**Dir:** *From Haverfordwest take B4327 towards Dale. Site 7m on right*

★ £12.75-£19 £12.75-£19 £12-£16.50

Open Mar-Dec (rs off-peak shop closed) Booking advisable BH & Jul-Aug Last arrival 21.00hrs Last departure 11.30hrs

A family owned and run park set in five acres of level grassland with tree-lined borders, close to many sandy beaches and the famous coastal footpath. Ideal for exploring the Pembrokeshire National Park. A 6-acre site with 60 touring pitches, 20 hardstandings.

**Facilities:**

**Services:** →

**Notes:** No commercial vans. Use of freezers, extra large tent pitches

## HAVERFORDWEST MAP 08 SM91

### ►► 78% Nolton Cross Caravan Park

*(SM879177)*
Nolton SA62 3NP
☎ 01437 710701 01437 710329
**email:** noltoncross@nolton.fsnet.co.uk
**web:** www.noltoncross-holidays.co.uk
**Dir:** *1m off A487 (Haverfordwest to St David's road) at Simpson Cross*

£8-£13 £8-£13

Open Mar-Dec Booking advisable high season Last arrival 22.00hrs Last departure noon

High grassy banks surround the touring area of this park next to the owners' working farm. It is located on open ground above the sea and St Bride's Bay which are both 1.5m away, and there is a coarse fishing lake close by. A 4-acre site with 15 touring pitches and 30 statics.

**Leisure:**

**Facilities:**

**Services:** → U

## LANDSHIPPING MAP 08 SN01

### ►► 76% *New Park Farm* *(SN026111)*

SA67 8BG
☎ 01834 891284 01834 891284
**Dir:** *7m W of Narberth, along unclass road off A4075*

Open Etr-Oct Booking advisable peak periods Last arrival 20.00hrs Last departure noon

A very pleasant, quiet farm site which has undergone considerable upgrading over the years. The touring area is well landscaped and terraced, and the basic facilities are adequate and very clean. A 2-acre site with 30 touring pitches, 20 hardstandings and 30 statics.

**Facilities:**

**Services:** → U

**Notes:**

## LITTLE HAVEN

*see Hasguard Cross*

WALES

## ROSEBUSH MAP 08 SN02

### ►► 70% **Rosebush Caravan Park** *(SN073293)*

Rhoslwyn SA66 7QT

☎ 01437 532206 & 07831 223166 Fax 01437 532206

**Dir:** *From A40 near Narbeth take B4313, between Haverfordwest and Cardigan B4329, 1m*

Open 14 Mar-Oct Booking advisable peak season Last arrival 23.00hrs Last departure noon

A most attractive park with a large ornamental lake at its centre and good landscaping. Set off the main tourist track, it offers lovely views of the Presely Hills which can be reached by a scenic walk. Rosebush is a quiet village with a handy pub, and the park owner also runs the village shop. Due to the deep lake on site, children are not accepted. A 12-acre site with 65 touring pitches and 15 statics.

**Facilities:**

**Services:** →

**Notes:** Adults only

## ST DAVID'S MAP 08 SM72

### ►►►► 79% **Caerfai Bay Caravan & Tent Park** *(SM759244)*

Caerfai Bay SA62 6QT

☎ 01437 720274 Fax 01437 720577

**email:** info@caerfaibay.co.uk

**web:** www.caerfaibay.co.uk

**Dir:** *At St David's turn off A487 at Visitor Centre/Grove Hotel. Follow signs for Caerfai Bay. Right at end of road*

Open Mar-mid Nov Booking advisable school hols Last arrival 21.00hrs Last departure 11.00hrs

Magnificent coastal scenery and an outlook over St Bride's Bay can be enjoyed from this delightful site, located just 300yds from a bathing beach. The facilities include four en suite family rooms which are an asset to the park. There is a farm shop very close by. A 10-acre site with 106 touring pitches, 14 hardstandings and 34 statics.

**Facilities:**

**Services:** →

**Notes:** No dogs in tent field mid Jul-Aug, no skateboards or rollerblades. Family washrooms

### ►►► 79% **Hendre Eynon Camping & Caravan Site** *(SM771284)*

SA62 6DB

☎ 01437 720474 Fax 01437 720474

**Dir:** *Take A487 (Fishguard road) from St David's, fork left at rugby club signed Llanrhian. Site 2m on right (NB do no take turn to Whitesands)*

Open May-Sep Booking advisable school hols Last arrival 21.00hrs Last departure noon

A peaceful country site on a working farm, with a modern toilet block including family rooms. Within easy reach of many lovely sandy beaches, and 2 miles from the cathedral city of St David's. A 7-acre site with 48 touring pitches.

**Facilities:**

**Services:** →

**Notes:** Maximum of two dogs per unit

### ►► 76% **St David's Camping & Caravanning Club Site** *(SM805310)*

Dwr Cwmdig, Berea SA62 6DW

☎ 01348 831376

**web:** www.campingandcaravanningclub.co.uk/stdavids

**Dir:** *S on A487, right at Glyncheryn Farmers Stores in Croesgoch. After 1m turn right follow signs to Abereiddy. At x-roads left. Site 75yds on left*

★ £14.05-£18.85 £14.05-£18.85 £14.05-£18.85

Open 28 Apr-29 Sep Booking advisable BH & peak periods Last arrival 21.00hrs Last departure noon

An immaculately kept small site in open country near the Pembrokeshire Coastal Path. The slightly sloping grass has a few hardstandings for motor homes, and plenty of electric hook-ups. A 4-acre site with 40 touring pitches, 4 hardstandings.

**Facilities:**

**Services:** →

**Notes:** Site gates closed 23.00hrs-07.00hrs

## ►► 76% Tretio Caravan & Camping Park

*(SM787292)*

SA62 6DE

☎ 01437 781600 01437 781594

**email:** info@tretio.com

**web:** www.tretio.com

**Dir:** *Leaving St David's keep left at Rugby Football Club, straight on 3m. Site signed on right*

Open Mar-Oct Booking advisable BH & mid Jul-Aug Last arrival 20.00hrs Last departure 10.00hrs

An attractive site in a very rural spot with distant country views, and beautiful local beaches. A mobile shop calls daily at peak periods, and the tiny cathedral city of St David's is only 3 miles away. A 6.5-acre site with 10 touring pitches and 30 statics.

**Leisure:** **Facilities:**

**Services:**

**Notes:** Dogs kept on leads at all times. Pitch & putt, ball games area

### TAVERNSPITE — MAP 08 SN11

## ►►► 76% Pantglas Farm Caravan Park

*(SN175122)*

SA34 0NS

☎ 01834 831618 01834 831193

**email:** pantglasfarm@btinternet.com

**web:** www.pantglasfarm.co.uk

**Dir:** *Leave A477 to Tenby at Red Roses x-roads onto B4314 to Tavernspite. Take middle road at village pumps. Site 0.5m on left*

Open Mar-end Oct Booking advisable Etr, Jul-Aug & BH Last arrival 20.00hrs Last departure 10.30hrs

A quiet site in a rural location with pitches located in three enclosures, and views across the rolling countryside towards Carmarthen Bay. There is a large activity play area for children, an indoor games room, and a licensed bar, and the toilet facilities are well maintained. The park is well situated for exploring this beautiful area with its lovely coastline. A 14-acre site with 86 touring pitches, 50 hardstandings.

**Leisure:**

**Facilities:**

**Services:**

**Notes:** No plastic ground sheets in awnings, no kites. Year-round caravan weekly storage

### TENBY — MAP 08 SN10

## 77% Kiln Park Holiday Centre *(SN119002)*

Marsh Rd SA70 7RB

☎ 01834 844121 01834 845387

**web:** www.kiln-park.co.uk

**Dir:** *Follow A477/A478 to Tenby for 6m, then follow signs to Penally, park is 0.5m on left*

★ £12-£84 £12-£84 £12-£60

Open mid Mar-Oct (rs mid Mar-May & Sep-Oct some facilities may be reduced) Booking advisable school hols Last arrival 22.00hrs Last departure 10.00hrs

A large holiday complex complete with leisure and sports facilities, and lots of entertainment for all the family. There are bars and cafés, and plenty of security. This site is on the outskirts of town, with a short walk through dunes to the sandy beach. The well-equipped toilet block is very clean. A 103-acre site with 240 touring pitches and 620 statics.

**Leisure:**

**Facilities:**

**Services:**

**Notes:** No dogs Jul & Aug. Entertainment complex, bowling & putting green

## ►►►► 77% *Trefalun* *(SN093027)*

Devonshire Dr, St Florence SA70 8RD

☎ 01646 651514 & 0500 655314 01646 651746

**email:** trefalun@aol.com

**web:** www.trefalunpark.co.uk

**Dir:** *1.5m NW of St Florence & 0.5m N of B4318*

Open Etr-Oct Booking advisable BH & Jul-Aug Last arrival 20.00hrs Last departure noon

Set within sheltered, well-kept grounds, this quiet country park offers well-maintained level grass pitches separated by bushes and trees, with plenty of space to relax in. Children can feed the park's friendly pets. Plenty of activities are available at the nearby Heatherton Country Sports Park, including go-karting, indoor bowls, golf and bumper boating. A 7-acre site with 90 touring pitches, 29 hardstandings and 10 statics.

**Leisure:**

**Facilities:**

**Services:**

*see advert on page 354*

WALES

**Facilities:** Bath · Shower · Electric Shaver · Hairdryer · Ice Pack Facility · Disabled Facilities · Public Telephone · Shop on Site or within 200yds · Mobile Shop (calls at least 5 days a week) · BBQ Area · Picnic Area · Dog Exercise Area

*TENBY* CONTINUED

►►►► 73% **Well Park Caravan & Camping Site** *(SN128028)*

SA70 8TL

☎ 01834 842179 01834 842179

**email:** enquiries@wellparkcaravans.co.uk

**web:** www.wellparkcaravans.co.uk

**Dir:** *Off A478 on right approx 1.5m before Tenby*

★ £10-£23 £10-£23 £10-£18

Open Mar-Oct (rs Mar-mid Jun & mid Sep-Oct bar, launderette, baby room may be closed) Booking advisable Spring BH & Jul-Aug Last arrival 22.00hrs Last departure 11.00hrs

An attractive park with good landscaping of trees, ornamental shrubs and attractive flower borders. The amenities include a launderette and indoor dishwashing, games room with table tennis, and an enclosed play area. A 10-acre site with 100 touring pitches, 14 hardstandings and 42 statics.

**Leisure:**

**Facilities:**

**Services:** →

**Notes:** Family parties only. TV hookups

►►► 74% **Wood Park Caravans** *(SN128025)*

New Hedges SA70 8TL

☎ 0845 129 8314 & 129 8344 (winter)

**email:** info@woodpark.co.uk

**web:** www.woodpark.co.uk

**Dir:** *At rdbt 2m N of Tenby follow A478 towards Tenby, then take 2nd right & right again*

Open Spring BH-Sep Booking advisable Spring BH & Jul-Aug Last arrival 22.00hrs Last departure 10.00hrs

Nestling in beautiful countryside between the popular seaside resorts of Tenby and Saundersfoot, and with Waterwynch Bay just a 15-minute walk away. This peaceful site provides a spacious and relaxing atmosphere for holidays. The slightly sloping touring area is partly divided by shrubs into three paddocks. A 10-acre site with 60 touring pitches and 90 statics.

**Leisure:**

**Facilities:**

**Services:** →

**Notes:** Only 1 car per unit, only small dogs accepted, no dogs Jul-Aug & BHs

# POWYS

## BRECON MAP 09 SO02

### ►►►► 76% ***Bishops Meadow Caravan Park*** *(SO060300)*

Bishops Meadow, Hay Rd LD3 9SW
☎ 01874 610000 01874 614922
**email:** enquiries@bishops-meadow.co.uk
**Dir:** *From A470 (just N of Brecon) take B4602. Site on right*

Open Mar-Oct Booking advisable BH

A family site with most pitches enjoying spectacular views of the Brecon Beacons. The site has its own outdoor swimming pool, and next door to the park is an all-day restaurant with a lounge bar open in the evenings. Facilities include two good quality amenity blocks. The attractions of Brecon are just under two miles from the park. A 3.5-acre site with 82 touring pitches, 24 hardstandings.

**Leisure:** **Facilities:**
**Services:** →

### ►►►► 90% **Brynich Caravan Park** *(SO069278)*

Brynich LD3 7SH
☎ 01874 623325 01874 623325
**email:** holidays@brynich.co.uk
**web:** www.brynich.co.uk
**Dir:** *2km E of Brecon on A470, 200mtrs from junct with A40*

Open 17 Mar-26 Oct Booking advisable BH & school hols, wknds Jun-Sep Last arrival 20.00hrs Last departure noon

An attractive and well-managed park with views across open countryside towards the Brecon Beacons. Families in particular will enjoy the facilities on offer here, including the centrally placed toddlers play area, large well equipped indoor play-barn, extensive recreation field and adventure playground for older children, and there's an excellent restaurant in a 17th-century converted barn. Brecon is 1.5 miles away. A 20-acre site with 130 touring pitches, 35 hardstandings.

**Leisure:** **Facilities:**
**Services:** →

**Notes:** No rollerskates, skateboards or motorized scooters, only environmentally friendly ground sheets, no commercial vehicles. Off licence

### ►►►► 92% **Pencelli Castle Caravan & Camping Park** *(SO096248)*

Pencelli LD3 7LX
☎ 01874 665451
**email:** aa@pencelli-castle.co.uk
**web:** www.pencelli-castle.co.uk
**Dir:** *Turn off A40 2m E of Brecon onto B4558, follow signs to Pencelli*

★ £17-£22 £17-£22 £17-£22

Open 30 Dec-3 Dec (rs 31 Dec-Etr shop closed) Booking advisable BH & school hols Last arrival 22.00hrs Last departure noon

Lying in the heart of the Brecon Beacons National Park, this charming park offers peace, beautiful scenery and high quality facilities. The park is bordered by the Brecon and Monmouth Canal. Attention to detail is superb, and the well-equipped heated toilets with en suite cubicles are matched by a drying room for clothes and boots, full laundry, and shop. A 10-acre site with 80 touring pitches, 40 hardstandings.

**Leisure:**
**Facilities:**
**Services:** →

**Notes:** Assistance dogs only permitted, no radios or music. Wi-fi. Bike hire, internet access

*see advert on this page*

## BRONLLYS MAP 09 SO13

### ►►► 75% Anchorage Caravan Park

*(SO142351)*
LD3 0LD
☎ 01874 711246 & 711230 📠 01874 711711
**web:** www.anchoragecp.co.uk
**Dir:** *8m NE of Brecon on A438, in Bronllys*

★ fr £10 fr £10 fr £10

Open all year (rs Nov-Mar TV room closed) Booking advisable BH & Aug Last arrival 23.00hrs Last departure 18.00hrs

A well-maintained site with a choice of south-facing, sloping grass pitches and superb views of the Black Mountains, or a more sheltered lower area with a number of excellent super pitches. The site is a short distance from the water sports centre at Llangorse Lake. An 8-acre site with 110 touring pitches, 8 hardstandings and 101 statics.

**Leisure:**

**Facilities:**

**Services:** →

**Notes:** Family room, post office, hairdresser

WALES

## BUILTH WELLS MAP 09 SO05

### ►►► 73% Fforest Fields Caravan & Camping Park *(SO100535)*

Hundred House LD1 5RT
☎ 01982 570406
**email:** office@fforestfields.co.uk

**web:** www.fforestfields.co.uk
**Dir:** *From town follow New Radnor signs on A481. 4m to signed entrance on right, 0.5m before Hundred House village*

★ £10 £10 £10

Open Etr & Apr-Oct Booking advisable BH & Jul-Aug Last arrival 21.00hrs Last departure 18.00hrs

A sheltered park in a hidden valley with wonderful views and plenty of wildlife. Set in unspoilt countryside, this is a peaceful park with delightful hill walks beginning on site. The historic town of Builth Wells and the Royal Welsh Showground are only 4 miles away, and there are plenty of outdoor activities in the vicinity. A 7-acre site with 60 touring pitches, 15 hardstandings.

**Facilities:** **Services:** →

**Notes:** No loud music or revellry. Some dairy produce & cured bacon available

## CHURCHSTOKE MAP 15 SO29

### ►►► 79% Mellington Hall Caravan Park

*(SO252934)*
Mellington SY15 6HX
☎ 01588 620011 📠 01588 620011
**email:** info@mellingtonhallcaravanpark.co.uk
**web:** www.mellingtonhallcaravanpark.co.uk
**Dir:** *Leave A489 1.5m W of Churchstoke turn onto B4385 to Mellington*

★ £16-£20 £16-£20 fr £10

Open all year Booking advisable BH Last arrival 20.00hrs

A small touring park set a mile down a wooded private drive in the grounds of Mellington Hall Hotel, with its attractive bistro. The 270 acres of park and farmland guarantee peace and seclusion, and there is plenty of wildlife and thousands of rare trees. Offa's Dyke footpath runs through the grounds, and this park is ideal for walking, cycling and fishing.
A 4-acre site with 40 touring pitches, 40 hardstandings and 95 statics.

**Leisure:**

**Facilities:**

**Services:** →

**Notes:** No cars by caravans or tents. Hiking maps

### ►► 74% *Bacheldre Watermill Touring & Camping Park* *(SO243928)*

Bacheldre Watermill SY15 6TE
☎ 01588 620489 📠 01588 620105
**email:** info@bacheldremill.co.uk
**web:** www.bacheldremill.co.uk
**Dir:** *Turn S off A489, 2m W of Churchstoke, site on right*

Open all year Booking advisable BH/summer Last departure noon

A secluded little park in the grounds of an 18th-century working watermill on the border of Wales and Shropshire. Tours of the mill can be arranged. A 2-acre site with 25 touring pitches.

**Facilities:**

**Services:** →

## CRICKHOWELL MAP 09 SO21

### ►►► 73% Riverside Caravan & Camping Park *(SO215184)*

New Rd NP8 1AY

☎ 01873 810397

**Dir:** *On A4077, well signed from A40*

★ fr £13 fr £13 fr £10

Open Mar-Oct Booking advisable for stays over 1 week Last arrival 22.00hrs

A very well tended adults-only park in delightful countryside on the edge of the small country town of Crickhowell. The adjacent riverside park is an excellent facility for all, including dog-walkers. Crickhowell has numerous specialist shops including a first-class delicatessen. Within a few minutes walk from the park are several friendly pubs with good restaurants. A 3.5-acre site with 35 touring pitches and 20 statics.

**Facilities:** **Services:** →

**Notes:** Adults only No hangliders or paragliders

## LLANDRINDOD WELLS MAP 09 SO06

### ►►► 78% Disserth Caravan & Camping Park *(SO035583)*

Disserth, Howey LD1 6NL

☎ 01597 860277

**email:** disserthcaravan@btconnect.com

**web:** www.disserth.com

**Dir:** *1m off A483, between Howey & Newbridge-on-Wye, by 13th-century church*

£10-£20 £10-£20 £5-£20

Open Mar-Oct Booking advisable BH & Royal Welsh Show Last arrival 22.00hrs Last departure noon

A delightfully secluded and predominantly adult park nestling in a beautiful valley on the banks of the River Ithon, a tributary of the River Wye. This little park is next to a 13th-century church, and has a small bar open at weekends and busy periods. The chalet toilet block offers spacious combined cubicles. A 4-acre site with 30 touring pitches and 23 statics.

**Facilities:**

**Services:** → **Notes:** Private trout fishing

### ►► 81% Dalmore Camping & Caravanning Park *(SO045568)*

Howey LD1 5RG

☎ 01597 822483 01597 822483

**Dir:** *3m S of Llandrindod Wells off A483. 4m N of Builth Wells, at top of the hill*

★ £8-£11 £8-£11 £8-£11

Open Mar-Oct Booking advisable Jun-Aug Last arrival 22.00hrs Last departure noon

An intimate, and well laid out adults-only park. Pitches are attractively terraced to ensure that all enjoy the wonderful views from this splendidly landscaped little park. Dogs are not allowed. A 3-acre site with 20 touring pitches, 11 hardstandings and 20 statics.

**Facilities:** **Services:** →

**Notes:** Adults only Gates closed 23.00hrs-07.00hrs, no ball games

## LLANGORS MAP 09 SO12

### ►►► 72% Lakeside Caravan Park *(SO128272)*

LD3 7TR

☎ 01874 658226 01874 658430

**email:** holidays@llangorselake.net.uk

**web:** www.llangorselake.net.uk

**Dir:** *Exit A40 at Bwlch onto B4560 towards Talgarth. Site signed towards lake in Llangors centre*

★ £9-£11 £9-£11 £9-£11

Open Etr/Apr-Oct (rs Mar-May & Oct clubhouse, restaurant, shop limited) Booking advisable Etr, May week, summer school hols Last arrival 21.30hrs Last departure 10.00hrs

Next to Llangors Common and Lake, this attractive park has launching and mooring facilities and is an ideal centre for water sports enthusiasts. Popular with families, and offering a clubhouse/bar, with a well-stocked shop and café/takeaway next door. Boats and windsurf equipment can be hired on site. A 2-acre site with 40 touring pitches and 72 statics.

**Leisure:**

**Facilities:**

**Services:** →

**Notes:** Bike hire, windsurfing, fishing from boats

### NEW ►►► 71% Llynfi Holiday Park

*(SO131277)*

LD3 7TR

☎ 01874 658283

**email:** brian.strawford@btinternet.com

**Dir:** *From A40 E of Brecon take B4560 towards Llangorse. Site on right*

With Llangors Common and Lake within walking distance, this is an ideal family location for those interested in water pursuits. It offers a clubhouse with entertainments most weekends, in a stylishly furnished bar and lounge. The two toilet facilities, including a portaloo serving the tent field, offer basic but adequate facilities. 150 touring pitches and 110 statics.

WALES

**Facilities:** Bath Shower Electric Shaver Hairdryer Ice Pack Facility Disabled Facilities Public Telephone Shop on Site or within 200yds Mobile Shop (calls at least 5 days a week) BBQ Area Picnic Area Dog Exercise Area

## MIDDLETOWN MAP 15 SJ31

### ►►► 76% Bank Farm Caravan Park

*(SJ293123)*
SY21 8EJ
☎ 01938 570526
**email:** gill@bankfarmcaravans.fsnet.co.uk
**web:** www.bankfarmcaravans.co.uk
**Dir:** *13m W of Shrewsbury, 5m E of Welshpool on A458*

★ £13 £13 fr £10

Open Mar-Oct Booking advisable BH Last arrival 20.00hrs

An attractive park on a small farm, maintained to a high standard. There are two touring areas, one on either side of the A458, and each with its own amenity block, and immediate access to hills, mountains and woodland. A pub serving good food, and a large play area are nearby. A 2-acre site with 40 touring pitches and 33 statics.

**Leisure:**

**Facilities:**

**Services:** →

**Notes:** Coarse fishing pool, jacuzzi, snooker room

## PRESTEIGNE MAP 09 SO36

### ►►► 72% Rockbridge Park *(SO294654)*

LD8 2NF
☎ 01547 560300 01547 560300
**email:** dustinrockbridge@hotmail.com
**Dir:** *1m W of Presteigne off B4356*

£10-£12 £10-£12 £8-£10

Open Apr-Oct Booking advisable public & school hols Last arrival 21.30hrs Last departure noon

A pretty little park set in meadowland with trees and shrubs along the banks of the River Lugg. A bridge across the stream gives good access to nearby footpaths. Facilities are very well maintained, and the owner is friendly and helpful. Dogs are not allowed on site. A 3-acre site with 35 touring pitches and 30 statics.

**Facilities:**

**Services:** →

**Notes:** Fishing

## RHAYADER MAP 09 SN96

### ►►► 75% Wyeside Caravan & Camping Park *(SO967690)*

Llangurig Rd LD6 5LB
☎ 01597 810183
**email:** info@wyesidecamping.co.uk
**web:** www.wyesidecamping.co.uk
**Dir:** *400mtrs N of Rhayader town centre on A470*

★ £12-£14.50 £12-£14.50 fr £7

Open Feb-Nov Booking advisable BH & school hols Last arrival 22.30hrs Last departure noon

With direct access from the A470, the park nestles on the banks of the River Wye. Situated just 400 metres from the centre of the market town of Rhayader, and next to a recreation park with tennis courts, bowling green and children's playground. There are good riverside walks from here, though the river is fast flowing and unfenced, and care is needed with young children. A 6-acre site with 140 touring pitches, 22 hardstandings and 39 statics.

**Facilities:**

**Services:** →

## TALYBONT-ON-USK MAP 09 SO12

### ►►► 75% Gilestone Camping & Caravan Park *(SO117228)*

Gilestone Farm LD3 7JE
☎ 01874 676236 & 07976 464965
**email:** gilestonefarm@aol.com
**web:** www.gilestonecaravanpark.co.uk
**Dir:** *from A40 onto B4558 to Talybont-on-Usk*

£17-£19 £17-£19 £6.50-£7.50

Open all year (rs 2 Nov-Feb EHU on generators) Booking advisable all year Last arrival anytime Last departure anytime

A family park in an open valley with panoramic views towards the surrounding hills. All pitches in the caravan/motorhome area have individual water points, with a number of fully serviced pitches also available. The separate tenting field has its own facilities and is well-served by electric points. The shop sells a wide range of locally produced products. A 30-acre site with 50 touring pitches, 22 hardstandings.

**Leisure:** **Facilities:**

**Services:** →

**Notes:** Wi-fi. Fishing, bike hire. Dogs on leads. Children must be supervised

WALES

**Services:** Toilet Fluid · Café/ Restaurant · Fast Food/Takeaway · Baby Care · Electric Hook Up · Motorvan Service Point · Launderette · Licensed Bar · Calor Gas · Camping Gaz · Battery Charging

# SWANSEA

## PONTARDDULAIS MAP 08 SN50

### AA Campsite of the Year for Wales 2008

►►►► 80% **River View Touring Park** *(SN578086)*

GOLD

The Dingle, Llanedi SA4 0FH

☎ 01269 844876

**email:** info@riverviewtouringpark.com

**web:** www.riverviewtouringpark.com

**Dir:** *From M4 junct 49 take A483 signed Llandeilo. 0.5m, 1st left after lay-by, follow lane to site*

★ £12-£17.50 £12-£17.50 £12-£17.50

Open Mar-early Dec Booking advisable at all times Last arrival 20.00hrs Last departure noon

This peaceful park is set on one lower and two upper levels in a sheltered valley with an abundance of wild flowers and wildlife. The River Gwli flows around the bottom of the park in which fishing for brown trout is possible. The excellent toilet facilities are an added bonus. This park is ideally situated for visiting the beaches of South Wales, The Black Mountains and the Brecon Beacons. A 6-acre site with 60 touring pitches, 30 hardstandings.

**Facilities:**

**Services:** → 

**Notes:** Dogs must be kept on leads. Outdoor activities organised, tourist information

## PORT EINON MAP 08 SS48

►►► 75% **Carreglwyd Camping & Caravan Park** *(SS465863)*

SA3 1NL

☎ 01792 390795 01792 390796

**Dir:** *A4118 to Port Einon, site adjacent to beach*

Open Mar-Dec Booking advisable Etr, Jul-Aug, BH Last arrival 18.00hrs Last departure 16.00hrs

Set in an unrivalled location alongside the safe sandy beach of Port Einon on the Gower Peninsula, this popular park is an ideal family holiday spot. Close to an attractive village with pubs and shops, most pitches offer sea views. The sloping ground has been partly terraced, and facilities are provided by two toilet blocks which might be stretched during busy periods. A 12-acre site with 150 touring pitches.

**Facilities:**

**Services:** →

**Notes:** Dogs must be kept on leads at all times

## RHOSSILI MAP 08 SS48

►►► 77% **Pitton Cross Caravan & Camping Park** *(SS434877)*

SA3 1PH

☎ 01792 390593 01792 391010

**email:** admin@pittoncross.co.uk

**web:** www.pittoncross.co.uk

**Dir:** *2m W of Scurlage on B4247*

Open all year Booking advisable at all times Last arrival 20.00hrs Last departure 11.00hrs

Surrounded by farmland close to sandy Menslade Bay, which is within walking distance across the fields. This grassy park is divided by hedging into paddocks. Nearby Rhossili Beach is popular with surfers. A 6-acre site with 100 touring pitches, 21 hardstandings.

**Leisure:** **Facilities:**

**Services:** →

**Notes:** Dogs must be kept on leads, quiet at all times. Motor caravan service bay, baby bath

## SWANSEA MAP 09 SS69

70% **Riverside Caravan Park** *(SS679991)*

Ynys Forgan Farm, Morriston SA6 6QL

☎ 01792 775587 01792 795751

**web:** www.riversideswansea.com

**Dir:** *Exit M4 junct 45 towards Swansea. Left into private road signed to park*

Open all year (rs winter months pool & club closed) Booking advisable BH & main school hols Last arrival mdnt Last departure noon

A large and busy park close to the M4 but in a quiet location beside the River Taw. This friendly family orientated park has a licensed club and bar with a full high-season entertainment programme. There is a choice of eating outlets with the clubhouse restaurant, takeaway or chip shop. The park has a good indoor pool. A 5-acre site with 90 touring pitches and 256 statics.

**Leisure:** **Facilities:**

**Services:** →

**Notes:** Dogs by arrangement only (no aggressive dog breeds permitted). Fishing on site by arrangement

WALES

WALES

## VALE OF GLAMORGAN

### LLANTWIT MAJOR MAP 09 SS96

**►►► 79% *Acorn Camping & Caravan Site*** *(SS973678)*

Ham Ln South CF61 1RP

☎ 01446 794024 🖷 01446 794024

**email:** info@acorncamping.co.uk

**web:** www.acorncamping.co.uk

**Dir:** *B4265 to Llantwit Major, follow camping signs. Approach site through Ham Manor residential park*

Open Feb-8 Dec Booking advisable BH, school hols, wknds May-Sep Last arrival 22.00hrs Last departure noon

A peaceful country site in level meadowland, with some individual pitches divided by hedges and shrubs. About one mile from the beach, which can be approached by a clifftop walk, and the same distance from the historic town of Llantwit Major. An internet station and a full size snooker table are useful amenities. A 4.5-acre site with 90 touring pitches, 10 hardstandings and 15 statics.

**Leisure:**

**Facilities:**

**Services:** →

**Notes:** No noise between 23.00hrs & 07.00hrs

## WREXHAM

### EYTON MAP 15 SJ34

## PREMIER PARK

**►►►►► 88% The Plassey Leisure Park** *(SJ353452)*

The Plassey LL13 0SP

☎ 01978 780277 🖷 01978 780019

**email:** enquiries@theplassey.co.uk

**web:** www.theplassey.co.uk

**Dir:** *From A483 at Bangor-on-Dee exit onto B5426 for 2.5m. Park entrance signed on left*

★ £12.50-£22 £12.50-£22 £12.50-£22

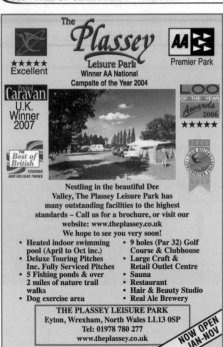

Open Jan-Nov Booking advisable wknds, BH & school hols Last arrival 21.00hrs Last departure 18.00hrs

A lovely park set in several hundred acres of quiet farm and meadowland in the Dee Valley. The superb toilet facilities include individual cubicles for total privacy and security, while the Edwardian farm buildings have been converted into a restaurant, coffee shop, beauty studio, and various craft outlets. There is plenty here to entertain the whole family, from scenic walks and swimming pool to free fishing, and use of the 9-hole golf course. A 10-acre site with 110 touring pitches, 45 hardstandings.

**Leisure:**

**Facilities:**

**Services:** →

**Notes:** No footballs, bikes or skateboards, dogs must be kept on leads. Wi-fi. Sauna, badminton & table tennis

*see advert on this page*

# Ireland

Lough Gur, Co. Limerick

# NORTHERN IRELAND

## CO ANTRIM

### ANTRIM MAP 01 D5

**►►► 78% Six Mile Water Caravan Park**

*(J 137870)*

Lough Rd BT41 4DG

028 9446 4963

**email:** sixmilewater@antrim.gov.uk

**web:** www.antrim.gov.uk/caravanpark

**Dir:** *1m from town centre, follow Antrim Forum/Loughshore Park signs. On Dublin road take Lough road (pass Antrim Forum on right). Park at end road*

★ fr £16 fr £16 £10-£16

Open Mar-Oct Booking advisable at all times Last arrival 21.45hrs Last departure noon

A pretty tree-lined site in a large municipal park, within walking distance of Antrim and the Antrim Forum leisure complex yet very much in the countryside. The modern toilet block is well equipped, and other facilities include a laundry and electric hook-ups. A 9.75-acre site with 44 touring pitches, 20 hardstandings.

**Leisure:**

**Facilities:**

**Services:**

**Notes:** Max stay 7 nights, no noise between 22.00hrs-08.00hrs, dogs must be under control & on leads. Watersport, angling stands & launching facilities

### BALLYMONEY MAP 01 C6

**►►►► 78% Drumaheglis Marina & Caravan Park** *(C 901254)*

36 Glenstall Rd BT53 7QN

028 2766 0280 & 2766 0227 028 2766 0222

**email:** helen.neill@ballymoney.gov.uk

**web:** www.ballymoney.gov.uk

**Dir:** *Signed off A26, approx 1.5m outside Ballymoney towards Coleraine. Off B66 S of Ballymoney*

£14-£17 £14-£17 £12.50

Open 17 Mar-Oct Booking advisable BH & summer months Last arrival 20.00hrs Last departure 13.00hrs

Exceptionally well-designed and laid out park beside the Lower Bann River, with very spacious pitches and two quality toilet blocks. Ideal base for touring Antrim or for watersports enthusiasts. A 16-acre site with 55 touring pitches, 55 hardstandings.

**Leisure:**

**Facilities:**

**Services:**

**Notes:** Dogs must be kept on leads. Wi-fi. Marina berthing, table tennis & volleyball

### BUSHMILLS MAP 01 C6

**►►►► 89% Ballyness Caravan Park**

*(C 944393)*

40 Castlecatt Rd BT57 8TN

028 2073 2393 028 2073 2713

**email:** info@ballynesscaravanpark.com

**web:** www.ballynesscaravanpark.com

**Dir:** *0.5m S of Bushmills on B66, follow signs.*

★ £17 £17 fr £10

Open 17 Mar-Oct Booking advisable Etr & Jun-Aug Last arrival 21.00hrs Last departure noon

A quality park with superb toilet and other facilities, on farmland beside St Columb's Rill, the stream that supplies the famous nearby Bushmills distillery. The friendly owners built this park with the discerning camper in mind. There is a pleasant walk around several ponds, and the park is peacefully located close to the beautiful north Antrim coast. A 16-acre site with 36 touring pitches, 30 hardstandings and 50 statics.

**Leisure:**

**Facilities:**

**Services:**

**Notes:** No skateboards or roller blades

### CUSHENDALL MAP 01 D6

**►► 70% Cushendall Caravan Camp**

*(D 244270)*

62 Coast Rd BT44 0QW

028 2177 1699 028 2076 2515

**email:** cushendallcp@moyle-council.org

**web:** www.moyle-council.org

**Dir:** *On A2, 1m S of town, start of main coast road by lifeboat station*

Open Apr-Sep Booking advisable at all times Last arrival 22.00hrs Last departure 12.30hrs

A pleasant site next to the beach and sailing club, on a spectacular stretch of the north Antrim coast. All touring pitches are fully serviced on hardstandings. 20 touring pitches and 64 statics.

**Facilities:**

**Services:**

**Notes:** Dogs must be kept on a lead at all times

**Services:** Toilet Fluid Café/ Restaurant Fast Food/Takeaway Baby Care Electric Hook Up Motorvan Service Point Launderette Licensed Bar Calor Gas Camping Gaz Battery Charging

### CUSHENDUN MAP 01 D6

**►►► 77% Cushendun Caravan Park**

*(D 256332)*

14 Glendun Rd BT44 0PX

☎ 028 2176 1254 028 2076 2515

**email:** cushenduncp@moyle-council.org

**web:** www.moyle-council.org

**Dir:** *From A2 take B92 for 1m towards Glenarm, clearly signed*

Open Apr-Sep Booking advisable at all times Last arrival 22.00hrs Last departure 12.30hrs

A pretty little grassy park surrounded by trees, with separate secluded areas offering some privacy, and static vans discreetly interspersed with tourers. The beautiful north Antrim coast is short drive away through scenic country. A 3-acre site with 12 touring pitches and 64 statics.

**Leisure:**

**Facilities:**

**Services:**

**Notes:** Dogs must be kept on leads at all times

### LARNE MAP 01 D5

**►► 58% Curran Court Caravan Park**

*(D 408028)*

131 Curran Rd BT40 1BD

☎ 028 2827 3797 028 2826 0096

**Dir:** *On A2, 0.25m from ferry. From town centre follow signs for Leisure Centre, opposite Curran Court Hotel*

Open Apr-Sep Booking advisable peak season

A handy site for the ferry. When the reception is closed, the owners can be contacted at the Curran Court Hotel across the road. A 3-acre site with 30 touring pitches.

**Leisure:**

**Facilities:**

**Services:**

**Notes:** Bowling & putting greens

## BELFAST

### DUNDONALD MAP 01 D5

**►►► 73% Dundonald Touring Caravan Park** *(J 410731)*

111 Old Dundonald Rd BT16 1XT

☎ 028 9080 9100 & 9080 9101 028 9048 9604

**email:** sales@castlereagh.gov.uk

**web:** www.theicebowl.com

**Dir:** *From Belfast city centre follow M3 & A20 to City Airport. Then A20 to Newtownards & follow signs to Dundonald & Ulster Hospital. At hospital right at sign for Dundonald Ice Bowl. Follow to end, turn right. (Ice Bowl on left)*

Open Apr-Sep (rs Oct-Mar open on request) Booking advisable Jul-Aug Last arrival 23.00hrs Last departure noon

A purpose-built park in a quiet corner of Dundonald Leisure Park on the outskirts of Belfast. This peaceful park is ideally located for touring County Down and exploring the capital. A 1.5-acre site with 22 touring pitches, 22 hardstandings.

**Leisure:**

**Facilities:**

**Services:**

**Notes:** Dogs must be kept on leads. Bowling, indoor play area

## CO DOWN

### CASTLEWELLAN MAP 01 D5

**►►► 77% Castlewellan Forest Park**

*(J 335365)*

BT31 9BU

☎ 028 4377 8664 028 4377 1762

**web:** www.forestserviceni.gov.uk

**Dir:** *Off A25, in Castlewellan turn right at Upper Square, turn into Forest Park, signed*

Open Etr-Oct Booking advisable at all times Last arrival 20.00hrs Last departure 15.00hrs

Attractive forest park site, situated down a long drive with views of the castle. The site is broken up into smaller areas by mature trees and shrubs. A 5-acre site with 140 touring pitches, 61 hardstandings.

**Facilities:**

**Services:**

**Notes:** No open fires, dogs must be on leads

IRELAND

## KILLYLEAGH MAP 01 D5

### ►►► 88% Delamont Country Park Camping & Caravanning Club Site

SILVER

*(J 511512)*

Delamont Country Park, Downpatrick Rd
BT30 9TZ

☎ 028 4482 1833

**web:** www.campingandcaravanningclub.co.uk/delamontcountrypark

**Dir:** *From Belfast take A22. Site 1m S of Killyleagh & 4m N of Downpatrick*

★ £15.45-£20.15 £15.45-£20.15 £15.45-£20.15

Open 13 Mar-3 Nov Booking advisable BH & peak periods Last arrival 21.00hrs Last departure noon

A spacious park enjoying superb views and walks, in a lovely and interesting part of the Province. The facilities are of a very high order, and include fully-serviced pitches and excellent toilets. The site is close to Strangford Loch Marine Water reserve, a medieval fairy fort, and a blue flag beach. A 4.5-acre site with 63 touring pitches, 63 hardstandings.

**Facilities:**

**Services:** →

**Notes:** Site gates closed 23.00hrs-07.00hrs

## NEWCASTLE MAP 01 D5

### ►►► 78% Tollymore Forest Park *(J 346328)*

Bryansford Rd BT33 0PW

☎ 028 4372 2428 028 4377 1762

**web:** www.forestserviceni.gov.uk

**Dir:** *From A2 at Newcastle take B180, site signed on right*

Open all year Booking advisable all year Last arrival 20.00hrs Last departure 15.00hrs

Popular site with a family field and a large tent area, set in a beautiful, extensive forest park. There are plenty of walks to be enjoyed, and the coast is a short drive away. A 7.5-acre site with 72 touring pitches, 72 hardstandings.

**Facilities:** **Services:** →

**Notes:** No open fires, dogs must be on leads

# CO FERMANAGH

## IRVINESTOWN MAP 01 C5

### ►►► 84% Castle Archdale Caravan Park & Camping Site *(H 176588)*

Lisnarick BT94 1PP

☎ 028 6862 1333 028 6862 1176

**email:** info@castlearchdale.com

**web:** www.castlearchdale.com

**Dir:** *Site off B82 (Enniskillen to Kesh road). 10m from Enniskillen*

£20-£25 £20-£25 £15-£20

Open Apr-Oct Last departure 14.00hrs

On the shores of Lower Loch Erne amidst very scenic countryside, this site is ideal for watersports enthusiasts with its marina and launching facilities. Other amenities available on the site include pony trekking, pedal go-karting, cycle hire and coarse fishing. An 11-acre site with 158 touring pitches, 58 hardstandings and 139 statics.

**Leisure:**

**Facilities:**

**Services:** →

**Notes:** Wi-fi

## LISNASKEA MAP 01 C5

### ►►► 81% Lisnaskea Caravan Park

*(H 297373)*

BT92 0NZ

☎ 028 6772 1040

**Dir:** *Exit Lisnaskea on B514 to Carrybridge, site signed*

Open Mar-Sep Booking advisable Jul-Aug Last arrival 21.00hrs Last departure 14.00hrs

A pretty riverside site set in peaceful countryside, with well-kept facilities and friendly owners. Fishing is available on the river, and this quiet area is an ideal location for touring the lakes of Fermanagh. A 6-acre site with 43 touring pitches, 43 hardstandings and 8 statics.

**Leisure:**

**Facilities:**

**Services:** →

**Notes:**

# CO TYRONE

## DUNGANNON MAP 01 C5

### ►►► 81% Dungannon Park *(H 805612)*

Circular Rd BT71 6DT

☎ 028 8772 8690 028 8772 9169

**email:** dpreception@dungannon.gov.uk

**Dir:** *M1 junct 15, then A29, left at 2nd lights*

Open Mar-Oct Booking advisable all wknds & BH Last arrival 20.30hrs Last departure noon

Modern caravan park in a quiet area of a public park with fishing lake and excellent facilities, especially for disabled. A 2-acre site with 20 touring pitches, 12 hardstandings.

**Leisure:**

**Facilities:**

**Services:** →

**Notes:** Hot & cold drinks, snacks

IRELAND

# REPUBLIC OF IRELAND

## CO CORK

### BALLINSPITTLE MAP 01 B2

**►►►► 74% *Garrettstown House Holiday Park*** *(W 588445)*

☎ 021 4778156 & 4775286 021 4778156

**email:** reception@garrettstownhouse.com

**web:** www.garrettstownhouse.com

**Dir:** *6m from Kinsale, through Ballinspittle, past school & football pitch on main road to beach. Beside stone estate entrance*

Open 4 May-9 Sep (rs early season shop closed) Last arrival 22.00hrs Last departure noon

Elevated holiday park with tiered camping areas and superb panoramic views. Plenty of on-site amenities, and close to beach and forest park. A 7-acre site with 60 touring pitches, 20 hardstandings and 80 statics.

**Leisure:**

**Facilities:**

**Services:** →

**Notes:** Children's club, crazy golf, video shows, snooker

*see advert on this page*

### BALLYLICKEY MAP 01 B2

**►►►► 77% *Eagle Point Caravan and Camping Park*** *(V 995535)*

☎ 027 50630

**email:** eaglepointcamping@eircom.net

**web:** www.eaglepointcamping.com

**Dir:** *N71 to Bandon, then R586 to Bantry, then N71 4m to Glengarriff, opposite petrol station*

Open 20 Apr-Sep Booking advisable Last arrival 22.00hrs Last departure noon

An immaculate park set in an idyllic position overlooking the rugged bays and mountains of West Cork. Boat launching facilities and small pebble beaches, in an Area of Outstanding Natural Beauty. A 20-acre site with 125 touring pitches.

**Leisure:**

**Facilities:**

**Services:** →

**Notes:** No commercial vehicles, bikes, skates, scooters or jet skis



## CO DONEGAL

### PORTNOO MAP 01 B5

**►► 62% Boyle's Caravan Park** *(G 702990)*

☎ 074 9545131 & 086 8523131

**Dir:** *Turn off N56 at Ardra onto R261 for 6m. Follow signs for Santaann Drive*

fr €20 fr €20 fr €20

Open 18 Mar-Oct Booking advisable Last arrival 23.00hrs Last departure 11.00hrs

Set at Narin Beach and close to a huge selection of water activities on a magnificent stretch of the Atlantic. This open park nestles among the sand dunes, and offers well-maintained facilities. A 1.5-acre site with 20 touring pitches and 80 statics.

**Facilities:**

**Services:** →

**Notes:** No skateboards

IRELAND

# CO DUBLIN

## CLONDALKIN MAP 01 D4

### ►►►► 73% Camac Valley Tourist Caravan & Camping Park *(O 056300)*

Naas Rd

☎ 01 4640644 01 4640643

**email:** info@camacvalley.com

**web:** www.camacvalley.com

**Dir:** *M50 junct 9, W on N7, site on right of dual carriageway after 2km. Site signed from N7*

Open all year Booking advisable Jul & Aug Last arrival anytime Last departure noon

A pleasant lightly wooded park with good layout, facilities and security, within an hour's drive or bus ride of city centre. A 15-acre site with 163 touring pitches, 113 hardstandings.

**Leisure:**

**Facilities:**

**Services:**

# CO KERRY

## CAHERDANIEL (CATHAIR D"NALL) MAP 01 A2

### ►►►► 70% *Wave Crest Caravan and Camping Park* *(V 550582)*

☎ 066 9475188 066 9475188

**email:** wavecrest@eircom.net

**web:** www.wavecrestcamping.com

**Dir:** *From Sneem on N70 (Ring of Kerry road), 1m before Caherdaniel on left*

Open 15 Mar-15 Oct (rs 15 Mar-1 May & Sep-15 Oct shop closed) Last arrival 22.00hrs Last departure noon

Seaside site, with pitches tucked away in the natural contours of the hillside, and offering plenty of privacy. Very good facilities, and an excellent shop. A 5.5-acre site with 120 touring pitches, 65 hardstandings and 2 statics.

**Leisure:**

**Facilities:**

**Services:**

**Notes:** Dogs must be kept on leads. Boat anchorage, fishing, pool, foreign exchange

# CO MAYO

## CASTLEBAR MAP 01 B4

### ►►►► 74% Lough Lannagh Caravan Park

*(M 140890)*

Old Westport Rd

☎ 094 9027111 094 9027295

**email:** llv@eircom.net

**web:** www.loughlannagh.ie

**Dir:** *N5 around Castlebar. 2nd exit at 3rd rdbt, past playground, 1st building on right.*

€21-€28 €21-€28 €21-€28

Open 14 Mar-Oct Booking advisable Jun-Aug Last arrival 20.00hrs Last departure 10.00hrs

This park is part of the Lough Lannagh Village which is situated in a wooded area a short walk form Castlebar town. Leisure facilities include a purpose built fitness and relaxation centre, tennis courts, kid's play area and café. A 2.5-acre site with 20 touring pitches, 20 hardstandings.

**Leisure:** **Facilities:**

**Services:**

**Notes:** No pets Jul & Aug. Use of fitness club, table tennis & boules

## KNOCK MAP 01 B4

### ►►► 77% Knock Caravan and Camping Park *(M 408828)*

Claremorris Rd

☎ 094 9388100 094 9388295

**email:** info@knock-shrine.ie

**web:** www.knock-shrine.ie/accommodation

**Dir:** *From rdbt in Knock, through town. Park entrance on left 1km, opp petrol station*

★ €19.75-€21.75 €19.75-€21.75 €19.75-€21.75

Open Mar-Nov Booking advisable Aug Last arrival 22.00hrs Last departure noon

A pleasant, very well maintained caravan park within the grounds of Knock Shrine, offering spacious terraced pitches and excellent facilities. A 10-acre site with 88 touring pitches, 88 hardstandings and 12 statics.

**Leisure:**

**Facilities:**

**Services:**

**Notes:** Dogs must be kept on leads

# CO ROSCOMMON

## BOYLE MAP 01 B4

### ►►►► 70% Lough Key Forest Park

*(G 846039)*

☎ 071 9662212

**web:** www.loughkey.ie

**Dir:** *Follow Lough Key Forest Park signs, site within grounds.*

★ €16-€20 €8-€10

Open 14 Apr-10 Sep Booking essential 3 weeks before arrival Last arrival 22.00hrs Last departure noon

Peaceful and very secluded site within the extensive grounds of a beautiful forest park. Lough Key offers boat trips and waterside walks, and there is a viewing tower. A 15-acre site with 72 touring pitches, 52 hardstandings.

**Leisure:**

**Facilities:**

**Services:**

**Notes:** No cars by tents

# CO WATERFORD

## CLONEA MAP 01 C2

### ►►► 76% Casey's Caravan Park *(X 320937)*

☎ 058 41919 058 41919

**Dir:** *From R675 (Dungarvan road), follow signs to Clonea Bay. Site at end of road*

€23-€26 €23-€26 €23-€26

Open 21 Mar-7 Sep Booking advisable May-Jun (ex BH wknds) Last arrival 22.00hrs Last departure noon

Spacious, well-kept park with excellent toilet facilities, next to beach. A 4.5-acre site with 108 touring pitches and 170 statics.

**Leisure:**

**Facilities:**

**Services:**

**Notes:** Dogs must be on leads at all times. Crazy golf & games room

IRELAND

**Leisure:** Indoor swimming pool · Outdoor swimming pool · Tennis court · Games room · Children's playground · Stables · 9/18 hole golf course · Boats for hire · Cinema · Fishing · Mini golf · Watersports · Separate TV room

# Index

Entries are listed alphabetically by town name, then campsite name. The following abreviations have been used: C&C - Caravan & Camping/Caravan & Campsite: HP - Holiday Park; CP - Caravan Park; C&C Club - Camping & Carvanning Club Site

# County Maps

The county map shown here will help you identify the counties within each country. You can look up each county in the guide using the county names at the top of each page. To find towns featured in the guide use the atlas and the index.

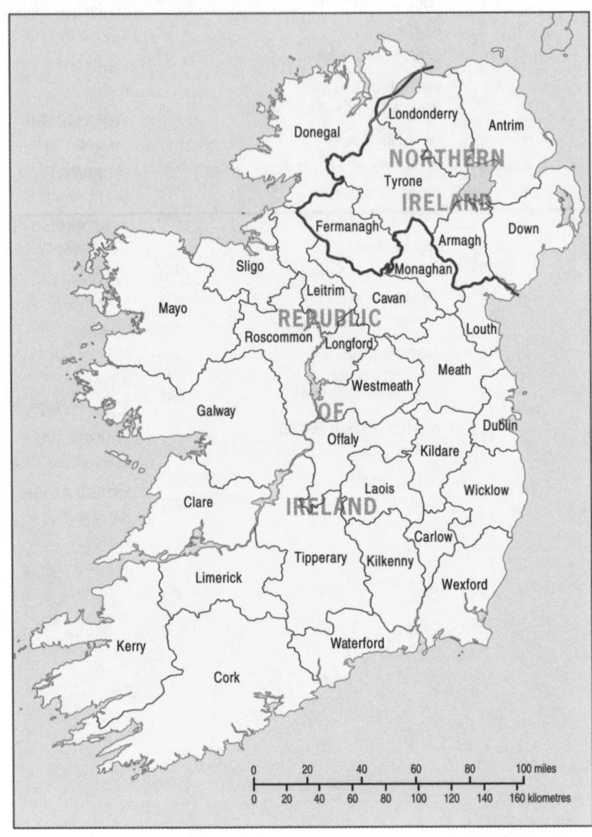


## England

1 Bedfordshire
2 Berkshire
3 Bristol
4 Buckinghamshire
5 Cambridgeshire
6 Greater Manchester
7 Herefordshire
8 Hertfordshire
9 Leicestershire
10 Northamptonshire
11 Nottinghamshire
12 Rutland
13 Staffordshire
14 Warwickshire
15 West Midlands
16 Worcestershire

## Scotland

17 City of Glasgow
18 Clackmannanshire
19 East Ayrshire
20 East Dunbartonshire
21 East Renfrewshire
22 Perth & Kinross
23 Renfrewshire
24 South Lanarkshire
25 West Dunbartonshire

## Wales

26 Blaenau Gwent
27 Bridgend
28 Caerphilly
29 Denbighshire
30 Flintshire
31 Merthyr Tydfil
32 Monmouthshire
33 Neath Port Talbot
34 Newport
35 Rhondda Cynon Taff
36 Torfaen
37 Vale of Glamorgan
38 Wrexham

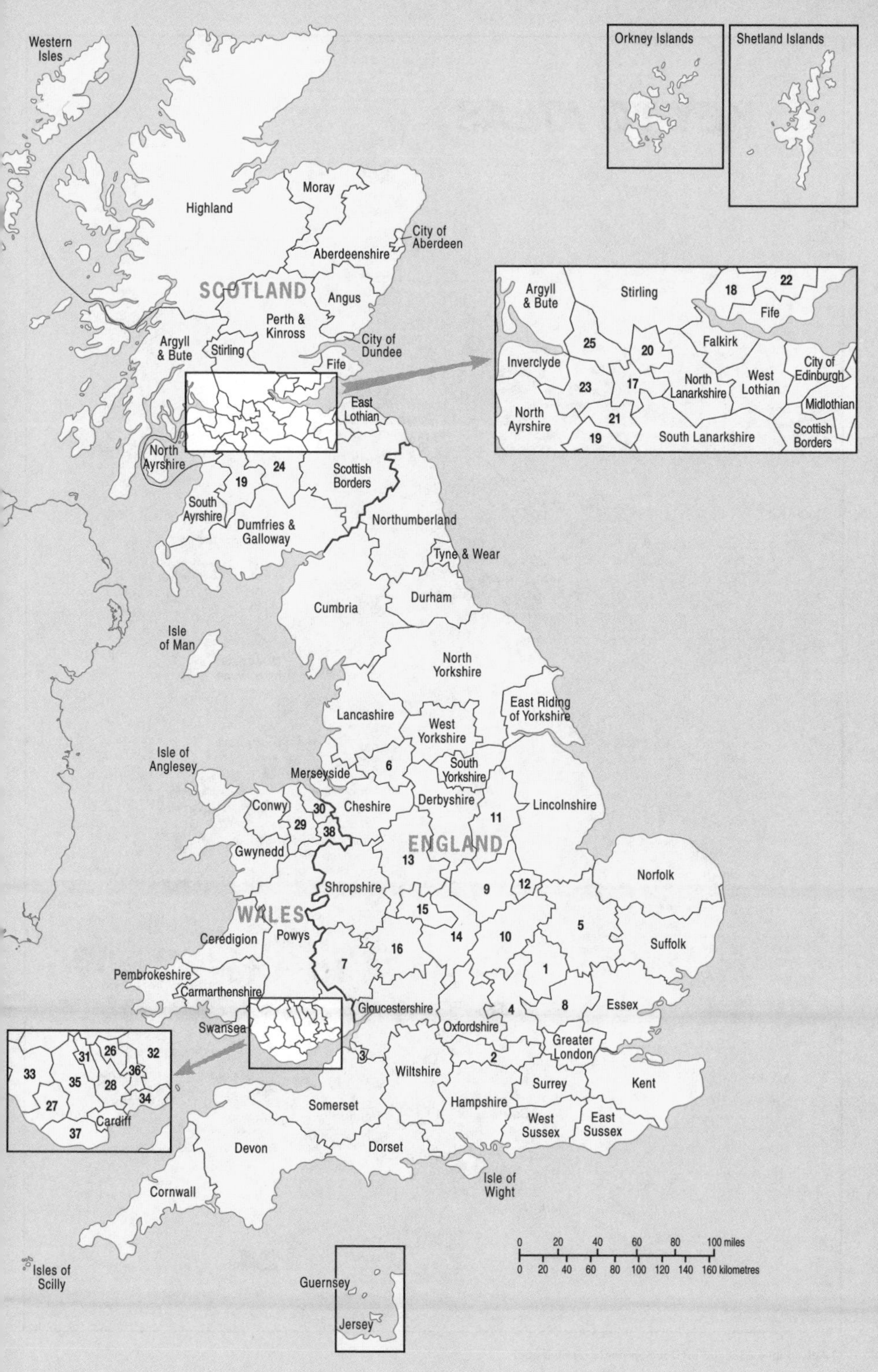

Western Isles
Orkney Islands
Shetland Islands
Highland
Moray
City of Aberdeen
Aberdeenshire
SCOTLAND
Angus
Perth & Kinross
Argyll & Bute
Stirling
City of Dundee
Fife
East Lothian
North Ayrshire
24
19
Scottish Borders
South Ayrshire
Dumfries & Galloway
Northumberland
Tyne & Wear
Durham
Cumbria
Isle of Man
North Yorkshire
East Riding of Yorkshire
Lancashire
West Yorkshire
Isle of Anglesey
6
South Yorkshire
Merseyside
Conwy
30
Cheshire
Derbyshire
11
Lincolnshire
29
38
Gwynedd
ENGLAND
13
Norfolk
Shropshire
9
12
15
WALES
5
Ceredigion
Powys
14
10
Suffolk
16
1
Pembrokeshire
7
Carmarthenshire
8
Essex
Gloucestershire
4
Swansea
Oxfordshire
Greater London
3
2
Wiltshire
Surrey
Kent
Somerset
Hampshire
West Sussex
East Sussex
Devon
Dorset
Isle of Wight
Cornwall
Isles of Scilly
Guernsey
Jersey
Argyll & Bute
Stirling
18
22
Fife
25
20
Falkirk
Inverclyde
City of Edinburgh
North Lanarkshire
West Lothian
23
17
Midlothian
North Ayrshire
21
Scottish Borders
19
South Lanarkshire
31
26
32
33
35
36
28
34
27
Cardiff
37
0 20 40 60 80 100 miles
0 20 40 60 80 100 120 140 160 kilometres

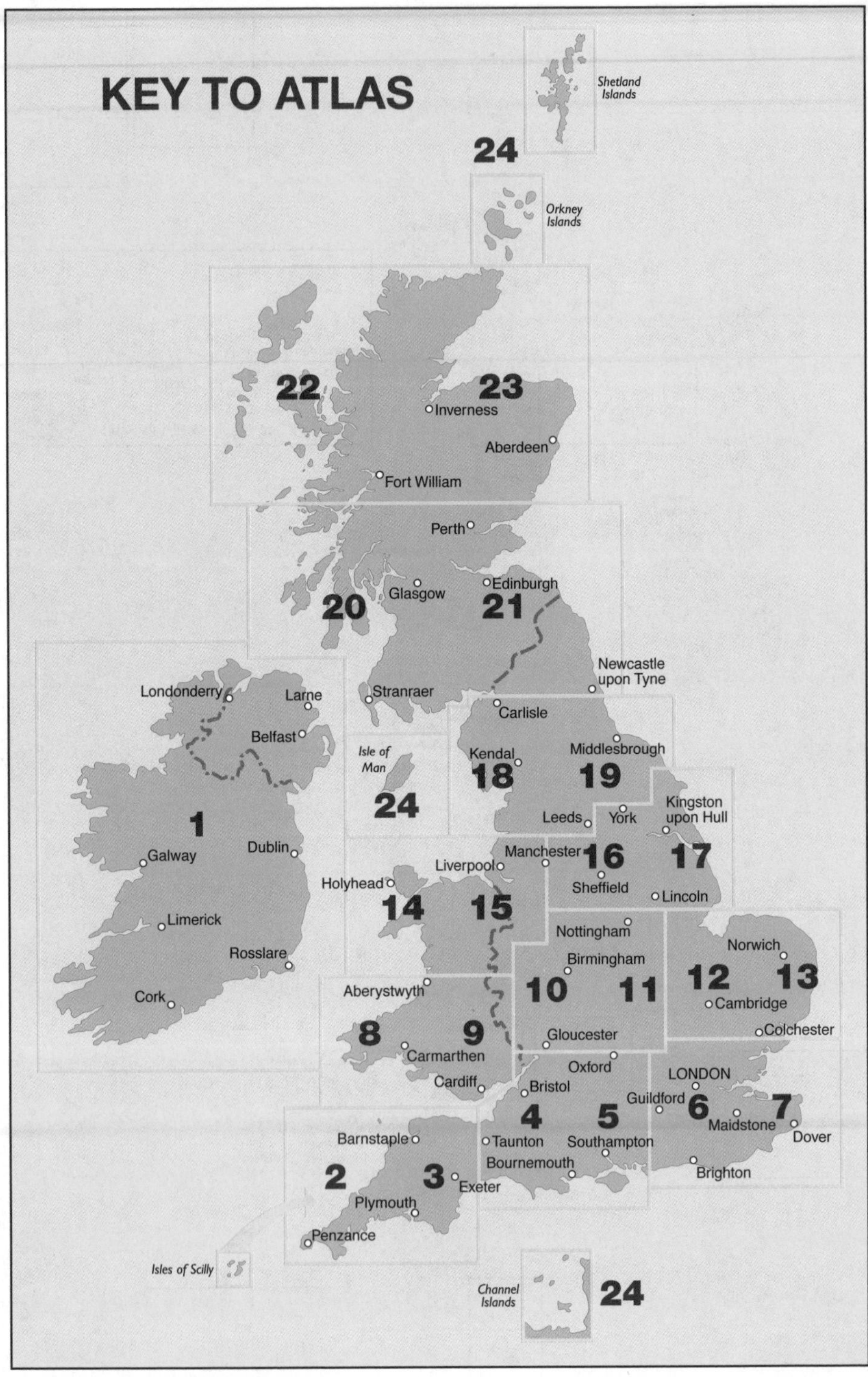
KEY TO ATLAS
Shetland Islands
24
Orkney Islands
22
23
Inverness
Aberdeen
Fort William
Perth
Edinburgh
Glasgow
20
21
Newcastle upon Tyne
Londonderry
Larne
Stranraer
Carlisle
Belfast
Isle of Man
24
Kendal
Middlesbrough
18
19
1
Leeds
York
Kingston upon Hull
Galway
Dublin
Manchester
16
17
Liverpool
Holyhead
Sheffield
Lincoln
14
15
Limerick
Nottingham
Norwich
Birmingham
Rosslare
12
13
10
11
Cork
Aberystwyth
Cambridge
Colchester
8
9
Gloucester
Carmarthen
Oxford
LONDON
Cardiff
Bristol
Guildford
6
7
4
5
Maidstone
Barnstaple
Taunton
Southampton
Dover
Bournemouth
2
3
Exeter
Brighton
Plymouth
Penzance
Isles of Scilly
Channel Islands
24

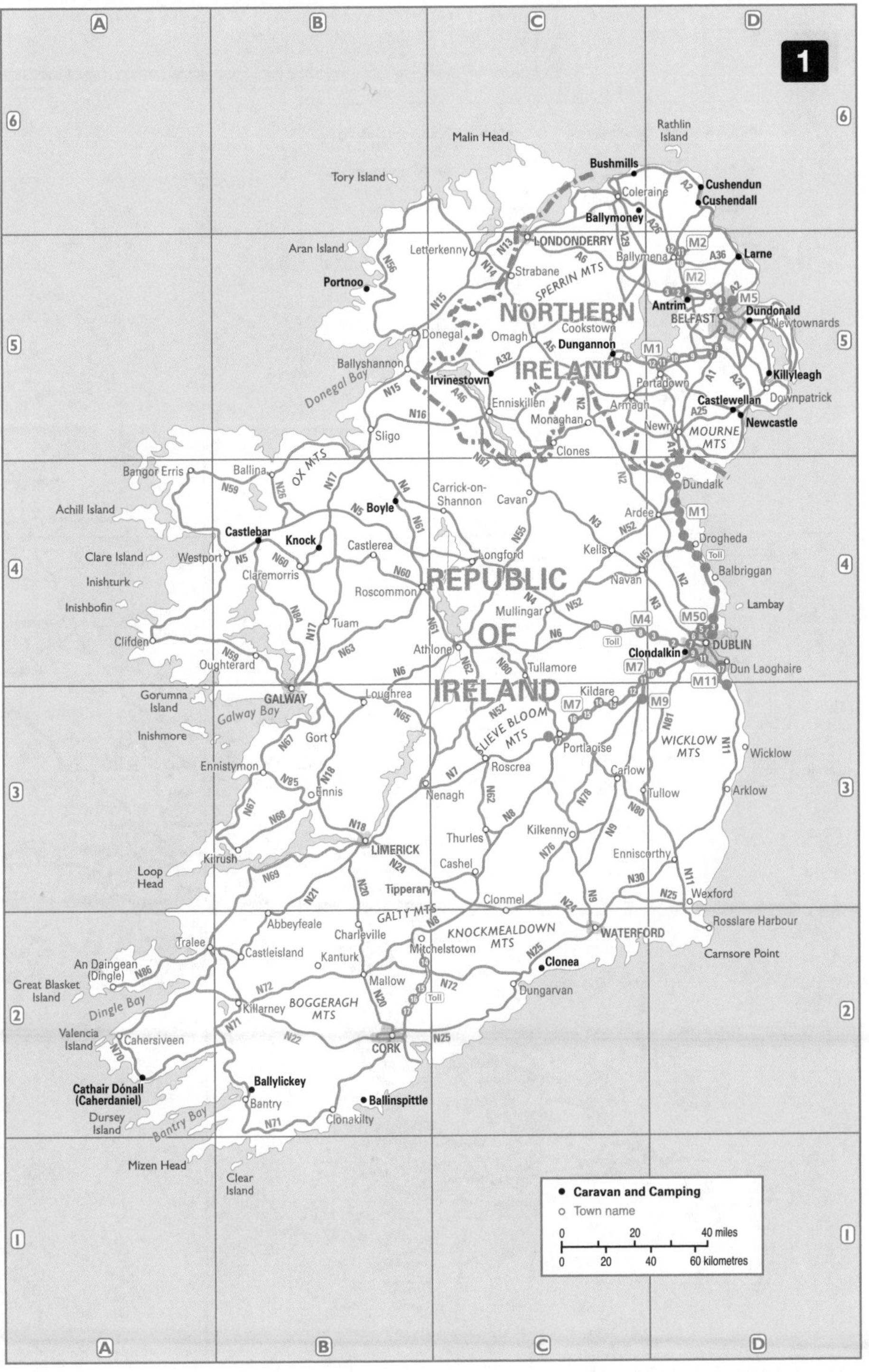
1
A
B
C
D
6
5
4
3
2
1
Malin Head
Rathlin Island
Tory Island
Bushmills
Cushendun
Cushendall
Coleraine
Ballymoney
Aran Island
Letterkenny
LONDONDERRY
Ballymena
Larne
Portnoo
Strabane
SPERRIN MTS
NORTHERN IRELAND
Antrim
BELFAST
Dundonald
Newtownards
Donegal
Omagh
Cookstown
Dungannon
Ballyshannon
Donegal Bay
Irvinestown
Portadown
Killyleagh
Enniskillen
Armagh
Downpatrick
Castlewellan
Newcastle
Monaghan
Newry
MOURNE MTS
Sligo
Clones
Bangor Erris
Ballina
OX MTS
Dundalk
Achill Island
Carrick-on-Shannon
Cavan
Boyle
Ardee
Castlebar
Knock
Drogheda
Clare Island
Westport
Castlerea
Kells
Longford
Balbriggan
Claremorris
REPUBLIC OF IRELAND
Inishturk
Roscommon
Navan
Inishbofin
Lambay
Mullingar
Tuam
Clifden
Athlone
DUBLIN
Clondalkin
Oughterard
Tullamore
Dun Laoghaire
GALWAY
Gorumna Island
Loughrea
Kildare
Galway Bay
Inishmore
Gort
SLIEVE BLOOM MTS
Portlaoise
WICKLOW MTS
Wicklow
Roscrea
Ennistymon
Carlow
Ennis
Nenagh
Tullow
Arklow
Thurles
Kilkenny
LIMERICK
Kilrush
Loop Head
Cashel
Enniscorthy
Tipperary
Wexford
Clonmel
GALTY MTS
Abbeyfeale
Rosslare Harbour
Tralee
Charleville
KNOCKMEALDOWN MTS
WATERFORD
Castleisland
Mitchelstown
Carnsore Point
An Daingean (Dingle)
Kanturk
Clonea
Great Blasket Island
Mallow
Dungarvan
Dingle Bay
Killarney
BOGGERAGH MTS
Valencia Island
Cahersiveen
CORK
Cathair Dónall (Caherdaniel)
Ballylickey
Bantry
Ballinspittle
Dursey Island
Bantry Bay
Clonakilty
Mizen Head
Clear Island
Caravan and Camping
Town name
0 20 40 miles
0 20 40 60 kilometres

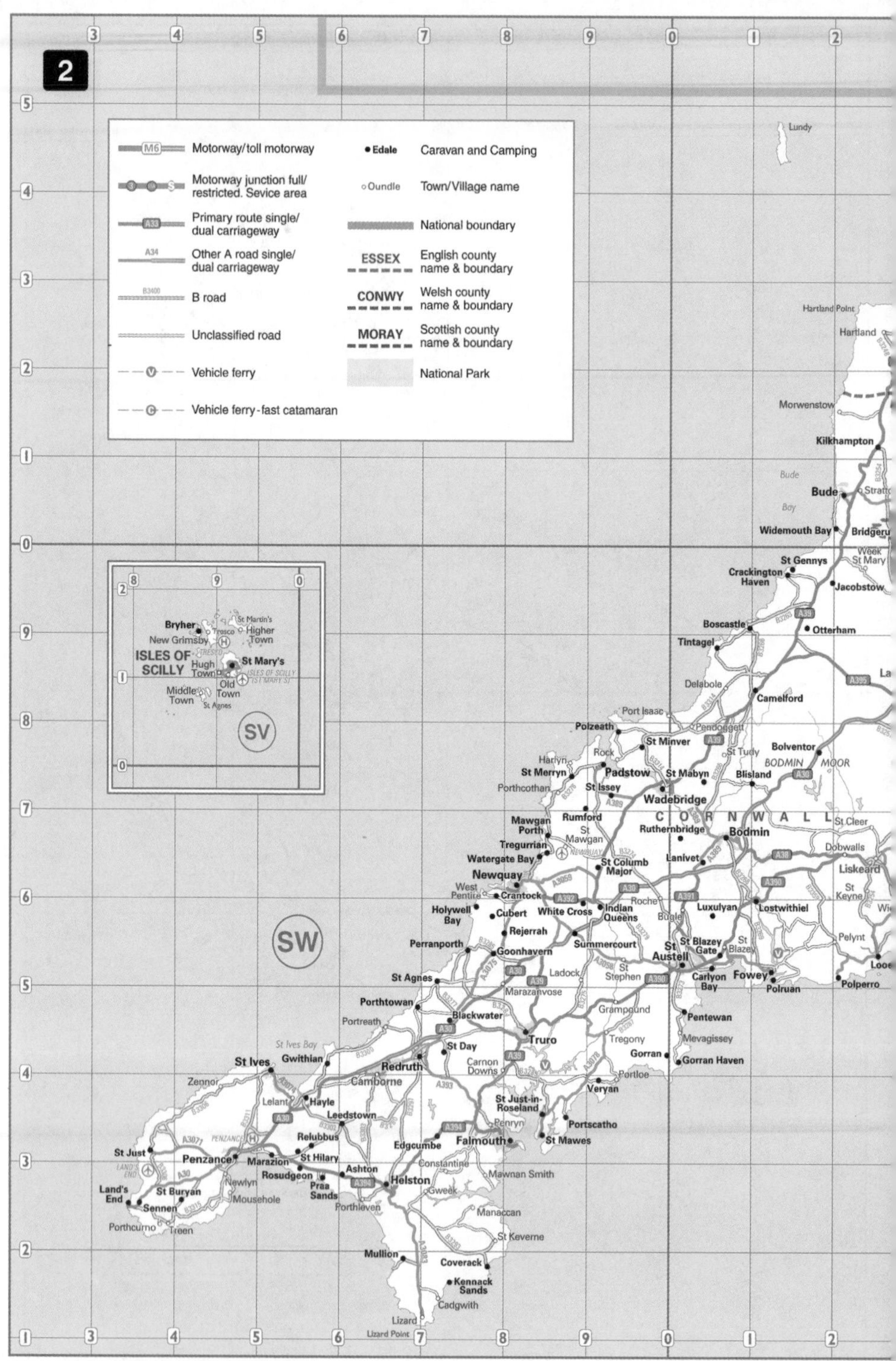


For continuation pages refer to numbered arrows

SUPER-MARE
Brean
Bridgwater Bay
3
9
Lynmouth
Lynton
Oare
Brendon
Porlock Weir
Porlock
Minehead
Ilfracombe
Combe Martin
Berrynarbor
Lee
Mortehoe
Woolacombe
Parracombe
EXMOOR
NATIONAL
PARK
Wootton Courtenay
Dunster
Blue Anchor
Watchet
Carhampton
Burnham-on-Sea
Highbridge
West Huntspill
Kilve
Stogursey
Sampford Brett
Nether Stowey
Cannington
QUANTOCK HILLS
Bridgwater
Crowcombe
Goathurst
North Petherton
Georgeham
Croyde Bay
Croyde
Saunton
Braunton
Chivenor
Muddiford
Bratton Fleming
Challacombe
Simonsbath
Exford
Wheddon Cross
Withypool
Winsford
Bridgetown
Brayford
Elworthy
Barnstaple
Bornstaple or Bideford Bay
Appledore
Instow
Northam
Westward Ho!
Bideford
Clovelly
Horns Cross
SS
North Molton
Molland
Dulverton
Brompton Regis
Wiveliscombe
Fitzhead
ST
Taunton
South Molton
East Anstey
Exbridge
Petton
Milverton
North Curry
Umberleigh
Bampton
Wellington
Sampford Arundel
Hatch Beauchamp
Monkleigh
Great Torrington
Chittlehamholt
Rackenford
Taunton Deane
Corfe
Staple Fitzpaine
Little Torrington
Burrington
Beaford
Stibb Cross
Chulmleigh
East Worlington
Witheridge
Sampford Peverell
Culmstock
Horton
Bradworthy
Chawleigh
Tiverton
Halberton
Uffculme
Hemyock
Dolton
Merton
Milton Damerel
Eggesford
Willand
Shebbear
Meeth
Winkleigh
Lapford
Cheriton Fitzpaine
Cullompton
Kentisbeare
Upottery
Chilsworthy
Black Torrington
Sheepwash
Morchard Bishop
Bickleigh
Yarcombe
Holsworthy
Highampton
Hatherleigh
Copplestone
Silverton
Tytherleigh
Halwill Junction
Crediton
Honiton
Fenny Bridges
Wilmington
Clawton
Beaworthy
DEVON
Newton St Cyres
Stoke Canon
Broadclyst
Whimple
Axminster
Ashwater
Okehampton
Tedburn St Mary
Shute
Chapmans Well
EXETER
Ottery St Mary
Colyton
Colyford
Uplyme
Bratton Clovelly
South Zeal
Crockernwell
Clyst St Mary
Broadwoodwidger
Sourton Cross
Sourton
Whiddon Down
Drewsteignton
Woodbury
Salterton
Axmouth
Seaton
Beer
Bridestowe
Dunsford
Topsham
Branscombe
Chagford
Kennford
Exminster
Sidmouth
DARTMOOR
Lydford
Moretonhampstead
Otterton
Lifton
Kenton
Milton Abbot
Budleigh Salterton
Chudleigh
Exmouth
Lamerton
Mary Tavy
Postbridge
Widecombe in the Moor
Bovey Tracey
Ideford
NATIONAL
Tavistock
Chudleigh Knighton
Dawlish
Princetown
Bishopsteignton
Teignmouth
Gunnislake
Hexworthy
Bickington
Kingsteignton
Shaldon
Pensilva
Callington
Horrabridge
Ashburton
Newton Abbot
Dousland
Holne
Kingskerswell
Maidencombe
Bere Alston
Yelverton
PARK
Buckfastleigh
SY
Pillaton
Bere Ferrers
Ipplepen
Shaugh Prior
Dartington
TORQUAY
Landrake
South Brent
Cornwood
Totnes
Paignton
Saltash
Wrangaton
Stoke Gabriel
Tor Bay
Plympton
Ivybridge
Churston Ferrers
Polbathic
Downderry
Harbertonford
Brixham
Torpoint
PLYMOUTH
Ugborough
Dittisham
Crafthole
Halwell
Millbrook
Heybrook Bay
Brixton
Yealmpton
Modbury
Kingswear
Cawsand
Holbeton
Dartmouth
Aveton Gifford
East Allington
Wembury
Newton Ferrers
Stoke Fleming
SX
Strete
Bigbury-on-Sea
Kingsbridge
Slapton
Bigbury Bay
Start Bay
Thurlestone
Chillington
Hope
Torcross
Malborough
Salcombe
Hallsands
Start Point
East Prawle
0
10 miles
0
10
20 kilometres

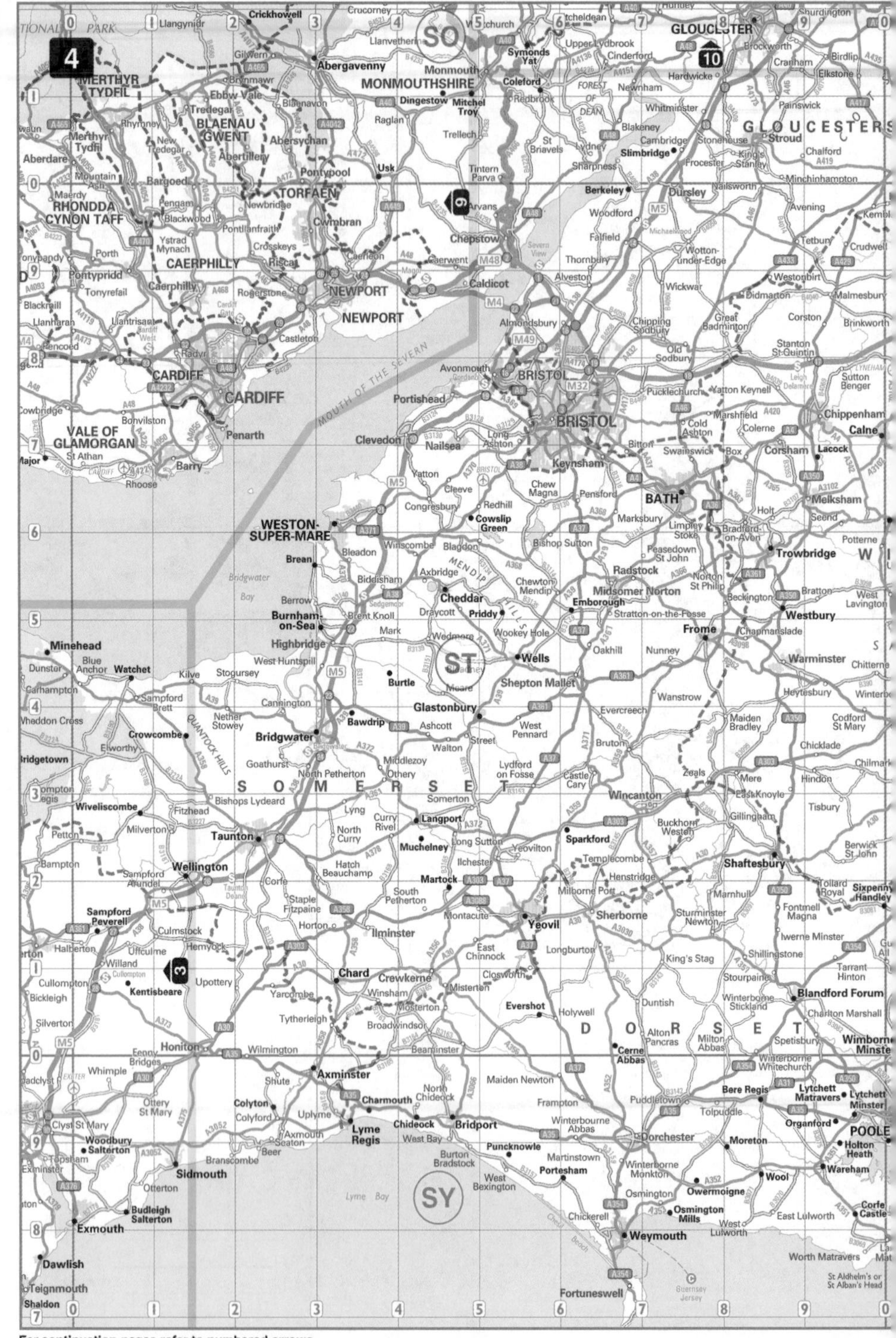


For continuation pages refer to numbered arrows

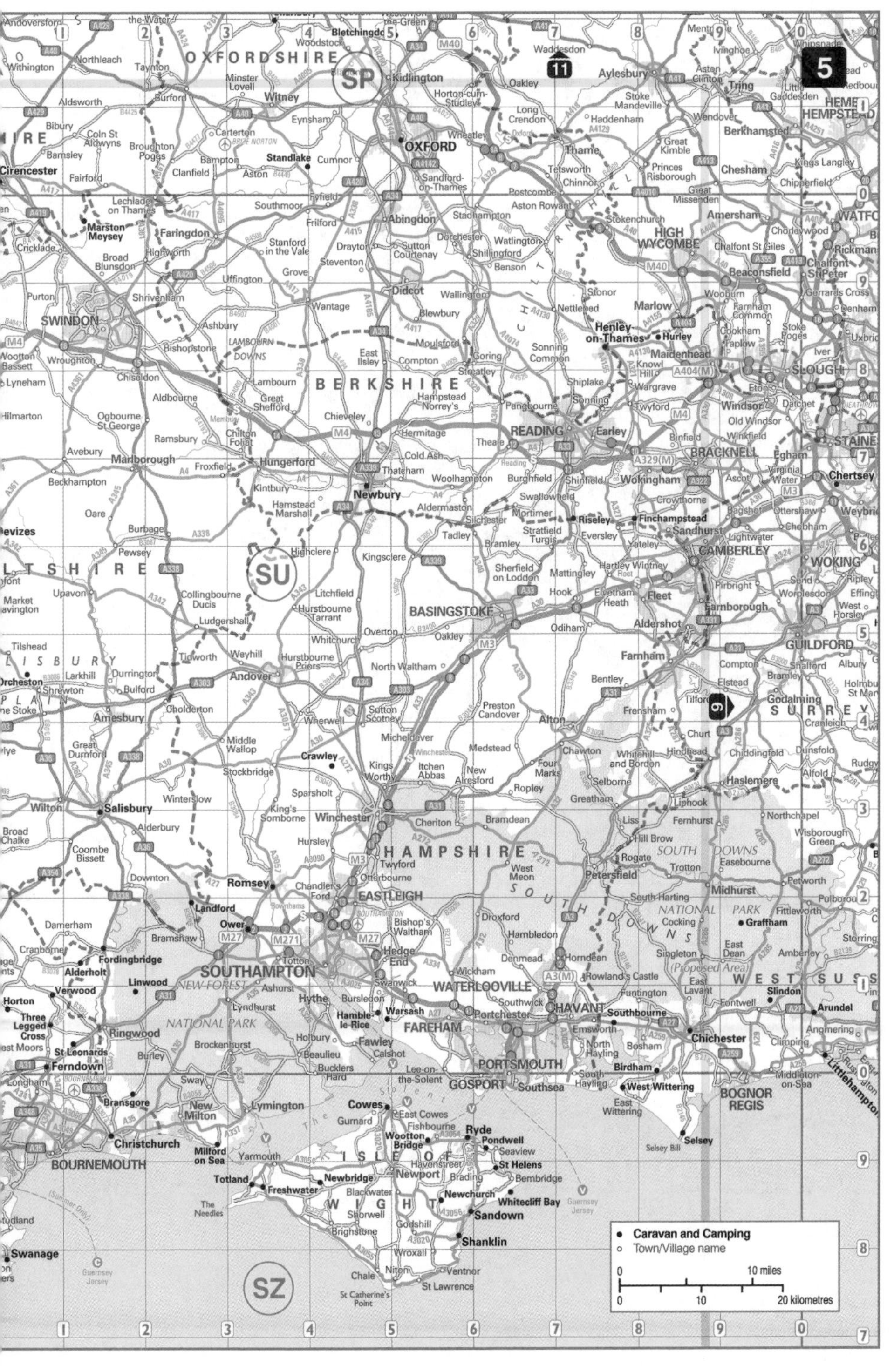

5
11
6
SP
SU
SZ
OXFORDSHIRE
BERKSHIRE
HAMPSHIRE
SURREY
WEST SUSSEX
ISLE OF WIGHT
SOUTH DOWNS NATIONAL PARK (Proposed Area)
NEW FOREST NATIONAL PARK
LAMBOURN DOWNS
CHILTERN HILLS
SALISBURY PLAIN
SOUTH DOWNS
The Solent
Withington
Northleach
Taynton
Minster Lovell
Witney
Woodstock
Bletchingdon
Kidlington
Oakley
Waddesdon
Aylesbury
Stoke Mandeville
Aston Clinton
Tring
Mentmore
Ivinghoe
Whipsnade
HEMEL HEMPSTEAD
Little Gaddesden
Aldsworth
Burford
Eynsham
Horton-cum-Studley
Long Crendon
Haddenham
Wendover
Berkhamsted
Bibury
Coln St Aldwyns
Carterton
Brize Norton
Barnsley
Broughton Poggs
Bampton
Standlake
Cumnor
OXFORD
Wheatley
Thame
Great Kimble
Princes Risborough
Chesham
Kings Langley
Cirencester
Fairford
Clanfield
Aston
Sandford-on-Thames
Tetsworth
Chinnor
Chipperfield
Lechlade on Thames
Southmoor
Fyfield
Abingdon
Postcombe
Aston Rowant
Great Missenden
Amersham
Marston Meysey
Faringdon
Frilford
Stadhampton
Stokenchurch
Chorleywood
Cricklade
Stanford in the Vale
Drayton
Sutton Courtenay
Dorchester
Watlington
HIGH WYCOMBE
Chalfont St Giles
Broad Blunsdon
Highworth
Steventon
Shillingford
Benson
Chalfont St Peter
Rickmansworth
Purton
Uffington
Grove
Didcot
Wallingford
Beaconsfield
Gerrards Cross
Shrivenham
Wantage
Blewbury
Stonor
Nettlebed
Marlow
Wooburn
Farnham Common
Denham
SWINDON
Ashbury
Henley-on-Thames
Hurley
Cookham
Stoke Poges
Bishopstone
Moulsford
Taplow
Uxbridge
Wootton Bassett
Wroughton
East Ilsley
Compton
Sonning Common
Maidenhead
Iver
Chiseldon
Goring
Streatley
Knowl Hill
SLOUGH
Lyneham
Lambourn
Shiplake
Wargrave
Eton
Aldbourne
Great Shefford
Hampstead Norrey's
Pangbourne
Sonning
Windsor
Datchet
Hilmarton
Ogbourne St George
Chieveley
Twyford
Old Windsor
Ramsbury
Chilton Foliat
Hermitage
READING
Earley
Binfield
Winkfield
STAINES
Avebury
Theale
BRACKNELL
Egham
Marlborough
Froxfield
Hungerford
Cold Ash
Thatcham
Woolhampton
Burghfield
Shinfield
Wokingham
Ascot
Virginia Water
Chertsey
Beckhampton
Kintbury
Newbury
Swallowfield
Crowthorne
Hamstead Marshall
Aldermaston
Mortimer
Riseley
Finchampstead
Bagshot
Ottershaw
Weybridge
Oare
Silchester
Chobham
Devizes
Burbage
Tadley
Stratfield Turgis
Eversley
Sandhurst
Lightwater
Pewsey
Highclere
Bramley
Yateley
CAMBERLEY
Kingsclere
WILTSHIRE
Sherfield on Loddon
Mattingley
Hartley Wintney
WOKING
Send
Ripley
Collingbourne Ducis
Litchfield
Fleet
Pirbright
Market Lavington
Upavon
Hook
Elvetham Heath
Worplesdon
Effingham
Hurstbourne Tarrant
BASINGSTOKE
West Horsley
Ludgershall
Farnborough
Aldershot
Overton
Oakley
Odiham
Whitchurch
GUILDFORD
Tilshead
Tidworth
Weyhill
Hurstbourne Priors
Farnham
Larkhill
Durrington
North Waltham
Compton
Shalford
Albury
Orcheston
Shrewton
Bulford
Andover
Bentley
Elstead
Bramley
Holmbury St Mary
Cholderton
Sutton Scotney
Preston Candover
Tilford
Godalming
Amesbury
Wherwell
Alton
Frensham
Cranleigh
Middle Wallop
Micheldever
Chawton
Churt
Great Durnford
Crawley
Medstead
Whitehill and Bordon
Hindhead
Chiddingfold
Dunsfold
Rudgwick
Stockbridge
Kings Worthy
Itchen Abbas
New Alresford
Four Marks
Alfold
Sparsholt
Ropley
Selborne
Haslemere
Winterslow
Greatham
Liphook
Wilton
Salisbury
King's Somborne
Winchester
Cheriton
Bramdean
Liss
Fernhurst
Northchapel
Broad Chalke
Alderbury
Hursley
Hill Brow
Wisborough Green
Coombe Bissett
Twyford
Rogate
Easebourne
West Meon
Petersfield
Trotton
Downton
Otterbourne
Romsey
Chandler's Ford
EASTLEIGH
South Harting
Midhurst
Petworth
Pulborough
Landford
Fittleworth
Damerham
Ower
Bishop's Waltham
Droxford
Cocking
Graffham
Bramshaw
Hambledon
Storrington
Cranborne
Fordingbridge
Totton
Hedge End
Singleton
East Dean
Amberley
Alderholt
Linwood
SOUTHAMPTON
Wickham
Denmead
Horndean
Ashurst
Swanwick
WATERLOOVILLE
Rowland's Castle
East Lavant
Slindon
Verwood
Hythe
Bursledon
Southwick
Funtington
Horton
Lyndhurst
Hamble-le-Rice
Warsash
Portchester
HAVANT
Southbourne
Fontwell
Arundel
Three Legged Cross
Ringwood
FAREHAM
Emsworth
Angmering
Holbury
West Moors
St Leonards
Brockenhurst
Beaulieu
Fawley
Calshot
North Hayling
Bosham
Chichester
Climping
Burley
Ferndown
Bucklers Hard
Lee-on-the-Solent
PORTSMOUTH
Birdham
Middleton-on-Sea
Littlehampton
Longham
Sway
GOSPORT
Southsea
South Hayling
West Wittering
BOGNOR REGIS
Bransgore
New Milton
Lymington
Cowes
East Cowes
East Wittering
Gurnard
Fishbourne
Christchurch
Wootton Bridge
Ryde
Pondwell
Seaview
Selsey
Selsey Bill
Milford on Sea
Yarmouth
Havenstreet
BOURNEMOUTH
Newbridge
Newport
St Helens
Brading
Bembridge
Totland
Freshwater
Blackwater
Newchurch
Whitecliff Bay
The Needles
Shorwell
Sandown
Godshill
Studland
Brighstone
Shanklin
Swanage
Wroxall
Chale
Niton
Ventnor
St Lawrence
St Catherine's Point
Guernsey Jersey
(Summer Only)
Caravan and Camping
Town/Village name
0
10 miles
0
10
20 kilometres

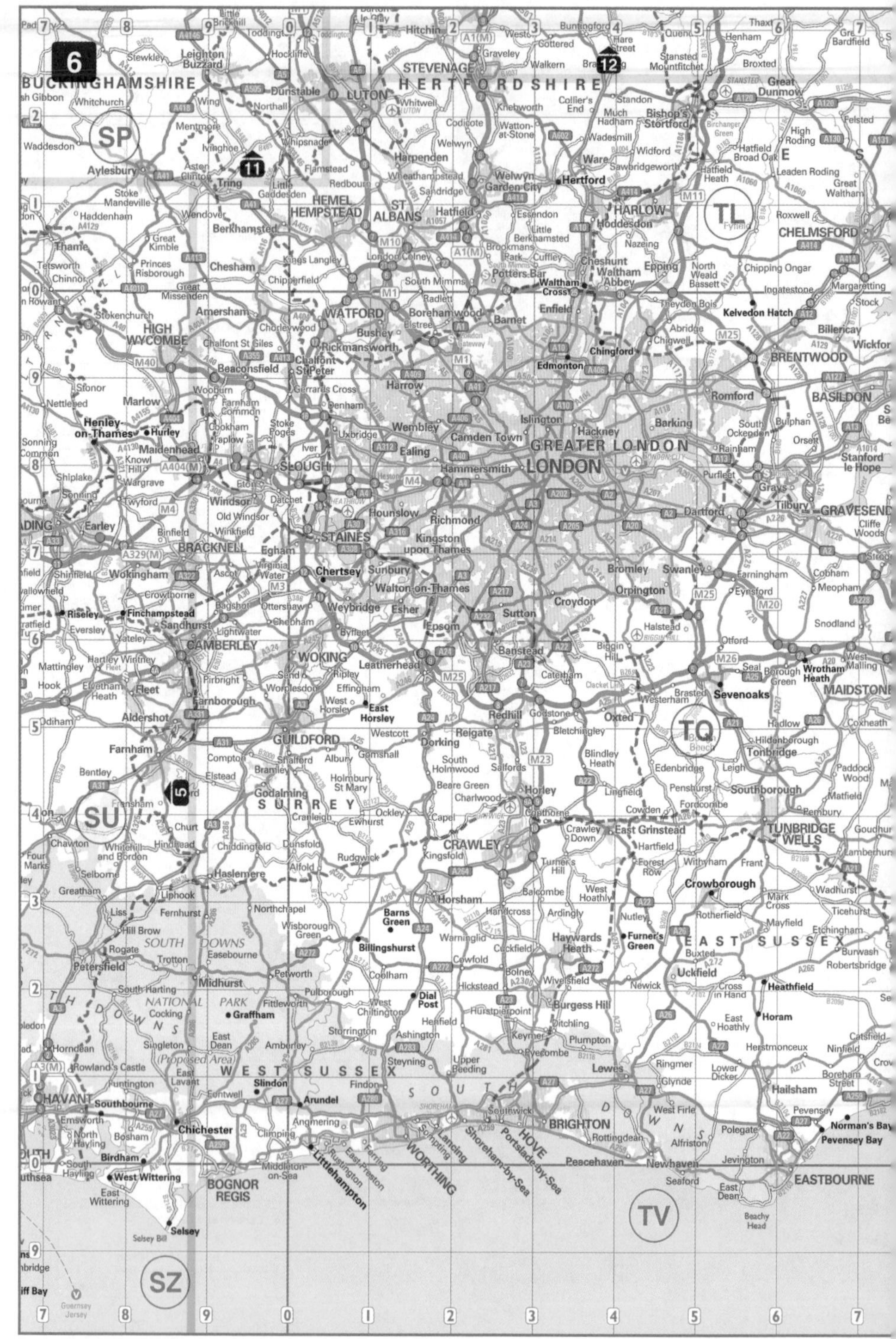


For continuation pages refer to numbered arrows

7
COLCHESTER
Walton on the Naze
CLACTON-ON-SEA
TM
Mersea Island
St Lawrence
Canewdon
SOUTHEND-ON-SEA
Eastchurch
Leysdown-on-Sea
MARGATE
Birchington
St Nicholas at Wade
Broadstairs
Ramsgate
Whitstable
Herne Bay
Canterbury
Sandwich
TR
Deal
DOVER
FOLKESTONE
KENT
Ashford
Biddenden
Camber
HASTINGS
STRAIT OF DOVER
Caravan and Camping
Town/Village name
10 miles
20 kilometres

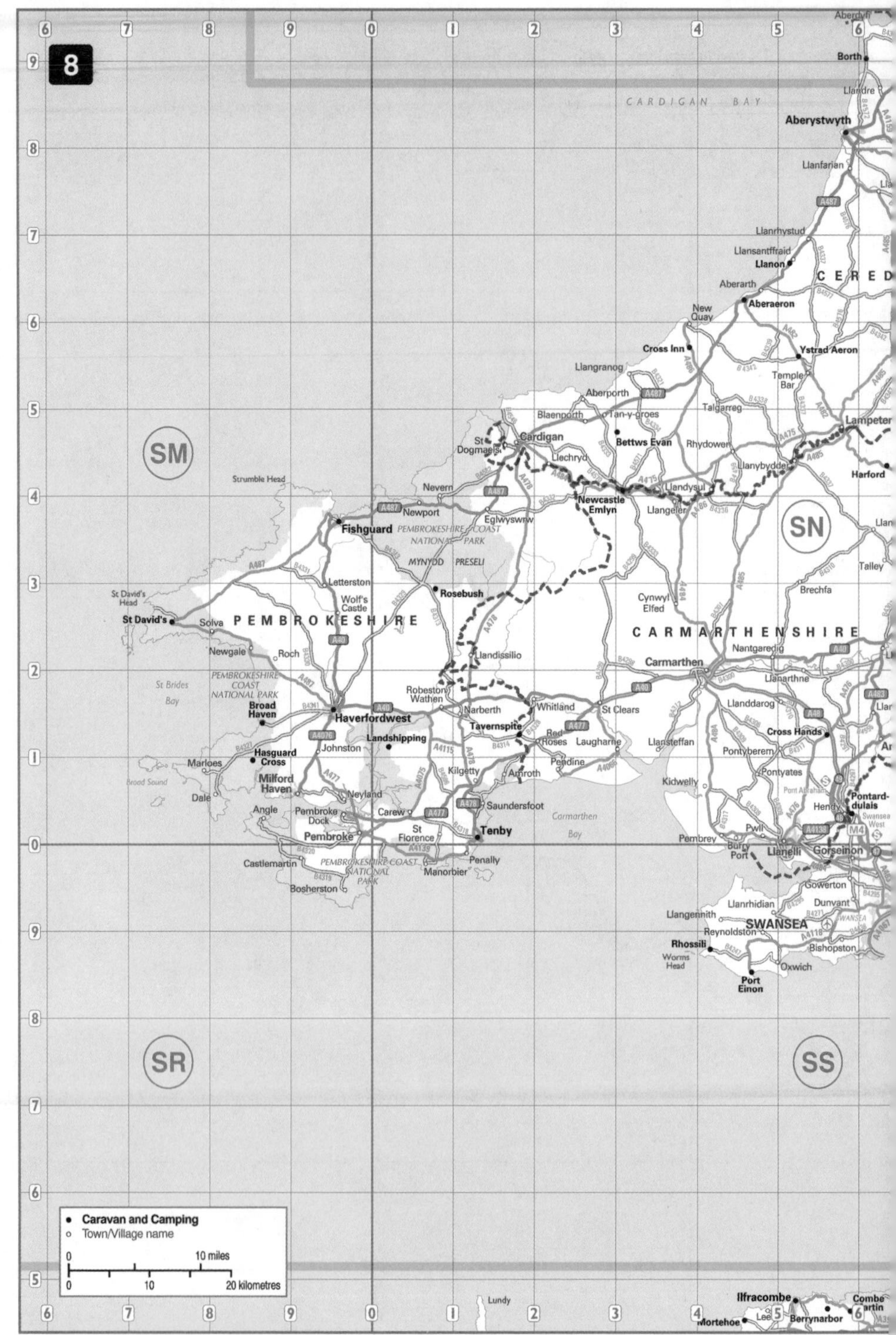


For continuation pages refer to numbered arrows

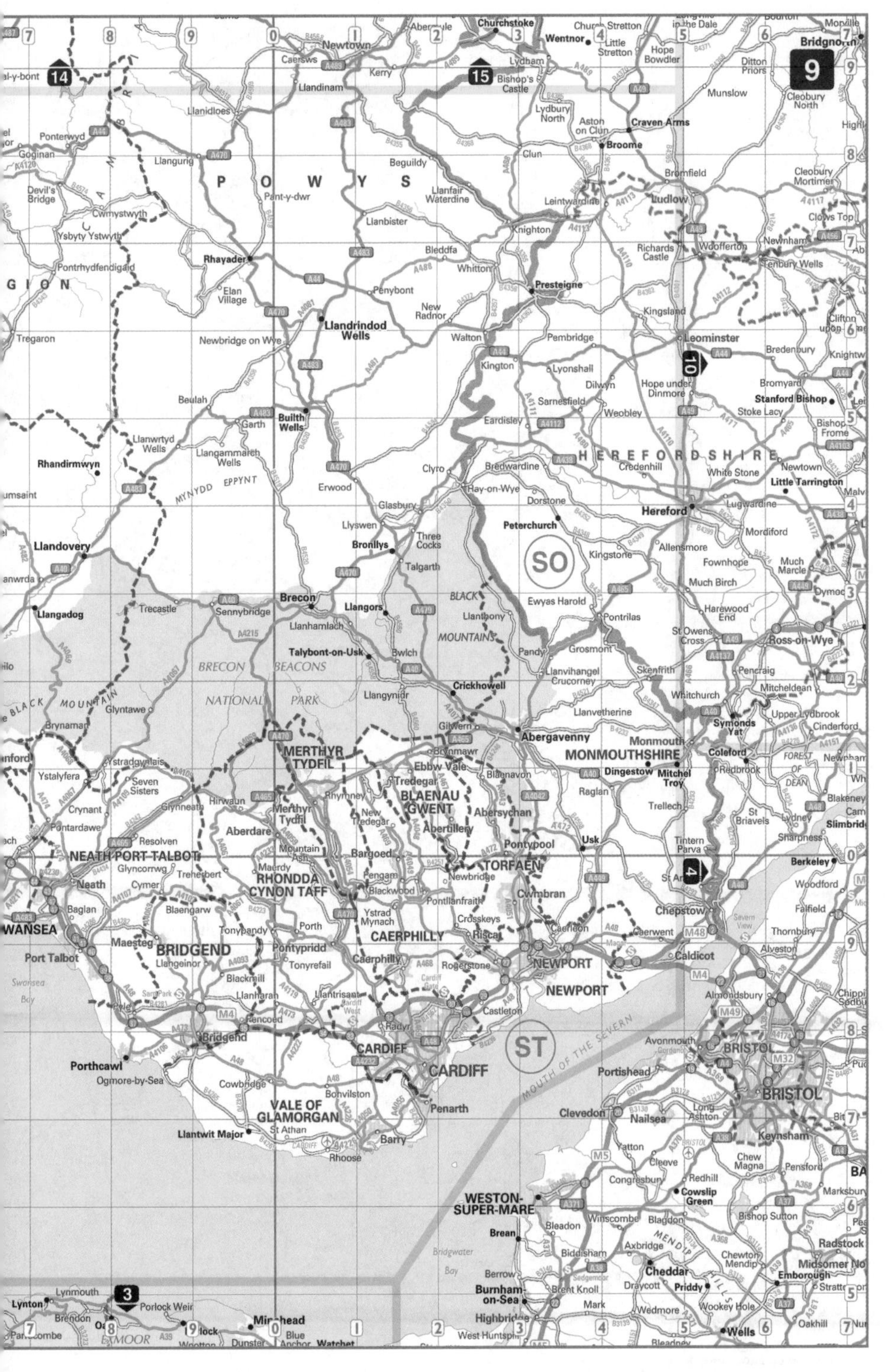

Churchstoke
Wentnor
Church Stretton
Little Stretton
Hope Bowdler
Morville
Bridgnorth
9
Abermule
Newtown
Caersws
Kerry
Lydham
15
Bishop's Castle
Ditton Priors
14
Llandinam
Munslow
Cleobury North
Lydbury North
Llanidloes
Aston on Clun
Craven Arms
Broome
Ponterwyd
Goginan
Llangurig
Clun
Beguildy
Bromfield
Cleobury Mortimer
Devil's Bridge
P O W Y S
Pant-y-dwr
Llanfair Waterdine
Leintwardine
Ludlow
Cwmystwyth
Llanbister
Clows Top
Ysbyty Ystwyth
Knighton
Newnham
Rhayader
Bleddfa
Whitton
Richards Castle
Woofferton
Tenbury Wells
Pontrhydfendigaid
Elan Village
Penybont
Presteigne
New Radnor
Kingsland
Llandrindod Wells
Tregaron
Newbridge on Wye
Walton
Pembridge
Leominster
Clifton upon Teme
Bredenbury
10
Kington
Lyonshall
Dilwyn
Hope under Dinmore
Bromyard
Beulah
Sarnesfield
Stanford Bishop
Builth Wells
Garth
Weobley
Stoke Lacy
Eardisley
Bishop's Frome
Llanwrtyd Wells
Llangammarch Wells
H E R E F O R D S H I R E
Rhandirmwyn
Clyro
Bredwardine
Credenhill
Newtown
White Stone
Little Tarrington
MYNYDD EPPYNT
Erwood
Hay-on-Wye
Dorstone
Hereford
Lugwardine
Glasbury
Peterchurch
Llyswen
Three Cocks
Mordiford
Llandovery
Bronllys
SO
Kingstone
Allensmore
Talgarth
Fownhope
Much Marcle
Much Birch
Ewyas Harold
Llangadog
Trecastle
Sennybridge
Brecon
Llangors
BLACK
Llanthony
Pontrilas
Harewood End
Llanhamlach
St Owens Cross
MOUNTAINS
Ross-on-Wye
BRECON
BEACONS
Talybont-on-Usk
Bwlch
Pandy
Grosmont
Llanvihangel Crucorney
Skenfrith
Pencraig
Crickhowell
Mitcheldean
NATIONAL
PARK
Llangynidr
Whitchurch
BLACK MOUNTAIN
Glyntawe
Llanvetherine
Upper Lydbrook
Brynaman
Symonds Yat
Cinderford
Gilwern
Abergavenny
Monmouth
MERTHYR TYDFIL
Brynmawr
MONMOUTHSHIRE
Coleford
Ystradgynlais
Ebbw Vale
Dingestow
Mitchel Troy
Redbrook
FOREST OF DEAN
Ystalyfera
Seven Sisters
Tredegar
Blaenavon
BLAENAU GWENT
Raglan
Crynant
Hirwaun
Glynneath
Rhymney
Trellech
Blakeney
Merthyr Tydfil
New Tredegar
Abersychan
St Briavels
Lydney
Pontardawe
Aberdare
Abertillery
Slimbridge
Resolven
Sharpness
NEATH PORT TALBOT
Mountain Ash
Bargoed
Pontypool
Usk
Tintern Parva
Glyncorrwg
Maerdy
TORFAEN
Berkeley
Neath
Cymer
Treherbert
RHONDDA CYNON TAFF
Pengam
Blackwood
Newbridge
4
Cwmbran
Woodford
Baglan
Pontllanfraith
Chepstow
Falfield
Blaengarw
Ystrad Mynach
Crosskeys
Porth
Risca
Caerleon
Caerwent
Thornbury
SWANSEA
Maesteg
Tonypandy
CAERPHILLY
Alveston
Port Talbot
BRIDGEND
Pontypridd
Caerphilly
Caldicot
Llangeinor
Tonyrefail
Rogerstone
NEWPORT
Swansea Bay
Blackmill
Almondsbury
Llanharan
Llantrisant
Castleton
Pyle
Pencoed
Radyr
Bridgend
CARDIFF
Avonmouth
BRISTOL
ST
Porthcawl
CARDIFF
Portishead
Ogmore-by-Sea
Cowbridge
MOUTH OF THE SEVERN
BRISTOL
Bonvilston
Penarth
Clevedon
Nailsea
Long Ashton
VALE OF GLAMORGAN
Llantwit Major
St Athan
Barry
Keynsham
Rhoose
Yatton
Chew Magna
Cleeve
Pensford
Congresbury
Redhill
Cowslip Green
WESTON-SUPER-MARE
Winscombe
Blagdon
Bishop Sutton
Bleadon
Brean
MENDIP HILLS
Axbridge
Biddisham
Chewton Mendip
Radstock
Bridgwater Bay
Cheddar
Midsomer Norton
Berrow
Emborough
Burnham-on-Sea
Brent Knoll
Draycott
Priddy
Lynmouth
Lynton
3
Porlock Weir
Mark
Wookey Hole
Brendon
Highbridge
Wedmore
Minehead
Blue Anchor
Watchet
West Huntspill
Wells
Oakhill
Dunster
EXMOOR

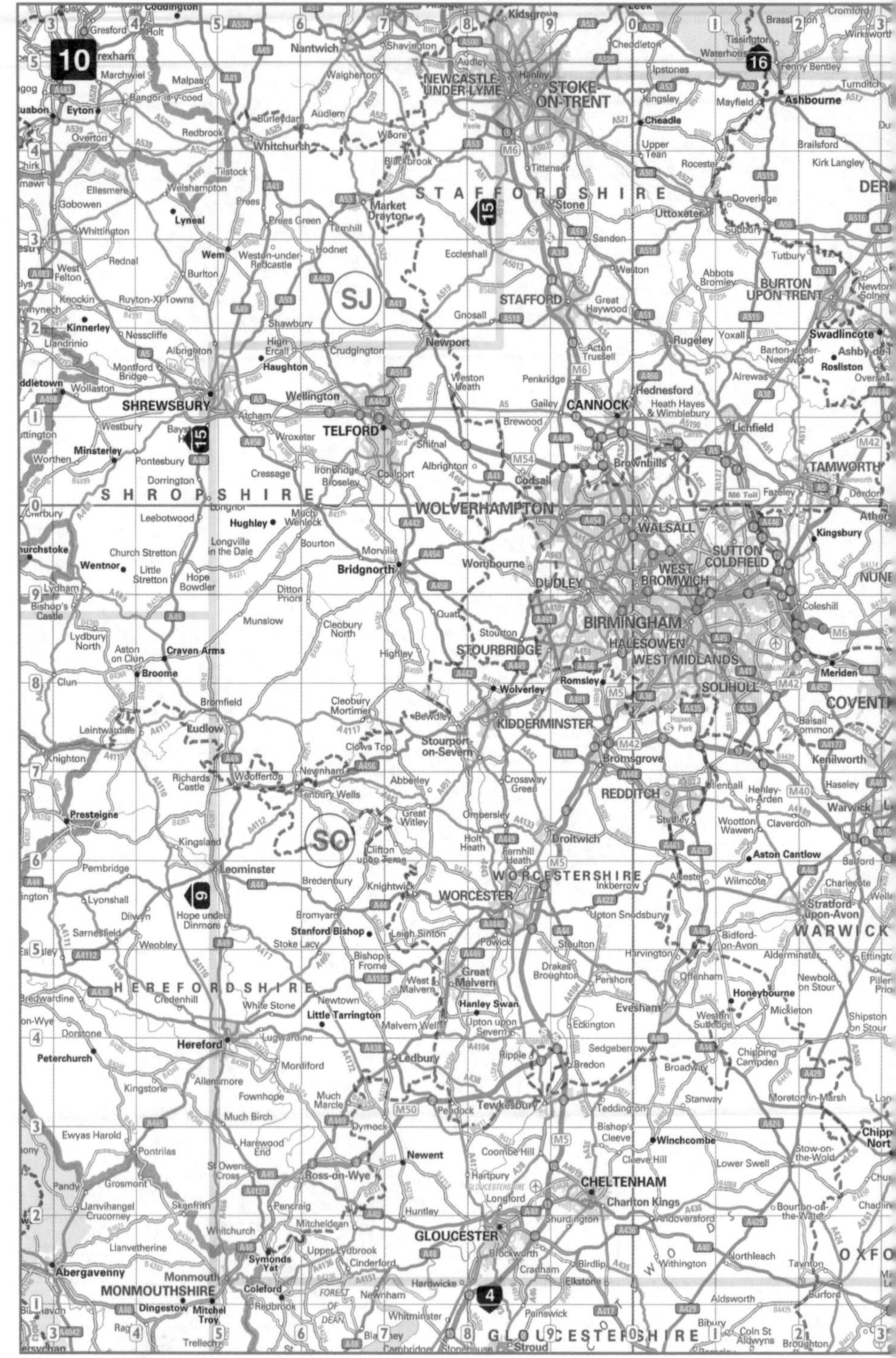


For continuation pages refer to numbered arrows

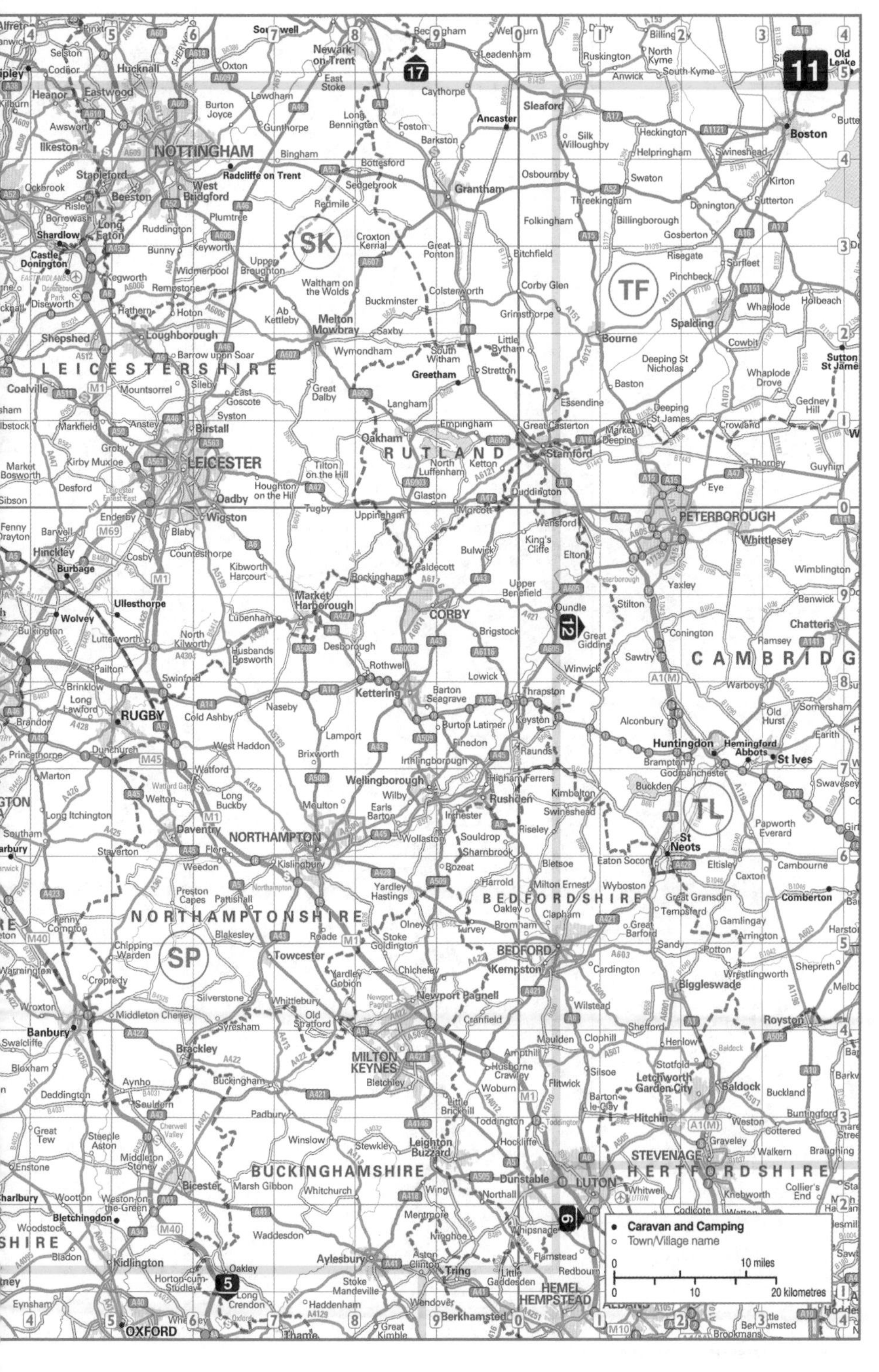

11
17
12
6
5
SK
TF
TL
SP
Newark-on-Trent
East Stoke
Caythorpe
Leadenham
Ruskington
North Kyme
South Kyme
Anwick
Old Leake
Boston
Sleaford
Ancaster
Silk Willoughby
Heckington
Helpringham
Swineshead
Kirton
Sutterton
Donington
Swaton
Osbournby
Threekingham
Billingborough
Gosberton
Risegate
Surfleet
Pinchbeck
Spalding
Whaplode
Holbeach
Cowbit
Whaplode Drove
Gedney Hill
Sutton St James
Crowland
Deeping St James
Deeping St Nicholas
Market Deeping
Bourne
Baston
Corby Glen
Grimsthorpe
Bitchfield
Folkingham
Grantham
Barkston
Foston
Long Bennington
Bottesford
Sedgebrook
Redmile
Croxton Kerrial
Great Ponton
Colsterworth
Buckminster
Waltham on the Wolds
Melton Mowbray
Saxby
Wymondham
South Witham
Little Bytham
Stretton
Greetham
Essendine
Great Casterton
Stamford
Empingham
Oakham
RUTLAND
North Luffenham
Ketton
Langham
Great Dalby
Tilton on the Hill
Glaston
Morcott
Duddington
Uppingham
Tugby
Caldecott
Rockingham
Bulwick
King's Cliffe
Wansford
Elton
Upper Benefield
CORBY
Oundle
Brigstock
Great Gidding
Stilton
Yaxley
PETERBOROUGH
Whittlesey
Eye
Thorney
Guyhirn
Wimblington
Benwick
Chatteris
Ramsey
Conington
Sawtry
CAMBRIDGESHIRE
Warboys
Somersham
Old Hurst
Earith
Alconbury
Huntingdon
Hemingford Abbots
St Ives
Godmanchester
Brampton
Swavesey
Buckden
St Neots
Papworth Everard
Eltisley
Caxton
Cambourne
Comberton
Eaton Socon
Great Gransden
Tempsford
Gamlingay
Great Barford
Sandy
Potton
Arrington
Wrestlingworth
Biggleswade
Shepreth
Royston
Baldock
Letchworth Garden City
Hitchin
Weston
Buckland
Graveley
STEVENAGE
Walkern
Braughing
HERTFORDSHIRE
Knebworth
Collier's End
Codicote
LUTON
Whitwell
Redbourn
Flamstead
HEMEL HEMPSTEAD
Berkhamsted
Tring
Little Gaddesden
Whipsnade
Dunstable
Northall
Ivinghoe
Mentmore
Wing
Leighton Buzzard
Hockliffe
Toddington
Little Brickhill
Woburn
Flitwick
Barton-le-Clay
Silsoe
Maulden
Clophill
Ampthill
Husborne Crawley
Shefford
Henlow
Stotfold
Wilstead
Cardington
Kempston
BEDFORD
Bromham
Clapham
Oakley
BEDFORDSHIRE
Milton Ernest
Wyboston
Bletsoe
Sharnbrook
Souldrop
Riseley
Swineshead
Kimbolton
Raunds
Higham Ferrers
Rushden
Irchester
Wollaston
Bozeat
Harrold
Turvey
Olney
Stoke Goldington
Chicheley
Newport Pagnell
Cranfield
MILTON KEYNES
Bletchley
Old Stratford
Yardley Gobion
Towcester
Roade
Yardley Hastings
Earls Barton
Wilby
Wellingborough
Irthlingborough
Finedon
Burton Latimer
Barton Seagrave
Kettering
Rothwell
Desborough
Thrapston
Keyston
Lowick
Winwick
NORTHAMPTON
NORTHAMPTONSHIRE
Moulton
Brixworth
Lamport
Kislingbury
Flore
Weedon
Daventry
Long Buckby
Watford
West Haddon
Naseby
Cold Ashby
Husbands Bosworth
North Kilworth
Lubenham
Market Harborough
Kibworth Harcourt
Welton
Preston Capes
Pattishall
Blakesley
Chipping Warden
Silverstone
Whittlebury
Syresham
Brackley
Middleton Cheney
Banbury
Cropredy
Warmington
Fenny Compton
Wroxton
Swalcliffe
Bloxham
Aynho
Deddington
Souldern
Great Tew
Steeple Aston
Middleton Stoney
Enstone
Bicester
Charlbury
Wootton
Weston-on-the-Green
Bletchingdon
Woodstock
Kidlington
Bladon
Eynsham
OXFORD
Wheatley
Horton-cum-Studley
Oakley
Long Crendon
Thame
Haddenham
Stoke Mandeville
Aylesbury
Great Kimble
Wendover
Aston Clinton
Waddesdon
Marsh Gibbon
Whitchurch
Winslow
Stewkley
Padbury
Buckingham
BUCKINGHAMSHIRE
RUGBY
Dunchurch
Brandon
Long Lawford
Brinklow
Pailton
Princethorpe
Marton
Long Itchington
Southam
Staverton
Wolvey
Bulkington
Ullesthorpe
Lutterworth
Swinford
Burbage
Hinckley
Barwell
Fenny Drayton
Sibson
Market Bosworth
Desford
Kirby Muxloe
Groby
Markfield
Ibstock
Coalville
Cosby
Countesthorpe
Blaby
Enderby
Wigston
Oadby
Houghton on the Hill
LEICESTER
Birstall
Anstey
Syston
East Goscote
Sileby
Mountsorrel
Barrow upon Soar
LEICESTERSHIRE
Loughborough
Shepshed
Hathern
Hoton
Diseworth
Kegworth
Castle Donington
Shardlow
Long Eaton
Rempstone
Widmerpool
Upper Broughton
Ab Kettleby
Bunny
Keyworth
Ruddington
Plumtree
West Bridgford
Beeston
Stapleford
Borrowash
Risley
Ockbrook
Ilkeston
NOTTINGHAM
Radcliffe on Trent
Bingham
Gunthorpe
Lowdham
Burton Joyce
Oxton
Hucknall
Eastwood
Heanor
Awsworth
Codnor
Selston
Kilburn
Caravan and Camping
Town/Village name
0
10 miles
10
20 kilometres

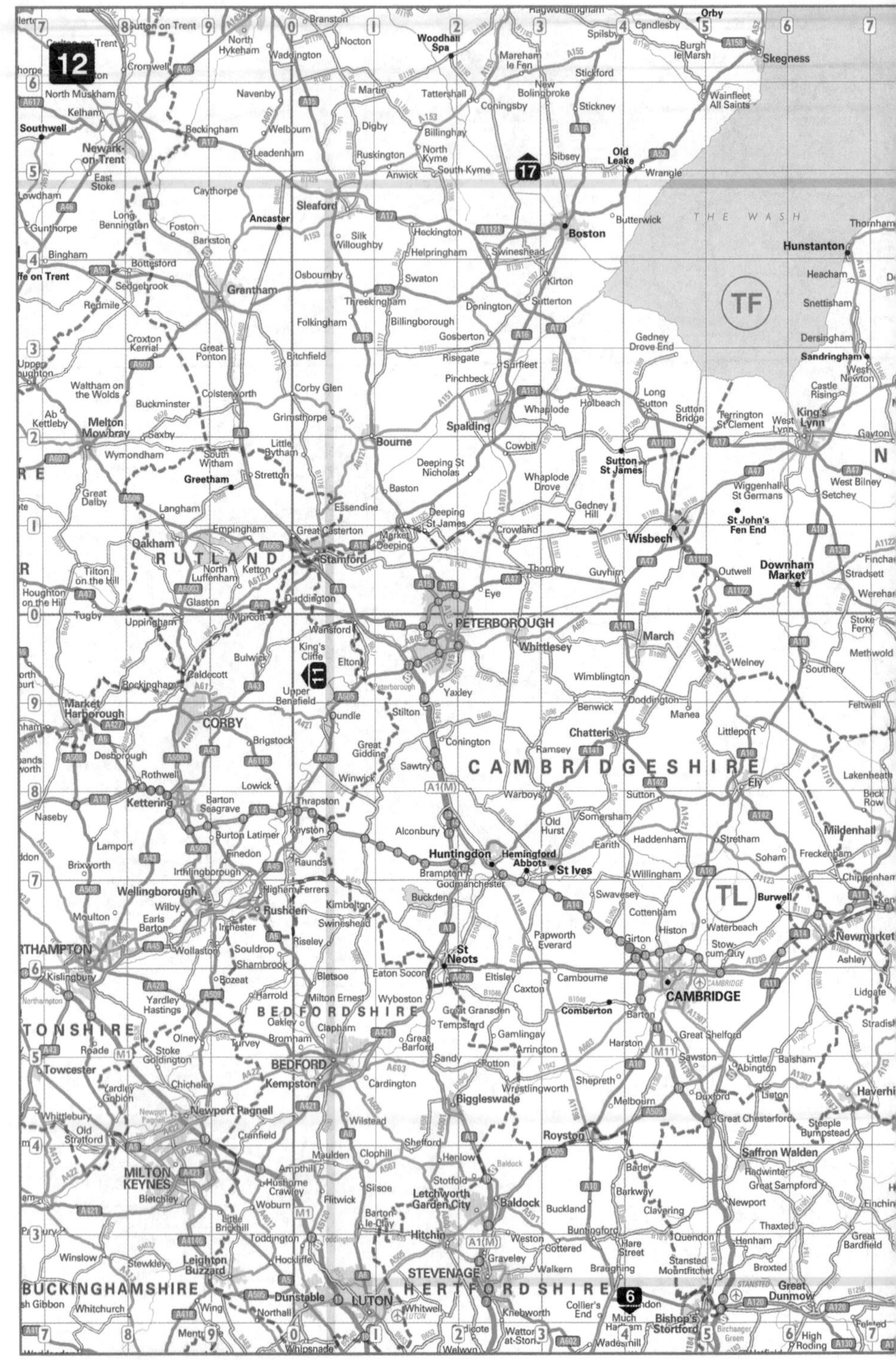


For continuation pages refer to numbered arrows

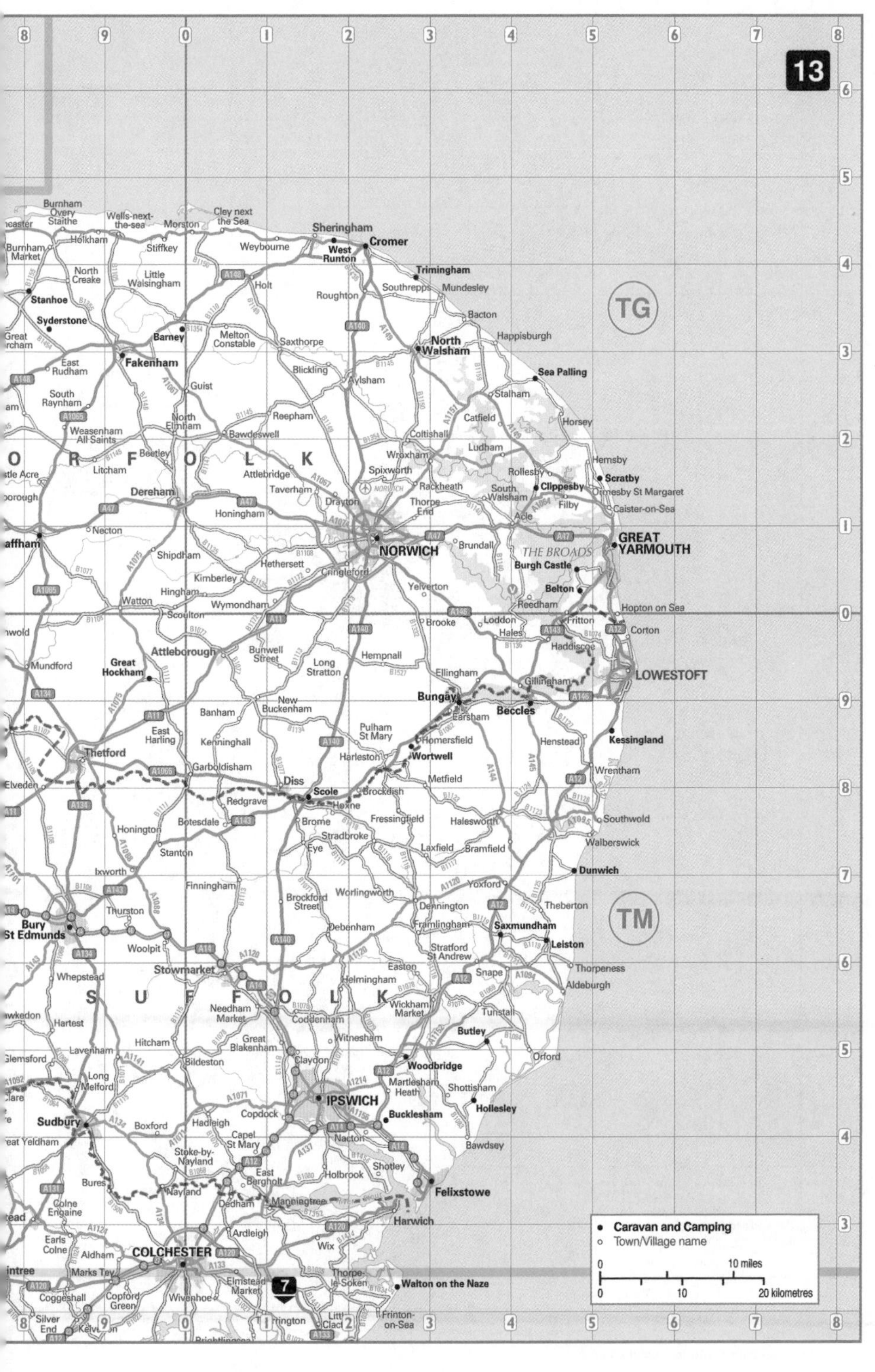
13
TG
TM
Burnham Overy Staithe
Wells-next-the-sea
Morston
Cley next the Sea
Sheringham
West Runton
Cromer
Burnham Market
Holkham
Stiffkey
Weybourne
North Creake
Little Walsingham
Holt
Trimingham
Stanhoe
Roughton
Southrepps
Mundesley
Syderstone
Bacton
Barney
Melton Constable
Saxthorpe
North Walsham
Happisburgh
East Rudham
Fakenham
Blickling
Aylsham
Sea Palling
South Raynham
Guist
Stalham
North Elmham
Reepham
Catfield
Horsey
Weasenham All Saints
Bawdeswell
Coltishall
Ludham
Hemsby
Beetley
Wroxham
Rollesby
Scratby
Litcham
Attlebridge
Spixworth
Rackheath
Clippesby
Ormesby St Margaret
Dereham
Taverham
NORWICH
South Walsham
Filby
Honingham
Drayton
Thorpe End
Acle
Caister-on-Sea
Necton
Brundall
GREAT YARMOUTH
Shipdham
THE BROADS
Burgh Castle
Hethersett
Cringleford
Kimberley
Yelverton
Belton
Hingham
Watton
Wymondham
Reedham
Hopton on Sea
Scoulton
Brooke
Loddon
Hales
Fritton
Corton
Haddiscoe
Attleborough
Bunwell Street
Hempnall
Mundford
Great Hockham
Long Stratton
Ellingham
LOWESTOFT
Gillingham
Bungay
Beccles
New Buckenham
Banham
Earsham
East Harling
Pulham St Mary
Homersfield
Henstead
Kessingland
Thetford
Kenninghall
Harleston
Wortwell
Garboldisham
Wrentham
Diss
Metfield
Elveden
Scole
Brockdish
Redgrave
Hoxne
Fressingfield
Halesworth
Southwold
Botesdale
Brome
Honington
Stradbroke
Walberswick
Stanton
Eye
Laxfield
Bramfield
Dunwich
Ixworth
Finningham
Worlingworth
Yoxford
Thurston
Brockford Street
Dennington
Theberton
Bury St Edmunds
Debenham
Framlingham
Saxmundham
Woolpit
Leiston
Stratford St Andrew
Stowmarket
Easton
Snape
Thorpeness
Whepstead
Helmingham
Aldeburgh
S U F F O L K
N O R F O L K
Needham Market
Wickham Market
Hartest
Coddenham
Tunstall
Hitcham
Witnesham
Butley
Lavenham
Great Blakenham
Glemsford
Bildeston
Claydon
Orford
Woodbridge
Long Melford
Martlesham Heath
IPSWICH
Shottisham
Hollesley
Copdock
Sudbury
Boxford
Hadleigh
Bucklesham
Capel St Mary
Nacton
Bawdsey
Stoke-by-Nayland
East Bergholt
Shotley
Bures
Holbrook
Felixstowe
Nayland
Colne Engaine
Dedham
Manningtree
Harwich
Ardleigh
Earls Colne
Aldham
COLCHESTER
Wix
Marks Tey
Elmstead Market
Thorpe-le-Soken
Walton on the Naze
Coggeshall
Copford Green
Wivenhoe
Silver End
Kelvedon
Frinton-on-Sea
7
A148
A140
A149
A47
A146
A143
A12
A11
A134
A1066
A14
A1120
A1214
A120
A133
A137
A131
A1065
A1075
A1094
A1095
● Caravan and Camping
○ Town/Village name
0
10 miles
0
10
20 kilometres

For continuation pages refer to numbered arrows

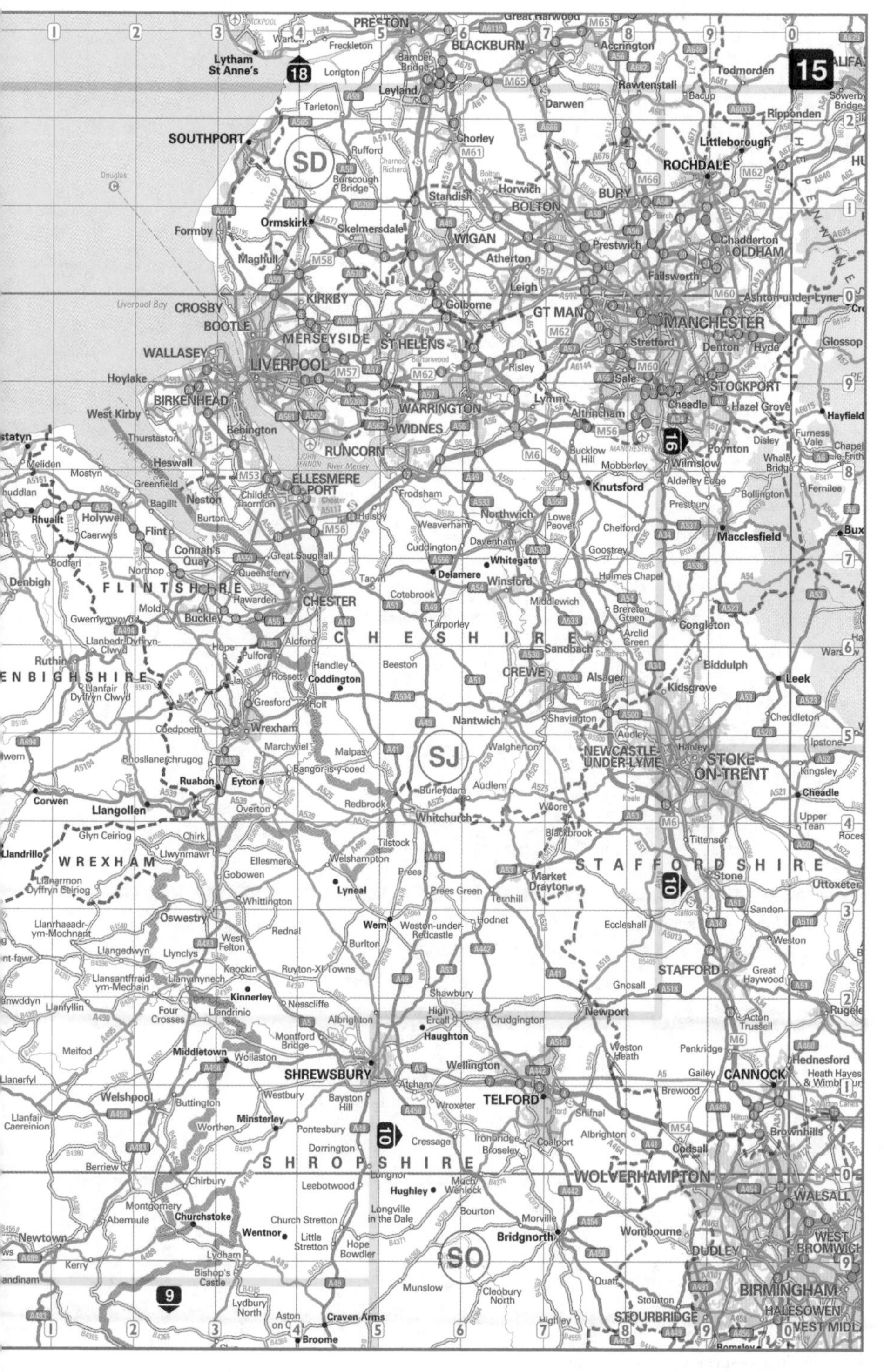

15
18
10
16
9
SD
SJ
SO
PRESTON
BLACKBURN
Great Harwood
Accrington
Lytham St Anne's
Warton
Freckleton
Longton
Bamber Bridge
Leyland
Tarleton
Todmorden
Rawtenstall
Bacup
Darwen
Ripponden
Littleborough
ROCHDALE
SOUTHPORT
Rufford
Chorley
Burscough Bridge
Standish
Horwich
BOLTON
BURY
Ormskirk
Skelmersdale
Formby
WIGAN
Prestwich
Chadderton
OLDHAM
Maghull
Atherton
Failsworth
Leigh
KIRKBY
Golborne
Liverpool Bay
CROSBY
BOOTLE
GT MAN
MANCHESTER
Ashton-under-Lyne
MERSEYSIDE
ST HELENS
Stretford
Denton
Hyde
Glossop
WALLASEY
LIVERPOOL
Risley
Sale
STOCKPORT
Hoylake
BIRKENHEAD
WARRINGTON
Lymm
Altrincham
Cheadle
Hazel Grove
Hayfield
West Kirby
WIDNES
Bebington
Thurstaston
RUNCORN
Bucklow Hill
Wilmslow
Poynton
Disley
Furness Vale
Chapel-en-le-Frith
Heswall
Mobberley
Whaley Bridge
Mostyn
Meliden
ELLESMERE PORT
Greenfield
Frodsham
Knutsford
Alderley Edge
Fernilee
Bollington
Neston
Bagillt
Holywell
Rhuallt
Flint
Helsby
Northwich
Lower Peover
Prestbury
Macclesfield
Caerwys
Burton
Weaverham
Chelford
Connah's Quay
Great Saughall
Cuddington
Davenham
Bodfari
Northop
Queensferry
Whitegate
Goostrey
Denbigh
FLINTSHIRE
Tarvin
Delamere
Winsford
Holmes Chapel
Hawarden
CHESTER
Cotebrook
Middlewich
Mold
Buckley
Tarporley
Brereton Green
Arclid Green
Congleton
Gwernymynydd
CHESHIRE
Sandbach
Llanbedr Dyffryn-Clwyd
Hope
Aldford
Ruthin
Pulford
Handley
Beeston
CREWE
Alsager
Biddulph
DENBIGHSHIRE
Rossett
Coddington
Kidsgrove
Leek
Llanfair Dyffryn Clwyd
Gresford
Holt
Nantwich
Shavington
Cheddleton
Coedpoeth
Wrexham
Audley
Marchwiel
Malpas
Walgherton
NEWCASTLE-UNDER-LYME
Hanley
STOKE-ON-TRENT
Ipstones
Kingsley
Rhosllanerchrugog
Bangor-is-y-coed
Ruabon
Eyton
Burleydam
Audlem
Cheadle
Corwen
Llangollen
Overton
Redbrook
Woore
Keele
Whitchurch
Upper Tean
Glyn Ceiriog
Chirk
Tilstock
Blackbrook
Tittensor
Llandrillo
WREXHAM
Llwynmawr
Ellesmere
Welshampton
STAFFORDSHIRE
Gobowen
Prees
Market Drayton
Stone
Llanarmon Dyffryn Ceiriog
Lyneal
Prees Green
Ternhill
Uttoxeter
Whittington
Sandon
Llanrhaeadr-ym-Mochnant
Oswestry
Rednal
Wem
Weston-under-Redcastle
Hodnet
Eccleshall
West Felton
Burlton
Weston
Llangedwyn
Llynclys
Knockin
Ruyton-XI-Towns
STAFFORD
Great Haywood
Llansantffraid-ym-Mechain
Llanymynech
Gnosall
Kinnerley
Shawbury
Llanfyllin
Four Crosses
Llandrinio
Nesscliffe
High Ercall
Newport
Rugeley
Albrighton
Crudgington
Acton Trussell
Haughton
Montford Bridge
Weston Heath
Penkridge
Meifod
Middletown
Wollaston
Hednesford
Wellington
SHREWSBURY
Gailey
CANNOCK
Heath Hayes & Wimblebury
Llanerfyl
Atcham
Welshpool
Westbury
Buttington
Bayston Hill
Wroxeter
TELFORD
Brewood
Shifnal
Llanfair Caereinion
Minsterley
Pontesbury
Cressage
Ironbridge
Broseley
Coalport
Albrighton
Brownhills
Worthen
Dorrington
Codsall
Berriew
SHROPSHIRE
Chirbury
Leebotwood
Much Wenlock
WOLVERHAMPTON
Montgomery
Hughley
WALSALL
Abermule
Churchstoke
Church Stretton
Longville in the Dale
Bourton
Morville
Newtown
Wentnor
Little Stretton
Hope Bowdler
Bridgnorth
Wombourne
WEST BROMWICH
Kerry
Lydham
DUDLEY
Bishop's Castle
Munslow
Quatt
BIRMINGHAM
Lydbury North
Cleobury North
Stourton
HALESOWEN
Aston on Clun
Craven Arms
Highley
STOURBRIDGE
WEST MIDLANDS
Broome
Romsley

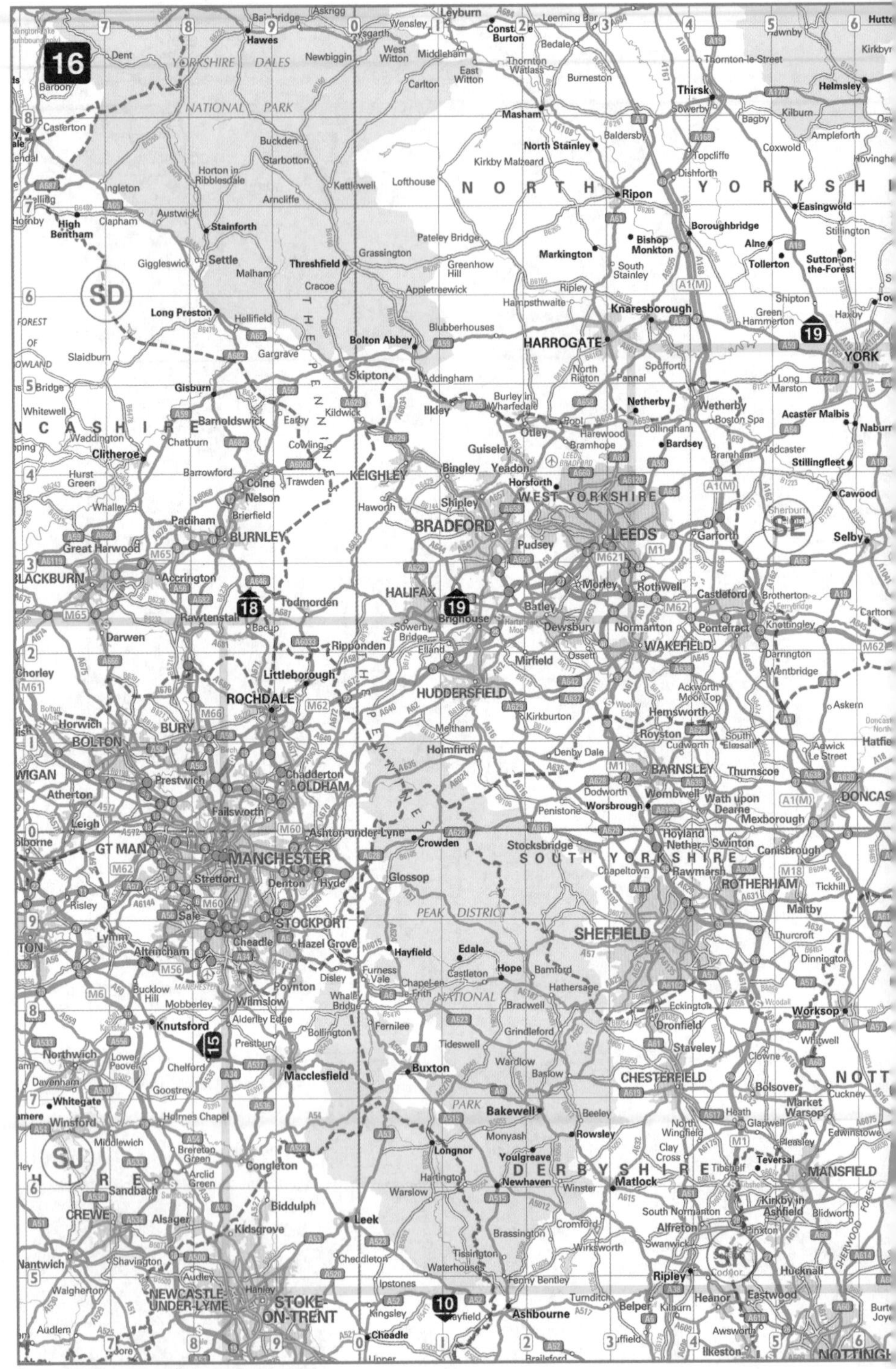

For continuation pages refer to numbered arrows

17
Caravan and Camping
Town/Village name
0
10 miles
0
10
20 kilometres
TA
TF
EAST RIDING OF YORKSHIRE
LINCOLNSHIRE
Lastingham
Cropton
Lockton
Hackness
Scalby
Scarborough
Wrelton
Pickering
Allerton
Thornton le Dale
Wykeham
East Ayton
Seamer
Cayton
Snainton
Brompton
Flixton
Filey
Kirby Misperton
Staxton
Slingsby
West Knapton
Sherburn
Hunmanby
Reighton
Malton
Norton
Rillington
Bempton
Flamborough Head
Flamborough
North Grimston
Burton Fleming
Rudston
Carnaby
Bridlington
Sledmere
Langtoft
Kilham
Burton Agnes
Fridaythorpe
Wetwang
Driffield
Barmston
Stamford Bridge
Skipsea
North Dalton
Bainton
North Frodingham
Beeford
Wilberfoss
Atwick
Pocklington
Middleton on the Wolds
Brandesburton
Hornsea
Barmby Moor
Leven
Shiptonthorpe
Market Weighton
Holme upon Spalding Moor
Beverley
Aldbrough
Walkington
Bubwith
North Cave
Little Weighton
Sproatley
South Cave
Cottingham
Howden
Ellougton
KINGSTON UPON HULL
Hedon
Withernsea
Hessle
Goole
Melton
North Ferriby
New Holland
Winteringham
Patrington
Barton upon-Humber
Goxhill
Burton upon Stather
Winterton
Easington
Immingham Dock
River Humber
Thorne
Wootton
Ulceby
Immingham
Crowle
Gunness
SCUNTHORPE
GRIMSBY
Spurn Head
Broughton
Wrawby
Keelby
Cleethorpes
Althorpe
Barnetby le Wold
Belton
Brigg
Laceby
Humberston
Scawby
Waltham
Epworth
Messingham
Hibaldstow
Holton le Clay
Caistor
Swallow
Tetney
North Cotes
Blaxton
Scotter
Finningley
Haxey
Kirton in Lindsey
Grainthorpe
North Somercotes
Ludborough
Misterton
Blyton
Waddingham
Saltfleet
Binbrook
Gringley on the Hill
Saltfleetby St Peter
Gainsborough
Glentham
Middle Rasen
Saundby
Market Rasen
Louth
Mablethorpe
Legbourne
Faldingworth
Ingham
Lissington
Sutton on Sea
Withern
East Barkwith
Retford
Torksey
Sturton by Stow
Wragby
Scamblesby
Church Laneham
Alford
Gamston
Huttoft
Newton on Trent
Saxilby
Bilsby
Elkesley
Langworth
Tetford
Markham Moor
Chapel St Leonards
Baumber
LINCOLN
Hogsthorpe
Tuxford
Skellingthorpe
Edlington
Washingborough
Bardney
Horncastle
Ingoldmells
Hagworthingham
Branston
Orby
Sutton on Trent
Candlesby
Carlton-on-Trent
North Hykeham
Nocton
Woodhall Spa
Spilsby
Burgh le Marsh
Waddington
Mareham le Fen
Skegness
Caunton
Cromwell
Stickford
Martin
Tattershall
New Bolingbroke
Wainfleet All Saints
North Muskham
Navenby
Coningsby
Stickney
Kelham
Digby
Billinghay
Southwell
Beckingham
Welbourn
Newark-on-Trent
Leadenham
Ruskington
North Kyme
Sibsey
Old Leake
Wrangle
Anwick
South Kyme
East Stoke
Caythorpe
Sleaford
Butterwick
THE WASH
Long Bennington
Foston
Ancaster
Silk Willoughby
Heckington
Boston
Thornham
Hunstanton
Helpringham
Swineshead
Barkston
Bingham
11
12
19

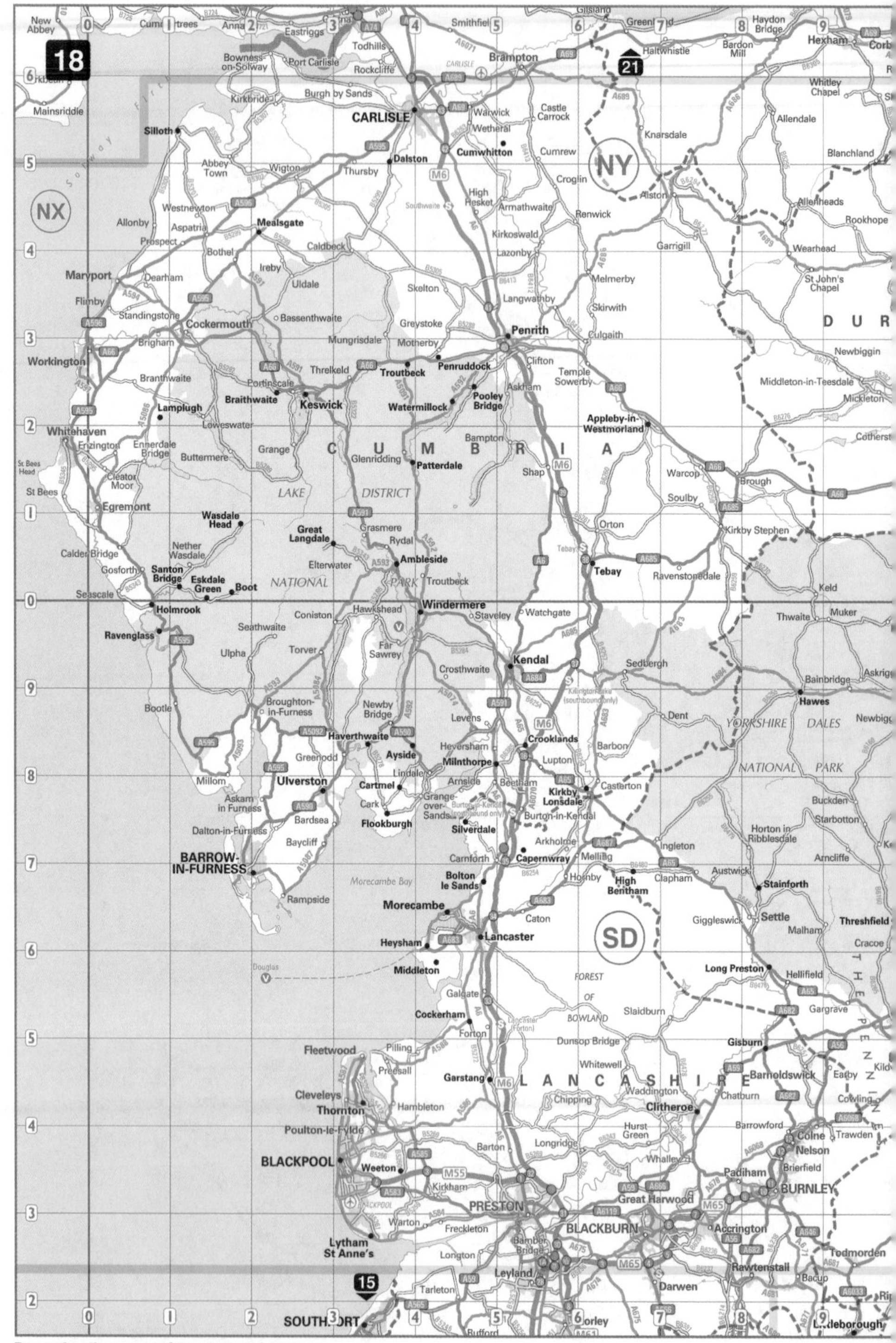

For continuation pages refer to numbered arrows

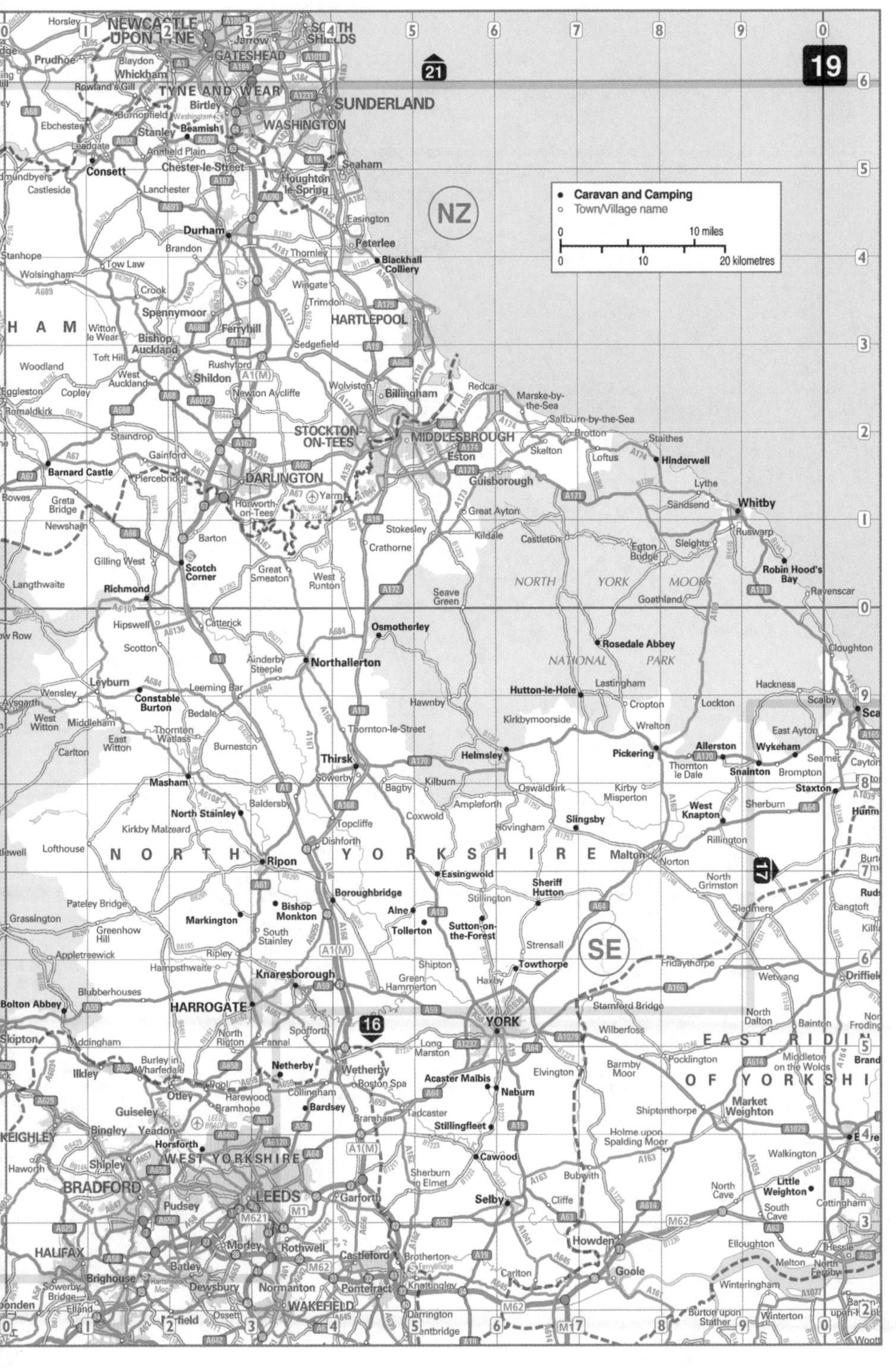
19
Caravan and Camping
Town/Village name
10 miles
20 kilometres
NZ
SE
NORTH YORKSHIRE
NORTH YORK MOORS NATIONAL PARK
TYNE AND WEAR
WEST YORKSHIRE
EAST RIDING OF YORKSHIRE
NEWCASTLE UPON TYNE
GATESHEAD
SUNDERLAND
WASHINGTON
HARTLEPOOL
STOCKTON-ON-TEES
MIDDLESBROUGH
DARLINGTON
YORK
HARROGATE
LEEDS
BRADFORD
WAKEFIELD
HALIFAX
KEIGHLEY
Durham
Consett
Beamish
Blackhall Colliery
Barnard Castle
Hinderwell
Whitby
Robin Hood's Bay
Rosedale Abbey
Hutton-le-Hole
Helmsley
Pickering
Allerston
Wykeham
Snainton
Staxton
West Knapton
Osmotherley
Northallerton
Richmond
Scotch Corner
Constable Burton
Masham
North Stainley
Ripon
Thirsk
Easingwold
Sheriff Hutton
Boroughbridge
Bishop Monkton
Markington
Alne
Tollerton
Sutton-on-the-Forest
Towthorpe
Knaresborough
Bolton Abbey
Netherby
Bardsey
Acaster Malbis
Naburn
Stillingfleet
Cawood
Selby
Horsforth
Little Weighton
Slingsby
Malton
Howden
Goole
16
17
21

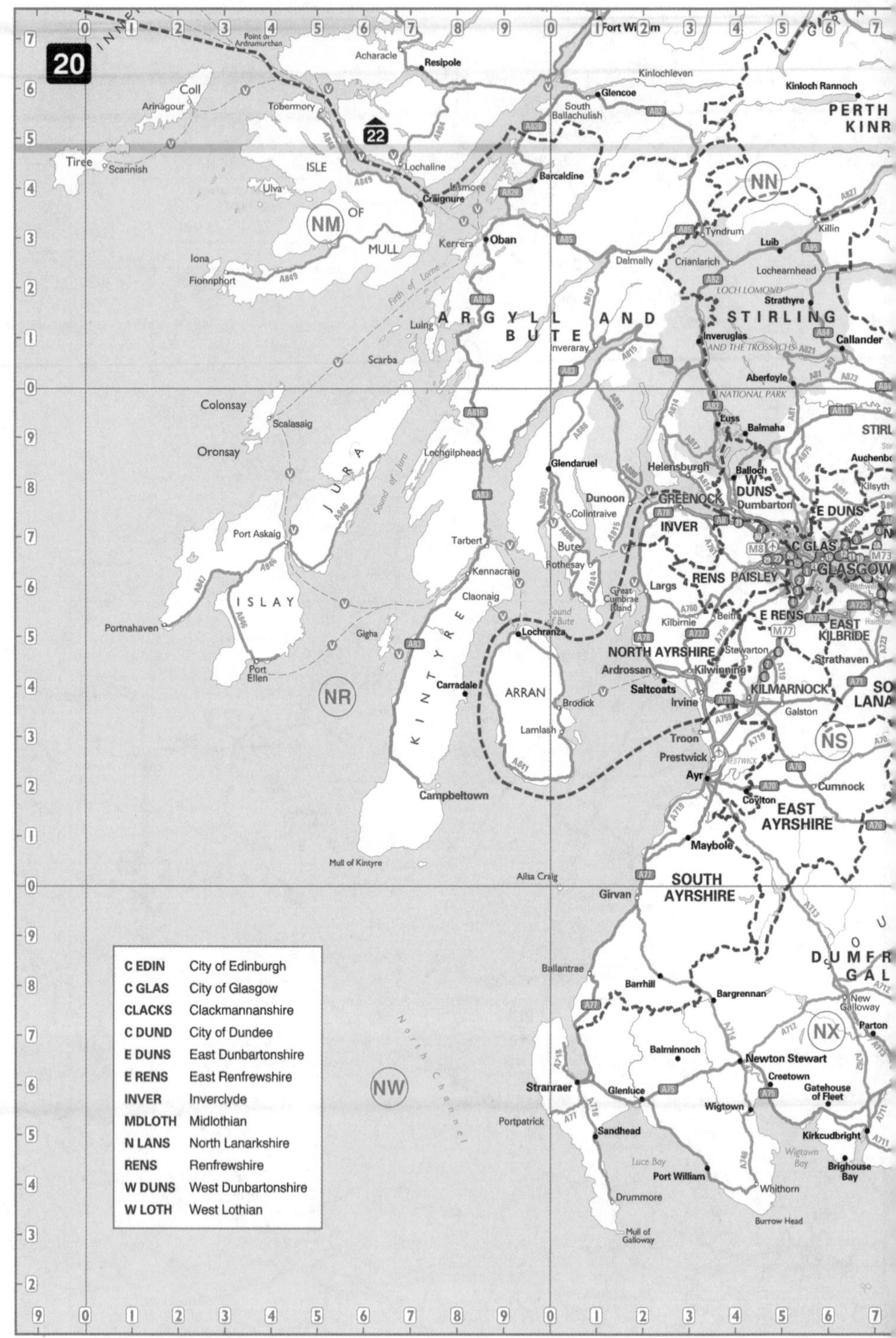


For continuation pages refer to numbered arrows

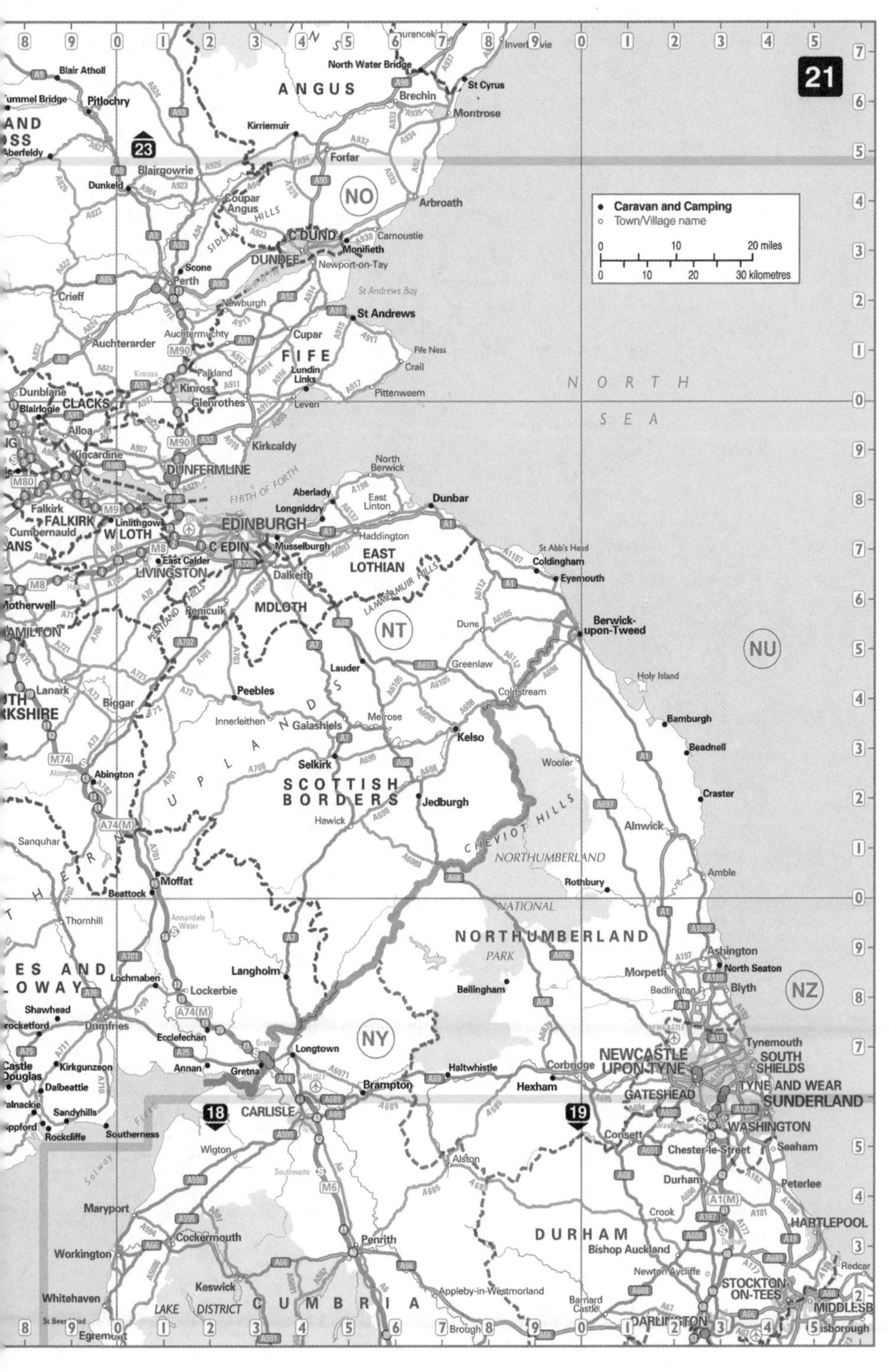
21
Caravan and Camping
Town/Village name
0 10 20 miles
0 10 20 30 kilometres
ANGUS
FIFE
EAST LOTHIAN
MDLOTH
SCOTTISH BORDERS
NORTHUMBERLAND
DURHAM
CUMBRIA
NORTH SEA
NO
NT
NU
NY
NZ
Blair Atholl
Pitlochry
Aberfeldy
Blairgowrie
Dunkeld
Kirriemuir
Forfar
Brechin
North Water Bridge
St Cyrus
Montrose
Arbroath
Carnoustie
Monifieth
DUNDEE
Newport-on-Tay
Coupar Angus
Scone
Perth
Crieff
Newburgh
St Andrews
Cupar
Auchtermuchty
Auchterarder
Fife Ness
Crail
Lundin Links
Leven
Pittenweem
Kinross
Glenrothes
Dunblane
Blairlogie
Alloa
Kirkcaldy
Kincardine
DUNFERMLINE
North Berwick
Aberlady
Longniddry
East Linton
Dunbar
Falkirk
Linlithgow
EDINBURGH
Musselburgh
Haddington
East Calder
LIVINGSTON
Dalkeith
St Abb's Head
Coldingham
Eyemouth
Motherwell
Penicuik
Berwick-upon-Tweed
Duns
Lauder
Greenlaw
Holy Island
Lanark
Peebles
Biggar
Coldstream
Innerleithen
Galashiels
Melrose
Kelso
Bamburgh
Beadnell
Abington
Selkirk
Wooler
Jedburgh
Craster
Hawick
Alnwick
Sanquhar
CHEVIOT HILLS
Moffat
Beattock
Rothbury
Amble
Thornhill
NORTHUMBERLAND NATIONAL PARK
Ashington
North Seaton
Langholm
Lochmaben
Lockerbie
Bellingham
Morpeth
Blyth
Bedlington
Shawhead
Dumfries
Ecclefechan
Tynemouth
Longtown
NEWCASTLE UPON TYNE
SOUTH SHIELDS
Kirkgunzeon
Annan
Gretna
Haltwhistle
Corbridge
Castle Douglas
Dalbeattie
Brampton
Hexham
TYNE AND WEAR
GATESHEAD
SUNDERLAND
Sandyhills
CARLISLE
Rockcliffe
Southerness
Consett
WASHINGTON
Wigton
Chester-le-Street
Seaham
Alston
Durham
Peterlee
Maryport
Crook
HARTLEPOOL
Cockermouth
Penrith
Bishop Auckland
Workington
Redcar
Newton Aycliffe
Keswick
Appleby-in-Westmorland
Barnard Castle
STOCKTON-ON-TEES
Whitehaven
LAKE DISTRICT
DARLINGTON
Egremont
Brough
MIDDLESB
23
18
19

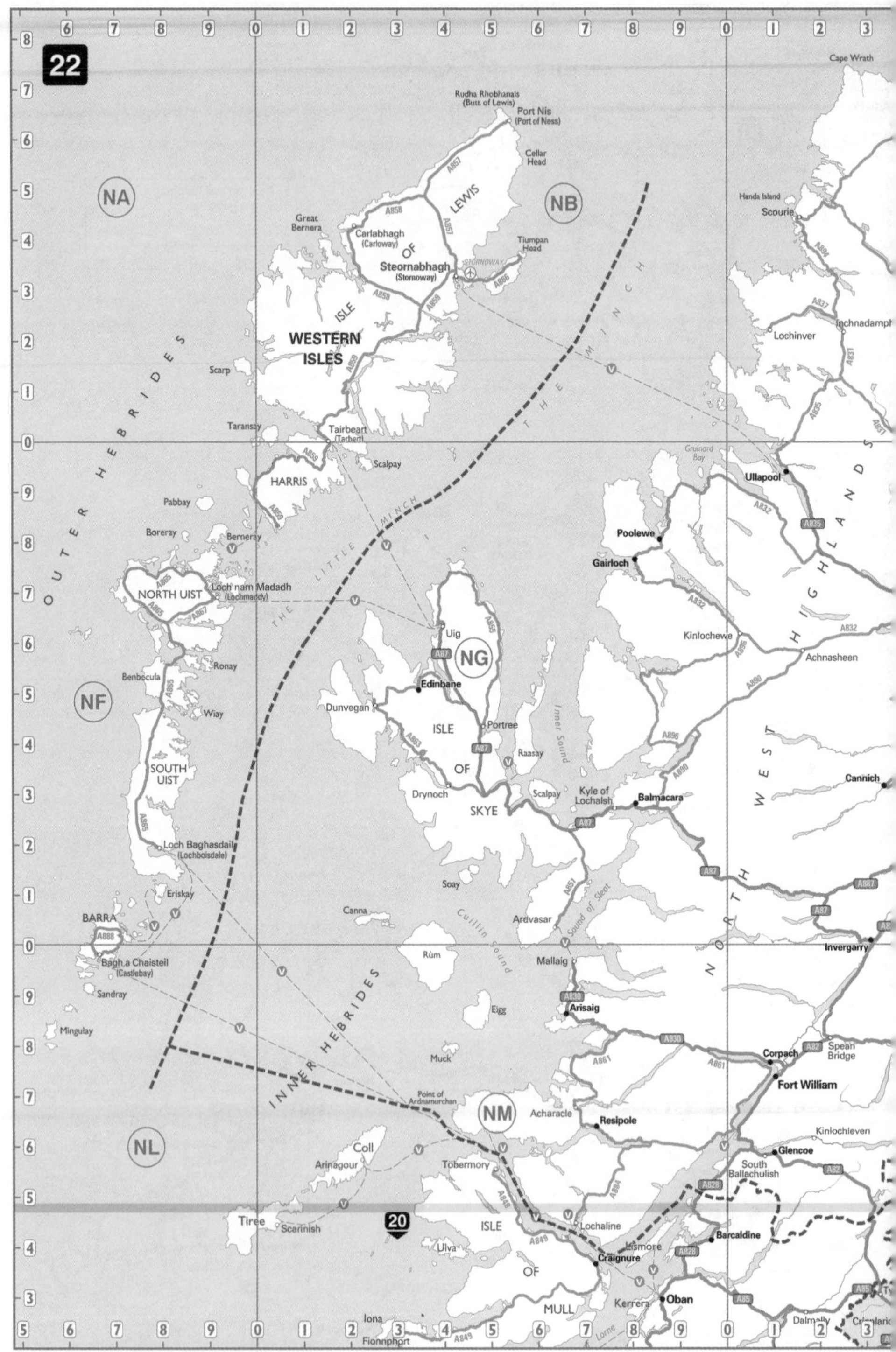


For continuation pages refer to numbered arrows

Caravan and Camping
Town/Village name
0 10 20 miles
0 10 20 30 kilometres
NC
ND
NH
NJ
NK
NN
NO
HIGHLAND
MORAY
ABERDEENSHIRE
ANGUS
PERTH AND KINROSS
CITY OF ABERDEEN
ABERDEEN
INVERNESS
DUNDEE
MORAY FIRTH
CAIRNGORMS NATIONAL PARK
GRAMPIAN MOUNTAINS
Monadhliath Mountains
John o' Groats
Thurso
Wick
Lairg
Dornoch
Tain
Dingwall
Rosemarkie
Nairn
Daviot
Findhorn
Alves
Lossiemouth
Cullen
Macduff
Fochabers
Craigellachie
Aberlour
Huntly
Grantown-on-Spey
Boat of Garten
Kintore
Tarland
Aboyne
Fordoun
North Water Bridge
St Cyrus
Kinloch Rannoch
Tummel Bridge
Blair Atholl
Pitlochry
Aberfeldy
Kirriemuir
Dunkeld
Luib
Monifieth
Scone
Stonehaven
Montrose
Arbroath
Brechin
Forfar
Peterhead
Fraserburgh
21

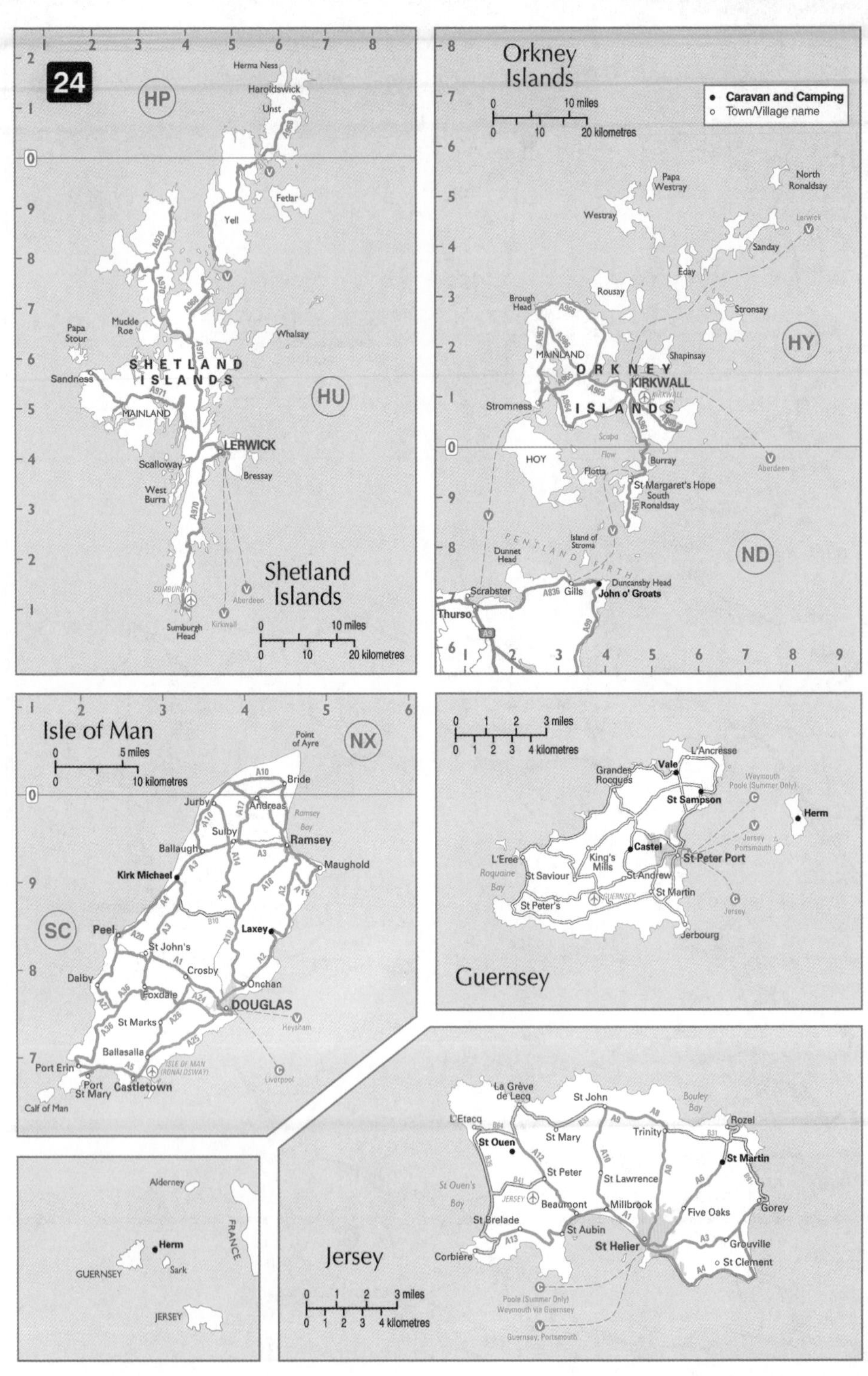
Shetland Islands
0 10 miles
0 10 20 kilometres
HP
HU
Herma Ness
Haroldswick
Unst
Fetlar
Yell
Whalsay
Papa Stour
Muckle Roe
SHETLAND ISLANDS
Sandness
MAINLAND
LERWICK
Scalloway
Bressay
West Burra
Aberdeen
Kirkwall
Sumburgh Head
SUMBURGH
Orkney Islands
0 10 miles
0 10 20 kilometres
Caravan and Camping
Town/Village name
Papa Westray
North Ronaldsay
Westray
Lerwick
Sanday
Eday
Rousay
Stronsay
Brough Head
MAINLAND
Shapinsay
HY
ORKNEY ISLANDS
KIRKWALL
Stromness
Scapa Flow
HOY
Flotta
Burray
Aberdeen
St Margaret's Hope
South Ronaldsay
PENTLAND FIRTH
Island of Stroma
Dunnet Head
ND
Duncansby Head
Scrabster
Gills
John o' Groats
Thurso
Isle of Man
0 5 miles
0 10 kilometres
Point of Ayre
NX
Bride
Jurby
Andreas
Ramsey Bay
Sulby
Ramsey
Ballaugh
Maughold
Kirk Michael
SC
Peel
Laxey
St John's
Crosby
Dalby
Onchan
Foxdale
DOUGLAS
St Marks
Heysham
Ballasalla
ISLE OF MAN (RONALDSWAY)
Port Erin
Port St Mary
Castletown
Liverpool
Calf of Man
0 1 2 3 miles
0 1 2 3 4 kilometres
L'Ancresse
Grandes Rocques
Vale
St Sampson
Weymouth Poole (Summer Only)
Herm
Castel
Jersey Portsmouth
L'Eree
King's Mills
St Peter Port
Roquaine Bay
St Saviour
St Andrew
St Martin
GUERNSEY
St Peter's
Jersey
Jerbourg
Guernsey
Alderney
FRANCE
Herm
GUERNSEY
Sark
JERSEY
La Grève de Lecq
St John
Bouley Bay
L'Etacq
Rozel
Trinity
St Ouen
St Mary
St Martin
St Peter
St Lawrence
St Ouen's Bay
JERSEY
Beaumont
Millbrook
Five Oaks
Gorey
St Brelade
St Aubin
St Helier
Grouville
Corbière
St Clement
Jersey
Poole (Summer Only) Weymouth via Guernsey
Guernsey, Portsmouth
0 1 2 3 miles
0 1 2 3 4 kilometres

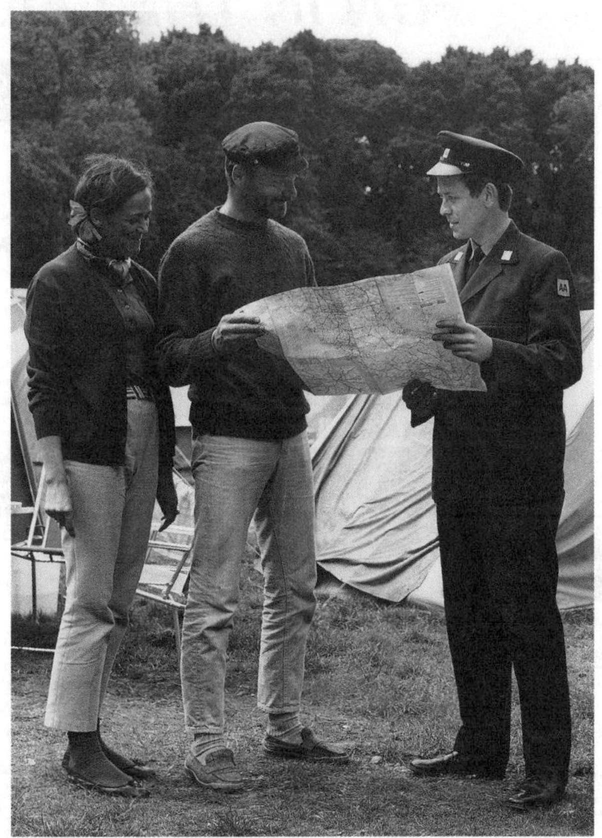

*Copyright Pace/AA Archive*

## Credits

The Automobile Association would like to thank the following photographers, companies and picture libraries for their assistance in the preparation of this book.

Abbreviations for the picture credits are as follows: (t) top; (b) bottom; (l) left; (r) right; (AA) AA World Travel Library.

1 AA/A Mockford & N Bonetti; 2l AA/D Forss; 3tr AA/S L Day; 3br AA/G Rowatt; 3bl AA/J A Tims; 4tl AA/T Mackie; 5tr AA/S L Day; 7tr AA/S L Day; 7b AA/S L Day; 8tl AA/T Mackie; 8bl AA/J Miller; 9tr AA/S L Day; 10tl AA/T Mackie; 11tr AA/S L Day; 13tr AA/S L Day; 13cl AA/J Wood; 15tr AA/S L Day; 16tl AA/T Mackie;17tr AA/S L Day; 18tl AA/T Mackie; 19tr AA/S L Day; 20tl AA/T Mackie; 21tr AA/S L Day; 22tl AA/T Mackie; 23tr AA/S L Day; 25tr AA/S L Day; 27tr AA/S L Day; 28tl AA/T Mackie; 28b AA/J Smith; 29tr AA/S L Day; 32/3 AA/P Sharpe; 290/1 AA/S L Day; 328/9 AA/N Jenkins; 362/3 AA/D Forss.
16cl AA Archive; 16br Pace/AA Archive; 17c AA Archive; 18tr Industrial News Photos/AA Archive; 18cr Hazel Harrod; 18b Maurice Broomfield/AA Archive; 19r Pace/AA Archive; 26b Hazel Harrod; 30b Philip Moorhouse; 409t Pace/ AA Archive

Every effort has been made to trace the copyright holders, and we apologise in advance for any accidental errors. We would be happy to apply the corrections in the following edition of this publication.

aravan &
railer Movers

Our expertise has enabled the design of the lightest caravan motorised mover with a fully radio controlled remote handset. The Rhyno system is made primarily for simple DIY fitting. A fitting service is available.

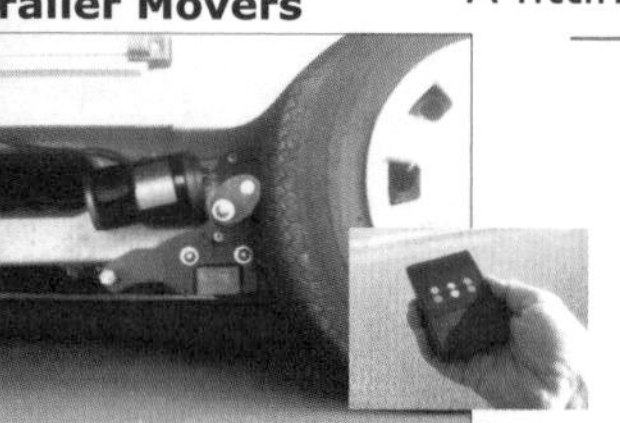

- *Lightweight construction - only 29 Kilos*
- *Non grit roller for ultimate reliability*
- *Fully remote controlled*
- *1800 Kilo capability*
- *Sits highest off the road*
- *5 Year Guarantee*
- *British made in the Midlands*

***et a Rhyno to move your caravan and never push that caravan again!***

**el: 02476 387 080 Email: sales@rhyno-uk.com www.rhyno-uk.com**

---

the largest choice at the best prices

**Breathable Groundsheet**

www.breathablegroundsheet.co.uk

**REE PHONE ORDER LINE (7 DAYS)**
**0800 043 0019**

E UKs All Brands Website

Softex •Ecomat
Aerotex •Comfimat
Ecotek •Questex
Carpetaire

SOFTEX - AEROTEX
ECOMAT - COMFIMAT
ARE OPEN WEAVE

Isabella Bolon •Carpetina
Kampa Easytread
Liteweave
Comficarpet

CARPETINA - COMFICARPET
LITEWEAVE - ISABELLA BOLON
ARE CLOSE WEAVE

NUFACTURERS 'SLIGHT SECONDS' AVAILABLE AT BARGAIN PRICES!

NEXT WORKING DAY DELIVERY STANDARD

I Zip Storage/Carry Bag with all orders over 12ft / 3.66m length

**ww.breathablegroundsheet.co.uk**

Morlands Industrial Park, Highbridge, Somerset TA9 3ET
Ebay Shop GROUNDSHEETMAN

---

caravan
finder.co.uk

the largest collection of UK caravans and motorhomes online

advertise from as little as £25 for 12 months

**Visit us at**
**www.caravanfinder.co.uk**

---

**ELECTRIC BIKES DIRECT**

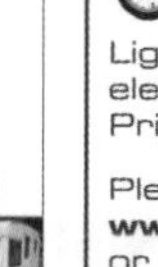

Lightweight folding bikes and electric bikes.
Prices start from £199

Please visit:
**www.electricbikesdirect.co.uk**
or phone:
**01903 765353/01903 753632**

---

**MAKE MONEY WITH YOUR MOTOR HOME**

ristol couple earnt £6,491 renting out their Hymer!

**WATCH OUR FREE VIDEO & FULL INCOME GUIDE**

ww.moneymotor.co.uk
lephone 0800-612-9418

---

**The Outdoor Superstores**

**Bursting with Stock for Caravans, Camping & all Outdoor Pursuits.**

| POOLE | WIMBORNE |
|---|---|
| MOOR-HITCH-N-PITCH | HITCH-N-PITCH |
| 12 Lagland St<br>Poole<br>BH15 1QG<br>01202676400 | Merley House<br>Lane. Wimborne<br>BH21 3AA<br>01202880888 |

**www.hitch-n-pitch.co.uk**

---

*Leisure Garden*

*For all your Camping and Gardening needs!!*

**Your premier garden and camping resource**

A range of products for your garden and accessories for your special caravan & camping holiday at home or abroad...

**...available for on-line purchase immediately**

0124 6281 628
www.leisuregarden.co.uk

# Notes

# Readers' Report Form

Please send this form to:
Editor, AA Caravan & Camping
Britain & Ireland,
Lifestyle Guides,
The Automobile Association,
Fanum House,
Basingstoke RG21 4EA

fax: 01256 491647
e-mail: lifestyleguides@theAA.com

Please use this form to tell us about any site you have visited, whether it is in the guide or not currently listed. Feedback from readers helps us to keep our guide accurate and up to date. However, if you have a complaint to make during your visit, we recommend that you discuss the matter with the management there and then, so that they have a chance to put things right before your visit is spoilt. The AA does not undertake to arbitrate between you and the site's management, or to obtain compensation or engage in protracted correspondence.

Date:

Your name (block capitals)

Your address (block capitals)

..........................................................................................................................................

..........................................................................................................................................

..........................................................................................................................................

..........................................................................................................................................

..........................................................................................................................................

..........................................................................................................................................

e-mail address:

Name of site/park:

Comments (Please include the address of the site/park) ..............................................................

..........................................................................................................................................

..........................................................................................................................................

..........................................................................................................................................

..........................................................................................................................................

..........................................................................................................................................

..........................................................................................................................................

..........................................................................................................................................

..........................................................................................................................................

..........................................................................................................................................

..........................................................................................................................................

(please attach a separate sheet if necessary)

Please tick here if you DO NOT wish to receive details of AA offers or products ☐

**PTO**

**Have you bought this Guide before?** Yes No

**How often do you visit a caravan park or camp site? (circle one choice)**
once a year twice a year 3 times a year
more than 3 times a year

**How long do you generally stay at a park or site? (circle one choice)**
one night up to a week 1 week
2 weeks over 2 weeks

**Do you have a:**
tent caravan motorhome

**Which of the following is most important when choosing a site? (circle one choice)**
location toilet/washing facilities personal recommendation
leisure facilities other ......................................................................

**Do you prefer self-contained cubicled washrooms with WC, shower and washhand basin to open-plan seperate facilities?**
yes no don't mind

**Do you buy any other camping guides? If so, which ones?** ..............................................
.....................................................................................................
.....................................................................................................

**Please answer these questions to help us make improvements to the guide:**

**Have you read the introductory pages and features in this guide?** Yes No

**Do you use the location atlas in this guide?** Yes No

**Which of the following most influences your choice of site/park from this guide? (circle one choice)**
gazetteer entry information and description photograph advertisement

**Do you have any suggestions to improve the guide?** ..............................................
.....................................................................................................
.....................................................................................................
.....................................................................................................

**Thank you for returning this form**

# Readers' Report Form

Please send this form to:
Editor, AA Caravan & Camping
Britain & Ireland,
Lifestyle Guides,
The Automobile Association,
Fanum House,
Basingstoke RG21 4EA

fax: 01256 491647
e-mail: lifestyleguides@theAA.com

Please use this form to tell us about any site you have visited, whether it is in the guide or not currently listed. Feedback from readers helps us to keep our guide accurate and up to date. However, if you have a complaint to make during your visit, we recommend that you discuss the matter with the management there and then, so that they have a chance to put things right before your visit is spoilt. The AA does not undertake to arbitrate between you and the site's management, or to obtain compensation or engage in protracted correspondence.

Date:

Your name (block capitals)

Your address (block capitals)

..................................................................................................................................

..................................................................................................................................

..................................................................................................................................

..................................................................................................................................

..................................................................................................................................

..................................................................................................................................

e-mail address:

Name of site/park:

Comments (Please include the address of the site/park) ..........................................................

..................................................................................................................................

..................................................................................................................................

..................................................................................................................................

..................................................................................................................................

..................................................................................................................................

..................................................................................................................................

..................................................................................................................................

..................................................................................................................................

..................................................................................................................................

..................................................................................................................................

(please attach a separate sheet if necessary)

Please tick here if you DO NOT wish to receive details of AA offers or products ☐

**PTO**

**Have you bought this Guide before?** Yes No

**How often do you visit a caravan park or camp site? (circle one choice)**
once a year twice a year 3 times a year
more than 3 times a year

**How long do you generally stay at a park or site? (circle one choice)**
one night up to a week 1 week
2 weeks over 2 weeks

**Do you have a:**
tent caravan motorhome

**Which of the following is most important when choosing a site? (circle one choice)**
location toilet/washing facilities personal recommendation
leisure facilities other ....................................................

**Do you prefer self-contained cubicled washrooms with WC, shower and washhand basin to open-plan seperate facilities?**
yes no don't mind

**Do you buy any other camping guides? If so, which ones?** ....................................................
....................................................................................................
....................................................................................................

**Please answer these questions to help us make improvements to the guide:**

**Have you read the introductory pages and features in this guide?** Yes No

**Do you use the location atlas in this guide?** Yes No

**Which of the following most influences your choice of site/park from this guide? (circle one choice)**
gazetteer entry information and description photograph advertisement

**Do you have any suggestions to improve the guide?** ....................................................
....................................................................................................
....................................................................................................
....................................................................................................

**Thank you for returning this form**